Guide to
Computer Forensics
and Investigations

Fourth Edition

Bill Nelson

Amelia Phillips

Christopher Steuart

COURSE TECHNOLOGY
CENGAGE Learning™

Australia • Brazil • Japan • Korea • Mexico • Singapore • Spain • United Kingdom • United States

COURSE TECHNOLOGY
CENGAGE Learning™

Guide to Computer Forensics and Investigations, Fourth Edition

Bill Nelson, Amelia Phillips, Christopher Steuart

Vice President, Career and Professional Editorial: Dave Garza

Executive Editor: Stephen Helba

Managing Editor: Marah Bellegarde

Senior Product Manager: Michelle Ruelos Cannistraci

Developmental Editor: Lisa M. Lord

Editorial Assistant: Sarah Pickering

Vice President, Career and Professional Marketing: Jennifer McAvey

Marketing Director: Deborah S. Yarnell

Senior Marketing Manager: Erin Coffin

Marketing Coordinator: Shanna Gibbs

Production Director: Carolyn Miller

Production Manager: Andrew Crouth

Content Project Manager: Jessica McNavich

Art Director: Jack Pendleton

Cover photo or illustration: Shutterstock

Production Technology Analyst: Tom Stover

Manufacturing Coordinator: Julio Esperas

Copyeditor: Ruth Bloom

Proofreader: Michele Callaghan

Compositor: Cadmus Communications

For product information and technology assistance, contact us at **Cengage Learning Customer & Sales Support, 1-800-354-9706**

For permission to use material from this text or product, submit all requests online at **cengage.com/permissions**

Further permissions questions can be emailed to **permissionrequest@cengage.com**

Library of Congress Control Number: 2009929885

ISBN-13: 978-1-435-49883-9
ISBN-10: 1-435-49883-6

Course Technology
20 Channel Center Street
Boston, MA 02210

Cengage Learning is a leading provider of customized learning solutions with office locations around the globe, including Singapore, the United Kingdom, Australia, Mexico, Brazil, and Japan. Locate your local office at: **international.cengage.com/region**

Cengage Learning products are represented in Canada by Nelson Education, Ltd.

For your lifelong learning solutions, visit **course.cengage.com**

Visit our corporate website at **cengage.com**.

Printed in the United States of America
2 3 4 5 6 7 12 11 10

Brief Table of Contents

Table of Contents

CHAPTER 6
Working with Windows and DOS Systems. 197

Preface

The rapid advance of technology has changed and influenced how we think about gathering digital evidence. Soon after the attacks on the World Trade Center in New York City on September 11, 2001, many young men and women volunteered to serve their country in different ways. For those who did not choose the military, options included positions with law enforcement and corporate security organizations. Ultimately, the combination of a renewed emphasis on homeland security along with the popularity of mainstream television shows, such as *CSI*, *Forensic Files*, and *NCIS*, has created a huge demand for highly educated specialists in the discipline of computer forensics. This demand is now being met by the advent of specialized forensics courses in colleges, universities, and even high schools throughout the United States.

Computer forensics, however, is by no means a new field of endeavor. During the early 1990s, while serving as a Special Agent with the Naval Criminal Investigative Service (NCIS), I realized that personal computers and, more specifically, unsecured personal computers posed a potential threat to national security. I became involved in conducting forensic investigations involving white collar crime, network intrusions, and telecommunications fraud. Recently, the U.S. government has taken significant steps to improve the quality and sophistication of the country's computer forensic capabilities, including the formation of the U.S. Cyber Command (CYBERCOM) in the Department of Defense. Today, most new computer forensics specialists can expect to be involved in a wide variety of investigations, including terrorism counterintelligence, financial fraud issues, intellectual property theft, data security breaches, and electronic data discovery.

The skill sets computer forensics specialists must have are varied. At a minimum, they must have an in-depth knowledge of the criminal justice system, computer hardware and software systems, and investigative and evidence-gathering protocols. The next generation of "digital detectives" will have to possess the knowledge, skills, and experience to conduct complex, data-intensive forensic examinations involving various operating systems, platforms, and file types with data sets in the multiple-terabyte range.

As time passes, the "hybrid discipline" of computer forensics is slowly evolving into a "hybrid science"—the science of digital forensics. Many colleges and universities in the United States and the United Kingdom have created multidiscipline curriculums that will offer undergraduate and graduate degrees in digital forensics. *Guide to Computer Forensics and Investigations*, now in its fourth edition, has emerged as a significant authoritative text for the computer and digital forensics communities. It's my belief that this book, designed to be used primarily in an academic setting with an enthusiastic and knowledgeable facilitator, will make for a fascinating course of instruction.

Today, it's not just computers that harbor the binary code of 1s and 0s, but an infinite array of personal digital devices. If one of these devices retains evidence of a crime, it will be up to newly trained and educated digital detectives to find the digital evidence in a forensically sound manner. This book will assist both students and practitioners in accomplishing this goal.

Respectfully,

John A. Sgromolo

As a Senior Special Agent, John was one of the founding members of the NCIS Computer Crime Investigations Group. John left government service to run his own company, Digital Forensics, Inc., and has taught hundreds of law enforcement and corporate students nationwide the art and science of computer forensics investigations. Currently, John serves as the senior forensics examiner for digital forensic investigations at Verizon.

Introduction

Computer forensics has been a professional field for many years, but most well-established experts in the field have been self-taught. The growth of the Internet and the worldwide proliferation of computers have increased the need for computing investigations. Computers can be used to commit crimes, and crimes can be recorded on computers, including company policy violations, embezzlement, e-mail harassment, murder, leaks of proprietary information, and even terrorism. Law enforcement, network administrators, attorneys, and private investigators now rely on the skills of professional computer forensics experts to investigate criminal and civil cases.

This book is not intended to provide comprehensive training in computer forensics. It does, however, give you a solid foundation by introducing computer forensics to those who are new to the field. Other books on computer forensics are targeted to experts; this book is intended for novices who have a thorough grounding in computer and networking basics.

The new generation of computer forensics experts needs more initial training because operating systems, computer hardware, and forensics software tools are changing more quickly. This book covers current and past operating systems and a range of computer hardware, from basic workstations to high-end network servers. Although this book focuses on a few forensics software tools, it also reviews and discusses other currently available tools.

The purpose of this book is to guide you toward becoming a skilled computer forensics investigator. A secondary goal is to help you pass the appropriate certification exams. As the field of computer forensics and investigations matures, keep in mind that certifications will change. You can find more information on certifications in Chapter 3 and Appendix A.

Intended Audience

Although this book can be used by people with a wide range of backgrounds, it's intended for those with an A+ and Network+ certification or equivalent. A networking background is necessary so that you understand how PCs operate in a networked environment and can work with a network administrator when needed. In addition, you must know how to use a computer from the command line and how to use popular operating systems, including Windows, Linux, and Mac OS, and their related hardware.

This book can be used at any educational level, from technical high schools and community colleges to graduate students. Current professionals in the public and private sectors can also use this book. Each group will approach investigative problems from a different perspective, but all will benefit from the coverage.

What's New in This Edition

The chapter flow of this book has been revised so that you're first exposed to what happens in a computer forensics lab and how to set one up before you get into the nuts and bolts. Coverage of several GUI tools has been added to give you a familiarity with some widely used software. In addition, Chapter 6 includes new information on interpreting the Windows NTFS Master File Table. The book's DVD includes video tutorials for each chapter that show how to perform the steps in in-chapter activities and explain how to use most of the forensics tools on the DVD. Corrections have been made to this edition based on feedback from users, and all software packages and Web sites have been updated to reflect what's current at the time of publication. A new lab manual is now offered to go with the new fourth edition textbook (ISBN: 1-4354-9885-2).

Chapter Descriptions

Here is a summary of the topics covered in each chapter of this book:

Chapter 1, "Computer Forensics and Investigations as a Profession," introduces you to the history of computer forensics and explains how the use of electronic evidence developed. It also introduces legal issues and compares public and private sector cases.

Chapter 2, "Understanding Computer Investigations," introduces you to tools used throughout the book and shows you how to apply scientific techniques to an investigative case. In addition, it covers procedures for corporate investigations, such as industrial espionage and employee termination cases.

Chapter 3, "The Investigator's Office and Laboratory," outlines physical requirements and equipment for computer forensics labs, from small private investigators' labs to the regional FBI lab. It also covers certifications for computing investigators and building a business case for a forensics lab.

Chapter 4, "Data Acquisition," explains how to prepare to acquire data from a suspect's drive and discusses available command-line and GUI acquisition tools. This chapter also discusses acquiring data from RAID systems and gives you an overview of tools for remote acquisitions.

Chapter 5, "Processing Crime and Incident Scenes," explains search warrants and the nature of a typical computer forensics case. It discusses when to use outside professionals, how to assemble a team, and how to evaluate a case and explains proper procedures for searching and seizing evidence. This chapter also introduces you to calculating hashes to verify data you collect.

Chapter 6, "Working with Windows and DOS Systems," discusses the most common operating systems. You learn what happens and what files are altered during computer startup and how each system deals with deleted and slack space. In addition, a new section on working with virtual machines has been added.

Chapter 7, "Current Computer Forensics Tools," explores current computer forensics software and hardware tools, including those that might not be readily available, and evaluates their strengths and weaknesses.

Chapter 8, "Macintosh and Linux Boot Processes and File Systems," continues the operating system discussion from Chapter 6 by examining Macintosh and Linux operating systems. It also covers CDs, DVDs, and SCSI, IDE/EIDE, and SATA drives.

Chapter 9, "Computer Forensics Analysis and Validation," covers determining what data to collect and analyze and refining investigation plans. It also explains validation with hex editors and forensics software, data-hiding techniques, and techniques for remote acquisitions.

Chapter 10, "Recovering Graphics Files," explains how to recover graphics files and examines data compression, carving data, reconstructing file fragments, and steganography and copyright issues.

Chapter 11, "Virtual Machines, Network Forensics, and Live Acquisitions" covers tools and methods for acquiring virtual machines, conducting network investigations, performing live acquisitions, and reviewing network logs for evidence. It also examines using UNIX/Linux tools and the Honeynet Project's resources.

Chapter 12, "E-mail Investigations," covers e-mail and Internet fundamentals and examines e-mail crimes and violations. It also reviews some specialized e-mail forensics tools.

Chapter 13, "Cell Phone and Mobile Device Forensics," covers investigation techniques and acquisition procedures for recovering data from cell phones and mobile devices. It also provides guidance on dealing with these constantly changing technologies.

Chapter 14, "Report Writing for High-Tech Investigations," discusses the importance of report writing in computer forensics examinations; offers guidelines on report content, structure, and presentation; and explains how to generate report findings with forensics software tools.

Chapter 15, "Expert Testimony in High-Tech Investigations," explores the role of an expert or technical/scientific witness, including developing a curriculum vitae, understanding the trial process, and preparing forensics evidence for testimony. It also offers guidelines for testifying in court and at depositions and hearings.

Chapter 16, "Ethics for the Expert Witness," provides guidance in the principles and practice of ethics for computer forensics investigators and examines other professional organizations' codes of ethics.

Appendix A, "Certification Test References," provides information on the National Institute of Standards and Technology (NIST) testing processes for validating computer forensics tools and covers computer forensics certifications and training programs.

Appendix B, "Computer Forensics References," lists recommended books, journals, e-mail lists, and Web sites for additional information and further study.

Appendix C, "Computer Forensics Lab Considerations," provides more information on considerations for forensics labs, including certifications, ergonomics, structural design, and communication and fire-suppression systems.

Appendix D, "DOS File System and Forensics Tools," reviews FAT file system basics and explains using DOS computer forensics tools, creating forensic boot media, and using scripts. It also reviews DriveSpy commands and X-Ways Replica.

Features

To help you fully understand computer forensics, this book includes many features designed to enhance your learning experience:

- *Chapter objectives*—Each chapter begins with a detailed list of the concepts to be mastered in that chapter. This list gives you a quick reference to the chapter's contents and is a useful study aid.

- *Figures and tables*—Screenshots are used as guidelines for stepping through commands and forensics tools. For tools not included with the book or that aren't offered in free demo versions, figures have been added to illustrate the tool's interface. Tables are used throughout the book to present information in an organized, easy-to-grasp manner.

- *Chapter summaries*—Each chapter's material is followed by a summary of the concepts introduced in that chapter. These summaries are a helpful way to review the ideas covered in each chapter.

- *Key terms*—Following the chapter summary, a list of all new terms introduced in the chapter with boldfaced text are gathered together in the Key Terms list, with full definitions for each term. This list encourages a more thorough understanding of the chapter's key concepts and is a useful reference.

- *Review questions*—The end-of-chapter assessment begins with a set of review questions that reinforce the main concepts in each chapter. These questions help you evaluate and apply the material you have learned.

- *Hands-on projects*—Although understanding the theory behind computer technology is important, nothing can improve on real-world experience. To this end, each chapter offers several hands-on projects with software supplied with this book or free downloads. You can explore a variety of ways to acquire and even hide evidence. For the conceptual chapters, research projects are provided.

- *Case projects*—At the end of each chapter are several case projects, including a running case example used throughout the book. To complete these projects, you must draw on real-world common sense as well as your knowledge of the technical topics covered to that point in the book. Your goal for each project is to come up with answers to problems similar to those you'll face as a working computer forensics investigator.

- *Video tutorials*—The book's DVD includes audio-video instructions to help with learning the tools needed to perform in-chapter activities. Each tutorial is a .wmv file that can be played in most OSs. The skills learned from these tutorials can be applied to hands-on projects at the end of each chapter.

- *Software and student data files*—This book includes a DVD containing student data files and free software demo packages for use with activities and projects in the chapters. (Additional software demos or freeware can be downloaded to use in some projects.) Four software companies have graciously agreed to allow including their products with this book: Technology Pathways (ProDiscover Basic), AccessData (Forensic Toolkit, Registry Viewer, and FTK Imager), X-Ways (WinHex Demo), and Runtime Software (DiskExplorer for FAT,

DiskExplorer for NTFS, and HDHOST). To check for newer versions or additional information, visit Technology Pathways, LLC at *www.techpathways.com*, AccessData Corporation at *www.accessdata.com*, X-Ways Software Technology AG at *www.x-ways.net*, and Runtime Software at *www.runtime.org*.

Text and Graphic Conventions

When appropriate, additional information and exercises have been added to this book to help you better understand the topic at hand. The following icons used in this book alert you to additional materials:

The Note icon draws your attention to additional helpful material related to the subject being covered.

Tips based on the authors' experience offer extra information about how to attack a problem or what to do in real-world situations.

The Caution icons warn you about potential mistakes or problems and explain how to avoid them.

Each hands-on project in this book is preceded by the Hands-On icon and a description of the exercise that follows.

These icons mark case projects, which are scenario-based assignments. In these extensive case examples, you're asked to apply independently what you have learned.

Instructor's Resources

The following additional materials are available when this book is used in a classroom setting. All the supplements available with this book are provided to instructors on a single CD (ISBN 1435498844). You can also retrieve these supplemental materials from the Cengage Web site, *www.cengage.com*, by going to the page for this book, under "Download Instructor Files & Teaching Tools."

- *Electronic Instructor's Manual*—The Instructor's Manual that accompanies this book includes additional instructional material to assist in class preparation, including suggestions for lecture topics, recommended lab activities, tips on setting up a lab for hands-on projects, and solutions to all end-of-chapter materials.

- *ExamView Test Bank*—This cutting-edge Windows-based testing software helps instructors design and administer tests and pretests. In addition to generating tests that can be printed and administered, this full-featured program has an online testing component that allows students to take tests at the computer and have their exams automatically graded.

- *PowerPoint presentations*—This book comes with a set of Microsoft PowerPoint slides for each chapter. These slides are meant to be used as a teaching aid for classroom presentations, to be made available to students on the network for chapter review, or to be printed for classroom distribution. Instructors are also at liberty to add their own slides for other topics introduced.

- *Figure files*—All the figures in the book are reproduced on the Instructor's Resources CD. Similar to the PowerPoint presentations, they're included as a teaching aid for classroom presentation, to make available to students for review, or to be printed for classroom distribution.

Student Resources

Lab Manual for Guide to Computer Forensics and Investigations (ISBN: 1-4354-9885-2)

- Companion to *Guide to Computer Forensics and Investigations, Fourth Edition*. This lab manual provides students with additional hands-on experience.

Web-Based Labs for Guide to Computer Forensics and Investigations (ISBN: 1-4354-9886-0)

- Using a real lab environment over the Internet, students can log on anywhere, anytime via a Web browser to gain essential hands-on experience in computer forensics using labs from *Guide to Computer Forensics and Investigations, Fourth Edition*.

Lab Requirements

The hands-on projects in this book help you apply what you have learned about computer forensics techniques. The following sections list the minimum requirements for completing all the projects in this book. In addition to the items listed, you must be able to download and install demo versions of software.

Minimum Lab Requirements

- Lab computers that boot to Windows XP
- Computers that dual-boot to Linux or UNIX
- At least one Macintosh computer running Mac OS X (although most projects are done in Windows or Linux/UNIX)
- An external USB, FireWire, or SATA drive larger than a typical 512 MB USB drive

The projects in this book are designed with the following hardware and software requirements in mind. The lab in which most of the work takes place should be a typical network training lab with a variety of operating systems and computers available.

Operating Systems and Hardware

Windows XP or Vista

Use a standard installation of Windows XP Professional or Vista. The computer running Windows XP or Vista should be a fairly current model that meets the following minimum requirements:

- USB ports
- CD-ROM/DVD-ROM drive

- VGA or higher monitor
- Hard disk partition of 10 GB or more
- Mouse or other pointing device
- Keyboard
- At least 512 MB RAM (more is recommended)

Linux

For this book, it's assumed you're using an Ubuntu, Red Hat Linux 9, or Fedora standard installation, although other Linux distributions will work with minor modifications. Also, some projects use specialized "live" Linux distributions, such as BackTrack. Some optional steps require the GIMP graphics editor, which must be installed separately in Red Hat Linux 9. Linux can be installed on a dual-boot computer as long as one or more partitions of at least 2 GB are reserved for the Linux OS.

- Hard disk partition of 2 GB or more reserved for Linux
- Other hardware requirements are the same as those listed for Windows computers

This book contains a dual-layered DVD with data files, demo software, and video tutorials. Some older computers and DVD drives might have difficulty reading data from this type of DVD. If you have any problems, make sure your computer has a DVD drive capable of reading dual-layer DVDs, and copy the data to an external USB or FireWire drive before transferring it to your computer.

Computer Forensics Software

Several computer forensics programs, listed previously under "Features," are supplied with this book. In addition, there are projects using the following software, most of which can be downloaded from the Internet as freeware, shareware, or free demo versions:

Because Web site addresses change frequently, use a search engine to find the following software online if URLs are no longer valid. Efforts have been made to provide information that's current at the time of writing, but things change constantly on the Web. Learning how to use search tools to find what you need is a valuable skill you'll use as a computer forensics investigator.

- BackTrack 3: Download from *www.remote-exploit.org/backtrack.html*.
- BitPim: Download from *www.bitpim.org*.
- BlackBag Technologies Macintosh Forensic Software: Download a trial version from *www.blackbagtech.com/support/downloads.html*. (Note that you must e-mail for a username and password before you can download the software. In addition, this URL has recently changed from the one given in Chapter 8.)
- HexWorkshop: Download from Breakpoint Software at *www.hexworkshop.com*.
- IrfanView: Download from *www.irfanview.com*.
- Knoppix-STD: Download the ISO image from *http://s-t-d.org* and burn it to a CD.

- Microsoft Virtual PC: Download from *www.microsoft.com/virtualpc*. (Check with your instructor about using an ISO image that the Microsoft Academic Alliance provides to schools.)
- OpenOffice (includes OpenCalc): Download from *www.openoffice.org*.
- PsTools: Download from *www.microsoft.com/technet/sysinternals/Utilities/PsTools.mspx*.
- SecureClean: Download from *www.whitecanyon.com/secureclean.php*.
- SIMCon: Download a commercial version from *www.simcon.no*.
- Sleuth Kit 2.08 and Autopsy Browser 2.07: Download from *www.sleuthkit.org*.
- S-Tools4: Download from *www.stegoarchive.com*.
- WinZip: Download an evaluation version from *www.winzip.com/download.htm*.
- Wireshark: Download from *www.wireshark.org*.

In addition, you use Microsoft Office Word (or other word processing software) and Excel (or other spreadsheet software) as well as a Web browser. You also need to have e-mail software installed on your computer, as explained in Chapter 12.

About the Authors

Bill Nelson has been a lead computer forensics investigator for a Fortune 50 company for more than 11 years and has developed high-tech investigation programs for professional organizations and colleges. His previous experience includes Automated Fingerprint Identification System (AFIS) software engineering and reserve police work. Bill has served as president and vice president for Computer Technology Investigators Northwest (CTIN) and is a member of Computer Related Information Management and Education (CRIME). He routinely lectures at several colleges and universities in the Pacific Northwest.

Amelia Phillips is a graduate of the Massachusetts Institute of Technology with B.S. degrees in astronautical engineering and archaeology and an MBA in technology management. After serving as an engineer at the Jet Propulsion Lab, she worked with e-commerce Web sites and began her training in computer forensics to prevent credit card numbers from being stolen from sensitive e-commerce databases. She designed certificate and AAS programs for community colleges in e-commerce, network security, computer forensics, and data recovery. She is currently tenured at Highline Community College in Seattle, Washington. Amelia is a Fulbright Scholar who taught at Polytechnic of Namibia in 2005 and 2006.

Christopher Steuart is a practicing attorney maintaining a general litigation practice, with experience in information systems security for a Fortune 50 company and the U.S. Army. He is also General Counsel for Computer Investigators Northwest (CTIN). He has presented computer forensics seminars in regional and national forums, including the American Society for Industrial Security (ASIS), Agora, Northwest Computer Technology Crime Analysis Seminar (NCT), and CTIN.

Acknowledgments

The team would like to express its appreciation to Acquisitions Editor Steve Helba, who has given us a great deal of moral support. We would like to thank the entire editorial and production staff for their dedication and fortitude during this project, including Michelle Ruelos Cannistraci, Senior Product Manager, and Jessica McNavich, Content Project Manager. Our special thanks go to Lisa Lord, the Developmental Editor. We also appreciate the careful reading and thoughtful suggestions of the

Technical Editor, John Bosco. We would like to thank the reviewers: Dean Farwood, Heald College, and Michael Goldner, ITT Technical Institute. We would also like to thank Franklin Clark, an investigator for the Pierce County Prosecutor in Tacoma, Washington, for his input, and Mike Lacey for his photos.

Bill Nelson

I want to express my appreciation to my wife, Tricia, for her support during the long hours spent writing, along with my mother, Celia, and in memory of my father, Harry for their encouragement these past years. I would also like to express appreciation to my coauthors along with our editors for the team effort in producing this book. And special thanks for the support and encouragement from my computer forensics colleagues: Franklin Clark of the Pierce County Prosecutor's Office, Tacoma, Washington; Detective Mike McNown, retired, Wichita PD; Scott Larson and Don Allison of Stoz Friedberg, LLC; Detectives Brian Palmer, Barry Walden, and Melissa Rogers of the King County Sheriff's Office, Seattle, Washington; John Sgromolo of Verizon; Art Ehuan of Digital First; Brett Shavers of e3Discovery; Clint Baker of the RCMP; Colin Cree of Forensic Data Recovery, Inc.; Chris Brown of Technology Pathways; Gordon Ross, formerly of Net Nanny; and Gordon Mitchell of Future Focus, Inc.

Amelia Phillips

My deepest gratitude goes to my coauthor Bill Nelson. I want to reiterate the thanks to Steve Helba and Lisa Lord for their patience and support. Acknowledgments go to my students who helped with research on determining what you can and can't do with a cell phone: Ron "Fry" Frymier, Rachel Sundstrom, Anne Weingart, Dave Wilson, Casey Draper, and Lynne Bowen. Acknowledgments also go to the fabulous group of students who put together the firestarter/arson case project used in the book. I would also like to thank the students from the Seattle area PDs and corporations who gave me a lot of case histories and insight. Thanks also go to Teressa Mobley, Detective Melissa Rogers, and Deb Buser who helped me with several cases and the cell phone software. Thanks go to my friends for their support, and special thanks to my aunties, who are all great teachers and set an excellent example for me.

Christopher K. Steuart

I would like to express my appreciation to my wife, Josephine, son, Alexander, and daughter, Isobel, for their enthusiastic support of my commitment to *Guide to Computer Forensics and Investigations*, even as it consumed time and energy that they deserved. I also want to express my thanks to my parents, William and Mary, for their support of my education and development of the skills needed for this project. I thank my coauthors for inviting me to join them in this project. I would like to express my appreciation to the Boy Scouts of America for providing me with the first of many leadership opportunities in my life. I want to recognize Lieutenant General (then Captain) Edward Soriano for seeing the potential in me as a young soldier and encouraging me in learning the skills required to administer, communicate with, and command an organization within the structure of law, regulation, and personal commitment. I must also thank the faculty of Drake University Law School, particularly Professor James A. Albert, for encouraging me to think and write creatively about the law. I also note the contribution of Diane Gagon and the staff of the Seattle Mission of the Church of Scientology in supporting my better understanding of commitment to myself and the others.

Photo Credits

Figure 1-3: 8088 computer courtesy of IBM Corporate Archives

chapter 1

Computer Forensics and Investigations as a Profession

After reading this chapter and completing the exercises, you will be able to:

- Define computer forensics
- Describe how to prepare for computer investigations and explain the difference between law enforcement agency and corporate investigations
- Explain the importance of maintaining professional conduct

In the past several years, the field of computer forensics and investigations has evolved significantly. This chapter introduces you to computer forensics and investigations and discusses some problems and concerns prevalent in the industry. This book blends traditional investigation methods with classic systems analysis problem-solving techniques and applies them to computer investigations. An understanding of these disciplines combined with the use of computer forensics tools will make you a highly skilled computer forensics examiner.

Understanding Computer Forensics

Computer forensics involves obtaining and analyzing digital information for use as evidence in civil, criminal, or administrative cases. The Federal Rules of Evidence (FRE) has controlled the use of digital evidence since 1970; from 1970 to 1985, state rules of evidence, as they were adopted by each state, controlled use of this type of evidence. The FBI Computer Analysis and Response Team (CART) was formed in 1984 to handle the increasing number of cases involving digital evidence. Figure 1-1 shows the home page for the FBI CART. By the late 1990s, CART had teamed up with the Department of Defense Computer Forensics Laboratory (DCFL) for research and training. Much of the early curriculum in this field came from the DCFL.

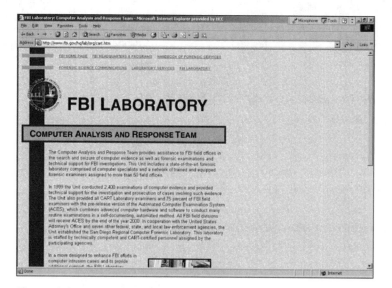

Figure 1-1 The FBI CART Web site

Documents maintained on a computer are covered by different rules, depending on the nature of the documents. Many court cases in state and federal courts have developed and clarified how the rules apply to digital evidence. The **Fourth Amendment** to the U.S. Constitution (and each state's constitution) protects everyone's rights to be secure in their person, residence, and property from search and seizure, for example. Continuing development of the jurisprudence of this amendment has played a role in determining whether the search for digital evidence has established a different precedent, so separate **search warrants** might not be necessary. However, when preparing to search for evidence in a criminal case, many investigators still include the suspect's computer and its components in the search warrant to avoid later admissibility problems.

In a significant case, the Pennsylvania Supreme Court addressed expectations of privacy and whether evidence is admissible (see *Commonwealth v. Copenhefer*, 587 A.2d 1353, 526 Pa. 555 [1991]). Initial investigations by the FBI, state police, and local police resulted in the discovery of a series of computer-generated notes and instructions, each one leading to another, which had been concealed in hiding places in and around Corry, Pennsylvania. The investigation also produced several possible suspects, including David Copenhefer, who owned a nearby bookstore and apparently had bad personal relations with the victim and her husband. Examination of trash discarded from Copenhefer's store revealed drafts of the ransom note and directions. Subsequent search warrants resulted in seizure of evidence against him. Copenhefer's computer contained several drafts and amendments of the text of the phone call to the victim on Thursday, the phone call to the victim's husband on Friday, the ransom note, the series of hidden notes, and a plan for the entire kidnapping scheme (*Copenhefer*, p. 559).

On direct appeal, the Pennsylvania Supreme Court concluded that the physical evidence, including the computer forensics evidence, was sufficient to support the bookstore owner's conviction. Copenhefer's argument was that "[E]ven though his computer was validly seized pursuant to a warrant, his attempted deletion of the documents in question created an expectation of privacy protected by the Fourth Amendment. Thus, he claims, under *Katz v. United States*, 389 U.S. 347, 357, 88 S.Ct. 507, 19 L.Ed.2d 576 (1967), and its progeny, Agent Johnson's retrieval of the documents, without first obtaining another search warrant, was unreasonable under the Fourth Amendment and the documents thus seized should have been suppressed" (*Copenhefer*, p. 561).

The Pennsylvania Supreme Court rejected this argument, stating "A defendant's attempt to secrete evidence of a crime is not synonymous with a legally cognizable expectation of privacy. A mere hope for secrecy is not a legally protected expectation. If it were, search warrants would be required in a vast number of cases where warrants are clearly not necessary" (*Copenhefer*, p. 562).

Almost every United States jurisdiction now has case law related to the admissibility of evidence recovered from computers. Canadian criminal law is primarily federal and generally enforced in provincial court.

The United States Department of Justice offers a useful guide to search and seizure procedures for computers and computer evidence at *www.usdoj.gov/criminal/cybercrime/s&smanual2002.htm*. This guide includes the 2006 update on search warrants and affidavits.

Computer Forensics Versus Other Related Disciplines

According to DIBS USA, Inc., a privately owned corporation specializing in computer forensics (*www.dibsusa.com*), computer forensics involves scientifically examining and analyzing data from computer storage media so that the data can be used as evidence in court. You can find a similar definition on the FBI's Web site (*www.fbi.gov/hq/lab/fsc/backissu/oct2000/computer.htm*). Typically, investigating computers includes collecting computer data securely, examining suspect data to determine details such as origin and content, presenting computer-based information to courts, and applying laws to computer practice.

In general, computer forensics investigates data that can be retrieved from a computer's hard drive or other storage media. Like an archaeologist excavating a site, computer investigators retrieve information from a computer or its component parts. The information you retrieve might already be on the drive, but it might not be easy to find or decipher. In contrast, network forensics yields information about how a perpetrator or an attacker gained access to a network.

Network forensics investigators use log files to determine when users logged on and determine which URLs users accessed, how they logged on to the network, and from what location. Keep in mind, however, that network forensics also tries to determine what tracks or new files were left behind on a victim's computer and what changes were made. In Chapter 11, you explore when and how network forensics should be used in your investigation.

Computer forensics is also different from **data recovery**, which involves recovering information from a computer that was deleted by mistake or lost during a power surge or server crash, for example. In data recovery, typically you know what you're looking for. Computer forensics is the task of recovering data that users have hidden or deleted, with the goal of ensuring that the recovered data is valid so that it can be used as evidence. The evidence can be **inculpatory** (in criminal cases, the expression is "incriminating") or **exculpatory**, meaning it might clear the suspect. Investigators often examine a computer disk not knowing whether it contains evidence. They must search storage media, and if they find data, they piece it together to produce evidence. Forensics software tools can be used for most cases. In extreme cases, investigators can use electron microscopes and other sophisticated equipment to retrieve information from machines that have been damaged or reformatted purposefully. This method is usually cost prohibitive, running from a low end of US$3,000 to more than US$20,000, so it's not normally used.

Like companies specializing in data recovery, companies specializing in **disaster recovery** use computer forensics techniques to retrieve information their clients have lost. Disaster recovery also involves preventing data loss by using backups, uninterruptible power supply (UPS) devices, and off-site monitoring.

Investigators often work as a team to make computers and networks secure in an organization. The computer investigations function is one of three in a triad that makes up computing security. In an enterprise network environment, the triad consists of the following parts (shown in Figure 1-2):

- Vulnerability assessment and risk management
- Network intrusion detection and incident response
- Computer investigations

Figure 1-2 The investigations triad

Each side of the triad in Figure 1-2 represents a group or department responsible for performing the associated tasks. Although each function operates independently, all three groups draw from one another when a large-scale computing investigation is being conducted. By combining these three groups into a team, all aspects of a high-technology investigation are addressed without calling in outside specialists.

The term **enterprise network environment** refers to large corporate computing systems that might include disparate or formerly independent systems. In smaller companies, one group might perform the tasks shown in the investigations triad, or a small company might contract with other companies for these services.

When you work in the **vulnerability assessment and risk management** group, you test and verify the integrity of standalone workstations and network servers. This integrity check covers the physical security of systems and the security of operating systems (OSs) and applications. People who work in this group test for known vulnerabilities of OSs and applications used in the network. This group also launches attacks on the network and its workstations and servers to assess vulnerabilities. Typically, people performing this task have several years of experience in UNIX and Windows administration.

Professionals in the vulnerability assessment and risk management group also need skills in **network intrusion detection and incident response**. This group detects intruder attacks by using automated tools and monitoring network firewall logs manually. When an external attack is detected, the response team tracks, locates, and identifies the intrusion method and denies further access to the network. If an intruder launches an attack that causes damage or potential damage, this team collects the necessary evidence, which can be used for civil or criminal litigation against the intruder. **Litigation** is the legal process of establishing criminal or civil liability in court.

If an internal user is engaged in illegal acts, the network intrusion detection and incident response group responds by locating the user and blocking his or her access. For example, someone at a community college sends inflammatory e-mails to other users on the network. The network team realizes that the e-mails are coming from a node on the internal network and dispatches a security team to the location. Vulnerability assessment staff often contribute significantly to computing investigations.

The **computer investigations** group manages investigations and conducts forensic analysis of systems suspected of containing evidence related to an incident or a crime. For complex casework, the computer investigations group draws on resources from those involved in vulnerability assessment, risk management, and network intrusion detection and incident response. This group resolves or terminates all case investigations.

A Brief History of Computer Forensics

Thirty years ago, most people didn't imagine that computers would be an integral part of everyday life. Now computer technology is commonplace, as are crimes in which a computer is the instrument of the crime, the target of the crime, and, by its nature, the location where evidence is stored or recorded.

By the 1970s, electronic crimes were increasing, especially in the financial sector. Most computers in this era were mainframes, used by trained people with specialized skills who worked in finance, engineering, and academia. White-collar fraud began when people in these industries saw a way to make money by manipulating computer data. One of the most well-known crimes of the mainframe era is the one-half cent crime. Banks commonly tracked money in accounts to the third decimal place or more. They used and still use the "rounding up" accounting method when paying interest. If the interest applied to an account resulted in a fraction of a cent, that fraction was used in the calculation for the next account until the total resulted in a whole cent. It was assumed that sooner or later every customer would benefit. Some computer programmers corrupted this method by opening an account for themselves and writing programs that diverted all the fractional monies into their accounts. In small banks, this practice amounted to only a few hundred dollars a month. In large banks with many branch offices, however, the amount reached hundreds of thousands of dollars.

During this time, most law enforcement officers didn't know enough about computers to ask the right questions or to preserve evidence for trial. Many began to attend the Federal Law Enforcement Training Center (FLETC) programs designed to train law enforcement in recovering digital data.

As PCs gained popularity and began to replace mainframe computers in the 1980s, many different OSs emerged. Apple released the Apple 2E in 1983 and then the Macintosh in 1984. Computers such as the TRS-80 and Commodore 64 were the machines of the day. CP/M machines, such as the Kaypro and Zenith, were also in demand.

Disk Operating System (DOS) was available in many varieties, including PC-DOS, QDOS, DR-DOS, IBM-DOS, and MS-DOS. Forensics tools at that time were simple, and most were generated by government agencies, such as the Royal Canadian Mounted Police (RCMP, which had its own investigative tools) and the U.S. Internal Revenue Service (IRS). Most tools were written in C and assembly language and weren't available to the general public.

In the mid-1980s, a new tool, Xtree Gold, appeared on the market. It recognized file types and retrieved lost or deleted files. Norton DiskEdit soon followed and became the preferred tool for finding deleted files. You could use these tools on the most powerful PCs of that time; IBM-compatible computers had 10 MB hard disks and two floppy drives, as shown in Figure 1-3.

Figure 1-3   An 8088 computer

In 1987, Apple produced the Mac SE, a Macintosh with an external EasyDrive hard disk with 60 MB of storage (see Figure 1-4). At this time, the popular Commodore 64 still used standard audiotapes to record data, so the Mac SE represented an important advance in computer technology.

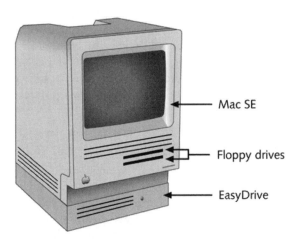

Mac SE

Floppy drives

EasyDrive

Figure 1-4   A Mac SE with an external EasyDrive hard disk

By the early 1990s, specialized tools for computer forensics were available. The **International Association of Computer Investigative Specialists (IACIS)** introduced training on software for forensics investigations, and the IRS created search-warrant programs. However, no commercial GUI software for computer forensics was available until ASR Data created Expert Witness for Macintosh. This software could recover deleted files and fragments of deleted files. One of the ASR Data partners later left and developed EnCase, which has become a popular computer forensics tool.

As computer technology continued to evolve, more computer forensics software was developed. The introduction of large hard disks posed new problems for investigators. Most DOS-based software didn't recognize a hard disk larger than 8 GB. Because contemporary computers have hard disks of 200 GB and larger, changes in forensics software were needed. Later in this book, you explore the challenges of using older software and hardware.

Other software, such as ILook, which is currently maintained by the IRS Criminal Investigation Division and limited to law enforcement, can analyze and read special files that are copies of a disk. AccessData Forensic Toolkit (FTK) has become a popular commercial product that performs similar tasks in the law enforcement and civilian markets, and you use it in several projects in this book.

As software companies become savvier about computer forensics and investigations, they are publishing more forensics tools to keep pace with technology. This book discusses as many tools as possible. You should also refer to trade publications and Web sites, such as *www. ctin.org* (Computer Technology Investigators Network) and *www.usdoj.gov* (U.S. Department of Justice), to stay current.

Understanding Case Law

The technology of computers and other digital devices is evolving at an exponential pace. Existing laws and statutes simply can't keep up with the rate of change. Therefore, when statutes or regulations don't exist, case law is used. Case law allows legal counsel to use previous cases similar to the current one and addresses the ambiguity in laws. Each new case is evaluated on its own merit and issues. The University of Rhode Island (*http://dfc. cs.uri.edu*) cites many cases in which problems occurred in the past. One example on the Web site is about an investigator viewing computer files by using a search warrant related to drug dealing. While viewing the files, he ran across images of child pornography. Instead of waiting for a new warrant, he kept searching. As a result, all evidence regarding the pictures was excluded. Investigators must be familiar with recent rulings to avoid making similar mistakes. Be aware that case law doesn't involve creating new criminal offenses, however.

Developing Computer Forensics Resources

To be a successful computer forensics investigator, you must be familiar with more than one computing platform. In addition to older platforms, such as DOS and Windows 9x, you should be familiar with Linux, Macintosh, and current Windows platforms. However, no one can be an expert in every aspect of computing. Likewise, you can't know everything about the technology you're investigating. To supplement your knowledge, you should develop and maintain contact with computing, network, and investigative professionals. Keep a log of contacts, and record the names of other professionals you've worked with, their areas of expertise, the most recent projects you worked on together, and their contributions.

Join computer user groups in both the public and private sectors. In the Pacific Northwest, for example, **Computer Technology Investigators Network (CTIN)** meets monthly to discuss problems that law enforcement and corporations face. This nonprofit organization also conducts free training. You can probably locate a similar group in your area, such as the **High Technology Crime Investigation Association (HTCIA)**, an organization that exchanges information about techniques related to computer investigations and security. (For more information, visit *www.htcia.org*.) In addition, build your own network of computer forensics experts and other professionals, and keep in touch through e-mail. Cultivate professional relationships with people who specialize in technical areas different from your own specialty. If you're a Windows expert, for example, maintain contact with experts in Linux, UNIX, and Macintosh.

User groups can be especially helpful when you need information about obscure OSs. For example, a user group helped convict a child molester in Pierce County, Washington, in 1996. The suspect installed video cameras throughout his house, served alcohol to young women to intoxicate them, and secretly filmed them playing strip poker. When he was accused of molesting a child, police seized his computers and other physical evidence. The investigator discovered that the computers used CoCo DOS, an OS that had been out of use for years. The investigator contacted a local user group, which supplied the standard commands and other information needed to gain access to the system. On the suspect's computer, the investigator found a diary detailing the suspect's actions over the past 15 years, including the molestation of more than 400 young women. As a result, the suspect received a longer sentence than if he had been convicted of molesting only one child.

Outside experts can provide detailed information you need to retrieve digital evidence. For example, a recent murder case involved a husband and wife who owned a Macintosh store. When the wife was discovered dead, apparently murdered, investigators found that she had wanted to leave her husband but didn't because of her religious beliefs. The police got a search warrant and confiscated the home and office computers. When the detective on the case examined the home Macintosh, he found that the hard drive had been compressed and erased. He contacted a Macintosh engineer, who determined the two software programs used to compress the drive. With this knowledge, the detective could retrieve information from the hard drive, including text files indicating that the husband spent $35,000 in business funds to purchase cocaine and prostitution services. This evidence proved crucial in making it possible to convict the husband of premeditated murder.

Take advantage of newsgroups, electronic mailing lists, and similar services devoted to computer forensics to solicit advice from experts. In one case, investigators couldn't access the hard disk of an Intel computer containing digital evidence without the password, which was hard-coded in the motherboard. When they began to run out of options and time, they posted a description of the problem on a mailing list. A list member told them that a dongle (a mechanical device) would bypass the password problem. As a result, the investigators were able to gather evidence to convict the perpetrator.

More recent cases involve laptops with specially designed ways of physically accessing the hard drives. Sometimes the manufacturer won't tell the average person who calls how to access a laptop's hard drive. Several investigators have had to go through law enforcement contacts to get this information—another example of the importance of developing good relationships with people in all aspects of the digital industry, not just other investigators.

Preparing for Computer Investigations

Computer investigations and forensics could be categorized several ways; for the purposes of this discussion, it falls into two distinct categories: public investigations and private or corporate investigations (see Figure 1-5).

Public investigations involve government agencies responsible for criminal investigations and prosecution. Government agencies range from local, county, and state or provincial police departments to federal regulatory enforcement agencies. These organizations must observe legal guidelines, such as Article 8 in the Charter of Rights of Canada, the Criminal Procedures Act of the Republic of Namibia, and U.S. Fourth Amendment issues of **search and seizure** (see Figure 1-6).

The law of search and seizure protects the rights of all people, including (and perhaps especially) people suspected of crimes; as a computer investigator, you must be sure to follow these laws. The Department of Justice (DOJ) updates information on computer search and seizure regularly (see *www.usdoj.gov/criminal/cybercrime/*).

Public investigations usually involve criminal cases and government agencies; private or corporate investigations, however, deal with private companies, non-law-enforcement government agencies, and lawyers. These private organizations aren't governed directly by **criminal law** or Fourth Amendment issues but by internal policies that define expected employee behavior and conduct in the workplace. Private corporate investigations can also involve litigation.

Private or corporate organizations
Company policy violations
Litigation disputes

Government agencies
Article 8 in the Charter of Rights of Canada
U.S. Fourth Amendment search
    and seizure rules

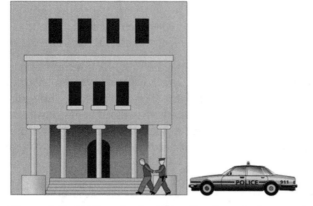
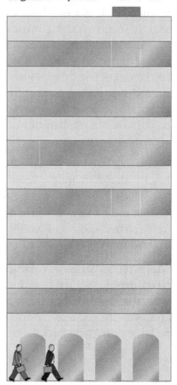

Figure 1-5 Public and private investigations

> *The right of the people to be secure in their persons, houses, papers, and effects, against unreasonable searches and seizures, shall not be violated, and no Warrants shall issue, but upon probable cause, supported by Oath or affirmation, and particularly describing the place to be searched, and the persons or things to be seized.*

Figure 1-6 The Fourth Amendment

Although private investigations are usually conducted in civil cases, a civil case can develop into a criminal case, and a criminal case can have implications leading to a civil case. If you follow good forensics procedures, the evidence found in your investigations can make the transition between civil and criminal cases.

Understanding Law Enforcement Agency Investigations

When conducting public computer investigations, you must understand city, county, state or province, and federal or national laws on computer-related crimes, including standard legal processes and how to build a criminal case. In a **criminal case**, a suspect is tried for a criminal offense, such as burglary, murder, molestation, or fraud. To determine whether there was a computer crime, an investigator asks questions such as the following: What was the tool used to commit the crime? Was it a simple trespass? Was it a theft, a burglary, or vandalism? Did the perpetrator infringe on someone else's rights by cyberstalking or e-mail harassment?

 Laws, including procedural rules, vary by jurisdiction and can be quite different. Therefore, this book points out when items accepted in U.S. courts don't stand up in other courts. Lately, a major issue has been European Union (EU) privacy laws as opposed to U.S. privacy laws. Issues related to international companies are still being defined. Over the past decade, more companies have been consolidating into global entities. As a result, internal corporate investigations can involve laws of multiple countries. For example, a company has a subsidiary operating in Australia. An employee at that subsidiary is suspected of fraud, and as part of your investigation, you need to seize his cell phone. Under U.S. law, you can if he used it on company property and synchronized it with the company network. Under Australian law, you cannot.

Computers and networks might be only tools used to commit crimes and are, therefore, no different from the lockpick a burglar uses to break into a house. For this reason, many states have added specific language to criminal codes to define crimes involving computers. For example, they have expanded the definition of laws for crimes such as theft to include taking data from a computer without the owner's permission, so computer theft is now on a par with shoplifting or car theft. Other states have instituted specific criminal statutes that address computer-related crimes but typically don't include computer-related issues in standard trespass, theft, vandalism, or burglary laws. The Computer Fraud and Abuse Act was passed in 1986, but specific state laws weren't formulated until later. To this day, many state laws on computer crime have yet to be tested in court.

Computers are involved in many serious crimes. The most notorious are those involving sexual exploitation of minors. Digital images are stored on hard disks, Zip disks, floppy disks, USB drives, removable hard drives, and other storage media and circulated on the Internet. Other computer crimes concern missing children and adults because information about missing people is often found on computers. Drug dealers often keep information about transactions on their computers or personal digital assistants (PDAs). This information is especially useful because it helps law enforcement officers convict the person they arrested and locate drug suppliers and other dealers. Additionally, in stalking cases, deleted e-mail, digital photos, and other evidence stored on a computer can help solve a case.

Following the Legal Processes

When conducting a computer investigation for potential criminal violations of the law, the legal processes you follow depend on local custom, legislative standards, and rules of evidence. In general, however, a criminal case follows three stages: the complaint, the investigation, and the prosecution (see Figure 1-7). Someone files a complaint; a specialist investigates the complaint and, with the help of a prosecutor, collects evidence and builds a case. If a crime has been committed, the case is tried in court.

Figure 1-7 The public-sector case flow

A criminal investigation can begin only when someone finds evidence of an illegal act or witnesses an illegal act. The witness or victim (often referred to as the "complainant") makes an **allegation** to the police, an accusation or supposition of fact that a crime has been committed.

A police officer interviews the complainant and writes a report about the crime. The police department processes the report, and management decides to start an investigation or log the information into a police blotter. The **police blotter** provides a record of clues to crimes that have been committed previously. Criminals often repeat actions in their illegal activities, and these habits can be discovered by examining police blotters. This historical knowledge is useful when conducting investigations, especially in high-technology crimes. Blotters now are generally electronic files, often databases, so they can be searched more easily than the old paper blotters.

Not every police officer is a computer expert. Some are computer novices; others might be trained to recognize what they can retrieve from a computer disk. To differentiate the training and experience officers have, CTIN has established three levels of law enforcement expertise:

- *Level 1*—Acquiring and seizing digital evidence, normally performed by a police officer on the scene.

- *Level 2*—Managing high-tech investigations, teaching investigators what to ask for, and understanding computer terminology and what can and can't be retrieved from digital evidence. The assigned detectives usually handle the case.

- *Level 3*—Specialist training in retrieving digital evidence, normally conducted by a data recovery or computer forensics expert, network forensics expert, or Internet fraud investigator. This person might also be qualified to manage a case, depending on his or her background.

If you're an investigator assigned to a case, recognize the level of expertise of police officers and others involved in the case. You should have Level 3 training to conduct the investigation and manage the computer forensics aspects of the case. You start by assessing the scope of the case, which includes the computer's OS, hardware, and peripheral devices. You then determine whether resources are available to process all the evidence. For example, collecting evidence is more difficult when information is stored on PDAs, cell phones, and other mobile devices. Determine whether you have the right tools to collect and analyze evidence and whether you need to call on other specialists to assist in collecting and processing evidence. After you have gathered the resources you need, your role is to delegate, collect, and process the information related to the complaint.

After you build a case, the information is turned over to the prosecutor. Your job is finished when you have used all known and available methods to extract data from the digital evidence that was seized. As an investigator, you must then present the collected evidence with a report to the government's attorney. Depending on the community and the nature of the crime, the prosecutor can be a prosecuting attorney, district attorney, state attorney, county attorney, Crown attorney, or U.S. attorney.

In a criminal or public case, if you have enough information to support a search warrant, the prosecuting attorney might direct you to submit an **affidavit**. This sworn statement of support of facts about or evidence of a crime is submitted to a judge with the request for a search warrant before seizing evidence. Figure 1-8 shows a typical affidavit. It's your responsibility to write the affidavit, which must include **exhibits** (evidence) that support the allegation to justify the warrant. You must then have the affidavit **notarized** under sworn oath to verify that the information in the affidavit is true. (You learn more about affidavits in Chapter 14.)

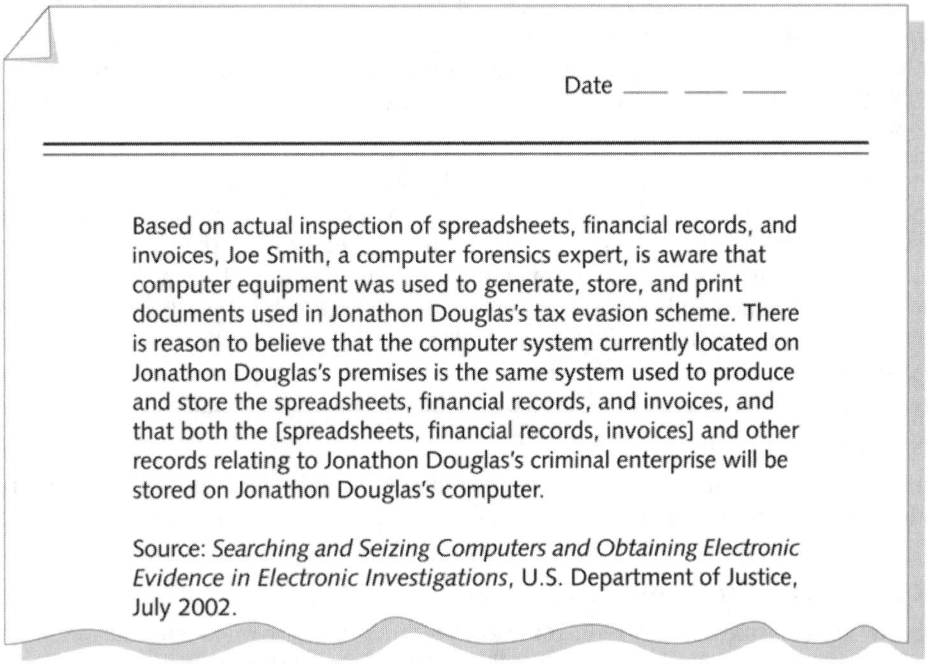

Date ___ ___ ___

Based on actual inspection of spreadsheets, financial records, and invoices, Joe Smith, a computer forensics expert, is aware that computer equipment was used to generate, store, and print documents used in Jonathon Douglas's tax evasion scheme. There is reason to believe that the computer system currently located on Jonathon Douglas's premises is the same system used to produce and store the spreadsheets, financial records, and invoices, and that both the [spreadsheets, financial records, invoices] and other records relating to Jonathon Douglas's criminal enterprise will be stored on Jonathon Douglas's computer.

Source: *Searching and Seizing Computers and Obtaining Electronic Evidence in Electronic Investigations*, U.S. Department of Justice, July 2002.

Figure 1-8   Typical affidavit language

After a judge approves and signs a search warrant, it's ready to be executed, meaning you can collect evidence as defined by the warrant. After you collect the evidence, you process and analyze it to determine whether a crime actually occurred. The evidence can then be presented in court in a hearing or trial. A judge or an administrative law judge then renders a judgment, or a jury hands down a **verdict** (after which a judge can enter a judgment).

Understanding Corporate Investigations

Private or corporate investigations involve private companies and lawyers who address company policy violations and litigation disputes, such as wrongful termination. When conducting a computer investigation for a private company, remember that business must continue with minimal interruption from your investigation. Because businesses usually focus on continuing their usual operations and making profits, many in a private corporate environment consider your investigation and apprehension of a suspect secondary to stopping the violation and minimizing damage or loss to the business. Businesses also strive to minimize or eliminate litigation, which is an expensive way to address criminal or civil issues. Corporate computer crimes can involve e-mail harassment, falsification of data, gender and age discrimination, embezzlement, sabotage, and **industrial espionage**, which involves selling sensitive or confidential company information to a competitor. Anyone with access to a computer can commit these crimes.

Embezzlement is a common computer crime, particularly in small firms. Typically, the owner is busy and trusts one person, such as the office manager, to handle daily transactions. When the office manager leaves, the owner discovers some clients were overbilled, others weren't billed at all, some payments weren't credited, or false accounts exist. Rebuilding the paper and electronic trail can be tedious. Collecting enough evidence to press charges might be beyond the owner's capabilities.

Corporate sabotage is most often committed by a disgruntled employee. For example, an employee decides to take a job at a competitor's firm and collects confidential files on a disk or USB drive before leaving. This type of crime can also lead to industrial espionage, which increases every year.

Investigators will soon be able to conduct digital investigations on site without a lab and without interrupting employees' work on a computer. Suppose an assisted-care facility has an employee involved in an insurance scam who is overcharging the insurance company and then funneling the monies into his or her own bank account. The facility's network server keeps track of patient billing and critical information, such as medication, medical conditions, and treatments, for each patient. Taking that system offline for more than a short time could result in harm to patients. For this reason, investigators can't seize the evidence; instead, they acquire a disk image and any other pertinent information and allow the system to go back online as quickly as possible.

Organizations can help prevent and address these crimes by creating and distributing appropriate policies, making employees aware of policies, and enforcing policies.

Establishing Company Policies

One way that businesses can reduce the risk of litigation is to publish and maintain policies that employees find easy to read and follow. The most important policies are those that set rules for using the company's computers and networks. Published company policies provide a **line of authority** for a business to conduct internal investigations. The line of authority states who has the legal right to initiate an investigation, who can take possession of evidence, and who can have access to evidence.

Well-defined policies give computer investigators and forensic examiners the authority to conduct an investigation. Policies also demonstrate that an organization intends to be fairminded and objective about how it treats employees and state that the organization will follow due process for all investigations. ("Due process" refers to fairness under the law and is meant to protect the innocent.) Without defined policies, a business risks exposing itself to litigation from current or former employees. The person or committee in charge of maintaining corporate policies must also stay current with local laws, which can vary depending on the city, state, and country.

Displaying Warning Banners

Another way a private or public organization can avoid litigation is to display a warning banner on computer screens. A **warning banner** usually appears when a computer starts or connects to the company intranet, network, or virtual private network (VPN) and informs end users that the organization reserves the right to inspect computer systems and network traffic at will. (An end user is a person using a computer to perform routine tasks other than system administration.) If this right isn't stated explicitly, employees might have an assumed right of privacy when using a company's computer systems and network accesses. With an assumed right of privacy, employees think their transmissions at work are protected in much the same way that mail sent via the U.S. Postal Service is protected. Figure 1-9 shows a sample warning banner.

Figure 1-9 A sample warning banner

A warning banner establishes the right to conduct an investigation. By displaying a strong, well-worded warning banner, an organization owning computer equipment doesn't need to obtain a search warrant or court order as required under Fourth Amendment search and seizure rules to seize the equipment. In a company with a well-defined policy, this right to inspect or search at will applies to both criminal activity and company policy violations. Keep in mind, however, that your country's laws might differ. For example, in some countries, even though the company has the right to seize computers at any time, if employees are suspected of a criminal act, they must be informed at that time.

Computer system users can include employees or guests. Employees can access the intranet, and guests can typically access only the main network. Companies can use two types of warning banners: one for internal employee access (intranet Web page access) and another for external visitor access (Internet Web page access). The following list recommends phrases to include in all warning banners. Before using these warnings, consult with the organization's legal department for other required legal notices for your work area or department. Depending on the type of organization, the following text can be used in internal warning banners:

- Access to this system and network is restricted.
- Use of this system and network is for official business only.
- Systems and networks are subject to monitoring at any time by the owner.
- Using this system implies consent to monitoring by the owner.
- Unauthorized or illegal users of this system or network will be subject to discipline or prosecution.

The DOJ document at *www.usdoj.gov/criminal/cybercrime/ s&smanual2002.htm* has several examples of warning banners.

An organization such as a community college might simply state that systems and networks are subject to observation and monitoring at any time because members of the local community who aren't staff or students might use the facilities. A for-profit organization, on the other hand, could have proprietary information on its network and use all the phrases suggested in the preceding list.

Guests, such as employees of business partners, might be allowed to use the system. The text that's displayed when a guest attempts to log on can include warnings similar to the following:

- This system is the property of Company X.
- This system is for authorized use only; unauthorized access is a violation of law and violators will be prosecuted.
- All activity, software, network traffic, and communications are subject to monitoring.

As a corporate computer investigator, make sure a company displays a well-defined warning banner. Without a banner, your authority to inspect might conflict with the user's expectation of privacy, and a court might have to determine the issue of authority to inspect. State laws vary on the expectation of privacy, but all states accept the concept of a waiver of the expectation of privacy. Additionally, the EU and its member nations impose strict fines for information that crosses national boundaries without the person's consent. So if your company is conducting an investigation in a subsidiary in the EU, you might not be able to acquire a network drive without notifying certain parties or making sure consent forms are in place.

Some might argue that written policies are all that are necessary. However, in the actual prosecution of cases, warning banners have been critical in determining that a system user didn't have an expectation of privacy for information stored on the system. A warning banner has the additional advantage of being easier to present in trial as an exhibit than a policy manual. Government agencies, such as the Department of Energy, Argonne National Labs, and Lawrence Livermore Labs, now require warning banners on all computer terminals on their systems. Many corporations also require warning banners as part of the logon/startup process.

Designating an Authorized Requester

As mentioned, investigations must establish a line of authority. In addition to using warning banners that state a company's rights of computer ownership, businesses are advised to specify an **authorized requester** who has the power to conduct investigations. Executive management should define this policy to avoid conflicts from competing interests between organizations or departments. In large organizations, competition for funding or management support can become so fierce that people sometimes create false allegations of misconduct to prevent a competing department from delivering a proposal for the same source of funds.

To avoid trivial or inappropriate investigations, executive management must also define and limit who is authorized to request a computer investigation and forensic analysis. Generally, the fewer groups with authority to request a computer investigation, the better. Examples of groups with authority to request computer investigations in a corporate environment include the following:

- Corporate security investigations
- Corporate ethics office
- Corporate equal employment opportunity office
- Internal auditing
- The general counsel or legal department

All other groups, such as the Human Resources Department, should coordinate their requests through the corporate security investigations group. This policy separates the investigative process from the process of employee discipline.

Conducting Security Investigations

Conducting a computer investigation in the private sector is not much different from conducting one in the public sector. During public investigations, you search for evidence to support criminal allegations. During private investigations, you search for evidence to support allegations of abuse of a company's assets and, in some cases, criminal complaints. Three types of situations are common in corporate environments:

- Abuse or misuse of computing assets
- E-mail abuse
- Internet abuse

Most computer investigations in the private sector involve misuse of computing assets. Typically, this misuse is referred to as "employee violation of company rules." Computing abuse complaints often center on e-mail and Internet misuse by employees but could involve other computing resources, such as using company software to produce a product for personal profit. The scope of an e-mail investigation ranges from excessive use of a company's e-mail system for personal use to making threats or harassing others via e-mail. Some common e-mail abuses involve transmitting offensive messages. These types of messages can create a **hostile work environment** that can result in an employee filing a civil lawsuit against a company that does nothing to prevent it (in other words, implicitly condones the e-mail abuse).

Computer investigators also examine Internet abuse. Employees' abuse of Internet privileges ranges from excessive use, such as spending all day Web surfing, to viewing pornographic pictures on the Web while at work. An extreme instance of Internet abuse is viewing contraband (illegal) pornographic images, such as child pornography. Viewing contraband images is a criminal act in most jurisdictions, and computer investigators must handle this situation with the highest level of professionalism. By enforcing policy consistently, a company minimizes its liability exposure. The role of a computer forensics examiner is to give management complete and accurate information so that they can verify and correct abuse problems in an organization. (In later chapters, you learn the procedures for conducting these types of investigations.)

Be sure to distinguish between a company's abuse problems and potential criminal violations. Abuse problems violate company policy but might not be illegal if performed at home. Criminal violations involve acts such as industrial espionage, embezzlement, and murder. However, actions that seem related to internal abuse could also have criminal or civil liability. Because any civil investigation can become a criminal investigation, you must treat all evidence you collect with the highest level of security and accountability. Later in this book, you learn the Federal Rules of Evidence (processes to ensure the chain of custody) and how to apply them to computing investigations.

Similarly, your private corporate investigation might seem to involve a civil, noncriminal matter, but as you progress through your analysis, you might identify a criminal matter, too. Because of this possibility, always remember that your work can come under the scrutiny of the civil or criminal legal system. The Federal Rules of Evidence are the same for civil and criminal matters. By applying the rules to all investigations uniformly, you eliminate any concerns. These standards are emphasized throughout this book.

Corporations can apply a principle similar to the **silver-platter doctrine** (no longer in effect between state law enforcement and the federal government) when a civilian or corporate investigative agent delivers evidence to a law enforcement officer. Remember that a police officer is a law enforcement agent. A corporate investigator's job is to minimize risk to the company. After you turn over evidence to law enforcement and begin working under their direction, you become an agent of law enforcement, subject to the same restrictions on search and seizure as a law enforcement agent. However, an agent of law enforcement can't ask you, as a private citizen, to obtain evidence that requires a warrant. The rules controlling the use of evidence collected by private citizens vary by jurisdiction, so check the law if you're investigating a case outside the United States.

Litigation is costly, so after you have assembled evidence, offending employees are usually disciplined or terminated with a minimum of fanfare. However, when you discover that a criminal act involving a third-party victim has been committed, generally you have a legal and moral obligation to turn the information over to law enforcement. In the next section, you learn about situations in which criminal evidence must be separated from any corporate proprietary information.

Distinguishing Personal and Company Property

Many company policies distinguish between personal and company computer property; however, making this distinction can be difficult with PDAs, cell phones, and personal notebook computers. For example, an employee has purchased a PDA and connects the device to his or her company computer. As the employee synchronizes information on the PDA with information in the company computer's copy of Microsoft Outlook, he or she copies some data in the PDA to the company network. During the synchronization, data on the company computer or network might be placed on the PDA, too. In this case, at least one question is "Does the information on the PDA belong to the company or the employee?"

Now suppose the company gave the employee the PDA as part of a holiday bonus. Can the company claim rights to the PDA? Similar issues come up when an employee brings in a personal notebook computer and connects it to the company network. What rules apply? As computers become more entrenched in daily life, you'll encounter these issues more often. These questions are still being debated, and companies are establishing their own policies to handle them. The safe policy is to not allow any personally owned devices to be connected to company-owned resources, thereby limiting the possibility of commingling personal and company data. This policy can be counterproductive; however, the risks should be identified and addressed in company policies. Other companies simply state that if you connect a personal device to the corporate network, it falls under the same rules as corporate property. At the time of this writing, this policy has yet to be tested in court.

Maintaining Professional Conduct

Your **professional conduct** as a computer investigation and forensics analyst is critical because it determines your credibility. Professional conduct, discussed in more detail in Chapters 15 and 16, includes ethics, morals, and standards of behavior. As a professional, you must exhibit the highest level of ethical behavior at all times. To do so, you must maintain objectivity and confidentiality during an investigation, expand your technical knowledge continuously, and conduct yourself with integrity. On any current crime drama, you can see how attorneys attack the character of witnesses, so your character and especially your reputation for honesty should be beyond reproach.

Maintaining objectivity means you must form and sustain unbiased opinions of your cases. Avoid making conclusions about your findings until you have exhausted all reasonable leads and considered the available facts. Your ultimate responsibility is to find digital evidence to support or refute the allegation. You must ignore external biases to maintain the integrity of your fact-finding in all investigations. For example, if you're employed by an attorney, do not allow the attorney's agenda to dictate the outcome of your investigation. Your reputation and long-term livelihood depend on being objective in all matters.

You must also maintain an investigation's credibility by keeping the case confidential. Discuss the case only with people who need to know about it, such as other investigators involved in the case or someone in the line of authority asking for an update. If you need advice from other professionals, discuss only the general terms and facts about the case without mentioning specifics. All investigations you conduct must be kept confidential, until you're designated as a witness or required by the attorney or court to release a report.

In the corporate environment, confidentiality is critical, especially when dealing with employees who have been terminated. The agreement between the company and the employee might have been to represent the termination as a layoff or resignation in exchange for no bad references. If you give case details and the employee's name to others, your company could be liable for breach of contract.

In some instances, your corporate case might become a criminal case as serious as murder. Because of the legal system, it could be years before the case goes to trial. If an investigator talks about the digital evidence with others, the case could be damaged because of pretrial publicity. When working for an attorney on an investigation, the attorney-work-product rule and attorney-client privilege apply to all communication. This means you can discuss the case only with the attorney or other members of the team working with the attorney. All communication about the case to other people requires the attorney's approval.

In addition to maintaining objectivity and confidentiality, you can enhance your professional conduct by continuing your training. The field of computer investigations and forensics is changing constantly. You should stay current with the latest technical changes in computer hardware and software, networking, and forensic tools. You should also learn about the latest investigation techniques you can use in your cases.

One way to enrich your knowledge of computer investigations is to record your fact-finding methods in a journal. A journal can help you remember how to perform tasks and procedures and use hardware and software tools. Be sure to include dates and important details that serve as memory triggers. Develop a routine of reviewing your journal regularly to keep your past achievements fresh in your mind.

To continue your professional training, you should attend workshops, conferences, and vendor courses. You might also need to continue your formal education. You enhance your professional standing if you have at least an undergraduate degree in computing or a related field. If you don't have an advanced degree, consider graduate-level studies in a complementary area of study, such as business law or e-commerce. Several colleges and universities now offer associate's, bachelor's, and master's degrees and certificate programs in computer forensics. Many companies are willing to reimburse your education costs, although some require commitment to a certain term of employment in exchange.

In addition to education and training, membership in professional organizations adds to your credentials. These organizations often sponsor training and offer information exchanges of the latest technical improvements and trends in computer investigations. Also, keep up to date with the most recent books and read as much as possible about computer investigations and forensics.

As a computer investigation and forensics professional, you're expected to maintain honesty and integrity. You must conduct yourself with the highest levels of integrity in all aspects of your life. Any indiscreet actions can embarrass you and give opposing attorneys opportunities to discredit you during your testimony in court or in depositions.

Chapter Summary

- Computer forensics applies forensics procedures to digital evidence. This process involves systematically accumulating and analyzing digital information for use as evidence in civil, criminal, or administrative cases. Computer forensics differs from network forensics, data recovery, and disaster recovery in scope, technique, and objective.

- Laws relating to digital evidence were established in the 1970s.

- To be a successful computer forensics investigator, you must be familiar with more than one computing platform. To supplement your knowledge, develop and maintain contact with computer, network, and investigative professionals.

- Public and private computer investigations differ, in that public investigations typically require a search warrant before seizing digital evidence. The Fourth Amendment to the U.S. Constitution and similar legislation in other countries apply to governmental search and seizure. During public investigations, you search for evidence to support criminal allegations. During private investigations, you search for evidence to support allegations of abuse of assets and, in some cases, criminal complaints.

- Warning banners should be used to remind employees and visitors of company policy on computer, e-mail, and Internet use.

- Companies should define and limit the number of authorized requesters who can start an investigation.

- Computer forensics investigators must maintain professional conduct to protect their credibility.

Key Terms

affidavit The document, given under penalty of perjury, that investigators create to detail their findings. This document is often used to justify issuing a warrant or to deal with abuse in a corporation.

allegation A charge made against someone or something before proof has been found.

authorized requester In a corporate environment, the person who has the right to request an investigation, such as the chief security officer or chief intelligence officer.

computer forensics The process of applying scientific methods to collect and analyze data and information that can be used as evidence.

computer investigations Conducting forensic analysis of systems suspected of containing evidence related to an incident or a crime.

Computer Technology Investigators Network (CTIN) A nonprofit group based in Seattle–Tacoma, WA, composed of law enforcement members, private corporation security professionals, and other security professionals whose aim is to improve the quality of high-technology investigations in the Pacific Northwest.

criminal case A case in which criminal law must be applied.

criminal law Statutes applicable to a jurisdiction that state offenses against the peace and dignity of the jurisdiction and the elements that define these offenses.

data recovery A specialty field in which companies retrieve files that were deleted accidentally or purposefully.

disaster recovery A specialty field in which companies perform real-time backups, monitoring, data recovery, and hot site operations.

enterprise network environment A large corporate computing system that can include formerly independent systems.

exculpatory Evidence that indicates the suspect is innocent of the crime.

exhibits Evidence used in court to prove a case.

Fourth Amendment The Fourth Amendment to the U.S. Constitution in the Bill of Rights dictates that the government and its agents must have probable cause for search and seizure.

High Technology Crime Investigation Association (HTCIA) A nonprofit association for solving international computer crimes.

hostile work environment An environment in which employees cannot perform their assigned duties because of the actions of others. In the workplace, these actions include sending threatening or demeaning e-mail or a co-worker viewing pornographic or hate sites.

inculpatory Evidence that indicates a suspect is guilty of the crime with which he or she is charged.

industrial espionage Selling sensitive or proprietary company information to a competitor.

International Association of Computer Investigative Specialists (IACIS) An organization created to provide training and software for law enforcement in the computer forensics field.

line of authority The order in which people or positions are notified of a problem; these people or positions have the legal right to initiate an investigation, take possession of evidence, and have access to evidence.

litigation The legal process leading to a trial with the purpose of proving criminal or civil liability.

network intrusion detection and incident response Detecting attacks from intruders by using automated tools; also includes the manual process of monitoring network firewall logs.

notarized Having a document witnessed and a person clearly identified as the signer by a notary public.

police blotter A log of criminal activity that law enforcement personnel can use to review the types of crimes currently being committed.

professional conduct Behavior expected of an employee in the workplace or other professional setting.

right of privacy The belief employees have that their transmissions at work are protected.

search and seizure The legal act of acquiring evidence for an investigation. *See also* Fourth Amendment.

search warrants Legal documents that allow law enforcement to search an office, a place of business, or other locale for evidence related to an alleged crime.

silver-platter doctrine A policy no longer in effect that allowed a state law enforcement officer to pass illegally obtained evidence to the federal government and allowed federal prosecution to use that evidence.

verdict The decision returned by a jury.

vulnerability assessment and risk management The group that determines the weakest points in a system. It covers physical security and the security of OSs and applications.

warning banner Text displayed on computer screens when people log on to a company computer; this text states ownership of the computer and specifies appropriate use of the machine or Internet access.

Review Questions

1. List two organizations mentioned in the chapter that provide computer forensics training.

2. Computer forensics and data recovery refer to the same activities. True or False?

3. Police in the United States must use procedures that adhere to which of the following?

    a. Third Amendment

    b. Fourth Amendment

    c. First Amendment

    d. None of the above

4. The triad of computing security includes which of the following?

    a. Detection, response, and monitoring

    b. Vulnerability assessment, detection, and monitoring

    c. Vulnerability assessment, intrusion response, and investigation

    d. Vulnerability assessment, intrusion response, and monitoring

5. List three common types of digital crime.

6. A corporate investigator must follow Fourth Amendment standards when conducting an investigation. True or False?

7. What is the purpose of maintaining a network of computer forensics specialists?

8. Policies can address rules for which of the following?

    a. When you can log on to a company network from home

    b. The Internet sites you can or cannot access

    c. The amount of personal e-mail you can send

    d. Any of the above

9. List two items that should appear on an internal warning banner.

10. Warning banners are often easier to present in court than policy manuals are. True or False?

11. Under normal circumstances, a corporate investigator is considered an agent of law enforcement. True or False?

12. List two types of computer investigations typically conducted in the corporate environment.

13. What is professional conduct and why is it important?

14. What is the purpose of maintaining a professional journal?

15. Laws and procedures for PDAs are which of the following?

    a. Well established

    b. Still being debated

    c. On the law books

    d. None of the above

16. Why should companies appoint an authorized requester for computer investigations?

17. What is the purpose of an affidavit?

18. What are the necessary components of a search warrant?

Hands-On Projects

Hands-On Project 1-1

Use a Web search engine, such as Google or Yahoo!, and search for companies specializing in computer forensics. Select three and write a two-to three-page paper comparing what each company does.

Hands-On Project 1-2

Research criminal law related to computer crime in a jurisdiction (the one where you live) that controls criminal law. If laws exist, list the source and how long they have been in existence. Identify cases that have been tried using these laws.

Hands-On Project 1-3

Start your own list of professional contacts in your area who do forensic analysis. Where would you begin to find these people? How can you verify that they're legitimate? How should you approach them?

Hands-On Project 1-4

Compare Article 8 of the Charter of Rights of Canada or any country of your choice to the U.S. Fourth Amendment. How do they differ? How are they similar? Use sources such as the U.S. Department of Justice Web site to justify your conclusions in a paper at least two pages long.

Hands-On Project 1-5

Search the Internet for articles on computer crime prosecutions. Find at least two. Write one to two pages summarizing the two articles and identify key features of the decisions you find in your search.

Hands-On Project 1-6

Is there a high-tech criminal investigation unit in or near your community? If so, who are the participants? E-mail the person in charge and let him or her know you are taking a course in computer forensics. Ask what the unit's policies and procedures are, and then write one to two pages summarizing your findings.

Hands-On Project 1-7

Start building a professional journal for yourself. Find at least two electronic mailing lists you can join and three Web sites and read them on a regular basis. The electronic mailing lists should contain areas for OSs, software and hardware listings, people contacted or worked with, user groups, other electronic mailing lists, and the results of any research you have done thus far.

Hands-On Project 1-8

Examine and summarize your community, state, or country's rules for search and seizure of criminal evidence. What concerns do you have after reading them?

Case Projects

CASE PROJECTS

Case Project 1-1

A lawyer in a law firm is suspected of embezzling money from a trust account. Who should conduct the investigation? If evidence is found to support the claim, what should be done? Write at least two pages explaining the steps to take, who is involved, and what items must be considered.

Case Project 1-2

A private corporation suspects an employee is using password-cracking tools to gain access to other accounts. The accounts include employees in the Payroll and Human Resources departments. Write a two-to three-page paper outlining what steps to take, who should be involved, and what should be considered.

Case Project 1-3

An employee is suspected of operating his llama business with a company computer. It's been alleged that he's tracking the sales price of the wool and the cost of feed and upkeep on spreadsheets. What should the employer do? Write at least two pages explaining the tasks an investigator should perform.

chapter 2

Understanding Computer Investigations

After reading this chapter and completing the exercises, you will be able to:

- Explain how to prepare a computer investigation
- Apply a systematic approach to an investigation
- Describe procedures for corporate high-tech investigations
- Explain requirements for data recovery workstations and software
- Describe how to conduct an investigation
- Explain how to complete and critique a case

This chapter gives you an overview of how to manage a computing investigation. You learn about the problems and challenges forensic examiners face when preparing and processing investigations, including the ideas and questions they must consider. This chapter introduces ProDiscover Basic, a GUI computer forensics tool. Throughout this chapter, you learn details about how other computer forensics tools are used in an investigation, too. You also explore standard problem-solving techniques.

As a basic computer user, you can solve most software problems by working with a GUI tool. A forensics professional, however, needs to interact with primary levels of the OS that are more fundamental than what can be accessed with GUI. Some computer forensics software tools involve working at the command line, and you should learn how to use these tools because in some cases, the command line is your only option. Appendix D includes examples of how to use DOS forensics tools.

In this chapter, you work with forensic disk images from small USB drives to perform the activities and projects in this chapter. After you know how to search for and find data on a small storage device, you can apply the same techniques to a large disk.

Preparing a Computer Investigation

Your role as a computer forensics professional is to gather evidence from a suspect's computer and determine whether the suspect committed a crime or violated a company policy. If the evidence suggests that a crime or policy violation has been committed, you begin to prepare a case, which is a collection of evidence you can offer in court or at a corporate inquiry. This process involves investigating the suspect's computer and then preserving the evidence on a different computer. Before you begin investigating, however, you must follow an accepted procedure to prepare a case. By approaching each case methodically, you can evaluate the evidence thoroughly and document the chain of evidence, or **chain of custody**, which is the route the evidence takes from the time you find it until the case is closed or goes to court.

The following sections present two sample cases—one involving a computer crime and another involving a company policy violation. Each example describes the typical steps of a forensics investigation, including gathering evidence, preparing a case, and preserving the evidence.

An Overview of a Computer Crime

Law enforcement officers often find computers and computer components as they're investigating crimes, gathering other evidence, or making arrests. Computers can contain information that helps law enforcement officers determine the chain of events leading to a crime or information providing evidence that's more likely to lead to a conviction. As an example of a case in which computers were involved in a crime, the police raided a suspected drug dealer's home and found a computer, several floppy disks and USB drives (also called keychain drives or memory sticks), a personal digital assistant (PDA), and a cell phone in a bedroom (see Figure 2-1). The computer was "bagged and tagged," meaning it was placed in evidence bags along with the storage media and then labeled with tags as part of the search and seizure.

Figure 2-1   The crime scene

The lead detective on the case wants you to examine the computer to find and organize data that could be evidence of a crime, such as files containing names of the drug dealer's contacts. The acquisitions officer gives you documentation of items the investigating officers collected with the computer, including a list of other storage media, such as removable disks and CDs. The acquisitions officer also notes that the computer is a Windows XP system, and the machine was running when it was discovered. Before shutting down the computer, the acquisitions officer photographs all open windows on the Windows desktop, including one showing Windows Explorer, and gives you the photos. (Before shutting down the computer, a live acquisition should be done to capture RAM, too. This procedure is discussed in Chapter 11.)

As a computer forensics investigator, you're grateful the officers followed proper procedure when acquiring the evidence. With digital evidence, it's important to realize how easily key data, such as the last access date, can be altered by an overeager investigator who's first on the scene. The U.S. Department of Justice (DOJ) has a document you can download that reviews proper acquisition of electronic evidence, including the search and seizure of computers (*www.usdoj.gov/criminal/cybercrime/s&smanual2002.htm*). If this link has changed because of site updates, use the search feature.

In your preliminary assessment, you assume that the hard disk and storage media include intact files, such as e-mail messages, deleted files, and hidden files. A range of software is available for use in your investigation; your office uses the tool Technology Pathways ProDiscover.

This chapter introduces you to the principles applied to computer forensics. In Chapter 7, you learn the strengths and weaknesses of several software packages.

Because some cases involve computers running legacy OSs, older versions of tools often need to be used in forensics investigations. For example, Norton DiskEdit is an older tool that was last available on the Norton System Works 2000 CD.

After your preliminary assessment, you identify the potential challenges in this case. Because drug dealers don't usually make information about their accomplices available, the files on the disks you received are probably **password protected**. You might need to acquire **password-cracking software** or find an expert who can help you decrypt a file.

Later, you perform the steps needed to investigate the case, including how to address risks and obstacles. Then you can begin the actual investigation and data retrieval.

An Overview of a Company Policy Violation

Companies often establish policies for employee use of computers. Employees surfing the Internet, sending personal e-mail, or using company computers for personal tasks during work hours can waste company time. Because lost time can cost companies millions of dollars, computer forensics specialists are often used to investigate policy violations. The following example describes a company policy violation.

Manager Steve Billings has been receiving complaints from customers about the job performance of one of his sales representatives, George Montgomery. George has worked as a representative for several years. He's been absent from work for two days but hasn't called in sick or told anyone why he wouldn't be at work. Another employee, Martha, is also missing and hasn't informed anyone of the reason for her absence. Steve asks the IT Department to confiscate George's hard drive and all storage media in his work area. He wants to know whether there's any information on George's computer and storage media that might offer a clue to George's whereabouts and job performance concerns. To help determine George and Martha's whereabouts, you must take a systematic approach, described in the following section, to examining and analyzing the data found on George's desk.

Taking a Systematic Approach

When preparing a case, you can apply standard systems analysis steps, explained in the following list, to problem solving. Later in this chapter, you apply these steps to cases.

- *Make an initial assessment about the type of case you're investigating*—To assess the type of case you're handling, talk to others involved in the case and ask questions about the incident. Have law enforcement or company security officers already seized the computer, disks, and other components? Do you need to visit an office or another location? Was the computer used to commit a crime, or does it contain evidence about another crime?

- *Determine a preliminary design or approach to the case*—Outline the general steps you need to follow to investigate the case. If the suspect is an employee and you need to acquire his or her system, determine whether you can seize the computer during work hours or have to wait until evening or weekend hours. If you're preparing a criminal case, determine what information law enforcement officers have already gathered.

- *Create a detailed checklist*—Refine the general outline by creating a detailed checklist of steps and an estimated amount of time for each step. This outline helps you stay on track during the investigation.

- *Determine the resources you need*—Based on the OS of the computer you're investigating, list the software you plan to use for the investigation, noting any other software or tools you might need.

- *Obtain and copy an evidence drive*—In some cases, you might be seizing multiple computers along with Zip disks, Jaz drives, CDs, USB drives, PDAs, and other removable media. (For the examples in this chapter, you're using only USB drives.) Make a forensic copy of the disk.

- *Identify the risks*—List the problems you normally expect in the type of case you're handling. This list is known as a standard risk assessment. For example, if the suspect seems knowledgeable about computers, he or she might have set up a logon scheme that shuts down the computer or overwrites data on the hard disk when someone tries to change the logon password.

- *Mitigate or minimize the risks*—Identify how you can minimize the risks. For example, if you're working with a computer on which the suspect has likely password-protected the hard drive, you can make multiple copies of the original media before starting. Then if you destroy a copy during the process of retrieving information from the disk, you have additional copies.

- *Test the design*—Review the decisions you've made and the steps you've completed. If you have already copied the original media, a standard part of testing the design involves comparing hash values (discussed in Chapters 4 and 5) to ensure that you copied the original media correctly.

- *Analyze and recover the digital evidence*—Using the software tools and other resources you've gathered, and making sure you've addressed any risks and obstacles, examine the disk to find digital evidence.

- *Investigate the data you recover*—View the information recovered from the disk, including existing files, deleted files, and e-mail, and organize the files to help prove the suspect's guilt or innocence.

- *Complete the case report*—Write a complete report detailing what you did and what you found.

- *Critique the case*—Self-evaluation is an essential part of professional growth. After you complete a case, review it to identify successful decisions and actions and determine how you could have improved your performance.

The amount of time and effort you put into each step varies, depending on the nature of the investigation. For example, in most cases, you need to create a simple investigation plan so that you don't overlook any steps. However, if a case involves many computers with complex issues to identify and examine, a detailed plan with periodic review and updates is essential. A systematic approach helps you discover the information you need for your case, and you should gather as much information as possible.

For all computing investigations, you must be prepared for the unexpected, so you should always have a contingency plan for the investigation. A contingency plan can consist of anything to help you complete the investigation, from alternative software and hardware tools to other methods of approaching the investigation.

Assessing the Case

As mentioned, identifying case requirements involves determining the type of case you're investigating. Doing so means you should outline the case details systematically, including the nature of the case, the type of evidence available, and the location of the evidence.

In the company-policy violation case, you have been asked to investigate George Montgomery. Steve Billings had the IT Department confiscate all of George's storage media that might contain information about his whereabouts. After talking to George's co-workers, Steve learned that George has been conducting a personal business on the side using company computers. Therefore, the focus of the case has changed from a missing person to a possible employee abuse of corporate resources. You can begin assessing this case as follows:

- *Situation*—Employee abuse case.
- *Nature of the case*—Side business conducted on the employer's computer.
- *Specifics of the case*—The employee is reportedly conducting a side business on his employer's computer that involves registering domain names for clients and setting up their Web sites at local ISPs. Co-workers have complained that he's been spending too much time on his own business and not performing his assigned work duties. Company policy states that all company-owned computing assets are subject to inspection by company management at any time. Employees have no expectation of privacy when operating company computer systems.
- *Type of evidence*—Small-capacity USB drive.
- *Operating system*—Microsoft Windows XP.
- *Known disk format*—FAT16.
- *Location of evidence*—One USB drive recovered from the employee's assigned computer.

Based on these details, you can determine the case requirements. You now know that the nature of the case involves employee abuse of company assets, and you're looking for evidence that an employee was conducting a side business using his employer's computers. On the USB drive retrieved from George's computer, you're looking for any information related to Web sites, ISPs, or domain names. You know that the computer OS is Windows XP, and the USB drive uses the FAT16 file system. To duplicate the USB drive and find deleted and hidden files, you need a reliable computer forensics tool. Because the USB drive has already been retrieved, you don't need to seize the drive yourself.

You call this case the Domain Name case and determine that your task is to gather data from the storage media seized to confirm or deny the allegation that George is conducting a side business on company time and computers. Remember that he's suspected only of asset abuse, and the evidence you obtain might be exculpatory—meaning it could prove his innocence. You must always maintain an unbiased perspective and be objective in your fact-findings. If you are systematic and thorough, you're more likely to produce consistently reliable results.

Planning Your Investigation

Now that you have identified the requirements of the Domain Name case, you can plan your investigation. You have already determined the kind of evidence you need; now you can identify the specific steps to gather the evidence, establish a chain of custody, and perform the forensic analysis. These steps become the basic plan for your investigation and indicate what you should do and when. To investigate the Domain Name case, you should perform the following general steps. Most of these steps are explained in more detail in the following sections.

1. Acquire the USB drive from George's manager.
2. Complete an evidence form and establish a chain of custody.
3. Transport the evidence to your computer forensics lab.
4. Place the evidence in an **approved secure container**.
5. Prepare your forensic workstation.
6. Retrieve the evidence from the secure container.
7. Make a forensic copy of the evidence drive (in this case, the USB drive).
8. Return the evidence drive to the secure container.
9. Process the copied evidence drive with your computer forensics tools.

TIP

The approved secure container you need in Step 4 should be a locked, fireproof locker or cabinet that has limited access. Limited access means that only you and other authorized personnel can open the evidence container.

The first rule for all investigations is to preserve the evidence, which means it should not be tampered with or contaminated. Because the IT Department staff confiscated the storage media, you need to go to them for the evidence. The IT Department manager confirms that the storage media has been locked in a secure cabinet since it was retrieved from George's desk. Keep in mind that even though this case is a corporate policy matter, many cases are thrown out because the chain of custody can't be proved or has been broken. When this happens, there's the possibility that the evidence has been compromised.

To document the evidence, you record details about the media, including who recovered the evidence and when and who possessed it and when. Use an **evidence custody form**, also called a chain-of-evidence form, which helps you document what has and has not been done with the original evidence and forensic copies of the evidence.

Depending on whether you're working in law enforcement or private corporate security, you can create an evidence custody form to fit your environment. This form should be easy to read and use. It can contain information for one or several pieces of evidence. Consider creating a **single-evidence form** (which lists each piece of evidence on a separate page) and a **multi-evidence form** (see Figure 2-2), depending on the administrative needs of your investigation.

If necessary, document how to use your evidence custody form. Clear instructions help users remain consistent when completing the form and ensure that everyone uses the same definitions for collected items. Standardization helps maintain consistent quality for all investigations and prevent confusion and mistakes about the evidence you collect.

Corporation X			
Security Investigations			
This form is to be used for one to ten pieces of evidence			
Case No.:		Investigating Organization:	
Investigator:			
Nature of Case:			
Location where evidence was obtained:			

	Description of evidence:	Vendor Name	Model No./Serial No.
Item #1			
Item #2			
Item #3			
Item #4			
Item #5			
Item #6			
Item #7			
Item #8			
Item #9			
Item #10			

Evidence Recovered by:		Date & Time:	
Evidence Placed in Locker:		Date & Time:	

Item #	Evidence Processed by	Disposition of Evidence	Date/Time
			Page ___ of ___

Figure 2-2   A sample multi-evidence form used in a corporate environment

An evidence custody form usually contains the following information:

- *Case number*—The number your organization assigns when an investigation is initiated.

- *Investigating organization*—The name of your organization. In large corporations with global facilities, several organizations might be conducting investigations in different geographic areas.

- *Investigator*—The name of the investigator assigned to the case. If many investigators are assigned, specify the lead investigator's name.

- *Nature of case*—A short description of the case. For example, in the corporate environment, it might be "Data recovery for corporate litigation" or "Employee policy violation case."

- *Location evidence was obtained*—The exact location where the evidence was collected. If you're using multi-evidence forms, a new form should be created for each location.

- *Description of evidence*—A list of the evidence items, such as "hard drive, 20 GB" or "one USB drive, 128 MB." On a multi-evidence form, write a description for each item of evidence you acquire.

- *Vendor name*—The name of the manufacturer of the computer evidence. List a 20 GB hard drive, for example, as a Maxtor 20 GB hard drive, or describe a USB drive as an

Attache 1 GB PNY Technologies drive. In later chapters, you see how differences among manufacturers can affect data recovery.

- *Model number or serial number*—List the model number or serial number (if available) of the computer component. Many computer components, including hard drives, memory chips, and expansion slot cards, have model numbers but not serial numbers.

- *Evidence recovered by*—The name of the investigator who recovered the evidence. The chain of custody for evidence starts with this information. If you insert your name, for example, you're declaring that you have taken control of the evidence. It's now your responsibility to ensure that nothing damages the evidence and no one tampers with it. The person placing his or her name on this line is responsible for preserving, transporting, and securing the evidence.

- *Date and time*—The date and time the evidence was taken into custody. This information establishes exactly when the chain of custody starts.

- *Evidence placed in locker*—Specifies which approved secure container is used to store evidence and when the evidence was placed in the container.

- *Item #/Evidence processed by/Disposition of evidence/Date/Time*—When you or another authorized investigator retrieves evidence from the evidence locker for processing and analysis, list the item number and your name, and then describe what was done to the evidence.

- *Page*—The forms used to catalog all evidence for each location should have page numbers. List the page number, and indicate the total number of pages for this group of evidence. For example, if you collected 15 pieces of evidence at one location and your form has only 10 lines, you need to fill out two multi-evidence forms. The first form is noted as "Page 1 of 2," and the second page is noted as "Page 2 of 2."

Figure 2-3 shows a single-evidence form, which lists only one piece of evidence per page. This form gives you more flexibility in tracking separate pieces of evidence for your chain-of-custody log. It also has more space for descriptions, which is helpful when finalizing the investigation and creating a case report. With this form, you can accurately account for what was done to the evidence and what was found. Use evidence forms as a reference for all actions taken during your investigative analysis.

You can use both multi-evidence and single-evidence forms in your investigation. By using two forms, you can keep the single-evidence form with the evidence and the multi-evidence form in your report file. Two forms also provide redundancy that can be used as a quality control for your evidence.

Securing Your Evidence

Computing investigations demand that you adjust your procedures to suit the case. For example, if the evidence for a case includes an entire computer system and associated storage media, such as floppy disks, Zip and Jaz cartridges, 4 mm DDS digital audio tape (DAT), and USB drives, you must be flexible when you account for all these items. Some evidence is small enough to fit into an evidence bag. Other items, such as the CPU cabinet, monitor, keyboard, and printer, are too large.

To secure and catalog the evidence contained in large computer components, you can use large **evidence bags**, tape, tags, labels, and other products available from police supply

Metropolis Police Bureau
High-tech Investigations Unit
This form is to be used for only one piece of evidence.
Fill out a separate form for each piece of evidence.

Case No.:		Unit Number:	
Investigator:			
Nature of Case:			
Location where evidence was obtained:			

Item # ID	Description of evidence:	Vendor Name	Model No./Serial No.
Evidence Recovered by:		Date & Time:	
Evidence Placed in Locker:		Date & Time:	

Evidence Processed by	Disposition of Evidence	Date/Time
		Page ___ of ___

Figure 2-3 A single-evidence form

vendors or office supply stores. When gathering products to secure your computer evidence, make sure they are safe and effective to use on computer components. Be cautious when handling any computer component to avoid damaging the component or coming into contact with static electricity, which can destroy digital data. For this reason, make sure you use antistatic bags when collecting computer evidence. Consider using an antistatic pad with an attached wrist strap, too. Both help prevent damage to computer evidence.

Be sure to place computer evidence in a well-padded container. Padding prevents damage to the evidence as you transport it to your secure evidence locker, evidence room, or computer lab. Save discarded hard drive boxes, antistatic bags, and packing material for computer hardware when you or others acquire computer devices.

Because you might not have everything needed to secure your evidence, you have to improvise. Securing evidence often requires building secure containers. If the computer component is large and contained in its own casing, such as a CPU cabinet, you can use evidence tape to seal all openings on the cabinet. Placing evidence tape over drive bays, insertion slots for power supply cords and USB cables, and any other openings ensures the security of evidence. As a standard practice, you should write your initials on the tape before applying it to the evidence. This practice makes it possible to prove later in court that the evidence hasn't been tampered with because the casing couldn't have been opened nor could power have been supplied to the closed casing with this tape in place. If the tape had been replaced, your initials wouldn't be present, which would indicate tampering. If you transport a CPU case, place new disks in disk drives to reduce possible drive damage while you're moving the computer.

Computer components require specific temperature and humidity ranges. If it's too cold, hot, or wet, computer components and magnetic media can be damaged. Even heated car seats can damage digital media, and placing a computer on top of a two-way car radio in the trunk can damage magnetic media. When collecting computer evidence, make sure you have a safe environment for transporting and storing it until a secure evidence container is available.

Procedures for Corporate High-Tech Investigations

As an investigator, you need to develop formal procedures and informal checklists to cover all issues important to high-tech investigations. These procedures are necessary to ensure that correct techniques are used in an investigation. Use informal checklists to be certain that all evidence is collected and processed properly. This section lists some sample procedures that computing investigators commonly use in corporate high-tech investigations.

Employee Termination Cases

The majority of investigative work for termination cases involves employee abuse of corporate assets. Incidents that create a hostile work environment, such as viewing pornography in the workplace and sending inappropriate e-mail messages, are the predominant types of cases investigated. The following sections describe key points for conducting an investigation that might lead to an employee's termination. Consulting with your organization's general counsel and Human Resources Department for specific directions on how to handle these investigations is recommended. Your organization must have appropriate policies in place, as described in Chapter 1.

Internet Abuse Investigations

The information in this section applies to an organization's internal private network, not a public ISP. Consult with your organization's general counsel after reviewing this list, and make changes according to their directions to build your own procedures. To conduct an investigation involving Internet abuse, you need the following:

- The organization's Internet proxy server logs
- Suspect computer's IP address obtained from your organization's network administrator
- Suspect computer's disk drive
- Your preferred computer forensics analysis tool (ProDiscover, Forensic Toolkit, EnCase, X-Ways Forensics, and so forth)

The following steps outline the recommended processing of an Internet abuse case:

1. Use the standard forensic analysis techniques and procedures described in this book for the disk drive examination.

2. Using tools such as DataLifter or Forensic Toolkit's Internet keyword search option, extract all Web page URL information.

3. Contact the network firewall administrator and request a proxy server log, if it's available, of the suspect computer's network device name or IP address for the dates of interest. Consult with your organization's network administrator to confirm that

these logs are maintained and how long the time to live (TTL) is set for the network's IP address assignments that use Dynamic Host Configuration Protocol (DHCP).

4. Compare the data recovered from forensic analysis to the proxy server log data to confirm that they match.

5. If the URL data matches the proxy server log and the forensic disk examination, continue analyzing the suspect computer's drive data, and collect any relevant downloaded inappropriate pictures or Web pages that support the allegation. If there are no matches between the proxy server logs, and the forensic examination shows no contributing evidence, report that the allegation is unsubstantiated.

Before investigating an Internet abuse case, research your state or country's privacy laws. Many countries have unique privacy laws that restrict the use of computer log data, such as proxy server logs or disk drive cache files, for any type of investigation. Some state or federal laws might supersede your organization's employee policies. Always consult with your organization's attorney. For companies with international business operations, jurisdiction is a problem; what is legal in the United States, such as examining and investigating a proxy server log, might not be legal in Germany, for example.

For investigations in which the proxy server log doesn't match the forensic analysis that found inappropriate data, continue the examination of the suspect computer's disk drive. Determine when inappropriate data was downloaded to the computer and whether it was through an organization's intranet connection to the Internet. Employees might have used their employer's laptop computers to connect to their own ISPs to download inappropriate Web content. For these situations, you need to consult your organization's employee policy guidelines for what's considered appropriate use of the organization's computing assets.

E-mail Abuse Investigations

E-mail investigations typically include spam, inappropriate and offensive message content, and harassment or threats. E-mail is subject to the same restrictions as other computer evidence data, in that an organization must have a defined policy, as described in Chapter 1. The following list is what you need for an investigation involving e-mail abuse:

- An electronic copy of the offending e-mail that contains message header data; consult with your e-mail server administrator

- If available, e-mail server log records; consult with your e-mail server administrator to see whether they are available

- For e-mail systems that store users' messages on a central server, access to the server; consult with your e-mail server administrator

- For e-mail systems that store users' messages on a computer as an Outlook .pst or .ost file, for example, access to the computer so that you can perform a forensic analysis on it

- Your preferred computer forensics analysis tool, such as Forensic Toolkit or ProDiscover

This is the recommended procedure for e-mail investigations:

1. For computer-based e-mail data files, such as Outlook .pst or .ost files, use the standard forensic analysis techniques and procedures described in this book for the drive examination.

2. For server-based e-mail data files, contact the e-mail server administrator and obtain an electronic copy of the suspect and victim's e-mail folder or data.

3. For Web-based e-mail investigations, such as Hotmail or Gmail, use tools such as Forensic Toolkit's Internet keyword search option to extract all related e-mail address information.

4. Examine header data of all messages of interest to the investigation.

Attorney-Client Privilege Investigations

When conducting a computer forensics analysis under **attorney-client privilege (ACP)** rules for an attorney, you must keep all findings confidential. The attorney you're working for is the ultimate authority over the investigation. For investigations of this nature, attorneys typically request that you extract all data from drives. It's your responsibility to comply with the attorney's directions. Because of the large quantities of data a drive can contain, the attorney will want to know about everything of interest on the drives.

Many attorneys like to have printouts of the data you have recovered, but printouts can present problems when you have log files with several thousand pages of data or CAD drawing programs that can be read only by proprietary programs. You need to persuade and educate many attorneys on how digital evidence can be viewed electronically. In addition, learn how to teach attorneys and paralegals to sort through files so that you can help them efficiently analyze the huge amount of data a forensic examination produces.

You can also encounter problems if you find data in the form of binary files, such as CAD drawings. Examining these files requires using the CAD program that created them. In addition, engineering companies often have specialized drafting programs. Discovery demands for lawsuits involving a product that caused injury or death requires extracting design plans for attorneys and expert witnesses to review. You're responsible for locating the programs for these design plans so that attorneys and expert witnesses can view the evidence files.

The following list shows the basic steps for conducting an ACP case:

1. Request a memorandum from the attorney directing you to start the investigation. The memorandum must state that the investigation is privileged communication and list your name and any other associates' names assigned to the case.

2. Request a list of keywords of interest to the investigation.

3. After you have received the memorandum, initiate the investigation and analysis. Any findings you made before receiving the memorandum are subject to discovery by the opposing attorney.

4. For drive examinations, make two bit-stream images (discussed later in this chapter) of the drive using a different tool for each image, such as EnCase for the first and ProDiscover or SafeBack for the second. If you have large enough storage drives, make each bit-stream image uncompressed so that if it becomes corrupt, you can still examine uncorrupted areas with your preferred forensic analysis tool.

5. If possible, compare hash values on all files on the original and re-created disks. Typically, attorneys want to view all data, even if it's not relevant to the case. Many GUI forensics tools perform this task during bit-stream imaging of the drive.

6. Methodically examine every portion of the drive (both allocated and unallocated data areas) and extract all data.

7. Run keyword searches on allocated and unallocated disk space. Follow up the search results to determine whether the search results contain information that supports the case.

8. For Windows OSs, use specialty tools to analyze and extract data from the Registry, such as AccessData Registry Viewer or a Registry viewer program (discussed in more detail in Chapter 6). Use the Edit, Find menu option in Registry Editor, for example, to search for keywords of interest to the investigation.

9. For binary files such as CAD drawings, locate the correct program and, if possible, make printouts of the binary file content. If the files are too large, load the specialty program on a separate workstation with the recovered binary files so that the attorney can view them.

10. For unallocated data (file slack space or free space, explained in Chapter 6) recovery, use a tool that removes or replaces nonprintable data, such as X-Ways Forensics Specialist Gather Text function.

11. Consolidate all recovered data from the evidence bit-stream image into well-organized folders and subfolders. Store the recovered data output, using a logical and easy-to-follow storage method for the attorney or paralegal.

Here are some other guidelines to remember for ACP cases:

- Minimize all written communication with the attorney; use the telephone when you need to ask questions or provide information related to the case.

- Any documentation written to the attorney must contain a header stating that it's "Privileged Legal Communication—Confidential Work Product," as defined under the attorney-work-product rule.

- Assist the attorney and paralegal in analyzing the data.

If you have difficulty complying with the directions or don't understand the directives from the memorandum, contact the attorney and explain the problem. Always keep an open line of verbal communication with the attorney during these types of investigations. If you're communicating via e-mail, use encryption (such as PGP) or another secure e-mail service for all messages.

Media Leak Investigations

In the corporate environment, controlling sensitive data can be difficult. Disgruntled employees, for example, might send an organization's sensitive data to a news reporter. The reasons for media leaks range from employees' efforts to embarrass management to a rival conducting a power struggle between other internal organizations. Another concern is the premature release of information about new products, which can disrupt operations and cause market share loss for a business if the information is made public too soon. Media leak investigations can be time consuming and resource intensive. Because management wants to find who leaked information, scope creep during the investigation is not uncommon.

Consider the following guidelines for media leak investigations:

- Examine e-mail, both the organization's e-mail servers and private e-mail accounts (Hotmail, Yahoo!, Gmail, and so on), on company-owned computers.

- Examine Internet message boards, and search the Internet for any information about the company or product. Use Internet search engines to run keyword searches related to the company, product, or leaked information. For example, you might search for "graphite-composite bicycle sprocket" for a bicycle manufacturer that was the victim of a media leak about a new product in development.

- Examine proxy server logs to check for log activities that might show use of free e-mail services, such as Gmail. Track back to the specific workstations where these messages originated and perform a forensic analysis on the drives to help determine what was communicated.

- Examine known suspects' workstations, perform computer forensics examinations on persons of interest, and develop other leads on possible associates.

- Examine all company phone records for any calls to known media organizations.

The following list outlines steps to take for media leaks:

1. Interview management privately to get a list of employees who have direct knowledge of the sensitive data.

2. Identify the media source that published the information.

3. Review company phone records to see who might have had contact with the news service.

4. Obtain a list of keywords related to the media leak.

5. Perform keyword searches on proxy and e-mail servers.

6. Discreetly conduct forensic disk acquisitions and analysis of employees of interest.

7. From the forensic disk examinations, analyze all e-mail correspondence and trace any sensitive messages to other people who haven't been listed as having direct knowledge of the sensitive data.

8. Expand the discreet forensic disk acquisition and analysis for any new persons of interest.

9. Consolidate and review your findings periodically to see whether new clues can be discovered.

10. Report findings to management routinely, and discuss how much further to continue the investigation.

Industrial Espionage Investigations

Industrial espionage cases, similar to media leaks, can be time consuming and are subject to the same scope creep problems. This section offers some guidelines on how to deal with industrial espionage investigations. Be aware that cases dealing with foreign nationals might be violations of International Traffic in Arms Regulations (ITAR) or Export Administration Regulations (EAR). For more information on ITAR, see the U.S. Department of State's Web site (*www.state.gov*; substitute the actual state name or a shortened version of it for *state*) or do an Internet search for "International Traffic in Arms Regulations." For EAR information, see the U.S. Department of Commerce Web site (*www.doc.gov*) or do an Internet search for "Export Administration Regulations."

Unlike the other corporate investigations covered in this section, all suspected industrial espionage cases should be treated as criminal investigations. The techniques described here are for private network environments and internal investigations that haven't yet been reported to law enforcement officials. Make sure you don't become an agent of law enforcement by filing a complaint of a suspected espionage case before substantiating the allegation. The following list includes staff you might need when planning an industrial espionage investigation. This list isn't exhaustive, so use your knowledge to improve on these recommendations:

- The computing investigator who is responsible for disk forensic examinations
- The technology specialist who is knowledgeable about the suspected compromised technical data
- The network specialist who can perform log analysis and set up network monitors to trap network communication of possible suspects
- The threat assessment specialist (typically an attorney) who is familiar with federal and state laws and regulations related to ITAR or EAR and industrial espionage

In addition, consider the following guidelines when initiating an international espionage investigation:

- Determine whether this investigation involves a possible industrial espionage incident, and then determine whether it falls under ITAR or EAR.
- Consult with corporate attorneys and upper management if the investigations must be conducted discreetly.
- Determine what information is needed to substantiate the allegation of industrial espionage.
- Generate a list of keywords for disk forensics and network monitoring.
- List and collect resources needed for the investigation.
- Determine the goal and scope of the investigation; consult with management and the company's attorneys on how much work you should do.
- Initiate the investigation after approval from management, and make regular reports of your activities and findings.

The following are planning considerations for industrial espionage investigations:

- Examine all e-mail of suspected employees, both company-provided e-mail and free Web-based services.
- Search Internet newsgroups or message boards for any postings related to the incident.
- Initiate physical surveillance with cameras on people or things of interest to the investigation.
- If available, examine all facility physical access logs for sensitive areas, which might include secure areas where smart badges or video surveillance recordings are used.
- If there's a suspect, determine his or her location in relation to the vulnerable asset that was compromised.
- Study the suspect's work habits.
- Collect all incoming and outgoing phone logs to see whether any unique or unusual places were called.

When conducting an industrial espionage case, follow these basic steps:

1. Gather all personnel assigned to the investigation and brief them on the plan and any concerns.

2. Gather the resources needed to conduct the investigation.

3. Start the investigation by placing surveillance systems, such as cameras and network monitors, at key locations.

4. Discreetly gather any additional evidence, such as the suspect's computer drive, and make a bit-stream image for follow-up examination.

5. Collect all log data from networks and e-mail servers, and examine them for unique items that might relate to the investigation.

6. Report regularly to management and corporate attorneys on your investigation's status and current findings.

7. Review the investigation's scope with management and corporate attorneys to determine whether it needs to be expanded and more resources added.

Interviews and Interrogations in High-Tech Investigations

Becoming a skilled interviewer and interrogator can take many years of experience. Typically, a corporate computing investigator is a technical person acquiring the evidence for an investigation. Many large organizations have full-time security investigators with years of training and experience in criminal and civil investigations and interviewing techniques. Few of these investigators have any computing or network technical skills, so you might be asked to assist in interviewing or interrogating a suspect when you have performed a forensic disk analysis on that suspect's machine.

An interrogation is different from an **interview**. An interview is usually conducted to collect information from a witness or suspect about specific facts related to an investigation. An **interrogation** is the process of trying to get a suspect to confess to a specific incident or crime. An investigator might change from an interview to an interrogation when talking to a witness or suspect. The more experience and training investigators have in the art of interviewing and interrogating, the more easily they can determine whether a witness is credible and possibly a suspect.

Your role as a computing investigator is to instruct the investigator conducting the interview on what questions to ask and what the answers should be. As you build rapport with the investigator, he or she might ask you to question the suspect. Watching a skilled interrogator is a learning experience in human relations skills.

If you're asked to assist in an interview or interrogation, prepare yourself by answering the following questions:

- What questions do I need to ask the suspect to get the vital information about the case?

- Do I know what I'm talking about, or will I have to research the topic or technology related to the investigation?

- Do I need additional questions to cover other indirect issues related to the investigation?

Common interview and interrogation errors include being unprepared for the interview or interrogation and not having the right questions or enough questions to increase your depth of knowledge. Make sure you don't run out of conversation topics; you need to keep the conversation friendly to gain the suspect's confidence. Avoid doubting your own skills, which might show the suspect you lack confidence in your ability.

Ingredients for a successful interview or interrogation require the following:

- Being patient throughout the session
- Repeating or rephrasing questions to zero in on specific facts from a reluctant witness or suspect
- Being tenacious

Understanding Data Recovery Workstations and Software

Now you know what's involved in acquiring and documenting evidence. In Chapter 3, you examine a complete setup of a computer forensics lab, which is where you conduct your investigations and where most of your equipment and software are located, including secure evidence containers. Be aware that some companies that perform computer investigations also do data recovery, which is the more well-known and lucrative side of the business.

Remember the difference between data recovery and computer forensics. In data recovery, you don't necessarily need a sterile target drive when restoring the forensic image. Typically, the customer or your company just wants the data back. The other key difference is that in data recovery, you usually know what you're trying to retrieve. In computer forensics, you might have an idea of what you're searching for, but not necessarily.

To conduct your investigation and analysis, you must have a specially configured PC known as a **forensic workstation**, which is a computer loaded with additional bays and forensics software. Depending on your needs, most computer forensics work can be performed on the following Microsoft OSs:

- MS-DOS 6.22
- Windows 95, 98, or Me
- Windows NT 3.5 or 4.0
- Windows 2000
- Windows XP
- Windows Vista

Chapters 3 and 7 cover the software resources you need and the forensics lab and workstation in detail. Visit *www.digitalintel.com* to examine the specifications of the Forensic Recovery of Evidence Device (F.R.E.D.) unit or *www.forensicpc.com* to examine the ForensicPC Dual Xeon Workstation and other current products.

In addition to the Windows OSs listed, you can use Linux or UNIX to conduct your analysis. Several open-source and freeware tools are available for this purpose. Some newer forensics tools, such as AccessData FTK, now require dual-core processors.

If you start Windows while you're examining a hard disk, Windows alters the evidence disk by writing data to the Recycle Bin and corrupts the quality and integrity of the evidence you're trying to preserve. Chapter 6 covers which files Windows updates automatically at startup. Windows XP and Vista systems also record the serial numbers of hard drives and CPUs in a file, which can be difficult to recover.

Of all the Microsoft OSs, the least intrusive (in terms of changing data) to disks is MS-DOS 6.22. With the continued evolution of Microsoft OSs, it's not always practical to use older MS-DOS platforms, however. Newer file system formats, such as NTFS, are accessible—that is, readable—only from Windows NT or newer OSs. You can use one of several write-blockers that enable you to boot to Windows without writing data to the evidence drive. In Chapter 4, you learn more about write-blockers and some inexpensive alternatives for preserving data during an acquisition.

There are many hardware write-blockers on the market. Some are inserted between the disk controller and the hard disk; others connect to USB or FireWire ports. Several vendors sell write-blockers, including Technology Pathways NoWrite FPU; Digital Intelligence Ultra-Kit, UltraBlock, FireFly, FireChief 800, and USB Write Blocker; WiebeTECH Forensic DriveDock; Guidance Software FastBloc2; Paralan's SCSI Write Blockers; and Intelligent Computer Solutions (*www.ics-iq.com*) Image LinkMaSSter Forensics Hard Case.

Many older computer forensics acquisition tools work in the MS-DOS environment. These tools can operate from an MS-DOS window in Windows 98 or from the command prompt in Windows 2000 and later. Some of their functions are disabled or generate error messages when run in these OSs, however.

Windows products are being developed that make performing disk forensics easier. However, because Windows has limitations in performing disk forensics, you might need to develop skills in acquiring data with MS-DOS and Linux. In later chapters, you learn more about using these other tools. Keep in mind that no single computer forensics tool can recover everything. Each tool and OS has its own strengths and weaknesses, so develop skills with as many tools as possible to become an effective computing investigator. Appendix D has additional information on how to use MS-DOS for data acquisitions.

Setting Up Your Workstation for Computer Forensics

With current computer forensics hardware and software, configuring a computer workstation or laptop as a forensic workstation is simple. All that's required are the following:

- A workstation running Windows XP or Vista
- A write-blocker device
- Computer forensics acquisition tool
- Computer forensics analysis tool

- A target drive to receive the source or suspect disk data
- Spare PATA or SATA ports
- USB ports

Additional useful items include the following:

- Network interface card (NIC)
- Extra USB ports
- FireWire 400/800 ports
- SCSI card
- Disk editor tool
- Text editor tool
- Graphics viewer program
- Other specialized viewing tools

In Chapter 3, you learn more about setting up and configuring a computer to be a forensic workstation.

Conducting an Investigation

Now you're ready to return to the Domain Name case. You have created a plan for the investigation, set up your forensic workstation, and installed the necessary forensic analysis software you need to examine the evidence. The type of software to install includes your preferred analysis tool, such as ProDiscover, EnCase, FTK, or X-Ways Forensics; an office suite, such as OpenOffice; and a graphics viewer, such as IrfanView. To begin conducting an investigation, you start by copying the evidence using a variety of methods. No single method retrieves all data from a disk, so using several tools to retrieve and analyze data is a good idea.

Start by gathering the resources you identified in your investigation plan. You need the following items:

- Original storage media
- Evidence custody form
- Evidence container for the storage media, such as an evidence bag
- Bit-stream imaging tool; in this case, the ProDiscover Basic acquisition utility
- Forensic workstation to copy and examine the evidence
- Secure evidence locker, cabinet, or safe

Gathering the Evidence

Now you're ready to gather evidence for the Domain Name case. Remember, you need anti-static bags and pads with wrist straps to prevent static electricity from damaging digital evidence. To acquire George Montgomery's storage media from the IT Department and then secure the evidence, you perform the following steps:

1. Arrange to meet the IT manager to interview him and pick up the storage media.

2. After interviewing the IT manager, fill out the evidence form, have him sign it, and then sign it yourself.

3. Store the storage media in an evidence bag, and then transport it to your forensic facility.

4. Carry the evidence to a secure container, such as a locker, cabinet, or safe.

5. Complete the evidence custody form. As mentioned, if you're using a multi-evidence form, you can store the form in the file folder for the case. If you're also using single-evidence forms, store them in the secure container with the evidence. Reduce the risk of tampering by limiting access to the forms.

6. Secure the evidence by locking the container.

Understanding Bit-stream Copies

A **bit-stream copy** is a bit-by-bit copy (also known as a sector copy) of the original drive or storage medium and is an exact duplicate. The more exact the copy, the better chance you have of retrieving the evidence you need from the disk. This process is usually referred to as "acquiring an image" or "making an image" of a suspect drive. A bit-stream copy is different from a simple backup copy of a disk. Backup software can only copy or compress files that are stored in a folder or are of a known file type. Backup software can't copy deleted files and e-mails or recover file fragments.

A **bit-stream image** is the file containing the bit-stream copy of all data on a disk or disk partition. For simplicity, it's usually referred to as an "image," "image save," or "image file." Some manufacturers also refer to it as a **forensic copy**. To create an exact image of an evidence disk, copying the image to a target disk that's identical to the evidence disk is preferable (see Figure 2-4). The target disk's manufacturer and model, in general, should be the same as the original disk's manufacturer and model. If the target disk is identical to the original, the size in bytes and sectors of both disks should also be the same. Some image acquisition tools can accommodate a target disk that's a different size than the original. These imaging tools are discussed in Chapter 4. Older computer forensics tools designed for MS-DOS work only on a copied disk. Current GUI tools can work on both a disk drive and copied data sets that many manufacturers refer to as "image saves."

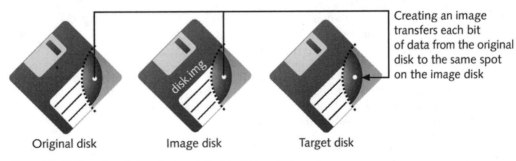

Creating an image transfers each bit of data from the original disk to the same spot on the image disk

Original disk   Image disk   Target disk

Figure 2-4 Transfer of data from original to image to target

Occasionally, the track and sector maps on the original and target disks don't match, even if you use disks of exactly the same size that are different makes or models. Tools such as Guidance EnCase and NTI SafeBack adjust for the target drive's geometry. Two other tools, X-Ways WinHex Specialist Edition and Technology Pathways ProDiscover, can copy sector by sector to equal-sized or larger disks without needing to force changes in the target disk's geometry.

Acquiring an Image of Evidence Media

After you retrieve and secure the evidence, you're ready to copy the evidence media and analyze the data. The first rule of computer forensics is to preserve the original evidence. Then conduct your analysis only on a copy of the data—the image of the original medium. Several vendors provide MS-DOS, Linux, and Windows acquisition tools. Windows tools, however, require a write-blocking device (discussed in Chapter 4) when acquiring data from FAT or NTFS file systems.

Using ProDiscover Basic to Acquire a USB Drive

ProDiscover Basic from Technology Pathways is a forensics analysis tool. You can use it to acquire and analyze data from several different file systems, such as Microsoft FAT and NTFS, Linux Ext2 and Ext3, and other UNIX file systems, from a Windows XP or older OS. To use ProDiscover Basic in Windows Vista, you need to run it in Administrator mode. See the Tip in the following steps for instructions on selecting this mode.

The DVD accompanying this book includes ProDiscover Basic. The installation program includes a user manual, ProDiscoverManual.pdf, in the C:\Program Files\Technology Pathways\ProDiscover folder (if the installation defaults are used). Read the user manual for instructions, and install ProDiscover Basic on your computer before you perform the following activity.

Before starting this activity, you need to create a work folder on your computer for data storage and other related files ProDiscover creates when acquiring and analyzing evidence. You can use any location and name for your work folder, but you'll see it referred to in activities as C:\Work or simply "your work folder." To keep your files organized, you should also create subfolders for each chapter. For this chapter, create a Work\Chap02\Chapter folder to store files from in-chapter activities. Note that you might see work folder pathnames in screenshots that are slightly different from your own pathname.

The following steps show how to acquire an image of a USB drive, but you can apply them to other media, such as disk drives and floppy disks. You can use any USB drive already containing files to see how ProDiscover acquires data. To perform an acquisition on a USB drive with ProDiscover Basic, follow these steps:

1. First, on the USB drive, locate the write-protect switch (if one is available) and place the drive in write-protect mode. Now connect the USB drive to your computer.

This activity is meant to introduce you to the ProDiscover Basic tool. Proper forensics procedures require write-protecting any evidence media to ensure that it's not altered. In Chapter 4, you learn how to use hardware and software write-blocking methods.

2. To start ProDiscover Basic, click **Start,** point to **All Programs,** point to **ProDiscover,** and click **ProDiscover Basic.** If the Launch Dialog dialog box opens (see Figure 2-5), click **Cancel.**

If you're using Windows Vista, right-click the ProDiscover Basic desktop icon (or menu item on the All Programs menu) and click Run as administrator. In the UAC message box, click Continue.

Tree view →

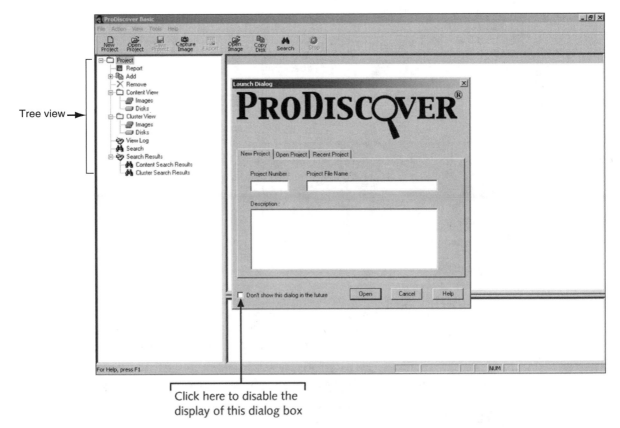

Click here to disable the display of this dialog box

Figure 2-5 The main window in ProDiscover

For convenience, you can disable the display of the Launch Dialog dialog box by clicking the check box indicated in Figure 2-5.

3. In the main window, click **Action, Capture Image** from the menu.

4. In the Capture Image dialog box shown in Figure 2-6, click the **Source Drive** list arrow, and select the USB drive.

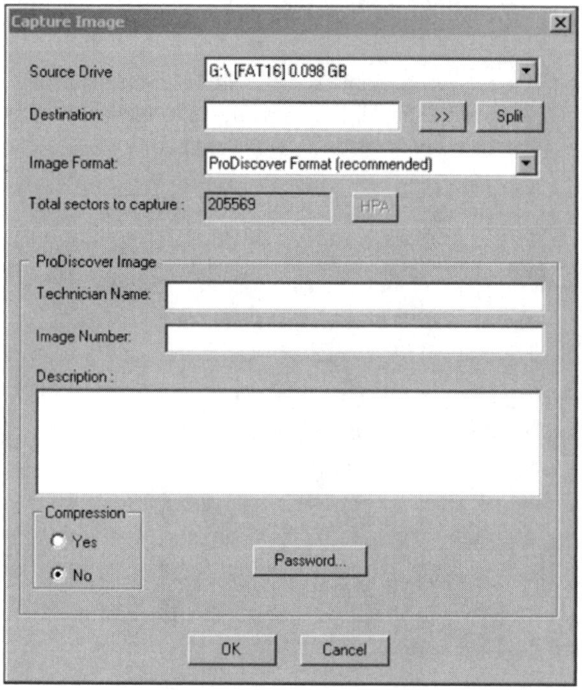

Capture Image

Source Drive	G:\ [FAT16] 0.098 GB
Destination:	[ ] >> Split
Image Format:	ProDiscover Format (recommended)
Total sectors to capture :	205569 HPA

ProDiscover Image

Technician Name: [ ]

Image Number: [ ]

Description :

[ ]

Compression

○ Yes

● No Password...

OK Cancel

Figure 2-6 The Capture Image dialog box

5. Click the >> button next to the Destination text box. When the Save As dialog box opens, navigate to your work folder (*Work*\Chap02\Chapter) and enter a name for the image you're making, such as **InChp-prac**. Click **Save** to save the file.

6. Next, in the Capture Image dialog box, type your name in the Technician Name text box and **InChp-prac-02** in the Image Number text box (see Figure 2-7). Click **OK**.

NOTE ProDiscover Basic then acquires an image of the USB drive. When it's finished, it displays a notice to check the log file created during the acquisition. This log file contains additional information if errors were encountered during the data acquisition. ProDiscover also creates an MD5 hash output file. In Chapters 4 and 5, you learn how to use MD5 for forensic analysis and evidence validation.

7. When ProDiscover is finished, click **OK** in the completion message box. Click **File, Exit** from the menu to exit ProDiscover.

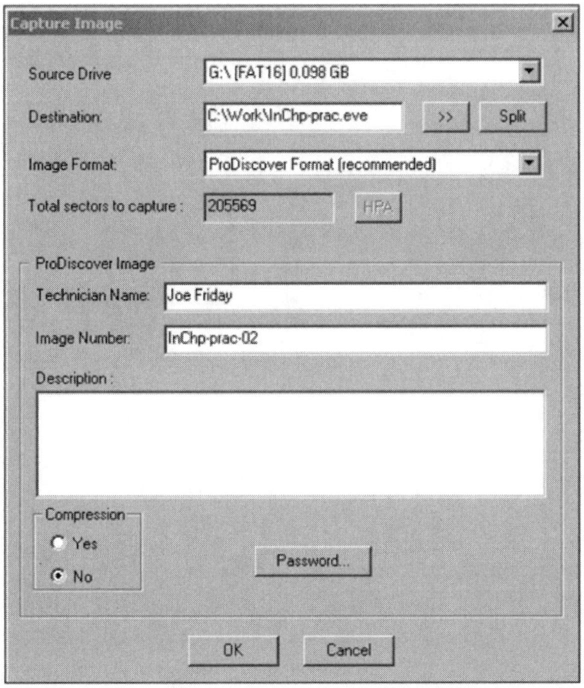

Figure 2-7 The completed Capture Image dialog box

This activity completes your first forensics data acquisition. Next, you learn how to locate data in an acquisition.

Analyzing Your Digital Evidence

When you analyze digital evidence, your job is to recover the data. If users have deleted or overwritten files on a disk, the disk contains deleted files and file fragments in addition to existing files. Remember that as files are deleted, the space they occupied becomes free space—meaning it can be used for new files that are saved or files that expand as data is added to them. The files that were deleted are still on the disk until a new file is saved to the same physical location, overwriting the original file. In the meantime, those files can still be retrieved. Forensics tools such as ProDiscover Basic can retrieve deleted files for use as evidence.

In the following steps, you analyze George Montgomery's USB drive. Before beginning, extract all compressed files from the Chap02 folder on the book's DVD to your work folder. The first task is loading the acquired image into ProDiscover Basic by following these steps:

1. Start ProDiscover Basic, as you did in the previous activity.
2. To create a new case, click **File, New Project** from the menu.
3. In the New Project dialog box, type **InChp02** in the Project Number text box and again in the Project File Name text box (see Figure 2-8), and then click **OK**.
4. In the tree view of the main window (see Figure 2-9), click to expand the **Add** item, and then click **Image File**.

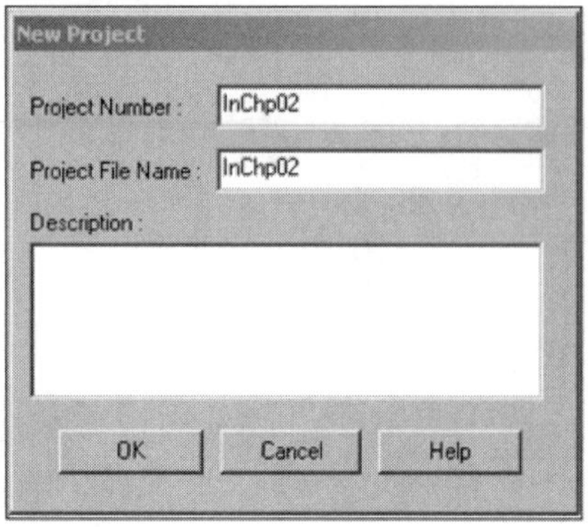

Figure 2-8   The New Project dialog box

Figure 2-9   The tree view in ProDiscover

5. In the Open dialog box, navigate to the folder containing the image, click the **InChp02.eve** file, and click **Open**. Click **Yes** in the Auto Image Checksum message box, if necessary.

The next task is to display the contents of the acquired data. Perform the following steps:

1. In the tree view, click to expand **Content View**, if necessary. Click to expand **Images**, click the image filename path **C:\Work\InChp02.eve** (substituting your folder path for "Work"—for example, C:\Work\Chap02\Chapter), and then click to expand the path.

2. Next, click **All Files** under the image filename path. When the CAUTION dialog box opens, click **Yes**. The InChp02.eve file is then loaded in the main window, as shown in Figure 2-10.

3. In the upper-right pane (the work area), click the **letter1** file to view its content in the data area (see Figure 2-11).

4. In the data area, you see the contents of the letter1 file. Continue to navigate through the work and data areas and inspect the contents of the recovered evidence. Note that many of these files are deleted files that haven't been overwritten. Leave ProDiscover Basic running for the next activity.

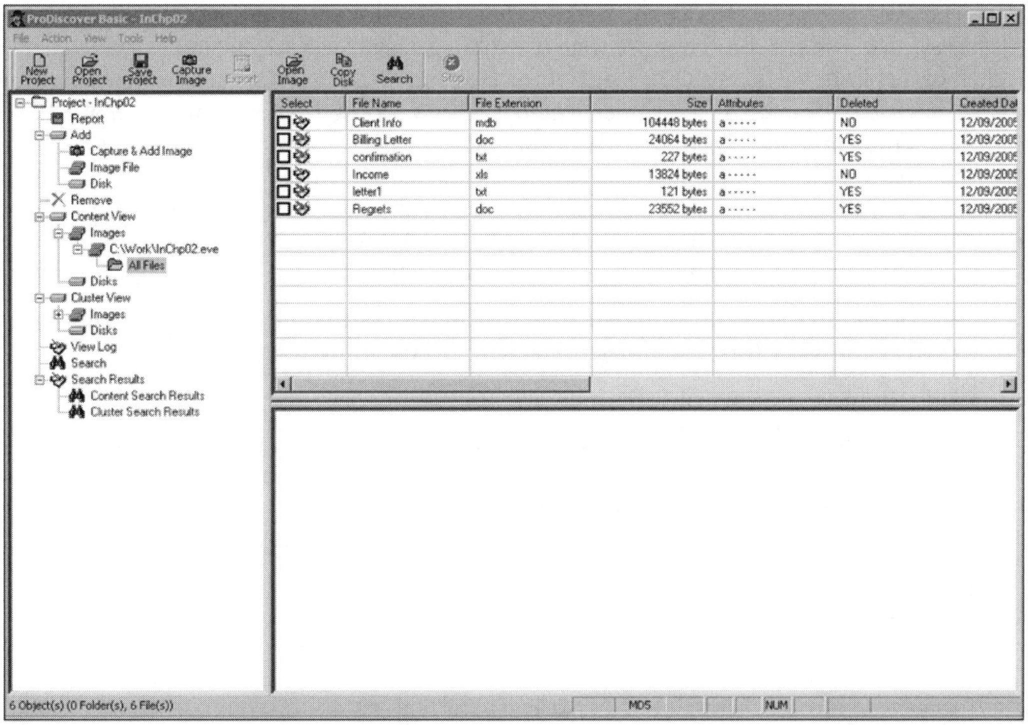

Figure 2-10 The loaded InChp02.eve file

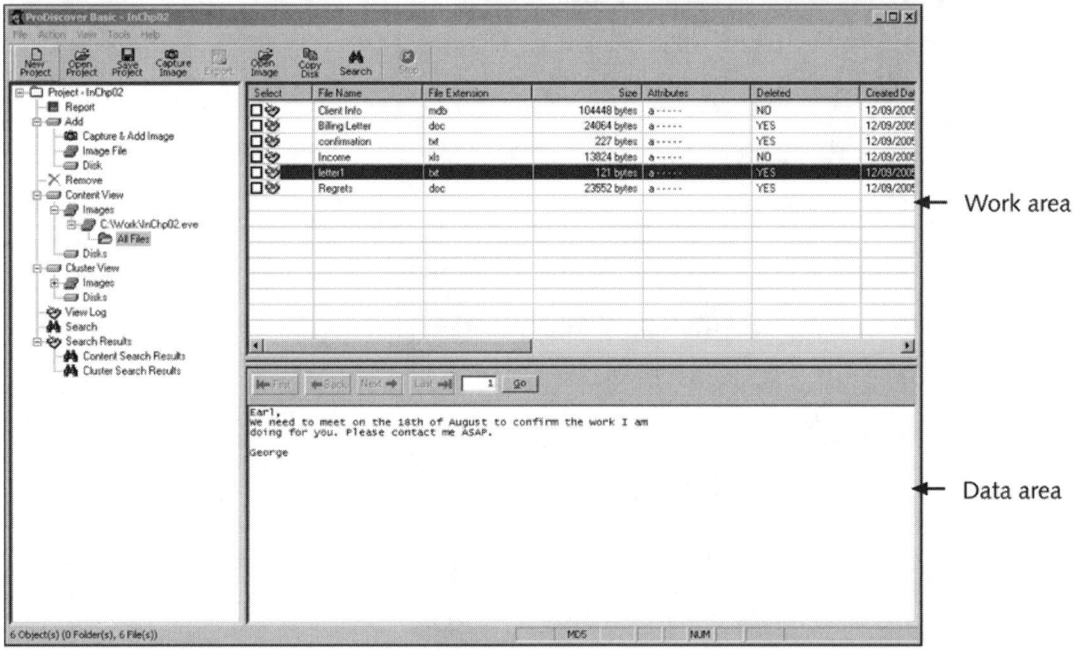

Figure 2-11 Selecting a file in the work area and viewing its contents in the data area

The next step is analyzing the data and searching for information related to the complaint. Data analysis can be the most time-consuming task, even when you know exactly what to look for in the evidence. The method for locating evidentiary artifacts is to search for specific known data values. Data values can be unique words or nonprintable characters, such as hexadecimal codes. There are also printable character codes that can't be generated from a keyboard, such as the copyright (©) or registered trademark (™) symbols. Many computer forensics programs can search for character strings (letters and numbers) and hexadecimal values, such as A9 for the copyright symbol or AE for the registered trademark symbol. All these searchable data values are referred to as "keywords."

With ProDiscover Basic, you can search for keywords of interest in the case. For this case, follow these steps to search for any reference to the name George:

1. In the tree view, click **Search**.

2. In the Search dialog box, click the **Content Search** tab, if necessary. Click the **Select all matches** check box, the **ASCII** option button, and the **Search for the pattern(s)** option button, if they aren't already selected.

3. Next, in the text box under the Search for the pattern(s) option button, type **George** (see Figure 2-12).

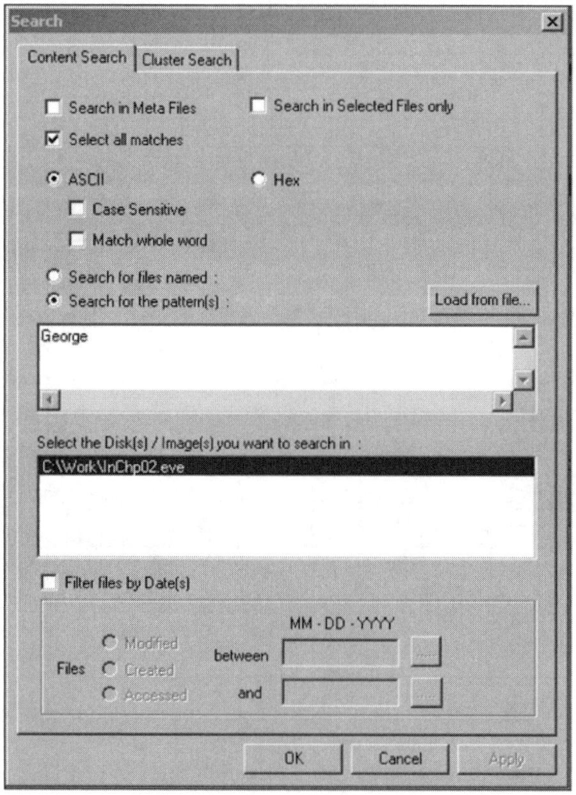

Figure 2-12 Entering a keyword in the Search dialog box

You can list keywords separately or combine words with the Boolean logic operators AND, OR, and NOT. Searching for a common keyword produces too many hits and makes it difficult to locate evidence of interest to the case. Applying Boolean logic can help reduce unrelated excessive hits, which are called "false-positive hits."

2

4. Under Select the Disk(s)/Image(s) you want to search in, click **C:*Work*\InChap02.eve** (substituting the path to your work folder), and then click **OK** to initiate the search. Leave ProDiscover Basic running for the next activity.

When the search is finished, ProDiscover displays the results in the search results pane in the work area. Note the tab labeled Search 1 in Figure 2-13. For each search you do in a case, ProDiscover adds a new tab to help catalog your searches.

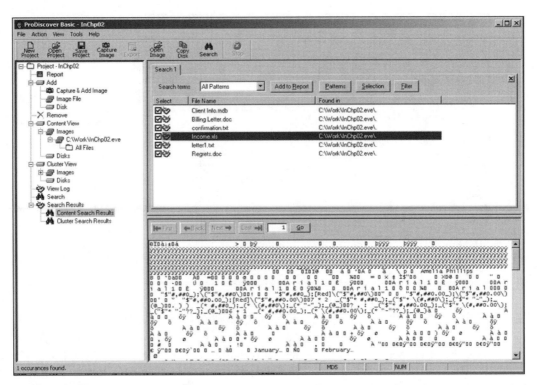

Figure 2-13   The search results pane

Click each file in the search results pane and examine its content in the data area. If you locate a file of interest that displays binary (nonprintable) data in the data area, you can double-click the file to display the data in the work area. Then you can double-click the file in the work area, and an associated program, such as Microsoft Excel for a spreadsheet, opens the file's content. If you want to extract the file, you can right-click it and click Copy File.

For this example, an Excel spreadsheet named Income.xls is displayed in the search results pane. The information in the data area shows mostly unreadable character data. To examine this data, you can export the data to a folder of your choice, and then open it for follow-up examination and analysis. To export the Income.xls file, perform the following steps:

1. In the search results pane, double-click the **Income.xls** file, which switches the view to the work area.

2. In the work area, right-click the **Income.xls** file and click **Copy File**.

3. In the Save As dialog box, navigate to the folder you've selected, and click **Save**.

4. Now that the Income.xls file has been copied to a Windows folder, start Excel (or another spreadsheet program, such as OpenOffice Calc) to examine the file's content. Figure 2-14 shows the extracted file open in OpenOffice Calc. Repeat this data examination and file export process for the remaining files in the search results pane. Then close all open windows except ProDiscover Basic for the next activity.

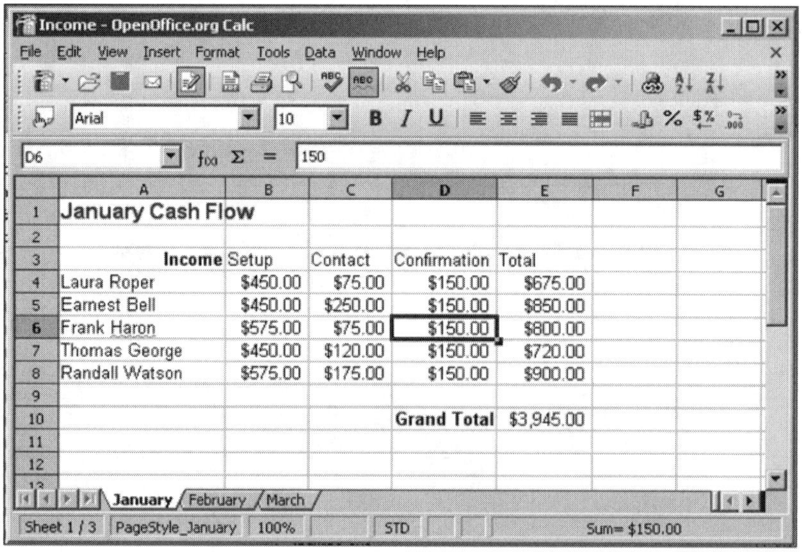

Figure 2-14   The extracted Income.xls file

With ProDiscover's Search feature, you can also search for specific filenames. To use this feature, click the "Search for files named" option button in the Search dialog box. When you're dealing with a very large drive with several thousand files, this useful feature minimizes human error in looking at data.

After completing the detailed examination and analysis, you can then generate a report of your activities. Several computer forensics programs provide a report generator or log file of actions taken during an examination. These reports and logs are typically text or HTML files. The text files are usually in plaintext or Rich Text Format (RTF). ProDiscover Basic offers a report generator that produces an RTF or a plaintext file that most word processing programs can read.

You can also select specific items and add them to the report. For example, to select a file in the work area, click the check box in the Select column next to the file to open the Add Comment dialog box. Enter a description and click OK. The descriptive comment is then added to the ProDiscover Basic report. To create a report in ProDiscover Basic, perform the following steps:

1. In the tree view, click **Report**. The report is then displayed in the right pane, as shown in Figure 2-15.

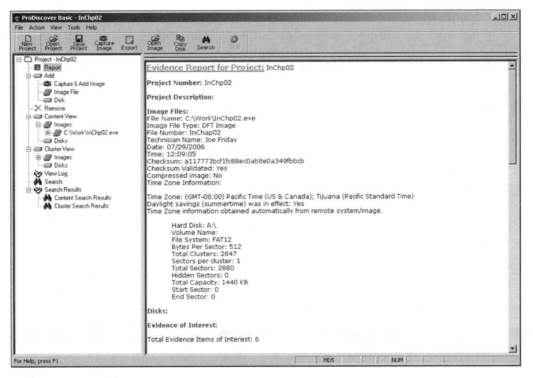

Figure 2-15   A ProDiscover report

2. To print the report, click **File, Print Report** from the menu.

3. In the Print dialog box, click **OK**.

If the report needs to be saved to a file, you use ProDiscover Basic's Export feature and choose RTF or plaintext for the file format. To export the report to a file, do the following:

1. In the tree view, click **Report**.

2. Click **Action, Export** from the menu.

3. In the Export dialog box, click the **RTF Format** or **Text Format** option button, type **InChp02** in the File Name text box, and then click **OK**.

To place the report in a different folder, click the Browse button and navigate to the folder where you want to save the report. Click Save, and then click OK in the Export dialog box.

4. Review the report, and then click **File, Exit** from the menu to exit ProDiscover Basic.

This activity completes your analysis of the USB drive. In the next section, you learn how to complete the case. In later chapters, you learn how to apply more search and analysis techniques.

Completing the Case

After analyzing the disk, you can retrieve deleted files, e-mail, and items that have been purposefully hidden, which you do in Chapters 9, 10, and 12. The files on George's USB drive indicate that he was conducting a side business on his company computer.

Now that you have retrieved and analyzed the evidence, you need to find the answers to the following questions to write the final report:

- How did George's manager acquire the disk?
- Did George perform the work on a laptop, which is his own property? If so, did he conduct business transactions on his break or during his lunch hour?
- At what times of the day was George using the non-work-related files? How did you retrieve that information?
- Which company policies apply?
- Are there any other items that need to be considered?

When you write your report, state what you did and what you found. The report you generated in ProDiscover gives you an account of the steps you took. As part of your final report, depending on guidance from management or legal counsel, include the ProDiscover report file to document your work. In any computing investigation, you should be able to repeat the steps you took and produce the same results. This capability is referred to as **repeatable findings**; without it, your work product has no value as evidence.

Keep a written journal of everything you do. Your notes can be used in court, so be mindful of what you write or e-mail, even to a fellow investigator. Often these journals start out as handwritten notes, but you can transcribe them to electronic format periodically.

Basic report writing involves answering the six Ws: who, what, when, where, why, and how. In addition to these basic facts, you must also explain computer and network processes. Typically, your reader is a senior personnel manager, a lawyer, or occasionally a judge who might have little computer knowledge. Identify your reader and write the report for that person. Provide explanations for processes and how systems and their components work.

Your organization might have templates to use when writing reports. Depending on your organization's needs and requirements, your report must describe the findings from your analysis. The report generated by ProDiscover lists your examination and data recovery findings. Other computer forensics tools generate a log file of all actions taken during your examination and analysis. Integrating a computer forensics log report from these other tools can enhance your final report. When describing the findings, consider writing your narrative first and then placing the log output at the end of the report, with references to it in the main narrative. Chapter 14 covers writing final reports for investigations in more detail.

In the Domain Name case, you want to show conclusive evidence that George had his own business registering domain names and list the names of his clients and his income from this business. You also want to show letters he wrote to clients about their accounts. The time and date stamps on the files are during work hours, so you should include this information, too. Eventually, you hand the evidence file to your supervisor or to Steve, George's manager, who then decides on a course of action.

Critiquing the Case

After you close the case and make your final report, you need to meet with your department or a group of fellow investigators and critique the case in an effort to improve your work. Ask yourself assessment questions such as the following:

- How could you improve your performance in the case?
- Did you expect the results you found? Did the case develop in ways you did not expect?
- Was the documentation as thorough as it could have been?
- What feedback has been received from the requesting source?
- Did you discover any new problems? If so, what are they?
- Did you use new techniques during the case or during research?

Make notes to yourself in your journal about techniques or processes that might need to be changed or addressed in future investigations. Then store your journal in a secure place.

Chapter Summary

- Always use a systematic approach to your investigations. Follow the checklist in this chapter as a guideline for your case.
- When planning a case, take into account the nature of the case, instructions from the requester, what additional tools and expertise you might need, and how you will acquire the evidence.
- Criminal cases and corporate-policy violations should be handled in much the same manner to ensure that quality evidence is presented. Both criminal cases and corporate-policy violations can go to court.
- When you begin a case, there might be unanticipated challenges that weren't obvious when applying a systematic approach to your investigation plan. For all investigations, you need to plan for contingencies for any unexpected problems you might encounter.
- You should create a standard evidence custody form to track the chain of custody of evidence for your case. There are two types of forms: a multi-evidence form and a single-evidence form.
- Internet and media leak investigations require examining server log data.
- For attorney-client privilege cases, all written communication should have a header label stating that it's privileged communication and a confidential work product.

- A bit-stream copy is a bit-by-bit duplicate of the original disk. You should use the duplicate, whenever possible, when analyzing evidence.

- Always maintain a journal to keep notes on exactly what you did when handling evidence.

- You should always critique your own work to determine what improvements you made during each case, what could have been done differently, and how to apply those lessons to future cases.

Key Terms

approved secure container A fireproof container locked by a key or combination.

attorney-client privilege (ACP) Communication between an attorney and client about legal matters is protected as confidential communications. The purpose of having confidential communications is to promote honest and open dialogue between an attorney and client. This confidential information must not be shared with unauthorized people.

bit-stream copy A bit-by-bit duplicate of data on the original storage medium. This process is usually called "acquiring an image" or "making an image."

bit-stream image The file where the bit-stream copy is stored; usually referred to as an "image," "image save," or "image file."

chain of custody The route evidence takes from the time the investigator obtains it until the case is closed or goes to court.

evidence bags Nonstatic bags used to transport removable media, hard drives, and other computer components.

evidence custody form A printed form indicating who has signed out and been in physical possession of evidence.

forensic copy Another name for a bit-stream image.

forensic workstation A workstation set up to allow copying forensic evidence, whether on a hard drive, USB drive, CD, or Zip disk. It usually has software preloaded and ready to use.

interrogation The process of trying to get a suspect to confess to a specific incident or crime.

interview A conversation conducted to collect information from a witness or suspect about specific facts related to an investigation.

multi-evidence form An evidence custody form used to list all items associated with a case. *See also* evidence custody form.

password-cracking software Software used to match the hash patterns of passwords or to simply guess passwords by using common combinations or standard algorithms.

password protected The method of requiring a password to limit access to certain files and areas of storage media; this method prevents unintentional or unauthorized use.

repeatable findings Being able to obtain the same results every time from a computer forensics examination.

single-evidence form A form that dedicates a page for each item retrieved for a case. It allows investigators to add more detail about exactly what was done to the evidence each time it was taken from the storage locker. *See also* evidence custody form.

Review Questions

1. What are some initial assessments you should make for a computing investigation?

2. What are some ways to determine the resources needed for an investigation?

3. List three items that should be on an evidence custody form.

4. Why should you do a standard risk assessment to prepare for an investigation?

5. You should always prove the allegations made by the person who hired you. True or False?

6. For digital evidence, an evidence bag is typically made of antistatic material. True or False?

7. Who should have access to a secure container?
   a. Only the primary investigator
   b. Only the investigators in the group
   c. Everyone on the floor
   d. Only senior-level management

8. For employee termination cases, what types of investigations do you typically encounter?

9. Why should your evidence media be write-protected?

10. List three items that should be in your case report.

11. Why should you critique your case after it's finished?

12. What do you call a list of people who have had physical possession of the evidence?

13. What two tasks is an acquisitions officer responsible for at a crime scene?

14. What are some reasons that an employee might leak information to the press?

15. When might an interview turn into an interrogation?

16. What is the most important point to remember when assigned to work on an attorney-client privilege case?

17. What are the basic guidelines when working on an attorney-client privilege case?

18. Data collected before an attorney issues a memorandum for an attorney-client privilege case is protected under the confidential work product rule. True or False?

Hands-On Projects

In the following Hands-On Projects, continue to work at the workstation you set up in this chapter. Extract the compressed files from the Chap02\Projects folder on the book's DVD to your *Work*\Chap02\Projects folder. (If necessary, create this folder on your system to store your files.)

If needed, refer to the directions in this chapter and the ProDiscover user manual, which is in C:\Program Files\ Technology Pathways\ProDiscover by default.

Hands-On Project 2-1

The case in this project involves a suspicious death. Joshua Zarkan found his girlfriend's dead body in her apartment and reported it. The first responding law enforcement officer seized a USB drive. A crime scene evidence technician skilled in data acquisition made an image of the USB drive with ProDiscover and named it C2Prj01.eve. Following the acquisition, the technician transported and secured the USB drive and placed it in a secure evidence locker at the police station. You have received the image file from the detective assigned to this case. He directs you to examine it and identify any evidentiary artifacts that might relate to this case. To process this case, follow these steps to evaluate what's on the image of the USB drive:

1. Start ProDiscover Basic. (If you're using Windows Vista, right-click the **ProDiscover** desktop icon and click **Run as administrator**.)

2. In the Launch Dialog dialog box, click the **New Project** tab, if necessary. Enter a project number. If your company doesn't have a standard numbering scheme, you can use the date followed by the number representing the case that day in sequence, such as 20090129_1.

3. Enter **C2Prj01** as the project name, enter a brief description of the case, and then click **Open**.

4. To add an image file, click **Action** from the menu, point to **Add**, and click **Image File**.

5. Navigate to your work folder, click **C2Prj01.eve**, and then click **Open**. If the Auto Image Checksum message box opens, click **Yes**.

6. In the tree view, click to expand **Content View**. Click to expand **Images**, and then click the pathname containing the image file. In the work area, notice the files that are listed.

7. Right-click any file and click **View** to start the associated program, such as Word or Excel. View the file, and then exit the program.

8. If you decide to export a file, right-click the file and click **Copy File**. (*Note*: Creating a separate folder for exports is a good idea to keep your files

organized.) In the Save As dialog box that opens, navigate to the location where you want to save the file, and then click **Save**.

9. To save the project to view later, click **File, Save Project** from the menu. The default project name is the one you entered in Step 3. Select the drive and folder (*Work*\Chap02\Projects, for example), and then click **Save**. After you have finished examining the files, exit ProDiscover Basic and save the project again, if prompted.

You need to export any files in this image and present them to the investigator. In addition, write a brief report (no more than two paragraphs) including any facts from the contents of the recovered data.

In ProDiscover Basic, you must exit the program before beginning a new case.

Hands-On Project 2-2

In this project, you work for a large corporation's IT security company. Your duties include conducting internal computing investigations and forensics examinations on company computing systems. A paralegal from the Law Department, Ms. Jones, asks you to examine a USB drive belonging to an employee who left the company and now works for a competitor. The Law Department is concerned that the former employee might possess sensitive company data. Ms. Jones wants to know whether the USB drive contains anything significant.

In addition, she informs you that the former employee might have had access to confidential documents because a co-worker saw him accessing his manager's computer on his last day of work. These confidential documents consist of 24 files with the text "book." She wants you to locate any occurrences of these files on the USB drive's bit-stream image.

To process this case, make sure you have extracted the C2Prj02.eve file to your work folder, and then follow these steps:

1. Start ProDiscover Basic. In the New Project tab, enter a project number, the project name **C2Prj02**, and a project description, and then click **Open**. It's a good idea to get in the habit of saving the project immediately, so click **File, Save Project** from the menu, and save the file in your work folder (*Work*\Chap02\Projects).

2. Click **Action** from the menu, point to **Add**, and click **Image File**. Navigate to and click **C2Prj02.eve** in your work folder, and then click **Open**. If the Auto Image Checksum message box opens, click **Yes**.

3. In the tree view, click to expand **Content View**. Click to expand **Images**, and then click the pathname containing the image file. In the work area, examine the files that are listed.

4. To search for the keyword "book," click the **Search** toolbar button (the binoculars) to open the Search dialog box.

5. Click the **Content Search** tab. If necessary, click the **ASCII** option button and the **Search for the pattern(s)** option button. Type **book** in the list box for search keywords. Under Select the Disk(s)/Image(s) you want to search in, click the drive you're searching (see Figure 2-16), and then click **OK**.

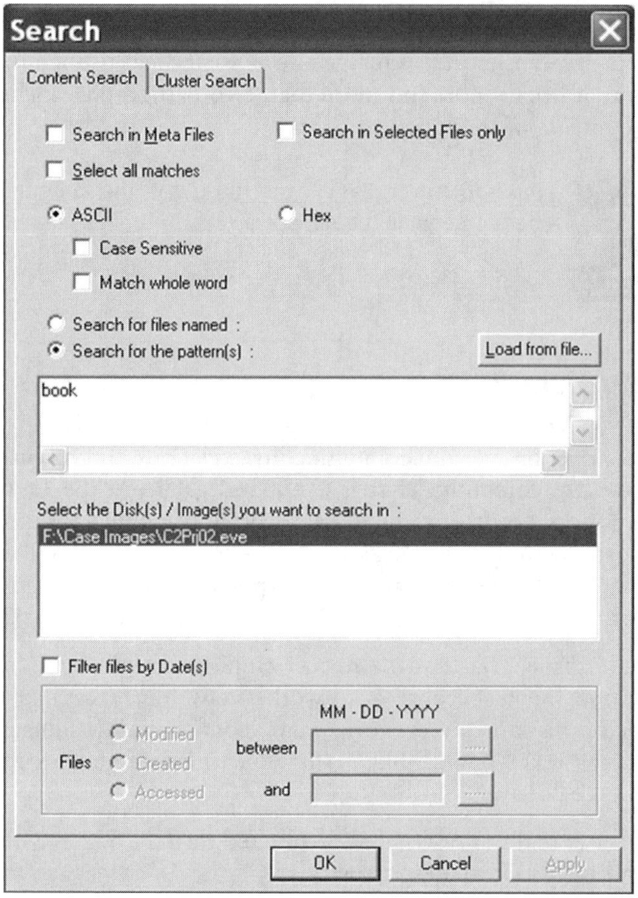

Figure 2-16 Entering search settings

6. In the tree view, click to expand **Search Results**, if necessary, and then click **Content Search Results** to specify the type of search. Figure 2-17 shows the search results pane.

7. Next, open the Search dialog box again, click the **Cluster Search** tab, and run the same search. Note that it takes longer because each cluster on the drive is searched.

8. In the tree view, click **Cluster Search Results**, and view the search results pane. Remember to save your project and exit ProDiscover Basic before starting the next case.

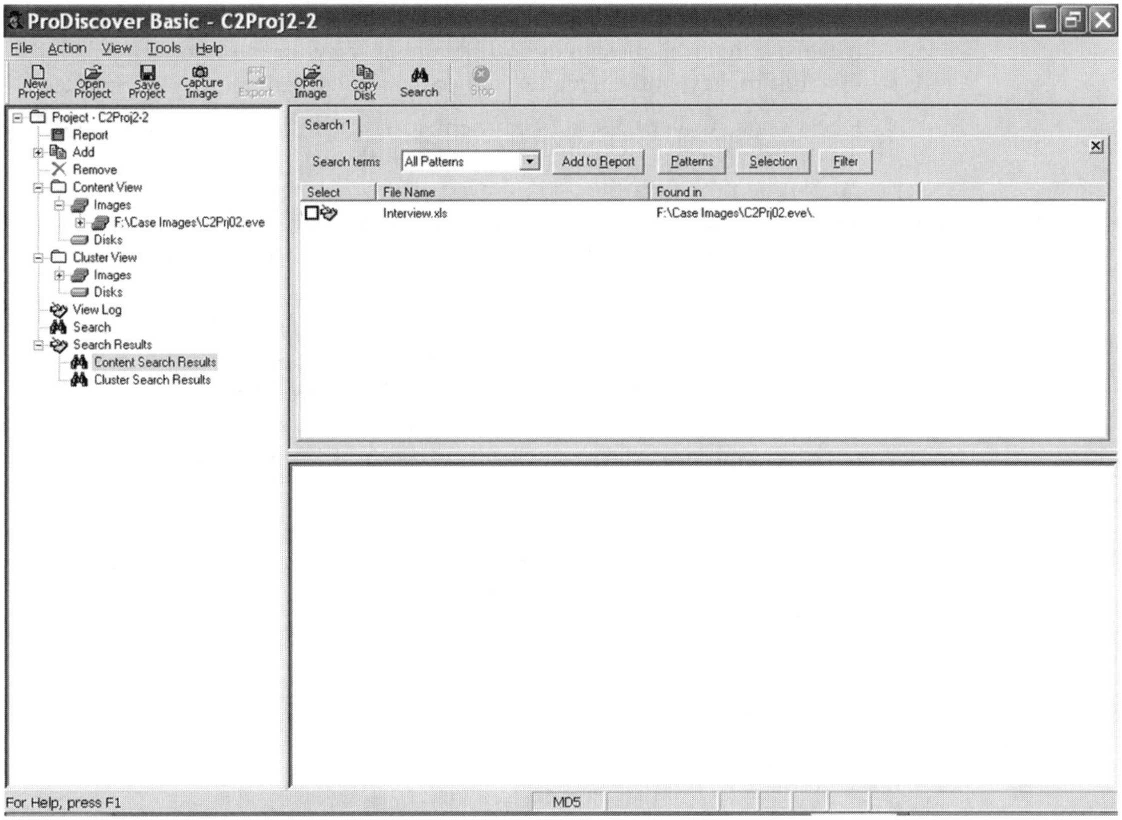

Figure 2-17 Viewing the search results

When you're finished, write a memo to Ms. Jones with the following information: the filenames in which you found a hit for the keyword and, if the hit occurred in unallocated space, the cluster number.

Hands-On Project 2-3

Ms. Jones notifies you that the former employee has used an additional drive. She asks you to examine this new drive to determine whether it contains an account number the employee might have had access to. The account number, 461562, belongs to the senior vice president and is used to access the company's banking service over the Internet.

1. Start ProDiscover Basic. In the New Project tab, enter a project number, the project name **C2Prj03**, and a brief description, and then click **Open**. Save the project in your work folder by clicking **File, Save Project** from the menu.

2. To add the evidence, click **Action** from the menu, point to **Add**, and click **Image File**. Navigate to your work folder, click the **C2Prj03.dd** file, and then click **Open**. Click **Yes** in the Auto Image Checksum message box, if necessary. Notice that the image file is a .dd file, not an .eve file. Like most forensics tools, ProDiscover can read standard UNIX .dd image files.

3. To aid in your investigation, you might want to view graphics files on the drive. To do this, click to expand **Content View** in the tree view, click to expand **Images,** and then click the pathname containing the image file.

4. Click **View, Gallery View** from the menu. Scroll through the graphics files on the drive image. You'll need to search through all folders, which can take some time. If a file is of interest, click the check box next to it in the Select column. In the Add Comment dialog box that opens, enter a description and click **OK.** These notes are added to the ProDiscover report.

5. This drive is related to the case in Hands-On Project 2-2, so you're still looking for occurrences of the word "book." Open the Search dialog box, and repeat Steps 5 through 8 of Hands-On Project 2-2 for this drive image. When you view the search results, click to select any files of interest (as described in Step 4), which opens the Add Comment dialog box where you can enter notes.

6. Next, search for the account number Ms. Jones gave you. Click the **Search** toolbar button. Click the **Content Search** tab, if necessary, and type **461562** as the search keyword. Click to select the drive you're searching, and then click **OK.** Click the **Cluster Search** tab, and repeat the search for the account number. Remember to select any files of interest and enter notes in the Add Comment dialog box.

Remember that text can be found in graphics files as well as in documents.

7. When you're finished, click **Report** in the tree view. Scroll through the report to make sure all the items you found are listed.

8. Next, click the **Export** toolbar button. In the Export dialog box, click the **RTF Format** option button, type **Ch2Prj03Report** in the File Name text box, and then click **OK.** (If you want to store the report in a different folder, click **Browse** and navigate to the new location.)

9. Write a short memo to summarize what you found. Save the project and exit ProDiscover Basic.

Hands-On Project 2-4

Sometimes discovery demands from law firms require you to recover only allocated data from a disk. This project shows you how to extract just the files that haven't been deleted from an image.

1. Start ProDiscover Basic. In the New Project tab, enter a project number, brief description, and the project name **C2Prj04,** and then click **Open.**

2. In the tree view, click to expand **Add,** and then click **Image File.** Navigate to your work folder, click the **C2Prj04.eve** file, and then click **Open.** Click **Yes** in the Auto Image Checksum message box, if necessary. Save the project in your work folder.

3. In the tree view, click to expand **Content View,** click to expand **Images,** and then click the pathname containing the image file. Notice the files visible in the work area.

4. Click the column header **Deleted** to sort the files into YES and NO groups (see Figure 2-18).

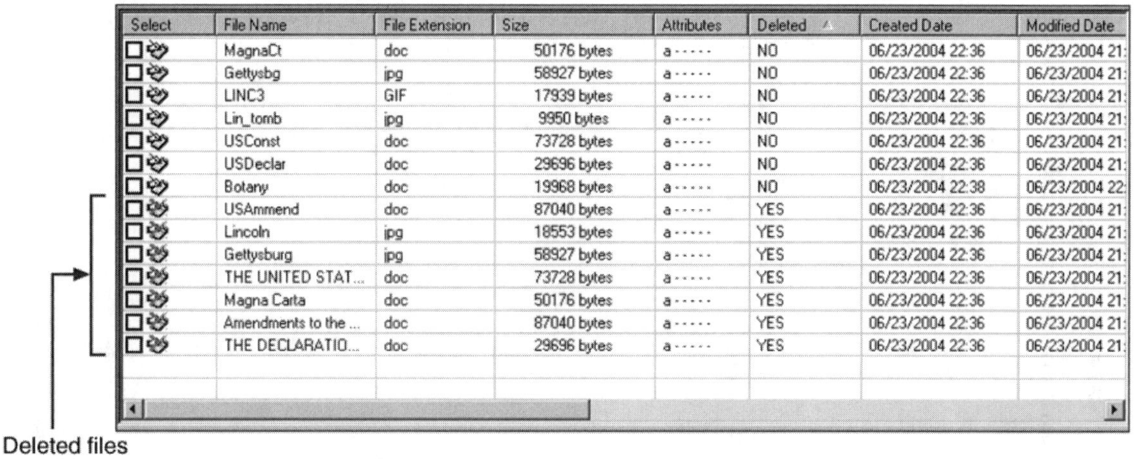

Select	File Name	File Extension	Size	Attributes	Deleted ▲	Created Date	Modified Date
☐ 🐾	MagnaCt	doc	50176 bytes	a - - - - -	NO	06/23/2004 22:36	06/23/2004 21:
☐ 🐾	Gettysbg	jpg	58927 bytes	a - - - - -	NO	06/23/2004 22:36	06/23/2004 21:
☐ 🐾	LINC3	GIF	17939 bytes	a - - - - -	NO	06/23/2004 22:36	06/23/2004 21:
☐ 🐾	Lin_tomb	jpg	9950 bytes	a - - - - -	NO	06/23/2004 22:36	06/23/2004 21:
☐ 🐾	USConst	doc	73728 bytes	a - - - - -	NO	06/23/2004 22:36	06/23/2004 21:
☐ 🐾	USDeclar	doc	29696 bytes	a - - - - -	NO	06/23/2004 22:36	06/23/2004 21:
☐ 🐾	Botany	doc	19968 bytes	a - - - - -	NO	06/23/2004 22:38	06/23/2004 22:
☐ 🐾	USAmmend	doc	87040 bytes	a - - - - -	YES	06/23/2004 22:36	06/23/2004 21:
☐ 🐾	Lincoln	jpg	18553 bytes	a - - - - -	YES	06/23/2004 22:36	06/23/2004 21:
☐ 🐾	Gettysburg	jpg	58927 bytes	a - - - - -	YES	06/23/2004 22:36	06/23/2004 21:
☐ 🐾	THE UNITED STAT...	doc	73728 bytes	a - - - - -	YES	06/23/2004 22:36	06/23/2004 21:
☐ 🐾	Magna Carta	doc	50176 bytes	a - - - - -	YES	06/23/2004 22:36	06/23/2004 21:
☐ 🐾	Amendments to the ...	doc	87040 bytes	a - - - - -	YES	06/23/2004 22:36	06/23/2004 21:
☐ 🐾	THE DECLARATIO...	doc	29696 bytes	a - - - - -	YES	06/23/2004 22:36	06/23/2004 21:

Deleted files

Figure 2-18 Deleted files displayed in the work area

5. To extract the allocated files from the image to your work folder, right-click each file containing NO in the Deleted column and click **Copy File.** (Note that in ProDiscover Basic, there's no way to select multiple files at once. You must copy each allocated file separately.) When you're finished, save the project and exit ProDiscover Basic.

Hands-On Project 2-5

This project is a continuation from the previous project; you'll create a report listing all the unallocated (deleted) files ProDiscover finds.

1. Start ProDiscover Basic. Click the **Open Project** tab, and navigate to your work folder.

2. Click the **C2Prj04.dft** file and click **Open.** Click **Yes** in the Auto Image Checksum message box, if necessary.

3. If necessary, sort the files in the work area again by clicking the **Deleted** column header. Click the check box in the Select column next to all unallocated (deleted) files, as shown in Figure 2-19. As you click each check box, the Add Comment dialog box opens, where you can enter a description of each file.

4. In the Investigator comments text box, add a comment noting that the file is deleted and indicating its file type, such as a Word document or an image file (.jpeg or .gif, for instance). Be sure to enter something meaningful by examining the file first.

5. When you're finished, click **Report** in the tree view. If you're satisfied, export the report by clicking the **Export** toolbar button. In the Export

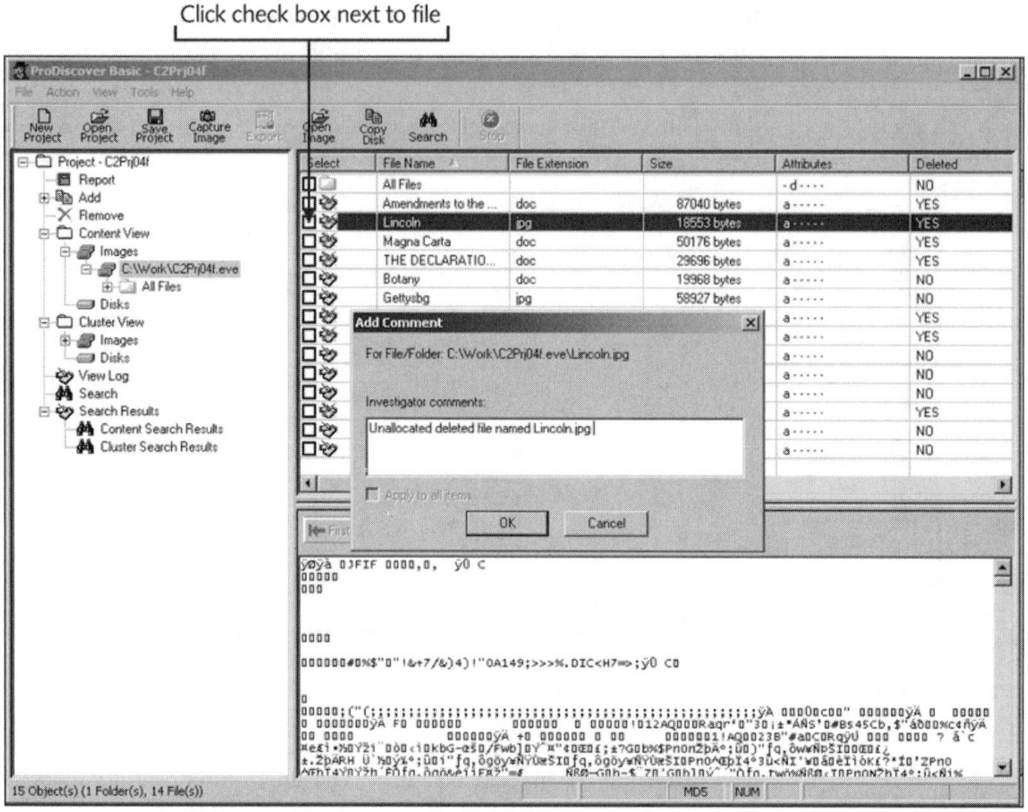

Click check box next to file

Figure 2-19   Selecting a file to include in a report

dialog box, select the format option you want, type **C2Prj05Report** in the File Name text box, and then click **OK**. Save the project and exit ProDiscover Basic.

Hands-On Project 2-6

In this project, another investigator asks you to examine an image and search for all occurrences of the following keywords:

- ANTONIO
- HUGH EVANS
- HORATIO

1. Start ProDiscover Basic. In the New Project tab, enter a project number, brief description, and the project name, and then click **Open**.

2. In the tree view, click to expand **Add**, and click **Image File**. Navigate to your work folder, click the **C2Prj06.eve** file, and click **Open**. Click **Yes** in the Auto Image Checksum message box, if necessary. Save the project in your work folder.

3. Click the **Search** toolbar button. In the Search dialog box, type all keywords in the list box (placing each on a separate line), click to select the drive containing the image, and click **OK**.

4. Examine the files in the search results pane. Select the ones that look interesting and enter notes in the Add Comment dialog box.

5. Generate a report and export it, as explained in previous projects. Save the project and exit ProDiscover Basic.

Case Projects

CASE PROJECTS

Case Project 2-1

An insurance company has asked your computer forensics firm to review a case for an arson investigation. The suspected arsonist has already been arrested, but the insurance company wants to determine whether there's any contributory negligence on the part of the victims. Two files were extracted to your work folder for this project. The first, CasePrj0201a.doc, is a memo about the case from the police department. The second, CasePrj0201b.doc, is a letter from the insurance company explaining what should be investigated. Review these files, and decide the course of action your firm needs to take. Write an outline for how your firm should approach the case.

Case Project 2-2

Jonathan Simpson owns a construction company. One day a subcontractor calls him, saying that he needs a replacement check for the job he completed at 1437 West Maple Avenue. Jonathan looks up the job on his accounting program and agrees to reissue the check for $12,750. The subcontractor says that the original check was for only $10,750. Jonathan looks around the office but can't find the company checkbook or ledger. Only one other person has access to the accounting program. Jonathan calls you to investigate. How would you proceed? Write a one-page report detailing the steps Jonathan needs to take to gather the necessary evidence and protect his company.

Case Project 2-3

You are the computer forensics investigator for a law firm. The firm acquired a new client, a young woman who was fired from her job for inappropriate files discovered on her computer. She swears she never accessed the files. What questions should you ask and how should you proceed? Write a one- to two-page report describing the computer the client used, who else had access to it, and any other relevant facts that should be investigated.

Case Project 2-4

A desperate employee calls because she has accidentally deleted crucial files from her hard drive and can't retrieve them from the Recycle Bin. What are your options? Write one to two pages explaining your capabilities and listing the questions you need to ask her about her system.

chapter 3

The Investigator's Office and Laboratory

After reading this chapter and completing the exercises, you will be able to:

- Describe certification requirements for computer forensics labs
- List physical requirements for a computer forensics lab
- Explain the criteria for selecting a basic forensic workstation
- Describe components used to build a business case for developing a forensics lab

This chapter details some options for setting up an effective computer forensics laboratory. Each computer forensics investigator in a lab should also have a private office where he or she can manage cases, conduct interviews, and communicate without eavesdropping concerns. Whether you are new to computer forensics or are an experienced examiner, your goal is to make your office and lab work smoothly and efficiently for all casework.

Computer forensics investigators must remember to consider budget and time when updating their labs to keep pace with computer technology changes. The workflow and processes you establish directly affect the quality of evidence you discover. You must balance cost, quality, and reliability when determining the kind of equipment, software, and other items you need to add to your lab. This chapter provides a foundation for organizing, controlling, and managing a safe, efficient computer forensics laboratory.

Understanding Forensics Lab Certification Requirements

A **computer forensics lab** is where you conduct investigations, store evidence, and do most of your work. You use the lab to house your instruments, current and legacy software, and forensic workstations. In general, you need a variety of computer forensics hardware and software to do your work.

You also need to make sure you have defined policies, processes, and prescribed procedures before beginning any casework to ensure the integrity of an analysis and its results. A number of organizations have created guidelines for devising your own processes and procedures. What's most important is that you follow the policies and procedures you have created to ensure consistency in your output.

 Be sure to research certifying bodies thoroughly before pursuing any certifications. Many certifications are offered by software vendors; others are specific for law enforcement or started by local groups.

The **American Society of Crime Laboratory Directors** (ASCLD; *www.ascld.org*) provides guidelines to members for managing a forensics lab and acquiring crime and forensics lab certification. ASCLD also certifies computer forensics labs that analyze digital evidence as they do other criminal evidence, such as fingerprints and DNA samples. This certification is based on the original crime lab certification, ASCLD/LAB (*www.ascld-lab.org*), which regulates how crime labs are organized and managed. The ASCLD/LAB program includes specific audits on all functions to ensure that lab procedures are being performed correctly and consistently for all casework. These audits should be performed in computer forensics labs to maintain the quality and integrity of analysis. The following sections discuss several key guidelines from the ASCLD/LAB program that you can apply to managing, configuring, and auditing your computer forensics lab.

Identifying Duties of the Lab Manager and Staff

The ASCLD states that each lab should have a specific set of objectives that a parent organization and the lab's director or manager determine. The lab manager sets up processes for managing cases and reviews them regularly. Besides performing general management tasks, such as promoting group consensus in decision making, maintaining fiscal responsibility for lab needs, and enforcing ethical standards (covered in Chapters 15 and 16) among staff members, the lab manager plans updates for the lab, such as new hardware and software purchases.

The lab manager also establishes and promotes quality assurance processes for the lab's staff to follow, such as outlining what to do when a case arrives, logging evidence, specifying who can enter the lab, and establishing guidelines for filing reports. To ensure the lab's efficiency, the lab manager also sets reasonable production schedules for processing work.

A typical case for an internal corporate investigation involves seizing a hard disk, making forensic copies of it, evaluating evidence, and filing a report. A forensics analysis of a 200 GB disk, for example, can take several days and often involves running imaging software overnight and on weekends. This means one of the forensic workstations in the lab is occupied for that time, which can be 20 hours or more. Based on past experience, the lab manager can estimate how many cases each investigator can handle and when to expect a preliminary and final report for each case.

The lab manager creates and monitors lab policies for staff and provides a safe and secure workplace for staff and evidence. Above all, the lab manager accounts for all activities the lab's staff conducts to complete its work. Tracking cases such as e-mail abuse, Internet misuse, and illicit activities can justify the funds spent on a lab.

Staff members in a computer forensics lab should have sufficient training to perform their tasks. Necessary skills include hardware and software knowledge, including OS and file types, and deductive reasoning. Their work is reviewed regularly by the lab manager and their peers to ensure quality. Staff members are also responsible for continuing technical training to update their investigative and computer skills and maintaining a record of the training they have completed. Many vendors and organizations hold annual or quarterly training seminars that offer certification exams.

The ASCLD Web site summarizes the requirements of managing a computer forensics lab, handling and preserving evidence, performing laboratory procedures, setting personnel requirements, and encouraging professional development. The site also provides a user license for printed and online manuals of lab management guidelines. ASCLD stresses that each lab should maintain an up-to-date library of resources in its field. For computer forensics, these resources include software, hardware information, and technical journals.

Lab Budget Planning

To conduct a professional computing investigation, you need to understand the cost of your lab operation. Lab costs can be broken down into daily, quarterly, and annual expenses. The better you understand these expenses, the better you can delegate resources for each investigation. Using a spreadsheet program helps you keep track of past investigation expenses so that you can extrapolate expected future costs. Remember, expenses include computer hardware and software, facility space, and trained personnel.

When creating a budget, start by estimating the number of computer cases your lab expects to examine and identifying the types of computers you're likely to examine, such as Windows PCs or Linux workstations. For example, suppose you work for a state police agency that's planning to provide computing investigation services for the entire state. You could start by collecting state crime statistics for the current year and several previous years to determine how many computers were used to commit a crime and the types of computers used in these crimes. Criminal behavior often reflects sales trends for certain computing systems. Because more than 90% of consumers use Intel and AMD PCs, and 90% of these computers run Microsoft Windows, the same statistics are likely true of computers used in crimes. Verify this trend by determining how often each type of system is used in a crime. List the number of crimes committed using DOS/Windows, Linux/UNIX, and Macintosh computers.

If you can't find detailed information on the types of computers and OSs used in computer crimes, gather enough information to make an educated guess. Your goal is to build a baseline for the types and numbers of systems you can expect to investigate. In addition to the historical data you compile, identify any future trends that could affect your lab, such as a new version of an OS or an increase in the number of computers involved in crime.

Next, estimate how many investigations you might conduct involving computer systems used less frequently to help determine how many tools you need to examine these systems. For example, if you learn that on average, one Macintosh computer running OS 9 or earlier is involved in a criminal investigation each month, you probably need only one or two software tools to conduct a forensic analysis on Macintosh file systems.

Figure 3-1 shows a table of statistics from a **Uniform Crime Report** that identifies the number of hard disk types, such as IDE or SCSI, and the OS used to commit crimes. Annual Uniform Crime Reports are generated at the federal, state, and local levels to show the types and frequency of crimes committed. For federal reports, see *www.fbi.gov/ucr/ucr.htm*, and for a summary of crimes committed at various levels, see *www.ojp.usdoj.gov/bjs/dtd.htm*.

You can also identify specialized software used with certain crimes. For example, if you find a check-writing software tool used in a large number of counterfeiting cases, you should consider adding this specialized software to your inventory.

If you're preparing to set up a computer forensics lab for a private company, you can determine your needs more easily because you're working in a contained environment. Start by obtaining an inventory of all known computing systems and applications used in the business. For example, an insurance company often has a network of Intel PCs and servers and specialized insurance software using a database for data storage. A large manufacturing company might use Intel PCs, UNIX workstations running a computer-aided design (CAD) system, super minicomputers, and mainframes. A publishing company might have a combination of Intel PCs and Apple Macintosh systems and a variety of word processing, imaging, and composition packages.

Next, check with your Management, Human Resource, and Security departments to determine the types of complaints and problems reported in the past year. Most companies using Internet connections, for example, receive complaints about employees accessing the Web excessively or for personal use, which generate investigations of Web misuse. Be sure to distinguish investigations of excessive Web use from inappropriate Web site access and e-mail harassment.

Your budget should also take future developments in computing technology into account because drive storage capabilities improve constantly. When examining a disk, you need a target disk to which you copy evidence data. This disk should be at least one and a half

	IDE Drive	SCSI Drive	Intel PC Platform			Linux	Apple Platform		UNIX H/W	Other H/W	Total Systems Examined	Total HDD Examined
			Win9x	WinNT /2k/ XP	MS Other O/S		OS 9.x & older	OS X				
Arson	5	3	3	1		1					5	8
Assault— Aggravated	78	5	31			14				1	47	83
Assault— Simple	180	3	77	6		1	32	44	2	1	163	183
Bribery	153		153								153	153
Burglary	1746		1487	259							1746	1746
Counterfeiting & Forgery	1390	4	543	331		309	21	186			1390	1394
Destruction, Damage, & Vandalism	976	48	142	45	29	127	325	90	217	1	976	1024
Drug, Narcotic	1939	24	1345	213		158	213	10			1939	1963
Embezzlement	1023		320	549		23	87	41		3	1023	1023
Extortion & Blackmail	77		2	61		10	3	1			77	77
Fraud	2002		638	932	9	173	55	190		5	2002	2002
Gambling	4910	5	1509	2634		136	138	498			4915	4915
Homicide	36		5	11	9	1	3	7			36	36
Kidnapping & Abduction	2		1	1							2	2
Larceny Theft	7342	56	2134	3093	5	935	127	982	1	21	7298	7398
Motor Vehicle Theft	1747		231	1508		5	1	2			1747	1747
Child Porn	593	2	98	162		68	105	160	2		595	595
Robbery	33		23	7		2		1			33	33
Sex Offense— Forcible	80		21	45		1	5	8			80	80
Sex Offense— Non-Forcible	900		324	437		6	90	43			900	900
Stolen Property Offenses	2711	10	800	1634	3	169	53	37	1	9	2706	2721
Weapons Violations	203	1	43	89	2	11	28	31			204	204
Totals Per System	28126	161	9930	12018	59	2179	1300	2289	222	40	28037	28287
			HDD FAT/NTFS	22007				HDD Mac O/S X/Linux/ UNIX	2511			

Figure 3-1 Uniform Crime Report statistics

times the size of the evidence (suspect) disk. For example, a lab equipped with 100 GB disks can effectively analyze disks up to 66 GB. If your company upgrades its computers to 200 GB disks, however, you need disks that are 300 GB or larger or a central secure server with at least 1 TB of storage. (Several forensic servers on the market are in the 20 TB and higher range.) Many businesses replace their desktop computer systems every 18 months to three years. You must be informed of computer upgrades and other changes in the computing environment so that you can prepare and submit your budget for needed resources.

Like computer hardware, OSs change periodically. If your current computer forensics tool doesn't work with the next release of a Microsoft OS or file system, you must upgrade your software tools. You should also monitor vendor product developments to learn about upgrades. File systems change, too. Forensics tools had their birth in DOS, and over the years, Windows hard disks evolved into a variety of file systems, including FAT16, FAT32, New Technology File System (NTFS), and Windows File System. Most DOS-based tools can't read NTFS disks. Now investigators must also address Vista, which has caused problems even with Windows forensics tools. In addition, the popularity and prevalence of the Xbox requires that investigators be familiar with the FATX file system.

Time management is a major issue when choosing software and hardware to purchase. For example, you've decided to purchase eight machines for your lab. Many commercial forensics software packages require a USB dongle to operate or have a site license of five concurrent users. You or the budget manager must decide whether you're using all the machines or need only two licensed copies of each software package. As another example, you can have a command-line tool running overnight for drive imaging; while it's running; investigators can use a commercial or freeware package to evaluate a drive. You choices depend on what tools you have verified and what's needed for your casework.

Another option is to use Helix (a Linux Live CD, discussed in Chapter 4) to view file systems, as it doesn't mount the hard drive automatically and, therefore, doesn't write to the drive. (A hardware write-blocker is still recommended to prevent errors caused by the forensics technician, if nothing else.) Examining PDAs, USB drives, and cell phones is routine now in cases from criminal investigations to civil litigation discovery demands. Computer investigators must be prepared to deal with constant change in these devices and know what tools are available to safely extract data from them for an investigation. In Chapter 13, you learn how to acquire data from these devices.

Acquiring Certification and Training

To continue a career in computing investigations and forensic analysis, you need to upgrade your skills through training. Several organizations have developed or are currently developing certification programs for computer forensics that usually test you after you have completed one or more training sessions successfully. Certifying organizations range from nonprofit associations to vendor-sponsored groups. All these programs charge fees for certification, and some require candidates to take vendor- or organization-sponsored training to qualify for the certification. More recently, some state and federal government agencies have been looking into establishing their own certification programs that address the minimum skills for conducting computing investigations at various levels.

Before enlisting in a certification program, thoroughly research the requirements, cost, and acceptability in your chosen area of employment. Most certification programs require continuing education credits or reexamination of candidates' skills, which can become costly.

International Association of Computer Investigative Specialists (IACIS)

Created by police officers who wanted to formalize credentials in computing investigations, IACIS is one of the oldest professional computer forensics organizations. It restricts membership to sworn law enforcement personnel or government employees working as computer forensics examiners. This restriction might change, so visit the IACIS Web site (*www.iacis.com*) to verify the requirements.

IACIS conducts an annual two-week training course for qualified members. Students must interpret and trace e-mail, acquire evidence properly, identify OSs, recover data, and understand encryption theory and other topics. Students must pass a written exam before continuing to the next level. Passing the exam earns the status of **Certified Electronic Evidence Collection Specialist (CEECS)**. The next level of training is completed through a correspondence course lasting up to one year. The IACIS certification process for this level consists of examining a variety of media and completing a written test. Some media must be examined by using a command-line tool. The testing agency plants files on these media that you must find, including easy-to-find items, data in unallocated space, RAM slack, file slack, and deleted files. Cell phones, PDAs, and other digital devices are being added as the field broadens.

Other topics include data hiding, determining file types of disguised files, and accessing password-protected files. You might also be asked to draw conclusions on a case based on evidence found on the media. Proficiency in technical tools and deductive reasoning is necessary. A detailed report demonstrating accepted procedures and evidence control must be submitted with each disk before proceeding to the next. The most basic test is the CEECS exam. Other candidates who complete all parts of the IACIS test successfully are designated as a **Certified Forensic Computer Examiner (CFCE)**. The CFCE process changes as technology changes. The description here is current as of this writing. IACIS requires recertification every three years to demonstrate continuing work in the field of computer forensics. Recertification is less intense than the original certification but does test examiners to make sure they're continuing their education and are still active in the field of computer forensics. For the latest information about IACIS and applying for CFCE certification or membership in IACIS, visit the IACIS Web site.

High-Tech Crime Network (HTCN) The **High-Tech Crime Network (HTCN)** also offers several levels of certification. Unlike IACIS, however, HTCN requires a review of all related training, including training in one of its approved courses, a written test for the specific certification, and a review of the candidate's work history. HTCN certification is open to anyone meeting the criteria in the profession of computing investigations. At the time of this writing, the HTCN Web site (*www.htcn.org*) specifies requirements for the certification levels discussed in the following paragraphs. Requirements are updated without notice, so make sure you check the site periodically.

Certified Computer Crime Investigator, Basic Level

- Candidates must have three years of experience directly related to investigating computer-related incidents or crimes.
- Candidates have successfully completed 40 hours of training from an approved agency, organization, or training company.
- Candidates must provide documentation of at least 10 cases in which they participated.

Certified Computer Crime Investigator, Advanced Level

- Candidates must have five years of experience directly related to investigating computer-related incidents or crimes.
- Candidates have successfully completed 80 hours of training from an approved agency, organization, or company.

- Candidates have served as lead investigator in at least 20 cases during the past three years and were involved in at least 40 other cases as a lead investigator or supervisor or in a supportive capacity. Candidates have at least 60 hours of involvement in cases in the past three years.

Certified Computer Forensic Technician, Basic

- Candidates must have three years of experience in computing investigations for law enforcement or corporate cases.
- Candidates must have completed 40 hours of computer forensics training from an approved organization.
- Candidates must provide documentation of at least 10 computing investigations.

Certified Computer Forensic Technician, Advanced

- Candidates must have five years of hands-on experience in computer forensics investigations for law enforcement or corporate cases.
- Candidates must have completed 80 hours of computer forensics training from an approved organization.
- Candidates must have been the lead computer forensics investigator in 20 or more investigations in the past three years and in 40 or more additional computing investigations as lead computer forensics technician, supervisor, or contributor. The candidate must have completed at least 60 investigations in the past three years.

EnCase Certified Examiner (EnCE) Certification   Guidance Software, the creator of EnCase, sponsors the EnCE certification program. EnCE certification is open to the public and private sectors and is specific to use and mastery of EnCase computer forensics analysis.

Requirements for taking the EnCE certification exam don't depend on taking the Guidance Software EnCase training courses. Candidates for this certificate are required to have a licensed copy of EnCase. For more information on EnCE certification requirements, visit *www.encase.com* or *www.guidancesoftware.com*.

AccessData Certified Examiner (ACE)   AccessData, the creator of Ultimate Toolkit, sponsors the ACE certification program. ACE certification is open to the public and private sectors and is specific to use and mastery of AccessData Ultimate Toolkit.

Requirements for taking the ACE exam include completing the AccessData BootCamp and Windows forensic courses. The exam has a knowledge base assessment (KBA) and a practical skills assessment (PSA), which is optional. For more information on this certification, visit *www.accessdata.com/acepreparation.html*.

Other Training and Certifications   Other organizations are considering certifications or have related training programs. Nonprofit high-technology organizations for public- and private-sector investigations that offer certification and training include the following:

- High Technology Crime Investigation Association (HTCIA), *www.htcia.org*
- SysAdmin, Audit, Network, Security (SANS) Institute, *www.sans.org*

- Computer Technology Investigators Network (CTIN), *www.ctin.org*
- New Technologies, Inc. (NTI), *www.forensics-intl.com*
- Southeast Cybercrime Institute at Kennesaw State University, *www.certifiedcomputerexaminer.com*

Organizations that offer training and certification for law enforcement personnel or qualified civilian government personnel include the following:

- Federal Law Enforcement Training Center (FLETC), *www.fletc.gov*
- National White Collar Crime Center (NW3C), *www.nw3c.org*

Determining the Physical Requirements for a Computer Forensics Lab

After you have the training to become a computer forensics investigator, you conduct most of your investigations in a lab. This section discusses the physical requirements for a computer forensics lab. Addressing these requirements can make a lab safer, more secure, and more productive.

Your lab facility must be physically secure so that evidence isn't lost, corrupted, or destroyed. As with hardware and software costs, you must consider what's needed to maintain a safe and secure environment when determining physical lab expenses. You must also use inventory control methods to track your computing assets, which means you should maintain a complete and up-to-date inventory of all major hardware and software items in the lab. For consumable items, such as cables and storage media, maintain an inventory so that you know when to order more supplies.

Identifying Lab Security Needs

All computer forensics labs need an enclosed room where a forensic workstation can be set up. You shouldn't use an open cubicle because it allows easy access to your evidence. You need a room you can lock to control your evidence and attest to its integrity. In particular, your lab should be secure during data analysis, even if it takes several weeks to analyze a disk drive. To preserve the integrity of evidence, your lab should function as an evidence locker or safe, making it a **secure facility** or a secure storage safe.

The following are the minimum requirements for a computer forensics lab of any size:

- Small room with true floor-to-ceiling walls
- Door access with a locking mechanism, which can be a regular key lock or combination lock; the key or combination must be limited to authorized users
- Secure container, such as a safe or heavy-duty file cabinet with a quality padlock that prevents drawers from opening
- Visitor's log listing all people who have accessed the lab

For daily work production, several examiners can work together in a large open area, as long as they all have the same level of authority and access need. This area should also have floor-to-ceiling walls and a locking door. In many public and private organizations, several investigators share a door to the lab that requires an ID card and entry code.

Computing investigators and forensics examiners must be briefed on the lab's security policy. Share information about a case investigation only with other examiners and personnel who need to know about the investigation.

Conducting High-Risk Investigations

High-risk investigations, such as those involving national security or murder, for example, demand more security than the minimum lab requirements provide. As technology improves and information circulates among computer attackers, keeping an investigation secure can be more difficult. For example, detecting computer eavesdropping is difficult and expensive, but sophisticated criminals and intelligence services in foreign countries can use equipment that detects network transmissions, wireless devices, phone conversations, and the use of computer equipment. Instructions for building a sniffing device that can collect computer emanations illegally can be found online and, therefore, are available to anyone. These devices can pick up anything you type on your computer.

Most electronic devices emit electromagnetic radiation (EMR). Certain kinds of equipment can intercept EMR, which can be used to determine the data the device is transmitting or displaying. The EMR from a computer monitor can be picked up as far away as a half mile.

During the Cold War, defense contractors were required to shield sensitive computing systems and prevent electronic eavesdropping of any computer emissions. The U.S. Department of Defense calls this special computer-emission shielding **TEMPEST**. (For a brief description of TEMPEST, see the National Industrial Security Program Operating Manual [NISPOM]. DoD 5220.22-M, Chapter 11, Section 1, Tempest, *http://nsi.org/Library/Govt/Nispom.html*. Another site listing reliable sources is *www.eskimo.com/~joelm/tempestintro.html*.)

To protect your investigations, you might consider constructing a TEMPEST-qualified lab, which requires lining the walls, ceiling, floor, and doors with specially grounded conductive metal sheets. Typically, copper sheeting is used because it conducts electricity well. TEMPEST facilities must include special filters for electrical power that prevent power cables from transmitting computer emanations. All heating and ventilation ducts must have special baffles to trap emanations. Likewise, telephones inside the TEMPEST facility must have special line filters. A TEMPEST facility usually has two doors separated by dead space. The first exterior door must be shut before opening the interior door. Each door also has special copper molding to enhance electricity conduction.

Because a TEMPEST-qualified lab facility is expensive and requires routine inspection and testing, it should be considered only for large regional computer forensics labs that demand absolute security from illegal eavesdropping. To avoid these costs, some vendors have built low-emanating workstations instead of TEMPEST facilities. These workstations are more expensive than average workstations but less expensive than a TEMPEST lab.

Using Evidence Containers

Evidence storage containers, also known as evidence lockers, must be secure so that no unauthorized person can access your evidence easily. You must use high-quality locks, such as padlocks, with limited duplicate-key distribution. Also, routinely inspect the contents of evidence storage containers to make sure only current evidence is stored. The evidence custody forms should indicate what's still in the locker. Evidence for closed cases should be moved to a secure off-site facility.

NISPOM Chapter 5, Section 3 (*http://nsi.org/Library/Govt/Nispom.html*) describes the characteristics of a safe storage container. Consult with your facility management or legal counsel, such as corporate or prosecuting attorneys, to determine what your lab should do to maintain evidence integrity. The following are recommendations for securing storage containers:

- The evidence container should be located in a restricted area that's accessible only to lab personnel.
- The number of people authorized to open the evidence container should be kept to a minimum. Maintain records on who's authorized to access each container.
- All evidence containers should remain locked when they aren't under the direct supervision of an authorized person.

If a combination locking system is used for your evidence container, follow these practices:

- Provide the same level of security for the combination as for the container's contents. Store the combination in another equally secure container.
- Destroy any previous combinations after setting up a new combination.
- Allow only authorized personnel to change lock combinations.
- Change the combination every six months, when any authorized personnel leave the organization, and immediately after finding an unsecured container—that is, one that's open and unattended.

If you're using a keyed padlock, follow these practices:

- Appoint a key custodian who's responsible for distributing keys.
- Stamp sequential numbers on each duplicate key.
- Maintain a registry listing which key is assigned to which authorized person.
- Conduct a monthly audit to ensure that no authorized person has lost a key.
- Take an inventory of all keys when the custodian changes.
- Place keys in a lockable container accessible only to the lab manager and designated key custodian.
- Maintain the same level of security for keys as for evidence containers.
- Change locks and keys annually; if a key is missing, replace all associated locks and the key.
- Do not use a master key for several locks.

The storage container or cabinet should be made of steel and include an internal cabinet lock or external padlock. If possible, purchase a safe, which provides superior security and protects your evidence from fire damage. Look for specialized safes, called media safes, designed to protect electronic media. Media safes are rated by the number of hours it takes before fire damages the contents. The higher the rating, the better the safe protects evidence.

An evidence storage room is also convenient, especially if it's part of your computer forensics lab. Security for an evidence room must integrate the same construction and securing devices as the general lab does. Large computer forensics operations also need an evidence custodian and a service counter with a securable metal roll-up window to control evidence. With a secure evidence room, you can store large computer components, such as computers, monitors, and other peripheral devices.

Be sure to maintain a log listing every time an evidence container is opened and closed. Each time the container is accessed, the log should indicate the date it was opened and the initials of the authorized person. These records should be maintained for at least three years or longer, as prescribed by your prosecuting or corporate attorneys. Logs are discussed in more detail in Chapter 5.

Overseeing Facility Maintenance

Your lab should be maintained properly at all times to ensure the safety and health of lab personnel. Any damage to the floor, walls, ceilings, or furniture should be repaired immediately. Also, be sure to escort cleaning crews into the facility and monitor them as they work.

Because static electricity is a major problem when handling computer parts, consider placing antistatic pads around electronic workbenches and workstations. In addition, floors and carpets should be cleaned at least once a week to help minimize dust that can cause static electricity.

Maintain two separate trash containers, one to store items unrelated to an investigation, such as discarded CDs or magnetic tapes, and the other for sensitive material that requires special handling to make sure it's destroyed. Using separate trash containers maintains the integrity of criminal investigation processes and protects trade secrets and attorney-client privileged communications in a private corporation. Several commercially bonded firms specialize in disposing of sensitive materials, and you should hire one to help maintain the integrity of your investigations.

Considering Physical Security Needs

In addition to your lab's physical design and construction, you need to enhance security by setting security policies. How much physical security you implement depends on the nature of your lab. A regional computer crime lab has high physical security needs because of the risks of losing, corrupting, or damaging evidence. The physical security needs of a large corporation are probably not as high because the risk of evidence loss or compromise is much lower. Determining the risk for your organization dictates how much security you integrate into your computer forensics lab.

When considering digital security needs, many companies neglect physical security.

Regardless of the security risk to your lab, maintain a paper or electronic sign-in log for all visitors. The log should list the visitor's name, date and time of arrival and departure, employer's name, purpose of the visit, and name of the lab member receiving the visitor. Consider anyone who's not assigned to the lab to be a visitor, including cleaning crews, facility maintenance personnel, friends, and family. All visitors should be escorted by an assigned authorized staff member throughout their visit to the lab to ensure that they don't accidentally or intentionally tamper with an investigation or evidence. As an added precaution, use a visible or audible alarm, such as a visitor badge, to let all investigators know that a visitor is in the area. If possible, hire a security guard or have an intrusion alarm system with a guard to ensure your lab's security. Alarm systems with guards can also be used after business hours to monitor your lab.

Auditing a Computer Forensics Lab

To make sure security policies and practices are followed, conduct routine inspections to audit your lab and evidence storage containers. Audits should include, but aren't limited to, the following facility components and practices:

- Inspect the lab's ceiling, floor, roof, and exterior walls at least once a month, looking for anything unusual or new.
- Inspect doors to make sure they close and lock correctly.
- Check locks to see whether they need to be replaced or changed.
- Review visitor logs to see whether they're being used properly.
- Review log sheets for evidence containers to determine when they have been opened and closed.
- At the end of every workday, secure any evidence that's not being processed on a forensic workstation.

Determining Floor Plans for Computer Forensics Labs

How you configure the work area for your computer forensics lab depends on your budget, the amount of available floor space, and the number of computers you assign to each computing investigator. For a small operation handling two or three cases a month, one forensic workstation should be enough to handle the workload. One workstation requires only the space an average desk takes up. If you're handling many more cases per month, you can probably process two or three investigations at a time, which requires more than one workstation. The ideal configuration for multiple workstations is to have two forensic workstations plus one nonforensic workstation with Internet access.

Because you need plenty of room around each workstation, a work area containing three workstations requires approximately 150 square feet of space, meaning the work area should be about 10 feet by 15 feet. This amount of space allows for two chairs so that the computing investigator can brief another investigator, paralegal, or attorney on the case.

Small labs usually consist of one or two forensic workstations, a research computer with Internet access, a workbench (if space allows), and storage cabinets, as shown in Figure 3-2.

Mid-size computer forensics labs, such as those in a private business, have more workstations. For safety reasons, the lab should have at least two exits, as shown in Figure 3-3. If possible, cubicles or even separate offices should be part of the layout to reinforce the need-to-know policy. These labs usually have more library space for software and hardware storage.

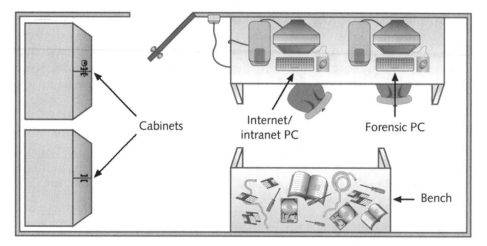

Figure 3-2 Small or home-based lab

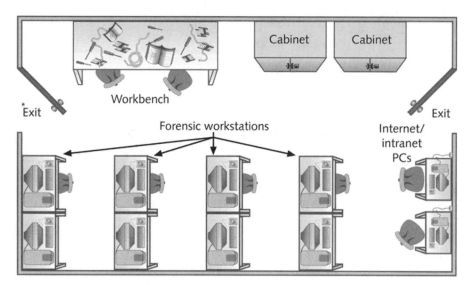

Figure 3-3 Mid-size computer forensics lab

State law enforcement or the FBI usually runs most large or regional computer forensics labs. As shown in Figure 3-4, these labs have a separate evidence room, which is typical in police investigations, except this room is limited to digital evidence. One or more custodians might be assigned to manage and control traffic in and out of the evidence room.

As discussed earlier, the evidence room needs to be secure. The lab should have at least two controlled exits and no windows. Separate offices for supervisors and cubicles for investigators are more practical in this configuration. Remember that forensic workstations are connected to an isolated LAN, and only a few machines are connected to an outside WAN or metropolitan area network (MAN).

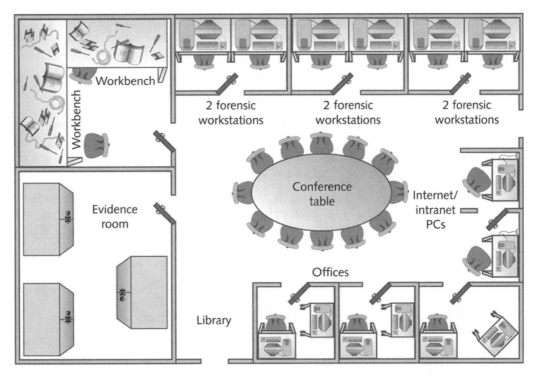

Figure 3-4 Regional computer forensics lab

Selecting a Basic Forensic Workstation

The computer workstation you use as a forensics analysis system depends on your budget and specific needs. Many well-designed forensic workstations are available that can handle most computing investigation needs. However, when you start processing a case, you use a workstation for the duration of the examination. Use less powerful workstations for mundane tasks and multipurpose workstations for higher-end analysis tasks.

Selecting Workstations for Police Labs

Police departments in major cities probably have the most diverse needs for computing investigation tools because the communities they serve use a wide assortment of computing systems. Not all computer users have the latest technology, so police departments usually need older machines and software, such as a Commodore 64, an Osbourne I, or a Kaypro running CP/M or Minix, to match what's used in their community. For small, local police departments, however, the majority of work involves Windows PCs and Apple Macintosh systems. A small police department's computer forensics lab could be limited to one multipurpose forensic workstation with one or two basic workstations.

One way to investigate older and unusual computing systems is to keep track of **special-interest groups (SIGs)** that still use these systems. SIGs, which you can find through an Internet search, can be a valuable source of support for recovering and analyzing uncommon systems. You can also coordinate with or subcontract to larger computer forensics labs. Like large police departments, a regional computer forensics lab must have diverse systems to serve its community and often receives work from smaller labs involving unusual computers or OSs.

Computing systems in a lab should be able to process typical cases in a timely manner. The time it takes to process a case usually depends on the size and type of industries in the region. For example, suppose your lab is located in a region with a large manufacturing firm that employs 50,000 people. Based on crime reports you've consulted, 10% of those employees might be involved in criminal behavior, meaning 5000 employees will commit crimes such as fraud, embezzlement, and so on. These statistics can help you estimate how much time is involved in processing these types of cases.

Until recently, the general rule was at least one law enforcement computer investigator for every 250,000 people in a geographic region. For example, if your community has 1,000,000 people, the regional computer forensics lab should have at least four computer investigators, each with at least one multipurpose forensic workstation and one general-purpose workstation. This rule is quickly changing, however, as the amount of data stored on digital devices increases.

Selecting Workstations for Private and Corporate Labs

For the private sector, such as a business conducting internal investigations or a commercial business providing computer forensics services to private parties, equipment resources are generally easy to determine.

Commercial businesses providing computer forensics analysis for other companies can tailor their services to specific markets. They can specialize in one or two platforms, such as an Intel PC running a Microsoft OS. They can also gather a variety of tools to meet a wider market. The type of equipment they need depends on their specialty, if any. For general computer forensics facilities, a multipurpose forensic workstation is sufficient.

Private companies conducting their own internal computing investigations can determine the type of forensic workstation they need based on the types of computers they use. If a company uses only Windows PCs, internal investigators don't need a wide variety of specialized equipment. If a company uses many kinds of computers, the Internal Computing Investigation Department needs systems and equipment that support the same types of computers. With some computer forensics programs, you can work from a Windows PC and examine both Windows and Macintosh disk drives.

Stocking Hardware Peripherals

In addition to workstations and software, all labs should have a wide assortment of cables and spare expansion slot cards. Consider stocking your computer forensics lab with the following peripheral devices:

- 40-pin 18-inch and 36-inch IDE cables, both ATA-33 and ATA-100 or faster
- Ribbon cables for floppy disks
- Extra SCSI cards, preferably ultra-wide
- Graphics cards, both Peripheral Component Interconnect (PCI) and Accelerated Graphics Port (AGP)

- Extra power cords
- A variety of hard drives (as many as you can afford and in as wide a variety as possible)
- At least two 2.5-inch adapters from notebook IDE hard drives to standard IDE/ATA drives, SATA drives, and so on
- Computer hand tools, such as Phillips and flathead screwdrivers, a socket wrench, and a small flashlight

Maintaining Operating Systems and Software Inventories

Operating systems are an essential part of your lab's inventory. You should maintain licensed copies of as many legacy OSs as possible to handle cases involving unusual systems. Microsoft OSs should include Windows XP, 2000, NT 4.0, NT 3.5, 9x, 3.11, and DOS 6.22. Macintosh OSs should include Mac OS X, 9.x, and 8 or older. Linux OSs can include Fedora, Caldera Open Linux, Slackware, and Debian. The most recent OSs, such as Windows Vista, should also be included.

Although most high-end computer forensics tools can open or display data files created with popular programs, they don't support all programs. Your software inventory should include current and older versions of the following programs. If you deal with both Windows PCs and Macintosh systems, you should have programs for both.

- Microsoft Office (including current and older versions)
- Quicken (if you handle a lot of financial investigations)
- Programming languages, such as Visual Basic and Visual C++
- Specialized viewers, such as QuickView, ACDSee, ThumbsPlus, and IrfanView
- Corel Office Suite
- StarOffice/OpenOffice
- Peachtree accounting applications

Using a Disaster Recovery Plan

Besides planning for equipment needs, you need to plan for disasters, such as hard disk crashes, lightning strikes, and power outages. A disaster recovery plan ensures that you can restore your workstations and file servers to their original condition if a catastrophic failure occurs.

A disaster recovery plan also specifies how to rebuild a forensic workstation after it has been severely contaminated by a virus from a drive you're analyzing. Central to any disaster recovery plan is a system for backing up investigation computers. Tools such as Norton Ghost are useful for restoring files directly. As a general precaution, consider backing up your workstation once a week. You can restore programs from the original disks or CDs, but recovering lost data without up-to-date backups is difficult.

Store your system backups where they are easily accessible. You should have at least one copy of backups on site and a duplicate copy or a previous copy of backups stored in a safe off-site facility. Off-site backups are usually rotated on a schedule that varies according to your needs, such as every day, week, or month.

In addition, record all updates you make to your workstation by using a process called **configuration management**. Some companies record updates in a configuration management database to maintain compliance with lab policy. Every time you add or update software on your workstation, enter the change in the database or in a simple notebook with handwritten entries to document the change.

A disaster recovery plan can also address how to restore a workstation you reconfigured for a specific investigation. For example, if you install a suite of applications, you might not have enough disk space for normal processing needs, so you could encounter problems during reconfigurations or even simple upgrades. The disaster recovery plan should outline how to uninstall software and delete any files the uninstall program hasn't removed so that you can restore your system to its original configuration.

For labs using high-end RAID servers (such as Digital Intelligence F.R.E.D.C. or F.R.E.D.M.), you must consider methods for restoring large data sets. These large-end servers must have adequate data backup systems available in the event of a major failure of more than one drive. When planning a recovery procedure for RAID servers, consider whether the amount of downtime it takes to restore backup data is acceptable to the lab operation.

Planning for Equipment Upgrades

Risk management involves determining how much risk is acceptable for any process or operation, such as replacing equipment. Identify the equipment your lab depends on, and create a schedule to replace that equipment. Also, identify equipment that you can replace when it fails.

Computing components are designed to last 18 to 36 months in normal business operations, and new versions of OSs and applications that take up more disk space are released frequently. Therefore, systems periodically need more RAM, disk space, and processing speed. To keep your lab current with updates in hardware technology, schedule hardware replacements at least every 18 months and preferably every 12 months.

Using Laptop Forensic Workstations

Recent important advances in hardware technology offer more flexibility in computer forensics. You can now use a laptop PC with FireWire (IEEE 1394B standard), USB 2.0, or PCMCIA SATA hard disks to create a lightweight, mobile forensic workstation. Improved throughput speeds of data transfer on laptops also make it easier to create images of suspect drives.

However, laptops are still limited as forensic workstations. Even with improved data transfer rates, acquiring data with a data compression imaging tool, such as EnCase or SafeBack, creates a bottleneck. The processor speed determines how quickly you can acquire an image of a hard disk. The faster the processor on your laptop (or other PC), the faster an image is created in a compressed mode.

Building a Business Case for Developing a Forensics Lab

Before you can set up a computer forensics lab, you must enlist the support of managers and other team members. To do so, you build a **business case**, a plan you can use to sell your services to management or clients. In the business case, you justify acquiring newer and better resources to investigate computer forensics cases.

How you develop a business case depends on the organization you support. If you're the sole proprietor, creating a business case is fairly simple. If you need money to buy tools, you can save your money for the purchase or negotiate with your bank for a loan. For a public entity such as a police department, business requirements can change drastically because budgets are planned a year or more in advance. Public agency department managers present their budget proposals to upper management. If the proposal is approved, upper management makes money available to acquire resources outlined in the budget. Some public organizations might have other funds available that can be spent immediately for special needs. Managers can divert these funds for emergency or unforeseen needs.

Keep in mind that a private-sector business, especially a large corporation, is motivated by the need to make money. A business case should demonstrate how computing investigations could save money and avoid risks that can damage profits, such as by preventing litigation involving the company. For example, recent court decisions have defined viewing pornographic images in the workplace as creating a hostile environment for other employees, which is related to employee harassment and computer misuse. An employer is responsible for preventing and investigating harassment of employees and non-employees associated with the workplace. A company is also liable if it doesn't actively prevent the creation of a hostile workplace by providing employee training and investigating allegations of computer misuse. A lawsuit, regardless of who wins, can cost an employer several hundred thousand dollars. In your business case, compare the cost of training and conducting computing investigations with the cost of a lawsuit.

The Internet makes it difficult for employers to provide a safe and secure environment for employees. In particular, employees can misuse free Web-based e-mail services. These free services give senders anonymity, making it possible for employees to send inappropriate e-mails, often in the form of sexual harassment. Because training rarely prevents this type of behavior, an employer needs to institute an investigation program that involves collecting network logs, such as proxy server logs, and examining computer disks to locate traces of message evidence. Chapter 12 discusses e-mail abuse and using e-mail server and network logs.

Your business case should also show how computing investigations can improve profits, such as by protecting intellectual property, trade secrets, and future business plans. For example, when employees leave one company for a competing company, they can reveal vital competitive information to their new employers. Suppose a company called Skateboard International (SI) has invested research and development funds into a new product that improves the stability of skateboards. Its main competitor is Better Skateboard; this company contacts Gwen Smith, a disgruntled SI employee, via e-mail and offers her a job. When Gwen leaves SI, she takes with her the plans for the new product. A few months later, Better Skateboard introduces a product similar to the skateboard Gwen had been researching at SI. SI recognizes that the new, improved skateboard is similar to the one Gwen had been developing and consults the noncompete agreement Gwen signed when she was hired. SI thinks the new technology Gwen might have given Better Skateboards belongs to its company. It suspects that Better Skateboard stole its trade secret and intellectual property.

SI could sue Better Skateboard and demand discovery on internal documents. Because Gwen and Better Skateboard corresponded via e-mail, a computing investigator needs to find data related to hiring and research engineering at Better Skateboard. Better Skateboard can also demand discovery on SI's research records to determine whether any discrepancies in product design could disprove the lawsuit. In this example, computing investigations can allow one company to generate revenue from a new product and prevent the other company from doing so. Information related to profit and loss makes a persuasive argument in a business case.

Preparing a Business Case for a Computer Forensics Lab

It's important to understand the need for planning in the creation and continued maintenance of a computer forensics lab. The reason for this demand is the constant cost-cutting efforts of upper management. Because of organizations' tendencies to constantly reduce costs, you must plan ahead to ensure that money is available for facilities, tools, supplies, and training for your computer forensics lab. The following sections describe some key elements for creating a computer forensics business case. It's a good idea to maintain a business case with annual updates.

Justification Before you can start, you need to justify to the person controlling the budget the reason a lab is needed. This justification step requires asking the following questions:

- What type of computing investigation service is needed for your organization?
- Who are the potential customers for this service, and how will it be budgeted—as an internal operation (police department or company security department, for instance) or an external operation (a for-profit business venture)?
- How will you advertise your services to customers?
- What time-management techniques will you use?
- Where will the initial and sustaining budget for business operations come from?

No matter what type of organization you work for—a public agency or a private business—operating a computer forensics lab successfully requires constant efforts to communicate, or advertise, the lab's services to previous, current, and future customers and clients. By using marketing to attract new customers or clients, you can justify future budgets for the lab's operation and staff.

Budget Development The budget needs to include all items described in the following sections. You must be as exact as possible when determining the true cost of these items. Making a mistake could cause delays and possible loss of the opportunity to start or improve your lab.

Facility Cost For a new computer forensics lab, startup costs might take most of the budget. Depending on how large the lab is, you must determine first how much floor space is needed. As mentioned, a good rule of thumb is 150 square feet per person. This amount of space might seem a bit larger than necessary, but consider how much storage space is needed to preserve evidence and to have enough supplies in stock. Check with your organization's facility manager on per-square-foot costs for your area or building. Here are some sample questions to answer to get started on calculating a budget:

- How many computer forensics examiners will you need?
- How much training will each examiner require per year?
- Will you need more than one lab?

- How many computer forensics examiners will use each lab? Will there be a need to accommodate other nonexaminers temporarily to inspect recovered evidence?
- What are the costs to construct a secure lab?
- Is there a suitable room that can be converted into a lab?
- Does the designated room have enough electrical power and heating, ventilation, and air-conditioning (HVAC) systems?
- Does the designated room have existing telephone lines and network cables? If not, how much will it cost to install these additional items?
- Is there an adequate door lock on the designated room's door?
- What will the furniture costs be?
- Will you need to install an alarm system?
- Are there any other facility costs, such as fees for janitorial services and facility maintenance services?

Computer Hardware Requirements Determining the types of investigations and data that will be analyzed in your computer forensics lab dictates what hardware equipment you need. If your organization is using Intel-based PCs with Windows XP, for instance, your forensic workstation should be a high-end Intel-based PC, too. For a small police department, determining the types of computers the public uses is more difficult. The diversity of a community's computer systems requires a police department to be more versatile in the tools needed to conduct investigations. To determine computer hardware budget needs, here are some questions to consider in your planning:

- What types of investigations and data recovery will be performed in the lab?
- How many investigations can be expected per month of operation?
- Will there be any time-sensitive investigations that demand rapid analysis of disk data?
- What sizes and how many drives will be needed to support a typical investigation?
- Will you need a high-speed backup system, such as tape backup or DVD burners?
- What is the predominant type of computer system you will investigate?
- What will you use to store digital evidence? How long do you need to store it?

Software Requirements In the past few years, many more computer forensics tools have become available. For the private sector, the cost for these tools ranges from about $300 and up. For the public sector, many computer forensics software vendors offer discounts. However, just as you select hardware for your computer forensics lab to fit specific needs, you must first determine what type of OSs and applications will be investigated and then make purchases that fit. Keep in mind that the more you spend on a computer forensics software package, the more function and flexibility will be available. To determine computer software budget needs, here are some questions to consider in your planning:

- What types of OSs will be examined?
- For less popular, uncommon, or older OSs (such as Mac OS 9.x, OS/2, and CP/M), how often will there be a need to investigate them?

- What are the minimum needs for forensics software tools? For example, how many copies of each tool will be needed? How often will each tool be used in an average week?

- What types of OSs will be needed to conduct routine examinations?

- Will there be a need for specialized software, such as QuickBooks or Peachtree?

- Is there a budget to purchase more than one forensics software tool, such as EnCase, FTK, or ProDiscover?

- Which disk-editing tool should be selected for general data analysis?

Miscellaneous Cost Needs For this section of the budget, you need to brainstorm on other items, tools, and supplies to consider purchasing for the lab, from general office supplies to specific needs for daily operations. To determine miscellaneous budget needs, here are some questions to consider in your planning:

- Will there be a need for errors and omission insurance for the lab's operation and staff?

- Will you need a budget for office supplies?

Approval and Acquisition The approval and acquisition phase for a computer forensics lab is a management function. It's your responsibility to create a business case with a budget to present to upper management for approval. As part of the approval process, you should include a risk analysis describing how the lab will minimize the risk of litigation, which is a persuasive argument for supporting the lab. You also need to make an educated guess of how many investigations are anticipated and how long they will take to complete on average. Remember, part of the approval process requires using negotiation skills to justify the business case. You might need to revise your case as needed to get approval.

As part of the business case, acquisition planning requires researching different products to determine which one is the best and most cost effective. You need to contact several vendors' sales staff and design engineers to learn more about each product and service. Another factor to investigate is annual maintenance costs. You need to budget for this expense, too, so that you can get support if you run into problems during an investigation. An additional item to research from others in the profession is the vendor's maintenance history. Do other computer forensics labs use the same product, and have they had any problems getting support for problems they encounter?

Another consideration is vendors' pricing structures. Vendor pricing isn't based on the cost of creating CDs and DVDs and packaging them. Product prices are based on cost for development, testing, documentation support, shipping, and research and development for future improvements. In addition, vendors are for-profit organizations; they have investors to pay, too. Keep in mind that for vendors to be around next year to provide products and services for you, they need to make money.

Implementation After approval and acquisition, you need to plan the implementation of facilities and tools. As part of your business case, describe how implementation of all approved items will be processed. A timeline showing expected delivery or installation dates and expected completion dates must be included. You should also have a coordination plan for delivery dates and times for materials and tools. Inspection of facility construction, equipment (including furniture and benches), and software tools should be included in the schedule. Make sure you schedule inspection dates, too, to ensure that what you ordered arrived and is functional.

Acceptance Testing Following the implementation scheduling and inspection, you need to develop an acceptance test plan for the computer forensics lab to make sure everything works correctly. When writing the acceptance test plan, consider the following items:

- Inspect the facility to see whether it meets the security criteria to contain and control digital evidence.

- Test all communications, such as phone and network connections, to make sure they work as expected.

- Test all hardware to verify that it operates correctly; for example, test a computer to make sure it boots to Windows.

- Install and start all software tools; make sure all software can run on the computers and OSs you have in the lab.

Correction for Acceptance The better you plan for your lab, the less likely you'll have problems. However, any lab operation has some problems during startup. Your business case must anticipate problems that can cause delays in lab production. In the business case, you need to develop contingencies to deal with system or facility failures. For example, devise workarounds for problems such as the wrong locks being installed on lab doors or electrical power needing additional filtering.

Production After all essential corrections have been made, your computer forensics lab can then go into production. At this time, you implement the lab operations procedures that have been described in this chapter.

For additional information on how to write a business case, see *www.sba.gov/smallbusinessplanner/plan/writeabusinessplan/index.html*.

Chapter Summary

- A computer forensics lab is where you conduct investigations, store evidence, and do most of your work. You use the lab to house your instruments, current and legacy software, and forensic workstations. In general, you need a variety of computer forensics hardware and software.

- To continue a career in computing investigations and forensic analysis, you need to upgrade your skills through training. Several organizations offer training and certification programs for computer forensics that test you after you have successfully completed training. Some state and federal government agencies are also considering establishing certification programs that address minimum skills needed to conduct computing investigations at different levels.

- Your lab facility must be physically secure so that evidence is not lost, corrupted, or destroyed.

- Police departments in major cities need a wide assortment of computing systems, including older, outdated technology. Most computer investigations in small, local police departments involve Windows PCs and Macintosh systems. As a general rule, there should be at least one law enforcement computer investigator for every 250,000 people in a geographic region. Commercial services providing computer forensics analysis for other businesses can tailor their services to specific markets.

- A forensic workstation needs to have adequate memory, storage, and ports to deal with the common types of cases that come through your lab.

- Before you can set up a computer forensics lab, you must enlist the support of your managers and other team members by building a business case, a plan you can use to sell your services to management or clients. In the business case, you justify acquiring newer and better resources to investigate computer forensics cases.

Key Terms

American Society of Crime Laboratory Directors (ASCLD) A national society that sets the standards, management, and audit procedures for labs used in crime analysis, including computer forensics labs used by the police, FBI, and similar organizations.

business case A document that provides justification to upper management or a lender for purchasing new equipment, software, or other tools when upgrading your facility. In many instances, a business case shows how upgrades will benefit the company.

Certified Electronic Evidence Collection Specialist (CEECS) A certificate awarded by IACIS at completion of the written exam.

Certified Forensic Computer Examiner (CFCE) A certificate awarded by IACIS at completion of all portions of the exam.

computer forensics lab A computer lab dedicated to computing investigations; typically, it has a variety of computers, OSs, and forensics software.

configuration management The process of keeping track of all upgrades and patches you apply to your computer's OS and applications.

High Tech Crime Network (HTCN) A national organization that provides certification for computer crime investigators and computer forensics technicians.

risk management The process of determining how much risk is acceptable for any process or operation, such as replacing equipment.

secure facility A facility that can be locked and allows limited access to the room's contents.

special-interest groups (SIGs) Associated with various operating systems, these groups maintain electronic mailing lists and might hold meetings to exchange information about current and legacy operating systems.

TEMPEST A term referring to facilities that have been hardened so that electrical signals from computers, the computer network, and telephone systems can't be monitored or accessed easily by someone outside the facility.

Uniform Crime Report Information collected at the federal, state, and local levels to determine the types and frequencies of crimes committed.

Review Questions

1. An employer can be held liable for e-mail harassment. True or False?

2. Building a business case can involve which of the following?

    a. Procedures for gathering evidence

    b. Testing software

    c. Protecting trade secrets

    d. All of the above

3. The ASCLD mandates the procedures established for a computer forensics lab. True or False?

4. The manager of a computer forensics lab is responsible for which of the following? (Choose all that apply.)

    a. Necessary changes in lab procedures and software

    b. Ensuring that staff members have sufficient training to do the job

    c. Knowing the lab objectives

    d. None of the above

5. To determine the types of operating systems needed in your lab, list two sources of information you could use.

6. What items should your business plan include?

7. List two popular certification systems for computer forensics.

8. The National Cybercrime Training Partnership is available only to law enforcement. True or False?

9. Why is physical security so critical for computer forensics labs?

10. If a visitor to your computer forensics lab is a personal friend, it's not necessary to have him or her sign the visitor's log. True or False?

11. What three items should you research before enlisting in a certification program?

12. Large computer forensics labs should have at least _____ exits.

13. Typically, a(n) _____ lab has a separate storage area or room for evidence.

14. Computer forensics facilities always have windows. True or False?

15. The chief custodian of evidence storage containers should keep several master keys. True or False?

16. Putting out fires in a computer lab usually requires a _____ rated fire extinguisher.

17. A forensic workstation should always have a direct broadband connection to the Internet. True or False?

18. Which organization provides good information on safe storage containers?

19. Which organization has guidelines on how to operate a computer forensics lab?

20. What term refers to labs constructed to shield EMR emissions?

Hands-On Projects

HANDS-ON PROJECTS

Hands-On Project 3-1

You have just been hired to perform digital investigations and forensics analysis for a company. You find that no policies, processes, or procedures are currently in place. Do an Internet search to find information, and then create a policy and processes document to provide the structure necessary for your lab environment. Be sure to cite your online sources.

Hands-On Project 3-2

As mentioned previously, new forensics certifications are constantly being offered. Research certifications online and find one not discussed in this chapter. Write a short paper stating what organization offers the certification, who endorses the certification, how long the organization has been in business, and so forth.

Hands-On Project 3-3

Physical security of a lab must always be maintained. In your classroom lab, get permission to make observations at different times of the day when classes are and aren't in session. Record how many people go in and out during a period. Do you know all the people or can you identify them? Are they all students or faculty? Who monitors the lab when classes aren't in session? Are the rooms locked? How often are things stolen from the labs? Write one to two pages about your observations. If it were a computer forensics lab, what changes would you have to make?

Hands-On Project 3-4

Write a disaster recovery plan of not more than three pages for a fictitious company's computer forensics lab. Include backup schedules, note the programs and OS installed on each machine, and list other information you would have to recover after a disaster. You should also note where the original disks and backups are located.

Hands-On Project 3-5

A law firm has hired you to assist with digital evidence cases involving divorces. The main evidence consists of e-mail, spreadsheets, and documents. Before hiring you, the firm used an outside group to conduct investigations. You have to decide what equipment and software to purchase. What would you do to build a business plan that would be approved?

Case Projects

Case Project 3-1

Based on your evaluation of the arson case in Case Project 2-1, build a business case for the resources you think you'll need to investigate it for the insurance company. Write a brief paper outlining the resources you'll need, and make sure to justify your needs.

Case Project 3-2

A new version of Windows has been released. What do you need to do to be ready in 6 to 10 months when you encounter cases involving the new OS? Include research, user groups, and others you need to contact. Write a one-page paper on the procedures you should use.

chapter 4

Data Acquisition

After reading this chapter and completing the exercises, you will be able to:

- List digital evidence storage formats
- Explain ways to determine the best acquisition method
- Describe contingency planning for data acquisitions
- Explain how to use acquisition tools
- Describe how to validate data acquisitions
- Describe RAID acquisition methods
- Explain how to use remote network acquisition tools
- List other forensics tools available for data acquisitions

Data acquisition is the process of copying data. For computer forensics, it's the task of collecting digital evidence from electronic media. There are two types of data acquisition: static acquisitions and live acquisitions. In this chapter, you learn how to perform static acquisitions from digital media.

The future of data acquisitions is shifting toward live acquisitions because of the use of disk encryption with newer operating systems (OSs). In addition to encryption concerns, collecting any data that's active in a suspect's computer RAM is becoming more important to digital investigations. Techniques for acquiring live disk and RAM data are covered in Chapter 11. The processes and data integrity requirements for static and live acquisitions are the same. The only shortcoming with live acquisitions is not being able to perform repeatable processes, which are critical for collecting digital evidence. With static acquisitions, if you have preserved the original media, making a second static acquisition should produce the same results. The data on the original disk is not altered, no matter how many times an acquisition is done. Making a second live acquisition while a computer is running collects new data because of dynamic changes in the OS.

Your goal when acquiring data for a static acquisition is to preserve the digital evidence. Many times, you have only one chance to create a reliable copy of disk evidence with a data acquisition tool. Although these tools are generally dependable, you should still take steps to make sure you acquire an image that can be verified. In addition, failures can and do occur, so you should learn how to use several acquisition tools and methods; you work with a few different tools in this chapter. Other data acquisition tools that work in Windows, MS-DOS 6.22, and Linux are described briefly in the last section, but the list of vendors and methods is by no means conclusive. You should always search for newer and better tools to ensure the integrity of your forensics acquisitions.

For additional information on MS-DOS acquisition methods and tools, see Appendix D. You can perform most digital acquisitions for your investigations with a combination of the tools discussed in this chapter.

Understanding Storage Formats for Digital Evidence

Chapter 2 introduced the process of acquiring data from a USB drive and storing it in a data file. The acquisition tool you used, ProDiscover Basic, performed a bit-by-bit (or sector-by-sector) copy of the USB drive and wrote it to an image file, which was an exact duplicate of the source device (the USB drive).

The data a computer forensics acquisition tool collects is stored as an image file in one of three formats. Two formats are open source and the third is proprietary. Each vendor has unique features, so several different proprietary formats are available. Depending on the proprietary format, many computer forensics analysis tools can read other vendors' formatted acquisitions.

Many computer forensics acquisition tools create a disk-to-image file in an older open-source format, known as raw, as well as their own proprietary format. The new open-source format, Advanced Forensic Format (AFF), is starting to gain recognition from computer forensics examiners. Because AFF is open source, many vendors should be including this format soon in their tools.

Each data acquisition format has unique features along with advantages and disadvantages. The following sections summarize each format to help you choose which one to use.

Raw Format

In the past, there was only one practical way of copying data for the purpose of evidence preservation and examination. Examiners performed a bit-by-bit copy from one disk to another disk the same size or larger. As a practical way to preserve digital evidence, vendors (and some OS utilities, such as the Linux/UNIX dd command) made it possible to write bit-stream data to files. This copy technique creates simple sequential flat files of a suspect drive or data set. The output of these flat files is referred to as a **raw format**. This format has unique advantages and disadvantages to consider when selecting an acquisition format.

The advantages of the raw format are fast data transfers and the capability to ignore minor data read errors on the source drive. In addition, most computer forensics tools can read the raw format, making it a universal acquisition format for most tools. One disadvantage of the raw format is that it requires as much storage space as the original disk or data set. Another disadvantage is that some raw format tools, typically freeware versions, might not collect marginal (bad) sectors on the source drive, meaning they have a low threshold of retry reads on weak media spots on a drive. Many commercial tools have a much higher threshold of retry reads to ensure that all data is collected.

Several commercial acquisition tools can produce raw format acquisitions and typically provide a validation check by using Cyclic Redundancy Check (CRC-32), Message Digest 5 (MD5), and Secure Hash Algorithm (SHA-1 or newer) hashing functions. These validation checks, however, usually create a separate file containing the hash value.

Proprietary Formats

Most commercial computer forensics tools have their own formats for collecting digital evidence. Proprietary formats typically offer several features that complement the vendor's analysis tool, such as the following:

- The option to compress or not compress image files of a suspect drive, thus saving space on the target drive
- The capability to split an image into smaller segmented files for archiving purposes, such as to CDs or DVDs, with data integrity checks integrated into each segment
- The capability to integrate metadata into the image file, such as date and time of the acquisition, hash value (for self-authentication) of the original disk or medium, investigator or examiner name, and comments or case details

Computer forensics examiners have several ways of referring to copying evidence data to files: bit-stream copy, bit-stream image, image, mirror, and sector copy, to name a few. For the purposes of this book, "image" is generally used to refer to all forensics acquisitions saved to a data file.

One major disadvantage of proprietary format acquisitions is the inability to share an image between different vendors' computer forensics analysis tools. For example, the ILook imaging tool IXimager produces three proprietary formats—IDIF, IRBF, and IEIF—that can be read only by ILook. (See *www.perlustro.com* for additional information on ILook, which is currently available only to law enforcement agencies.) If necessary, IXimager can copy IDIF, IRBF, and IEIF formats to a raw format image file that can be read by other tools.

Another problem with proprietary and raw formats is a file size limitation for each segmented volume. Typically, proprietary format tools produce a segmented file of 650 MB. The file size can be adjusted up or down, with a maximum file size per segment of no more than 2 GB. Most proprietary format tools go up to only 2 GB because many examiners use a target drive formatted as FAT, which has a file size limit of 2 GB.

Of all the proprietary formats for image acquisitions, the Expert Witness format is currently the unofficial standard. This format, the default for Guidance Software EnCase, produces both compressed and uncompressed image files. These files (or volumes) write an extension starting with .E01 and incrementing it for each additional segmented image volume.

Several computer forensics analysis tools can generate generic versions of the Expert Witness format and analyze it, including X-Ways Forensics, AccessData Forensic Toolkit (FTK), and SMART. For more information on the Expert Witness format, see *www.asrdata.com/ SMART/whitepaper.html*.

Advanced Forensic Format

Dr. Simson L. Garfinkel of Basis Technology Corporation recently developed a new open-source acquisition format called **Advanced Forensic Format (AFF)**. This format has the following design goals:

- Creating compressed or uncompressed image files
- No size restriction for disk-to-image files
- Providing space in the image file or segmented files for metadata
- Simple design with extensibility
- Open source for multiple computing platforms and OSs
- Offer internal consistency checks for self-authentication

File extensions include .afd for segmented image files and .afm for AFF metadata. Because AFF is open source, computer forensics vendors will have no implementation restrictions on this format. Expect AFF to become the future standard for forensically sound acquisition formats. For more information on AFF, see *www.afflib.org* and *www.basistech.com/digital-forensics/aff.html*.

For more information on acquisition file formats, see *www.sleuthkit.org/informer*, issues #19 and #23.

Determining the Best Acquisition Method

As mentioned, there are two types of acquisitions: **static acquisitions** and **live acquisitions**. Typically, a static acquisition is done on a computer seized during a police raid, for example. If the computer has an encrypted drive, a live acquisition is done if the password or passphrase is available—meaning the computer is powered on and has been logged on to by the suspect. Static acquisitions are always the preferred way to collect digital evidence. However, they do have limitations in some situations, such as an encrypted drive that's readable only when the computer is powered on or a computer that's accessible only over a network.

In Chapter 11, you learn how to perform live acquisitions, including collection of digital media and dynamic/volatile memory (RAM) on a computing system.

For both types of acquisitions, data can be collected with four methods: creating a disk-to-image file, creating a disk-to-disk copy, creating a logical disk-to-disk or disk-to-data file, or creating a sparse copy of a folder or file. Determining the best acquisition method depends on the circumstances of the investigation.

Creating a disk-to-image file is the most common method and offers the most flexibility for your investigation. With this method, you can make one or many copies of a suspect drive. These copies are bit-for-bit replications of the original drive. In addition, you can use other forensics tools, such as ProDiscover, EnCase, FTK, SMART, Sleuth Kit, X-Ways Forensics, and ILook, to read the most common types of disk-to-image files you create. These programs read the disk-to-image file as though it were the original disk. MS-DOS tools can only read data from a drive. To use MS-DOS tools, you have to duplicate the original drive to perform the analysis. The newer GUI programs save time and disk resources because they can read and interpret directly from the disk-to-image file of a copied drive.

Sometimes you can't make a disk-to-image file because of hardware or software errors or incompatibilities. This problem is more common when you have to acquire older drives. For these drives, you might have to create a disk-to-disk copy of the suspect drive. Several imaging tools can copy data exactly from an older disk to a newer disk. These programs can adjust the target disk's geometry (its cylinder, head, and track configuration) so that the copied data matches the original suspect drive. These imaging tools include EnCase and SafeBack (*www.forensics-intl.com/safeback.html*). SafeBack must run from an MS-DOS system. See the vendors' manuals for instructions on using these tools for disk-to-disk copying.

For more information about current and older drives, see *www.t13.org*.

Collecting evidence from a large drive can take several hours. If your time is limited, consider using a **logical acquisition** or **sparse acquisition** data copy method. A logical acquisition captures only specific files of interest to the case or specific types of files. A sparse acquisition is similar but also collects fragments of unallocated (deleted) data; use this method only when you don't need to examine the entire drive. An example of a logical acquisition is an e-mail investigation that requires collecting only Outlook .pst or .ost files. Another example is collecting only specific records from a large RAID server. If you have to recover data from a RAID server with several terabytes (TBs) of data storage, the logical method might be the only way you can acquire the evidence. In electronic discovery for the purpose of litigation, a logical acquisition is becoming the preferred method, especially with large data storage systems.

To determine which acquisition method to use for an investigation, consider the size of the source (suspect) disk, whether you can retain the source disk as evidence or must return it to the owner, how much time you have to perform the acquisition, and where the evidence is located.

If the source disk is very large, such as 500 GB or more, make sure you have a target disk that can store a disk-to-image file of the large disk. If you don't have a target disk of comparable size, review alternatives for reducing the size of data to create a verifiable copy of the suspect drive. Older Microsoft disk compression tools, such as DoubleSpace or DriveSpace, eliminate only slack disk space between files. Other compression methods use an algorithm to reduce file size. Popular archiving tools, such as PKZip, WinZip, and WinRAR, use an algorithm referred to as lossless compression. Compression algorithms for graphics files use what's called lossy compression, which can change data. For example, lossy compression is used with .jpeg files to reduce file size and doesn't affect image quality when the file is restored and viewed. Because lossy compression alters original data, however, it isn't used for forensics acquisitions. Both compression methods are discussed in more detail in Chapter 10.

Most imaging tools have an option to use lossless compression to save disk space, which means the target drive doesn't have to be as large as the suspect drive. For example, if you have a SATA 1.5 TB suspect drive, you might be able to use lossless compression to create the disk-to-image file on a 500 GB target drive. Image files can be reduced by as much as 50% of the original. If the suspect drive already contains compressed data, such as several large zipped files, the imaging tool can't compress the data any further, however.

An easy way to test lossless compression is to perform an MD5 or SHA-1 hash on a file before and after it's compressed. If the compression is done correctly, both versions have the same hash value. If the hashes don't match, that means something corrupted the compressed file, such as a hardware or software error. As an added precaution, perform two separate hashes with different algorithms, such as MD5 and SHA-1. This step isn't mandatory; however, it's a good way to establish that nothing has changed during data processing.

When working with large drives, an alternative is using tape backup systems, such as Super Digital Linear Tape (SDLT) or Digital Audio Tape/Digital Data Storage (DAT/DDS). Snap-Back and SafeBack have special software drivers designed to write data from a suspect drive to a tape backup system through standard PCI SCSI cards. The advantage of this type of acquisition is that there's no limit to the size of data that can be acquired. The one big disadvantage, especially with microprocessor systems, is that it can be slow and time consuming.

If you can't retain the original evidence drive and must return it to the owner, as in a discovery demand for a civil litigation case, check with the requester, such as your lawyer or supervisor, and ask whether a logical acquisition is acceptable. If not, you have to refer the matter back to your lawyer or supervisor. When performing an acquisition under these conditions, make sure you have a good copy because most discovery demands give you only one chance to capture data. In addition, make sure you have a reliable forensics tool that you know how to use.

Contingency Planning for Image Acquisitions

Because you're working with electronic data, you need to take precautions to protect your digital evidence. You should also make contingency plans in case software or hardware doesn't work or you encounter a failure during an acquisition. The most common and time-consuming technique for preserving evidence is creating a duplicate of your disk-to-image file. Many computer investigators don't make duplicates of their evidence because they don't have enough time or resources to make a second image. However, if the first copy doesn't work correctly, having a duplicate is worth the effort and resources. Be sure you take steps to minimize the risk of failure in your investigation.

As a standard practice, make at least two images of the digital evidence you collect. If you have more than one imaging tool, such as ProDiscover, FTK, and X-Ways Forensics, make the first copy with one tool and the second copy with the other tool. If you have only one tool, consider making two images of the drive with the same tool, especially for critical investigations. With tools such as EnCase and ProDiscover, you can make one copy with no compression and compress the other copy. Remember that Murphy's Law applies to computer forensics, too: If anything can go wrong, it will.

Many acquisition tools don't copy data in the host protected area (HPA) of a disk drive. (Refer to Chapter 8 for more information on host protected areas.) For these situations, consider using a hardware acquisition tool that can access the drive at the BIOS level, such as ProDiscover with the NoWrite FPU write-blocker, ImageMASSter Solo, or X-Ways Replica. These tools can read a disk's HPA.

Microsoft has recently added **whole disk encryption** in Windows Vista Ultimate and Enterprise Editions, which makes performing static acquisitions more difficult. (Utimaco Software SafeGuard Easy also uses whole disk encryption.) As part of your contingency planning, you must be prepared to deal with encrypted drives. A static acquisition on most whole disk encrypted drives currently involves decrypting the drives, which requires the user's cooperation in providing the decryption key. Most whole disk encrypted tools at least have a manual process for decrypting data, which is converting the encrypted disk to an unencrypted disk. This process can take several hours, depending on the disk size. One good thing about encryption use is that data isn't altered, in that free and slack space aren't changed. The biggest concern with whole disk encryption is getting the decryption key. In criminal investigations, this might be impossible because if a disk contains evidence supporting the crime, a suspect has a strong motivation *not* to supply the decryption key. Researchers at Princeton University have produced a technique to recover passwords and passphrases from RAM, however; for more information, visit *http://citp. princeton.edu/pub/coldboot.pdf*.

Using Acquisition Tools

Many computer forensics software vendors have developed acquisition tools that run in Windows. These tools make acquiring evidence from a suspect drive more convenient, especially when you use them with hot-swappable devices, such as USB-2, FireWire 1394A and 1394B, or SATA, to connect disks to your workstation.

However, Windows acquisition tools have some drawbacks. Because Windows can easily contaminate your evidence drive, you must protect it with a well-tested write-blocking hardware device. (Chapter 7 discusses write-blocking devices in more detail.) Another drawback is that most Windows tools can't acquire data from a disk's host protected area. In addition, some countries haven't yet accepted the use of write-blocking devices for data acquisitions. Check with your legal counsel for evidence standards in your community or country.

Windows XP Write-Protection with USB Devices

When Microsoft updated Windows XP with Service Pack 2 (SP2), a new feature was added to the Registry: The USB write-protection feature blocks any writing to USB devices. This feature is still available in Windows Vista SP1. The only additional hardware device needed for an acquisition is a USB external drive or a cable-connecting device (see Figure 4-1). On your acquisition workstation, simply connect the suspect drive to the USB external drive or connector after you've modified the Windows Registry to enable write-protection. The advantage of this Registry modification is that you don't need an expensive physical write-blocker to make a disk acquisition from Windows. The disadvantage is that your target drive needs to be connected to an internal PATA (IDE), SATA, or SCSI controller, not another USB external drive.

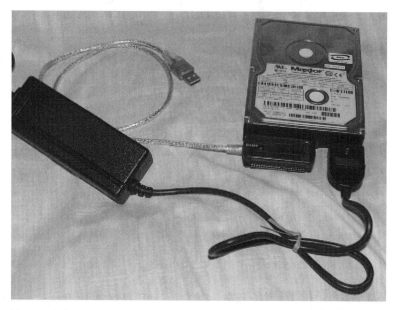

Figure 4-1 A typical inexpensive USB IDE/SATA external connector

To update the Registry, you need to perform three tasks. First, back up the Registry in case something fails while you're modifying it. Second, modify the Registry with the write-protection feature. Third, create two desktop icons to automate switching between enabling and disabling writes to the USB device.

Backing Up the Registry Activities for updating the Registry are written for Windows Vista. If you're using Windows XP, you'll notice slight differences in dialog boxes, and you won't see the User Account Control (UAC) message box.

Before updating the Registry for the write-blocking feature or any other task, backing it up is crucial. To back up your Registry, follow these steps:

1. Click **Start,** point to **All Programs,** point to **Accessories,** point to **System Tools,** and click **System Restore.** When the UAC message box opens, click **Continue.**

2. In the first window of the System Restore Wizard (see Figure 4-2), click the **open System Protection** link to create a restore point. (Note that if you haven't created a restore point previously, you must click the **System Protection** link.)

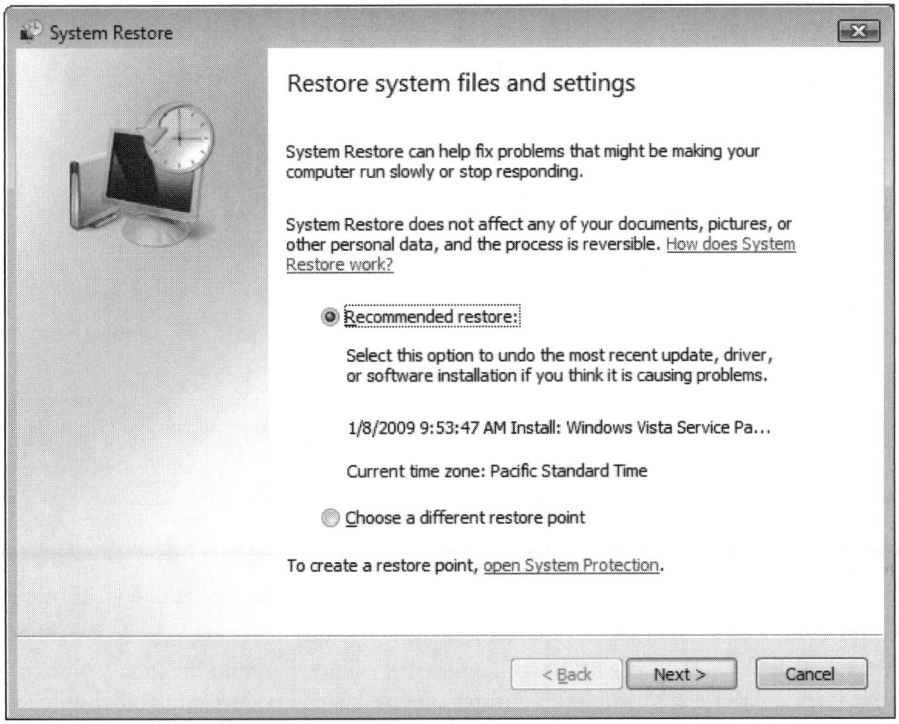

Figure 4-2   The System Restore Wizard

3. In the System Properties dialog box (see Figure 4-3), click the **Create** button. In the Create a restore point window, enter a name for the restore point (such as Primary Restore), click **Create,** and then click **OK** twice. Click **Cancel** in the System Restore Wizard.

Modifying the Registry for USB Write-Blocking After you have created a restore point for the Registry, perform the following steps to enable the write-blocking feature:

1. Click **Start,** type **regedit** in the Start Search text box, and then press **Enter.** If the UAC message box opens, click **Continue.** (In Windows XP, click **Start, Run,** type **regedit,** and click **OK.**)

2. In Registry Editor, navigate to and click to expand the **\HKEY_LOCAL_MACHINE\ SYSTEM\CurrentControlSet** key.

3. Under the CurrentControlSet item, right-click the **Control** subkey, point to **New,** and then click **Key.**

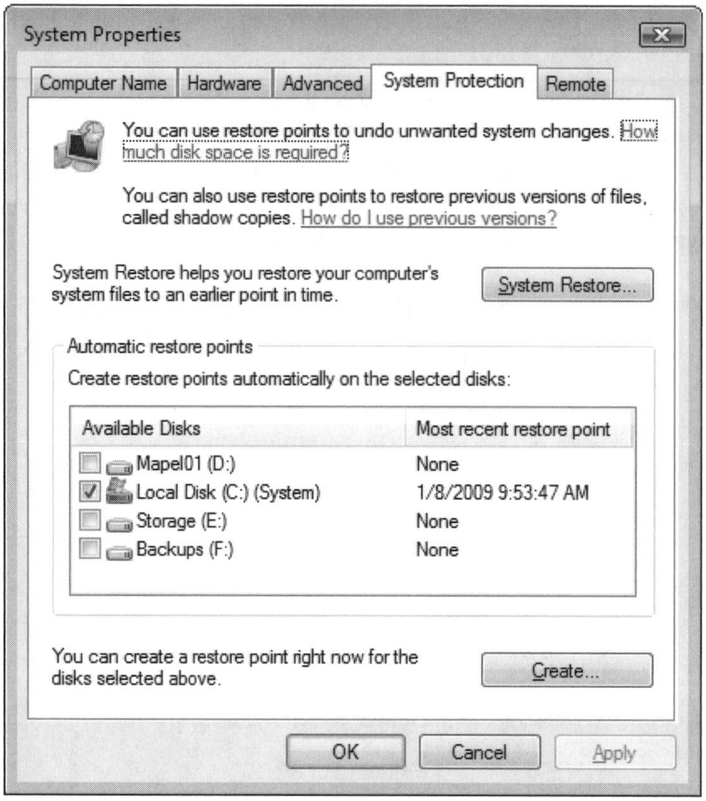

Figure 4-3 The System Properties dialog box

4. Registry Editor then prompts you for a key name. Type **StorageDevicePolicies** and press **Enter**.

5. Right-click the newly created **StorageDevicePolicies** descendent key, point to **New**, and click **DWORD Value**. (Depending on the Vista version you're running, you might see selections for a 32-bit value and a 64-bit value. If so, select the 32-bit value.)

6. A new prompt appears in the key data area at the right. Type **WriteProtect** and press **Enter**.

7. Next, in the key data area, right-click **WriteProtect DWORD** (or just **WriteProtect**, depending on the Vista version) and click **Modify**.

8. In the Edit DWORD Value dialog box, change the Value Data setting from 0 to **1**, and then click **OK** to activate write-blocking to USB devices. Keep Registry Editor open for the next task.

Automating USB Write-Blocking To minimize errors in updating the Registry every time you need to write-block a USB device, exporting the Registry is recommended. To do this, you create a .reg file and save it to your workstation's desktop. To make it easier to switch between writing and blocking modes for the Registry, follow these steps in Registry Editor:

1. Right-click the **StorageDevicePolicies** descendent key and click **Export**.

2. In the Export Registry File dialog box, click **Desktop** in the Save in list box. In the File name text box, type **Write Protect USB ON**, and click **Save**.

3. In Registry Editor, click **StorageDevicePolicies**. In the key data area, right-click **Write-Protect DWORD** and click **Modify**.

4. Next, in the Edit DWORD Value dialog box, change the Value Data setting from 1 to 0, and then click **OK** to deactivate write-blocking to USB devices.

5. Right-click the **StorageDevicePolicies** descendent key again and click **Export**.

6. In the Export Registry File dialog box, click **Desktop** in the Save in list box. In the File name text box, type **Write Protect USB OFF**, and click **Save**. Close Registry Editor.

Now that you have made this Registry modification, you should see two desktop icons named Write Protect USB ON.reg and Write Protect USB OFF.reg. When you need to set your workstation so that it write-blocks (prevents writes to USB devices), double-click the Write Protect USB ON icon. When a dialog box opens, asking whether you want to modify the Registry, click OK, and then click OK again in the message box stating the Registry has been modified successfully. To undo write-blocking (allow writes to USB devices), double-click the Write Protect USB OFF icon. Click OK to modify the Registry and OK again to finish.

For a more information on this Registry modification procedure and other useful guides, do an Internet search for "USB Registry write-blocker."

Acquiring Data with a Linux Boot CD

The Linux OS has many features that are applicable to computer forensics, especially data acquisitions. One unique feature is that Linux can access a drive that isn't mounted. Physical access for the purpose of reading data can be done on a connected media device, such as a disk drive, a USB drive, or other storage devices. In Windows OSs and newer Linux kernels, when you connect a drive via USB, FireWire, external SATA, or even internal PATA or SATA controllers, both OSs automatically mount and access the drive. For example, a Windows XP or Linux kernel 2.6 or later workstation automatically accesses a suspect drive when connecting to it, which could alter data. On Windows drives, an acquisition workstation can access and alter data in the Recycle Bin; on Linux drives, the workstation most likely alters metadata, such as mount point configurations for an Ext2 or Ext3 drive.

In static acquisitions, this automatic access corrupts the integrity of evidence. When acquiring data with Windows, you must use a write-blocking device or Registry utility. With a correctly configured Linux OS, such as a forensic Linux Live CD, media aren't accessed automatically, which eliminates the need for a write-blocker. If you need to acquire a USB drive that doesn't have a write-lock switch, use one of the forensic Linux Live CDs (discussed in the next section) to access the device.

Use caution when working with newer Linux distributions with KDE or Gnome GUIs. Many newer distributions mount most media devices automatically. If you're using a nonforensic Linux distribution, you should test it before using it on actual evidence to see how it handles attached storage devices. If in doubt, always use a physical write-blocker for an acquisition from Linux.

Using Linux Live CD Distributions Several Linux distributions, such as Knoppix (*www.knoppix.org*), provide an ISO image that can be burned to a CD or DVD. Linux ISO images are referred to as Live CDs. Most of these Linux distributions are for Linux OS recovery, not for computer forensics acquisition and analysis. For a list of the most current Linux Live CDs, see *www.frozentech.com*.

A few Linux ISO images are specifically designed for computer forensics, however. These special Linux ISO images contain additional utilities that aren't typically installed in normal Linux distributions. They are also configured not to mount, or to mount as read-only, any connected storage media, such as disk drives. This feature protects the media's integrity for the purpose of acquiring and analyzing data. To access media, you have to give specific instructions to the Live CD boot session through a GUI utility or a shell command prompt. Mounting drives from a shell gives you more control over them. See the man page for the mount command (by typing "man mount" at the shell prompt) to learn what options are available for your Linux distribution.

The man command displays pages from the online help manual for information on Linux commands and their options.

Linux can read data from a physical device without having to mount it. As a usual practice, don't mount a suspect media device as a precaution against any writes to it. Later in this section, you learn how to make a forensics acquisition in Linux without mounting the device.

The following are well-designed Linux Live CDs for computer forensics:

- Helix (*www.e-fense.com/helix/*; English interface)
- Penguin Sleuth (*www.linux-forensics.com*; English interface)
- FCCU (*www.d-fence.be*; French interface)

You can download these ISO images to any computer, including a Windows system, and then burn them to CD/DVD with burner software, such as Roxio or Nero. Creating a bootable image from an ISO file is different from copying data or music files to a CD or DVD, however. If you aren't familiar with how to do it, see the Help menu in your burner software for instructions on creating a bootable CD or DVD. For example, Roxio Creator Classic has a Burn from Disc Image File option in the File menu, and Nero Express has a Bootable CD option.

After creating a Linux Live CD, test it on your workstation. Remember to check your workstation's BIOS to see whether it boots first from the CD or DVD on the system. To test the Live CD, simply place it in the CD or DVD drive and reboot your system. If successful, Linux loads into your computer's memory, and a common GUI for Linux appears on the screen. If you have problems with the video display on your workstation, try another computer with a different video card. No one Live CD distribution has all video drivers. Linux Live CDs load the OS into the computer's RAM, so performance can be affected when you're using GUI tools. The following sections explain how to use Linux to make forensically sound data acquisitions.

Preparing a Target Drive for Acquisition in Linux The Linux OS provides many tools that you can use to modify non-Linux file systems. Current Linux distributions can create Microsoft FAT and NTFS partition tables. Linux kernel version 2.6.17.7 and earlier can format and read only the FAT file system, although an NTFS driver, ntfs-3g, is available that allows Linux to mount and write data only to NTFS partitions. You can download this driver from *www.linux-ntfs.org* or *www.ntfs-3g.org*, where you can also find information about NTFS and instructions for installing the driver.

In this section, you learn how to partition and format a Microsoft FAT drive from Linux so that you don't have to switch OSs or computers to prepare a FAT target disk. After you make the acquisition, you can then transfer the FAT disk to a Windows system to use a Windows analysis tool.

When preparing a drive to be used on a Linux system for forensics acquisition or analysis, do it in a separate boot session with no suspect drive attached.

Linux/UNIX commands are case sensitive, so make sure you type commands exactly as shown in this section's steps.

Assuming you have a functioning Linux computer or one running with a Linux Live CD, perform the following steps from a shell prompt:

1. First, boot Linux on your computer.
2. Connect the USB, FireWire, or SATA external drive to the Linux computer and power it on.
3. If a shell window isn't already open, start one.
4. At the shell prompt, type **su** and press **Enter** to log in as the superuser (root). Then type the root password and press **Enter**.

If you're using one of the Live CDs listed previously, these distributions are typically already in superuser (root) mode, so there's no need to use the su command. Other Linux Live CDs might have no password set and simply require pressing Enter.

5. To list the current disk devices connected to the computer, type **fdisk -l** (lowercase L) and press **Enter**. You should see output similar to the following:

Linux lists all IDE (also known as PATA) drives as hda, hdb, and so on. All SCSI, SATA, FireWire, and USB connected drives are listed as sda, sdb, and so forth.

```
Disk /dev/hda: 40.0 GB, 40007761920 bytes
255 heads, 63 sectors/track, 4864 cylinders
Units = cylinders of 16065 * 512 = 8225280 bytes
```

```
Device Boot      Start     End      Blocks       Id      System
/dev/hda1  *     1         13       104391       83      Linux
/dev/hda2        14        4864     38965657+    8e      Linux LVM
```

```
Disk /dev/sda: 6448 MB, 6448619520 bytes
199 heads, 62 sectors/track, 1020 cylinders
Units = cylinders of 12338 * 512 = 6317056 bytes
```

Disk /dev/sda doesn't contain a valid partition table

 In the preceding output, the /dev/sda device has no partition listed. These steps show how to create a Microsoft FAT partition on this disk. If there's a partition on this drive, it can be deleted with the Linux fdisk utility. For additional information on fdisk, refer to the man page.

6. Type **fdisk /dev/sda** and press **Enter** to partition the disk drive as a FAT file system. You should see output similar to the following:

```
Device contains neither a valid DOS partition table, nor Sun, SGI or OSF disk label
Building a new DOS disk label. Changes will remain in memory only, until you
decide to write them. After that, of course, the previous content won't be
recoverable.
```

```
Warning: invalid flag 0x0000 of partition table 4 will be
corrected by write)
```

7. Display fdisk menu options by typing **m** and pressing **Enter**. You should see output similar to the following:

```
Command action
a   toggle a bootable flag
b   edit bsddisklabel
c   toggle the dos compatibility flag
d   delete a partition
l   list known partition types
m   print this menu
n   add a new partition
o   create a new empty DOS partition table
p   print the partition table
q   quit without saving changes
s   create a new empty Sun disk label
t   change a partition's system id
u   change display/entry units
v   verify the partition table
w   write table to disk and exit
x   extra functionality (experts only)
```

8. Determine whether there are any partitions on /dev/sda by typing **p** and pressing **Enter**. You should see output similar to the following:

```
Disk /dev/sda: 6448 MB, 6448619520 bytes
199 heads, 62 sectors/track, 1020 cylinders
Units = cylinders of 12338 * 512 = 6317056 bytes


Device Boot    Start    End    Blocks    Id    System
```

In this example, the disk has no previously configured partitions. If it did, there would be data under each column heading describing each partition's configuration.

9. Next, you create a new primary partition on /dev/sda. To use the defaults and select the entire drive, type **n** and press **Enter**. To create a primary partition table, type **p** and press **Enter**, and then type **1** (the numeral) to select the first partition and press **Enter**. At the remaining prompts, press **Enter**. Your output should be similar to the following:

```
Command action
e   extended
p   primary partition (1-4)
p
Partition number (1-4): 1
First cylinder (1-1020, default 1):
Using default value 1
Last cylinder or +size or +sizeM or +sizeK (1-1020, default 1020):
Using default value 1020
```

In Linux, the first logical partition created after the primary and extended partitions is numbered 5; any additional logical partitions are numbered 6, 7, and so on. For example, the C partition is typically /dev/hda1, and the D partition is /dev/hda2.

10. List the newly defined partitions by typing **p** and pressing **Enter**, which produces the following output:

```
Disk /dev/sda: 6448 MB, 6448619520 bytes
199 heads, 62 sectors/track, 1020 cylinders
Units = cylinders of 12338 * 512 = 6317056 bytes


Device Boot    Start    End    Blocks     Id    System
/dev/sda1      1        1020   6292349    83    Linux
```

11. To list the menu again so that you can select the change partition ID, type **m** and press **Enter**. You should see output similar to the following:

```
Command action
a   toggle a bootable flag
b   edit bsddisklabel
```

```
c   toggle the dos compatibility flag
d   delete a partition
l   list known partition types
m   print this menu
n   add a new partition
o   create a new empty DOS partition table
p   print the partition table
q   quit without saving changes
s   create a new empty Sun disk label
t   change a partition's system id
u   change display/entry units
v   verify the partition table
w   write table to disk and exit
x   extra functionality (experts only)
```

12. To change the newly created partition to the Windows 95 FAT32 file system, first type **t** and press **Enter,** which produces the following output:

```
Selected partition 1
Hex code (type L to list codes):
```

13. List available file systems and their code values by typing **l** (lowercase L) and pressing **Enter.** You should see output similar to the following:

```
0    Empty 1c  Hidden W95 FAT3 70 DiskSecureMult bb Boot Wizard hid
1    FAT12     1e  Hidden W95 FAT1 75  PC/IX       be  Solaris boot
2    XENIX root  24  NEC DOS     80  Old Minix    c1  DRDOS/sec (FAT-
3    XENIXusr 39  Plan 9    81  Minix / old Lin c4  DRDOS/sec (FAT-
4    FAT16 <32M 3c PartitionMagic 82  Linux swap c6  DRDOS/sec (FAT-
5    Extended    40  Venix 80286     83  Linux         c7  Syrinx
6    FAT16    41  PPC PReP Boot  84  OS/2 hidden C:  da  Non-FS data
7    HPFS/NTFS    42  SFS      85  Linux extended  db  CP/M / CTOS / .
8    AIX      4d  QNX4.x     86  NTFS volume set de  Dell Utility
9    AIX bootable 4e  QNX4.x 2nd part 87  NTFS volume set dfBootIt
a    OS/2 Boot Manag 4f QNX4.x 3rd part 8e  Linux LVM  e1 DOS access
b    W95 FAT32  50  OnTrack DM     93  Amoeba        e3  DOS R/O
c    W95 FAT32 (LBA) 51 OnTrack DM6 Aux 94  Amoeba BBT e4 SpeedStor
e    W95 FAT16 (LBA) 52  CP/M    9f  BSD/OS     eb  BeOS fs
f    W95Ext'd (LBA) 53 OnTrack DM6 Aux a0 IBM Thinkpad hi ee  EFI GPT
10   OPUS     54  OnTrackDM6    a5  FreeBSD     ef  EFI (FAT-12/16/
11   Hidden FAT12  55  EZ-Drive    a6  OpenBSD  f0  Linux/PA-RISC b
12   Compaqdiagnost 56  Golden Bow  a7  NeXTSTEP  f1  SpeedStor
14   Hidden FAT16 <3 5c  PriamEdisk  a8  Darwin UFS  f4 SpeedStor
16   Hidden FAT16   61  SpeedStor a9  NetBSD  f2  DOS secondary
17   Hidden HPFS/NTF 63 GNU HURD or Sys ab Darwin boot fd Linux raid auto
18   ASTSmartSleep 64  Novell Netware  b7  BSDI fsfeLANstep
1b   Hidden W95 FAT3 65  Novell Netware  b8  BSDI swap  ff  BBT
```

14. Change the newly created partition to the Windows 95 FAT32 file system by typing **c** and pressing **Enter**. Your output should look similar to the following:

```
Changed system type of partition 1 to b (W95 FAT32)
```

15. To display partitions of the newly changed drive, type **p** and press **Enter**, which produces the following output:

```
Disk /dev/sda: 6448 MB, 6448619520 bytes
199 heads, 62 sectors/track, 1020 cylinders
Units = cylinders of 12338 * 512 = 6317056 bytes

Device Boot    Start    End    Blocks    Id    System
/dev/sda1      1        1020   6292349   b     W95 FAT32
```

4

16. Save (write) the newly created partition to the /dev/sda drive by typing **w** and pressing **Enter**. Your output should look similar to the following:

```
The partition table has been altered!

Calling ioctl() to re-read partition table.

WARNING: If you have created or modified any DOS 6.x partitions,
please see the fdisk manual page for additional information.
Syncing disks.
```

Fdisk exits back to the shell prompt after updating the partition table on the /dev/sda drive.

17. Show the known drives connected to your computer by typing **fdisk -l** and pressing **Enter**, which produces the following output:

```
Disk /dev/hda: 40.0 GB, 40007761920 bytes
255 heads, 63 sectors/track, 4864 cylinders
Units = cylinders of 16065 * 512 = 8225280 bytes

Device Boot    Start    End    Blocks       Id    System
/dev/hda1  *   1        13     104391       83    Linux
/dev/hda2      14       4864   38965657+    8e    Linux LVM

Disk /dev/sda: 6448 MB, 6448619520 bytes
199 heads, 62 sectors/track, 1020 cylinders
Units = cylinders of 12338 * 512 = 6317056 bytes

Device Boot    Start    End    Blocks       Id    System
/dev/sda1      1        1020   6292349      b     W95 FAT32
```

18. To format a FAT file system from Linux, type **mkfs.msdos -vF32 /dev/sda1** and press **Enter**, which produces the following output:

```
mkfs.msdos 2.8 (28 Feb 2001)
Selecting 8 sectors per cluster
/dev/sde1 has 33 heads and 61 sectors per track,
logical sector size is 512,
using 0xf8 media descriptor, with 2047966 sectors;
file system has 2 32-bit FATs and 8 sectors per cluster.
FAT size is 1997 sectors, and provides 255492 clusters.
Volume ID is 420781ea, no volume label.
```

Newer Linux distributions automatically sync the newly created partition and format the drive. The sync feature eliminates the need to reboot the computer, unlike with Microsoft OSs.

19. Close the shell window for this session by typing **exit** and pressing **Enter**.

This drive can now be mounted and used to receive an image of a suspect drive. Later in this section, you learn how to mount and write to this Microsoft FAT target drive.

Acquiring Data with dd in Linux A unique feature of a forensic Linux Live CD is that it can mount and read most drives. To perform a data acquisition on a suspect computer, all you need are the following:

- A forensic Linux Live CD

- A USB, FireWire, or SATA external drive with cables

- Knowledge of how to alter the suspect computer's BIOS to boot from the Linux Live CD

- Knowledge of which shell commands to use for the data acquisition

The dd command, available on all UNIX and Linux distributions, means "data dump." This command, with many functions and switches, can be used to read and write data from a media device and a data file. The dd command is not bound by a logical file system's data structures, meaning the drive doesn't have to be mounted for dd to access it. For example, if you list a physical device name, the dd command copies the entire device—all data files, slack space, and free space (unallocated data) on the device. The dd command creates a raw format file that most computer forensics analysis tools can read, which makes it useful for data acquisitions.

Use extreme caution with the dd command. Make sure you know which drives are the suspect drive and target drive. Although you might not have mounted the suspect drive, if you reverse the input field (if=) of the suspect and target drives with the output field (of=), data is written to the wrong drive, thus destroying the original evidence drive.

As powerful as this command is, it does have some shortcomings. One major problem is that it requires more advanced skills than the average computer user might have. Also, because it doesn't compress data, the target drive needs to be equal to or larger than the suspect drive. It's possible to divide the output to other drives if a large enough target drive isn't available, but this process can be cumbersome and prone to mistakes when you're trying to keep track of which data blocks to copy to which target drive.

The dd command combined with the split command segments output into separate volumes. Use the split command with the -b switch to adjust the size of segmented volumes the dd command creates. As a standard practice for archiving purposes, creating segmented volumes that fit on a 650 MB CD is convenient. For additional information on dd and split, see their man pages.

Perform the following steps to make an image of an NTFS disk on a FAT32 disk by using the dd command:

1. Assuming that your workstation is the suspect computer and is booted from a Linux Live CD, connect the USB, FireWire, or SATA external drive containing the FAT32 target drive, and turn the external drive on.

2. If you're not at a shell prompt, start a shell window, switch to superuser (su) mode, type the root password, and press **Enter**.

3. At the shell prompt, list all drives connected to the computer by typing **fdisk -l** and pressing **Enter**, which produces the following output:

```
Disk /dev/hda: 40.0 GB, 40007761920 bytes
255 heads, 63 sectors/track, 4864 cylinders
Units = cylinders of 16065 * 512 = 8225280 bytes
```

Device Boot		Start	End	Blocks	Id	System
/dev/hda1	*	1	13	104391	83	Linux
/dev/hda2		14	4864	38965657+	8e	Linux LVM

```
Disk /dev/sda: 163.9 GB, 163928605184 bytes
255 heads, 63 sectors/track, 19929 cylinders
Units = cylinders of 16065 * 512 = 8225280 bytes
```

Device Boot	Start	End	Blocks	Id	System
/dev/sda1	1	12000	96389968+	b	W95 FAT32
/dev/sda2	12001	19929	63689692+	5	Extended
/dev/sda5	12001	19929	63689661	c	W95 FAT32 (LBA)

```
Disk /dev/sdb: 6448 MB, 6448619520 bytes
199 heads, 62 sectors/track, 1020 cylinders
Units = cylinders of 12338 * 512 = 6317056 bytes
```

Device Boot	Start	End	Blocks	Id	System
/dev/sdb1	1	1020	6292349	7	HPFS/NTFS

4. To create a mount point for the USB, FireWire, or SATA external drive and partition, make a directory in /mnt by typing **mkdir /mnt/sda5** and pressing **Enter**.

5. To mount the target drive partition, type **mount -t vfat /dev/sda5 /mnt/sda5** and press **Enter**.

6. To change your default directory to the target drive, type **cd /mnt/sda5** and press **Enter**.

7. List the contents of the target drive's root level by typing **ls -al** and pressing **Enter**. Your output should be similar to the following:

```
total 40
drwxr-xr-x  2 root root 32768 Dec 31  1969 .
drwxr-xr-x  5 root root  4096 Feb  6 17:22 ..
```

8. To make a target directory to receive image saves of the suspect drive, type **mkdir case01** and press **Enter**.

9. To change to the newly created target directory, type **cd case01** and press **Enter**. Don't close the shell window.

Next, you perform a raw format image of the entire suspect drive to the target directory. To do this, you use the split command with the dd command. The split command creates a two-letter extension for each segmented volume. The -d switch creates numeric rather than letter extensions. As a general rule, if you plan to use a Windows forensics tool to examine a dd image file created with this switch, the segmented volumes shouldn't exceed 2 GB each because of FAT32 file size limits. This 2 GB limit allows you to copy only up to 198 GB of a suspect's disk. If you need to use the dd command, it's better to use the split command's default of incremented letter extensions and make smaller segments. To adjust the segmented volume size, change the value for the -b switch from the 650 MB used in the following example to 2000 MB.

1. First, type **dd if=/dev/sdb | split -b 650m - image_sdb.** and press **Enter**. You should see output similar to the following:

```
12594960+0 records in
12594960+0 records out
```

When using the split command, type a period at the end of the line as shown, with no space between it and the filename. Otherwise, the extension is appended to the filename with no "." delimiter.

2. Now list the raw images that have been created from the dd and split commands by typing **ls -l** and pressing **Enter**. You should see output similar to the following:

```
total 6297504
-rwxr-xr-x  1 root root 681574400 Feb  6 17:26 image_sdb.aa
-rwxr-xr-x  1 root root 681574400 Feb  6 17:28 image_sdb.ab
-rwxr-xr-x  1 root root 681574400 Feb  6 17:29 image_sdb.ac
-rwxr-xr-x  1 root root 681574400 Feb  6 17:30 image_sdb.ad
-rwxr-xr-x  1 root root 681574400 Feb  6 17:32 image_sdb.ae
-rwxr-xr-x  1 root root 681574400 Feb  6 17:33 image_sdb.af
-rwxr-xr-x  1 root root 681574400 Feb  6 17:34 image_sdb.ag
-rwxr-xr-x  1 root root 681574400 Feb  6 17:36 image_sdb.ah
```

```
-rwxr-xr-x  1 root root 681574400 Feb  6 17:37 image_sdb.ai
-rwxr-xr-x  1 root root 314449920 Feb  6 17:37 image_sdb.aj
```

3. To complete this acquisition, dismount the target drive by typing **umount /dev/sda5** and pressing **Enter**.

Depending on the Windows forensics analysis tool you're using, renaming each segmented volume's extension with incremented numbers instead of letters might be necessary. For example, rename image_sdb.aa as image_sdb.01, and so on. Several Windows forensics tools can read only disk-to-image segmented files that have numeric extensions. Most Linux forensics tools can read segments with numeric or lettered extensions.

Acquiring a specific partition on a drive works the same way as acquiring the entire drive. Instead of typing /dev/sdb as you would for the entire drive, add the partition number to the device name, such as /dev/sdb1. For drives with additional partitions, use the number that would be listed in the fdisk -l output. For example, to copy only the partition of the previous NTFS drive, you use the following dd command:

```
dd if=/dev/sdb1 | split -b 650m - image_sdb1
```

Remember to use caution with the dd command in your forensics data acquisitions.

Acquiring Data with dcfldd in Linux The dd command is intended as a data management tool; it's not designed for forensics acquisitions. Because of these shortcomings, Nicholas Harbour of the Defense Computer Forensics Laboratory (DCFL) developed a tool that can be added to most UNIX/Linux OSs. This tool, the dcfldd command, works similarly to the dd command but has many features designed for computer forensics acquisitions. The following are important functions dcfldd offers that aren't possible with dd:

- Specify hexadecimal patterns or text for clearing disk space.
- Log errors to an output file for analysis and review.
- Use the hashing options MD5, SHA-1, SHA-256, SHA-384, and SHA-512, with logging and the option of specifying the number of bytes to hash, such as specific blocks or sectors.
- Refer to a status display indicating the acquisition's progress in bytes.
- Split data acquisitions into segmented volumes with numeric extensions (unlike dd's limit of 99).
- Verify the acquired data with the original disk or media data.

When using dcfldd, you should follow the same precautions as with dd. The dcfldd command can also write to the wrong device, if you aren't careful.

The following examples show how to use the dcfldd command to acquire data from a 64 MB USB drive, although you can use the command on a larger media device. All commands need to be run from a privileged root shell session. To acquire an entire media device in one image file, you type the following command at the shell prompt:

```
dcfldd if=/dev/sda of=usbimg.dat
```

If the suspect media or disk needs to be segmented, use the dcfldd command with the split command, placing split before the output file field (of=), as shown here:

```
dcfldd if=/dev/sda split=2M of=usbimg hash=md5
```

This command creates segmented volumes of 2 MB each. To create segmented volumes that fit on a CD of 650 MB, change the split=2M to split=650M. This command also displays the MD5 value of the acquired data.

For additional information on the dcfldd command, see *http://dcfldd.sourceforge.net*. Information on how to download and install dcfldd is available for many UNIX, Linux, and Macintosh OSs. You can also use the man page to find more information on dcfldd's features and switches.

Capturing an Image with ProDiscover Basic

In Chapter 2, you learned how to acquire an image of a USB drive. ProDiscover automates many acquisition functions, unlike current Linux tools. Because USB drives are typically small, a single image file can be acquired with no need to segment it. In this section, you learn how to make an image of a larger drive and use the Split function in ProDiscover Basic to create segmented files of 650 MB each that can be archived to CDs.

Before acquiring data directly from a suspect drive with ProDiscover Basic, always use a hardware write-blocker device or the write-protection method for USB-connected drives described earlier in this chapter.

The following activity assumes you have removed the suspect drive and connected it to a USB or FireWire write-blocker device connected to your forensic workstation. The acquisition is written to a work folder on your C drive, assuming it has enough free space for the acquired data. Follow these steps to perform the first task of connecting the suspect's drive to your workstation:

1. Document the chain of evidence for the drive you plan to acquire.

2. Remove the drive from the suspect's computer.

3. Configure the suspect drive's jumpers as needed, if it's a PATA (IDE) disk. (*Note*: This step doesn't apply to SATA drives.)

4. Connect the suspect drive to the USB or FireWire write-blocker device.

5. Create a storage folder on the target drive. For this activity, you use your work folder (C:*Work*\\Chap04\\Chapter), but in real life, you'd use a folder name such as C:\\Evidence.

The work folder shown in screenshots might differ from the work folder you've created for this chapter's activities.

Using ProDiscover's Proprietary Acquisition Format Follow these 11 steps to perform the second task, starting ProDiscover Basic and configuring settings for the acquisition:

1. Start ProDiscover Basic. (Remember to select the Run as administrator option if you're using Windows Vista.) If the Launch Dialog dialog box opens, click **Cancel**.

2. In the ProDiscover Basic window, click **Action, Capture Image** from the menu.

3. In the Capture Image dialog box, click the **Source Drive** list arrow, and then click **PhysicalDrive1**.

Selecting PhysicalDrive1 assumes there's only the system disk (drive C) and the suspect drive connected to your workstation. If you have additional drives connected, start the Computer Management utility from the Computer window, and click Disk Management. Identify the target and suspect drive to determine the physical disk numbers.

4. Click the >> button next to the Destination text box. In the Save As dialog box, navigate to the work folder you set up. In the File name text box, type **InChp041**, and then click **Save**.

5. Click the **Split** button. In the Split Image dialog box shown in Figure 4-4, type **650** in the Split into equal sized image of text box, click **Split**, and then click **OK**.

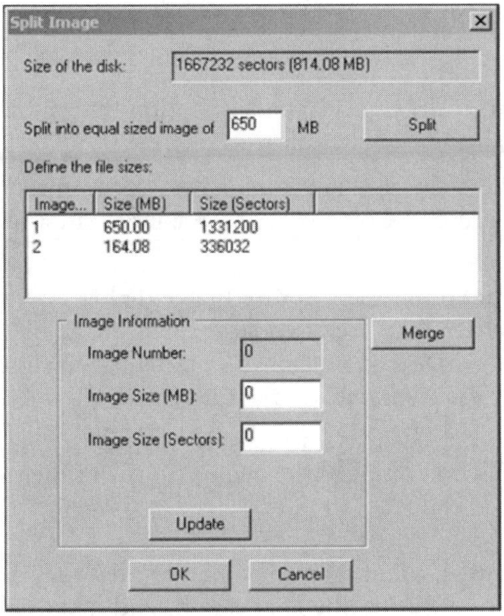

Figure 4-4 The Split Image dialog box

6. In the Capture Image dialog box, click the **Image Format** list arrow, and click **ProDiscover Format (recommended)**, if it's not already selected.

7. In the Technician Name text box, type your name, and in the Image Number text box, type **InChp04**. If you like, in the Description text box, type any comments related to the case (see Figure 4-5).

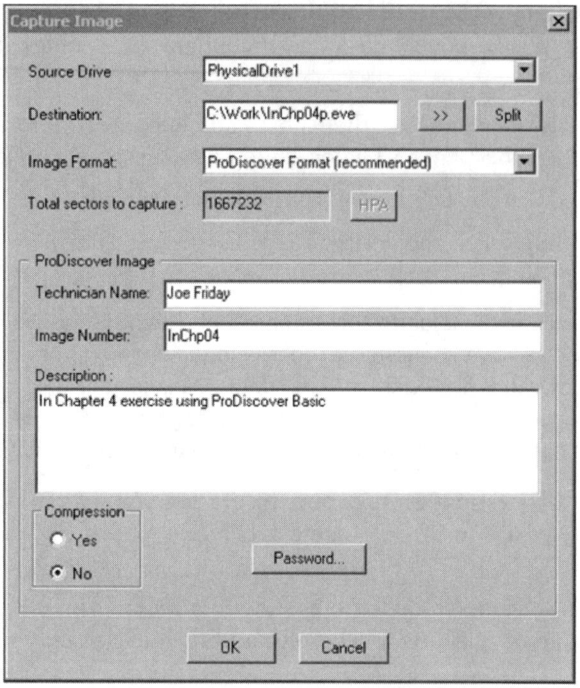

Figure 4-5 The Capture Image dialog box

8. If you need to save space on your target drive, click the **Yes** option button in the Compression section.

9. If additional security is needed for the acquired image, click **Password**. In the Password dialog box, enter a new password once, type it again to confirm it, and then click **OK**.

10. When you're finished entering information in the Capture Image dialog box, click **OK** to begin the acquisition. ProDiscover then creates a segmented image file in your work folder. During this acquisition, ProDiscover displays a status bar in the lower-right corner to show the progress for each volume segment it's creating.

11. When the acquisition is done, ProDiscover displays a message box instructing you to examine a log file for errors. Click **OK** to complete the acquisition, and then exit ProDiscover Basic.

ProDiscover then creates image files (segmented volumes) with an .eve extension, a log file (.log extension) listing any errors that occurred during the acquisition, and a special inventory file (.pds extension) that tells ProDiscover how many segmented volumes were created. All these files have the prefix you specified in the Capture Image dialog box. ProDiscover uses the .pds file to load all segmented volumes in the correct order for analysis.

For this activity, ProDiscover produced four files. Two are segments of the split image of the suspect drive, one is the log file, and one is the .pds file. A larger drive would have more than two segmented volumes. The first segmented volume (volume one) has the extension .eve, and all other segmented volumes have the suffix -Split1, -Split2, -Split3, and so on before the .eve extension. If the compression option was selected, ProDiscover uses a .cmp rather than an .eve extension on all segmented volumes.

Using ProDiscover's Raw Acquisition Format For versatility, ProDiscover can produce raw format acquisitions that many other forensics tools can read. To perform a raw format acquisition, follow the same steps as for the proprietary format in the Capture Image dialog box, but select the UNIX style dd format in the Image Format list box. When you select this option, the input fields at the bottom of the Capture Image dialog box are grayed out. To segment the image acquisition, click the Split button as you would for the proprietary format.

To initiate the raw acquisition, click OK, and then click Proceed in the warning box, which simply advises you that the raw acquisition saves only the image data and hash value. When the raw acquisition is finished, click OK in the message box.

The raw format creates a log file (.pds extension) and segmented volume files, just like the proprietary format acquisition. Another file with the .md5 extension is also created, which contains the MD5 hash for the acquired drive. In the proprietary format, the hash value, the time zone where the acquisition occurred, the password if it was specified, the investigator's name, and any comments entered in the Description text box are stored in the .eve file.

Capturing an Image with AccessData FTK Imager

FTK Imager is a Windows data acquisition program that's included with a licensed copy of AccessData Forensic Toolkit. FTK Imager, like most Windows data acquisition tools, requires using a device such as a USB or parallel port dongle for licensing. However, a version of FTK Imager has been provided on this book's DVD for you to use for activities and projects.

FTK Imager is designed for viewing evidence disks and disk-to-image files created from other proprietary formats. FTK Imager can read AccessData .ad1, Expert Witness (EnCase) .e01, SafeBack (up to version 2.0), SMART .s01, and raw format files. In addition to disk media, FTK Imager can read CD and DVD file systems. This program provides a view of a disk partition or an image file as though it's a mounted partition, with additional panes showing the contents of the selected file (see Figure 4-6).

FTK Imager can make disk-to-image copies of evidence drives and enables you to acquire an evidence drive from a logical partition level or a physical drive level. You can also define the size of each disk-to-image file volume, allowing you to segment the image into one or many split volumes. For example, you can specify 650 MB volume segments if you plan to store volumes on 650 MB CD-Rs or 2.0 GB volume segments so that you can record volumes on DVD-/+Rs.

Because FTK Imager is designed to run in Windows, the evidence drive from which you're acquiring data must have a hardware write-blocking device or the USB write-protection Registry feature enabled between your workstation and the evidence drive.

FTK Imager can't acquire a drive's host protected area, however. In other words, if the drive's specifications indicate it has 11,000,000 sectors and the BIOS display indicates 9,000,000, a host protected area of 2,000,000 sectors might be assigned to the drive. If you suspect an evidence drive has a host protected area, you must use an advanced acquisition tool, such as ProDiscover, X-Ways Replica, NTI SafeBack, or SnapBack DatArrest, to

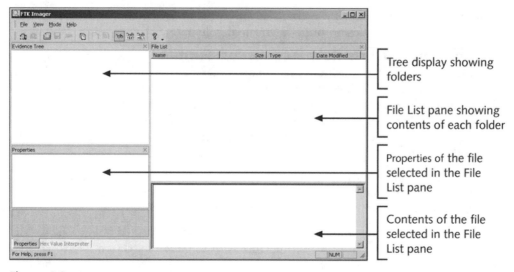

Tree display showing folders

File List pane showing contents of each folder

Properties of the file selected in the File List pane

Contents of the file selected in the File List pane

Figure 4-6 The FTK Imager main window

include this area when copying data. With MS-DOS tools, you might have to define the exact sector count to make sure you include more than what the BIOS shows as the number of known sectors on a drive. Review vendor product manuals to determine how to account for a drive's host protected area.

In the following activity, you use FTK Imager to make an image file. Use a write-blocking device or the USB write-protection method to protect the suspect drive, and then follow these steps:

1. Boot your forensic workstation to Windows, using an installed write-blocker or the USB write-protection Registry method. If you're using the USB Registry method, connect a target drive to an internal PATA or SATA controller.

2. Connect the evidence drive to a write-blocking device or USB device.

3. Connect the target drive to a USB external drive, if you're using a write-blocker.

4. To start FTK Imager, click **Start,** point to **All Programs,** point to **AccessData,** point to **FTK Imager,** and then right-click **FTK Imager** and click **Run as administrator.** (In Windows XP, click **Start,** point to **All Programs,** point to **AccessData,** point to **FTK Imager,** and then click **FTK Imager.**)

5. In the FTK Imager main window, click **File, Create Disk Image** from the menu.

6. In the Select Source dialog box, click the **Physical Drive** option button (see Figure 4-7), and then click **Next.**

7. In the Select Drive dialog box, click the **Drive Selection** list arrow, click the suspect drive, and then click **Finish.**

8. In the Create Image dialog box, click to select the **Verify images after they are created** check box, and then click **Add.** In the Select Image Type dialog box that opens (see Figure 4-8), click the **Raw (dd)** option button, and then click **Next.**

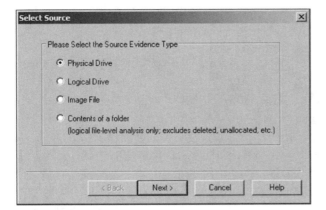

Figure 4-7 The Select Source dialog box

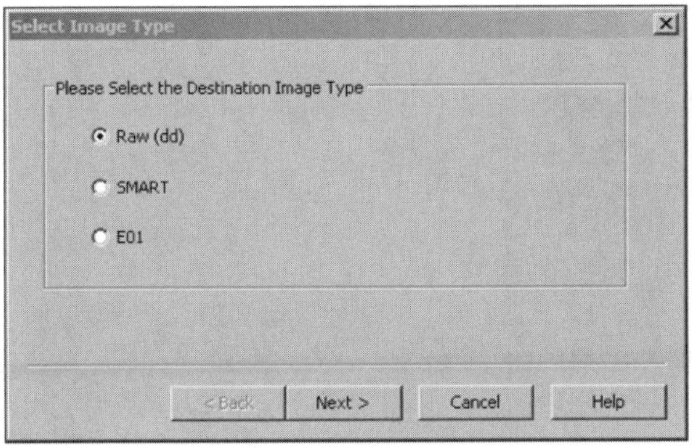

Figure 4-8 The Select Image Type dialog box

9. In the Select Image Destination dialog box (see Figure 4-9), click **Browse**, navigate to the location for the image file (your work folder), and then click **OK**.

10. In the Image filename (excluding extension) text box, type **InChp04-ftk**, and then click **Finish**.

You can adjust the segmented volume size in this dialog box, but for this activity, accept the default of 650 MB.

11. Next, in the Create Image dialog box, click **Start** to initiate the acquisition.

12. When FTK Imager finishes the acquisition, click **Close** in the Drive/Image Verify Results dialog box, and then click **Close** again in the Creating Image dialog box (see Figure 4-10).

13. Exit FTK Imager by clicking **File, Exit** from the menu.

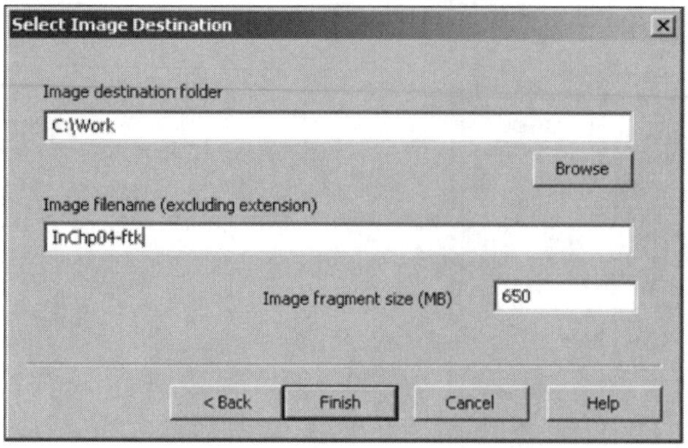

Select Image Destination ☒

Image destination folder

C:\Work

Browse

Image filename (excluding extension)

InChp04-ftk

Image fragment size (MB)   650

< Back   Finish   Cancel   Help

Figure 4-9   Selecting where to save the image file

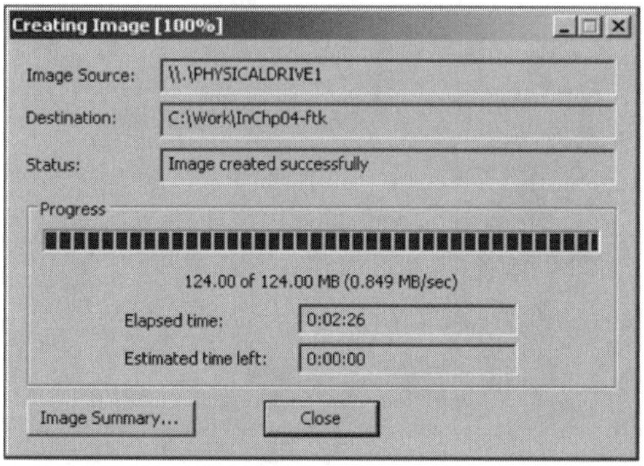

Creating Image [100%] _ ☐ ☒

Image Source: \\.\PHYSICALDRIVE1

Destination: C:\Work\InChp04-ftk

Status: Image created successfully

Progress

████████████████████████████████████

124.00 of 124.00 MB (0.849 MB/sec)

Elapsed time: 0:02:26

Estimated time left: 0:00:00

Image Summary...   Close

Figure 4-10   A completed image save

For additional information, see the Help menu in FTK Imager to learn more about its many features.

Validating Data Acquisitions

Probably the most critical aspect of computer forensics is validating digital evidence. The weakest point of any digital investigation is the integrity of the data you collect, so validation is essential. In this section, you learn how to use several tools to validate data acquisitions.

Validating digital evidence requires using a hashing algorithm utility, which is designed to create a binary or hexadecimal number that represents the uniqueness of a data set, such as a file or disk drive. This unique number is referred to as a "digital fingerprint." Because hash values are unique, if two files have the same hash values, they are identical, even if they have different filenames. Making any alteration in one of the files—even changing one letter from uppercase to lowercase—produces a completely different hash value, however.

In recent years, researchers have discovered that MD5 can produce collisions. For forensic examinations of data files on a disk drive, however, collisions are of little concern. If two files with different content have the same MD5 hash value, a comparison of each byte of a file can be done to see the differences. Currently, several tools can do a byte-by-byte comparison of files. Programs such as X-Ways Forensics, X-Ways WinHex, and IDM Computing Solution's UltraCompare can analyze and compare data files. For more information on MD5 collisions, see *www.x-ways.net/md5collision.html* or *www.mscs.dal.ca/~selinger/md5collision/*. Chapter 5 discusses methods of using MD5 and SHA-1.

For imaging an evidence drive, many tools offer validation techniques ranging from CRC-32, MD5, and SHA-1 to SHA-512. The advantage of older validation utilities, such as CRC-32, is speed because it takes less CPU processing time to compute hash values. More advanced validation utilities, such as MD5 and the SHA series, require far more CPU cycles to complete. The higher the level of hashing done on an acquisition, the longer the calculation takes.

These hashing algorithm utilities are available as standalone programs or are integrated into many acquisition tools. The following sections discuss how to perform validation with some currently available acquisition programs.

Linux Validation Methods

Linux and UNIX are rich in commands and functions. The two Linux shell commands shown earlier in this chapter, dd and dcfldd, have several options that can be combined with other commands to validate data. The dcfldd command has additional options that validate data collected from an acquisition. Validating acquired data with the dd command requires using other shell commands.

Current distributions of Linux include two hashing algorithm utilities: md5sum and sha1-sum. Both utilities can compute hashes of a single file, multiple files, individual or multiple disk partitions, or an entire disk drive.

Validating dd Acquired Data
As shown earlier, the following command produces segmented volumes of the /dev/sdb drive, with each segmented volume named image_sdb and an incrementing extension of .aa, .ab, .ac, and so on:

```
dd if=/dev/sdb | split -b 650m - image_sdb
```

To validate all segmented volumes of a suspect drive with the md5sum utility, you use the Linux shell commands in the following steps. For the saved images, remember to change to the directory where the data was saved, or list the exact path for the saved images. To use sha1sum instead of md5sum, just replace all md5sum references in commands with sha1-sum. The drive should still be connected to your acquisition workstation.

1. If necessary, start Linux, open a shell window, and navigate to the directory where image files are saved. To calculate the hash value of the original drive, type **md5sum /dev/sdb > md5_sdb.txt** and press **Enter**.

The redirect (>) option saves the computed MD5 hash value in the md5_sdb.txt file. This file should be saved with image files as validation of the evidence.

2. To compute the MD5 hash value for the segmented volumes and append the output to the md5_sdb.txt file, type **cat image_sdb. | md5sum >> md5_sdb.txt** and press **Enter**.

By using the cat (concatenate) command with an asterisk (*) as the extension value, all segmented volumes are read sequentially as one big contiguous file, as though they were the original drive or partition. The pipe (|) function outputs the cat command read data to the input of the md5sum command. The >> option adds the md5sum hash results at the end of the md5_sdb.txt file's content.

3. Examine the md5_sdb.txt file to see whether both hashes match by typing **cat md5_sdb.txt** and pressing **Enter**. If the data acquisition is successful, the two hash numbers should be identical. If not, the acquisition didn't work correctly. You should see output similar to the following:

```
34963884a4bc5810b130018b00da9de1  /dev/sdb
34963884a4bc5810b130018b00da9de1
```

4. Close the Linux shell window by typing **exit** and pressing **Enter**.

With the dd command, the md5sum or sha1sum utilities should be run on all suspect disks and volumes or segmented volumes.

Validating dcfldd Acquired Data

Because dcfldd is designed for forensic data acquisition, it has validation options integrated: hash and hashlog. You use the hash option to designate a hashing algorithm of md5, sha1, sha256, sha384, or sha512. The hashlog option outputs hash results to a text file that can be stored with the image files.

To create an MD5 hash output file during a dcfldd acquisition, you enter the following command at the shell prompt:

```
dcfldd if=/dev/sda split=2M of=usbimg hash=md5
hashlog=usbhash.log
```

To see the results of files generated with the split command, you enter the list directory (ls) command at the shell prompt. You should see the following output:

```
usbhash.logusbimg.004 usbimg.010 usbimg.016 usbimg.022 usbimg.028
usbseghash.logusbimg.005 usbimg.011 usbimg.017 usbimg.023 usbimg.029
usbimg.000 usbimg.006 usbimg.012 usbimg.018 usbimg.024 usbimg.030
usbimg.001 usbimg.007 usbimg.013 usbimg.019 usbimg.025
usbimg.002 usbimg.008 usbimg.014 usbimg.020 usbimg.026
usbimg.003 usbimg.009 usbimg.015 usbimg.021 usbimg.027
```

Note that the first segmented volume has an extension of .000 rather than .001. Some Windows forensics tools might not be able to read segmented file extensions starting with .000. They are typically looking for .001. If your forensics tool requires starting with a

.001 extension, the files need to be renamed incrementally. So segmented file .000 should be renamed .001, .001 should be renamed .002, and so on.

Another useful dcfldd command is the vf (verify file) option, which compares the image file to the original medium, such as a partition or drive. The vf option applies only to a nonsegmented image file. To validate segmented files from dcfldd, use the md5sum command described previously. To use the vf option, you enter the following command at the shell prompt:

```
dcfldd if=/dev/sdavf=sda_hash.img
```

4

For additional information on dcfldd, see the man page.

Windows Validation Methods

Unlike Linux and UNIX, Windows has no built-in hashing algorithm tools for computer forensics. However, many Windows third-party programs do provide a variety of built-in tools. These third-party programs range from hexadecimal editors, such as X-Ways WinHex or Breakpoint Software Hex Workshop, to computer forensics programs, such as ProDiscover, EnCase, and FTK. In Chapter 9, you learn how to hash specific data by using a hexadecimal editor to locate and verify groups of data that have no file association or are sections within a file.

Commercial computer forensics programs also have built-in validation features. Each program has its own validation technique used with acquisition data in its proprietary format. For example, ProDiscover's .eve files contain metadata in the acquisition file or segmented files, including the hash value for the suspect drive or partition. Image data loaded into ProDiscover is hashed and then compared to the hash value in the stored metadata. If the hashes don't match, ProDiscover notifies you that the acquisition is corrupt and can't be considered reliable evidence. This function is called Auto Verify Image Checksum.

In ProDiscover and many other computer forensics tools, however, raw format image files don't contain metadata. As mentioned previously, a separate manual validation is recommended for all raw acquisitions at the time of analysis. The previously generated validation file for raw format acquisitions is essential to the integrity of digital evidence. The saved validation file can be used later to check whether the acquisition file is still good.

In FTK Imager, when you select the Expert Witness (.e01) or the SMART (.s01) format, additional options for validation are displayed. This validation report also lists the MD5 and SHA-1 hash values. The MD5 hash value is added to the proprietary format image or segmented files. When this image is loaded into FTK, SMART, or X-Ways Forensics (X-Ways Forensics can read only .e01 and raw files), the MD5 hash is read and compared to the image to verify whether the acquisition is correct.

Performing RAID Data Acquisitions

Acquisitions of RAID drives can be challenging and frustrating for computing forensics examiners because of how RAID systems are designed, configured, and sized. Size is the biggest concern because many RAID systems are now pushing into many terabytes of data. The following sections review common RAID configurations and discuss ways to acquire data on these large storage devices.

Understanding RAID

Redundant array of independent disks (RAID) is a computer configuration involving two or more disks. Originally, RAID was developed as a data-redundancy measure to minimize data loss caused by a disk failure. As technology improved, RAID also provided increased storage capabilities.

Several levels of RAID can be implemented through software or special hardware controllers. For Windows XP, 2000, and NT servers and workstations, RAID 0 or 1 is available. For a high-end data-processing environment, RAID 5 is common and is often based in special RAID towers. These high-end RAID systems usually have integrated controllers that connect to high-end servers or mainframes. These systems provide redundancy and high-speed data access and can make many small disks appear as one very large drive.

 Other variations of RAID besides 0, 1, and 5 are specific to their vendor or application.

RAID 0 provides rapid access and increased data storage (see Figure 4-11). In RAID 0, two or more disk drives become one large volume, so the computer views the disks as a single disk. The tracks of data on this mode of storage cross over to each disk. The logical addressing scheme makes it seem as though each track of data is continuous throughout all disks. If you have two disks configured as RAID 0, track one starts on the first physical disk and continues to the second physical disk. When viewed from a booted OS, such as Windows XP, the two disks appear as one large disk. The advantage of RAID 0 is increased speed and data storage capability spread over two or more disks that can be one large disk partition. Its biggest disadvantage is lack of redundancy; if a disk fails, data isn't continuously available.

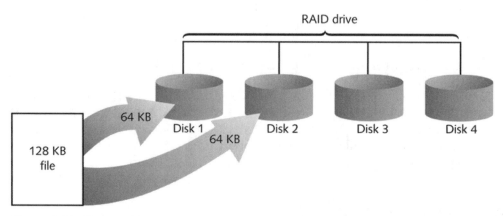

Figure 4-11   RAID 0: Striping

RAID 1, shown in Figure 4-12, is made up of two disks for each volume and is designed for data recovery in the event of a disk failure. The contents of the two disks in RAID 1 are

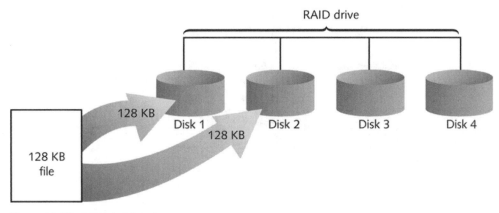

Figure 4-12 RAID 1: Mirroring

identical. When data is written to a volume, the OS writes the data twice—once to each disk at the same time. If one drive fails, the OS switches to the other disk.

RAID 1 ensures that data isn't lost and helps prevent computer downtime. The only disadvantage of RAID 1 is that it takes two disks for each volume, which doubles the cost of disk storage.

Like RAID 1, RAID 2 (see Figure 4-13) provides rapid access and increased storage by configuring two or more disks as one large volume. The difference with RAID 2 is that data is written to disks on a bit level. An error-correcting code (ECC) is used to verify whether the write is successful. RAID 2, therefore, has better data integrity checking than RAID 0. Because of the bit-level writes and the ECC, however, RAID 2 is slower than RAID 0.

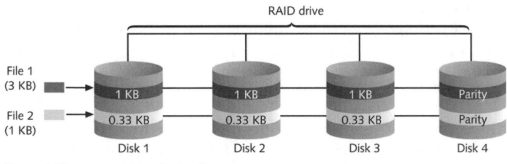

Figure 4-13 RAID 2: Striping (bit level)

RAID 3 uses data striping and dedicated parity and requires at least three disks. Similar to RAID 0, RAID 3 stripes tracks across all disks that make up one volume. RAID 3 also implements dedicated parity of data to ensure recovery if data is corrupted. Dedicated parity is stored on one disk in the RAID 3 array. Like RAID 3, RAID 4 uses data striping and dedicated parity (block writing), except data is written in blocks rather than bytes.

RAID 5 (see Figure 4-14) is similar to RAIDs 0 and 3 in that it uses distributed data and distributed parity and stripes data tracks across all disks in the RAID array. Unlike RAID 3, however, RAID 5 places parity data on each disk. If a disk in a RAID array has a data

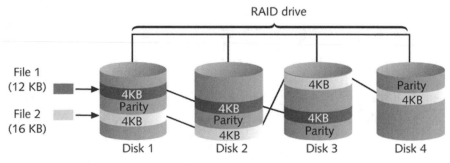

Figure 4-14   RAID 5: Block-level striping with distributed parity

failure, the parity on other disks rebuilds the corrupt data automatically when the failed drive is replaced.

In RAID 6, distributed data and distributed parity (double parity) function the same way as RAID 5, except each disk in the RAID array has redundant parity. The advantage of RAID 6 over RAID 5 is that it recovers any two disks that fail because of the additional parity stored on each disk.

RAID 10, or mirrored striping, also known as RAID 1+0, is a combination of RAID 1 and RAID 0. It provides fast access and redundancy of data storage. RAID 15, or mirrored striping with parity, also known as RAID 1+5, is a combination of RAID 1 and RAID 5. It offers the most robust data recovery capability and speed of access of all RAID configurations and is also more costly.

Acquiring RAID Disks

There's no simple method for getting an image of a RAID server's disks. You need to address the following concerns:

- How much data storage is needed to acquire all data for a forensics image?
- What type of RAID is used? Is it Windows RAID 0 or 1 or an integrated hardware-firmware vendor's RAID 5, 10, or 15? Is it another unknown configuration or OS (Linux, UNIX, mainframe)?
- Do you have an acquisition tool capable of copying the data correctly?
- Can the tool read a forensically copied RAID image?
- Can the tool read split data saves of each RAID disk, and then combine all images of each disk into one RAID virtual drive for analysis?

With the larger disks now available, copying small RAID systems to one large disk is possible, similar to the way non-RAID suspect drives are copied. For example, a small server running eight 36 GB SCSI drives in a RAID 0 tower requires about a 300 GB SATA or IDE (PATA) drive. Less data storage is needed if a proprietary format acquisition is used with compression applied. All forensics analysis tools can analyze an image because they see the acquired data as one large drive, not eight separate drives.

Older hardware-firmware RAID systems can be a challenge when you're making an image. For example, you're making an acquisition of an older HP/Compaq ProLiant system configured as RAID 1. A software implementation of RAID 1 has two identical disks, but making an acquisition requires only one of the two disks. However, with older ProLiant systems, you must have both mirrored disks to make the acquisition. In addition, the acquisition needs to be performed on a ProLiant server. Copying only one disk from this type of system produces unexpected results because of ProLiant's proprietary format.

For a HP/Compaq ProLiant RAID 1 acquisition, Guidance Software EnCase is capable of performing a static image acquisition. The EnCase DOS program En.exe requires using a forensic MS-DOS boot floppy or CD and a network crossover cable. The network crossover cable is connected to the suspect ProLiant server and your acquisition workstation. Using EnCase with a network crossover cable is reliable but slow at copying data, even on a 100 Mbps network connection.

Several computer forensics vendors have added RAID recovery features. These vendors typically specialize in one or two types of RAID formats. The following are some vendors offering RAID acquisition functions:

- Technologies Pathways ProDiscover
- Guidance Software EnCase
- X-Ways Forensics
- Runtime Software
- R-Tools Technologies

You should know which vendor supports which RAID format and keep up to date on the latest improvements in these products.

ProDiscover can acquire RAID disks at the physical level. After all disks have been acquired, a ProDiscover Group file (.pdg extension) is created, which includes instructions for how ProDiscover should load each physical disk's image data. It also lists the paths to each physical disk's image data if the RAID acquisition takes several storage drives.

Being able to separate each physical disk into smaller save sets eliminates the need to have one large drive for storing acquired data. Acquiring RAID data requires only similar sized drives that match each disk in the RAID array. For example, with a RAID 0 array of three 250 GB disks, all you need are three target drives of the same size. If each acquisition is compressed, you might be able to get by with slightly smaller target drives.

With ProDiscover, all you need are three 250 GB target drives to collect the image's segmented files for each disk. This feature eliminates the need for a 750 GB drive to collect the combined data from all three 250 GB drives. EnCase and X-Ways Forensics also have similar features for RAID 0 and 5 acquisitions.

Other tools, such as Runtime Software (*www.runtime.org*) and R-Tools Technologies (*www.r-tt.com*), are designed as data recovery tools. Although not intended as forensics acquisition tools, they have unique features that can aid in recovering corrupted RAID data and can perform raw format acquisitions and repair broken RAID 0 and 5 systems. The Runtime RAID Reconstructor tool copies the original RAID to a raw format file, which must then be restored on another RAID-configured system where repairs can be performed. It also scans and corrects errors on the newly copied RAID. R-Tools R-Studio creates a virtual volume of the RAID image file. All repairs are made on the virtual volume, which can then be restored to the original RAID.

Occasionally, a RAID system is too large for a static acquisition. Under ideal circumstances, your goal is to collect a complete image of evidence drives. Because RAID systems can have dozens or more terabytes of data storage, copying all data isn't always practical, as you would for a small desktop or laptop computer. For these occasions, retrieving only the data relevant to the investigation with the sparse or logical acquisition method is the only practical solution. When dealing with very large RAID servers, consult with the computer forensics vendor to determine how to best capture RAID data.

Using Remote Network Acquisition Tools

Recent improvements in computer forensics tools include the capability to acquire disk data or data fragments (sparse or logical) remotely. With this feature, you can connect to a suspect computer remotely via a network connection and copy data from it. Remote acquisition tools vary in configurations and capabilities. Some require manual intervention on remote suspect computers to initiate the data copy. Others can acquire data surreptitiously through an encrypted link by pushing a remote access program to the suspect's computer. From an investigation perspective, being able to connect to a suspect's computer remotely to perform an acquisition has tremendous appeal. It saves time because you don't have to go to a suspect's computer, and it minimizes the chances of a suspect discovering that an investigation is taking place. Most remote acquisitions have to be done as live acquisitions, not static acquisitions.

There are some drawbacks to consider, however. For example, if you have access to the same LAN as the suspect's computer, data transfer speeds and routing table conflicts could cause problems. On a WAN, you have the problem of gaining the permissions needed to access more secure subnets. In addition, heavy traffic on the network could cause delays and errors during the acquisition, no matter what tool you're using. Another problem is the remote access program being detected by antivirus, antispyware, and firewall tools. Most of these security programs can be configured to ignore remote access programs. However, if suspects have administrator rights on their computers, they could easily install their own security tools that trigger an alarm to notify them of remote access intrusions.

The following section describes how to perform remote acquisitions in ProDiscover. Chapter 11 covers other resources for data copying and explains how to perform a live forensics acquisition.

Remote Acquisition with ProDiscover

Two versions of ProDiscover can perform remote acquisitions: ProDiscover Investigator and ProDiscover Incident Response. When connected to a remote computer, both tools use the same ProDiscover acquisition method described previously. After the connection is established, the remote computer is displayed in the Capture Image dialog box.

ProDiscover Investigator is designed to capture data from a suspect's computer while the user is operating it, which is a live acquisition. Being able to connect to a suspect's computer directly allows the following capabilities:

- Preview a suspect's drive remotely while it's in use or powered on.
- Perform a live acquisition (also called a "smear" because with an active computer, disk data is being altered) while the suspect's computer is powered on.

- Encrypt the connection between the suspect's and examiner's computers.
- Copy the suspect computer's RAM while the computer is powered on.
- Use the optional stealth mode to hide the remote connection from the suspect while data is previewed or acquired.

ProDiscover Incident Response is designed to be integrated as a network intrusion analysis tool. It offers all the functions and features of other tools in the ProDiscover suite plus the following:

- Capture volatile system state information.
- Analyze current running processes on a remote system.
- Locate unseen files and processes on a remote system that might be running malware or spyware.
- Remotely view and listen to IP ports on a compromised system.
- Run hash comparisons on a remote system to search for known Trojans and rootkits.
- Create a hash inventory of all files on a system remotely (a negative hash search capability) to establish a baseline if it gets attacked.

The ProDiscover utility for remote access is the PDServer remote agent, which must be loaded on the suspect computer before ProDiscover Investigator or ProDiscover Incident Response can access it. This remote agent can be installed in three different ways:

- *Trusted CD*—For this manual installation method, ProDiscover can create a special CD containing the PDServer remote agent. This CD is used to load PDServer manually on the suspect computer.
- *Preinstallation*—For networks with a configured OS, PDServer remote agent can be added to the standard installation of high-risk computers, which enables network security administrators to respond to network attacks and malware contaminations quickly. Any network management tool, such as Dameware (*www.dameware.com*) or Hyena (*www.systemtools.com/hyena/*), can be used to initiate a connection with ProDiscover. This is a remote method of installing the remote acquisition tool.
- *Pushing out and running remotely*—Downloading PDServer to a remote computer helps investigators respond quickly to incidents. Data is collected in real time when using this function. This is a remote method of installing the remote acquisition tool.

With both remote methods of installing PDServer, you have the option of running it in a stealth mode to hide it from the suspect. Note that Windows Task Manager lists the process as PDServer. To disguise it, you can change the process name so that it appears to be an OS function in the suspect computer's Task Manager. In addition, the following security features are available for remote connections:

- *Password Protection*—PDServer on the target computer is password-protected, and the password is encrypted at all times.
- *Encryption*—All communication between PDServer on the suspect's and investigator's computers can be encrypted. ProDiscover provides 256-bit Advanced Encryption Standard (AES) or Twofish encryption for the connection.

- *Secure Communication Protocol*—All connections between the suspect's and examiner's computers have globally unique identifiers (GIUDs) to prevent inserting packets in the data stream.

- *Write Protected Trusted Binaries*—PDServer can run from a write-protected device, such as a CD.

- *Digital Signatures*—PDServer and its removal device driver, PARemoval.sys, are digitally signed to verify that they haven't been tampered with before and during the remote connection.

 For more information on PDServer, see *www.techpathways.com*

Remote Acquisition with EnCase Enterprise

Guidance Software was the first computer forensics vendor to develop a remote acquisition and analysis tool based on its desktop tool EnCase. This remote tool, EnCase Enterprise, comes with several capabilities. The following are some of its remote acquisition features:

- Remote data acquisition of a computer's media and RAM data

- Integration with intrusion detection system (IDS) tools that copy evidence of intrusions to an investigation workstation automatically for further analysis over the network

- Options to create an image of data from one or more systems

- Preview of systems to determine whether future actions, such as an acquisition, are needed

- A wide range of file system formats, such as NTFS, FAT, Ext2/3, Reiser, Solaris UFS, AIX Journaling File System (JFS), LVM8, FFS, Palm, Macintosh HFS/HFS+, CDFS, ISO 9660, UDF, DVD, and more

- RAID support for both hardware and software

EnCase Enterprise is set up with an Examiner workstation and a Secure Authentication for EnCase (SAFE) workstation. Acquisition and analysis are conducted on the Examiner workstation. The SAFE workstation provides secure encrypted authentication for the Examiner workstation and the suspect's system.

The remote access program in EnCase Enterprise is Servlet, a passive utility installed on the suspect computer. Servlet connects the suspect computer to the Examiner and SAFE workstations. A unique feature is that Servlet can run in stealth mode on the suspect computer. For more information on EnCase Enterprise, see *www.guidancesoftware.com/downloads/ Review_Security_Schema.pdf*.

Remote Acquisition with R-Tools R-Studio

The R-Tools suite of software is designed for data recovery. As part of this recovery capability, the R-Studio network edition can remotely access networked computer systems. Its remote connection uses Triple Data Encryption Standard (3DES) encryption. Data acquired with R-Studio network edition creates raw format acquisitions, and it's capable of recovering the following file systems:

- FAT12, FAT16, FAT32
- NTFS, NTFS5
- Ext2FS, Ext3FS
- UFS1, USF2

For more information on R-Studio, see *www.r-tt.com*.

Remote Acquisition with WetStone LiveWire

LiveWire, part of a suite of tools developed by WetStone, can connect to a networked computer remotely and perform a live acquisition of all drives connected to it. LiveWire's acquisition file format is raw (.dd). In addition to being able to copy disk data, LiveWire can capture RAM data from remote systems. You can find more information on LiveWire at *www.wetstonetech.com/cgi-bin/shop.cgi?view,14*.

Remote Acquisition with F-Response

F-Response (*www.f-response.com*) is a vendor-neutral specialty remote access utility designed to work with any computer forensics program. When installed on a remote computer, it sets up a security read-only connection that allows the computer forensics examiner to access it. With F-Response, examiners can access remote drives at the physical level and view raw data. After the F-Response connection has been set up, any computer forensics acquisition tool can be used to collect digital evidence.

F-Response is sold in three different versions: Field Kit Edition, Consultant Edition, and Enterprise Edition. The Consultant and Enterprise editions allow accessing remote systems over longer distances.

Remote Acquisition with Runtime Software

Runtime Software offers several compact shareware programs for data recovery. For remote acquisitions, Runtime has created these utilities:

- DiskExplorer for FAT
- DiskExplorer for NTFS
- HDHOST

Runtime has designed its tools to be file system specific, so DiskExplorer versions for both FAT and NTFS are available. These tools offer the following features for acquisition needs:

- Create a raw format image file.
- Segment the raw format or compressed image for archiving purposes.
- Access network computers' drives.

HDHOST is a remote access program that allows communication between two computers. The connection is established between systems by using the DiskExplorer program corresponding to the suspect (remote) computer's drives. There are two types of connections in HDHOST. The first is between two computers using serial (RS232) ports and a null-modem cable. The second is with a NIC using TCP/IP with a standard network connection through a hub, router, or crossover network cable between the two computers. In Chapter 9, you learn how to use Runtime's DiskExplorer and HDHOST utilities to make a remote acquisition.

Using Other Forensics Acquisition Tools

In addition to ProDiscover, FTK Imager, and X-Ways Forensics, you can use other commercial acquisition tools, described in the following sections. Prices for some tools are discounted for law enforcement officers working in computer forensics, and two tools are freeware.

SnapBack DatArrest

SnapBack DatArrest (*www.intersys-group.com/snapback/datarrest_overview.htm*) from Columbia Data Products is an older forensics acquisition program that runs from a true MS-DOS boot floppy disk. It can make an image of an evidence drive in three ways: disk to SCSI drive (magnetic tape or Jaz disk), disk to network drive, and disk to disk. Each method is a separate program that fits on a forensic boot floppy disk. SnapBack DatArrest provides network drivers so that you can boot from a forensic boot floppy disk and access a remote network server's drive. You can then save an image file directly to a remote network server's drive or restore image files created on a network drive or removable media to a new target drive for follow-up examination and analysis.

NTI SafeBack

SafeBack, another reliable MS-DOS acquisition tool, is small enough to fit on a forensic boot floppy disk. It performs an SHA-256 calculation for each sector copied to ensure data integrity. During the acquisition, SafeBack creates a log file of all transactions it performs. The log file includes a comment field where you can identify the investigation and data you collect. SafeBack does the following:

- Creates image files
- Copies from a suspect drive to an image on a tape drive
- Copies from a suspect drive to a target drive (disk-to-disk copy), adjusting the target drive's geometry to match the suspect drive
- Copies from a suspect drive to a target drive by using a parallel port laplink cable
- Copies a partition to an image file
- Compresses image files to reduce the number of volume segments

AccessData FTK and ILook can read SafeBack version 2 and older image files. For more information on SafeBack, see *www.forensics-intl.com/safeback.html*.

DIBS USA RAID

DIBS USA has developed Rapid Action Imaging Device (RAID) to make forensically sound disk copies. DIBS USA RAID is a portable computer system designed to make disk-to-disk images. The copied disk can then be attached to a write-blocker device connected to a forensic workstation for analysis. For more information on RAID, see *www.dibsusa.com/products/raid.asp*.

ILook Investigator IXimager

IXimager runs from a bootable floppy disk or CD. It's a standalone proprietary format acquisition tool designed to work only with ILook Investigator. It can acquire single drives and RAID drives. It supports IDE (PATA), SCSI, USB, and FireWire devices. The IXimager proprietary format can be converted to a raw format if other analysis tools are used. IXimager has three format options:

- *IDIF*—A compressed format
- *IRBF*—A raw format
- *IEIF*—An encrypted format for added security

For more information on IXimager, see *www.perlustro.com.*

ASRData SMART

ASRData SMART is a Linux forensics analysis tool that can make image files of a suspect drive. SMART can produce proprietary or raw format images and includes the following capabilities:

- Robust data reading of bad sectors on drives
- Mounting suspect drives in write-protected mode
- Mounting target drives, including NTFS drives, in read/write mode
- Optional compression schemes to speed up acquisition or reduce the amount of storage needed for acquired digital evidence

For more information on SMART, see *www.asrdata.com.*

Australian Department of Defence PyFlag

The Australian Department of Defence created the PyFlag tool. Intended as a network forensics analysis tool, PyFlag can create proprietary format Expert Witness image files and uses sgzip and gzip in Linux. For more information, see *www.pyflag.net.*

Chapter Summary

- Forensics data acquisitions are stored in three different formats: raw, proprietary, and AFF. Most proprietary formats and AFF store metadata about the acquired data in the image file.
- The four methods of acquiring data for forensics analysis are disk-to-image file, disk-to-disk copy, logical disk-to-disk or disk-to-data file, or sparse data copy of a folder or file.
- Large disks might require using tape backup devices. With enough tapes, any size drive or RAID drive can be backed up. Tape backups run more slowly but are a reliable method for forensics acquisitions.
- Lossless compression for forensics acquisitions doesn't alter the data when it's restored, unlike lossy compression. Lossless compression can compress up to 50% for

most data. If data is already compressed on a drive, lossless compression might not save much more space.

- If there are time restrictions or too much data to acquire from large drives or RAID drives, a logical or sparse acquisition might be necessary. Consult with your lead attorney or supervisor first to let them know that collecting all the data might not be possible.

- You should have a contingency plan to ensure that you have a forensically sound acquisition and make two acquisitions if you have enough data storage. The first acquisition should be compressed, and the second should be uncompressed. If one acquisition becomes corrupt, the other one is available for analysis.

- Write-blocking devices or utilities must be used with GUI acquisition tools in both Windows and Linux. Practice with a test drive rather than suspect drive, and use a hashing tool on the test drive to verify that no data was altered.

- Always validate your acquisition with built-in tools from a forensics acquisition program, a hexadecimal editor with MD5 or SHA-1 hashing functions, or the Linux md5sum or sha1sum commands.

- A Linux Live CD provides many useful tools for computer forensics acquisitions.

- The preferred Linux acquisition tool is dcfldd instead of dd because it was designed for forensics acquisition. Always validate the acquisition with the hashing features of dcfldd and md5sum or sha1sum.

- When using the Linux dd or dcfldd commands, remember that reversing the output field (of=) and input field (if=) of suspect and target drives could write data to the wrong drive, thus destroying your evidence. If available, you should always use a physical write-blocker device for acquisitions.

- To acquire RAID disks, you need to determine the type of RAID and then which acquisition tool to use. With a firmware-hardware RAID, acquiring data directly from the RAID server might be necessary.

- Remote network acquisition tools require installing a remote agent on the suspect's computer. The remote agent can be detected if suspects install their own security programs, such as a firewall.

Key Terms

Advanced Forensic Format (AFF) A new data acquisition format developed by Simson L. Garfinkel and Basis Technology. This open and extensible format stores image data and metadata. File extensions include .afd for segmented image files and .afm for AFF metadata.

live acquisitions A data acquisition method used when a suspect computer can't be shut down to perform a static acquisition. Data is collected from the local computer or over a remote network connection. The captured data might be altered during the acquisition because it's not write-protected. Live acquisitions aren't repeatable because data is continually being altered by the suspect computer's OS.

logical acquisition This data acquisition method captures only specific files of interest to the case or specific types of files, such as Outlook PST files. *See also* sparse acquisition.

raw format A data acquisition format that creates simple sequential flat files of a suspect drive or data set.

redundant array of independent disks (RAID) Two or more disks combined into one large drive in several configurations for special needs. Some RAID systems are designed for redundancy to ensure continuous operations if one disk fails. Another configuration spreads data across several disks to improve access speeds for reads and writes.

sparse acquisition Like logical acquisitions, this data acquisition method captures only specific files of interest to the case, but it also collects fragments of unallocated (deleted) data. *See also* logical acquisition.

static acquisitions A data acquisition method used when a suspect drive is write-protected and can't be altered. If disk evidence is preserved correctly, static acquisitions are repeatable.

whole disk encryption An encryption technique that performs a sector-by-sector encryption of an entire drive. Each sector is encrypted in its entirety, making it unreadable when copied with a static acquisition method.

Review Questions

1. What is the primary goal of a static acquisition?

2. Name the three formats for computer forensics data acquisitions.

3. What are two advantages and disadvantages of the raw format?

4. List two features common with proprietary format acquisition files.

5. Of all the proprietary formats, which one is the unofficial standard?

6. Name two commercial tools that can make a forensic sector-by-sector copy of a drive to a larger drive.

7. What does a logical acquisition collect for an investigation?

8. What does a sparse acquisition collect for an investigation?

9. What should you consider when determining which data acquisition method to use?

10. What is the advantage of using a tape backup system for forensic acquisitions of large data sets?

11. When is a standard data backup tool, such as Norton Ghost, used for a computing investigation?

12. Why is it a good practice to make two images of a suspect drive in a critical investigation?

13. When you perform an acquisition at a remote location, what should you consider to prepare for this task?

14. What is the disadvantage of using the Windows XP/Vista USB write-protection Registry method?

15. With newer Linux kernel distributions, what happens if you connect a hot-swappable device, such a USB drive, containing evidence?

16. In a Linux shell, the fdisk -1 command lists the suspect drive as /dev/hda1. Is the following dcfldd command correct?

    ```
    dcfldd if=image_file.img of=/dev/hda1
    ```

17. What is the most critical aspect of computer evidence?

18. What is a hashing algorithm?

19. Which hashing algorithm utilities can be run from a Linux shell prompt?

20. In the Linux dcfldd command, which three options are used for validating data?

21. What's the maximum file size when writing data to a FAT32 drive?

22. What are two concerns when acquiring data from a RAID server?

23. R-Studio and DiskExplorer are used primarily for computer forensics. True or False?

24. With remote acquisitions, what problems should you be aware of?
    a. Data transfer speeds
    b. Access permissions over the network
    c. Antivirus, antispyware, and firewall programs
    d. All of the above

25. How does ProDiscover Investigator encrypt the connection between the examiner's and suspect's computers?

26. What is the EnCase Enterprise remote access program?

27. What is the ProDiscover remote access program?

28. What is the Runtime Software utility used to acquire data over a network connection?

29. HDHost is automatically encrypted when connected to another computer. True or False?

30. List two types of connections in HDHOST.

31. Which computer forensics tools can connect to a suspect's remote computer and run surreptitiously?

32. EnCase, FTK, SMART, and ILook treat an image file as though it were the original disk. True or False?

33. When possible, you should make two copies of evidence. True or False?

34. FTK Imager can acquire data in a drive's host protected area. True or False?

Hands-On Projects

If necessary, extract all data files in the Chap04\Projects folder on the book's DVD to the *Work*\Chap04\Projects folder on your system. (If necessary, create this folder on your system before starting the projects.)

Hands-On Project 4-1

In this project, you learn how to restore an image file to a drive. Subsequent projects in this book require using these steps. To prepare for this project, you need the following items:

- A USB or FireWire drive that can hold up to 100 MB or a secondary internally connected drive
- ProDiscover Basic installed on your workstation
- The **GCFI-datacarve-FAT.eve** data file extracted from Chap04\Projects on the book's DVD

The first task is to transfer data from the GCFI-datacarve-FAT.eve file to the target drive. Follow these steps:

1. Boot your acquisition workstation.
2. Connect a hot-swappable media storage device to receive the data, such as a 100+ MB USB drive, a FireWire drive, or an internally connected drive. This device is referred to as the target drive.
3. Start ProDiscover Basic, and in the main window, click **Tools, Copy Disk** from the menu.
4. In the Copy source disk or image to destination disk dialog box, click the **Image to Disk** tab.
5. Click **Browse** next to the Image File text box, and navigate to the location where you copied this chapter's data files (*Work*\Chap04\Projects). Click the **GCFI-datacarve- FAT.eve** file, and then click **Open**.
6. In the Copy source disk or image to destination disk dialog box, click in the space under the Disk Name column at the bottom, as shown in Figure 4-15.

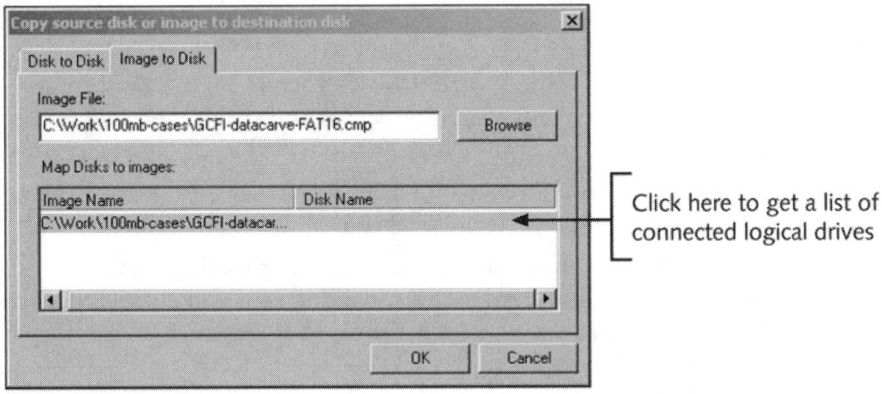

Figure 4-15   The Copy source disk or image to destination disk dialog box

7. Click the **Disk Name** list arrow, click the target drive, and then click **OK**.

8. In the Copy dialog box that opens, click the **Write All 0's** option button (see Figure 4-16), and then click **OK** to start the data loading.

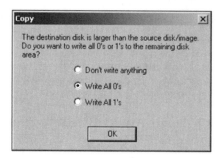

Figure 4-16 Selecting the writing method

9. Click **OK** in the completion dialog box to terminate the loading.

10. Exit ProDiscover Basic, shut down your acquisition workstation, and remove the target drive.

Hands-On Project 4-2

In this project, you make a ProDiscover image file of the data load in Hands-On Project 4-1. To prepare, you need to do the following:

- Make sure you have the suspect drive containing the data load from Hands-On Project 4-1.

- Use a hardware write-blocker or the USB write-protection Registry method for the suspect drive.

- Review the steps in "Using ProDiscover's Raw Acquisition Format" for creating an image file.

- Verify that you have enough free space on your computer's internal drive to receive the image file (about 120 MB).

To make this acquisition on a USB or FireWire drive using the USB write-protection Registry method, follow these steps:

1. Turn on your acquisition workstation, if necessary.

2. Double-click the **Write Protect USB ON** icon on your desktop to protect the suspect drive. If necessary, click **Yes** and then **OK** in the two confirmation dialog boxes that follow.

3. Connect the suspect drive to the USB or FireWire cable, and then connect the cable to your acquisition workstation.

4. Start ProDiscover Basic. Follow the steps in this chapter for making a raw format acquisition in ProDiscover, making sure you click **UNIX style dd** in the Image Format drop-down list box. Then click **OK** in the Capture Image dialog box.

5. When the acquisition is finished, exit ProDiscover. Dismount the USB or FireWire device, remove the suspect drive, and secure it as evidence.

6. Next, click the **Write Protect USB OFF** icon on your desktop, and then shut down the acquisition workstation.

To make this acquisition on an internally connected drive, follow these steps:

1. Use a write-blocking hardware device to protect the suspect drive.

2. Turn on your acquisition workstation.

3. Start ProDiscover. Follow the steps in this chapter for making a raw format acquisition, making sure you click **UNIX style dd** in the Image Format drop-down list box. Then click **OK** in the Capture Image dialog box.

4. When the acquisition is finished, exit ProDiscover. Shut down the acquisition workstation, remove the suspect drive, and secure it as evidence.

Hands-On Project 4-3

In this project, you prepare a drive and create a FAT32 disk partition using Linux. You need the following:

• A Linux distribution or Linux Live CD

• A disk drive

• A method of connecting a disk drive to your workstation, such as USB, FireWire, external SATA, or internal connections, such as PATA or SATA

• Review steps in the "Preparing a Target Drive for Acquisition in Linux" section

To format a drive as FAT32 in Linux, follow these steps:

1. Connect the target drive to be partitioned and formatted as FAT32 to your workstation.

2. Start your workstation, and log on to Linux or boot the Linux Live CD.

3. Follow the steps in the "Preparing a Target Disk for Acquisition in Linux" section.

4. When you're done formatting the target drive, leave it connected for the next project.

Hands-On Project 4-4

In this project, you learn how to use the Linux dd command to make an acquisition split into 30 MB segmented volumes. Then you validate the data by using the Linux md5sum command on the original drive and the image files. The output for md5sum is then redirected to a data file kept with the image files. For this project, you need the following:

• A Linux distribution or Linux Live CD

• The FAT32 drive partitioned and formatted in Hands-On Project 4-3

- A method of connecting the FAT32 drive and the drive created in Hands-On Project 4-1 to your workstation, such as USB, FireWire, external SATA, or internal connections, such as PATA or SATA

- A review of the "Acquiring Data with dd in Linux" and "Validating dd Acquired Data" sections

Follow these steps:

1. Make sure you've connected the drive you prepared in Hands-On Project 4-3 to your Linux workstation.

2. Start your workstation, if necessary, and log on to Linux or boot the Linux Live CD.

3. Perform the dd acquisition, following the steps in "Acquiring Data with dd in Linux." For the split -b command, make the segmented size **30m**, and use the **-d** switch to create numeric extensions for each segmented file.

4. When the acquisition is done, perform a validation of the suspect drive and the acquired image files. Follow the steps in the "Validating dd Acquired Data" section. When you're finished, close the shell window, and log off Linux.

Case Projects

CASE PROJECTS

Case Project 4-1

Your supervisor has asked you to research current acquisition tools. Using your preferred Internet search engine and the vendors listed in this chapter, prepare a report containing the following information for each tool and stating which tool you would prefer to use:

- Computer forensics vendor name

- Acquisition tool name and latest version number

- Features of the vendor's product

With this data collected, prepare a spreadsheet listing vendors in the rows. For the column headings, list the following features:

- Raw format

- Proprietary format

- AFF format

- Other proprietary formats the tool can read

- Compression of image files

- Remote network acquisition capabilities

- Method used to validate (MD5, SHA-1, and so on)

Case Project 4-2

At a murder scene, you have started making an image of a computer's drive. You're in the back bedroom of the house, and a small fire has started in the kitchen. If the fire can't be extinguished, you have only a few minutes to acquire data from a 10 GB hard disk. Write one to two pages outlining your options for preserving the data.

Case Project 4-3

You need to acquire an image of a disk on a computer that can't be removed from the scene, and you discover that it's a Linux computer. What are your options for acquiring the image? Write a brief paper specifying the hardware and software you would use.

Case Project 4-4

A bank has hired your firm to investigate employee fraud. The bank uses four 20 TB servers on a LAN. You are permitted to talk to the network administrator, who is familiar with where the data is stored. What diplomatic strategies should you use? Which acquisition method should you use? Write a two-page report outlining the problems you expect to encounter, explaining how to rectify them, and describing your solution. Be sure to address any customer privacy issues.

Case Project 4-5

You're investigating a case involving a 2 GB drive that you need to copy at the scene. Write one to two pages describing three options you have to copy the drive accurately. Be sure to include your software and media choices.

chapter 5

Processing Crime and Incident Scenes

After reading this chapter and completing the exercises, you will be able to:

- Explain the rules for controlling digital evidence
- Describe how to collect evidence at private-sector incident scenes
- Explain guidelines for processing law enforcement crime scenes
- List the steps in preparing for an evidence search
- Describe how to secure a computer incident or crime scene
- Explain guidelines for seizing digital evidence at the scene
- List procedures for storing digital evidence
- Explain how to obtain a digital hash
- Review a case to identify requirements and plan your investigation

In this chapter, you learn how to process a computer investigation scene. Because this chapter focuses on investigation needs for computing systems, you should supplement your training by studying police science or U.S. Department of Justice (DOJ) procedures to understand field-of-evidence recovery tasks. If you're in another country, be aware of laws relating to privacy, searches, and the rules of evidence for your region and consult your local authorities.

Evidence rules are critical, whether you're on a corporate or a criminal case. As you'll see, a civil case can quickly become a criminal case, and a criminal case can have civil implications larger than the criminal case. This chapter examines rules of evidence in the United States, but similar procedures apply in most courts worldwide. This chapter also describes differences between a business (private entity) and a law enforcement organization (public entity) in needs and concerns and discusses incident-scene processing for both types of investigations. Private-sector security officers often begin investigating corporate computer crimes and then coordinate with law enforcement as they complete the investigation. Law enforcement investigators should, therefore, know how to process and manage incident scenes. Because public agencies usually don't have the funding to train officers continuously in technology advances, they must learn to work with private-sector investigators, whose employers can often afford to maintain their investigators' computing skills.

This chapter also discusses how the Fourth Amendment relates to corporate and law enforcement computing investigations in the United States. Many countries have similar statutes or charters. As the world becomes more global or "flat" in nature, you need to be aware of how laws are interpreted in other countries. As more countries establish e-laws and more cases go to court, the laws must be applied consistently. Cases of fraud and money laundering are becoming more of a global or an international issue, and crimes against consumers can originate from anywhere in the world. Computers and digital evidence seized in one U.S. jurisdiction might affect a case that's worldwide in scope.

To address these issues, this chapter explains how to apply standard crime scene practices and rules for handling evidence to corporate and law enforcement computing investigations. You must handle digital evidence systematically so that you don't inadvertently alter or lose data. In addition, you should apply the same security controls to evidence for a civil lawsuit as evidence for a major crime. The same rules of evidence govern civil and criminal cases. These rules are similar in English-speaking countries because they have a common ancestor in English common law (judge-made law), dating back to the late Middle Ages.

Identifying Digital Evidence

Digital evidence can be any information stored or transmitted in digital form. Because you can't see or touch digital data directly, it's difficult to explain and describe. Is digital evidence real or virtual? Does data on a disk or other storage medium physically exist, or does it merely represent real information? U.S. courts accept digital evidence as physical evidence, which means that digital data is treated as a tangible object, such as a weapon, paper document, or visible injury, that's related to a criminal or civil incident. Courts in other countries are still updating their laws to take digital evidence into account. Some require that all digital evidence be printed out to be presented in court. Groups such as the **Scientific Working Group on Digital Evidence (SWGDE;** *www.swgde.org*) and the **International Organization on**

Computer Evidence (IOCE; *www.ioce.org*) set standards for recovering, preserving, and examining digital evidence.

For more information on digital evidence, visit *www.ojp.usdoj.gov/nij/pubs-sum/187736.htm* and read "Electronic Crime Scene Investigation: A Guide for First Responders," which provides guidelines for U.S. law enforcement and other responders who protect an electronic crime scene and search for, collect, and preserve electronic evidence.

Following are the general tasks investigators perform when working with digital evidence:

- Identify digital information or artifacts that can be used as evidence.
- Collect, preserve, and document evidence.
- Analyze, identify, and organize evidence.
- Rebuild evidence or repeat a situation to verify that the results can be reproduced reliably.

Collecting computers and processing a criminal or incident scene must be done systematically. To minimize confusion, reduce the risk of losing evidence, and avoid damaging evidence, only one person should collect and catalog digital evidence at a crime scene or lab, if practical. If there's too much evidence or too many systems to make it practical for one person to perform these tasks, all examiners must follow the same established operating procedures, and a lead or managing examiner should control collecting and cataloging evidence. You should also use standardized forms (discussed later in "Documenting Evidence") for tracking evidence to ensure that you consistently handle evidence in a safe, secure manner.

An important challenge investigators face today is establishing recognized standards for digital evidence. For example, cases involving several police raids are being conducted simultaneously in several countries. As a result, you have multiple sites where evidence was seized and hundreds of pieces of digital evidence, including hard drives, cell phones, memory sticks, PDAs, and other storage devices. If law enforcement and civil organizations in those countries have agreed on proper procedures (generally, the highest control standard should be applied to evidence collection in all jurisdictions), the evidence can be presented in any jurisdiction confidently.

Understanding Rules of Evidence

Consistent practices help verify your work and enhance your credibility, so you must handle all evidence consistently. Apply the same security and accountability controls for evidence in a civil lawsuit as in a major crime to comply with your state's rules of evidence or with the Federal Rules of Evidence. Also, keep in mind that evidence admitted in a criminal case might also be used in a civil suit, and vice versa. For example, suppose someone is charged with murder and acquitted at the criminal trial because the jury isn't convinced beyond a reasonable doubt of the person's guilt. If enough evidence shows that the accused's negligence contributed to a wrongful death, however, the victim's relatives can use the evidence in a civil lawsuit to recover damages.

You can review the Federal Rules of Evidence at *www.law.cornell.edu/rules/fre/.*

As part of your professional growth, keep current on the latest rulings and directives on collecting, processing, storing, and admitting digital evidence. The following sections discuss some key concepts of digital evidence. You can find additional information at the U.S. Department of Justice Web site (*www.usdoj.gov*) and by searching the Internet for "digital evidence," "best evidence rule," "hearsay," and other relevant keywords. Consult with your prosecuting attorney, Crown attorney, corporate general counsel, or the attorney who retained you to learn more about managing evidence for your investigation.

In Chapter 2, you learned how to make an image of a disk as part of gathering digital evidence. The data you discover from a forensic examination falls under your state's rules of evidence or the Federal Rules of Evidence. However, digital evidence is unlike other physical evidence because it can be changed more easily. The only way to detect these changes is to compare the original data with a duplicate. Furthermore, distinguishing a duplicate from the original electronically is impossible, so digital evidence requires special legal consideration.

Most courts have interpreted computer records as hearsay evidence. The rule against hearsay evidence is deceptively simple and full of exceptions. Hearsay is any out-of-court statement presented in court to prove the truth of an assertion. In other words, hearsay is evidence of a statement made other than by a witness while testifying at the hearing and is offered to prove the truth of a statement. The definition of hearsay isn't difficult to understand, but it can become confusing when considering all the exceptions to the general rule against hearsay.

Twenty-four exceptions in the federal rules don't require proof that the person who made the statement is unavailable. The following are the ones most applicable to computer forensics practice:

- Business records, including those of a public agency.
- Certain public records and reports.
- Evidence of the absence of a business record or entry.
- Learned treatises used to question an expert witness.
- Statements of the absence of a public record or entry.
- The catchall rule, which doesn't require that the declarant be unavailable to testify. It does say that evidence of a hearsay statement not included in one of the other exceptions can be admitted if it meets the following conditions:
  - It has sound guarantees of trustworthiness.
  - It is offered to help prove a material fact.
  - It is more probative than other equivalent and reasonably obtainable evidence.
  - Its admission would forward the cause of justice.
  - The other parties have been notified that it will be offered into evidence.

The business-record exception, for example, allows "records of regularly conducted activity," such as business memos, reports, records, or data compilations. Business records are authenticated by verifying that they were created "at or near the time by, or from information transmitted by, a person with knowledge ..." and are admissible "if the record was kept in the course of a regularly conducted business activity, and it was the regular practice of that business activity to make the record" (Federal Rules of Evidence, 803(6); see Section V,

"Evidence," in *Searching and Seizing Computers and Obtaining Electronic Evidence in Criminal Investigations, www.usdoj.gov/criminal/cybercrime/s&smanual2002.htm*).

Generally, computer records are considered admissible if they qualify as a business record. Computer records are usually divided into **computer-generated records** and **computer-stored records**. Computer-generated records are data the system maintains, such as system log files and proxy server logs. They are output generated from a computer process or algorithm, not usually data a person creates. Computer-stored records, however, are electronic data that a person creates and saves on a computer, such as a spreadsheet or word processing document. Some records combine computer-generated and computer-stored evidence, such as a spreadsheet containing mathematical operations (computer-generated records) generated from a person's input (computer-stored records).

Computer records must also be shown to be authentic and trustworthy to be admitted into evidence. Computer-generated records are considered authentic if the program that created the output is functioning correctly. These records are usually considered exceptions to the hearsay rule. For computer-stored records to be admitted into court, they must also satisfy an exception to the hearsay rule, usually the business-record exception, so they must be authentic records of regularly conducted business activity. To show that computer-stored records are authentic, the person offering the records (the "offeror"—the plaintiff, or defense) must demonstrate that a person created the data and the data is reliable and trustworthy—in other words, that it wasn't altered when it was acquired or afterward.

Collecting evidence according to the proper steps of evidence control helps ensure that the computer evidence is authentic, as does using established computer forensics software tools. Courts have consistently ruled that computer forensics investigators don't have to be subject matter experts on the tools they use. In *United States v. Salgado* (250 F.3d 438, 453, 6th Cir., 2001), the court stated, "It is not necessary that the computer programmer testify in order to authenticate computer-generated records." In other words, the witness must have firsthand knowledge only of facts relevant to the case. If you have to testify about your role in acquiring, preserving, and analyzing evidence, you don't have to know the inner workings of the tools you use, but you should understand their purpose and operation. For example, Message Digest 5 (MD5) and Secure Hash Algorithm (SHA-1) tools use complex algorithms. During a cross-examination, an opposing attorney might ask you to describe how these forensics tools work. You can safely testify that you don't know how the MD5 hashing algorithm works, but you should know how to describe the steps for using the MD5 function in AccessData Forensic Toolkit, for instance.

When attorneys challenge digital evidence, often they raise the issue of whether computer-generated records were altered or damaged after they were created. Attorneys might also question the authenticity of computer-generated records by challenging the program that created them. To date, courts have been skeptical of unsupported claims about digital evidence. Asserting that the data changed without specific evidence is not sufficient grounds to discredit the digital evidence's authenticity. Most federal courts that evaluate digital evidence from computer-generated records assume that the records contain hearsay. Federal courts then apply the business-records exception to hearsay as it applies to digital evidence.

As mentioned, one test to prove that computer-stored records are authentic is to demonstrate that a specific person created the records. Establishing who created digital evidence can be difficult, however, because records recovered from slack space or unallocated disk space usually don't identify the author. The same is true for other records, such as anonymous e-mail messages or text messages from instant-messaging programs. To establish authorship of digital evidence in these cases, attorneys can use circumstantial evidence, which requires finding other clues associated with the suspect's computer or location. The circumstantial evidence might be that the computer has a password consistent with the password the suspect used on other systems, a witness saw the suspect at the computer at the time the offense occurred, or additional trace evidence associates the suspect with the computer at the time of the incident. In a recent case, the attorney chose not to use the digital evidence because although it could be proved that a particular camera was used to create the suspect's movies, CDs, and DVDs, there was no way to prove that the suspect was the person using the camera. Therefore, there was no circumstantial or corroborating evidence to prove that the suspect was guilty.

Although some files might not contain the author's name, in the arrest of the BTK strangler, the author of a Microsoft Word document was identified by using file metadata. In February 2005, the man claiming to be the BTK strangler sent a floppy disk to FOX News in Wichita. The police he had been taunting told him that they wouldn't be able to trace him via the floppy disk. Forensics analysis of the disk came back with the name of the church and a user named Dennis, who turned out to be Dennis Radar, president of the congregation. The police had enough physical evidence to link him to the crimes. They arrested him, and he confessed to the murders of 10 people over the course of 30 years. He was sentenced to nine life terms. (For the full story, visit the TruTV Web site at *www.crimelibrary.com/serial_killers/unsolved/btk/index_1.html*.)

The following activity shows an easy way to identify this file metadata. Follow these steps in the demo version of AccessData Forensic Toolkit:

These steps are designed for FTK Demo, which has been provided on this book's DVD. If you haven't installed it, do so now. In addition, create a *Work*\Chap05\Chapter work folder on your system. Then extract all compressed files from the Chap05 folder on the book's DVD to your work folder. The work folder path shown in screenshots might differ slightly from yours.

1. Start Microsoft Word, and in a new document, type **By creating a file, you can identify the author with file metadata**. Save it in your work folder as **InChp05-01. doc**, and then exit Microsoft Word.

2. To start FTK, click **Start**, point to **All Programs**, point to **AccessData**, point to **Forensic Toolkit**, and click **Forensic Toolkit**. If you're prompted with a warning dialog box and/or notification, click **OK** to continue, and click **OK**, if necessary, in the message box thanking you for evaluating the program.

3. Click **Go directly to working in program**, and then click **OK**. Click **File, Add Evidence** from the menu.

4. In the Add Evidence dialog box, enter your name as the investigator, and then click **Next**. In the Evidence Processing Options dialog box, accept the default setting, and then click **Next**.

5. In the main Add Evidence to Case dialog box, click the **Add Evidence** button. In the next Add Evidence to Case dialog box, click the **Individual File** option button, and then click **Continue**.

6. In the Browse for Folder dialog box, navigate to your work folder, click **InChp05-01.doc**, click **Open**, and then click **OK**. Click **Next**, and then click **Finish**.

7. In the main window, click the **Overview** tab, if necessary. Under the File Category heading, click the **Documents** button. Click to select the **InChp05-01.doc** file in the bottom pane; its contents are then displayed in the upper-right pane. Figure 5-1 shows an example (although the filename in this figure is different).

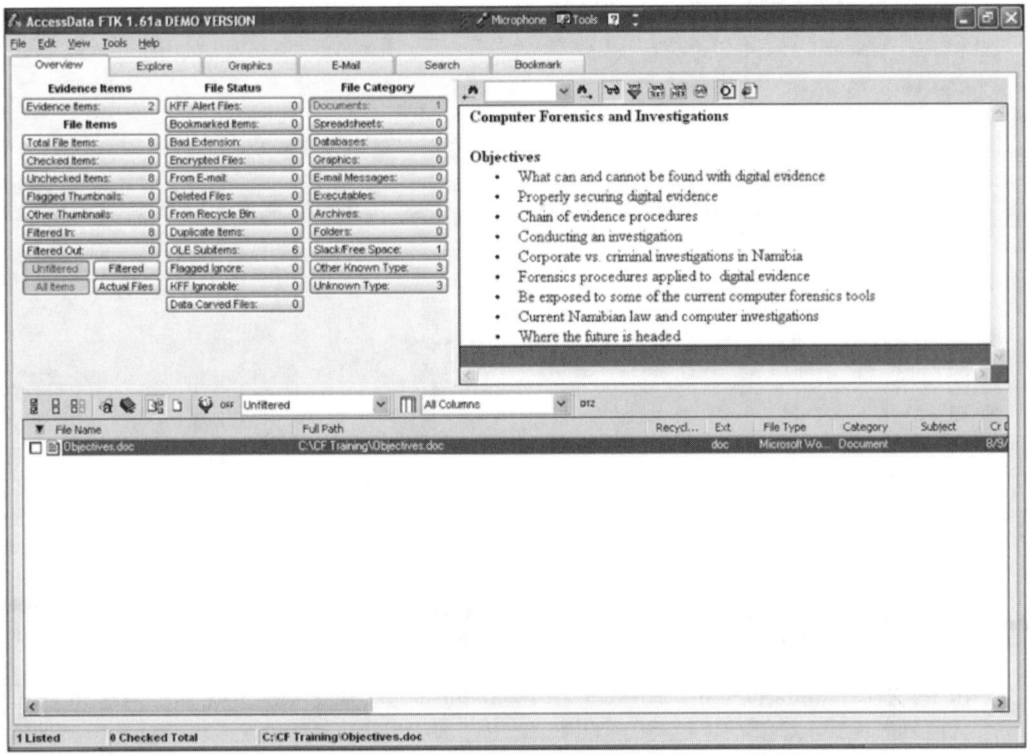

Figure 5-1 Selecting a document

8. On the File List toolbar at the upper right, click the **View files in native format** button, if the button isn't already selected. (*Hint*: Hover your mouse over buttons to see their names displayed.)

9. Next, click the **View files in filtered text format** button. If you entered your username and organization when you installed Word, that information is displayed (see Figure 5-2).

10. Exit FTK, clicking **No** if prompted to back up your work.

In addition to revealing the author, computer-stored records must be proved authentic, which is the most difficult requirement to prove when you're trying to qualify evidence as an exception to the hearsay rule. The process of establishing digital evidence's trustworthiness originated with written documents and the best evidence rule, which states that to prove the content of a written document, recording, or photograph, ordinarily the original writing, recording, or photograph is required (see Federal Rules of Evidence, 1002). In other words, the original of a document is preferred to a duplicate. The best evidence, therefore, is the document created and saved on a computer's hard disk.

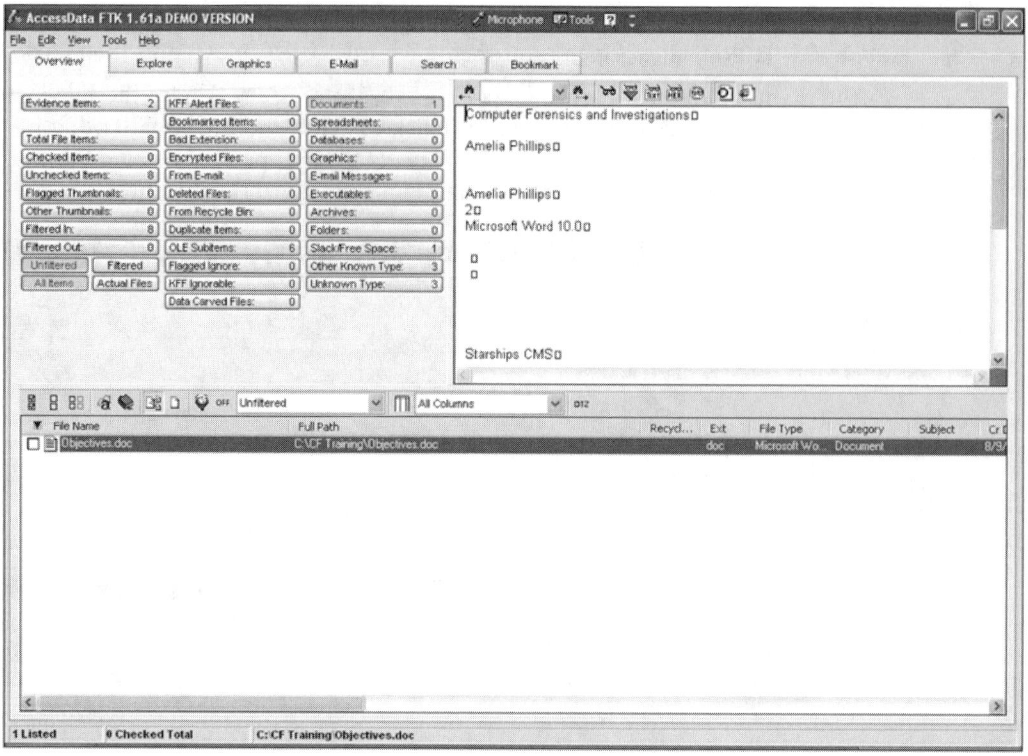

Figure 5-2 Viewing file metadata

Agents and prosecutors occasionally express concern that a printout of a computer-stored electronic file might not qualify as an original document, according to the best evidence rule. In its most fundamental form, the original file is a collection of 0s and 1s; in contrast, the printout is the result of manipulating the file through a complicated series of electronic and mechanical processes (Federal Rules of Evidence, 803(6); see *Searching and Seizing from Computers and Obtaining Electronic Evidence in Criminal Investigations*, p. 152). To address this concern about original evidence, the Federal Rules of Evidence state: "[I]f data are stored in a computer or similar device, any printout or other output readable by sight, shown to reflect the data accurately, is an 'original.'" Instead of producing hard disks in court, attorneys can submit printed copies of files as evidence. In contrast, some countries allow *only* the printed version to be presented in court, not hard disks.

In addition, the Federal Rules of Evidence, 1001(4), allow duplicates instead of originals when the duplicate is "produced by the same impression as the original ... by mechanical or electronic re-recording ... or by other equivalent techniques which accurately reproduce the original." Therefore, as long as bit-stream copies of data are created and maintained properly, the copies can be admitted in court, although they aren't considered best evidence. The copied evidence can be a reliable working copy, but it's not considered the original. Courts understand that the original evidence might not be available, however. For example, you could make one image of the evidence drive successfully but lose access to the original drive because it has a head crash when you attempt to make a backup image. Your first successful copy then becomes secondary evidence. The attorney must be able to explain to the judge that circumstances beyond the examiner's control resulted in loss of the original evi[...] this case, the hard drive is no longer available to be examined or imaged. Mishaps w[...] dence happen routinely in all aspects of evidence recovery.

Another example of not being able to use original evidence is investigations involving net work servers. Removing a server from the network to acquire evidence data could cause harm to a business or its owner, who might be an innocent bystander to a crime or civil wrong. For example, Steve Jackson Games was the innocent party in a case in which evidence of criminal activity had been stored in e-mail on company computers. The network administrator had reported evidence of a crime committed by users of the company's bulletin board system (BBS) to the Secret Service. Secret Service agents seized all the computers at Steve Jackson Games and effectively put the company out of business. SJG sued the Secret Service, which was found liable for damages under the Privacy Protection Act and Title II of the Electronic Communications Privacy Act. For more information, see *Steve Jackson Games v. United States Secret Service and United States of America* (36 F.3d 457, USCA 5, 1994). In this situation, you might not have the authority to create an image or remove the original drive. Instead, make your best effort to acquire the digital evidence with a less intrusive or disruptive method. In this context, the recovered materials become the best evidence because of the circumstances.

In summary, computer-generated records, such as system logs or the results of a mathematical formula in a spreadsheet, aren't hearsay. Computer-stored records that a person generates are subject to rules governing hearsay, however. For the evidence to qualify as a business-record exception to the hearsay rule, a person must have created the computer-stored records, and the records must be original. The Federal Rules of Evidence treat images and printouts of digital files as original evidence.

Collecting Evidence in Private-Sector Incident Scenes

Private-sector organizations include businesses and government agencies that aren't involved in law enforcement. In the United States, these agencies must comply with state public disclosure and federal Freedom of Information Act (FOIA) laws and make certain documents available as public records. State public disclosure laws define state public records as open and available for inspection. For example, divorces recorded in a public office, such as a courthouse, become matters of public record unless a judge orders the documents sealed. Anyone can request a copy of a public divorce decree. Figure 5-3 shows an excerpt of a public disclosure law for the state of Idaho.

State public disclosure laws apply to state records, but the FOIA allows citizens to request copies of public documents created by federal agencies. The FOIA was originally enacted in the 1960s, and several subsequent amendments have broadened its laws. Some Web sites now provide copies of publicly accessible records for a fee.

A special category of private-sector businesses includes ISPs and other communication companies. ISPs can investigate computer abuse committed by their employees, but not by customers. ISPs must preserve customer privacy, especially when dealing with e-mail. However, federal regulations related to the Homeland Security Act and the Patriot Act of 2001 have redefined how ISPs and large corporate Internet users operate and maintain their records.

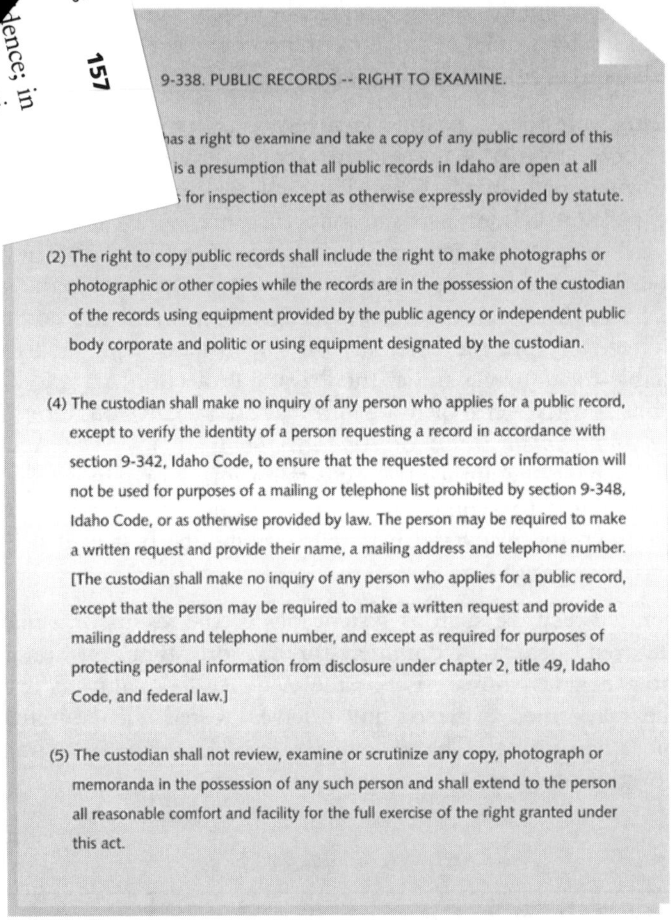

9-338. PUBLIC RECORDS -- RIGHT TO EXAMINE.

has a right to examine and take a copy of any public record of this
is a presumption that all public records in Idaho are open at all
for inspection except as otherwise expressly provided by statute.

(2) The right to copy public records shall include the right to make photographs or
photographic or other copies while the records are in the possession of the custodian
of the records using equipment provided by the public agency or independent public
body corporate and politic or using equipment designated by the custodian.

(4) The custodian shall make no inquiry of any person who applies for a public record,
except to verify the identity of a person requesting a record in accordance with
section 9-342, Idaho Code, to ensure that the requested record or information will
not be used for purposes of a mailing or telephone list prohibited by section 9-348,
Idaho Code, or as otherwise provided by law. The person may be required to make
a written request and provide their name, a mailing address and telephone number.
[The custodian shall make no inquiry of any person who applies for a public record,
except that the person may be required to make a written request and provide a
mailing address and telephone number, and except as required for purposes of
protecting personal information from disclosure under chapter 2, title 49, Idaho
Code, and federal law.]

(5) The custodian shall not review, examine or scrutinize any copy, photograph or
memoranda in the possession of any such person and shall extend to the person
all reasonable comfort and facility for the full exercise of the right granted under
this act.

Figure 5-3 Idaho public disclosure law

ISPs and other communication companies now can investigate customers' activities that are
deemed to create an emergency situation. An emergency situation under the Patriot Act is the
immediate risk of death or personal injury, such as finding a bomb threat in an e-mail message. Some provisions of those laws have been revised over the past few years, so you should
stay abreast of their implications.

Investigating and controlling computer incident scenes in the corporate environment is much
easier than in the criminal environment. In the private sector, the incident scene is often a
workplace, such as a contained office or manufacturing area, where a policy violation is
being investigated. Everything from the computers used to violate a company policy to the
surrounding facility is under a controlled authority—that is, company management. Typically,
businesses have inventory databases of computer hardware and software. Having access to
this database and knowing what applications are on suspected computers help identify the
computer forensics tools needed to analyze a policy violation and the best way to conduct
the analysis. For example, most companies use a single Web browser, such as Microsoft Internet Explorer, Mozilla Firefox, or KDE Konqueror. Knowing which browser a suspect used

helps you develop standard examination procedures to identify data downloaded to the suspect's workstation.

To investigate employees suspected of improper use of company computing assets, a corporate policy statement about misuse of computing assets allows corporate investigators to conduct covert surveillance with little or no cause and access company computer systems without a warrant, which is an advantage for corporate investigators. Law enforcement investigators cannot do the same, however, without sufficient reason for a warrant.

However, if a company doesn't display a warning banner or publish a policy stating that it reserves the right to inspect computing assets at will, employees have an expectation of privacy (as explained in Chapter 1). When an employee is being investigated, this expected privacy prevents the employer from legally conducting an intrusive investigation. A well-defined corporate policy, therefore, should state that an employer has the right to examine, inspect, or access any company-owned computing assets. If a company issues a policy statement to all employees, the employer can investigate computing assets at will without any privacy right restrictions; this practice applies in most countries. As a standard practice, companies should use both warning banners and policy statements. For example, if an incident is escalated to a criminal complaint, prosecutors prefer showing juries warning banners rather than a policy manual. A warning banner leaves a much stronger impression on a jury.

5

In addition to making sure a company has a policy statement or a warning banner, corporate investigators should know under what circumstances they can examine an employee's computer. With a policy statement, an employer can freely initiate any inquiry necessary to protect the company or organization. However, every organization must also have a well-defined process describing when an investigation can be initiated. At a minimum, most corporate policies require that employers have a "reasonable suspicion" that a law or policy is being violated. For example, if a policy states that employees may not use company computers for outside business and a supervisor notices a change in work behavior that could indicate an employee is violating this rule, generally it's enough to warrant an investigation. Note that some countries require notifying employees that they're being investigated if they are suspected of criminal behavior at work.

If a corporate investigator finds that an employee is committing or has committed a crime, the employer can file a criminal complaint with the police. Some businesses, such as banks, have a regulatory requirement to report crimes. In the United States, the employer must turn over all evidence to the police for prosecution. If this evidence had been collected by a law enforcement officer, it would require a warrant, which would be difficult to obtain without sufficient probable cause. In "Processing Law Enforcement Crime Scenes," you learn more about probable cause and how it applies to a criminal investigation.

Employers are usually interested in enforcing company policy, not seeking out and prosecuting employees, so typically they approve computer investigations only to identify employees who are misusing company assets. Corporate investigators are, therefore, primarily concerned with protecting company assets. Finding evidence of a criminal act during an investigation escalates the investigation from an internal civil matter to an external criminal complaint.

If you discover evidence of a crime during a company policy investigation, first determine whether the incident meets the elements of criminal law. You might have to consult with your corporate attorney to determine whether the situation is a potential crime. Next, inform management of the incident; they might have other concerns, such as protecting confidential business data that might be included with the criminal evidence (referred to as "commingled data"). In this case, coordinate with management and the corporate attorney to determine the best way to protect commingled data. After you submit evidence containing sensitive information to the police, it becomes public record. Public record laws do include exceptions for protecting sensitive corporate information; ultimately, however, a judge decides what to protect.

After you discover illegal activity and document and report the crime, stop your investigation to make sure you don't violate Fourth Amendment restrictions on obtaining evidence. If the information you supply is specific enough to meet the criteria for a search warrant, the police are responsible for obtaining a warrant that requests any new evidence. If you follow police instructions to gather additional evidence without a search warrant after you have reported the crime, you run the risk of becoming an agent of law enforcement. Instead, consult with your corporate attorney on how to respond to a police request for information. The police and prosecutor should issue a subpoena for any additional new evidence, which minimizes your exposure to potential civil liability. In addition, you should keep all documentation of evidence collected to investigate an internal company policy violation. Later in this section, you learn more about using affidavits in an internal investigation.

One example of a company policy violation involves employees observing another employee accessing pornographic Web sites. If your organization's policy requires you to determine whether any evidence supports this accusation, you could start by extracting log file data from the proxy server (used to connect a company LAN to the Internet) and conducting a forensic examination of the subject's computer. Suppose that during your examination, you find adult and child pornography. Further examination of the subject's hard disk reveals that the employee has been collecting child pornography in separate folders on his workstation's hard drive. In the United States, possessing child pornography is a crime under federal and state criminal statutes. These situations aren't uncommon and make life difficult for investigators who don't want to be guilty of possession of contraband, such as child pornography, on their forensic workstations.

You survey the remaining content of the subject's drive and find that he's a lead engineer for the team developing your company's latest high-tech bicycle. He placed the child pornography images in a subfolder where the bicycle plans are stored. By doing so, he has commingled contraband with the company's confidential design plans for the bicycle. Your discovery poses two problems in dealing with this contraband evidence. First, you must report the crime to the police; many states require reporting evidence of sexual exploitation of children. Second, you must also protect sensitive company information. Letting the high-tech bicycle plans become part of the criminal evidence might make it public record, and the design work will then be available to competitors. Your first step is to ask your corporate attorney how to deal with the commingled contraband data and sensitive design plans.

Your next step is to work with the corporate attorney to write an affidavit confirming your findings. The attorney should indicate in the affidavit that the evidence is commingled with company secrets and releasing the information will be detrimental to the company's financial health. When the affidavit is completed, you sign it before a notary, and then deliver the affidavit and the recovered evidence with log files to the police, where you make a criminal complaint. At the same time, the corporate attorney goes to court and requests that all evidence recovered from the hard disk that's not related to the complaint and is a company trade secret be protected from public viewing. You and the corporate attorney have reported the crime and taken steps to protect the sensitive data.

Now suppose the detective assigned to the case calls you. In the evidence you've turned over to the police, the detective notices that the suspect is collecting most of his contraband from e-mail attachments. The prosecutor instructed the detective to ask you to collect more evidence to determine whether the suspect is transmitting contraband pictures to other potential suspects. In this case, you should immediately inform the detective that collecting more evidence might make you an agent of law enforcement and violate the employee's Fourth Amendment rights. Before collecting any additional information, consult with your corporate attorney or wait until you receive a subpoena or other court order.

5

Processing Law Enforcement Crime Scenes

To process a crime scene properly, you must be familiar with criminal rules of search and seizure. You should also understand how a search warrant works and what to do when you process one. For all criminal investigations in the United States, the Fourth Amendment limits how governments search and seize evidence. A law enforcement officer can search for and seize criminal evidence only with **probable cause**. Probable cause refers to the standard specifying whether a police officer has the right to make an arrest, conduct a personal or property search, or obtain a warrant for arrest. With probable cause, a police officer can obtain a search warrant from a judge that authorizes a search and the seizure of specific evidence related to the criminal complaint.

The Fourth Amendment states that only warrants "particularly describing the place to be searched, and the persons or things to be seized" can be issued. Note that this excerpt uses the word "particularly." The courts have determined that this phrase means a warrant can authorize a search only of a specific place for a specific thing. Without *specific* evidence and the description of a particular location, a warrant might be weak and create problems later during prosecution. For example, stating that the evidence is in a house located on Elm Avenue between Broadway and Main Street is too general, unless only one house fits that description, because several houses might be located in that area. Instead, provide specific information, such as "123 Elm Avenue." Most courts have allowed more generality for computer evidence. For example, you can state that you want to seize a "computer" rather than specify a "Dell Optiplex GXA." Figure 5-4 shows sample search warrant language for computer evidence that the state of Maryland makes available for computer crime investigators (available at *http://ccu.mdsp.org*; do a search for guidelines on seizing digital evidence).

Although several court cases have allowed latitude when searching and seizing computer evidence, making your warrant as specific as possible to avoid challenges from defense attorneys is a good practice. Often a warrant is written and issued in haste because of the nature of the investigation. Law enforcement officers might not have the time to research the correct language for stating the nature of the complaint to meet probable cause requirements. However, because a judge can exclude evidence obtained from a poorly worded warrant, you should review these issues with your local prosecutor before investigating a case.

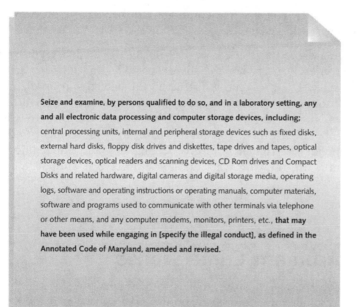

Seize and examine, by persons qualified to do so, and in a laboratory setting, any
and all electronic data processing and computer storage devices, including:
central processing units, internal and peripheral storage devices such as fixed disks,
external hard disks, floppy disk drives and diskettes, tape drives and tapes, optical
storage devices, optical readers and scanning devices, CD Rom drives and Compact
Disks and related hardware, digital cameras and digital storage media, operating
logs, software and operating instructions or operating manuals, computer materials,
software and programs used to communicate with other terminals via telephone
or other means, and any computer modems, monitors, printers, etc., **that may
have been used while engaging in [specify the illegal conduct], as defined in the
Annotated Code of Maryland, amended and revised.**

Figure 5-4 Sample search warrant wording for computer evidence

Understanding Concepts and Terms Used in Warrants

You should be familiar with warrant terminology that governs the type of evidence that can
be seized. Many computing investigations involve large amounts of data you must sort
through to find evidence; the Enron case, for example, involved terabytes of information.
Unrelated information (referred to as **innocent information**) is often included with the evidence you're trying to recover. This unrelated information might be personal and private
records of innocent people or confidential business information. When you find commingled
evidence, judges often issue a **limiting phrase** to the warrant, which allows the police to separate innocent information from evidence. The warrant must list which items can be seized.

When approaching or investigating a crime scene, you might find evidence related to the
crime but not in the location the warrant specifies. You might also find evidence of another
unrelated crime. In these situations, this evidence is subject to the **plain view doctrine**. The
plain view doctrine states that objects falling in the direct sight of an officer who has the
right to be in a location are subject to seizure without a warrant and can be introduced into
evidence. For the plain view doctrine to apply, three criteria must be met:

- The officer is where he or she has a legal right to be.
- Ordinary senses must not be enhanced by advanced technology.
- Any discovery must be by chance.

For the officer to seize the item, he or she must have probable cause to believe the item is evidence of a crime or is contraband. In addition, the police aren't permitted to move objects to
get a better view. In *Arizona v. Hicks* (480 U.S. 321, 1987), the officer was found to have
acted unlawfully because he moved stereo equipment, without probable cause, to record the

serial numbers. The plain view doctrine has also been expanded to include the subdoctrines of plain feel, plain smell, and plain hearing.

In *Horton v. California* (496 U.S. 128, 1990), the court eliminated the requirement that the discovery of evidence in plain view be inadvertent. Previously, "inadvertent discovery" was required, which led to difficulties in defining this term. The three-prong Horton test requires the following:

- The officer must be lawfully present at the place where the evidence can be plainly viewed.
- The officer must have a lawful right of access to the object.
- The incriminating character of the object must be "immediately apparent."

The plain view doctrine does not extend to supporting a general exploratory search from one object to another unless something incriminating is found (*Coolidge v. New Hampshire*, 403 U.S. 443, 466, 1971).

The plain view doctrine's applicability in the digital forensics world is subject to development. Only the United States Court of Appeals for the Ninth Circuit has directly addressed this doctrine and has used it to give wide latitude to law enforcement (*United States v. Wong*, 334 F.3d 831, 9th Cir., 2003). Other circuit courts have been less willing to address applying the doctrine to computer searches. For example, police investigating a case have a search warrant authorizing the search of a computer for evidence related to illegal drug trafficking; during the search, the examiner observes an .avi file, opens it, and sees that it's child pornography. At that point, he must get an additional warrant or an expansion of the existing warrant to continue the search for child pornography. This approach is consistent with rulings in *United States v. Carey* (172 F.3d 1268, 10th Cir., 1999) and *United States v. Walser* (275 F.3d 981, 10th Cir. 2001).

Preparing for a Search

Preparing for a computer search and seizure is probably the most important step in computing investigations. The better you prepare, the smoother your investigation will be. The following sections discuss the tasks you should complete before you search for evidence. To perform these tasks, you might need to get answers from the victim (the complainant) and an informant, who could be a police detective assigned to the case, a law enforcement witness, or a manager or co-worker of the **person of interest** to the investigation.

Identifying the Nature of the Case

Recall from Chapter 2 that when you're assigned a computing investigation case, you start by identifying the nature of the case, including whether it involves the private or public sector. For example, a corporate investigation might involve an employee abusing Internet privileges by surfing the Web excessively or an employee who has filed an equal employment opportunity (EEO) or ethics complaint. Serious cases might involve an employee abusing company computing assets to acquire or deliver contraband. Law enforcement cases could range from a check fraud ring to a homicide. The nature of the case dictates how you proceed and what types of assets or resources you need to use in the investigation (discussed in more detail in "Determining the Tools You Need" later in this chapter).

Identifying the Type of Computing System

Next, determine the type of computing systems involved in the investigation. For law enforcement, this step might be difficult because the crime scene isn't controlled. You might not know what kinds of computers were used to commit a crime or how or where they were used. In this case, you must draw on your skills, creativity, and sources of knowledge, such as the Uniform Crime Report discussed in Chapter 3, to deal with the unknown.

If you can identify the computing system, estimate the size of the drive on the suspect's computer and how many computers you have to process at the scene. Also, determine which OSs and hardware might be involved and whether the evidence is located on a Microsoft, Linux, UNIX, Macintosh, or mainframe computer. For corporate investigators, configuration management databases (discussed in Chapter 3) make this step easier. Consultants to the private sector or law enforcement officers might have to investigate more thoroughly to determine these details.

Determining Whether You Can Seize a Computer

Generally, the ideal situation for incident or crime scenes is seizing the computers and taking them to your lab for further processing. However, the type of case and location of the evidence determine whether you can remove computers from the scene. Law enforcement investigators need a warrant to remove computers from a crime scene and transport them to a lab. If removing the computers will irreparably harm a business, the computers should not be taken offsite, unless you have disclosed the effect of the seizure to the judge. An additional complication is files stored offsite that are accessed remotely. You must decide whether the drives containing those files need to be examined. Another consideration is the availability of online data storage services that rent space, which essentially can't be located physically. The data is stored on drives where data from many other subscribers might be stored.

If you aren't allowed to take the computers to your lab, determine the resources you need to acquire digital evidence and which tools can speed data acquisition. With large drives, such as a 200 GB drive, acquisition times can increase to several hours. In Chapter 4, you examined data acquisition software and learned which tools meet specific needs for acquiring disk images. Some software, such as EnCase, compresses data while making forensic images. For large drives, this compression might be necessary.

Obtaining a Detailed Description of the Location

The more information you have about the location of a computer crime, the more efficiently you can gather evidence from a crime scene. Environmental and safety issues are the primary concerns during this process. Before arriving at an incident or crime scene, identify potential hazards to your safety as well as that of other examiners.

Some computer cases involve dangerous settings, such as a drug bust of a methamphetamine lab or a terrorist attack using biological, chemical, or nuclear contaminants. For these types of investigations, you must rely on the skills of **hazardous materials (HAZMAT)** teams to recover evidence from the scene. The recovery process might include decontaminating computing components needed for the investigation, if possible. If the decontamination procedure might destroy electronic evidence, a HAZMAT specialist or an investigator in HAZMAT gear should make an image of a suspect's drive. If you have to rely on a HAZMAT specialist to acquire data, coach the specialist on how to connect cables between the computer and drives and how to run the software. You must be exact and articulate in your instructions.

Ambiguous or incorrect instructions could destroy evidence. Ideally, a computer forensics investigator trained in dealing with HAZMAT environments should acquire drive images. However, not all organizations have funds available for this training.

Whether you or a HAZMAT technician is the one acquiring an image, you should keep some guidelines in mind. Before acquiring the data, a HAZMAT technician might suggest that you put the target drive in a special HAZMAT bag, leaving the IDE and power cables out of the bag but providing an airtight seal around the cables to prevent any contaminants from entering the bag and affecting the target drive. When the data acquisition is completed, power down the computer and then cut the IDE and power cables from the target drive. The HAZMAT technician can then decontaminate the bag. When dealing with extreme conditions, such as biological or chemical hazardous contaminants, you might have to sacrifice equipment, such as IDE and power cables, to accomplish a task. In certain instances, such as a meth lab bust, the contaminants might be so toxic that hazards to the safety of others prohibit acquiring any digital evidence.

In addition, if the temperature in the contaminated room is higher than 80 degrees, you should take measures to avoid damage to the drive from overheating. In a dry desert region, consider cooling the target drive by using sealed ice packs or double-wrapped bags of ice so that moisture doesn't leak out and damage the drive. In extreme conditions, consider the risks to evidence and your equipment. You'll need to brainstorm for solutions to overcome these problems. Moving the equipment to a controlled environment is ideal; however, doing so isn't always possible.

Determining Who Is in Charge

Corporate computing investigations usually require only one person to respond to an incident or crime scene. Processing evidence involves acquiring an image of a subject's drive. In law enforcement, however, many investigations require additional staff to collect all evidence quickly. For large-scale investigations, a crime or incident scene leader should be designated. Anyone assigned to a large-scale investigation scene should cooperate with the designated leader to ensure that the team addresses all details when collecting evidence.

Using Additional Technical Expertise

After you collect evidence data, determine whether you need specialized help to process the incident or crime scene. For example, suppose you're assigned to process a crime scene at a data center running Microsoft Windows servers with several RAID drives and high-end UNIX servers. If you're the leader of this investigation, you must identify the additional skills needed to process the crime scene, such as enlisting help with a high-end server OS. Other concerns are how to acquire data from RAID servers and how much data you can acquire. RAID servers typically process several terabytes of data, and standard imaging tools might not be able to handle these large data sets.

When working at high-end computing facilities, identify the applications the suspect uses, such as Oracle databases. You might need to recruit an Oracle specialist or site support staff to help extract data for the investigation. Finding the right person can be an even bigger challenge than conducting the investigation.

If you do need to recruit a specialist who's not an investigator, develop a training program to educate the specialist in proper investigative techniques. This advice also applies to specialists you plan to supervise during search-and-seizure tasks. When dealing with computer evidence, an untrained specialist can easily and unintentionally destroy evidence, no matter how careful you are in providing instructions and monitoring his or her activities.

Determining the Tools You Need

After you have gathered as much information as possible about the incident or crime scene, you can start listing what you need at the scene. Being overprepared is better than being underprepared, especially when you determine that you can't transfer the computer to your lab for processing.

To manage your tools, consider creating an initial-response field kit and an extensive-response field kit. Using the right kit makes processing an incident or crime scene much easier and minimizes how much you have to carry from your vehicle to the scene.

Your **initial-response field kit** should be lightweight and easy to transport. With this kit, you can arrive at a scene, acquire the data you need, and return to the lab as quickly as possible. Figure 5-5 shows some items you might need, and Table 5-1 lists the tools you might need in an initial-response field kit.

Computer forensics kit

Laptop computer

Digital camera

Flashlight

Figure 5-5 Items in an initial-response field kit

Table 5-1 Tools in an initial-response field kit

Number needed	Tools
1	Small computer toolkit
1	Large-capacity drive
1	IDE ribbon cable (ATA-33 or ATA-100)
1	SATA cable
1	Forensic boot media containing your preferred acquisition utility
1	Laptop IDE 40- to 44-pin adapter, other adapter cables
1	Laptop computer
1	FireWire or USB dual write-protect external bay
1	Flashlight
1	Digital or 35mm camera with film and flash
10	Evidence log forms
1	Notebook or dictation recorder
10	Computer evidence bags (antistatic bags)
20	Evidence labels, tape, and tags
1	Permanent ink marker
10	External USB devices or a portable hard drive

An **extensive-response field kit** should include all the tools you can afford to take to the field. When you arrive at the scene, you should extract only those items you need to acquire evidence. Doing so protects your equipment and minimizes how many items you have to keep track of at the scene. Table 5-2 lists the tools you might need in an extensive-response field kit, including external USB drives.

Table 5-2 Tools in an extensive-response field kit

Number needed	Tools
Varies	Assorted technical manuals, ranging from OS references to forensics analysis guides
1	Initial-response field kit
1	Portable PC with SCSI card for DLT tape drive or suspect's SCSI drive
2	Electrical power strips
1	Additional hand tools, including bolt cutters, pry bar, and hacksaw
1	Leather gloves and disposable latex gloves (assorted sizes)
1	Hand truck and luggage cart
10	Large garbage bags and large cardboard boxes with packaging tape
1	Rubber bands of assorted sizes

Table 5-2 Tools in an extensive-response field kit (*continued*)

Number needed	Tools
1	Magnifying glass
1	Ream of printer paper
1	Small brush for cleaning dust from suspect's interior CPU cabinet
10	USB drives of varying sizes
2	External hard drives (200 GB or larger) with power cables
Assorted	Converter cables
5	Additional assorted hard drives for data acquisition

When deciding what items to include in initial-response and extensive-response field kits, you need to analyze your specific needs in your region or organization. Refer to Tables 5-1 and 5-2 for guidelines.

Preparing the Investigation Team

Before you initiate the search and seizure of digital evidence at an incident or crime scene, you must review all the available facts, plans, and objectives with the investigation team you have assembled. The goal of scene processing is to collect and secure digital evidence successfully. The better prepared you are, the fewer problems you encounter when you carry out the plan to collect data.

Keep in mind that digital evidence is volatile. Develop the skills to assess the facts quickly, make your plan, gather the needed resources, and collect data from the incident or crime scene. In some computing investigations, responding slowly might result in the loss of important evidence for the case.

Securing a Computer Incident or Crime Scene

Investigators secure an incident or crime scene to preserve the evidence and to keep information about the incident or crime confidential. Information made public could jeopardize the investigation. If you're in charge of securing a computer incident or crime scene, use yellow barrier tape to prevent bystanders from accidentally entering the scene. Use police officers or security guards to prevent others from entering the scene. Legal authority for a corporate incident scene includes trespassing violations; for a crime scene, it includes obstructing justice or failing to comply with a police officer. Access to the scene should be restricted to only those people who have a specific reason to be there. The reason for the standard practice of securing an incident or crime scene is to expand the area of control beyond the scene's immediate location. In this way, you avoid overlooking an area that might be part of the scene. Shrinking the scene's perimeter is easier than expanding it.

For major crime scenes, computer investigators aren't usually responsible for defining a scene's security perimeter. These cases involve other specialists and detectives who are collecting physical evidence and recording the scene. For incidents primarily involving computers, the computers can be a crime scene within a crime scene, containing evidence to be processed. The evidence is in the computer, but the courts consider it physical evidence. Computers can also contain actual physical evidence, such as DNA evidence or fingerprints on keyboards. Crime labs can use special vacuums to extract DNA residue from a keyboard to compare with other DNA samples. In a major crime scene, law enforcement usually retains the keyboard.

Evidence is commonly lost or corrupted because of **professional curiosity**, which involves police officers and other professionals who aren't part of the crime scene processing team. They just have a compelling interest in seeing what happened. Their presence could contaminate the scene directly or indirectly. Keep in mind that even those authorized and trained to search crime scenes can inadvertently alter the scene or evidence.

For example, during one homicide investigation, the lead detective collected a good latent fingerprint from the crime scene. He compared it with the victim's fingerprints and those of others who knew the victim. He couldn't find a fingerprint matching the latent fingerprint from the scene. The detective suspected he had the murderer's fingerprint and kept it on file for several years until his police department purchased an **Automated Fingerprint Identification Systems (AFIS)** computer. During acceptance testing, the software vendor processed sample fingerprints to see how quickly and accurately the system could match fingerprints in the database. The detective asked the acceptance testing team to run the fingerprint he found at the homicide scene. He believed the suspect's fingerprints were in the AFIS database. The acceptance testing team complied and within minutes, AFIS found a near-perfect match of the latent fingerprint: It belonged to the detective.

Always remember that professional curiosity can destroy or corrupt evidence, including digital evidence. When working at an incident or crime scene, be aware of what you're doing and what you have touched, physically or virtually. A police detective can take elimination prints of everyone who had access to the crime scene to identify the fingerprints of known people; computer evidence doesn't have an equivalent elimination process. You must protect all digital evidence, so make sure no one examines a suspect's computer before you can capture and preserve an image of the hard disk. Starting a computer without forensic boot media alters important data, such as the date and time stamps of last access to certain files.

Seizing Digital Evidence at the Scene

With proper search warrants, law enforcement can seize all computing systems and peripherals. In corporate investigations, you might have similar authority; however, you might have the authority only to make an image of the suspect's drive. Depending on company policies, corporate investigators rarely have the authority to seize all computers and peripherals.

When seizing computer evidence in criminal investigations, follow the U.S. DOJ standards for seizing digital data (described later in this chapter, or see *www.usdoj.gov/criminal/cybercrime/searching.html*). For civil investigations, follow the same rules of evidence as for criminal investigation. You might be looking for specific evidence, such a particular e-mail message or spreadsheet. In a criminal matter, investigators seize entire drives to preserve as much information as possible and ensure that no evidence is overlooked. If you have any questions, doubts, or concerns, consult with your attorney for additional guidance.

Preparing to Acquire Digital Evidence

The evidence you acquire at the scene depends on the nature of the case and the alleged crime or violation. For a criminal case involving a drug dealer's computer, for example, you need to take the entire computer along with any peripherals and media in the area, including cell phones, USB devices, CDs, DVDs, printers, cameras, and scanners. Seizing peripherals and other media ensures that you leave no necessary system components behind; often, predicting what components might be critical to the system's operation is difficult. On the other hand, if you're investigating employee misconduct, you might need only a few specific items.

Before you collect digital evidence, ask your supervisor or senior forensics examiner in the organization the following questions:

- Do you need to take the entire computer and all peripherals and media in the immediate area? How are you going to protect the computer and media while transporting them to your lab?

- Is the computer powered on when you arrive? (This question is discussed in more detail later in "Processing an Incident or Crime Scene.")

- Is the suspect you're investigating in the immediate area of the computer? Is it possible the suspect damaged or destroyed the computer, peripherals, or media? Will you have to separate the suspect from the computer?

For example, suppose a company employee, Edward Braun, is suspected of using a company computer at his desk to write a book. You suspect that Edward is saving personal files on the computer's hard drive. Using imaging software, such as Norton Ghost from Symantec, you can copy the hard drive onto another drive, install the duplicate hard drive in the computer, and take the original drive to your forensics lab for examination. This procedure doesn't create a bit-for-bit copy; you're creating a working copy for continued business operations and taking the original for examination.

Because Edward's supervisors don't want him to know he's being investigated, you must create the working copy when he's not at his desk and isn't expected to return. Because most people notice when something is out of order on their desks, you should photograph the scene, measure the height of his chair, and record the position of items on his desk you need to move before removing the hard drive. (The following section has more tips on photographing and documenting the scene.) After you create an image of his hard drive and substitute the copy, return Edward's belongings to their original locations.

Processing an Incident or Crime Scene

The following guidelines offer suggestions on how to process an incident or crime scene. As you gain experience in performing searches and seizures, you can add to or modify these guidelines to meet the needs of specific cases. Use your judgment to determine what steps to take when processing a civil or criminal investigation. For any difficult issues, seek out legal counsel or other technical experts.

Keep a journal to document your activities. Include the date and time you arrive on the scene, the people you encounter, and notes on every important task you perform. Update the journal as you process the scene.

To secure the scene, use whatever is practical to make sure that only authorized people can access the area. Remove anyone who isn't investigating the scene unless you need his or her help to process the scene. For example, the company's network administrator might need to help you collect and recover data. As mentioned earlier, you should secure a wider scene perimeter than necessary. Make sure nothing in this area, including computer evidence, moves until you have had time to record it. Be professional and courteous to any curious onlookers, but don't offer information about the investigation or incident or answer questions. Refer journalists to a public information officer or the organization's public relations manager.

Take video and still recordings of the area around the computer. Start by recording the overall scene, and then record details with close-up shots, including the back of all computers. Before recording the back of each computer, place numbered or lettered labels on each cable to help identify which cable is connected to which plug, in case you need to reassemble components at the lab. Make sure you take close-ups of all cable connections, including keyloggers (devices used to record keystrokes) and dongle devices used with software as part of the licensing agreement. Record the area around the computer, including the floor and ceiling, and all access points to the computer, such as doors and windows. Be sure to look under any tables or desks for anything taped to the underside of a table or desk drawer or on the floor out of view. If the area has ceiling panels—false ceiling tiles—remove them and record that area, too. Slowly pan or zoom the camera to prevent blurring in the video image, and maintain a camera log for all shots you take.

When you finish videotaping or photographing the scene, sketch the incident or crime scene. This sketch is usually a rough draft with notes on objects' dimensions and distances between fixed objects. For example, a note might read "The suspect's computer is on the south wall, three meters from the southeast corner of the room." When you prepare your report, you can make a clean, detailed drawing from your sketch, preferably using a computer drawing program so that the sketch is in electronic form.

Because computer data is volatile, check the state of each computer at the scene as soon as possible. Determine whether the computer is powered on or off or in hibernation or sleep mode. If it's off, leave it off. If it's on, use your professional judgment on what to do next. Standard computer forensics practice has been to kill the computer's power to make sure data doesn't become corrupt through covert means. Typically, this procedure is still acceptable on legacy Windows and MS-DOS systems because turning off the power usually preserves data. On Windows XP/Vista, UNIX, and Linux computers, generally you should perform an orderly shutdown first. Every shutdown process has inherent risks, however; to avoid data loss, you or your supervisor might have to determine the best shutdown procedure.

In addition, there are many urban legends about criminals placing self-destruct mechanisms—both hardware and software devices—in computers. Many years ago, a common trick was altering the DOS program Command.com by changing the Dir (directory) command to the Deltree (delete the directory tree) command. When an investigator entered the Dir command on a suspect's computer, he would inadvertently start the Deltree command, which deletes all files and folders and their contents. More advanced computer criminals have been known to create similar command-altering methods that overwrite a drive's contents. In addition, computer owners who suspect someone will investigate their computers might set the computer to delete the hard drive's contents if the correct screensaver password isn't entered.

As a general rule, don't cut electrical power to a running system unless it's an older Windows 9x or MS-DOS system. However, it's a judgment call because of recent trends in computer crimes. More computing investigations now revolve around network- and Internet-related cases, which rely heavily on log file data. Certain files, such as the Event log and Security log in Windows XP, might lose essential network activity records if power is terminated without a proper shutdown.

If you're working on a network or Internet investigation and the computer is on, save data in any current applications as safely as possible and record all active windows or shell sessions. Don't examine folders or network connections or press any keys unless it's necessary. For systems that are powered on and running, photograph the screens. If windows are open but minimized, expanding them so that you can photograph them is safe. As a precaution, write down the contents of each window.

As you're copying data on a live suspect computer, make notes in your journal about everything you do so that you can explain your actions in your formal report to prosecutors and other attorneys. When you've finished recording screen contents, save them to external media. For example, if one screen shows a Word file, save it to an external drive. Keep in mind that the suspect might have changed the file since last using the Save command. If another screen is a Web browser, take a screenshot or save the Web page to a USB drive or an external hard drive. If the suspect computer has an active connection to a network server with enough storage, you can save large files to a folder on the server. To do so, you need the cooperation of the network administrator to help direct you to the correct server and folder for storing the file.

If you can't save an open application to external media, save the open application to the suspect drive with a new filename. Changing the filename avoids overwriting an existing file that might not have been updated already. This method isn't ideal and should be done only in extreme emergency conditions. Remember that your goal is to preserve as much evidence in as good a condition as is practical.

After you have saved all active files on the suspect computer, you can close all applications. If an application prompts you to save before closing, don't save the files. When all applications are closed, perform an orderly shutdown. If you're not familiar with the correct shutdown method for the computer you're examining, consult someone who has expertise in this procedure.

After you record the scene and shut down the system, bag and tag the evidence, following these steps:

1. Assign one person, if possible, to collect and log all evidence. Minimize the number of people handling evidence to ensure its integrity.

2. Tag all the evidence you collect with the current date and time, serial numbers or unique features, make and model, and name of the person who collected it.

3. Maintain two separate logs of collected evidence to be reconciled for audit control purposes and to verify everything you have collected.

4. Maintain constant control of the collected evidence and the crime or incident scene.

If the nature of the case doesn't permit you to seize the computer, create an image of the hard drive, as you learned in Chapter 4.

In Chapter 11, you learn how to use forensics tools to acquire RAM. Many studies are being conducted on how to analyze RAM systematically, in an effort to find relevant information in what appears to look like random garbage data.

During the data acquisition or immediately after collecting the evidence, look for information related to the investigation, such as passwords, passphrases, personal identification numbers (PINs), and bank account numbers (particularly offshore bank accounts, often used to hide evidence of financial transactions). This information might be in plain view or out of sight in a drawer or trash can. At the scene, collect as much personal information as possible about the suspect or victim. Collect all information related to facts about the crime or incident, particularly anything that connects the suspect to the victim.

To complete your analysis and processing of a scene, collect all documentation and media related to the investigation, including the following material:

- Hardware, including peripheral devices
- Software, including OSs and applications
- All media, such as backup tapes and disks
- All documentation, manuals, printouts, and handwritten notes

Processing Data Centers with RAID Systems

Computer investigators sometimes perform forensics analysis on RAID systems or server farms, which are rooms filled with extremely large disk systems and are typical of large business data centers, such as the Department of Motor Vehicles (DMV), banks, insurance companies, and ISPs. As you learned in Chapter 4, one technique for extracting evidence from large systems is called sparse acquisition. This technique extracts only data related to evidence for your case from allocated files and minimizes how much data you need to analyze. A drawback of this technique is that it doesn't recover data in free or slack space. If you have a computer forensics tool that accesses unallocated space on a RAID system, work with the tool on a test system first to make sure it doesn't corrupt the RAID system.

Using a Technical Advisor

When working with advanced technologies, recruit a technical advisor who can help you list the tools you need to process the incident or crime scene. At large data centers, the technical advisor is the person guiding you about where to locate data and helping you extract log records or other evidence from large RAID servers. In law enforcement cases, the technical advisor can help create the search warrant by itemizing what you need for the warrant. If you use a technical advisor for this purpose, you should list his or her name in the warrant. At the scene, a technical advisor can help direct other investigators to collect evidence correctly. Technical advisors have the following responsibilities:

- Know all aspects of the system being seized and searched.
- Direct investigators on how to handle sensitive media and systems to prevent damage.
- Help ensure security of the scene.
- Help document the planning strategy for the search and seizure.
- Conduct ad hoc training for investigators on the technologies and components being seized and searched.
- Document activities during the search and seizure.
- Help conduct the search and seizure.

Documenting Evidence in the Lab

After you collect digital evidence at the scene, you transport it to a forensics lab, which should be a controlled environment that ensures the security and integrity of digital evidence. In any investigative work, be sure to record your activities and findings as you work. To do so, you can maintain a journal to record the steps you take as you process evidence. Your goal is to be able to reproduce the same results when you or another investigator repeat the steps you took to collect evidence.

If you get different results when you repeat the steps, the credibility of your evidence becomes questionable. At best, the evidence's value is compromised; at worst, the evidence will be disqualified. Because of the nature of electronic components, failures do occur. For example, you might not be able to repeat a data recovery because of a hardware failure, such as a disk drive head crash. Be sure to report all facts and events as they occur.

Besides verifying your work, a journal serves as a reference that documents the methods you used to process digital evidence. You and others can use it for training and guidance on other investigations.

Processing and Handling Digital Evidence

You must maintain the integrity of digital evidence in the lab as you do when collecting it in the field. Your first task is to preserve the disk data. If you have a suspect computer that hasn't been copied with an imaging tool, you must create a copy. When you do, be sure to make the suspect drive read-only (typically by using a write-blocking device), and document this step. If the disk has been copied with an imaging tool, you must preserve the image files. With most imaging tools, you can create smaller, compressed volume sets to make archiving your data easier.

In Chapter 4, you learned how to use imaging tools, and in Chapter 2, you examined the steps for preserving digital evidence with chain-of-custody controls. You use the following steps to create image files:

1. Copy all image files to a large drive. Most forensics labs have several machines set up with disk-imaging software and multiple hard drives that can be exchanged as needed for your cases. You can use these resources to copy image files to large drives. Some might be equipped with large network storage devices for ongoing cases.

2. Start your forensics tool to analyze the evidence.

3. Run an MD5 or SHA-1 hashing algorithm on the image files to get a digital hash. Later in "Obtaining a Digital Hash," you learn how to compare MD5 or SHA-1 hashes to make sure the evidence hasn't changed.

4. When you finish copying image files to a larger drive, secure the original media in an evidence locker. Don't work with the original media; it should be stored in a locker that has an evidence custody form. Be sure to fill out the form and date it.

Storing Digital Evidence

With digital evidence, you need to consider how and on what type of media to save it and what type of storage device is recommended to secure it. The media you use to store digital evidence usually depends on how long you need to keep it. If you investigate criminal matters, store the evidence as long as you can. The ideal media on which to store digital data are CD-Rs or DVDs. These media have long lives, but copying data to them takes a long time. Older CDs had lives up to five years. Research is currently being done on CD-Rs and CD-RWs with lifespans of only one or two years. Today's larger drives demand more storage capacity; 200 GB drives are common, and DVDs can store up to only 17 GB of data.

You can also use magnetic tape to preserve evidence data. The **4-mm DAT** magnetic tapes store between 40 to 72 GB or more of data, but like CD-Rs, they are slow at reading and writing data. If you're using these tapes, test your data by copying the contents from the tape back to a disk drive. Then verify that the data is good by examining it with your computer forensics tools or doing an MD5 hash comparison of the original data set and the newly restored data set.

If a 30-year lifespan for data storage is acceptable for your digital evidence, older DLT magnetic tape cartridge systems are a good choice. Keep in mind that you never know how long it will take for a case to go to trial. Figure 5-6 shows a 4-mm DAT drive and tape and a DLT tape drive.

4-mm DAT drive and tape   DLT tape drive

Figure 5-6 4-mm DAT and DLT tape drives

DLT systems have been used with mainframe computers for several decades and are reliable data-archiving systems. Depending on the size of the DLT cartridge, one cartridge can store up to 80 GB of data in compressed mode. Speed of data transfer from your hard drive to a DLT tape is also faster than transferring data to a CD-R or DVD. The only major drawback of a DLT drive and tapes is cost. A drive can cost from $400 to $800, and each tape is about $40. However, with the current large disk drives, the DLT system does offer significant labor savings over other systems. Recently, manufacturers such as Quantum Corp. have introduced a high-speed, high-capacity tape cartridge drive system called Super Digital Linear Tape (Super-DLT or SLDT). These systems are specifically designed for large RAID data backups and can store more than 1 TB of data. Smaller external Super-DLT drives can connect to a workstation through a SCSI card.

However, don't rely on one media storage method to preserve your evidence—be sure to make two copies of every image to prevent data loss. Also, if practical, use different tools to create the two images. For example, you can use the Linux dd command to create the first image and ProDiscover to create the second image.

Evidence Retention and Media Storage Needs

To help maintain the chain of custody for digital evidence so that it's accepted in court or by arbitration, restrict access to your lab and evidence storage area. When your lab is open for operations, authorized personnel must keep these areas under constant supervision. When your lab is closed, at least two security workers should guard evidence storage cabinets and lab facilities.

As a good security practice, your lab should have a sign-in roster for all visitors. Most labs use a manual log system that an authorized technician maintains when an evidence storage container is opened and closed. These logs should be maintained for a period based on legal requirements, including the statute of limitations, the maximum sentence, and expiration of appeal periods. Make the logs available for management to inspect. The evidence custody form should contain an entry for every person who handles the evidence (see Figure 5-7).

Item description:				
Item tag number:				
Person	Date logged out	Time logged out	Date logged in	Time logged in

Figure 5-7 A sample log file

If you're supporting a law enforcement agency, you might need to retain evidence indefinitely, depending on the type of crime. Check with your local prosecuting attorney's office or state laws to make sure you're in compliance. For the private sector or corporate environments, check with your company's legal department (the general counsel), which is responsible for setting your organization's standards for evidence retention. Cases involving child pornography are the exception: The evidence must be turned over to law enforcement. This material is contraband and must not be stored by any person or organization other than a law enforcement agency.

Documenting Evidence

To document evidence, create or use an evidence custody form, as shown in Chapter 2. Because of constant changes in technologies and methods for acquiring data, create an electronic evidence custody form that you can modify as needed. An evidence custody form serves the following functions:

- Identifies the evidence
- Identifies who has handled the evidence
- Lists dates and times the evidence was handled

After you have established these pieces of information, you can add others to your form, such as a section listing MD5 and SHA-1 hash values. Include any detailed information you might need to reference.

Evidence bags also include labels or evidence forms you can use to document your evidence. Commercial companies offer a variety of sizes and styles of paper and plastic evidence bags. Be sure to write on the bag when it's empty, not when it contains digital evidence, to make sure your writing is legible and to avoid possibly damaging the evidence. You should use antistatic bags for electronic components.

5

Obtaining a Digital Hash

To verify data integrity, different methods of obtaining a unique identity for file data have been developed. One of the first methods, the **Cyclic Redundancy Check (CRC)** is a mathematical algorithm that determines whether a file's contents have changed. The most recent version is CRC-32. CRC, however, is not considered a forensic hashing algorithm. The first algorithm for computer forensics use was **Message Digest 5 (MD5)**. Like CRC, MD5 is a mathematical formula that translates a file into a hexadecimal code value, or a hash value. If a bit or byte in the file changes, it alters the **hash value**, a unique hexadecimal value that identifies a file or drive. (Before you process or analyze a file, you can use a software tool to calculate its hash value.) After you process the file, you produce another digital hash. If it's the same as the original one, you can verify the integrity of your digital evidence with mathematical proof that the file didn't change.

According to work done by Wang Xiaoyun and her associates from Beijing's Tsinghua University and Shandong University of Technology, there are three rules for forensic hashes:

- You can't predict the hash value of a file or device.
- No two hash values can be the same. (Note: Collisions have occurred in research using supercomputers.)
- If anything changes in the file or device, the hash value must change.

A newer hashing algorithm is **Secure Hash Algorithm version 1 (SHA-1)**, developed by the **National Institute of Standards and Technology (NIST)**. SHA-1 is slowly replacing MD5 and CRC-32, although MD5 is still widely used. (For more information on SHA-1, see *http://csrc.nist.gov/publications/fips/fips180-2/fips180-2.pdf*.) In both MD5 and SHA-1, collisions have occurred, meaning two different files have the same hash value. Collisions are rare, however, and despite flaws in MD5 and SHA-1, both are still useful for validating digital evidence collected from files and storage media. If a collision is suspected, you can do a byte-by-byte comparison to verify that all bytes are identical. Byte-by-byte comparisons can be performed with the MS-DOS Comp command or the Linux/UNIX diff command. New developments in this field are constant, however, so staying current by investigating the NIST Web site and reading related journals is a good idea.

Most computer forensics hashing needs can be satisfied with a **nonkeyed hash set**, which is a unique hash number generated by a software tool, such as the Linux md5sum command. The advantage of this type of hash is that it can identify known files, such as executable programs or viruses, that hide themselves by changing their names. For example, many people who view or transmit pornographic material change filenames and extensions to obscure the nature of the contents. However, even if a file's name and extension change, the hash value doesn't.

The alternative to a nonkeyed hash is a **keyed hash set**, which is created by an encryption utility's secret key. You can use the secret key to create a unique hash value for a file. Although a keyed hash set can't identify files as nonkeyed hash methods can, it can produce a unique hash set for your digital evidence.

You can use the MD5 function in FTK Imager to obtain the digital signature of a file or an entire drive. In the following activity, you use a thumb drive, although you often work with hard drives in actual investigations. First, you create a test file and then generate an MD5 hash value for it. Then you change the file and produce another MD5 hash value, this time noting the change in the hash value. You need a blank, formatted USB drive and a Windows computer to complete the following steps:

1. Power on your forensic workstation, booting it to Windows.

2. Insert a blank, formatted USB drive into your computer.

3. Next, start Notepad. In a new text file, type **This is a test to see how an MD5 digital hash works.**

4. Click **File, Save As** from the menu. In the File name text box, type **InChap05.txt**. Click your thumb drive in the Save in drop-down list, and then click **Save**.

5. Exit Notepad.

Next, you use FTK Imager to determine the MD5 and SHA-1 hash values:

 If you didn't install FTK Imager in Chapter 4, do so before performing these steps.

1. If the FTK Imager icon is not on your desktop, click **Start**, point to **All Programs**, point to **AccessData**, point to **FTK Imager**, and click **FTK Imager**.

2. Click **File, Add Evidence Item** from the menu. In the Select Source dialog box, click the **Logical Drive** option button, and then click **Next**.

3. In the Select Drive dialog box, click the **Drive Selection** list arrow, click your USB drive in the drop-down list, and then click **Finish**.

4. Right-click the USB drive at the upper left and click **Verify Drive/Image**. The verification process takes a few minutes. When it finishes, you should see a window similar to Figure 5-8. Copy the MD5 and SHA-1 hash values for this file to a text file in Notepad, and then click **Close**. Save the text file in your work folder with a filename of your choosing, and then exit Notepad.

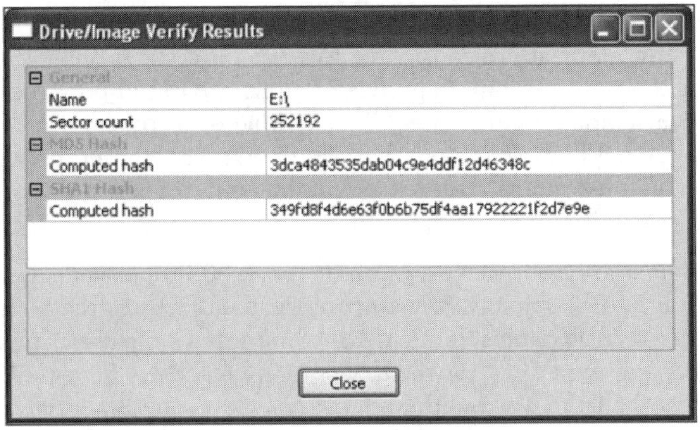

Figure 5-8   Using FTK Imager to verify hash values

5. In FTK Imager, click **File, Remove Evidence Item** from the menu. (You're about to make changes to the file and don't want it open in FTK Imager while you do so.) Leave FTK Imager running for the next set of steps.

Now you change the text file:

1. Start Notepad, and open the **InChap05.txt** file.

2. Delete one word from the sentence. Save the file with the same filename, and exit Notepad.

3. Repeat the previous steps in FTK Imager to generate MD5 and SHA-1 hash values. They should be different from the original hash values you found for this file. When you're finished, exit FTK Imager.

Reviewing a Case

Chapter 2 introduced tasks for planning your investigation, some of which are repeated in the following list. Later in this section, you apply each task to a hypothetical investigation to create a preparation plan for searching an incident or crime scene. The following are the general tasks you perform in any computer forensics case:

- Identify the case requirements.
- Plan your investigation.
- Conduct the investigation.
- Complete the case report.
- Critique the case.

The following sections give you an example of civil and criminal investigations, and then you review how to perform some of these general tasks in a case involving a hypothetical company.

Sample Civil Investigation

Most cases in the corporate environment are considered **low-level investigations,** or noncriminal cases. This doesn't mean corporate computing investigations are less important; it means they require less effort than a major criminal case. The example of a low-level civil investigation in this section is an e-mail investigation that resulted in a lawsuit between two businesses. An investigation of this nature requires examining only e-mail messages, not a complete disk forensics analysis.

Mr. Jones at Company A claims to have received an order for $200,000 in widgets from the purchasing manager, Mr. Smith, at Company B. Company A manufactures the widgets and notifies Company B that they're ready for shipment. Mr. Smith at Company B replies that they didn't order any widgets and won't pay for them. Company A locates an e-mail requesting the widgets that appears to be from Mr. Smith and informs Company B about the e-mail. Company B tells Company A that the e-mail didn't originate from its e-mail server, and it won't pay for the widgets.

Company A files a lawsuit against Company B based on the widget order in Mr. Smith's e-mail. The lawyers for Company A contact the lawyers for Company B and discuss the lawsuit. Company A's lawyers make discovery demands to conduct a computer forensics analysis on Mr. Smith's computer in hopes of finding the original message that caused the problem. At the same time, Company B's lawyers demand discovery on Mr. Jones's computer because they believe the e-mail is a fake.

As a computing investigator, you receive a call from your boss asking you to fulfill the discovery demands from Company B's lawyers to locate and determine whether the e-mail message on Mr. Jones's computer is real or fake. Because it's an e-mail investigation, not a major crime involving computers, you're dispatched to Company A. When you get there, you find Mr. Jones's computer powered on and running Microsoft Outlook. The discovery order authorizes you to recover only Mr. Jones's Outlook e-mail folder, the .pst file. You aren't authorized to do anything else. You would take the following steps in this situation:

1. Close the Outlook program on Mr. Jones's computer.

2. Use Windows Explorer to locate the Outlook .pst file containing his business e-mail. You might need to use the Windows Search feature to find files with the .pst extension.

3. Determine how large the .pst file is and connect the appropriate media device, such as an external USB drive, to Mr. Jones's computer.

4. Copy the .pst file to your external USB drive, and then remove the USB drive.

5. Fill out your evidence form, stating where on Mr. Jones's disk you located the .pst file, along with the date and time you performed this task.

6. Leave Company A and return to your computer forensics lab. Place the USB drive in your evidence safe.

For most civil investigations, you collect only specific items that have been determined germane by lawyers or the Human Resources Department.

Another activity common in the corporate computing environment is **covert surveillance** of employees who are abusing their computing and network privileges. The use of covert surveillance of employees must be well defined in company policy before it can be carried out. If a company doesn't have a policy that informs employees they have no privacy rights when using company computers, no surveillance can be conducted without exposing the company to civil or even criminal liability. If no policy exists, the company must create a policy and notify all employees about the new rules. Your legal department should create policy language appropriate for your state or country and define the rights and authority the company has in conducting surveillance of employees according to provincial, state, or country privacy laws.

For covert surveillance, you set up monitoring tools that record a suspect's activity in real time. Real-time surveillance requires **sniffing** data transmissions between a suspect's computer and a network server. Sniffing software allows network administrators and others to determine what data is being transmitted over the network. Other data-collecting tools (called keylogger programs—Spector and WinWhatWhere, for example) are screen capture programs that collect most or all screens and keystrokes on a suspect's computer. Most of these tools run on Windows and usually collect data through remote network connections. The tools are hidden or disguised as other programs in Windows Task Manager and process logs.

Another covert surveillance product is Guidance Software EnCase Enterprise Edition (EEE), which is a centrally located server with specialized software that can activate servlets over a network to remote workstations. Computing investigators can perform forensics examinations in real time through this remote connection to a suspect's computer.

Sample Criminal Investigation

Crime scenes involving computers range from fraud cases to homicides. Because high-quality printers are now available, one of the most common computer-related crimes is check fraud. Many check fraud cases also involve making and selling false ID cards, such as driver's licenses.

In one recent case, the police received a tip that a check-forging operation was active in an apartment building. After the detective contacted a reliable informant, he had enough information for a search warrant and asked the patrol division to assist him in serving the warrant. When the detective entered the suspect's apartment and conducted a preliminary search, he found a network of six high-end workstations with cables connected to devices in the adjacent apartment through a hole in the wall (see Figure 5-9). Unfortunately, the warrant specified a search of only one apartment.

The detective contacted the deputy prosecutor, who instructed him to stand guard at both apartments until she could have a judge issue an additional warrant for the neighboring apartment. When he received the second search warrant, the detective entered the adjoining apartment and continued his search, finding more computers, high-quality color laser printers, checks, and stolen blank driver's licenses. The outcome of the investigation revealed that the perpetrators were three enterprising high school students who were selling fake IDs to fellow students. The check fraud scheme was a new sideline they were developing to improve their cash flow.

Reviewing Background Information for a Case

A company called Superior Bicycles, with a Web site at *www.superiorbicycles.biz*, specializes in creating new and inventive modes of human-driven transportation. Two employees, Chris

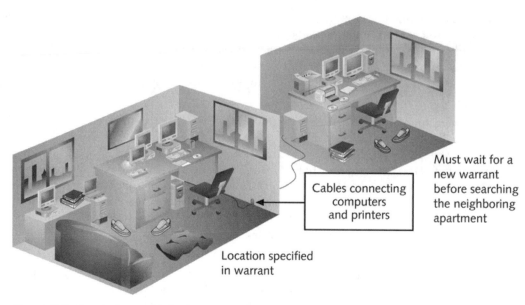

Figure 5-9 Search warrant limits

Murphy and Nau Tjeriko, have been missing for several days. A USB drive has been recovered from Chris's office with evidence that he had been conducting a side business using company computers. Steve, a manager, talks to other employees, but no one knows why Chris and Nau aren't at work. To learn where Nau might be, Steve searches the surface of her desk and notices travel brochures for European tours. Steve also looks around Chris's office again and finds notes about a Swiss supplier Steve once used and another USB drive with the supplier's name on the label. Steve suspects the USB drive contains more information and calls you, the computing investigator for his company. He describes Chris and Nau's absence from the company and asks you to examine the USB drive to see whether it identifies their whereabouts.

Identifying the Case Requirements

Before you analyze the USB drive, answer the following basic questions to start your investigation:

- *What is the nature of the case?* Two people are missing or overdue at work.
- *What are their names?* Chris Murphy and Nau Tjeriko.
- *What do they do?* Chris works in the Financial Records Department, and Nau is a nurse who does ergonomic work for Superior Bicycles.
- *What is the OS of the suspect computer?* Microsoft Windows XP.
- *What type of media needs to be examined?* One USB drive.
- *What is the suspect computer's configuration, such as type, CPU speed, and hard drive size?* An AMD dual-core processor, 3 GB RAM, and a 200 GB Western Digital hard drive.

Planning the Investigation

To find information about Chris and Nau's whereabouts, list what you can assume or already know about the case:

- Chris and Nau's absences might or might not be related.
- Chris's computer might contain information explaining their absence.
- No one else has used Chris's computer since he disappeared.

You need to make an image of Chris's USB drive and attempt to retrieve evidence related to the case. The following section explains how to use AccessData FTK to examine the drive's contents.

5

Conducting the Investigation: Acquiring Evidence with AccessData FTK

In the following activity, you use AccessData FTK to extract and analyze an image file. In Chapters 2 and 4, you learned how to acquire an image of a drive with ProDiscover Basic and other tools. To prepare FTK for analyzing the image of a suspect drive, follow these steps:

1. Make sure you have extracted data files from the Chap05 folder on the book's DVD to your work folder for this chapter.

2. To start FTK, click **Start**, point to **All Programs**, point to **AccessData**, point to **Forensic Toolkit**, and click **Forensic Toolkit**. If you're prompted with a warning dialog box and/or notification, click **OK** to continue, and click **OK**, if necessary, in the message box thanking you for evaluating the program.

3. In the AccessData FTK Startup dialog box, click the **Start a new case** option button, and then click **OK**.

4. In the New Case dialog box, enter your name as the investigator, **InChp05** as the case number, and a suitable case name, and then click **Next**.

5. Fill out the information in the Forensic Examiner Information dialog box as you want it to appear in your final report, and then click **Next** until you reach the Evidence Processing Options dialog box. Make sure the Data Carve check box is *not* selected because this option makes processing take much longer; you can always do data carving later, if necessary. Then click **Next**.

6. In the Refine Case - Default dialog box, click the **Include All Items** button (see Figure 5-10), and then click **Next**.

7. In the Refine Index - Default dialog box, accept the default settings, and then click **Next**.

8. In the main Add Evidence to Case dialog box, click the **Add Evidence** button.

9. In the second Add Evidence to Case dialog box, click the **Acquired Image of Drive** option button, and then click **Continue**.

10. In the Open dialog box, navigate to your work folder, click to select the **InChap05.001** file, and then click **Open**.

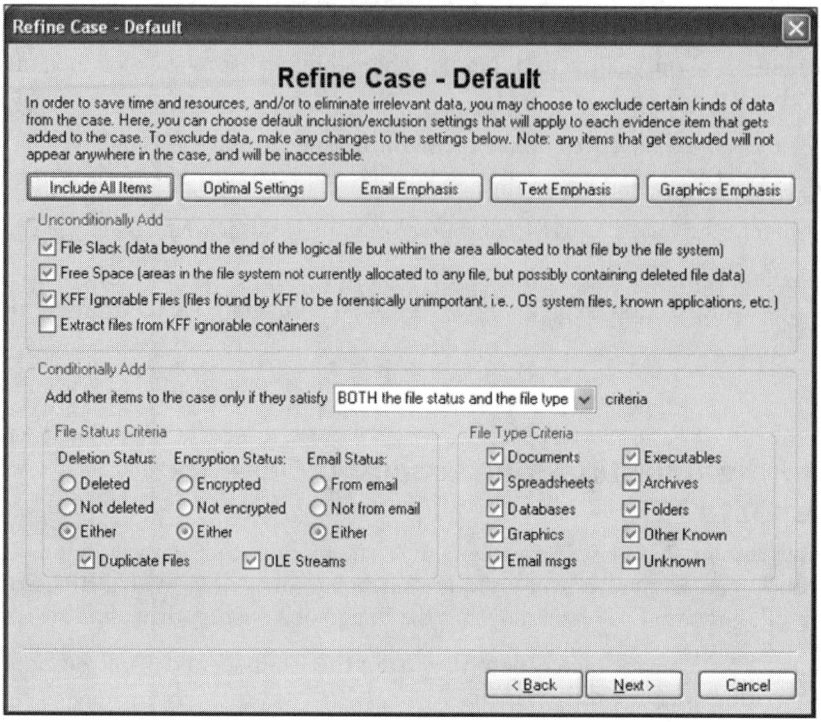

Figure 5-10 The Refine Case - Default dialog box

11. In the Evidence Information dialog box, enter the additional information, using Figure 5-11 as a guideline. Click the **Local Evidence Time Zone** list arrow at the bottom, click the suspect's time zone in the drop-down list, and then click **OK**.

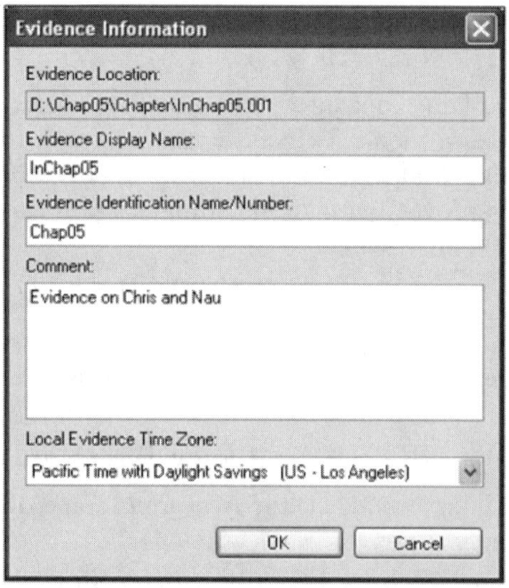

Figure 5-11 The Evidence Information dialog box

12. In the main Add Evidence to Case dialog box, shown in Figure 5-12, accept the default settings, and then click **Next**.

Add Evidence to Case

Add Evidence

Any number of evidence items can be added to the case. There are several types of evidence items:

Acquired image of drive:	Several formats supported; can be an image of a logical or physical drive
Local drive:	Can be a logical or physical drive
Folder:	Adds all files in the specified folder, including contents of subfolders
Individual File:	Adds a single file. NOTE: Disk image files should be added as acquired images.

The default refinement options, set previously, can be overridden independently for each evidence item, and additional types of refinements can also be made. These refinements can include the exclusion of date/size ranges, as well as specific folders. To make these further refinements, highlight an evidence item in the list and press Refine Evidence - Advanced...

[Add Evidence...] [Edit Evidence...] [Remove Evidence] [Refine Evidence - Advanced...]

Display Name	Source	Name/N...	Type	Refined	Time Zone	Comment
InChap05\NO NAME-FAT16	D:\Chap05\C...	Chap05	FAT16	N	America/L...	Evidence ...

[< Back] [Next >] [Cancel]

Figure 5-12 The Add Evidence to Case dialog box with image file listed

13. In the Case Summary dialog box (see Figure 5-13), click **Finish** to initiate the analysis. FTK then performs several steps of cataloging data and indexing every word in the InChap05.001 image file. The cataloging process organizes and lists each file in its own section for follow-up analysis (see Figure 5-14). The indexing feature creates a database of every word in the image file with its exact location so that you can easily look up keywords of interest to the investigation.

14. When FTK finishes cataloging and indexing, the FTK window opens to the Overview tab. To analyze an image with FTK, click the **Explore** tab. In the upper-left pane (the tree view), click to expand a folder, if needed, and then click the **List all descendants** check box.

 When you're navigating between the Explore, Graphics, and E-Mail tabs in the FTK window, only the folder tree is displayed. If you click to expand a folder in the upper-left pane, its contents (files) are displayed in the lower pane. The List all descendants option enables you to view all files, regardless of which folder they're in, and you can scroll through all files at once.

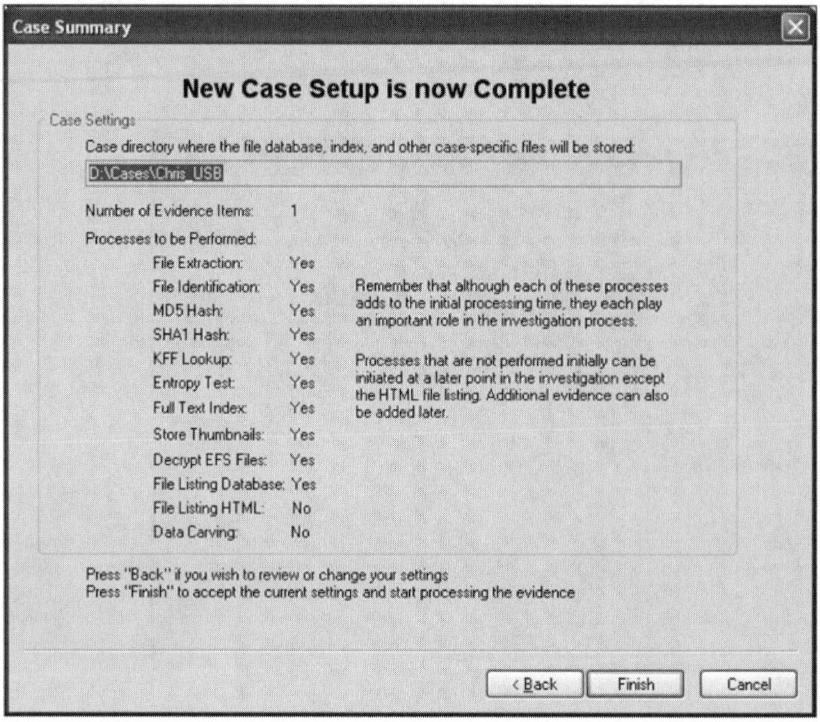

Figure 5-13 The Case Summary dialog box

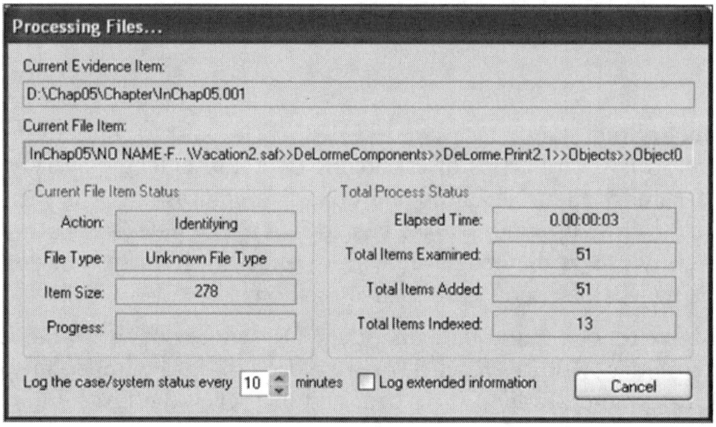

Figure 5-14 The Processing Files dialog box

15. Navigate through each file in the lower pane by clicking the filenames one at a time. The upper-right pane displays any data in the files. For example, Figure 5-15 shows the data for the PICT0032.jpg file selected in the lower pane. Review this data to see what information can be retrieved from this image.

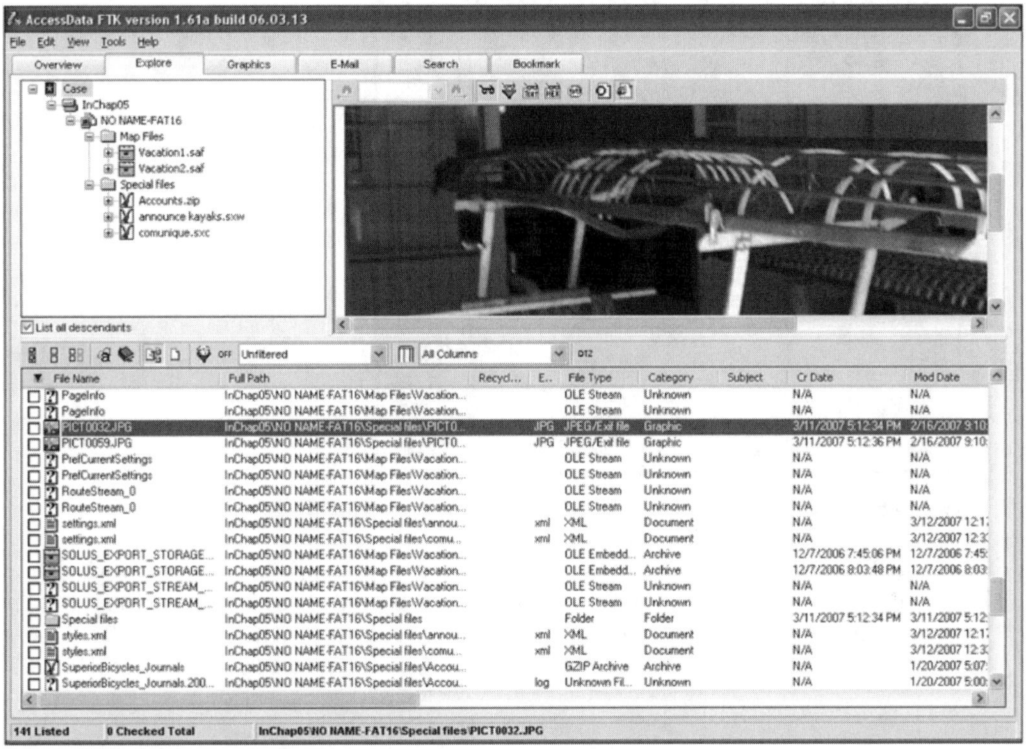

Figure 5-15 Selecting files of interest

16. When you have located a file containing information you think is important, click the check box next to the filename in the lower pane. Continue searching for more information, and select any additional files of interest.

17. After you have selected all files of interest, click **Tools, Create Bookmark** from the menu. In the Create New Bookmark dialog box, type a bookmark name and any comments. Then click the **All checked items** button, click the **Include in report** and **Export files** check boxes (see Figure 5-16), and click **OK**.

> The purpose of bookmarks in FTK is to provide a way to copy information of evidentiary value to a report.
>
> **NOTE**

18. After you have bookmarked key files containing possible evidence, click **File, Report Wizard** from the menu. In the Case Information dialog box, click to select the **Include Investigator Information in report** check box (if necessary), click to select the investigator's name in the drop-down list box, and then click **Next**.

19. In the Bookmarks - A window, click **Next**. Continue clicking **Next** through the remaining report wizard windows until you reach the Report Location window, and then click **Finish**.

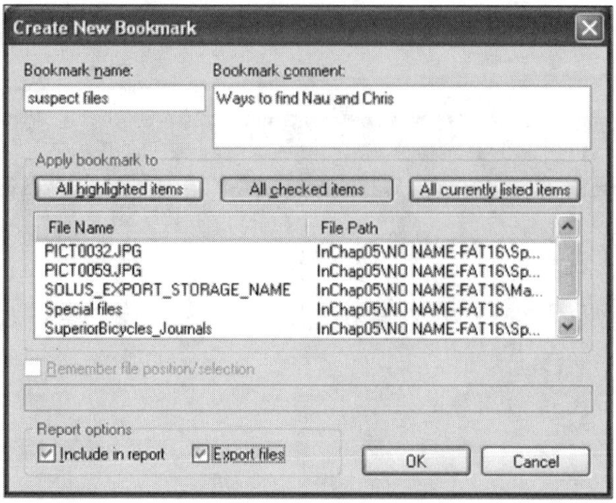

Figure 5-16   The Create New Bookmark dialog box

20. When the Report Wizard displays a prompt asking whether you want to view the report, click **Yes** to see the report in your default Web browser. Click the links to view the report's contents, and then close your browser. When you're done, exit FTK by clicking **File, Exit** from the menu. If prompted to back up your case, click **No**.

Chapter Summary

- Digital evidence is anything stored or transmitted on electronic or optical media. It's extremely fragile and easily altered.

- In the private sector, an incident scene is often a place of work, such as a contained office or manufacturing area. Because everything from the computers used to violate a company policy to the surrounding facility is under a controlled authority, investigating and controlling the scene are easier than at a crime scene.

- Companies should publish policies stating that they reserve the right to inspect computing assets at will; otherwise, employees' expectation of privacy prevents an employer from legally conducting an intrusive investigation or covert surveillance. A well-defined corporate policy states that an employer has the right to examine, inspect, or access any company-owned computing asset.

- Proper procedure needs to be followed even in private-sector investigations because civil cases can easily become criminal cases. If an internal corporate case is turned over to law enforcement because of criminal activity, the corporate investigator must avoid becoming an agent of law enforcement.

- Criminal cases require a properly executed and well-defined search warrant. A specific crime and location must be spelled out in the warrant. For all criminal investigations in the United States, the Fourth Amendment specifies that a law enforcement officer can search for and seize criminal evidence only with probable cause, which is facts or circumstances that lead a reasonable person to believe a crime has been committed or is about to be committed.

- The plain view doctrine applies when investigators find evidentiary items that aren't specified in a warrant or under probable cause.

- When preparing for a case, describe the nature of the case, identify the type of OS, determine whether you can seize the computer, and obtain a description of the location.

- When dealing with a hazardous materials (HAZMAT) situation, you might need to obtain HAZMAT certification or have someone else with that certification collect the evidence.

- Always take pictures or use a video camera to document the scene. Prevent professional curiosity from contaminating evidence by limiting who enters the scene.

- As you collect digital evidence, guard against physically destroying or contaminating it. Take precautions to prevent static electricity discharge to electronic devices. If possible, bag or box digital evidence and any hardware you collect from the scene. As you collect hardware, sketch the equipment, including exact markings of where components are located. Tag and number each cable, port, and other connection and record its number and description in a log.

- Selecting a medium for storing digital evidence usually depends on how long you need to keep the evidence. The ideal storage media are CD-Rs or DVDs. You can also use magnetic tape, such as 4-mm DAT and DLT magnetic tapes.

- Forensic hash values are used to verify that data or storage media have not been altered. The two most common hashing algorithms for forensics purposes are currently MD5 and SHA-1, although both are being replaced slowly as more research is done. A forensic hash can't be predicted, no two files can have the same hash value, and if the file changes, the hash value must change.

- To analyze computer forensics data, learn to use more than one vendor tool. Different vendors offer varying methods for recovering data from magnetic media. AccessData FTK is a Windows GUI tool for recovering data from FAT, NTFS, and Ext2 file systems and has a unique method of cataloging and indexing data that speeds up the examination process.

- You must handle all evidence the same way every time you handle it. Apply the same security and accountability controls for evidence in a civil lawsuit as for evidence from a crime scene to comply with state or federal rules of evidence.

- After you determine that an incident scene has digital evidence, identify the digital information or artifacts that can be used as evidence. Next, catalog or document the evidence you find. Your goal is to preserve evidence integrity, which means you must not modify the evidence as you collect and catalog it. An incident scene should be photographed and sketched, and then each item labeled and put in an evidence bag. Collect, preserve, document, analyze, identify, and organize the evidence. Then rebuild evidence or repeat a situation to verify that you get the same results every time.

Key Terms

4-mm DAT Magnetic tapes that store about 4 GB of data, but like CD-Rs, are slow to read and write data.

Automated Fingerprint Identification Systems (AFIS) A computerized system for identifying fingerprints that's connected to a central database; used to identify criminal suspects and review thousands of fingerprint samples at high speed.

computer-generated records Data generated by a computer, such as system log files or proxy server logs.

computer-stored records Digital files generated by a person, such as electronic spreadsheets.

covert surveillance Observing people or places without being detected, often using electronic equipment, such as video cameras or key stroke/screen capture programs.

Cyclic Redundancy Check (CRC) A mathematical algorithm that translates a file into a unique hexadecimal value.

digital evidence Evidence consisting of information stored or transmitted in electronic form.

extensive-response field kit A portable kit designed to process several computers and a variety of operating systems at a crime or incident scene involving computers. This kit should contain two or more types of software or hardware computer forensics tools, such as extra storage drives.

hash value A unique hexadecimal value that identifies a file or drive.

hazardous materials (HAZMAT) Chemical, biological, or radiological substances that can cause harm to people.

initial-response field kit A portable kit containing only the minimum tools needed to perform disk acquisitions and preliminary forensics analysis in the field.

innocent information Data that doesn't contribute to evidence of a crime or violation.

International Organization on Computer Evidence (IOCE) A group that sets standards for recovering, preserving, and examining digital evidence.

keyed hash set A value created by an encryption utility's secret key.

limiting phrase Wording in a search warrant that limits the scope of a search for evidence.

low-level investigations Corporate cases that require less effort than a major criminal case.

Message Digest 5 (MD5) An algorithm that produces a hexadecimal value of a file or storage media. Used to determine whether data has been changed.

National Institute of Standards and Technology (NIST) One of the governing bodies responsible for setting standards for various U.S. industries.

nonkeyed hash set A unique hash numbered generated by a software tool and used to identify files.

person of interest Someone who might be a suspect or someone with additional knowledge that can provide enough evidence of probable cause for a search warrant or arrest.

plain view doctrine When conducting a search and seizure, objects in plain view of a law enforcement officer, who has the right to be in position to have that view, are subject to seizure without a warrant and can be introduced as evidence. As applied to executing searches of computers, the plain view doctrine's limitations are less clear.

probable cause The standard specifying whether a police officer has the right to make an arrest, conduct a personal or property search, or obtain a warrant for arrest.

professional curiosity The motivation for law enforcement and other professional personnel to examine an incident or crime scene to see what happened.

Scientific Working Group on Digital Evidence (SWGDE) A group that sets standards for recovering, preserving, and examining digital evidence.

Secure Hash Algorithm version 1 (SHA-1) A forensic hashing algorithm created by NIST to determine whether data in a file or on storage media has been altered.

sniffing Detecting data transmissions to and from a suspect's computer and a network server to determine the type of data being transmitted over a network.

5

Review Questions

1. Corporate investigations are typically easier than law enforcement investigations for which of the following reasons?

   a. Most companies keep inventory databases of all hardware and software used.

   b. The investigator doesn't have to get a warrant.

   c. The investigator has to get a warrant.

   d. Users can load whatever they want on their machines.

2. In the United States, if a company publishes a policy stating that it reserves the right to inspect computing assets at will, a corporate investigator can conduct covert surveillance on an employee with little cause. True or False?

3. If you discover a criminal act, such as murder or child pornography, while investigating a corporate policy abuse, the case becomes a criminal investigation and should be referred to law enforcement. True or False?

4. As a corporate investigator, you can become an agent of law enforcement when which of the following happens? (Choose all that apply.)

   a. You begin to take orders from a police detective without a warrant or subpoena.

   b. Your internal investigation has concluded, and you have filed a criminal complaint and turned over the evidence to law enforcement.

   c. Your internal investigation begins.

   d. None of the above.

5. The plain view doctrine in computer searches is well-established law. True or False?

6. If a suspect computer is located in an area that might have toxic chemicals, you must do which of the following? (Choose all that apply.)

   a. Coordinate with the HAZMAT team.

   b. Determine a way to obtain the suspect computer.

   c. Assume the suspect computer is contaminated.

   d. Do not enter alone.

7. What are the three rules for a forensic hash?

8. In forensic hashes, a collision occurs when _____.

9. List three items that should be in an initial-response field kit.

10. When you arrive at the scene, why should you extract only those items you need to acquire evidence?

11. Computer peripherals or attachments can contain DNA evidence. True or False?

12. If a suspect computer is running Windows 2000, which of the following can you perform safely?

    a. Browsing open applications

    b. Disconnecting power

    c. Either of the above

    d. None of the above

13. Describe what should be videotaped or sketched at a computer crime scene.

14. Which of the following techniques might be used in covert surveillance?

    a. Keylogging

    b. Data sniffing

    c. Network logs

15. Commingling evidence means what in a corporate setting?

16. List two hashing algorithms commonly used for forensic purposes.

17. Small companies rarely need investigators. True or False?

18. If a company doesn't distribute a computing use policy stating an employer's right to inspect employees' computers freely, including e-mail and Web use, employees have an expectation of privacy. True or False?

19. You have been called to the scene of a fatal car crash where a laptop computer is still running. What type of field kit should you take with you?

20. You should always answer questions from onlookers at a crime scene. True or False?

Hands-On Projects

There are no data files to extract for this chapter's projects, but create a *Work*\Chap05\ Projects folder on your system before starting the projects.

Hands-On Project 5-1

In the past few years, there have been challenges to and changes in the way the Patriot Act is applied and what information ISPs must supply. Research these recent changes online, making sure to check the date of any articles you find. Write a one- to two-page paper explaining how the Patriot Act originally affected ISPs and what changes have taken place since then.

Hands-On Project 5-2

You're investigating an internal policy violation when you find an e-mail about a serious assault for which a police report needs to be filed. What should you do? Write a two-page paper specifying who in your company you need to talk to first and what evidence must be turned over to the police.

Hands-On Project 5-3

You're at a crime scene, which is the home of a suspected drug dealer. You find a computer turned on with three applications running. An online session is also open through a DSL connection. Write a one- to two-page paper outlining what you should do to document the crime scene and collect and package the evidence.

Hands-On Project 5-4

In this project, you create a file on a USB drive and calculate its hash value in FTK Imager. Then you change the file and calculate the hash value again to compare the files. You need a Windows computer and a USB drive.

1. Create a folder called **C5Prj04** on your USB drive, and then start Notepad.
2. In a new text file, type **This is a test of hash values. One definition of a forensic hash is that if the file changes, the hash value changes.**
3. Save the file as **hash1.txt** in the **C5Prj04** folder on your USB drive, and then exit Notepad.
4. Start FTK Imager, and click **File, Add Evidence Item** from the menu. In the Select Source dialog box, click the **Logical Drive** option button, and then click **Next**.
5. In the Select Drive dialog box, click the **Drive Selection** list arrow, click to select your USB drive, and then click **Finish**.
6. In the upper-left pane, click to expand your USB drive and continue expanding until you can click the C5Prj04 folder. In the upper-right pane, you should see the hash1.txt file you created.
7. Right-click the file and click **Export File Hash List**. Save the file as **original hash** in the C5Prj04 folder on your USB drive. FTK Imager saves it as a .csv file. Exit FTK Imager, and start Notepad.
8. Open **hash1.txt** in Notepad. Add one letter to the end of the file, save it, and exit Notepad.
9. Start FTK Imager again. Repeat Steps 4 to 7 (but without starting Notepad again), but this time when you export the file hash list, save the file as **changed hash**.

10. Open the **original hash** and **changed hash** files on your USB drive in Excel (or another spreadsheet program). Compare the hash values in both files to see whether they are different, and then exit Excel.

Hands-On Project 5-5

In this project, you create a file on your USB drive and calculate its hash values in FTK Imager. Then you change the filename and extension and calculate the hash values again to compare them. You need a Windows computer and a USB drive.

1. Create a folder called **C5Prj05** on your USB drive, and then start Notepad.

2. In a new text file, type **This project shows that the file, not the filename, has to change for the hash value to change.**

3. Click **File, Save As** from the menu, and save the file as **testhash.txt** in the C5Prj05 folder on your USB drive. Exit Notepad, and start FTK Imager.

4. Click **File, Add Evidence Item** from the menu. In the Select Source dialog box, click the **Logical Drive** option button, and then click **Next**.

5. In the Select Drive dialog box, click the **Drive Selection** list arrow, click to select your USB drive, and then click **Finish**.

6. In the upper-left pane, click to expand your USB drive and continue expanding until you can click the C5Prj05 folder. In the upper-right pane, you should see the testhash.txt file you created.

7. Right-click the file and click **Export File Hash List**. Save the file as **original hash value** in the C5Prj05 folder on your USB drive. FTK Imager saves it as a .csv file.

8. Click to select your USB drive in the upper-left pane, if necessary, and then click **File, Remove Evidence Item** from the menu. Exit FTK Imager.

9. Open Windows Explorer. Right-click the **testhash.txt** file on your USB drive, and rename it as **testhash.doc**. In the error message about the change in extension, click **Yes**.

10. Start FTK Imager. Follow Steps 4 to 7, but this time when you export the file hash list, right-click the **testhash.doc** file, and save it as **changed hash value**. Exit FTK Imager.

11. Open **original hash value** and **changed hash value** in Excel (or another spreadsheet program). Compare the hash values in both files to see whether they are different, and then exit Excel.

Case Projects

Case Project 5-1

In the arson running case project, what information do you need about the crime scene and how the digital evidence was acquired? Review the memos you received from the Seattle Police Department and the Legatima Insurance Company, and write a short paper outlining what information might be missing and what you need to find out.

Case Project 5-2

You're a detective for the local police. Thomas Brown, the primary suspect in a murder investigation, works at a large local firm and is reported to have two computers at work in addition to one at home. What do you need to do to gather evidence from these computers, and what obstacles can you expect to encounter during this process? Write a two- to three-page report stating what you would do if the company had its own Computer Forensics and Investigations Department and what you would do if the company did not.

Case Project 5-3

A murder in a downtown office building has been widely publicized. You're a police detective and receive a phone call from a computer forensics investigator, Gary Owens, who says he has information that might relate to the murder case. Gary says he ran across a few files while investigating a policy violation at a company in the same office building. Considering the silver-platter doctrine, what procedures might you, as a public official, have to follow? Write a one-page paper detailing what you might do.

Case Project 5-4

Your spouse works at a middle school and reports rumors of a teacher, Zane Wilkens, molesting some students and taking illicit pictures of them. Zane allegedly viewed these pictures in his office. Your spouse wants you to take a disk image of Zane's computer and find out whether the rumors are true. Write a one- to two-page paper outlining how you would tell your spouse and school administrators to proceed. Also, explain why walking into Zane's office to acquire a disk image wouldn't preserve the integrity of the evidence.

Case Project 5-5

As a computing investigator for your local sheriff's department, you have been asked to go with a detective to a local school that received a bomb threat in an anonymous e-mail. The detective already has information from a subpoena sent to the last known ISP where the anonymous e-mail originated, and the message was sent from a residence in the school's neighborhood. The detective tells you the school principal also stated that the school's Web server had been defaced by an unknown computer attacker. The detective has just obtained a warrant for the search and seizure of a computer at the residence the ISP identified. Prepare a list of what items should be included in an initial-response field kit to ensure the preservation of computer evidence when the warrant is carried out.

Working with Windows and DOS Systems

After reading this chapter and completing the exercises, you will be able to:

- Explain the purpose and structure of file systems

- Describe Microsoft file structures

- Explain the structure of New Technology File System (NTFS) disks

- List some options for decrypting drives encrypted with whole disk encryption

- Explain how the Windows Registry works

- Describe Microsoft startup tasks

- Describe MS-DOS startup tasks

- Explain the purpose of a virtual machine

Chapters 6 and 8 provide an overview of computer data and drives. This chapter reviews how data is stored and managed on Microsoft operating systems (OSs). To become proficient in recovering data for computer investigations, you should understand file systems and their OSs, including legacy (MS-DOS, Windows 9x, and Windows Me, for example) and current OSs, such as Windows 2000, XP, and Vista. In this chapter, you examine the tasks an OS performs when it starts so that you can avoid altering evidence when you examine data on a drive. You also learn how to use a Virtual PC environment to further analyze Windows digital evidence. Chapter 8 discusses Macintosh and Linux file systems and covers hardware devices such as CDs, CD-RWs, and SCSI, IDE, and SATA drives.

Understanding File Systems

To investigate computer evidence effectively, you must understand how the most commonly used OSs work and how they store files. In addition to this section on file systems, you should review books on Computer Technology Industry Association (CompTIA) A+ certifications in hardware and firmware startup tasks and operations.

A **file system** gives an OS a road map to data on a disk. The type of file system an OS uses determines how data is stored on the disk. A file system is usually directly related to an OS, although some vendors grandfather in previous OSs so that newer ones can read them. For example, most current Linux releases can access disks configured in the older Linux Ext2fs and Ext3fs file systems.

No matter which platform you use, you need to know how to access and modify system settings when necessary. When you need to access a suspect's computer to acquire or inspect data related to your investigation, you should be familiar with the computer's platform. This chapter examines Windows and DOS in detail; Chapter 8 covers information on Macintosh and Linux. For other computer systems, consult system administrators and vendor manuals.

Understanding the Boot Sequence

To ensure that you don't contaminate or alter data on a suspect's Windows or DOS PC, you must know how to access and modify a PC's Complementary Metal Oxide Semiconductor (CMOS) and Basic Input/Output System (BIOS) settings. A computer stores system configuration and date and time information in the CMOS when power to the system is off. The system BIOS contains programs that perform input and output at the hardware level.

When a subject's computer starts, you must make sure it boots to a forensic floppy disk or CD, as described in Chapters 2 and 4, because booting to the hard disk overwrites and changes evidentiary data. To do this, you access the CMOS setup by monitoring the subject's computer during the initial **bootstrap process** to identify the correct key or keys to use. The bootstrap process is contained in ROM and tells the computer how to proceed. As the computer starts, the screen usually displays the key or keys, such as the Delete key, you press to open the CMOS setup screen. You can also try unhooking the keyboard to force the system to tell you what keys to use. The key you press to access

CMOS depends on the computer's BIOS. The popular BIOS manufacturers Award and AMI use the Delete key to access CMOS; other manufacturers use Ctrl+Alt+Insert, Ctrl+A, Ctrl+S, or Ctrl+F1, F2, and F10.

Figure 6-1 shows a typical CMOS setup screen, where you check a computer's boot sequence. If necessary, you can change the boot sequence so that the OS accesses the CD/DVD drive or a floppy drive (if available) before any other boot device. Each BIOS vendor's screen is different, but you can refer to the vendor's documentation or Web site for instructions on changing the boot sequence.

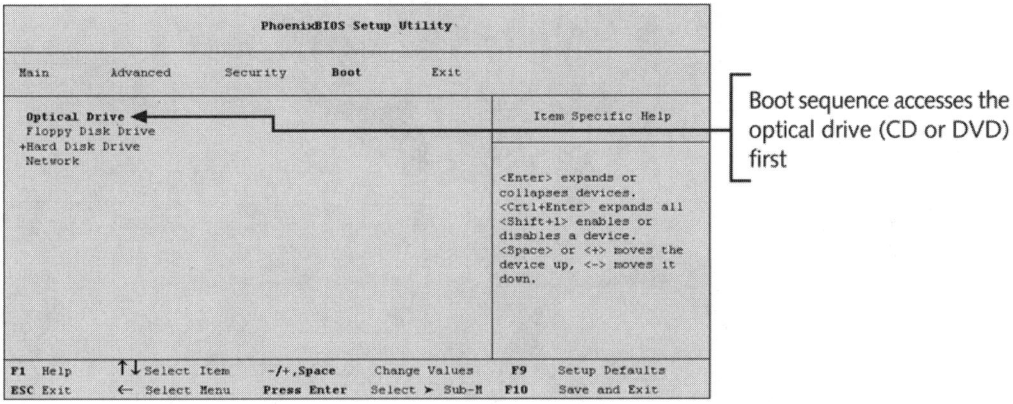

Figure 6-1 A typical CMOS setup screen

Understanding Disk Drives

You should be familiar with disk drives and how data is organized on a disk so that you can find data effectively. Disk drives are made up of one or more platters coated with magnetic material, and data is stored on platters in a particular way. For additional information on disk drive configurations, see *www.storagereview.com/guide2000/ref/hdd/index.html*. Following is a list of disk drive components, illustrated in Figure 6-2:

- *Geometry*—**Geometry** refers to a disk's structure of platters, tracks, and sectors.
- *Head*—The **head** is the device that reads and writes data to a drive. There's one head per platter.
- *Tracks*—**Tracks** are concentric circles on a disk platter where data is located.
- *Cylinders*—A **cylinder** is a column of tracks on two or more disk platters. Typically, each platter has two surfaces: top and bottom.
- *Sectors*—A **sector** is a section on a track, usually made up of 512 bytes.

The manufacturer engineers a disk to have a certain number of sectors per track, and a typical disk drive stores 512 bytes per sector. To determine the total number of addressable bytes on a disk, multiply the number of cylinders by the number of heads (actually tracks) and by the number of sectors (groups of 512 or more bytes), as shown

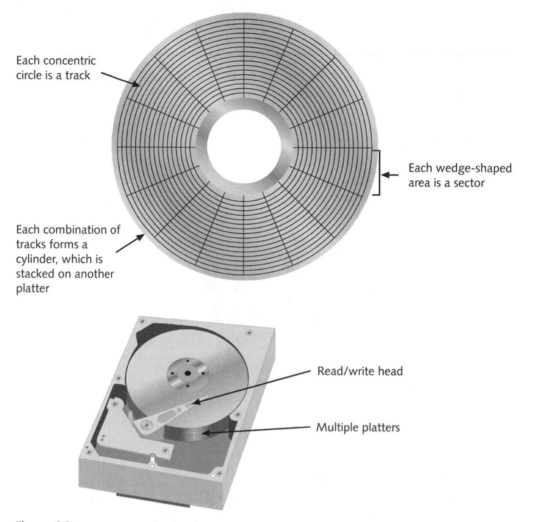

Each concentric circle is a track

Each wedge-shaped area is a sector

Each combination of tracks forms a cylinder, which is stacked on another platter

Read/write head

Multiple platters

Figure 6-2 Components of a disk drive

in Figure 6-3. Disk drive vendors refer to this formula as a cylinder, head, and sector (CHS) calculation. Tracks also follow a numbering scheme starting from 0, which is the first value in computing. If a disk lists 79 tracks, you actually have 80 tracks from 0 to 79.

Other disk properties, such as **zoned bit recording (ZBR)**, **track density**, **areal density**, and **head and cylinder skew**, are handled at the drive's hardware or firmware level. ZBR is how most manufacturers deal with a platter's inner tracks being shorter than its outer tracks. Grouping tracks by zones ensures that all tracks hold the same amount of data.

Track density is the space between each track. As with old vinyl records, the smaller the space between each track, the more tracks you can place on the platter. On older disks, the space was wider, which allowed heads to wander, making it possible for specialists to retrieve data from previous writes to a platter.

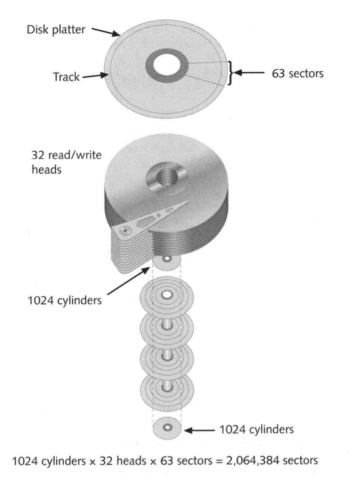

Disk platter

Track

63 sectors

32 read/write heads

1024 cylinders

1024 cylinders

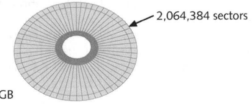

1024 cylinders × 32 heads × 63 sectors = 2,064,384 sectors

2,064,384 sectors

512 bytes per sector
1,056,964,608 or 1.056 GB

Figure 6-3 CHS calculation

Areal density refers to the number of bits in one square inch of a disk platter. This number includes the unused space between tracks. Head and cylinder skew are used to improve disk performance. As the read-write head moves from one track to another, starting sectors are offset to minimize lag time.

Exploring Microsoft File Structures

Because most PCs use Microsoft software products, you should understand Microsoft file systems so that you know how Windows and DOS computers store files. In particular, you need to understand clusters, File Allocation Table (FAT), and New Technology File System (NTFS). The method an OS uses to store files determines where data can be hidden. When you examine a computer for forensic evidence, you need to explore these hiding places to determine whether they contain files or parts of files that might be evidence of a crime or policy violation.

In Microsoft file structures, sectors are grouped to form **clusters**, which are storage allocation units of one or more sectors. Clusters are typically 512, 1024, 2048, 4096, or more bytes each. Combining sectors minimizes the overhead of writing or reading files to a disk. The OS groups one or more sectors into a cluster. The number of sectors in a cluster varies according to the disk size. For example, a double-sided floppy disk has one sector per cluster; a hard disk has four or more sectors per cluster.

Clusters are numbered sequentially starting at 2 because the first sector of all disks contains a system area, the boot record, and a file structure database. The OS assigns these cluster numbers, which are referred to as **logical addresses**. These addresses point to relative cluster positions; for example, cluster address 100 is 98 clusters from cluster address 2. Sector numbers, however, are referred to as **physical addresses** because they reside at the hardware or firmware level and go from address 0 (the first sector on the disk) to the last sector on the disk. Clusters and their addresses are specific to a logical disk drive, which is a disk partition.

Disk Partitions

Many hard disks are partitioned, or divided, into two or more sections. A **partition** is a logical drive. For example, an 8 GB hard disk might contain four partitions or logical drives. FAT16 does not recognize disks larger than 2 MB, so these disks have to be partitioned into smaller sections for FAT to recognize the additional space. Someone who wants to hide data on a hard disk can create hidden partitions or voids—large unused gaps between partitions on a disk drive. For example, partitions containing unused space (voids) can be created between the primary partition and the first logical partition. This unused space between partitions is called the **partition gap**. If data is hidden in a partition gap, a disk editor utility could also be used to alter information in the disk's partition table. Doing so removes all references to the hidden partition, concealing it from the computer's OS. Another technique is to hide incriminating digital evidence at the end of a disk by declaring a smaller number of bytes than the actual drive size. With disk-editing tools, however, you can access these hidden or empty areas of the disk.

One way to examine a partition's physical level is to use a disk editor, such as Norton Disk-Edit, WinHex, or Hex Workshop. These tools enable you to view file headers and other critical parts of a file. Both tasks involve analyzing the key hexadecimal codes the OS uses to identify and maintain the file system. Table 6-1 lists the hexadecimal codes in a partition table and identifies some common file system structures.

Table 6-1 Hexadecimal codes in the partition table

Hexadecimal code	File system
01	DOS 12-bit FAT
04	DOS 16-bit FAT for partitions smaller than 32 MB
05	Extended partition

Table 6-1 Hexadecimal codes in the partition table (*continued*)

Hexadecimal code	File system
06	DOS 16-bit FAT for partitions larger than 32 MB
07	NTFS
08	AIX bootable partition
09	AIX data partition
0B	DOS 32-bit FAT
0C	DOS 32-bit FAT for interrupt 13 support
17	Hidden NTFS partition (XP and earlier)
1B	Hidden FAT32 partition
1E	Hidden VFAT partition
3C	Partition Magic recovery partition
66–69	Novell partitions
81	Linux
82	Linux swap partition (can also be associated with Solaris partitions)
83	Linux native file systems (Ext2, Ext3, Reiser, Xiafs)
86	FAT16 volume/stripe set (Windows NT)
87	High Performance File System (HPFS) fault-tolerant mirrored partition or NTFS volume/stripe set
A5	FreeBSD and BSD/386
A6	OpenBSD
A9	NetBSD
C7	Typical of a corrupted NTFS volume/stripe set
EB	BeOS

In some instances, you might need to identify the OS on an unknown disk. You can use Norton DiskEdit, WinHex, or Hex Workshop for this task. The following steps show you how to determine a disk's OS by using Hex Workshop:

1. If necessary, download Hex Workshop from BreakPoint Software (*www.hexworkshop.com*) and install it. Check with your instructor about where you should install it on your computer.

2. Insert a USB drive into a USB port.

3. Start Hex Workshop by right-clicking the **Hex Workshop** desktop icon and clicking **Run as administrator**, and then clicking the **Continue** button in the UAC message box. (In Windows XP or an older Windows OS, simply double-click the Hex Workshop desktop icon.)

4. In Hex Workshop, click **Disk, Open Drive** from the menu to see a list of your logical drives. Click the **C:** drive (or your working drive), and click **OK**. Figure 6-4 shows a typical hard disk in the Hex Workshop window.

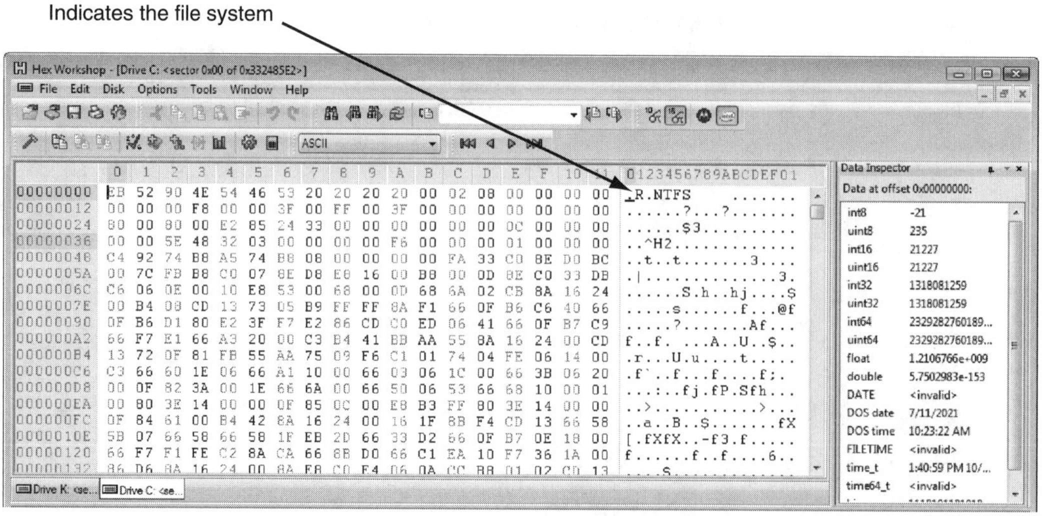

Indicates the file system

Figure 6-4 Hex Workshop identifying the file system

The C drive displays ".R.NTFS" if the partition is formatted as an NTFS drive. If it's a FAT drive, it displays MSDOS5.0 or MSWIN4.1 in the first logical sector.

5. Click **Disk, Open Drive** again, but this time, in the Open Drive drop-down list, click your USB drive, and then click **OK**. Compare the file system label for this drive to the one you saw in Step 4. Leave Hex Workshop open for the next activity.

With tools such as Hex Workshop, you can also identify file headers to identify file types with or without an extension. Before performing the following steps in Hex Workshop, use Windows Explorer or My Computer to find a folder on your system containing a bitmap (.bmp) file and a folder containing a Word document (.doc). Then follow these steps:

1. To open a bitmap file on your computer, click **File, Open** from the Hex Workshop menu. Navigate to a folder containing a bitmap (.bmp) file, and then double-click the .bmp file. (If you're prompted to select any bookmarks, click **Cancel** and continue with this activity.)

2. As shown in Figure 6-5, the Hex Workshop window identifies the file type for the graphic. For .bmp files, it shows "BM6," "BM," or "BMF." As shown in the figure, "42 4D" is also displayed to indicate a .bmp file.

3. To open a Word document, click **File, Open** from the menu. Navigate to a folder containing a Word document (.doc) file, and then double-click the .doc file. As shown in Figure 6-6, the first line contains a row of 0s followed by "D0 CF 11 E0 A1 B1 1A E1," which identifies the file as a Microsoft Office document. The same file header is displayed for an Excel or a PowerPoint file but doesn't apply to Access databases.

4. Exit Hex Workshop.

Depending on the hexadecimal editor, hex values can be grouped in sets of two or four digits.

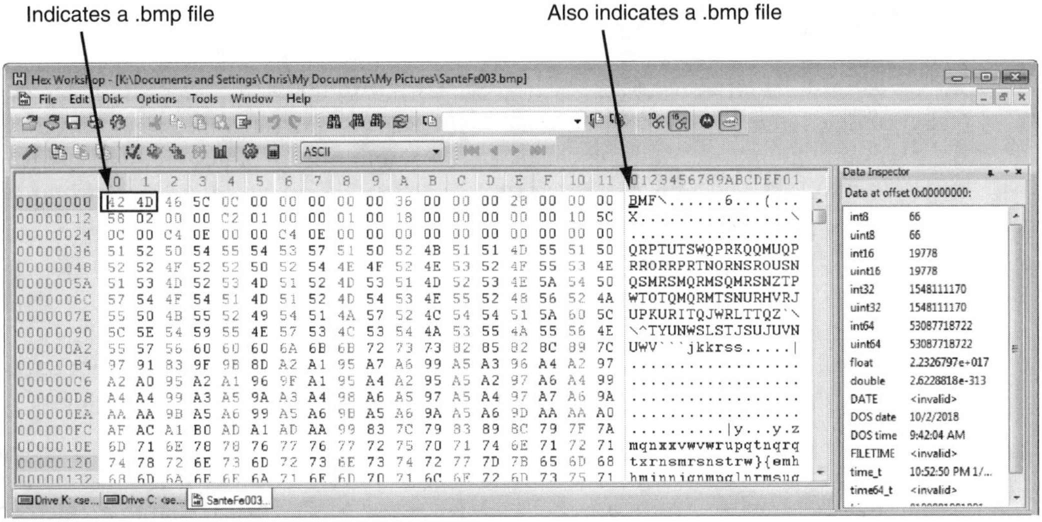

Indicates a .bmp file   Also indicates a .bmp file

Figure 6-5   Hex Workshop indicating a .bmp file

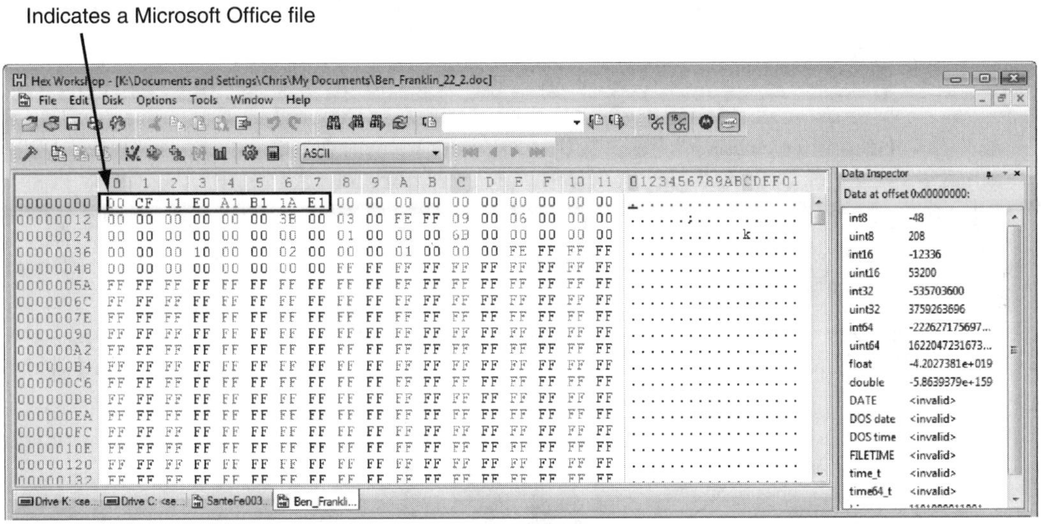

Indicates a Microsoft Office file

Figure 6-6   Hex Workshop indicating a Microsoft Office file

In the Hands-On Projects, you apply these techniques to other file types.

Master Boot Record

On Windows and DOS computer systems, the boot disk contains a file called the **Master Boot Record (MBR)**, which stores information about partitions on a disk and their locations, size, and other important items. Several software products can modify the MBR, such as Partition Magic's Boot Magic. These boot partition utilities can interfere with some computer forensics acquisition tools, which is another reason you need several data acquisition tools.

Examining FAT Disks

File Allocation Table (FAT) is the file structure database that Microsoft originally designed for floppy disks. FAT is used on file systems before Windows NT and 2000. The FAT database is typically written to a disk's outermost track and contains filenames, directory names, date and time stamps, the starting cluster number, and file attributes (archive, hidden, system, and read-only). PCs use FAT to organize files on a disk so that the OS can find the files it needs.

There are four versions of FAT—FAT12, FAT16, FAT32, and FATX (used by Xbox game systems)—and a variation called Virtual File Allocation Table (VFAT). Microsoft developed VFAT to handle long filenames when it released Windows 95 and Windows for Workgroups. The FAT version in Microsoft DOS 6.22 had a limitation of eight characters for filenames and three characters for extensions. The following list summarizes the evolution of FAT versions:

- *FAT12*—This version is used specifically for floppy disks, so it has a limited amount of storage space. It was originally designed for MS-DOS 1.0, the first Microsoft OS, used for floppy disk drives and drives up to 16 MB.

- *FAT16*—To handle large disks, Microsoft developed FAT16, which is still used on older Microsoft OSs, such as MS-DOS 3.0 through 6.22, Windows 95 (first release), and Windows NT 3.5 and 4.0. FAT16 supports disk partitions with a maximum storage capacity of 2 GB.

- *FAT32*—When disk technology improved and disks larger than 2 GB were created, Microsoft developed FAT32, which is used on Microsoft OSs such as Windows 95 (second release), 98, Me, 2000, XP, and Vista. FAT32 can access up to 2 TB of disk storage. One disk can have multiple partitions in FAT16, FAT32, or NTFS.

- *FATX*—Xbox media is stored in the FATX format and can be read by any Windows system. The date stamps start at the year 2000, unlike the other FAT formats that start at 1980.

Cluster sizes vary according to the hard disk size and file system. Table 6-2 lists the number of sectors and bytes assigned to a cluster on FAT16 disk according to hard disk size. For

Table 6-2 Sectors and bytes per cluster

Drive size	Sectors per cluster	FAT16
0–32 MB	1	512 bytes
33–64 MB	2	1 KB
65–128 MB	4	2 KB
129–255 MB	8	4 KB
256–511 MB	16	8 KB
512–1023 MB	32	16 KB
1024–2047 MB	64	32 KB
2048–4095 MB	128	68 KB

FAT32 file systems, cluster sizes are determined by the OS. Clusters can range from 1 sector consisting of 512 bytes to 128 sectors of 64 KB.

Microsoft OSs allocate disk space for files by clusters. This practice results in **drive slack**, composed of the unused space in a cluster between the end of an active file and the end of the cluster. Drive slack includes **RAM slack** (found primarily in older Microsoft OSs) and **file slack**.

For example, suppose you create a text document containing 5000 characters—that is, 5000 bytes of data. If you save this file on a FAT16 1.6 GB disk, a Microsoft OS reserves one cluster for it automatically. For a 1.6 GB disk, the OS allocates about 32,000 bytes, or 64 sectors (512 bytes per sector), for your file. The unused space, 27,000 bytes, is the file slack (see Figure 6-7). RAM slack is created in the unused space on a sector. The 5000-byte text document uses up 10 sectors, or 5120 bytes, so 120 bytes of a sector aren't used; however, DOS must write in full 512-byte chunks of data (sectors). The data to fill the 120-byte void is pulled from RAM and placed in the area between the end of the file (EOF) and the end of the last sector used by the active file in the cluster. Any information in RAM at that point, such as logon IDs or passwords, is placed in RAM slack on older Microsoft OSs when you save a file. File fragments, deleted e-mails, and passwords are often found in RAM and file slack.

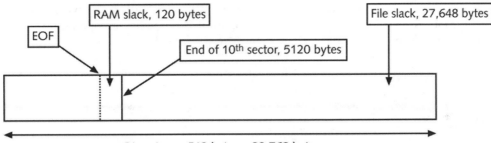

Figure 6-7 File slack space

An unintentional side effect of FAT16 having large clusters was that it reduced fragmentation as cluster size increased. The OS added extra data to the end of the file and allowed the file to expand to this assigned cluster until it consumed the remaining reserved 27,000 bytes. This increased cluster size resulted in inefficient use of disk space. Because of this inefficient allocation of sectors to clusters, when nearly full FAT16 drives were converted to FAT32, users discovered they had a lot of extra free disk space because the files wasted less space.

When you run out of room for an allocated cluster, the OS allocates another cluster for your file, which creates more slack space on the disk. As files grow and require more disk space, assigned clusters are chained together. Typically, chained clusters are contiguous on the disk. However, as some files are created and deleted and other files are expanded, the chain can be broken or fragmented. With a tool such as ProDiscover, you can view the cluster-chaining sequence and see how FAT addresses linking clusters to one another (see Figure 6-8).

When the OS stores data in a FAT file system, it assigns a starting cluster position to a file. Data for the file is written to the first sector of the first assigned cluster. When this first assigned cluster is filled and runs out of room, FAT assigns the next available cluster to the

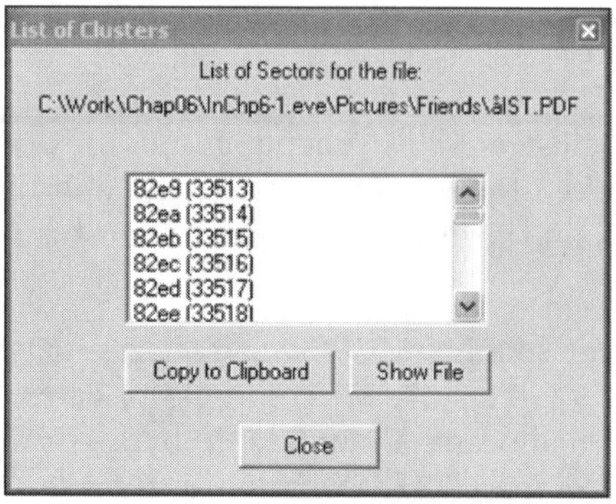

List of Clusters

List of Sectors for the file:
C:\Work\Chap06\InChp6-1.eve\Pictures\Friends\åIST.PDF

```
82e9 (33513)
82ea (33514)
82eb (33515)
82ec (33516)
82ed (33517)
82ee (33518)
```

Copy to Clipboard   Show File

Close

Figure 6-8 Chained sectors associated with clusters as a result of increasing file size

file. If the next available cluster isn't contiguous to the current cluster, the file becomes fragmented. In the FAT for each cluster on the **volume** (the partitioned disk), the OS writes the next assigned cluster, which is the number to the right of [0] in the FAT cluster assignment. Think of clusters as buckets that can hold a specific number of bytes. When a cluster (or bucket) fills up, the OS allocates another cluster to collect the extra data.

On rare occasions, such as a system failure or sabotage, these cluster chains can break. If they do, data can be lost because it's no longer associated with the previous chained cluster. FAT looks forward for the next cluster assignment but doesn't provide pointers to the previous cluster. Rebuilding these broken chains can be difficult.

Many recent disk forensics tools have automated much of the file-rebuilding process. These improved features make recovering data easier.

Deleting FAT Files When a file is deleted in Windows Explorer or with the MS-DOS Delete command, the OS inserts a HEX E5 (0xE5), which many hex-editing programs reflect as the lowercase Greek letter sigma (σ) in the filename's first letter position in the FAT database. The sigma symbol tells the OS that the file is no longer available and a new file can be written to the same cluster location.

In Microsoft OSs, when a file is deleted, the only modifications made are that the directory entry is marked as a deleted file, with the HEX E5 character replacing the first letter of the filename, and the FAT chain for that file is set to 0. The data in the file remains on the disk drive. The area of the disk where the deleted file resides becomes **unallocated disk space** (also called "free disk space"). The unallocated disk space is now available to receive new data from newly created files or other files needing more space as they grow. Most forensics tools can recover data still residing in this area.

Examining NTFS Disks

New Technology File System (NTFS) was introduced when Microsoft created Windows NT and is the primary file system for Windows Vista. Each generation of Windows since NT has included minor changes in NTFS configuration and features. The NTFS design was partially based on, and incorporated many features from, Microsoft's project for IBM with the OS/2 operating system; in this OS, the file system was **High Performance File System** (**HPFS**). When Microsoft created Windows NT, it provided backward compatibility so that NT could read OS/2 HPFS disk drives. Since the release of Windows 2000, this backward compatibility is no longer available. For a detailed explanation of NTFS structures, see *www.linux-ntfs.org*.

To be an effective computer forensics investigator, you should maintain a library of old OSs and application software. Also, keep older hardware that's in good working condition. You might need old software and hardware to do an analysis because some forensics tasks can't be performed with modern tools on older OSs and hardware.

NTFS offers significant improvements over FAT file systems. It provides more information about a file, including security features, file ownership, and other file attributes. With NTFS, you also have more control over files and folders (directories) than with FAT file systems.

NTFS was Microsoft's move toward a journaling file system. The system keeps track of transactions such as file deleting or saving. This journaling feature is helpful because it records a transaction before the system carries it out. That way, in a power failure or other interruption, the system can complete the transaction or go back to the last good setting.

In NTFS, everything written to the disk is considered a file. On an NTFS disk, the first data set is the **Partition Boot Sector**, which starts at sector [0] of the disk and can expand to 16 sectors. Immediately after the Partition Boot Sector is the **Master File Table** (**MFT**). The MFT, similar to FAT in earlier Microsoft OSs, is the first file on the disk. An MFT file is created at the same time a disk partition is formatted as an NTFS volume and usually consumes about 12.5% of the disk when it's created. As data is added, the MFT can expand to take up 50 % of the disk. (The MFT is covered in more detail in "NTFS System Files.")

An important advantage of NTFS over FAT is that it results in much less file slack space. Compare the cluster sizes in Table 6-3 to Table 6-2, which showed FAT cluster sizes. Clusters are smaller for smaller disk drives. This feature saves more space on all disks using NTFS.

Table 6-3 Cluster sizes in an NTFS disk

Drive size	Sectors per cluster	Cluster size
0–512 MB	1	512 bytes
512 MB–1 GB	2	1024 bytes
1–2 GB	4	2048 bytes
2–4 GB	8	4096 bytes
4–8 GB	16	8192 bytes
8–16 GB	32	16,384 bytes
16–32 GB	64	32,768 bytes
More than 32 GB	128	65,536 bytes

NTFS also uses **Unicode,** an international data format. Unlike the **American Standard Code for Information Interchange (ASCII)** 8-bit configuration, Unicode uses an 8-bit, a 16-bit, or a 32-bit configuration. These configurations are known as **UTF-8 (Unicode Transformation Format),** UTF-16, and UTF-32. For Western-language alphabetic characters, UTF-8 is identical to ASCII (see *www.unicode.org/versions* for more details). Knowing this feature of Unicode comes in handy when you perform keyword searches for evidence on a disk drive. (This feature is discussed in more detail in Chapter 9.) Because NTFS offers many more features than FAT, more utilities are used to manage it.

NTFS System Files

Because everything on an NTFS disk is a file, the first file, the MFT, contains information about all files on the disk, including the system files the OS uses. In the MFT, the first 15 records are reserved for system files. Records in the MFT are referred to as **metadata.** Table 6-4 lists the first 16 metadata records you find in the MFT.

Table 6-4   Metadata records in the MFT

Filename	System file	Record position	Description
$Mft	MFT	0	Base file record for each folder on the NTFS volume; other record positions in the MFT are allocated if more space is needed.
$MftMirr	MFT 2	1	The first four records of the MFT are saved in this position. If a single sector fails in the first MFT, the records can be restored, allowing recovery of the MFT.
$LogFile	Log file	2	Previous transactions are stored here to allow recovery after a system failure in the NTFS volume.
$Volume	Volume	3	Information specific to the volume, such as label and version, is stored here.
$AttrDef	Attribute definitions	4	A table listing attribute names, numbers, and definitions.
$	Root filename index	5	This is the root folder on the NTFS volume.
$Bitmap	Boot sector	6	A map of the NTFS volume showing which clusters are in use and which are available.
$Boot	Boot sector	7	Used to mount the NTFS volume during the bootstrap process; additional code is listed here if it's the boot drive for the system.
$BadClus	Bad cluster file	8	For clusters that have unrecoverable errors, an entry of the cluster location is made in this file.
$Secure	Security file	9	Unique security descriptors for the volume are listed in this file. It's where the access control list (ACL) is maintained for all files and folders on the NTFS volume.

Table 6-4 Metadata records in the MFT (*continued*)

Filename	System file	Record position	Description
$Upcase	Upcase table	10	Converts all lowercase characters to uppercase Unicode characters for the NTFS volume.
$Extend	NTFS extension file	11	Optional extensions are listed here, such as quotas, object identifiers, and reparse point data.
		12–15	Reserved for future use.

MFT and File Attributes

When Microsoft introduced NTFS, the way the OS stores data on disks changed significantly. In the NTFS MFT, all files and folders are stored in separate records of 1024 bytes each. Each record contains file or folder information. This information is divided into record fields containing metadata about the file or folder and the file's data or links to the file's data. A record field is referred to as an **attribute ID**.

File or folder information is typically stored in one of two ways in an MFT record: resident and nonresident. For very small files, about 512 bytes or less, all file metadata and data are stored in the MFT record. These types of records are called resident files because all their information is stored in the MFT record.

Files larger than 512 bytes are stored outside the MFT. The file or folder's MFT record provides cluster addresses where the file is stored on the drive's partition. These cluster addresses are referred to as **data runs**. This type of MFT record is called nonresident because the file's data is stored in its own separate file outside the MFT.

Each MFT record starts with a header identifying it as a resident or nonresident attribute. The first 4 bytes (characters) for all MFT records are FILE. The header information contains additional data specifying where the first attribute ID starts, which is typically at offset 0x14 from the beginning of the record. Each attribute ID has a length value in hexadecimal defining where it ends and where the next attribute starts. The length value is located 4 bytes from the attribute ID.

Table 6-5 list the types of attributes in an MFT record. For more details on how the MFT is configured, search on MFT and NTFS at *http://technet.microsoft.com/en-us/library/cc781134. aspx* and *http://sourceforge.net/project/showfiles.php?group_id=13956&package_ id=16543& release_id=244298.*

Table 6-5 Attributes in the MFT

Attribute ID	Purpose
0x10	$Standard Information This field contains data on file creation, alterations, MFT changes, read dates and times, and DOS file permissions.
0x20	$Attribute_List Attributes that don't fit in the MFT (nonresident attributes) are listed here along with their locations.

Table 6-5 Attributes in the MFT (*continued*)

Attribute ID	Purpose
0x30	$File_Name The long and short names for a file are contained here. Up to 255 Unicode bytes are available for long filenames. For POSIX requirements, additional names or hard links can also be listed. Files with short filenames have only one attribute ID 0x30. Long filenames have two attribute ID 0x30s in the MFT record: one for the short name and one for the long name.
0x40	$Object_ID (for Windows NT, it's named $Volume_Version) Ownership and who has access rights to the file or folder are listed here. Every MFT record is assigned a unique GUID. Depending on your NTFS setup, some file records might not contain this attribute ID.
0x50	$Security_Descriptor Contains the access control list (ACL) for the file.
0x60	$Volume_Name The volume-unique file identifier is listed here. Not all files need this unique identifier.
0x70	$Volume_Information This field indicates the version and state of the volume.
0x80	$Data File data or data runs to nonresident files.
0x90	$Index_Root Implemented for use of folders and indexes.
0xA0	$Index_Allocation Implemented for use of folders and indexes.
0xB0	$Bitmap Implemented for use of folders and indexes.
0xC0	$Reparse_Point This field is used for volume mount points and Installable File System (IFS) filter drivers. For the IFS, it marks specific files used by drivers.
0xD0	$EA_Information For use with OS/2 HPFS.
0xE0	$EA For use with OS/2 HPFS.
0x100	$Logged_Utility_Stream This field is used by EFS in Windows 2000, XP, and Vista.

Figure 6-9 is an MFT record showing the resident attributes of a small file viewed in a hexadecimal editor. Note that on line 035B3530 near the bottom, there's text data in the right pane. In Figure 6-10, the bottom half of the hexadecimal editor window shows the remaining portion of this resident file's MFT record.

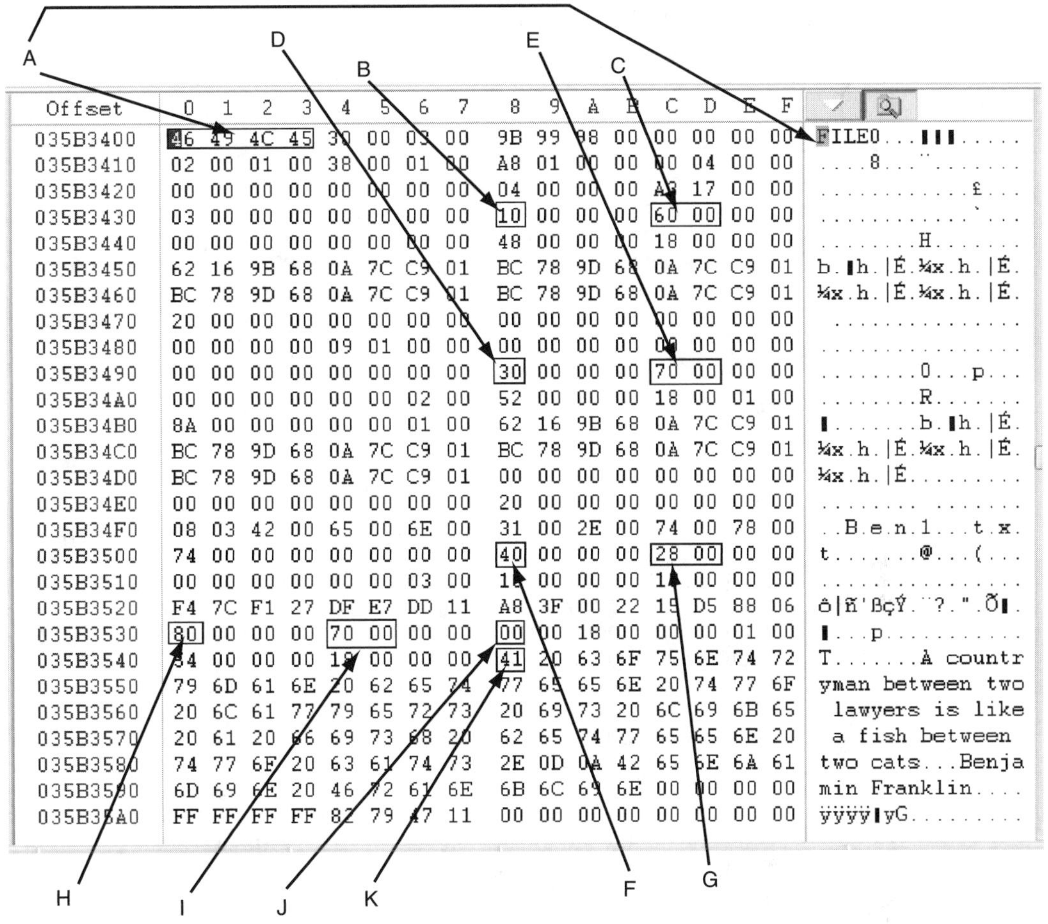

A: All MFT records start with FILE0
B: Start of attribute 0x10
C: Length of attribute 0x10 (value 60)
D: Start of attribute 0x30
E: Length of attribute 0x30 (value 70)
F: Start of attribute 0x40
G: Length of attribute 0x40 (value 28)
H: Start of attribute 0x80
I: Length of attribute 0x80 (value 70)
J: Attribute 0x80 resident flag
K: Starting position of resident data

Figure 6-9 Resident file in an MFT record

Figure 6-11 is an example of a nonresident file's hexadecimal view. Note that on line 35B3D50 near the bottom, there's no text data. This file is a longer version of the file shown in Figure 6-9. Current computer forensics tools, such as ProDiscover, EnCase, FTK, and X-Ways Forensics, can interpret the MFT from an image file.

A: Starting position of attribute 0x80 $Data

B: Length of attribute 0x80 in little endian format

C: Interpreted little endian value

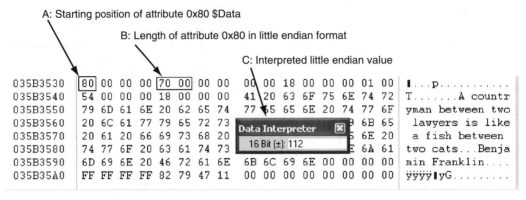

```
035B3530   80 00 00 00 70 00 00 00   00 00 18 00 00 00 01 00   ▌...p...........
035B3540   54 00 00 00 18 00 00 00   41 20 63 6F 75 6E 74 72   T.......A countr
035B3550   79 6D 61 6E 20 62 65 74   77 65 65 6E 20 74 77 6F   yman between two
035B3560   20 6C 61 77 79 65 72 73                    6B 65      lawyers is like
035B3570   20 61 20 66 69 73 68 20                    6E 20     a fish between
035B3580   74 77 6F 20 63 61 74 73                    6A 61   two cats...Benja
035B3590   6D 69 6E 20 46 72 61 6E   6B 6C 69 6E 00 00 00 00   min Franklin....
035B35A0   FF FF FF FF 82 79 47 11   00 00 00 00 00 00 00 00   ÿÿÿÿ‚yG.........
```

Data Interpreter [X]

16 Bit (±): 112

Figure 6-10 File data for a resident file

```
Offset      0  1  2  3  4  5  6  7   8  9  A  B  C  D  E  F      ✓  🔍
035B3C00   46 49 4C 45 30 00 03 00   D3 BD 98 00 00 00 00 00   FILE0...Ó½˜.....
035B3C10   02 00 01 00 38 00 01 00   80 01 00 00 00 04 00 00   ....8...▌......
035B3C20   00 00 00 00 00 00 00 00   05 00 00 00 A5 17 00 00   ............¥...
035B3C30   03 00 00 00 00 00 00 00   10 00 00 00 60 00 00 00   ............`...
035B3C40   00 00 00 00 00 00 00 00   48 00 00 00 18 00 00 00   ........H......
035B3C50   10 C0 13 88 0B 7C C9 01   6A 22 16 88 0B 7C C9 01   .À.ˆ.|É.j".ˆ.|É.
035B3C60   6A 22 16 88 0B 7C C9 01   6A 22 16 88 0B 7C C9 01   j".ˆ.|É.j".ˆ.|É.
035B3C70   20 00 00 00 00 00 00 00   00 00 00 00 00 00 00 00    ...............
035B3C80   00 00 00 00 09 01 00 00   00 00 00 00 00 00 00 00   ...............
035B3C90   00 00 00 00 00 00 00 00   30 00 00 00 70 00 00 00   ........0...p...
035B3CA0   00 00 00 00 00 00 02 00   52 00 00 00 18 00 01 00   ........R......
035B3CB0   8A 00 00 00 00 00 01 00   10 C0 13 88 0B 7C C9 01   Š........À.ˆ.|É.
035B3CC0   6A 22 16 88 0B 7C C9 01   6A 22 16 88 0B 7C C9 01   j".ˆ.|É.j".ˆ.|É.
035B3CD0   6A 22 16 88 0B 7C C9 01   00 00 00 00 00 00 00 00   j".ˆ.|É.........
035B3CE0   00 00 00 00 00 00 00 00   20 00 00 00 00 00 00 00   ........ .......
035B3CF0   08 03 42 00 65 00 6E 00   32 00 2E 00 72 00 74 00   ..B.e.n.2...r.t.
035B3D00   66 00 00 00 00 00 00 00   40 00 00 00 28 00 00 00   f.......@...(...
035B3D10   00 00 00 00 00 00 04 00   10 00 00 00 18 00 00 00   ...............
035B3D20   F7 7C F1 27 DF E7 DD 11   A8 3F 00 22 15 D5 88 06   ÷|ñ'ßçÝ.¨?.".Õˆ.
035B3D30   80 00 00 00 48 00 00 00   01 00 00 00 00 00 03 00   ▌...H..........
035B3D40   00 00 00 00 00 00 00 00   02 00 00 00 00 00 00 00   ...............
035B3D50   40 00 00 00 00 00 00 00   00 06 00 00 00 00 00 00   @..............
035B3D60   78 05 00 00 00 00 00 00   78 05 00 00 00 00 00 00   x.......x.......
035B3D70   31 03 15 55 01 00 01 00   FF FF FF FF 82 79 47 11   1..U....ÿÿÿÿ‚yG.
```

A   D   B   C   E

A: Start of nonresident attribute 0x80
B: Length of nonresident attribute 0x80
C: Attribute 0x80 nonresident flag
D: Starting point of data run
E: End-of-record marker (FF FF FF FF) for the MFT record

Figure 6-11 Nonresident file in an MFT record

To understand how data runs are assigned for nonresident MFT records, you should know that when a disk is created as an NTFS file structure, the OS assigns logical clusters to the entire disk partition. These assigned clusters, called **logical cluster numbers (LCNs)**, are sequentially numbered from the beginning of the disk partition, starting with the value 0. LCNs become the addresses that allow the MFT to link to nonresident files (files outside the MFT) on the disk's partition.

When data is initially written to nonresident files, an LCN address is assigned to the MFT (attribute 0x80 field); it's the first data run for a nonresident file. If the file can't be stored contiguously on the disk (because of excessive file fragmentation), another data run is added. The second and all other data runs have a **virtual cluster number (VCN)** assigned. A VCN is the offset position from the previous LCN value in the data run. VCNs are signed integers so that if the next largest unused disk space is at a lower address than the previous LCN, the lower value address can be computed by simply adding a negative number to the VCN. For example, if the previous LCN data run is at offset 3000000 and the next available open area to receive data is at LCN 2900000, the VCN is -100000 (3000000 + [-100000] = 2900000).

The following two sections explain the basic configuration of resident and nonresidents files managed by the MFT. By learning how data is stored in the MFT, a computer forensics examiner can manually reconstruct any residual data on NTFS-formatted disk media. The following descriptions aren't exhaustive, as far as the values and functions of NTFS and the MFT. Be aware that future Windows updates could change these configurations. This discussion should be used as a quick reference for locating and interpreting data artifacts where you might find residual fragments from partially overwritten MFT records.

MFT Structures for File Data

When viewing an MFT record with a hexadecimal editor, such as WinHex, the data is displayed in little endian format, meaning it's read from right to left. For example, the hexadecimal value 400 is displayed as 00 04 00 00, and the number 0x40000 is displayed as 00 00 04 00.

The first section of an MFT record is the header that defines the size and starting position of the first attribute. Following the header are the attributes that are specific for the file type, such as an application file or a data file. MFT records for directories and system files have additional attributes that don't appear in a file MFT record. The following sections explain how data files are configured in the MFT.

MFT Header Fields For the header of all MFT records, the record fields of interest are as follows:

- *At offset 0x00*—The MFT record identifier FILE; the letter F is at offset 0.
- *At offset 0x1C to 0x1F*—Size of the MFT record; the default is 0x400 (1024) bytes, or two sectors.
- *At offset 0x14*—Length of the header, which indicates where the next attribute starts; it's typically 0x38 bytes.
- *At offset 0x32 and 0x33*—The update sequence array, which stores the 2 two bytes of the first sector of the MFT record. It's used only when MFT data exceeds 512 bytes. The update sequence array is used as a checksum for record integrity validation.

Figure 6-12 shows these fields and their relationships in the MFT record.

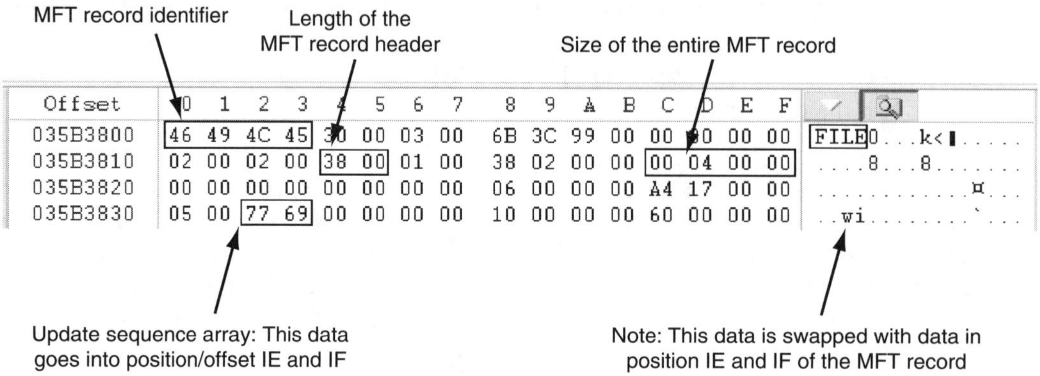

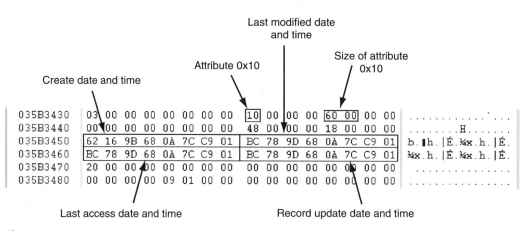

Figure 6-12 An MFT header

Attribute 0x10: Standard Information Following the MFT header for a data file is the Standard Information attribute, 0x10, which has the following fields (see Figure 6-13):

Figure 6-13 Attribute 0x10: Standard Information

- *At offset 0x38 from the beginning of the MFT record*—The start of attribute 0x10.
- *At offset 0x04 and 0x05 from the beginning of attribute 0x10*—Size of the 0x10 attribute.
- *At offset 0x18 to 0x1F*—The file's create date and time; all dates and times are stored in the Win32 Filetime format.
- *At offset 0x20 to 0x27*—The last modified date and time for the file.
- *At offset 0x28 to 0x2F*—The last access date and time.
- *At offset 0x30 to 0x37*—The record update date and time.

Attribute 0x30: File_Name For files with filenames that are eight characters or less, the MFT record has only one attribute 0x30. If a filename is longer than eight characters, there are two attribute 0x30s. The following description shows an MFT record with a short and long filename in attribute 0x30. The fields of interest for the short filename attribute 0x30 are as follows:

- *At offset 0x04 and 0x05 from the beginning of attribute 0x30*—The size of attribute 0x30.
- *At offset 0x5A from the 0x30 attribute's starting position*—The short filename; note that it's in Unicode.
- *At offset 0x20 to 0x27*—The file's create date and time; all dates and times are stored in Win32 Filetime format.
- *At offset 0x28 to 0x2F*—The last modified date and time for the file.
- *At offset 0x30 to 0x37*—The last access date and time.
- *At offset 0x38 to 0x3F*—The record update date and time.

The date and time values in attribute 0x30 are usually the same as in attribute 0x10. On occasion, depending how data is copied to a disk and the Windows OS version, these values might differ significantly.

The following are fields of interest for the long filename attribute 0x30:

- *At offset 0x04 and 0x05 from the beginning of attribute 0x30*—The size of attribute 0x30.
- *At offset 0x5A from the 0x30 attribute's starting position*—The long filename; note that it's in Unicode.
- *At offset 0x20 to 0x27*—The file's create date and time; all dates and times are stored in Win32 Filetime format.
- *At offset 0x28 to 0x2F*—The last modified date and time for the file.
- *At offset 0x30 to 0x37*—The last access date and time.
- *At offset 0x38 to 0x3F*—The record update date and time.

Figure 6-14 shows these fields and their relationships in the MFT record.

Attribute 0x40: Object_ID Depending on the Windows version, sometimes attribute 0x40 is listed in the MFT. This attribute contains file ownership and access control information and has the following fields:

- *At offset 0x04 and 0x05 from the beginning of attribute 0x40*—The size of attribute 0x40
- *At offset 0x14*—Starting offset position for GUID data
- *At offset 0x18 to 0x27*—Starting position for GUID Object_ID data

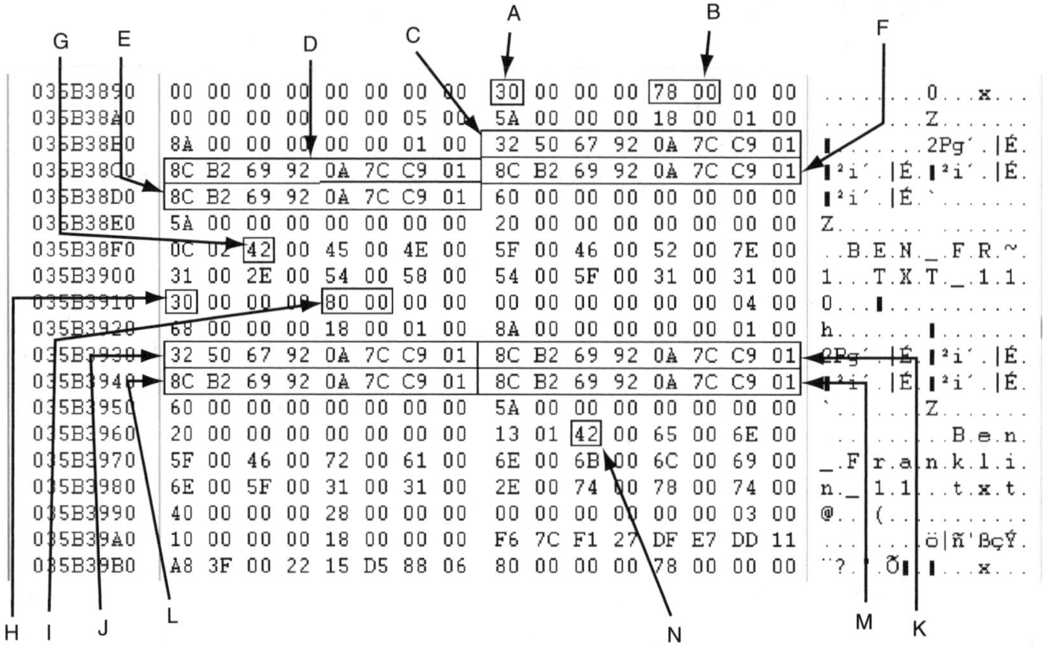

Figure 6-14 Attributes 0x30: short and long filenames

A: Attribute 0x30 short filename
B: Size of attribute 0x30 short filename
C: Short create date and time
D: Short last modified date and time
E: Short last access date and time
F: Short record update date and time
G: Starting position of short filename
H: Attribute 0x30 long filename
I: Size of attribute 0x30 long filename
J: Long create date and time
K: Long last modified date and time
L: Long last access date and time
M: Long record update date and time
N: Starting position of long filename

In this example, only the GUID Object_ID is listed. In large enterprise systems, typically additional information is listed, such as the following:

- GUID Birth Volume ID
- GUID Birth Object ID
- GUID Birth Domain ID

Figure 6-15 shows these fields and their relationships in the MFT record.

Attribute 0x80: Data for a Resident File For a resident file's attribute 0x80, the fields of interest are as follows (see Figure 6-16):

- *At offset 0x04 and 0x05 from the beginning of attribute 0x80*—Size of the attribute.
- *At offset 0x08*—The resident/nonresident flag; for resident data, it's set to 0x00.

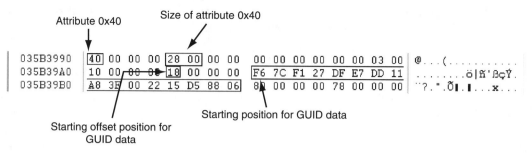

Figure 6-15 Attribute 0x40: Object_ID

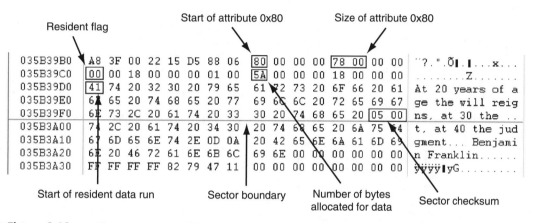

Figure 6-16 Attribute 0x80: Data for a resident file

- *At offset 0x10*—Number of bytes in the data run.
- *At offset 0x18*—Start of the resident data run.
- *At offset 0x1E and 0x1F from the beginning of the MFT header*—The sector checksum value, used to validate the first 512 bytes of the MFT record. The break between the first and second sectors is referred to as the sector boundary. The 2 bytes at positions 0x32 and 0x33 of the MFT header in the update sequence array field are where the actual values for these bytes are stored.

The end of the MFT record is indicated by the hexadecimal values FF FF FF FF at the end of the record.

Attribute 0x80: Data for a Nonresident File
For a nonresident file, the fields of interest for attribute 0x80 are as follows:

- *At offset 0x04 and 0x05 from the beginning of attribute 0x80*—Size of the attribute.
- *At offset 0x08*—The resident/nonresident flag; for nonresident data, it's set to 0x01.
- *At offset 0x40*—The start of the data run. The first run is the LCN; if the file is fragmented, additional data runs follow, as shown in Figure 6-17. In this example, there are a total of six data runs, which means this file has several fragments.

Following the last data run, the value 0x00 indicates the end of the Data attribute. Figure 6-17 shows these fields and their relationships in the MFT record.

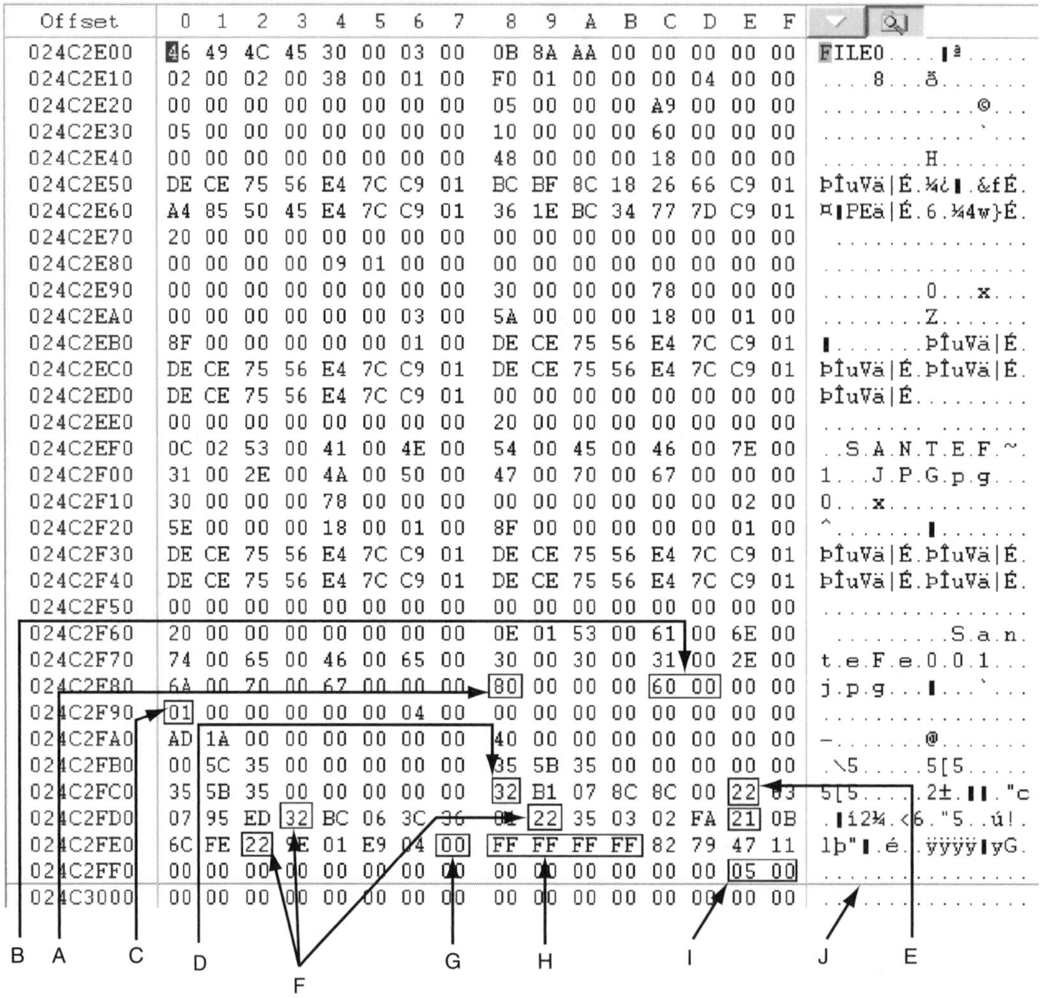

Figure 6-17 Attribute 0x80: Data for a nonresident file

A: Start of attribute 0x80
B: Size of attribute 0x80
C: Nonresident flag
D: First data run
E: Second data run
F: Additional data runs
G: End of data run
H: End of MFT record
I: Sector checksum
J: Sector boundary

Interpreting a Data Run As discussed, the first data run for a nonresident attribute 0x80 field starts at offset 0x40 from the beginning of the attribute. In this discussion, a file called SanteFe001.jpg is used as an example of how data runs are interpreted. Data runs have three components: The first component declares how many bytes in the attribute field are needed to store the values for the second and third components. The second component stores the number of clusters assigned to the data run, and the third component contains the starting cluster address value (the LCN or the VCN). This discussion uses a file with six fragments (data runs).

For the first component—the 32 shown in Figure 6-18 as the data run's starting position—the second digit, 2, means that the next 2 bytes contain the number of clusters assigned to this data run. The first digit, 3, means that the next 3 bytes (after the number of clusters assigned) contain the cluster address value; for the first data run, this value is the LCN. The next and all other data runs contain the VCN value rather than the LCN value.

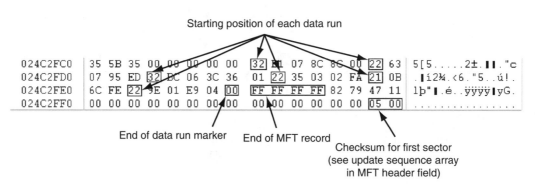

Figure 6-18 Multiple data runs

In Figure 6-19, the second component shows the 2 bytes needed to store the hexadecimal value (in little endian) for the number of clusters assigned to this data run. The number of clusters assigned to this data run is 7B1 (hexadecimal) or 1969 in decimal.

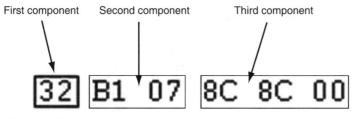

Figure 6-19 Data run components

As shown in Figure 6-20, for the third component, the starting assigned cluster address is 0x8C8C (hexadecimal), or 35980 in decimal. Because it's the first data run of the file, this address is the LCN.

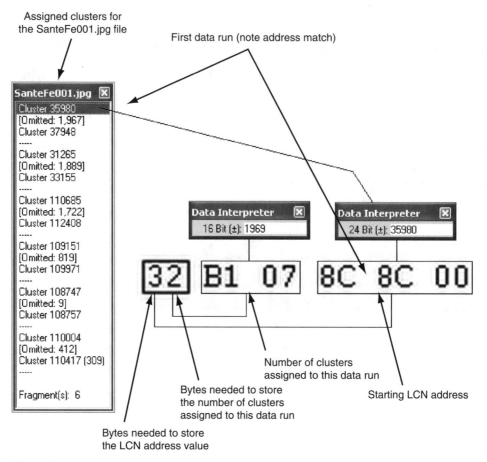

Figure 6-20   First data run with an LCN address

Figures 6-21 and 6-22 show the second and third data runs for the SanteFe001.jpg file. For the second and all other data runs, the third component is a signed integer; for example, in Figure 6-21, this value is converted from a hexadecimal number to a negative decimal number. In NTFS, if the next available open area of a highly fragmented disk is at a lower address, a negative number is assigned as the VCN value. The way NTFS navigates to this second open area is by adding the VCN to the previous LCN. For example, the first data run has the LCN address 35980, and the second data run has a value of -4715. The OS adds the two numbers, but because the second data run has a negative number, they're actually subtracted: 35980 + (-4715) = 31265.

As you can see in the assigned cluster lists in Figure 6-22, the second fragment has a starting cluster number (an LCN) of 31265. In the third data run, the VCN value is a positive number.

For additional information on NTFS and its design, see *http://data. linux-ntfs.org/ntfsdoc.pdf*.

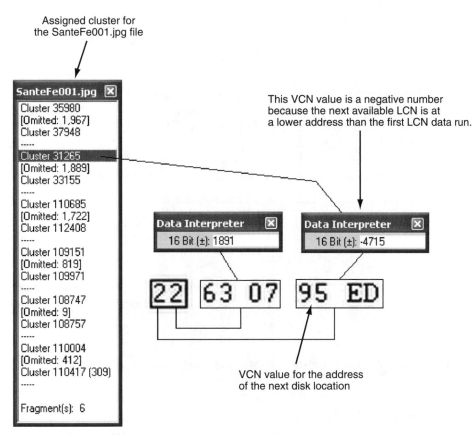

Assigned cluster for
the SanteFe001.jpg file

This VCN value is a negative number
because the next available LCN is at
a lower address than the first LCN data run.

VCN value for the address
of the next disk location

Figure 6-21 Second data run with a VCN address

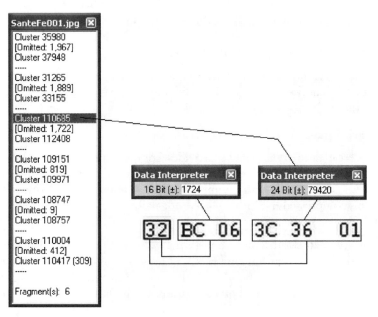

Figure 6-22 Third data run with a VCN address

6

NTFS Data Streams

Of particular interest when you're examining NTFS disks are **data streams**, which are ways data can be appended to existing files. When you're examining a disk, be aware that data streams can obscure valuable evidentiary data, intentionally or by coincidence.

In NTFS, a data stream becomes an additional file attribute and allows the file to be associated with different applications. As a result, it remains one data unit. You can also store information about a file in a data stream. In its resource documentation Web page, Microsoft states: "For example, a graphics program can store a thumbnail image of a bitmap in a named data stream within the NTFS file containing the image." From a Windows NT and later command prompt, you can create a data stream with this MS-DOS command:

```
C:\echo text_string > myfile.txt:stream_name
```

You can also use the following Type command to redirect the contents of a small file to a data stream:

```
C:\type textfile.txt > myfile.txt:stream1
```

In these commands, the data stream is defined in the MFT by the colon between the file extension and the data stream label. To display a data stream's content as a simple text string, use this command:

```
C:\more < myfile.txt:stream1
```

Be aware that if you save a file with data streams attached to a FAT volume, the data streams aren't transferred.

If you perform a keyword search and retrieve a file associated with a keyword, you might not be able to open the data stream. A data stream isn't displayed when you open a file in a text editor. The only way you can tell whether a file has a data stream attached is by examining that file's MFT record entry. Figure 6-23 shows the MFT record of a file containing a text data stream. Note that there are two attribute 0x80 fields.

Figure 6-24 shows what larger files that are nonresident look like in an MFT record. Note that the sector boundary's checksum value (item R) must be swapped with the update sequence array's value (item C).

NTFS Compressed Files

To improve data storage on disk drives, NTFS provides compression similar to FAT Drive-Space 3, a Windows 98 compression utility. Under NTFS, files, folders, or entire volumes can be compressed. With FAT16, you can compress only a volume. On a Windows Vista, XP, 2000, or NT system, compressed data is displayed normally when you view it in Windows Explorer or applications such as Microsoft Word.

During an investigation, typically you work from an image of a compressed disk, folder, or file. Most computer forensics tools can uncompress and analyze compressed Windows data, including data compressed with the Lempel-Ziv-Huffman (LZH) algorithm and in formats such as PKZip, WinZip, and GNU gzip. Forensics tools might have difficulty with third-party compression utilities, such as the RAR format. If you identify third-party compressed data, you need to uncompress it with the utility that created it.

Offset	0	1	2	3	4	5	6	7		8	9	A	B	C	D	E	F		
024C0E00	46	49	4C	45	30	00	03	00		41	FD	AA	00	00	00	00	00	FILE0...Aýª.....
024C0E10	03	00	01	00	38	00	01	00		B8	01	00	00	00	04	00	00	....8...,.....
024C0E20	00	00	00	00	00	00	00	00		07	00	00	00	A1	00	00	00	...........¡...
024C0E30	07	00	00	00	00	00	00	00		10	00	00	00	60	00	00	00	............`...
024C0E40	00	00	00	00	00	00	00	00		48	00	00	00	18	00	00	00	........H......
024C0E50	B2	4C	07	BB	D3	7C	C9	01		14	4A	A3	3D	C8	7D	C9	01	²L.»Ó	É..J£=È}É.
024C0E60	14	4A	A3	3D	C8	7D	C9	01		96	75	F5	6A	54	7E	C9	01	.J£=È}É.	uõjT~É.
024C0E70	20	00	00	00	00	00	00	00		00	00	00	00	00	00	00	00	....
024C0E80	00	00	00	00	09	01	00	00		00	00	00	00	00	00	00	00	....
024C0E90	00	00	00	00	00	00	00	00		30	00	00	00	70	00	00	00	........0...p...
024C0EA0	00	00	00	00	00	00	02	00		54	00	00	00	18	00	01	00	........T......
024C0EB0	8A	00	00	00	00	00	01	00		B2	4C	07	BB	D3	7C	C9	01	|.......²L.»Ó|É.
024C0EC0	B2	4C	07	BB	D3	7C	C9	01		B2	4C	07	BB	D3	7C	C9	01	²L.»Ó|É.²L.»Ó|É.
024C0ED0	B2	4C	07	BB	D3	7C	C9	01		00	00	00	00	00	00	00	00	²L.»Ó	É........
024C0EE0	00	00	00	00	00	00	00	00		20	00	00	00	00	00	00	00	....
024C0EF0	09	03	42	00	46	00	31	00		5F	00	34	00	2E	00	74	00	..B.F.1._.4...t.
024C0F00	78	00	74	00	00	00	00	00		80	00	00	00	50	00	00	00	x.t....	...P...
024C0F10	00	00	18	00	00	00	05	00		38	00	00	00	18	00	00	00	........8......
024C0F20	57	65	6C	6C	20	64	6F	6E		65	20	69	73	20	62	65	74	Well done is bet
024C0F30	74	65	72	20	74	68	61	6E		20	77	65	6C	6C	20	73	61	ter than well sa
024C0F40	69	64	2E	0D	0A	20	20	42		65	6E	6A	61	6D	69	6E	20	id... Benjamin
024C0F50	46	72	61	6E	6B	6C	69	6E		80	00	00	00	58	00	00	00	Franklin	...X...
024C0F60	01	06	40	00	00	00	06	00		00	00	00	00	00	00	00	00	..@...........
024C0F70	00	00	00	00	00	00	00	00		50	00	00	00	00	00	00	00	.......P......
024C0F80	00	02	00	00	00	00	00	00		3B	00	00	00	00	00	00	00	........;.....
024C0F90	3B	00	00	00	00	00	00	00		68	00	69	00	64	00	64	00	;......h.i.d.d.
024C0FA0	65	00	6E	00	00	00	00	00		31	01	31	A2	00	00	21	E4	e.n.....1.1¢..!ä
024C0FB0	FF	FF	FF	FF	82	79	47	11		00	00	00	00	00	00	00	00	ÿÿÿÿ	yG........

Second attribute 0x80

Start of data run for second attribute
0x80 (location of hidden data stream)

Size of second attribute 0x80

Figure 6-23   A text data stream

NTFS Encrypting File System (EFS)

When Microsoft introduced Windows 2000, it added built-in encryption to NTFS called
Encrypting File System (EFS). EFS implements a **public key** and **private key** method of
encrypting files, folders, or disk volumes (partitions). Only the owner or user who encrypted
the data can access encrypted files. The owner holds the private key, and the public key is
held by a certificate authority, such as a global registry, network server, or company such as
VeriSign.

When EFS is used in Windows Vista Business Edition or higher, XP Professional, or 2000, a
recovery certificate is generated and sent to the local Windows administrator account. The
purpose of the recovery certificate is to provide a mechanism for recovering encrypted files
under EFS if there's a problem with the user's original private key. The recovery key is stored
in one of two places. When the user of a network workstation initiates EFS, the recovery key
is sent to the local domain server's administrator account. If the workstation is standalone,
the recovery key is sent to the workstation's administrator account.

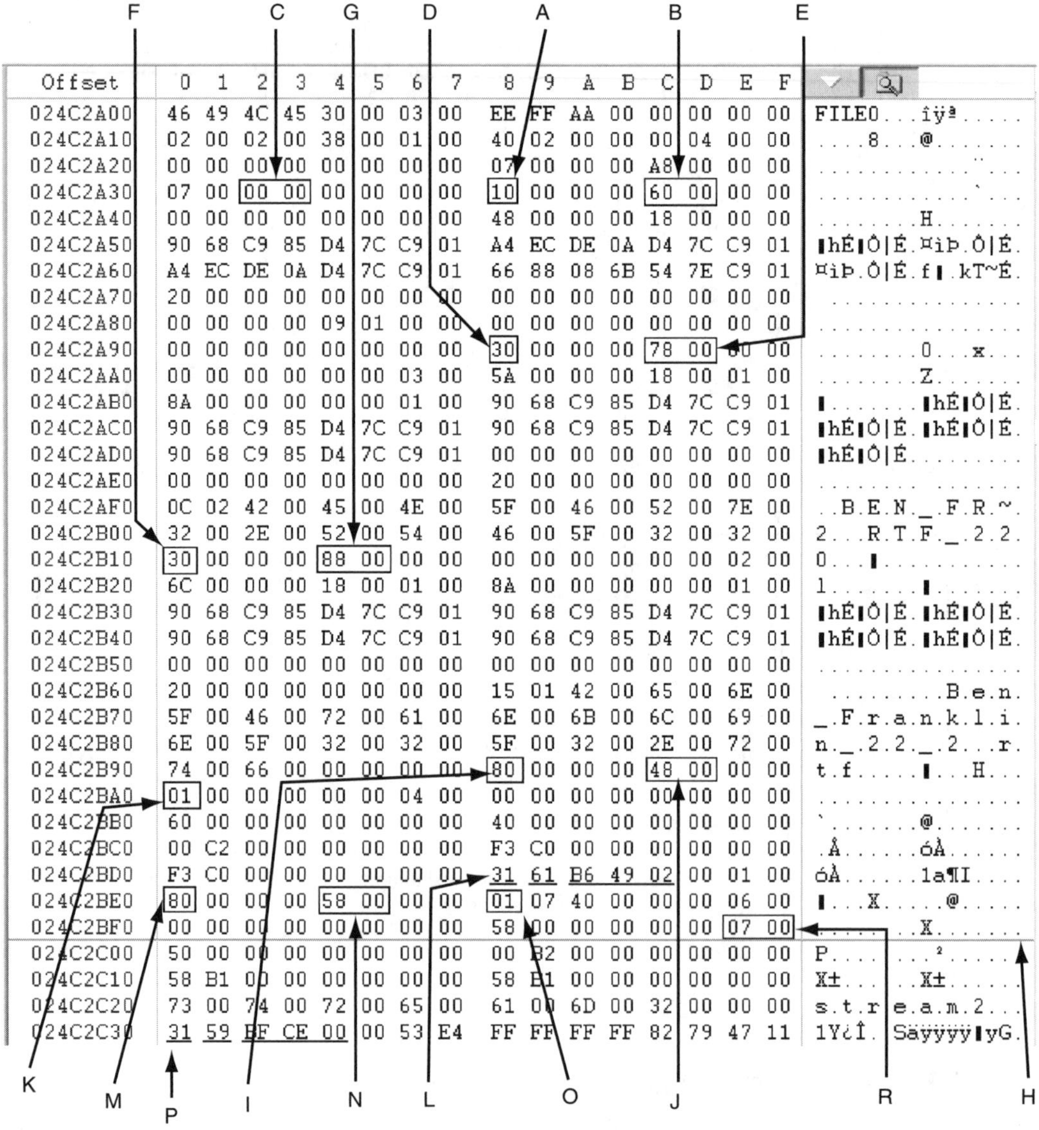

```
         F        C   G    D       A         B          E
Offset   0  1  2  3  4  5  6  7  8  9  A  B  C  D  E  F
024C2A00 46 49 4C 45 30 00 03 00 EE FF AA 00 00 00 00 00  FILE0...îÿª.....
024C2A10 02 00 02 00 38 00 01 00 40 02 00 00 00 04 00 00  ....8...@.....
024C2A20 00 00 00 00 00 00 00 00 07 00 00 00 A8 00 00 00  ................
024C2A30 07 00 00 00 00 00 00 00 10 00 00 00 60 00 00 00  ............`...
024C2A40 00 00 00 00 00 00 00 00 48 00 00 00 18 00 00 00  ........H.......
024C2A50 90 68 C9 85 D4 7C C9 01 A4 EC DE 0A D4 7C C9 01  ▌hÉ▌Ô|É.¤ìÞ.Ô|É.
024C2A60 A4 EC DE 0A D4 7C C9 01 66 88 08 6B 54 7E C9 01  ¤ìÞ.Ô|É.f▌.kT~É.
024C2A70 20 00 00 00 00 00 00 00 00 00 00 00 00 00 00 00   ...............
024C2A80 00 00 00 00 09 01 00 00 00 00 00 00 00 00 00 00  ................
024C2A90 00 00 00 00 00 00 00 00 30 00 00 00 78 00 00 00  ........0...x...
024C2AA0 00 00 00 00 00 03 00 00 5A 00 00 00 18 00 01 00  ........Z.......
024C2AB0 8A 00 00 00 00 00 01 00 90 68 C9 85 D4 7C C9 01  ▌.......▌hÉ▌Ô|É.
024C2AC0 90 68 C9 85 D4 7C C9 01 90 68 C9 85 D4 7C C9 01  ▌hÉ▌Ô|É.▌hÉ▌Ô|É.
024C2AD0 90 68 C9 85 D4 7C C9 01 00 00 00 00 00 00 00 00  ▌hÉ▌Ô|É........
024C2AE0 00 00 00 00 00 00 00 00 20 00 00 00 00 00 00 00  ........ .......
024C2AF0 0C 02 42 00 45 00 4E 00 5F 00 46 00 52 00 7E 00  ..B.E.N._.F.R.~.
024C2B00 32 00 2E 00 52 00 54 00 46 00 5F 00 32 00 32 00  2...R.T.F._.2.2.
024C2B10 30 00 00 00 88 00 00 00 00 00 00 00 00 00 02 00  0...▌..........
024C2B20 6C 00 00 00 18 00 01 00 8A 00 00 00 00 00 01 00  l.......▌......
024C2B30 90 68 C9 85 D4 7C C9 01 90 68 C9 85 D4 7C C9 01  ▌hÉ▌Ô|É.▌hÉ▌Ô|É.
024C2B40 90 68 C9 85 D4 7C C9 01 90 68 C9 85 D4 7C C9 01  ▌hÉ▌Ô|É.▌hÉ▌Ô|É.
024C2B50 00 00 00 00 00 00 00 00 00 00 00 00 00 00 00 00  ................
024C2B60 20 00 00 00 00 00 00 00 15 01 42 00 65 00 6E 00   .........B.e.n.
024C2B70 5F 00 46 00 72 00 61 00 6E 00 6B 00 6C 00 69 00  _.F.r.a.n.k.l.i.
024C2B80 6E 00 5F 00 32 00 32 00 5F 00 32 00 2E 00 72 00  n._.2.2._.2..r.
024C2B90 74 00 66 00 00 00 00 00 80 00 00 00 48 00 00 00  t.f.....▌...H...
024C2BA0 01 00 00 00 00 00 04 00 00 00 00 00 00 00 00 00  ................
024C2BB0 60 00 00 00 00 00 00 00 40 00 00 00 00 00 00 00  `.......@.......
024C2BC0 00 C2 00 00 00 00 00 00 F3 C0 00 00 00 00 00 00  .Â......óÀ......
024C2BD0 F3 C0 00 00 00 00 00 00 31 61 B6 49 02 00 01 00  óÀ......1a¶I....
024C2BE0 80 00 00 00 58 00 00 00 01 07 40 00 00 00 06 00  ▌...X.....@.....
024C2BF0 00 00 00 00 00 00 00 00 58 00 00 00 00 00 07 00  ........X.....X.
024C2C00 50 00 00 00 00 00 00 00 00 B2 00 00 00 00 00 00  P........²......
024C2C10 58 B1 00 00 00 00 00 00 58 B1 00 00 00 00 00 00  X±......X±......
024C2C20 73 00 74 00 72 00 65 00 61 00 6D 00 32 00 00 00  s.t.r.e.a.m.2...
024C2C30 31 59 BF CE 00 00 53 E4 FF FF FF FF 82 79 47 11  1Y¿Î..Säÿÿÿÿ▌yG.
```

        K   M   P   I   N   L   O   J   R   H

A: Attribute 0x10
B: Attribute 0x10 size
C: Update sequence array
D: Attribute 0x30 short filename
E: Attribute 0x30 size short filename
F: Attribute 0x30 long filename
G: Attribute 0x30 size long filename
H: Sector boundary
I: First attribute 0x80

J: Size of attribute
K: Nonresident flag
L: Start of first data run
M: Second attribute 0x80
N: Size of attribute
O: Nonresident flag
P: Start of second data run
R: Sector boundary's checksum

Figure 6-24 A nonresident data stream

Users can apply EFS to files stored on their local workstations or a remote server. Windows 2000 and XP decrypt the data automatically when the user or an application the user runs accesses an EFS file, folder, or disk volume. In Windows Server 2003 and 2008, users can grant other users access to their EFS data. If a user copies a file encrypted with EFS to a folder that isn't encrypted, the copied data is saved in unencrypted format.

EFS Recovery Key Agent

The Recovery Key Agent implements the recovery certificate, which is in the Windows administrator account. Windows administrators can recover a key in two ways: through Windows or from an MS-DOS command prompt. These three commands are available from the MS-DOS command prompt:

- Cipher
- Copy
- Efsrecvr (used to decrypt EFS files)

For information on how to use these commands, enter the question mark switch after each command. For example, type cipher /? and press Enter. Encrypted files aren't part of FAT12, FAT16, or FAT32 file systems, so Cipher and Efsrecvr work only on NTFS systems running Windows 2000 Professional, XP Professional, and Vista Business Edition or higher. The Copy command, however, works in both FAT and NTFS.

In Vista Business Edition and higher, Microsoft has added features to the Cipher command that aren't available when encrypting data in Windows Explorer. One is the /w switch that overwrites all deleted files, making them impossible to recover with data recovery or forensics carving tools.

If you copy an encrypted file from an EFS-enabled NTFS disk or folder to a non-EFS storage media or folder, it's unencrypted automatically.

To recover an encrypted EFS file, a user can e-mail it or copy the file to the administrator. The administrator can then run the Recovery Key Agent function to restore the file. For additional information, review the Microsoft Windows Resource Kit documentation (*www.microsoft.com/windows/reskits/default.asp*) for the latest procedures on how to recover EFS files.

Deleting NTFS Files

Typically, you use Windows Explorer to delete files from a disk. When a file is deleted in Windows NT and later, the OS renames it and moves it to the Recycle Bin. Another method is using the Del (delete) MS-DOS command. This method doesn't rename and move the file to the Recycle Bin, but it eliminates the file from the MFT listing in the same way FAT does.

When you delete a file in Windows Explorer, you can restore it from the Recycle Bin. The OS takes the following steps when you delete a file or a folder in Windows Explorer:

1. Windows changes the filename and moves the file to a subfolder with a unique identity in the Recycle Bin.

2. Windows stores information about the original path and filename in the **Info2 file**, which is the control file for the Recycle Bin. It contains ASCII data, Unicode data, and the date and time of deletion for each file or folder.

NTFS files deleted at an MS-DOS command prompt function much like FAT files. (The following steps also apply when a user empties the Recycle Bin.) The OS performs the following tasks:

1. The associated clusters are designated as free—that is, marked as available for new data.

2. The $Bitmap file attribute in the MFT is updated to reflect the file's deletion, showing that this space is available.

3. The file's record in the MFT is marked as being available.

4. VCN/LCN cluster locations linked to deleted nonresident files are then removed from the original MFT record.

5. A run list is maintained in the MFT of all cluster locations on the disk for nonresident files. When the list of links is deleted, any reference to the links is lost.

NTFS is more efficient than FAT at reclaiming deleted space. Deleted files are overwritten more quickly.

Understanding Whole Disk Encryption

In recent years, there has been more concern about loss of **personal identity information (PII)** and trade secrets caused by computer theft. Company PII might consist of employees' full names, home addresses, and Social Security numbers. With this information, criminals could easily apply for credit card accounts in these employees' names. Trade secrets are any information a business keeps confidential because it provides a competitive edge over other companies. The inadvertent public release of this information could devastate a business's competitive edge.

Of particular concern is the theft of laptop computers and other handheld devices, such as PDAs. If data on these devices isn't secured properly, the owners could be liable for any damages incurred, such as stolen identities, credit card fraud, or loss of business caused by the release of trade secrets to the competition. Because of the PII problem, many states have enacted laws requiring any person or business to notify potential victims of the loss as soon as possible. To help prevent loss of information, software vendors, including Microsoft, now provide whole disk encryption (WDE, introduced in Chapter 4). This feature creates new challenges in examining and recovering data from drives.

Current whole disk encryption tools offer the following features that computer forensics examiners should be aware of:

- Preboot authentication, such as a single sign-on password, fingerprint scan, or token (USB device)
- Full or partial disk encryption with secure hibernation, such as activating a password-protected screen saver
- Advanced encryption algorithms, such as AES and IDEA
- Key management function that uses a challenge-and-response method to reset passwords or passphrases
- A **Trusted Platform Module (TPM)** microchip to generate encryption keys and authenticate logins

Whole disk encryption tools encrypt each sector of a drive separately. Many of these tools encrypt the drive's boot sector to prevent any efforts to bypass the secured drive's partition. To examine an encrypted drive, you must decrypt it first. An encryption tool's key management function typically uses a challenge-and-response method for decryption, which means you must run a vendor-specific program to decrypt the drive. Many vendors use a bootable CD or USB drive that prompts for a **one-time passphrase** generated by the key management function. If you need to decrypt the same computer a second time, you need a new one-time passphrase.

The biggest drawback to decrypting a drive is the several hours required to read, decrypt, and write each sector. The larger the drive, the longer decryption takes. After you've decrypted the drive, however, you can use standard acquisition methods to retrieve data.

Examining Microsoft BitLocker

Microsoft's utility for protecting drive data is called BitLocker, available only with Vista Enterprise and Ultimate editions. BitLocker's current hardware and software requirements are as follows:

- A computer capable of running Windows Vista
- The TPM microchip, version 1.2 or newer
- A computer BIOS compliant with **Trusted Computing Group (TCG)**
- Two NTFS partitions for the OS and an active system volume with 1.5 GB available space
- The BIOS configured so that the hard drive boots first before checking the CD/DVD drive or other bootable peripherals

For more information on BitLocker, see *http://technet.microsoft.com/ en-us/windows/aa905065.aspx* or go to *http://technet.microsoft.com* and search on BitLocker.

Examining Third-Party Disk Encryption Tools

Several vendors offer third-party WDE utilities that often have more features than BitLocker. For example, BitLocker can encrypt only NTFS drives. If you want to encrypt a FAT drive, you need a third-party solution. Decrypting with third-party utilities typically follows the same process as in BitLocker, with some exceptions. Before using one of these utilities, make sure you investigate its features thoroughly. The following list describes some available third-party WDE utilities:

- PGP Whole Disk Encryption (*www.pgp.com/products/wholediskencryption/index.html*) can be used on PCs, laptops, and removable media to secure an entire disk volume. This tool works in Windows 2000, XP Professional (SP1 and SP2), and Mac OS X 10.4 and can also encrypt FAT volumes.

- Voltage SecureDisk (*www.voltage.com/products/index.htm*) is designed for an enterprise computing environment.

- Utimaco SafeGuard Easy (*http://americas.utimaco.com/safeguard_easy/*) provides whole disk encryption for NTFS and FAT file systems.

- Jetico BestCrypt Volume Encryption (*www.jetico.com*) provides whole disk encryption for older MS-DOS and Windows NTFS systems.

- SoftWinter Sentry 2020 for Windows XP (*www.softwinter.com/sentry_nt.html*) is an inexpensive disk encryption tool. It doesn't encrypt the entire drive. To secure data, it creates a virtual drive saved to a large data file. This virtual file is similar to MS-DOS DoubleSpace, Stacker, or DriveSpace. Recovering deleted data from this type of encrypted volume file might be difficult or impossible because volume file space is overwritten quickly.

In addition to commercial tools, several open-source tools are available to encrypt files, folders, and entire disk volumes on Microsoft file systems. These tools have no standards other than meeting the requirements of open-source software. Most create a virtual encrypted disk volume, similar to the commercial product Sentry 2020. The following list describes some available open-source encryption tools:

- TrueCrypt (*www.truecrypt.org*) creates a virtual encrypted volume—a file mounted as though it were a disk drive. Data is encrypted automatically and in real time.

- CrossCrypt (*www.scherrer.cc/crypt/*) also creates a virtual encrypted volume and provides Filedisk, a command-line utility with options for creating, mounting, dismounting, and encrypting volumes.

- FreeOTFE (on-the-fly encryption, *www.freeotfe.org*), like other open-source encryption tools, creates a virtual disk that can encrypt data with several popular algorithms. FreeOTFE can be used in Windows 2000, XP, and Vista as well as with PDAs.

With improved encryption methods, extracting digital evidence will become more difficult. Because of these challenges, you need to know how to make remote live acquisitions, discussed in Chapter 11.

Understanding the Windows Registry

When Microsoft created Windows 95, it consolidated initialization (.ini) files into the **Registry**, a database that stores hardware and software configuration information, network connections, user preferences (including usernames and passwords), and setup information. The Registry has been updated and is still used in Windows Vista.

For investigative purposes, the Registry can contain valuable evidence. To view the Registry, you can use the Regedit (Registry Editor) program for Windows 9x and Regedt32 for Windows 2000, XP, and Vista. For more information on how to use Regedit and Regedt32, see the Microsoft Windows Resource Kit documentation for the OS. You can find information at *http://support.microsoft.com/kb/256986* and *http://technet.microsoft.com/en-us/library/cc775519(WS.10).aspx*.

For more information on Regedit and Regedt32, visit *http://support. microsoft.com/kb/141377* and *http://msdn.microsoft.com/en-us/library/ aa965884(VS.85).aspx.*

In general, you can use the Edit, Find menu command in Registry Editor to locate entries that might contain trace evidence, such as information identifying the last person who logged on to the computer, which is usually stored in user account information. Windows 9x systems don't record a user's logon information reliably, but you can find related user information, such as network logon data, by searching for all occurrences of "username" or application licenses. You can also use the Registry to determine the most recently accessed files and peripheral devices. In addition, all installed programs store information in the Registry, such as Web sites accessed, recent files, and even chat rooms accessed.

As a computing investigator, you should explore the Registry of all Windows systems. On a live system, be careful not to alter any Registry setting to avoid corrupting the system and possibly making it unbootable.

Several third-party tools, such as FTK Registry Viewer, are also available for accessing the Registry.

Exploring the Organization of the Windows Registry

The Windows Registry is organized in a specific way that has changed slightly with each new version of Windows. However, the major Registry sections have been consistent, with some minor changes, since Windows 2000; they're slightly different in Windows 9x/Me. Before proceeding, review the following list of Registry terminology:

- *Registry*—A collection of files containing system and user information.

- *Registry Editor*—A Windows utility for viewing and modifying data in the Registry. There are two Registry Editors: Regedit and Regedt32 (introduced in Windows 2000).

- *HKEY*—Windows splits the Registry into categories with the prefix HKEY_. Windows 9x systems have six HKEY categories and Windows 2000 and later have five. Windows programmers refer to the "H" as the handle for the key.

- *Key*—Each HKEY contains folders referred to as keys. Keys can contain other key folders or values.

- *Subkey*—A key displayed under another key is a subkey, similar to a subfolder in Windows Explorer.

- *Branch*—A key and its contents, including subkeys, make up a branch in the Registry.

- *Value*—A name and value in a key; it's similar to a file and its data content.

- *Default value*—All keys have a default value that may or may not contain data.

- *Hives*—Hives are specific branches in HKEY_USER and HKEY_LOCAL_MACHINE. Hive branches in HKEY_LOCAL_MACHINE\Software are SAM, Security, Components, and System. For HKEY_USER, each user account has its own hive link to Ntuser.dat.

The next piece of the puzzle is learning where data files that the Registry reads are located. The number of files the Registry uses depends on the Windows version. In Windows 9x/Me, it uses only two files; in Windows NT, 2000, XP, and Vista, it uses six files. When examining Registry data from a suspect drive, you need to know where these files are located so that you can extract them and analyze their content. You can find these files with tools such as AccessData Registry Viewer. Table 6-6 shows how Registry data files are organized and explains these files' purposes in different versions of Windows.

Table 6-6 Registry file locations and purposes

Filename and location	Purpose of file
Windows 9x/Me	
Windows\System.dat	User-protected storage area; contains installed program settings, usernames and passwords associated with installed programs, and system settings
Windows\User.dat Windows\profile*UserAccount*	Contains the most recently used (MRU) files list and desktop configuration settings; every user account created on the system has its own user data file
Windows NT, 2000, XP, and Vista	
Documents and Settings*user-account*\Ntuser.dat (in Vista, Users*UserAccount*\Ntuser.dat)	User-protected storage area; contains the MRU files list and desktop configuration settings
Winnt\system32\config\Default	Contains the computer's system settings
Winnt\system32\config\SAM	Contains user account management and security settings
Winnt\system32\config\Security	Contains the computer's security settings
Winnt\system32\config\Software	Contains installed programs settings and associated usernames and passwords
Winnt\system32\config\System	Contains additional computer system settings

When viewing the Registry with Registry Editor, you can see the HKEYs used in Windows (see Figure 6-25).

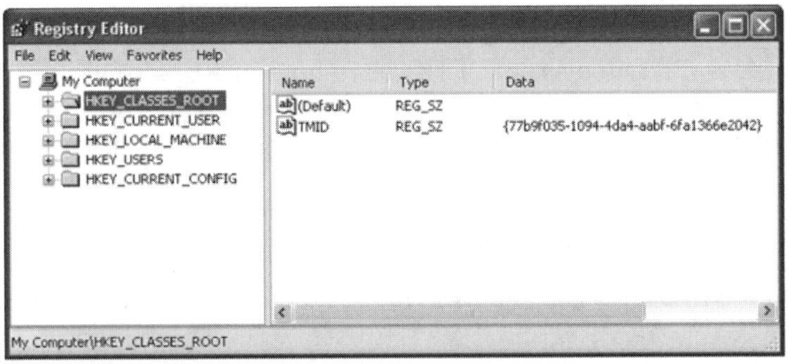

Figure 6-25   Viewing HKEYs in Windows XP Registry Editor

Table 6-7 describes the functions of Registry HKEYs.

Table 6-7   Registry HKEYs and their functions

HKEY	Function
HKEY_CLASS_ROOT	A symbolic link to HKEY_LOCAL_MACHINE\SOFTWARE\Classes; provides file type and file extension information, URL protocol prefixes, and so forth
HKEY_CURRENT_USER	A symbolic link to HKEY_USERS; stores settings for the currently logged-on user
HKEY_LOCAL_MACHINE	Contains information about installed hardware and software
HKEY_USERS	Stores information for the currently logged-on user; only one key in this HKEY is linked to HKEY_CURRENT_USER
HKEY_CURRENT_CONFIG	A symbolic link to HKEY_LOCAL_MACHINE\SYSTEM\CurrentControlSet\ Hardware Profile\xxxx (with xxxx representing the current hardware profile); contains hardware configuration settings
HKEY_DYN_DATA	Used only in Windows 9x/Me systems; stores hardware configuration settings

> **TIP**
>
> For additional information on the Registry, see *http://support.microsoft.com/default.aspx?scid=kb;EN-US;256986* and *www.computerhope.com/registry.htm*.

Although you can examine the Registry in a variety of ways, one of the easiest is loading an image of a Windows machine into AccessData FTK and then clicking File, Registry Viewer from the menu, which enables you to view HKEY data. The demo version of Registry Viewer disables the following features, however:

- *Common areas*—Registry keys containing useful information, such as usernames, passwords, and Web browser history information
- *Report window*—Displaying certain keys selected for a report
- *Generating a report*—Copying and adding selected keys to an FTK report
- *Protected storage*—Viewing Registry areas containing confidential user information, such as password-protected Web sites, username/password combinations, and e-mail passwords

Examining the Windows Registry

Some forensics tools, such as ProDiscover and FTK, have built-in Registry viewers. For this next activity, your company's Legal Department has asked you to search for any references to the Superior Bicycles company and e-mail addresses containing the name Denise. A paralegal tells you the home page for Superior Bicycles (*www.superiorbicycles.biz*) and gives you a ProDiscover .eve file containing the image of a Windows 98 computer belonging to a Superior Bicycle employee named Denise Robinson.

For this activity, you use ProDiscover Basic to extract System.dat and User.dat from the image file, and then use AccessData Registry Viewer to see what information you can find in these files. If you find any items of interest, you copy the Registry path and name to a text file that you can give to the paralegal. Although the file is an image of a Windows 98 computer, you can use Windows XP or Vista to run ProDiscover Basic and AccessData Registry Viewer in the following activities. Registry Viewer can run in Windows 9x and later and analyze all Windows Registry versions.

Before beginning this activity, extract compressed files from the Chap06 folder on the book's DVD to your *Work*\Chap06\Chapter folder. If necessary, create the Chap06 and Chapter folders first. The work folder pathname you see in screenshots might differ.

To extract Registry files with ProDiscover Basic, follow these steps:

1. Start ProDiscover Basic with the **Run as administrator** option. If the Launch Dialog dialog box opens, click **Cancel**.

2. Click **File, New Project** from the menu.

3. In the New Project dialog box, type **InChap06** in the Project Number text box and the Project File Name text box, and then click **OK**.

4. In the tree view of the main window, click to expand **Add** and then click **Image File**.

5. In the Open dialog box, navigate to your work folder, click the **GCFI-Win98.eve** image file, and click **Open**. Click **Yes** in the Auto Image Checksum message box, if necessary.

6. Click the **Search** toolbar button. In the Search dialog box, click the **Content Search** tab. Click the **Search for files named** option button, and in the Search text box, type **system.dat** and **user.dat**. Under Select the Disk(s)/Image(s) you want to search in, click the image file (see Figure 6-26), and then click **OK**.

7. In the search results, click the check box next to the SYSTEM.DAT file. When the Add Comment dialog box opens, type **Registry files to extract**, click the **Apply to all items** check box, and then click **OK** (see Figure 6-27).

8. Click the check box next to the USER.DAT file, and then click **Tools, Copy Selected Files** from the menu. In the Choose Destination dialog box, click **Browse**. In the Browse for Folder dialog box, navigate to and click your work folder, and then click **OK**. Click **OK** again in the Choose Destination dialog box.

9. Exit ProDiscover Basic, saving the project if prompted.

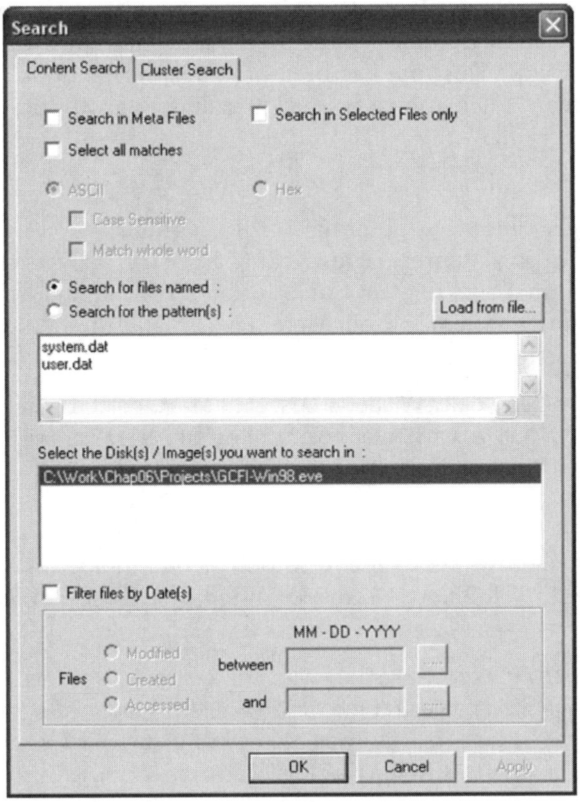

Figure 6-26 Searching for Registry files

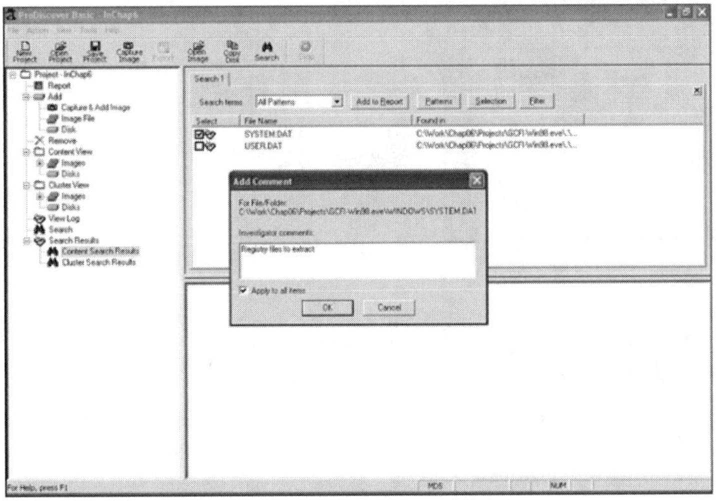

Figure 6-27 Selecting files in the search results

To extract Registry files for other Windows OSs, refer to Table 6-6 for the filenames and path locations. Next, you learn how to examine extracted Registry files with the demo version of AccessData Registry Viewer. This tool has been provided on the book's DVD, so copy and install it on your system. When you've finished installing Registry Viewer, follow these steps to examine a Registry file:

1. Start Notepad or another text editor.

2. Start Registry Viewer by clicking **Start**, pointing to **All Programs**, pointing to **AccessData**, pointing to **Registry Viewer**, right-clicking **Registry Viewer**, clicking **Run as administrator**, and then clicking **Continue**. If you see a message stating "...cannot find ... C:\windows\system32\CodeMeter.exe..." and then "No dongle found," click **OK** to start the program.

In Windows XP and older Windows OSs, click **Start**, point to **All Programs**, point to **AccessData**, point to **Registry Viewer**, and click **Registry Viewer**.

3. In Registry Viewer's main window, click the **Open** toolbar button and navigate to *Work*\Chap06\Chapter\GCFI-Win98.eve Recovered\Windows. Click **USER.DAT**, and then click **Open**.

When ProDiscover extracts Registry files, it creates a subfolder with the image file's name and the suffix Recovered, followed by the folder path where the file was recovered. In the previous activity, the Registry files were originally located on the suspect's drive at   C:\Windows. ProDiscover maintains this directory path prefaced by the image filename.

4. Click **Edit, Find** from the menu. In the Find dialog box, type **superior** in the Find what text box (see Figure 6-28), and then click **Find Next**.

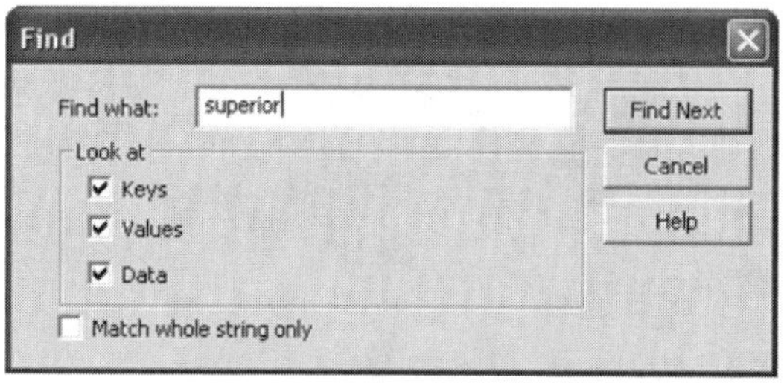

![Find dialog box with "superior" typed in the Find what text box. Look at section shows Keys, Values, and Data checked. Match whole string only is unchecked. Buttons: Find Next, Cancel, Help.]

Figure 6-28   Entering a search term in Registry Viewer

5. When the search results are displayed, right-click the folder in the left pane containing the key and click **Copy Key Name** (see Figure 6-29). Paste it into Notepad.

6. Back in Registry Viewer, press **F3** to search for the next occurrence of the keyword "superior," and copy and paste the key name as before. Repeat this step until you find no more occurrences.

7. Click **USER.DAT** in the left pane, and then click **Edit, Find** from the menu again. This time, type **denise** in the Find what text box and click **Find Next**.

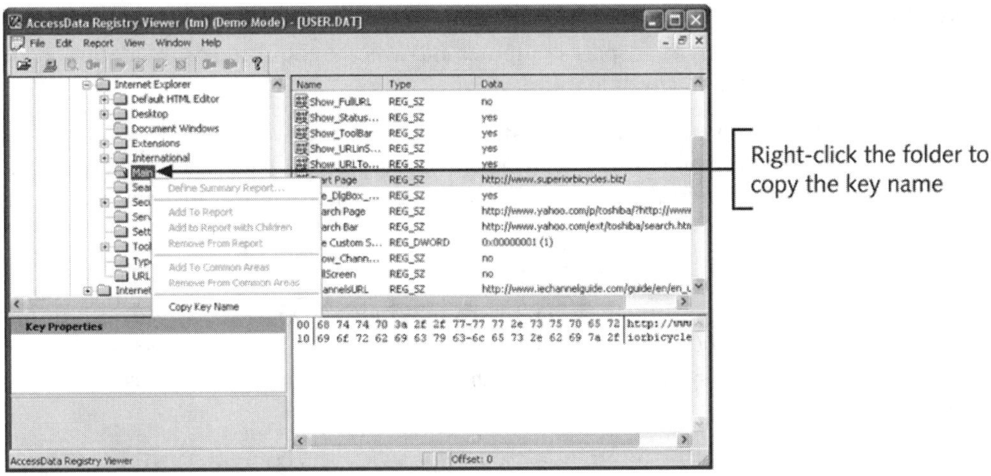

Right-click the folder to copy the key name

Figure 6-29 Copying a key name in Registry Viewer

8. When the search results are displayed, right-click the folder in the left pane containing the key, click **Copy Key Name**, and paste it into Notepad. Press **F3** to search for the next occurrence of the keyword "denise," and copy and paste the key name as before. Repeat until no more occurrences are found.

9. Exit Registry Viewer by clicking **File, Exit** from the menu, and then clicking **Yes** in the Exit Registry Viewer dialog box.

10. Delete any redundant folder names in Notepad (refer to Figure 6-30), and save this text document as **InChap6-reg-search.txt**. Exit Notepad.

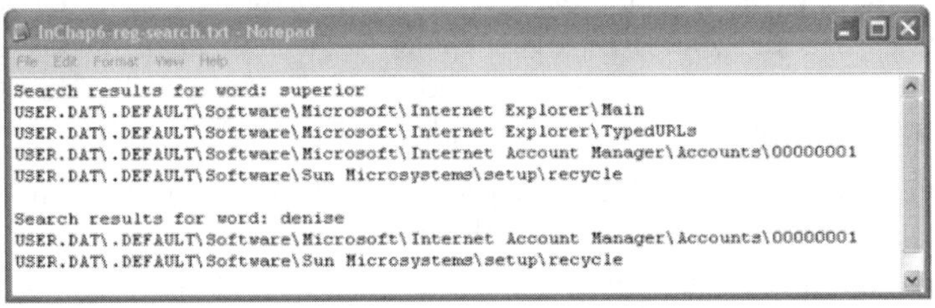

Figure 6-30 The search results showing paths for keys of interest

An extensive amount of information is stored in the Registry. With Registry data, you can ascertain when users went online, when they accessed a printer, and many other events. A lot of the information in the Registry is beyond the scope of this book, so you're encouraged to expand your knowledge by attending training sessions or classes.

Understanding Microsoft Startup Tasks

You should have a good understanding of what happens to disk data at startup. In some investigations, you must preserve data on the disk exactly as the suspect last used it. Any access to a computer system after it was used for illicit purposes alters your disk evidence. As you learned in Chapter 4, altering disk data lessens its evidentiary quality considerably. In some instances, accessing a suspect computer incorrectly could make the digital evidence corrupt and less credible for any litigation.

In the following sections, you learn what files are accessed when Windows starts. This information helps you determine when a suspect's computer was last accessed, which is particularly important with computers that might have been used after an incident was reported.

Startup in Windows NT and Later

Although Windows NT is much different from Windows 95 and 98, the startup method for the NT OSs—NT, 2000, XP, and Vista—is about the same. There are some minor differences in how certain system start files function, but basically, they accomplish the same orderly startup.

All NTFS computers perform the following steps when the computer is turned on:

- Power-on self test (POST)
- Initial startup
- Boot loader
- Hardware detection and configuration
- Kernel loading
- User logon

Windows OSs use the files discussed in the following sections to start. These files can be located on the system partition or boot partition.

Startup Files for Windows Vista
When Microsoft developed Vista, it updated the boot process to use the new Extensible Firmware Interface (EFI) as well as the older BIOS system. The EFI boot firmware is designed to provide better protection against malware than BIOS does. EFI Vista's boot processes have also changed since Windows XP. The Ntldr program in Windows XP used to load the OS has been replaced with these three boot utilities:

- *Bootmgr.exe*—The Windows Boot Manager program controls boot flow and allows booting multiple OSs, such as booting Vista along with XP.
- *Winload.exe*—The Windows Vista OS loader installs the kernel and the Hardware Abstraction Layer (HAL) and loads memory with the necessary boot drivers.
- *Winresume.exe*—This tool restarts Vista after the OS goes into hibernation mode.

Windows Vista also includes a tool for modifying boot options called Boot Configuration Data (BCD); it replaces Windows XP's Boot.ini file. For additional information on EFI, see *www.microsoft.com/whdc/system/platform/firmware/bcd.mspx*.

Startup Files for Windows XP
Unless otherwise specified, most startup files for Windows XP are located in the root folder of the system partition. The **NT Loader (Ntldr)** file loads the OS. When the system is powered on, Ntldr reads the **Boot.ini** file, which displays a boot menu. After you select the mode to boot to, Boot.ini runs Ntoskrnl.exe and reads Bootvid.dll, Hal.dll, and startup device drivers. Boot.ini specifies the Windows XP path installation and contains options for selecting the Windows version.

If a system has multiple boot OSs, including older ones such as Windows 9x or DOS, Ntldr reads **BootSect.dos** (a hidden file), which contains the address (boot sector location) of each OS.

When the boot selection is made, Ntldr runs **NTDetect.com**, a 16-bit real-mode program that queries the system for device and configuration data, and then passes its findings to Ntldr. This program identifies components and values on the computer system, such as the following:

- CMOS time and date value
- Buses attached to the motherboard, such as Industry Standard Architecture (ISA) or Peripheral Component Interconnect (PCI)
- Disk drives connected to the system
- Mouse input devices connected to the system
- Parallel ports connected to the system

NTBootdd.sys is the device driver that allows the OS to communicate with SCSI or ATA drives that aren't related to the BIOS. (On some workstations, a SCSI disk is used as the primary boot disk.) Controllers that don't use Interrupt 13 (INT-13) use NTBootdd.sys. It runs in privileged processor mode with direct access to hardware and system data.

Ntoskrnl.exe is the Windows XP OS kernel, located in the *%system-root%*\Windows\ System32 folder.

Hal.dll is the Hardware Abstraction Layer (HAL) dynamic link library, located in the *%system-root%*\Windows\System32 folder. The HAL allows the OS kernel to communicate with the computer's hardware.

At startup, data and instruction code are moved in and out of the **Pagefile.sys** file to optimize the amount of physical RAM available.

The HKEY_LOCAL_MACHINE\SYSTEM Registry key contains information the OS requires to start system services and devices. This system Registry file is located in the *%system-root%*\Windows\System32\Config\System folder.

Device drivers contain instructions for the OS for hardware devices, such as the keyboard, mouse, and video card, and are stored in the *%system-root%*\Windows\System32\Drivers folder.

To identify the specific path for *%system-root%* at a DOS prompt, type Set with no switches or parameters and press Enter. This command displays all current *%system-root%* paths.

Windows XP System Files Next, you need to examine the core OS files that Windows XP, 2000, and NT use, usually located in *%system-root%*\Windows\System32 or *%system-root%*\Winnt\System32. Table 6-8 lists the essential files Windows XP uses. Although a few of these files are repeats of previous table entries, you should be aware of their key roles.

Table 6-8 Windows XP system files

Filename	Description
Ntoskrnl.exe	The XP executable and kernel
Ntkrnlpa.exe	The physical address support program for accessing more than 4 GB of physical RAM
Hal.dll	The Hardware Abstraction Layer (described earlier)
Win32k.sys	The kernel-mode portion of the Win32subsystem
Ntdll.dll	System service dispatch stubs to executable functions and internal support functions
Kernel32.dll	Core Win32 subsystem DLL file
Advapi32.dll	Core Win32 subsystem DLL file
User32.dll	Core Win32 subsystem DLL file
Gdi32.dll	Core Win32 subsystem DLL file

Contamination Concerns with Windows XP When you start a Windows XP NTFS workstation, several files are accessed immediately. When any of these or other related OS files are accessed at startup, the last access date and time stamp for the files change to the current date and time. This change destroys any potential evidence that shows when a Windows XP workstation was last used. For this reason, you should have a strong working knowledge of the startup process.

Startup in Windows 9x/Me

Like Windows XP, system files in Windows 9x/Me containing valuable information can be altered easily during startup, which affects their evidentiary value and integrity. Windows 9x OSs have similar boot processes. Windows Me is similar, too, with one important exception: You can't boot to a true MS-DOS mode. When you're conducting a computing investigation, being able to boot to MS-DOS is preferred, especially if you're running a later version of Windows 95 OEM SR2 (version 4.00.1111) or a newer one in which the MS-DOS boot mode can read and write to a FAT32 disk.

Windows 9x OSs have two modes: **DOS protected-mode interface (DPMI)** and **protected-mode GUI** (serves the same purpose as Config.sys in MS-DOS). Many older computer forensics tools use DPMI mode and can't be run from a Windows command prompt window because they use certain disk accesses that conflict with the GUI. (See *www.webopedia.com/ TERM/D/DOS_Protected_Mode_Interface.html* for more details.)

The system files Windows 9x uses have their origin in MS-DOS 6.22. The **Io.sys** file communicates between a computer's BIOS, the hardware, and the OS kernel. During the boot phase of a Windows 9x system, Io.sys monitors the keyboard for an F8 keystroke. If F8 is pressed during startup, Io.sys loads the Windows Startup menu, which has options such as booting to Windows normally and running in Safe mode to perform maintenance.

Option 5 in the Windows Startup menu (see Figure 6-31) is "Command prompt only." By selecting this option, you can go directly to a Windows 9x version of MS-DOS.

You need to be familiar with MS-DOS 6.22 or Windows 9x MS-DOS. **Msdos.sys** is a hidden text file containing startup options for Windows 9x. In MS-DOS 6.22, this file is the actual OS kernel. In Windows 9x, Msdos.sys has a different role; it has replaced the Autoexec.bat and Config.sys files used in MS-DOS 6.22. The Msdos.sys file is usually located in the root folder of the C drive.

Microsoft Windows 98 Startup Menu

1. Normal
2. Logged (\BOOTLOG.TXT)
3. Safe mode
4. Step-by-step confirmation
5. Command prompt only
6. Save mode command prompt only

Enter a choice: 1

Figure 6-31   Windows 9x startup options

The **Command.com** file provides a command prompt when booting to MS-DOS mode (DPMI). You can run a limited number of MS-DOS commands built into Command.com, called internal MS-DOS commands and described in the following list:

- *Dir*—List directories.
- *Cd (Chdir)*—Change directory location.
- *Cls*—Clear the screen of all output.
- *Date*—Display the CMOS calendar value.
- *Copy*—Copy a file from one location to another.
- *Del (Erase)*—Erase a file.
- *Md (Mkdir)*—Create a subdirectory.
- *Path*—Define where to find other commands and programs.
- *Prompt*—Define what your MS-DOS prompt looks like.
- *Rd (Rmdir)*—Erase a directory or folder.
- *Set*—Define or remove environmental variables.
- *Time*—Display the CMOS clock value.
- *Type*—List the content of a text file on screen.
- *Ver*—Get the MS-DOS version number in which you're working.
- *Vol*—Display the volume label of the disk drive.

Understanding MS-DOS Startup Tasks

MS-DOS uses three files when starting, with the same names as in Windows 9x/Me: Io.sys, Msdos.sys, and Command.com. Two other files are then used to configure MS-DOS at startup: Config.sys and Autoexec.bat. Although MS-DOS and Windows 9x use some of the same startup filenames, there are some important differences between the files in these OSs.

Io.sys is the first file loaded after the ROM bootstrap loader finds the disk drive. Io.sys then resides in RAM and provides the basic input and output service for all MS-DOS functions.

Msdos.sys is the second program to load into RAM immediately after Io.sys. As mentioned, this file is the actual OS kernel, not a text file as in Windows 9x and Me. After Msdos.sys finishes setting up DOS services, it looks for the Config.sys file to configure device drivers and other settings. **Config.sys** is a text file containing commands that typically run only at system startup to enhance the computer's DOS configuration.

Msdos.sys then loads Command.com, which contains the same internal DOS commands in MS-DOS 6.22 as in Windows 9x. As the loading of Command.com nears completion, Msdos.sys looks for and loads **Autoexec.bat**, a batch file containing customized settings for MS-DOS that runs automatically. In this batch file, you can define the default path and set environmental variables, such as temporary directories. MS-DOS then accesses and resets the last access dates and times on files when powered up.

Other Disk Operating Systems

Years ago, other microcomputer OSs, such as Control Program for Microprocessors (CP/M), Digital Research Disk Operating System (DR-DOS), and Personal Computer Disk Operating System (PC-DOS) were used. Of these OSs, only DR-DOS is still available. As mentioned in Chapter 1, if you encounter an old computer running one of these OSs, you might need to call on your network of experts to research, explore, and test the OS. This section summarizes some features of these OSs.

In the 1970s, Digital Research created the first nonspecific microcomputer OS, CP/M, which had a unique file system. Computers using CP/M had 8-inch floppy drives and didn't support hard drives. The CPU was the Zilog Z-80, which could access up to 64 KB RAM. In the early 1980s, IBM supplied an expansion card with a built-in Z-80 CPU that allowed users to process applications available for CP/M.

After Microsoft developed MS-DOS, Digital Research created DR-DOS in 1988 to compete with that OS; it used FAT12 and FAT16 and had a richer command environment than MS-DOS. DR-DOS is now sold primarily as an embedded OS for out-of-the-box ROM or Flash ROM systems.

When IBM created the first PC using the Intel 8088 processor, it contracted with Microsoft, then a startup company, to create an OS. In 1981, Microsoft purchased 86-DOS from Seattle Computing; it could run on the Intel 8088 16-bit processor and was a modification of CP/M. Microsoft supplied 86-DOS to IBM for use on its PCs, and IBM called it PC-DOS. IBM maintained upgrades to PC-DOS until Microsoft released Windows 95.

PC-DOS works much like MS-DOS, although its OS files are slightly different. For example, Io.sys is called Ibmio.sys, and Msdos.sys is called Ibmdos.sys. However, PC-DOS uses FAT12 and FAT16, so accessing data is no different from working with MS-DOS.

For more information on DOS commands and batch files, see Appendix D.

Understanding Virtual Machines

New versions of OSs and applications are released frequently, but older versions are still widely used. As an investigator, you'll be faced with the challenge of having enough resources to support the variety of software you're likely to encounter. More companies are turning to virtualization to reduce the cost of hardware purchases, so the number of investigations involving virtual machines will increase as this practice continues.

As an investigator, you might need a virtual server to view legacy systems, and you might need to forensically examine suspects' virtual machines. **Virtual machines** enable you run another OS on an existing physical computer (known as the host computer) by emulating a computer's hardware environment. Figure 6-32 shows a VMware Server virtual machine running Windows XP Professional on the desktop of a host computer. Typically, a virtual machine consists of several files. The two main files are the configuration file containing hardware settings, such as RAM, network configurations, port settings, and so on, and the virtual hard disk file, which contains the boot loader program, OS files, and users' data files. (Depending on the virtualization software, these files might be organized differently.)

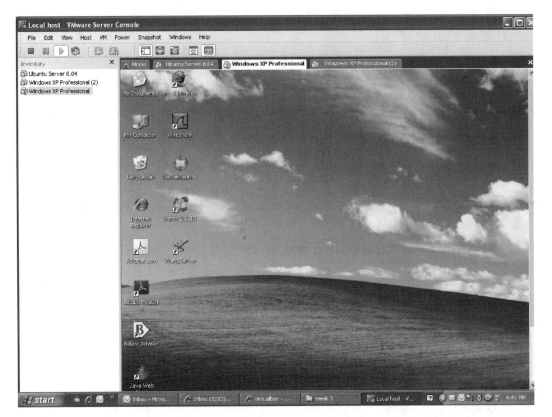

Figure 6-32 A virtual machine running on the host computer's desktop

A virtual machine acts like any other file but with a twist: It performs all the tasks the OS running on the physical computer can, up to a certain point. The virtual machine recognizes hardware components of the host computer it's loaded on, such as the mouse, keyboard, and CD/DVD drive. However, the guest OS (the one running on a virtual machine) is limited by the host computer's OS, which might block certain operations. For example, most virtual machines recognize a CD/DVD drive because the host computer defaults to auto-detect. Some virtual machines don't recognize a USB drive; this capability varies with the virtualization software. Although networking capabilities are beyond the scope of this book, be aware that virtual machines can use bridged, Network Address Translation (NAT), or other network configurations to determine how they access the Internet and communicate with systems on the local network.

Say your company has upgraded to Windows Vista, but you still have a few applications that require Windows 98. Not a problem! Choose your virtualization software, install the Windows 98 OS and the applications you want to run, and you're ready to go. Depending on the host computer's hard drive size and amount of RAM, you can have an entire virtual network running on one physical computer. One advantage is that if you're running several virtual machines, you can pause some of the guest OSs to keep them from consuming CPU cycles and then resume them when needed.

In computer forensics, virtual machines make it possible to restore a suspect drive on a virtual machine and run nonstandard software the suspect might have loaded, for example. You can browse through the drive's contents, and then go back to the forensic image and test the items you found. Remember that in forensics, everything should be reproducible. Therefore, anything you found in the virtual machine re-creation of the suspect drive should exist in the forensic image, too.

From a network forensics standpoint, you need to be aware of some potential issues, such as a virtual machine used to attack another system or network. The technology is still developing, so it's unclear how much of the physical drive is represented in the virtual disk file. File slack, unallocated space, and so forth don't exist on a virtual machine, so many standard items don't work on virtual drives. Malware can be tested on virtual machines with little fear of infecting the host computer, but some malware, unfortunately, can detect that it's on a virtual machine and won't activate. You learn more about forensics procedures with virtual machines in Chapter 11.

Creating a Virtual Machine

Some common applications for creating virtual machines are VMware Server and VMware Workstation, Sun Microsystems VirtualBox, and Microsoft Virtual PC, although others are available. VirtualBox is an open-source program that can be downloaded at *www.virtualbox.org*. Virtual PC 2007 can be downloaded free from *www.microsoft.com/virtualpc*. (This version of Virtual PC doesn't run on Vista Home Edition.)

 The Microsoft Academic Alliance issues ISO images to schools and students for an inexpensive annual fee.

Consult with your instructor before doing the following activity. You must download and install Virtual PC first, and you need an ISO image of an OS because no OSs are provided with Virtual PC. Follow these steps to create a virtual machine:

1. If you haven't already done so, install Microsoft Virtual PC.

2. Start Virtual PC. In Virtual PC 2007, the New Virtual Machine Wizard starts automatically. (If it doesn't, click **File**, **New Virtual Machine Wizard** from the menu.)

3. In the welcome window of the New Virtual Machine Wizard, click **Next**.

4. In the Options window, click the **Create a virtual machine** option button, as shown in Figure 6-33, and click **Next**.

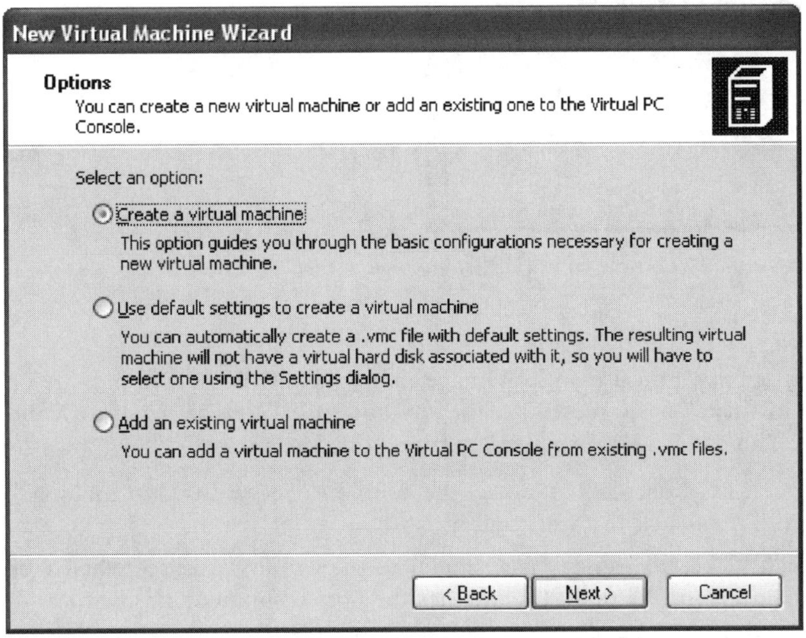

New Virtual Machine Wizard

Options
You can create a new virtual machine or add an existing one to the Virtual PC Console.

Select an option:

◉ Create a virtual machine
This option guides you through the basic configurations necessary for creating a new virtual machine.

○ Use default settings to create a virtual machine
You can automatically create a .vmc file with default settings. The resulting virtual machine will not have a virtual hard disk associated with it, so you will have to select one using the Settings dialog.

○ Add an existing virtual machine
You can add a virtual machine to the Virtual PC Console from existing .vmc files.

[< Back] [Next >] [Cancel]

Figure 6-33 Creating a new virtual machine

5. In the Virtual Machine Name and Location window, type **Windows Server 2003** for the virtual machine name. Note that the default location for Vista is Documents\ Virtual Machines. Your instructor might tell you to use a different location. Click **Next**.

6. In the Operating System window, click **Windows Server 2003** in the Operating system list box, and then click **Next**.

7. In the Memory window, you allocate the amount of RAM. You can increase the amount of RAM if needed, but for now, leave it at the recommended level, and then click **Next**.

8. In the Virtual Hard Disk Options window, click the **A new virtual hard disk** option button, and then click **Next**.

9. In the Virtual Hard Disk Location window, accept the default location (generated by your selection in Step 5), and then click **Next**.

10. Click **Finish**. The Virtual PC Console should look like Figure 6-34.

Microsoft Virtual PC isn't as easy to use when you're trying to load non-Microsoft OSs. For Linux and SUN systems, another virtual platform is recommended.

Figure 6-34 The Virtual PC Console with a virtual machine available

In the following activity, you use an ISO image that your instructor will provide on the network or a CD for installing a guest OS. For any guest OS, you must have a valid product key to install it. You can get the product key from your instructor.

1. In the Virtual PC Console, make sure the Windows Server 2003 virtual machine is selected, and then click the **Start** button.

2. The Virtual PC user console opens, similar to the window you see when a physical computer starts, and Virtual PC examines the host computer's hardware.

3. This book assumes you know how to install an OS, so detailed steps aren't given. Virtual PC treats an ISO image the same as an installation CD, so when you're prompted for the source disk, enter the location of the ISO image. For the name of the owner, type **Sally Freidman**, and for the company name, type **ABC Corporation**.

4. Create a domain name of **MainHost**.

5. Create an administrator password and make a note of it.

6. After the OS is installed, log on. Note that pressing Ctrl+Alt+Delete activates the host computer. To log on to the virtual machine, press **right Alt+Delete**. (You can also use Alt+Enter for full screen.)

7. You should be able to navigate through the contents of the Windows Server 2003 virtual server as though it were a real computer. To switch between the virtual machine window and the desktop, press **right Alt** and move the cursor.

8. To exit Virtual PC, click **File, Close** from the menu, and then click **Turn off** in the drop-down list.

In Virtual PC, the virtual hard disk file has a .vhd extension, and the configuration file has a .vmc extension (see the right pane in Figure 6-35).

To see what type of physical computer the virtual machine thinks it's running, open the Virtual PC Console, and click the Settings button. You should see a dialog box similar to the one in Figure 6-36, which shows you the settings for the virtual machine's emulated hardware. Notice that you can rename the virtual machine.

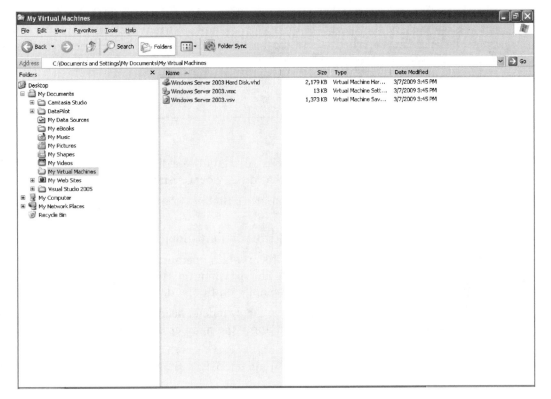

Figure 6-35 Virtual machine configuration files

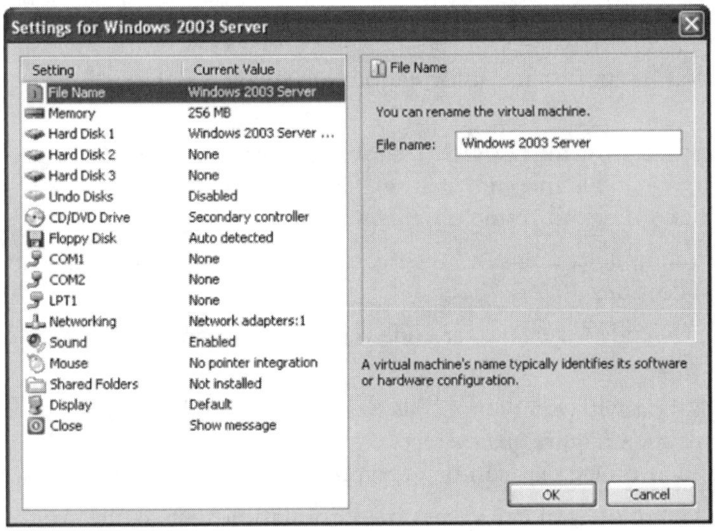

Figure 6-36 Properties of a virtual machine

Be aware that as you install software and perform other tasks, you might encounter problems with recognition of the CD/DVD drive, for example. Virtual machines present some challenges because they are limited by the host computer they're loaded on. For this reason, many legal issues need to be addressed before these systems are accepted for use in court.

Chapter Summary

- When booting a suspect's computer, using boot media, such as forensic boot floppies or CDs, is important to ensure that disk evidence isn't altered.

- You should access a suspect computer's BIOS to configure the computer to boot to a floppy disk or CD first.

- The Master Boot Record (MBR) stores information about partitions on a disk.

- Microsoft used FAT12 and FAT16 on older operating systems, such as MS-DOS, Windows 3.x, and Windows 9x. The maximum partition size is 2 GB. Newer systems use FAT32. FAT12 is now used mainly on floppy disks and small USB drives.

- To find a hard disk's capacity, use the cylinders, heads, and sectors (CHS) calculation. To find a disk's byte capacity, multiply the number of heads, cylinders, and sectors.

- Sectors are grouped into clusters and clusters are chained because the OS can track only a given number of allocation units (65,536 in FAT16 and 4,294,967,296 in FAT32).

- When files are deleted in a FAT file system, the Greek letter sigma (0x05) is inserted in the first character of the filename in the directory.

- New Technology File System (NTFS) is more versatile because it uses the Master File Table (MFT) to track file information. Approximately the first 512 bytes of data for small files (called resident files) are stored in the MFT. Data for larger files (called nonresident files) is stored outside the MFT and linked by using cluster addresses.

- Records in the MFT contain attribute IDs that store metadata about files.

- In NTFS, data streams can obscure information that might be of evidentiary value to an investigation.

- File slack, random access memory (RAM) slack (in older Windows OSs), and drive slack are areas in which valuable information, such as downloaded files, swap files, passwords, and logon IDs, can reside on a drive.

- To be an effective computer forensics investigator, you need to maintain a library of older OSs and applications.

- NTFS uses 16-bit Unicode for character code representation instead of the 8-bit configuration that ASCII uses.

- NTFS can encrypt data with Encrypting File System (EFS) and BitLocker. Decrypting data with these methods requires using recovery certificates. BitLocker is Microsoft's whole disk encryption utility that can be decrypted by using a one-time passphrase.

- With a hexadecimal editor, you can determine information such as file type and OS configurations.

- NTFS can compress files, folders, or an entire volume. FAT16 can compress entire volumes.

- The Registry in Windows keeps a record of attached hardware, user prefere. work connections, and installed software. It also contains information such as passwords in two binary files: System.dat and User.dat.

- User information in Windows is stored in User.dat for Windows 9x/Me and Ntuser.dat for Windows 2000 and later. Every user with an account on a Windows computer has his or her own User.dat or Ntuser.dat file.

- Virtualization software enables you to run other OSs on a host computer. Virtual machines are beneficial if, for example, you need to run a previous OS to test old software that won't run on newer OSs.

Key Terms

American Standard Code for Information Interchange (ASCII) An 8-bit coding scheme that assigns numeric values to up to 256 characters, including letters, numerals, punctuation marks, control characters, and other symbols.

areal density The number of bits per square inch of a disk platter.

attribute ID In NTFS, an MFT record field containing metadata about the file or folder and the file's data or links to the file's data.

Autoexec.bat A batch file containing customized settings for MS-DOS that runs automatically. It includes the default path and environmental variables, such as temporary directories.

Boot.ini A file that specifies the Windows path installation and a variety of other startup options.

BootSect.dos If a machine has multiple booting OSs, NTLDR reads BootSect.dos, which is a hidden file, to determine the address (boot sector location) of each OS. *See also* NT Loader (Ntldr).

bootstrap process Information contained in ROM that a computer accesses during startup; this information tells the computer how to access the OS and hard drive.

clusters Storage allocation units composed of groups of sectors. Clusters are 512, 1024, 2048, or 4096 bytes each.

Command.com This system file provides a command prompt when booting to MS-DOS mode.

Config.sys A text file containing commands that typically run only at system startup to enhance the computer's DOS configuration.

cylinder A column of tracks on two or more disk platters.

data runs Cluster addresses where files are stored on a drive's partition outside the MFT record. Data runs are used for nonresident MFT file records. A data run record field consists of three components; the first component defines the size in bytes needed to store the second and third components' content.

data streams Ways in which data can be appended to a file (intentionally or not). In NTFS, data streams become an additional file attribute.

device drivers Files containing instructions for the OS for hardware devices, such as the keyboard, mouse, and video card.

DOS protected-mode interface (DPMI) Used by many computer forensics tools that don't operate in the Windows environment. It allows DOS programs to access extended memory while protecting the system.

drive slack Unused space in a cluster between the end of an active file and the end of the cluster. It can contain deleted files, deleted e-mail, or file fragments. Drive slack is made up of both file slack and RAM slack. *See also* file slack *and* RAM slack.

Encrypting File System (EFS) A public/private key encryption first used in Windows 2000 on NTFS-formatted disks. The file is encrypted with a symmetric key, and then a public/private key is used to encrypt the symmetric key.

File Allocation Table (FAT) The original Microsoft file structure database. It's written to the outermost track of a disk and contains information about each file stored on the drive. PCs use the FAT to organize files on a disk so that the OS can find the files it needs. The variations are FAT12, FAT16, FAT32, and FATX.

file slack The unused space created when a file is saved. If the allocated space is larger than the file, the remaining space is slack space and can contain passwords, logon IDs, file fragments, and deleted e-mails.

file system The way files are stored on a disk; gives an OS a road map to data on a disk.

geometry A disk drive's internal organization of platters, tracks, and sectors.

Hal.dll The Hardware Abstraction Layer dynamic link library allows the OS kernel to communicate with hardware.

head The device that reads and writes data to a disk drive.

head and cylinder skew A method manufacturers use to minimize lag time. The starting sectors of tracks are slightly offset from each other to move the read-write head.

High Performance File System (HPFS) The file system IBM uses for its OS/2 operating system.

Info2 file In Windows NT through Vista, the control file for the Recycle Bin. It contains ASCII data, Unicode data, and date and time of deletion.

Io.sys This MS-DOS file communicates between a computer's BIOS, the hardware, and the OS kernel.

logical addresses When files are saved, they are assigned to clusters, which the OS numbers sequentially starting at 2. Logical addresses point to relative cluster positions, using these assigned cluster numbers.

logical cluster numbers (LCNs) The numbers sequentially assigned to each cluster when an NTFS disk partition is created and formatted. The first cluster on an NTFS partition starts at count 0. LCNs become the addresses that allow the MFT to read and write data to the disk's nonresident attribute area. *See also* virtual cluster number (VCN) *and* data runs.

Master Boot Record (MBR) On Windows and DOS computers, this boot disk file contains information about partitions on a disk and their locations, size, and other important items.

Master File Table (MFT) NTFS uses this database to store and link to files. It contains information about access rights, date and time stamps, system attributes, and other information about files.

metadata In NTFS, this term refers to information stored in the MFT. *See also* Master File Table (MFT).

Msdos.sys A hidden text file containing startup options for Windows 9x. In MS-DOS 6.22 and earlier, it was an actual OS executable.

New Technology File System (NTFS) The file system Microsoft created to replace FAT. NTFS uses security features, allows smaller cluster sizes, and uses Unicode, which makes it a more versatile system. NTFS is used mainly on newer OSs, starting with Windows NT.

NTBootdd.sys A device driver that allows the OS to communicate with SCSI or ATA drives that aren't related to the BIOS.

NTDetect.com A 16-bit program that identifies hardware components during startup and sends the information to Ntldr.

NT Loader (Ntldr) A program located in the root folder of the system partition that loads the OS. *See also* Bootsect.dos.

Ntoskrnl.exe The kernel for the Windows XP OS.

one-time passphrase A password used to access special accounts or programs requiring a high level of security, such as a decryption utility for an encrypted drive. This passphrase can be used only once, and then it expires.

Pagefile.sys At startup, data and instruction code are moved in and out of this file to optimize the amount of physical RAM available during startup.

partition A logical drive on a disk. It can be the entire disk or part of the disk.

Partition Boot Sector The first data set of an NTFS disk. It starts at sector [0] of the disk drive and can expand up to 16 sectors.

partition gap Unused space or void between the primary partition and the first logical partition.

personal identity information (PII) Any information that can be used to create bank or credit card accounts, such as name, home address, Social Security number, and driver's license number.

physical addresses The actual sectors in which files are located. Sectors reside at the hardware and firmware level.

private key In encryption, the key used to decrypt the file. The file owner keeps the private key.

protected-mode GUI Provides the same functional startup process for Windows that Config.sys provided for DOS. It loads all the device drivers.

public key In encryption, the key used to encrypt a file; it's held by a certificate authority, such as a global registry, network server, or company such as VeriSign.

RAM slack The unused space between the end of the file (EOF) and the end of the last sector used by the active file in the cluster. Any data residing in RAM at the time the file is saved, such as logon IDs and passwords, can appear in this area, whether the information was saved or not. RAM slack is found primarily in older Microsoft OSs.

recovery certificate A method NTFS uses so that a network administrator can recover encrypted files if the file's user/creator loses the private key encryption code.

Registry A Windows database containing information about hardware and software configurations, network connections, user preferences, setup information, and other critical information.

sector A section on a track, typically made up of 512 bytes.

track density The space between tracks on a disk. The smaller the space between tracks, the more tracks on a disk. Older drives with wider track densities allowed the heads to wander.

tracks Concentric circles on a disk platter where data is stored.

Trusted Computing Group (TCG) A nonprofit organization that develops support standards for trusted computer access across multiple platforms.

Trusted Platform Module (TPM) A microchip that stores encryption key data used to encrypt and decrypt drive data.

unallocated disk space Partition disk space that isn't allocated to a file. This space might contain data from files that have been deleted previously.

Unicode A character code representation that's replacing ASCII. It's capable of representing more than 64,000 characters and non-European-based languages.

UTF-8 (Unicode Transformation Format) One of three formats Unicode uses to translate languages for digital representation.

virtual cluster number (VCN) When a large file is saved in NTFS, it's assigned a logical cluster number specifying a location on the partition. Large files are referred to as nonresident files. If the disk is highly fragmented, VCNs are assigned and list the additional space needed to store the file. The LCN is a physical location on the NTFS partition; VCNs are the offset from the previous LCN data run. *See also* logical cluster numbers (LCNs) *and* data runs.

virtual machines Emulated computer environments that simulate hardware and can be used for running OSs separate from the physical (host) computer. For example, a computer running Windows Vista could have a virtual Windows 98 OS, allowing the user to switch between OSs.

volume Any storage media, such as a floppy disk, a partition on a hard drive, the entire drive, or several drives. On Intel systems, a volume is any partitioned disk.

zoned bit recording (ZBR) The method most manufacturers use to deal with a platter's inner tracks being shorter than the outer tracks. Grouping tracks by zones ensures that all tracks hold the same amount of data.

Review Questions

1. In DOS and Windows 9.x, Io.sys is the first file loaded after the ROM bootstrap loader finds the disk. True or False?

2. On a Windows system, sectors typically contain how many bytes?
   a. 256
   b. 512
   c. 1024
   d. 2048

3. What does CHS stand for?

4. Zoned bit recording is how disk manufacturers ensure that a platter's outer tracks store as much data as possible. True or False?

5. Areal density refers to which of the following?

    a. Number of bits per disk

    b. Number of bits per partition

    c. Number of bits per square inch of a disk platter

    d. Number of bits per platter

6. Clusters in Windows always begin numbering at what number?

7. What is the ratio of sectors per cluster in a floppy disk?

    a. 1:1

    b. 2:1

    c. 4:1

    d. 8:1

8. List three items stored in the FAT database.

9. Windows 2000 can be configured to access which of these file formats? (Choose all that apply.)

    a. FAT12

    b. FAT16

    c. FAT32

    d. NTFS

10. In FAT32, a 123 KB file uses how many sectors?

11. What is the space on a drive called when a file is deleted? (Choose all that apply.)

    a. Disk space

    b. Unallocated space

    c. Drive space

    d. Free space

12. List two features NTFS has that FAT does not.

13. What does MFT stand for?

14. In NTFS, files smaller than 512 bytes are stored in the MFT. True or False?

15. RAM slack can contain passwords. True or False?

16. A virtual cluster consists of what kind of clusters?

17. The Windows Registry in Windows 9x consists of what two files?

18. HPFS is used on which OS?

19. Device drivers contain what kind of information?

20. Which of the following Windows XP files contains user-specific information?

    a. User.dat

    b. Ntuser.dat

    c. System.dat

    d. Sam.dat

21. Virtual machines have which of the following limitations when running on a host computer?

    a. Internet connectivity is restricted to virtual Web sites.

    b. Applications can be run on the virtual machine only if they're resident on the physical machine.

    c. Virtual machines are limited to the host computer's peripheral configurations, such as mouse, keyboard, CD/DVD drives, and other devices.

    d. Virtual machines can run only OSs that are older than the physical machine's OS.

22. An image of a suspect drive can be loaded on a virtual machine. True or False?

23. EFS can encrypt which of the following?

    a. Files, folders, and volumes

    b. Certificates and private keys

    c. The global Registry

    d. Network servers

24. To encrypt a FAT volume, which of the following utilities can you use?

    a. Microsoft BitLocker

    b. EFS

    c. PGP Whole Disk Encryption

    d. FreeOTFE

25. What are the functions of a data run's field components in an MFT record?

Hands-On Projects

There are no data files to extract for this chapter's projects, but create a *Work\Chap06\Projects* folder on your system before starting the projects.

Hands-On Project 6-1

In this project, you compare two files created in Microsoft Office to determine whether the files are different at the hexadecimal level. Keep a log of what you find. Use a Windows XP or Vista computer, and follow these steps:

1. Start Word, and in a new document, type **This is a test.**

2. Save the file as **Mywordnew.doc** in your work folder, using **Word 97 - 2003 (*.doc)** as the file type. Exit Word.

3. Start Excel, and in a new workbook, enter a few random numbers. Save the file in your work folder as **Myworkbook.xls**, using **Excel 97 - 2003** (***.xls**) as the file type.

4. Exit Excel, and start Hex Workshop (which you downloaded earlier).

5. Click **File, Open** from the menu. In the Open dialog box, navigate to your work folder and double-click **Mywordnew.doc**.

6. In Hex Workshop, there are two upper panes: the Editor pane and the Data Inspector pane. The Editor pane is divided into three columns: Offset, Hex, and Text. (*Note*: If needed, click **Help, Contents** from the menu, and read the Layout and Editing section.) You should see eight 0s in the Offset column. The file header D0 CF 11 E0 A1 B1 1A E1 should be in the first row of the Hex column.

7. When you've finished examining this information, print just the first page of the document.

8. Click **File, Close** from the menu to close Mywordnew.doc.

9. Click **File, Open** from the menu. In the Open dialog box, navigate to your work folder and double-click **Myworkbook.xls**.

10. Examine the information in the Hex Workshop window, and then print the first page.

11. Close Myworkbook.xls, and compare the two printouts. There should be no difference between any files created in Microsoft Office, except in Microsoft Access files. Describe any differences you see in the Office 2007 header. Exit Hex Workshop.

Hands-On Project 6-2

In this project, you explore the MFT and learn how to locate date and time values in the metadata of a file you create. These steps help you identify fragments of MFT records, which you might find in unallocated disk space or Pagefile.sys. You need the following for this project:

- Windows 2000 or later with the C drive configured as NTFS
- Notepad to create a small text file
- ProDiscover Basic to copy the MFT to your work folder (*Note*: Vista users, remember to use the Run as administrator option.)
- WinHex Demo to analyze the metadata in the MFT (provided on the book's DVD, so copy and install it on your system first, if necessary)

1. Start Notepad, and create a text file with one or more of the following lines:
   - A countryman between two lawyers is like a fish between two cats.
   - A slip of the foot you may soon recover, but a slip of the tongue you may never get over.
   - An investment in knowledge always pays the best interest.
   - Drive thy business or it will drive thee.

2. Save the file in your work folder as **C6Prj02.txt,** and exit Notepad. (If your work folder isn't on the C drive, make sure you save the C6Prj02.txt file on your C drive to have it entered in the $MFT files you copy later.)

3. Next, review the material in "MFT and File Attributes," paying particular attention to attributes 0x10 and 0x30 for file dates and times. The following charts show the offset byte count starting at position FILE of the file's MFT record for the date and time stamps:

The offsets listed in the following charts are from the first byte of the MFT record, not the starting position of the specific attributes 0x10 and 0x30.

0x10 $Standard Information (data starts at offset 0x18)

Description of field	Offset position	Byte size
C Time (file creation)	0x50	8
A Time (file altered)	0x58	8
M Time (MFT change)	0x60	8

0x30 $File_Name (data starts at offset 0x18)

Description of field	Offset position	Byte size
C Time (file creation)	0xB8	8
A Time (file altered)	0xC0	8
M Time (MFT change)	0xC8	8
R Time (file read)	0XD0	8

4. Start ProDiscover Basic, and start a new project, using **C6Prj02** for the project number and filename.

5. Click **Action** from the menu, point to **Add,** and click **Disk.**

6. In the Add Disk to Project dialog box, click **PhysicalDrive0.** Type **c-drive** in the Please enter unique name for physical disk text box, and then click **Add.** If you see the Add Disk warning message, click **OK.**

7. In the tree view, click to expand **Content View, Disks,** and **PhysicalDrive0.** Then click to select the C drive.

8. In the work area, scroll down, if necessary, and then right-click **$MFT** and click **Copy File.** In the Save As dialog box, navigate to your work folder, and then click **Save.**

9. When the $MFT file has been copied to your work folder, exit ProDiscover Basic, saving the project if prompted.

Next, you examine the copied $MFT file to learn how metadata is stored. Follow these steps:

1. Start WinHex Demo by clicking **Start**, pointing to **All Programs**, and clicking **WinHex**. If you see an evaluation warning message, click **OK**.

2. Click the **Open** toolbar button. In the Open dialog box, navigate to your work folder, click the **$MFT** file, and then click **Open**. If you see another evaluation warning message, click the **Do not display this kind of message again** check box, and then click **OK**.

3. Click **Search, Find Text** from the menu.

4. In the text box for specifying the text string to search, type **C6Prj02.txt**. Click the **Format Code** list arrow (next to the list box containing the text "ASCII"), click **Unicode**, and then click **OK**.

By default, WinHex displays a floating Data Interpreter window that converts hex values to decimal values and can also convert date and time codes. If you don't see this window, activate it by clicking View, pointing to Show, and clicking Data Interpreter.

NOTE

6

5. Right-click the **Data Interpreter** window and click **Options**. In the Data Interpreter Options dialog box, click the **Win32 FILETIME (64 bit)** check box, and then click **OK**. The Data Interpreter should then have FILETIME as an additional display.

6. In the WinHex window, scroll up so that the MFT record label FILE for C6Prj02.txt is the first line at the top of the hexadecimal and text displays.

7. Click at the beginning of the record, on the letter **F** in FILE, and then drag down and to the right while you monitor the hexadecimal counter in the lower-right corner. When the counter reaches 50, release the mouse button.

8. Move the cursor one position to the left (to the next byte), and record the date and time of the Data Interpreter's FILETIME values.

9. Repeat Steps 7 and 8, using the offset positions plus 1 byte to see the values for the remaining date and time positions. Write down these values.

10. When you're finished, exit WinHex and hand in the date and time values you recorded.

Hands-On Project 6-3

In this project, you use Hex Workshop to become familiar with different file types. Follow these steps on a Windows XP or Vista computer:

1. On your hard drive, locate or create Microsoft Excel (.xls), Microsoft Word (.doc), .gif, .jpg, and .avi files.

2. Start Hex Workshop.

3. Open each file by clicking **File, Open** from the menu, and then print just the first page of each file.

4. On each printout, circle the item that identifies the file type. Do this for all five file types.

5. Exit Hex Workshop.

Hands-On Project 6-4

In this project, you generate a word list based on an in-chapter activity. If you didn't do the activity in "Examining the Windows Registry," go back and perform those steps now. This word list could be used later with a password recovery program. When you're finished, follow these steps:

1. Start AccessData Registry Viewer and open the User.dat file you retrieved from GCFI-Win98.eve earlier in this chapter.

2. Click **Report, Export Word List** from the menu.

3. In the Generate Word List dialog box, navigate to your work folder, and then click **Save**.

4. After the word list has been generated, exit Registry Viewer and turn the report file in to your instructor.

Case Projects

CASE PROJECTS

Case Project 6-1

For the arson running case project, decide whether you're going to work from the image or restore it to a drive. Next, determine the file system type, such as FAT32 or NTFS, and investigate whether any files used EFS or another encryption method. Write a short paper on your findings, and if any encryption methods were used, include a discussion of what forensics tools you could use to open those files.

Case Project 6-2

An employee suspects that his password has been compromised. He changed it two days ago, yet it seems someone has used it again. What might be going on?

chapter 7

Current Computer Forensics Tools

After reading this chapter and completing the exercises, you will be able to:

- Explain how to evaluate needs for computer forensics tools
- Describe available computer forensics software tools
- List some considerations for computer forensics hardware tools
- Describe methods for validating and testing computer forensics tools

Chapter 3 outlined how to set up a computer forensics laboratory. This chapter explores many software and hardware tools used during computer forensics investigations. No specific tools are recommended; instead, the goal is to explain how to select tools for computing investigations based on specific criteria.

Computer forensics tools are constantly being developed, updated, patched, and revised. Therefore, checking vendors' Web sites routinely to look for new features and improvements is important. These improvements might address a difficult problem you're having in an investigation.

Before purchasing any forensics tools, consider whether the tool can save you time during investigations and whether that time savings affects the reliability of data you recover. Many GUI forensics tools are resource intensive and demand computers with more memory and faster processor speeds. Sometimes they require more resources than a typical workstation has because of other applications, such as antivirus programs, running in the background. These background programs compete for resources with a computer forensics program, and a GUI forensics tool or the OS can stop running or hang, causing delays in your investigation.

Finally, when planning purchases for your computer forensics lab, determine what a new forensics tool can do better than one you're currently using. In particular, assess how well the software performs in validation tests, and then verify the integrity of the tool's results.

Evaluating Computer Forensics Tool Needs

As described in Chapter 3, you need to develop a business plan to justify the acquisition of computer forensics hardware and software. When researching tools, strive for versatile, flexible, and robust tools that include technical support. The goal is to find the best value for as many features as possible. Some questions to ask when evaluating tools include the following:

- On which OS does the forensics tool run?
- Is the tool versatile? For example, does it work in Windows 98, XP, and Vista and produce the same results in all three OSs?
- Can the tool analyze more than one file system, such as FAT, NTFS, and Ext2fs?
- Can a scripting language be used with the tool to automate repetitive functions and tasks?
- Does the tool have any automated features that can help reduce the time needed to analyze data?
- What is the vendor's reputation for providing product support?

As you learn more about computing investigations, you'll have more questions about tools for conducting these investigations. When you search for tools, keep in mind what file types you'll be analyzing. For example, if you need to analyze Microsoft Access databases, look for a product designed to read these files. If you're analyzing e-mail messages, look for a forensics tool capable of reading e-mail content.

When you're selecting tools for your lab, keep an open mind, and compare platforms and applications for different tasks. Although many investigators are most comfortable using Microsoft platforms, you're encouraged to check into other options, such as Linux and Macintosh platforms.

Types of Computer Forensics Tools

Computer forensics tools are divided into two major categories: hardware and software. Each category has additional subcategories discussed in more depth later in this chapter. The following sections outline basic features required and expected of most computer forensics tools.

Hardware Forensics Tools Hardware forensics tools range from simple, single-purpose components to complete computer systems and servers. Single-purpose components can be devices, such as the ACARD AEC-7720WP Ultra Wide SCSI-to-IDE Bridge, which is designed to write-block an IDE drive connected to a SCSI cable.

Some examples of complete systems are Digital Intelligence F.R.E.D. systems, DIBS Advanced Forensic Workstations, and Forensic Computers Forensic Examination Stations and portable units. To see photos of these tower and portable units, go to the Forensic Computers Web site at *www.forensic-computers.com* and do a search.

Software Forensics Tools Software forensics tools are grouped into command-line applications and GUI applications. Some tools are specialized to perform one task, such as SafeBack, a command-line disk acquisition tool from New Technologies, Inc. (NTI). Other tools are designed to perform many different tasks. For example, Technology Pathways ProDiscover, X-Ways Forensics, Guidance Software EnCase, and AccessData FTK are GUI tools designed to perform most computer forensics acquisition and analysis functions.

Software forensics tools are commonly used to copy data from a suspect's drive to an image file. Many GUI acquisition tools can read all structures in an image file as though the image were the original drive. Many analysis tools, such as ProDiscover, EnCase, FTK, X-Ways Forensics, ILook, and others, have the capability to analyze image files. In Chapter 4, you learned how some of these tools are used to acquire data from suspects' drives.

Tasks Performed by Computer Forensics Tools

All computer forensics tools, both hardware and software, perform specific functions. These functions are grouped into five major categories, each with subfunctions for further refining data analysis and recovery:

- Acquisition
- Validation and discrimination
- Extraction
- Reconstruction
- Reporting

In the following sections, you learn how these five functions and associated subfunctions apply to computing investigations.

Acquisition Acquisition, the first task in computer forensics investigations, is making a copy of the original drive. As described in Chapter 4, this procedure preserves the original drive to make sure it doesn't become corrupt and damage the digital evidence. In Chapter 5, you learned how to handle digital evidence correctly, and in Chapter 9, you learn more about using acquisition tools. Subfunctions in the acquisition category include the following:

- Physical data copy
- Logical data copy

- Data acquisition format
- Command-line acquisition
- GUI acquisition
- Remote acquisition
- Verification

Some computer forensics software suites, such as AccessData FTK and EnCase, provide separate tools for acquiring an image. However, some investigators opt to use hardware devices, such as the Logicube Talon, VOOM HardCopy 3, or ImageMASSter Solo III Forensic unit from Intelligent Computer Solutions, Inc., for acquiring an image. These hardware devices have their own built-in software for data acquisition. No other device or program is needed to make a duplicate drive; however, you still need forensics software to analyze the data.

To see a photo of the Logicube Talon, go to *www.logicube.com/ products/hd_duplication/talon.asp*. To see the ImageMASSter Solo III unit, search at *www.icsforensic.com*. To see VOOM HardCopy 3, search at *www.voomtech.com*.

Other acquisition tools require combining hardware devices and software programs to make disk acquisitions. For example, Guidance Software has a DOS program, En.exe, and a function in its Windows application, EnCase, for making data acquisitions. Making an acquisition with En.exe requires a PC running MS-DOS, a 12-volt hard drive power connector (Molex, SATA, or one specified for the hard drive you're acquiring), and a data cable, such as an IDE (PATA), a SATA, or a SCSI connector cable. The Windows EnCase application requires a write-blocker device, such as FastBloc, to prevent Windows from accessing and corrupting a suspect drive. Later in "Using a Write-Blocker," you learn more about these devices.

If you use a Linux/UNIX platform for data acquisitions, an EnCase program called LinEn.exe is supported.

Two types of data-copying methods are used in software acquisitions: physical copying of the entire drive and logical copying of a disk partition. Most software acquisition tools include the option of imaging an entire physical drive or just a logical partition. The situation dictates whether you make a physical or logical acquisition. One reason to choose a logical acquisition is drive encryption. With the increasing emphasis on data security, drive encryption is used more commonly now. As mentioned in Chapter 4, making a physical acquisition of a drive with whole disk encryption results in unreadable data. With a logical acquisition, however, you can still read and analyze the files. Of course, this method requires a live acquisition (covered in Chapter 11) because you need to log on to the system.

Disk acquisition formats vary from raw data to vendor-specific proprietary, as you learned in Chapter 4. The raw data format, typically created with the UNIX/Linux dd command, is a simple bit-for-bit copy of a data file, a disk partition, or an entire drive. A raw imaging tool can copy data from one drive to another disk or to segmented files. Because it's a true unaltered copy, you can view a raw image file's contents with any hexadecimal editor, such as

Hex Workshop or WinHex. Hexadecimal editors, also known as disk editors (such as Norton DiskEdit), provide a hexadecimal view and a plaintext view of the data (see Figure 7-1).

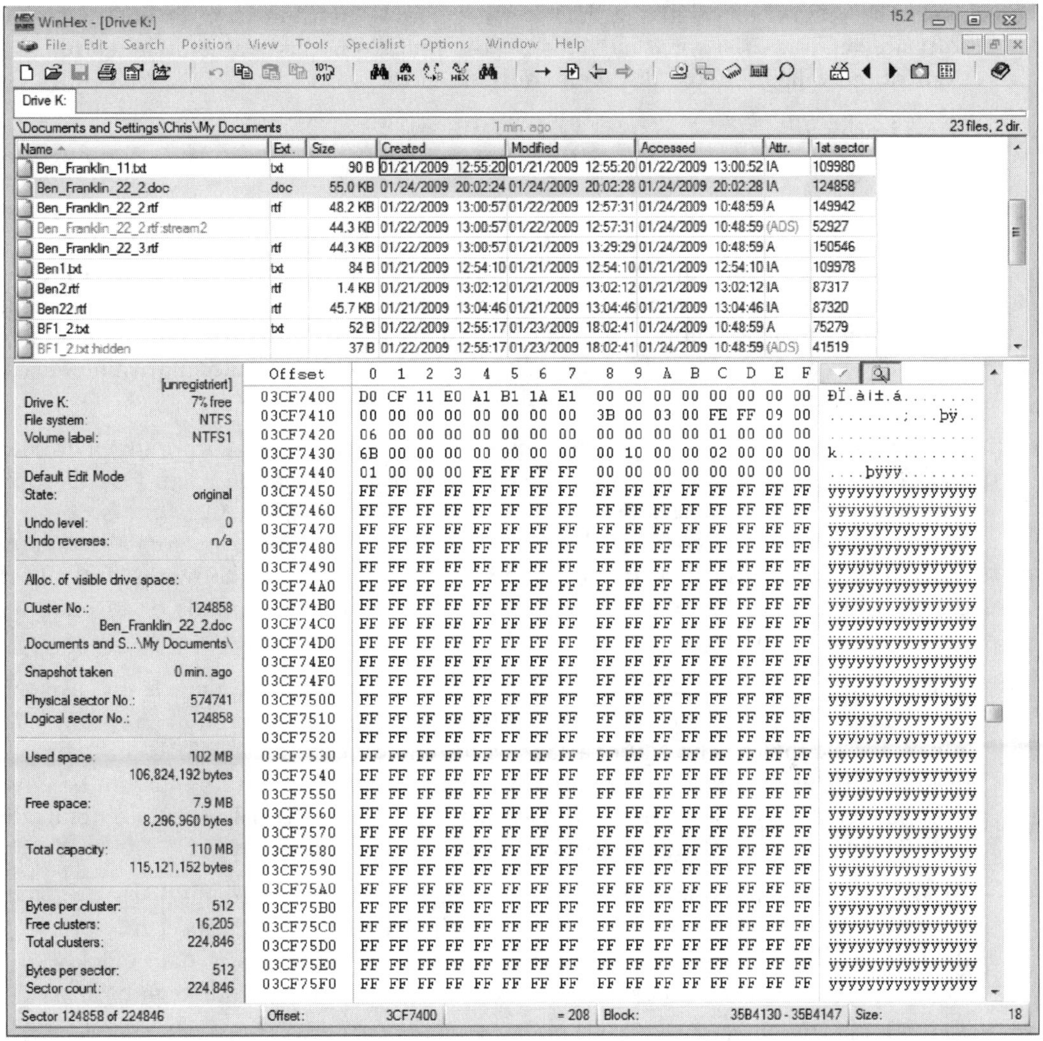

Figure 7-1 Viewing data in a hexadecimal editor

Creating smaller segmented files is a typical feature in vendor acquisition tools. The purpose of segmented files is to make it easier to store acquired data on smaller media, such as CD-Rs or DVD-Rs.

All computer forensics acquisition tools have a method for verification of the data-copying process that compares the original drive with the image. For example, EnCase prompts you to obtain the MD5 hash value of acquired data, FTK validates MD5 and SHA-1 hash sets during data acquisition, and SafeBack runs an SHA-256 hash while acquiring data. Hardware acquisition tools, such as ImageMASSter Solo, can perform simultaneous MD5 and CRC-32 hashing during data acquisition. Whether you choose a software or hardware solution for your acquisition needs, make sure the tool has a hashing function for verification purposes.

Validation and Discrimination Two issues in dealing with computer evidence are critical. First is ensuring the integrity of data being copied—the **validation** process. Second is the **discrimination** of data, which involves sorting and searching through all investigation data. The process of validating data is what allows discrimination of data. Many forensics software vendors offer three methods for discriminating data values. These are the subfunctions of the validation and discrimination function:

- Hashing
- Filtering
- Analyzing file headers

Validating data is done by obtaining hash values. As a standard feature, most forensics tools and many disk editors have one or more types of data hashing. How data hashing is used depends on the investigation, but using a hashing algorithm on the entire suspect drive and all its files is a good idea. This method produces a unique hexadecimal value for data, used to make sure the original data hasn't changed.

This unique value has other potential uses. For example, in the corporate environment, you could create a known good hash value list of a fresh installation of an OS, all applications, and all known good images and documents (spreadsheets, text files, and so on). With this information, an investigator could ignore all files on this known good list and focus on other files on the disk that aren't on this list. This process is known as filtering. Filtering can also be used to find data for evidence in criminal investigations or to build a case for terminating an employee.

The primary purpose of data discrimination is to remove good data from suspicious data. Good data consists of known files, such as OS files and common programs (Microsoft Word, for example). The National Software Reference Library (NSRL) has compiled a list of known file hashes for a variety of OSs, applications, and images that can be downloaded from *www.nsrl.nist.gov/Downloads.htm* (see Figure 7-2). You learn more about the NSRL in "Validating and Testing Forensics Software" later in this chapter.

Several computer forensics programs can integrate known good file hash sets, such as the ones from the NSRL, and compare them to file hashes from a suspect drive to see whether they match. With this process, you can eliminate large amounts of data quickly so that you can focus your evidence analysis. You can also begin building your own hash sets.

Another feature to consider for hashing functions is hashing and comparing sectors of data. This feature is useful for identifying fragments of data in slack and free disk space that might be partially overwritten.

An additional method of discriminating data is analyzing and verifying header values for known file types. Similar to the hash values of known files, many computer forensics programs include a list of common header values. With this information, you can see whether a file extension is incorrect for the file type. Renaming file extensions is a common way to try to hide data, and you could miss pertinent data if you don't check file headers. For example, in the file header for ForensicData.doc, you see the letters "JFIF" (see Figure 7-3).

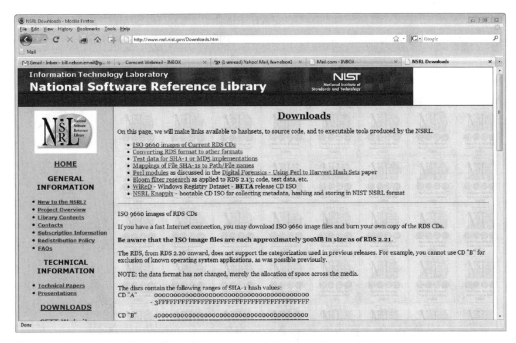

Figure 7-2 The download page of the National Software Reference Library

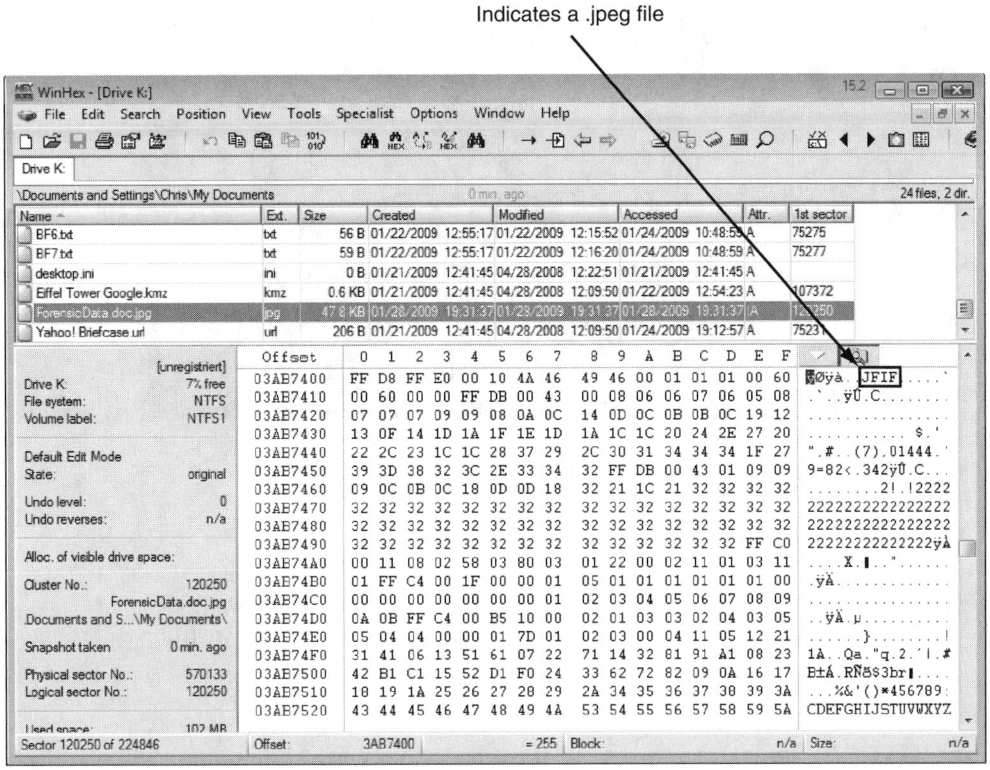

Indicates a .jpeg file

Figure 7-3 The file header indicates a .jpeg file

After some practice in viewing file headers, you'll learn to recognize common header values. In this example, .jpeg files, not .doc files, are known to have "JFIF" in the header. Therefore, ForensicData.doc is a .jpeg image, not a .doc file. If you try to view ForensicData.doc in Microsoft Word, you see the error message shown in Figure 7-4.

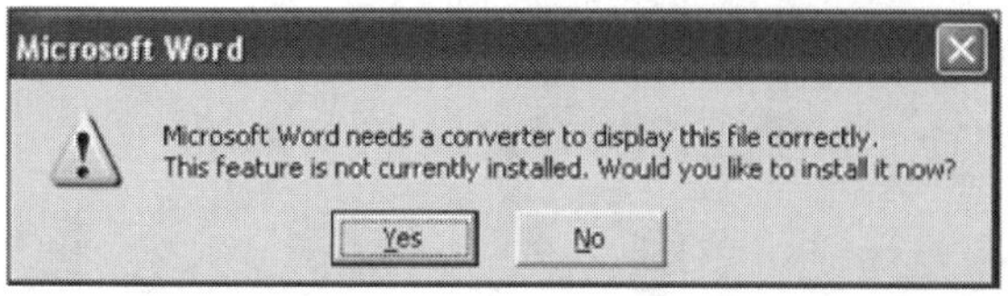

Figure 7-4 Error message displayed when trying to open a .jpeg file in Word

If you try to open the file with an image viewer, such as Windows Picture and Fax Viewer, you see the image shown in Figure 7-5.

Figure 7-5 ForensicData.doc open in an image viewer

Most forensics tools can identify header values. Searching and comparing file headers rather than file extensions improves the data discrimination function. With this feature, you can locate files that might have been altered intentionally. In Chapters 10 and 12, you see how to use this feature to locate hidden data.

Extraction The **extraction** function is the recovery task in a computing investigation and is the most challenging of all tasks to master. In Chapter 2, you learned how system analysis applies to an investigation. Recovering data is the first step in analyzing an investigation's data. The following subfunctions of extraction are used in investigations:

- Data viewing
- Keyword searching
- Decompressing
- Carving
- Decrypting
- Bookmarking

Many computer forensics tools include a data-viewing mechanism for digital evidence. How data is viewed depends on the tool. Tools such as ProDiscover, X-Ways Forensics, FTK, EnCase, SMART, ILook, and others offer several ways to view data, including logical drive structures, such as folders and files. These tools also display allocated file data and unallocated disk areas with special file and disk viewers. Being able to view this data in its normal form makes analyzing and collecting clues for the investigation easier.

A common task in computing investigations is searching for and recovering key data facts. Computer forensics programs have functions for searching for keywords of interest to the investigation. Using a **keyword search** speeds up the analysis process for investigators, if used correctly; however, a poor selection of keywords generates too much information. For example, the name "Ben" is a poor search term because it generates a large number of false-positive hits. To reduce false-positive hits, you need to refine the search scope. One way is to search on combinations of words, in which one word is within so many words of the next. For example, with FTK's Indexed Search feature (see Figure 7-6), you could search for the word "Ben" within one word of the word "Franklin" by entering "Ben w/1 Franklin" and narrow the search further with the word "Son" as a separate entry in the Search Term text box.

With some tools, you can set filters to select the file types to search, such as searching only PDF documents. Another function in some forensics tools is indexing all words on a drive. X-Ways Forensics and FTK 1.6x and earlier offer this feature, using the binary index (B-tree) search engine from dtSearch. FTK 2.0 also includes indexing but has switched to an Oracle database and takes advantage of this database program's indexing capabilities. These features make instant lookup for keywords possible, which speeds up analysis.

Another function to consider for extraction is the format the forensics tool can read. For example, FTK has a built-in function that reads and indexes data from Microsoft .pst and. ost files; EnCase has a third-party add-on that performs indexing and analyzes Microsoft .pst files. In addition, EnCase, X-Ways Forensics, and ProDiscover enable you to create scripts for extracting data, but FTK doesn't have this feature. Keep in mind that you have to use a combination of tools to retrieve and report on evidence from digital devices accurately.

Part of the investigation process also involves reconstructing fragments of files that have been deleted from a suspect drive. In North America, this reconstruction is referred to as "carving"; in Europe, it's called "salvaging." (Carving is covered in more depth in Chapter 10.) Investigators often need to be able to extract data from unallocated disk space. Locating file header information, as mentioned previously in "Validation and Discrimination," is

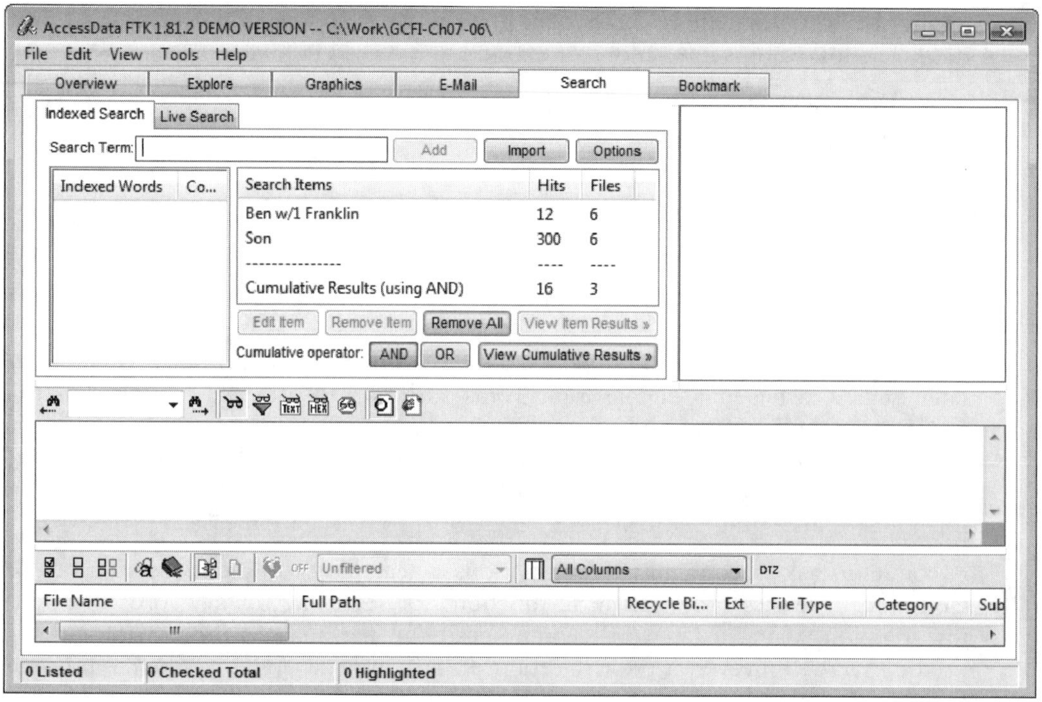

Figure 7-6   The Indexed Search feature in FTK

a reliable method for carving data. Most forensics tools analyze unallocated areas of a drive or an image file and locate fragments or entire file structures that can be carved and copied into a newly reconstructed file. Some investigators prefer carving fragmented data manually with a command-line tool, but advanced GUI tools, such as X-Ways Forensics, EnCase, FTK, and ProDiscover, with built-in functions for carving are used more commonly now. For example, Figure 7-7 shows an option in FTK for adding carved files to a case automatically.

Some tools, such as DataLifter and Davory, are specifically designed to carve known data types from exported unallocated disk space. DataLifter includes a customization feature that enables you to add other header values.

A major challenge in computing investigations is analyzing, recovering, and decrypting data from encrypted files or systems. Encryption can be used on a drive, disk partition, or file. Many e-mail services, such as Microsoft Outlook, provide encryption protection for .pst folders and messages. The types of encryption range from platform specific, such as Windows Encrypting File System (EFS), to third-party vendors, such as Pretty Good Privacy (PGP) and GnuPG.

From an investigation perspective, encrypted files and systems are a problem. Many password recovery tools have a feature for generating potential password lists for a **password dictionary attack**. FTK, for example, produces a list of possible passwords for an encrypted file from a suspect drive. The password could also have been written to a temporary file or system file, such as Pagefile.sys. FTK's generated password list can be loaded into the AccessData Password Recovery Toolkit (PRTK) dictionary, and PRTK runs the password

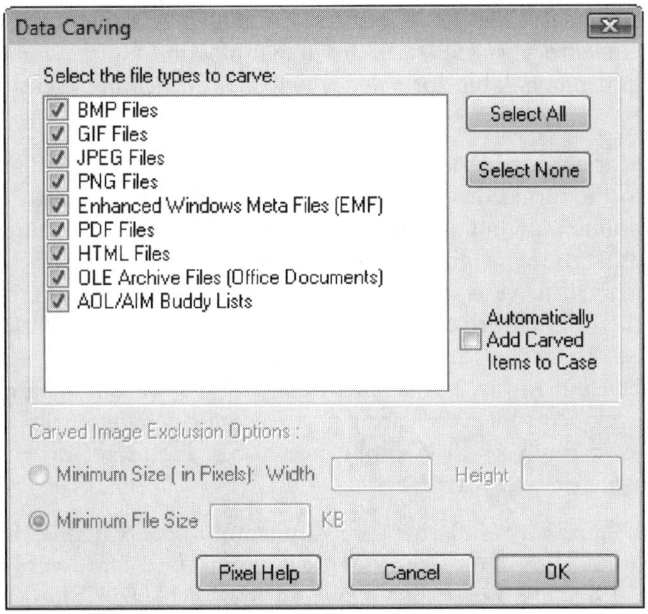

Figure 7-7 Data-carving options in FTK

list against the encrypted file. If it fails to match the password's hash values, it runs a **brute-force attack** on the encrypted file.

AccessData has also created an advanced password-cracking software suite called Distributed Network Attack (DNA) that allows multiple machines to attempt cracking a password. AccessData DNA can also take advantage of AccessData Rainbow Tables, which are a collection of tables containing hash values of plaintext passwords.

After locating the evidence, the next task is to bookmark it so that you can refer to it later when needed. Many forensics tools use bookmarks to insert digital evidence into a report generator, which produces a technical report in HTML or RTF format of the examination's findings. When the report generator is launched, bookmarks are loaded into the report.

Reconstruction The purpose of having a **reconstruction** feature in a forensics tool is to re-create a suspect drive to show what happened during a crime or an incident. Another reason for duplicating a suspect drive is to create a copy for other computer investigators, who might need a fully functional copy of the drive so that they can perform their own acquisition, test, and analysis of the evidence. These are the subfunctions of reconstruction:

- Disk-to-disk copy
- Image-to-disk copy
- Partition-to-partition copy
- Image-to-partition copy

There are several ways to re-create an image of a suspect drive. Under ideal circumstances, the best and most reliable method is obtaining the same make and model drive as the suspect drive, as discussed in Chapter 4. If the suspect drive has been manufactured recently, locating an identical drive is fairly easy. However, because computer manufacturers use just-in-time delivery systems for inventory supplies, a drive manufactured three months ago might be out of production and unavailable for sale, which makes locating identical older drives more difficult.

The simplest method of duplicating a drive is using a tool that makes a direct disk-to-disk copy from the suspect drive to the target drive. Many tools can perform this task. One free tool is the UNIX/Linux dd command, but it has a major disadvantage: The target drive being written to must be identical to the original (suspect) drive, with the same cylinder, sector, and track count. If an identical drive is unavailable, manipulating the drive's cylinders, sectors, and tracks to match the original drive might be possible through your workstation's BIOS. Be aware, however, that other issues might prevent this technique from working correctly because of the target drive's firmware. To address the problem of matching a suspect drive, several vendors have developed tools that can force a geometry change from a suspect drive to a target drive. For most forensics disk duplication tools, the target drive must be equal in size to or larger than the suspect drive.

For a disk-to-disk copy, both hardware and software duplicators are available; hardware duplicators are the fastest way to copy data from one disk to another. Hardware duplicators, such as Logicube Talon, Logicube Forensic MD5, and ImageMASSter Solo III Forensics Hard Drive Duplicator, adjust the target drive's geometry to match the suspect drive's cylinder, sectors, and tracks. Software duplicators, although slower than hardware duplicators, include SnapBack, SafeBack, EnCase, and X-Ways Forensics.

For image-to-disk and image-to-partition copies, many more tools are available, but they are considerably slower in transferring data. The following are some tools that perform an image-to-disk copy:

- SafeBack
- SnapBack
- EnCase
- FTK Imager
- ProDiscover
- X-Ways Forensics

All these tools have proprietary formats that can be restored only by the same application that created them. For example, a ProDiscover image (.eve format) can be restored only by using ProDiscover.

When you must demonstrate in court how criminal activity was carried out on a suspect's computer, you need a product that shadows the suspect drive. This shadowing technique requires a hardware device such as Voom Technologies Shadow Drive. This device connects the suspect drive to a read-only IDE port and another drive to a read-write port. The read-write port drive is referred to as a "shadow drive." When the Voom device with drives is connected to a computer, you can access and run applications on the suspect drive. All data that would normally be written to the suspect drive is redirected to the shadow drive. This tool saves time and helps solve problems you might encounter when trying to make a working duplicate of a suspect drive.

Reporting To complete a forensics disk analysis and examination, you need to create a report. Before Windows forensics tools were available, this process required copying data from a suspect drive and extracting the digital evidence manually. The investigator then copied the evidence to a separate program, such as a word processor, to create a report. File data that couldn't be read in a word processor—databases, spreadsheets, and graphics, for example—made it difficult to insert nonprintable characters, such as binary data, into a report. Typically, these reports weren't stored electronically because investigators had to collect printouts from several different applications to consolidate everything into one large paper report.

Newer Windows forensics tools can produce electronic reports in a variety of formats, such as word processing documents, HTML Web pages, or Acrobat PDF files. These are the subfunctions of the reporting function:

- Log reports
- Report generator

As part of the validation process, often you need to document the steps you took to acquire data from a suspect drive. Many forensics tools, such as FTK, ILook, and X-Ways Forensics, can produce a log report that records activities the investigator performed. Then a built-in report generator is used to create a report in a variety of formats. The following tools are some that offer report generators displaying bookmarked evidence:

- EnCase
- FTK
- ILook
- X-Ways Forensics
- ProDiscover

The log report can be added to your final report as additional documentation of the steps you took during the examination, which can be useful if repeating the examination is necessary. For a case that requires peer review, log reports confirm what activities were performed and what results were found in the original analysis and examination.

Tool Comparisons

To help determine which computer forensics tool to purchase, a comparison table of functions, subfunctions, and vendor products is useful. Cross-referencing functions and subfunctions with vendor products makes it easier to identify the computer forensics tool that best meets your needs. Table 7-1 is an example of how to compare forensics vendors' tools. Your needs might differ from the functions and subfunctions listed in this table. When developing your own table, add other functions and subfunctions you think are necessary to determine which tools you should acquire for an investigation.

Table 7-1 Comparison of forensics tool functions

Function	ProDiscover Basic	ProDiscover Investigator	AccessData Ultimate Toolkit	Guidance Software EnCase
Acquisition				
Physical data copy	✓	✓	✓	✓

Table 7-1 Comparison of forensics tool functions (*continued*)

Function	ProDiscover Basic	ProDiscover Investigator	AccessData Ultimate Toolkit	Guidance Software EnCase
Logical data copy	✓	✓	✓	✓
Data acquisition formats	✓	✓	✓	✓
Command-line process				✓
GUI process	✓	✓	✓	✓
Remote acquisition		✓		✓*
Verification	✓	✓	✓	✓
Validation and discrimination				
Hashing	✓	✓	✓**	✓**
Filtering		✓	✓	✓
Analyzing file headers		✓	✓	✓
Extraction				
Data viewing	✓	✓	✓***	✓***
Keyword searching	✓	✓	✓	✓
Decompressing			✓	✓
Carving		✓	✓	✓
Decrypting			✓	
Bookmarking	✓	✓	✓	✓
Reconstruction				
Disk-to-disk copy	✓	✓	✓	✓
Image-to-disk copy	✓	✓	✓	✓
Partition-to-partition copy	✓	✓		✓
Image-to-partition copy	✓	✓		✓
Reporting				
Log reports		✓	✓	✓
Report generator	✓	✓	✓	
Automation features				
Scripting language		✓		✓

*Must purchase EnCase Enterprise Edition for this feature.
**Both MD5 and SHA-1 hashing are available.
***Supported file formats vary.

Other Considerations for Tools

As part of the business planning for your lab, you should determine which tools offer the most flexibility, reliability, and future expandability. The software tools you select should be compatible with the next generation of OSs. For example, Windows Vista has a new file structure, Windows File Structure (WFS). As an investigator, it's your responsibility to find information on changes in new hardware or software releases and changes planned for the next release. Because OS vendors don't always supply adequate information about future file system upgrades, you must research and prepare for these changes and develop resources for finding new specifications if the vendor fails to provide them. For example, when NTFS was introduced with Windows NT, forensics software vendors revised their products for this new file system, but addressing the file system changes took some time. Therefore, investigators had to look for alternatives to getting the data they needed, such as consulting Microsoft resource kits for Windows NT.

Another consideration when maintaining a computer forensics lab is creating a software library containing older versions of forensics utilities, OSs, and other programs. When purchasing newer and more versatile tools, you should also ensure that your lab maintains older versions of software and OSs, such as Windows and Linux. If a new software version fixes one bug but introduces another, you can use the previous version to overcome problems caused by the new bug.

Computer Forensics Software Tools

Whether you use a suite of tools or a task-specific tool, you have the option of selecting one that enables you to analyze digital evidence through the command line or in a GUI. The following sections explore some options for command-line and GUI tools in both Windows and UNIX/Linux.

Command-Line Forensics Tools

As mentioned in Chapter 1, computers used several OSs before MS-DOS dominated the market. During this time, computer forensics wasn't a major concern. After people started using PCs, however, they figured out how to use them for illegal and destructive purposes and to commit crimes and civil infractions. Software developers began releasing computer forensics tools to help private- and public-sector investigators examine PCs. The first tools that analyzed and extracted data from floppy disks and hard disks were MS-DOS tools for IBM PC file systems.

One of the first MS-DOS tools used for computer investigations was Norton DiskEdit. This tool used manual processes that required investigators to spend considerable time on a typical 500 MB drive. Eventually, programs designed for computer forensics were developed for DOS, Windows, Apple, NetWare, and UNIX systems. Some of these early programs could extract data from slack and free disk space; others were capable only of retrieving deleted files. Current programs are more robust and can search for specific words or characters, import a keyword list to search, calculate hash values, recover deleted items, conduct physical and logical analyses, and more.

One advantage of using command-line tools for an investigation is that they require few system resources because they're designed to run in minimal configurations. In fact, most tools fit on bootable media (floppy disk, USB drive, CD, or DVD). Conducting an initial inquiry or a complete investigation with bootable media can save time and effort. Most tools also produce a text report small enough to fit on a floppy disk.

Some command-line forensics tools are created specifically for DOS/Windows platforms; others are created for Macintosh and UNIX/Linux. Because there are many different versions of UNIX and Linux, these OSs are often referred to as *nix platforms. In Chapter 4, you were introduced to using some command-line tools in Linux, such as the dd and dcfldd commands. For DOS/Windows platforms, a number of companies, such as NTI, Digital Intelligence, MaresWare, DataLifter, and ByteBack, are well recognized for their work in command-line forensics tools.

As software continues to evolve and investigators develop new needs, vendors will address these needs. The tools listed in this chapter are in *no* way a complete list of tools available for DOS/Windows or *nix platforms.

Some tools that are readily available in the command line are often overlooked. For example, in Windows 2000, XP, and Vista, the Dir command shows you the file owner if you have multiple users on the system or network. Try it by following these steps:

1. First, open a command prompt window. In Windows Vista, click **Start**, type **cmd** in the Start Search text box, and then press **Enter**. In Windows XP, click **Start, Run**, type **cmd**, and click **OK**.

2. At the command prompt, type **cd ** and press **Enter** to take you to the root directory.

3. Type **dir /q > C:\Fileowner.txt** and press **Enter**.

4. In any text editor, open Fileowner.txt to see the results. When you're finished, exit the text editor and close the command prompt window.

UNIX/Linux Forensics Tools

The *nix platforms have long been the primary command-line OSs, but typical end users haven't used them widely. However, with GUIs now available with *nix platforms, these OSs are becoming more popular with home and corporate end users.

This newfound popularity and the staggering number of versions give investigators a challenge: learning the *nix command line and investigating the *nix environment. In Chapter 8, you learn more about several *nix tools for forensics analysis, such as SMART, BackTrack, Autopsy with Sleuth Kit, and Knoppix-STD.

This book isn't geared toward the Linux platform for forensics analysis, but using a Linux tool for the processes described in this book works as well as on a Microsoft platform.

SMART SMART is designed to be installed on numerous Linux versions, including Gentoo, Fedora, SUSE, Debian, Knoppix, Ubuntu, Slackware, and more. You can analyze a variety of file systems with SMART; for a list of file systems or to download an evaluation ISO image for SMART and SMART Linux, go to *www.asrdata2.com*.

SMART includes several plug-in utilities. This modular approach makes it possible to upgrade SMART components easily and quickly. SMART can also take advantage of multithreading capabilities in OSs and hardware, a feature lacking in other forensics utilities.

This tool is one of the few that can mount different file systems, such as journaling file systems, in a read-only format.

Another useful option in SMART is the hex viewer. Hex values are color-coded to make it easier to see where a file begins and ends. SMART also offers a reporting feature. Everything you do during your investigation with SMART is logged, so you can select what you want to include in a report, such as bookmarks.

Helix One of the easiest suites to use is Helix because of its user interface. Although Helix is no longer a free package, you can visit *www.e-fense.com* to learn more about it. What's unique about Helix is that you can load it on a live Windows system, and it loads as a bootable Linux OS from a cold boot. Its Windows component is used for live acquisitions. Be aware, however, that some international courts have *not* accepted live acquisitions as a valid forensics practice.

During corporate investigations, often you need to retrieve RAM and other data, such as the suspect's user profile, from a workstation or server that can't be seized or turned off. This data is extracted while the system is running and captured in its state at the time of extraction. Make sure to keep a journal to record what you're doing, however. To do a live acquisition, insert the Helix CD into the suspect's machine. After clicking I ACCEPT in the licensing window, you see the Helix menu shown in Figure 7-8.

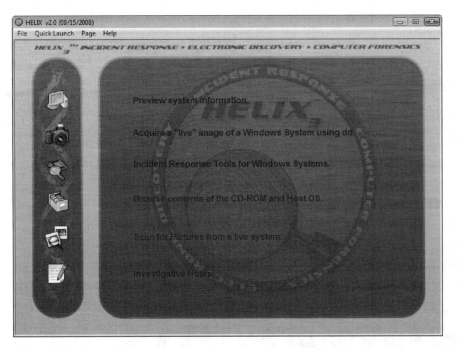

Figure 7-8 The Helix menu

BackTrack BackTrack is another Linux Live CD used by many security professionals and forensics investigators. It includes a variety of tools and has an easy-to-use KDE interface. You can download the ISO image from *www.remote-exploit.org/backtrack.html*. Autopsy and Sleuth Kit, discussed next, are included with the BackTrack tools as well as Foremost (covered in Chapter 8), dcfldd, Pasco, MemFetch, and MBoxGrep. You work with some BackTrack tools in Chapter 11.

Autopsy and Sleuth Kit Sleuth Kit is a Linux forensics tool, and Autopsy is the GUI browser interface for accessing Sleuth Kit's tools. Chapter 8 explains how to install these tools, but if you're accessing them from Helix, for example, shut down your Windows computer with the Helix disc in the CD/DVD drive, making sure your system is set to boot from the CD/DVD drive before the hard drive. Then do a hard boot to the computer. In the options that are displayed, select Expert Mode. (Note that this mode is forensically sound.) If you're booting from a laptop, you might have display issues. You can select "scan" to have Helix find the correct settings. (If Helix fails to find these settings, experiment until you find a setting that works.) After the correct display setting is applied, a GUI with a blue background is displayed. If prompted, specify whether to load SCSI modules or additional modules from a floppy disk.

On your desktop, you should see what drives have been detected. For example, say that /mnt/hda1 and /mnt/hda2 are displayed at the upper left. If you click the Helix button, which is similar to the Start button in Windows, you see the GUI selection. When you select Forensic Tools, the Autopsy option is displayed. From here, you can open an existing case or start a new case. For more information on these tools, visit *www.sleuthkit. org*.

Knoppix-STD Knoppix Security Tools Distribution (STD) is a collection of tools for configuring security measures, including computer and network forensics. Note that Knoppix-STD is forensically sound, so it doesn't allow you to alter or damage the system you're analyzing. You can download the ISO image at *www.knoppix-std.org* and create a bootable CD with it. If you boot this CD into Windows, Knoppix lists available tools. Although many of the tools have GUI interfaces, some are still command line only. If you right-click each category while booted in Linux, a section called rtfm has a README file for each application. Figure 7-9 shows what you see if you load the Knoppix-STD CD in Windows. You can scroll through this window and see some of the available tools (see Figure 7-10).

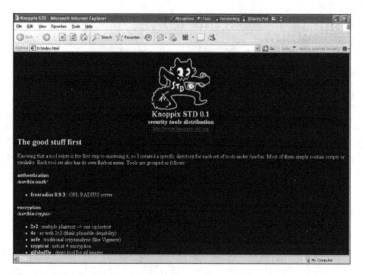

Figure 7-9 The Knoppix-STD information window in Windows

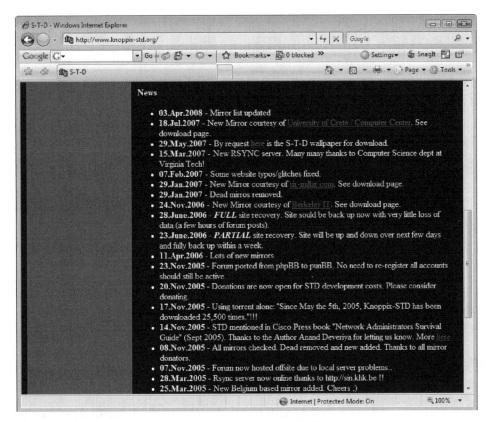

Figure 7-10 A list of forensics tools available in Knoppix-STD

Like Helix, Knoppix-STD is a Linux bootable CD. If you shut down Windows and reboot with the Knoppix-STD disc in the CD/DVD drive, your system boots into Linux.

Other GUI Forensics Tools

Several software vendors have introduced forensics tools that work in Windows. Because GUI forensics tools don't require the same understanding of MS-DOS and file systems as command-line tools, they can simplify computer forensics investigations. These GUI tools have also simplified training for beginning examiners; however, you should continue to learn about and use command-line tools because some GUI tools might miss critical evidence.

Most GUI tools are put together as suites of tools. For example, the largest GUI tool vendors—Technology Pathways, AccessData, and Guidance Software—offer tools that perform most of the tasks discussed in this chapter. As with all software, each suite has its strengths and weaknesses.

GUI tools have several advantages, such as ease of use, the capability to perform multiple tasks, and no requirement to learn older OSs. Their disadvantages range from excessive resource requirements (needing large amounts of RAM, for example) and producing inconsistent results because of the type of OS used, such as Windows Vista 32-bit or 64-bit systems. Another concern with using GUI tools is that they create investigators' dependence on using only one tool. In some situations, GUI tools don't work and a command-line tool is required, so investigators must be familiar with more than one type of tool.

Computer Forensics Hardware Tools

This section discusses computer hardware used for forensics investigations. Technology changes rapidly, and hardware manufacturers have designed most computer components to last about 18 months between failures. Hardware is hardware; whether it's a rack-mounted server or a forensic workstation, eventually it fails. For this reason, you should schedule equipment replacements periodically—ideally, every 18 months if you use the hardware full-time. Most computer forensics operations use a workstation 24 hours a day for a week or longer between complete shutdowns.

You should plan your hardware needs carefully, especially if you have budget limitations. Include the amount of time you expect the forensic workstation to be running, how often you expect hardware failures, consultant and vendor fees to support the hardware, and how often to anticipate replacing forensic workstations. The longer you expect the forensic work-station to be running, the more you need to anticipate physical equipment failure and the expense of replacement equipment.

Forensic Workstations

Many computer vendors offer a wide range of forensic workstations that you can tailor to meet your investigation needs. The more diverse your investigation environment, the more options you need. In general, forensic workstations can be divided into the following categories:

- *Stationary workstation*—A tower with several bays and many peripheral devices
- *Portable workstation*—A laptop computer with a built-in LCD monitor and almost as many bays and peripherals as a stationary workstation
- *Lightweight workstation*—Usually a laptop computer built into a carrying case with a small selection of peripheral options

When considering options to add to a basic workstation, keep in mind that PCs have limitations on how many peripherals they can handle. The more peripherals you add, the more potential problems you might have, especially if you're using an older version of Windows. You must learn to balance what you actually need with what your system can handle.

If you're operating a computer forensics lab for a police agency, you need as many options as possible to handle any investigation. If possible, use two or three configurations of PCs to handle diverse investigations. You should also keep a hardware inventory in addition to your software library. In the corporate environment, however, consider streamlining your workstation to meet the needs of only the types of systems used in your business.

Building Your Own Workstation
To decide whether you want to build your own workstation, first ask "How much do I have to spend?" Building a forensic work-station isn't as difficult as it sounds but can quickly become expensive if you aren't careful. If you have the time and skill to build your own forensic workstation, you can

customize it to your needs and save money, although you might have trouble finding support for problems that develop. For example, peripheral devices might conflict with one another, or components might fail. If you build your own forensic workstation, you should be able to support the hardware. You also need to identify what you intend to analyze. If you're analyzing SPARC disks from workstations in a corporate network, for example, you need to include a SPARC drive with a write-protector on your forensic workstation.

If you decide that building a forensic workstation is beyond your skills, several vendors offer workstations designed for computer forensics, such as the F.R.E.D. unit from Digital Intelligence or the Dual Xeon Workstation from ForensicPC. Having a vendor-supplied workstation has its advantages. If you aren't skilled in computer hardware maintenance and repair, having vendor support can save you time and frustration when you have problems. Of course, you can always mix and match components to get the capabilities you need for your forensic workstation.

 If you don't have the skills to build and support a PC, you might want to consider taking an A+ certification course.

Using a Write-Blocker

The first item you should consider for a forensic workstation is a **write-blocker**. Write-blockers protect evidence disks by preventing data from being written to them. Software and hardware write-blockers perform the same function but in a different fashion.

Software write-blockers, such as PDBlock from Digital Intelligence, typically run in a shell mode (for example, DOS). PDBlock changes interrupt 13 of a workstation's BIOS to prevent writing to the specified drive. If you attempt to write data to the blocked drive, an alarm sounds, advising that no writes have occurred. PDBlock can run only in a true DOS mode, however, not in a Windows MS-DOS shell.

With hardware write-blockers, you can connect the evidence drive to your workstation and start the OS as usual. Hardware write-blockers are ideal for GUI forensics tools. They prevent Windows or Linux from writing data to the blocked drive. Hardware write-blockers act as a bridge between the suspect drive and the forensic workstation.

In the Windows environment, when a write-blocker is installed on an attached drive, the drive appears as any other attached disk. You can navigate to the blocked drive with any Windows application, such as Windows Explorer, to view files or use Word to read files. When you copy data to the blocked drive or write updates to a file with Word, Windows shows that the data copy is successful. However, the write-blocker actually discards the written data—in other words, data is written to null. When you restart the workstation and examine the blocked drive, you won't see the data or files you copied to it previously.

Many vendors have developed write-blocking devices that connect to a computer through FireWire, USB 2.0, SATA, and SCSI controllers. Most of these write-blockers enable you to remove and reconnect drives without having to shut down your workstation, which saves time in processing the evidence drive. For more information on write-blocker specifications, visit *www.cftt.nist.gov*. The following vendors provide write-blocking devices:

- *www.digitalintelligence.com*
- *www.forensicpc.com*
- *www.guidancesoftware.com*
- *www.voomtech.com*
- *www.mykeytech.com*
- *www.lc-tech.com*
- *www.logicube.com*
- *www.forensic-computers.com*
- *www.wiebetech.com*
- *www.paraben-forensics.com*
- *www.usbgear.com/USB-FORENSIC.html*

Recommendations for a Forensic Workstation

Before you purchase or build a forensic workstation, determine where your data acquisitions will take place. If you acquire data in the field, consider streamlining the tools you use. With the newer FireWire and USB 2.0 write-blocking devices, you can acquire data easily with Digital Intelligence FireChief and a laptop computer, for example. If you want to reduce the hardware you carry, consider a product such as the WiebeTech Forensic DriveDock with its regular DriveDock FireWire bridge or the Logicube Talon.

When choosing a computer as a stationary or lightweight forensic workstation, you want a full tower to allow for expansion devices, such as a 2.5-inch drive converter to analyze a laptop hard drive on a 3.5-inch IDE write-protected drive controller. You want as much memory and processor power as your budget allows and various sizes of hard drives. In addition, consider a 400-watt or better power supply with battery backup, extra power and data cables, a SCSI controller card, external FireWire and USB ports, an assortment of drive adapter bridges to connect SATA to IDE (PATA) drives, an ergonomic keyboard and mouse, and a good video card with at least a 17-inch monitor. If you plan to conduct many investigations, a high-end video card and monitor are recommended. If you have a limited budget, one option for outfitting your lab is to use high-end game PCs from a local computer store. With some minor modifications and additions of hardware components, these systems perform extremely well.

As with any technology, what your forensic workstation includes is often a matter of preference. Whatever vendor you choose, make sure the devices you select perform the functions you expect to need as an investigator.

Validating and Testing Forensics Software

Now that you have selected some tools to use, you need to make sure the evidence you recover and analyze can be admitted in court. To do this, you must test and validate your software. The following sections discuss validation tools available at the time of this writing and how to develop your own validation protocols.

Using National Institute of Standards and Technology (NIST) Tools

The National Institute of Standards and Technology publishes articles, provides tools, and creates procedures for testing and validating computer forensics software. Software should be verified to improve evidence admissibility in judicial proceedings. NIST sponsors the **Computer Forensics Tool Testing (CFTT)** project to manage research on computer forensics tools. For additional information on this testing project, visit *www.cftt.nist.gov*.

NIST has created criteria for testing computer forensics tools, which are included in the article "General Test Methodology for Computer Forensic Tools" (version 1.9, November 7, 2001), available at *www.cftt.nist.gov/testdocs.html*. The article addresses the lack of specifications for what forensics tools should do and the importance of tools meeting judicial scrutiny. The criteria are based on standard testing methods and ISO 17025 criteria for testing items that have no current standards. Your lab must meet the following criteria and keep accurate records so that when new software and hardware become available, testing standards are in place for your lab:

- *Establish categories for computer forensics tools*—Group computer forensics software according to categories, such as forensics tools designed to retrieve and trace e-mail.

- *Identify computer forensics category requirements*—For each category, describe the technical features or functions a forensics tool must have.

- *Develop test assertions*—Based on the requirements, create tests that prove or disprove the tool's capability to meet the requirements.

- *Identify test cases*—Find or create types of cases to investigate with the forensics tool, and identify information to retrieve from a sample drive or other media. For example, use the image of a closed case file created with a trusted forensics tool to test a new tool in the same category and see whether it produces the same results.

- *Establish a test method*—Considering the tool's purpose and design, specify how to test it.

- *Report test results*—Describe the test results in a report that complies with ISO 17025, which requires accurate, clear, unambiguous, and objective test reports.

Another standards document, ISO 5725, demands accuracy for all aspects of the testing process, so results must be repeatable and reproducible. "Repeatable results" means that if you work in the same lab on the same machine, you generate the same results. "Reproducible results" means that if you're in a different lab working on a different machine, the tool still retrieves the same information.

NIST has also developed several tools for evaluating drive-imaging tools. These tools are posted on the CFTT Web site at *www.cftt.nist.gov/disk_imaging.htm*.

In addition, NIST created the **National Software Reference Library (NSRL)** project (*www.nsrl.nist.gov*) with the goal of collecting all known hash values for commercial software and OS files. The primary hash NSRL uses is SHA-1, which generates a known set of digital signatures called the Reference Data Set (RDS). SHA-1 provides better accuracy than other hashing methods, such as MD5 or CRC-32.

The purpose of collecting known hash values is to reduce the number of known files, such as OS or program files, included in a forensics examination of a drive so that only unknown files are left. You can also use the RDS to locate and identify known bad files, such as illegal images and computer viruses, on a suspect drive.

Using Validation Protocols

After retrieving and examining evidence data with one tool, you should verify your results by performing the same tasks with other similar forensics tools. For example, after you use one forensics tool to retrieve disk data, you use another to see whether you retrieve the same information. Although this step might seem unnecessary, you might be asked on the witness stand "How did you verify your results?" To satisfy the need for verification, you need at least two tools to validate software or hardware upgrades. The tool you use to validate the results should be well tested and documented. You perform a tool validation exercise in the Hands-On Projects at the end of this chapter.

Investigators must be confident in a tool's capability to produce consistent and accurate findings during analysis. Understanding how the tool works is equally important, as you might not have vendor support in a courtroom. One way to compare results and verify a new tool is by using a disk editor, such as Hex Workshop or WinHex, to view data on a disk in its raw format. Disk editors typically show files, file headers, file slack, RAM slack, and other data on the physical disk. Although disk editors aren't known for their flashy interfaces, they are reliable and capable of accessing sectors of the digital evidence to verify your findings.

 Although a disk editor gives you the most flexibility in testing, it might not be capable of examining a compressed file's contents, such as a .zip file or an Outlook .pst file. This is another reason that testing and validating your tools' capabilities are essential.

If you decide to use a GUI computer forensics tool, use the recommended steps in the following sections to validate your findings.

Computer Forensics Examination Protocol

1. First, conduct your investigation of the digital evidence with one GUI tool.

2. Then perform the same investigation with a disk editor to verify that the GUI tool is seeing the same digital evidence in the same places on the test or suspect drive's image.

3. If a file is recovered, obtain the hash value with the GUI tool and the disk editor, and then compare the results to verify whether the file has the same value in both tools.

Many investigators in both the public and private sectors use FTK and EnCase as their choice of "flagship" forensics software suites, but they don't rely on them solely; investigators' software libraries often include other forensics utilities to supplement these tools' capabilities.

Computer Forensics Tool Upgrade Protocol In addition to verifying your results by using two disk-analysis tools, you should test all new releases and OS patches and upgrades to make sure they're reliable and don't corrupt evidence data. New releases and OS upgrades and patches can affect the way your forensics tools perform. If you determine that a patch or upgrade isn't reliable, don't use it on your forensic workstation until the problem has been fixed. If you have a problem, such as not being able to read old image files with the new release or the disk editor generating errors after you apply the latest service pack, you can file an error report with the vendor. In most cases, the vendor addresses the problem and provides a new patch, which you should check with another round of validation testing.

One of the best ways to test patches and upgrades is to build a test hard disk to store data in unused space allocated for a file, also known as file slack. You can then use a forensics tool to retrieve it. If you can retrieve the data with that tool and verify your findings with a second tool, you know the tool is reliable.

As computer forensics tools continue to evolve, you should check the Web for new editions, updates, patches, and validation tests for your tools. Always validate what the hardware or software tool is doing as opposed to what it's supposed to be doing. Be confident and knowledgeable about the capabilities of your forensics toolbox. Remember to test and document why a tool does or doesn't work the way it's supposed to.

7

Chapter Summary

- Consult your business plan to get the best hardware and software solution for your computer investigation needs.

- The five functions required for computer forensics tools are acquisition, validation and discrimination, extraction, reconstruction, and reporting.

- For your computer forensics lab, you should create a software library for older versions of forensics utilities, OSs, and applications and maintain older versions of software you have used and retired, such as previous versions of Windows and Linux.

- Some computer forensics tools run in a command-line interface, including those that can find file slack and free space, recover data, and search by keyword. They are designed to run in minimal configurations and can fit on a bootable disk.

- Hardware required for computer forensics includes workstations and devices, such as write-blockers, to prevent contamination of evidence. Before you purchase or build a forensic workstation, consider where you acquire data, which determines the hardware configuration you need.

- Tools that run in Windows and other GUI environments don't require the same level of computing expertise as command-line tools and can simplify training and investigations.

- Before upgrading to a new version of a computer forensics tool, run a validation test on the new version. The National Institute of Standards and Technology has standard guidelines for verifying forensics tools.

Key Terms

acquisition The process of creating a duplicate image of data; one of the five required functions of computer forensics tools.

brute-force attack The process of trying every combination of characters—letters, numbers, and special characters typically found on a keyboard—to find a matching password or passphrase value for an encrypted file.

Computer Forensics Tool Testing (CFTT) A project sponsored by the National Institute of Standards and Technology to manage research on computer forensics tools.

discrimination The process of sorting and searching through investigation data to separate known good data from suspicious data; along with validation, one of the five required functions of computer forensics tools.

extraction The process of pulling relevant data from an image and recovering or reconstructing data fragments; one of the five required functions of computer forensics tools.

keyword search A method of finding files or other information by entering relevant characters, words, or phrases in a search tool.

National Software Reference Library (NSRL) A NIST project with the goal of collecting all known hash values for commercial software and OS files.

password dictionary attack An attack that uses a collection of words or phrases that might be passwords for an encrypted file. Password recovery programs can use a password dictionary to compare potential passwords to an encrypted file's password or passphrase hash values.

reconstruction The process of rebuilding data files; one of the five required functions of computer forensics tools.

validation The process of checking the accuracy of results; along with discrimination, one of the five required functions of computer forensics tools.

write-blocker A hardware device or software program that prevents a computer from writing data to an evidence drive. Software write-blockers typically alter interrupt 13 write functions to a drive in a PC's BIOS. Hardware write-blockers are usually bridging devices between a drive and the forensic workstation.

Review Questions

1. What are the five required functions for computer forensics tools?

2. A disk partition can be copied only with a command-line acquisition tool. True or False?

3. What two data-copying methods are used in software data acquisitions?
   a.   Remote and local
   b.   Local and logical
   c.   Logical and physical
   d.   Physical and compact

4. During a remote acquisition of a suspect drive, RAM data is lost. True or False?

5. Hashing, filtering, and file header analysis make up which function of computer forensics tools?

    a. Validation and discrimination

    b. Acquisition

    c. Extraction

    d. Reporting

6. Sleuth Kit is used to access Autopsy's tools. True or False?

7. When considering new forensics software, you should do which of the following?

    a. Uninstall other forensics software.

    b. Reinstall the OS.

    c. Test and validate the software.

    d. None of the above.

8. What are the subfunctions of the extraction function?

9. Data can't be written to the disk with a command-line tool. True or False?

10. Hash values are used for which of the following purposes? (Choose all that apply.)

    a. Determining file size

    b. Filtering known good files from potentially suspicious data

    c. Reconstructing file fragments

    d. Validating that the original data hasn't changed

11. What's the name of the NIST project established to collect all known hash values for commercial software and OS files?

12. Many of the newer GUI tools use a lot of system resources. True or False?

13. Building a forensic workstation is more expensive than purchasing one. True or False?

14. A live acquisition is considered an accepted forensics practice. True or False?

15. Which of the following is true of most drive-imaging tools? (Choose all that apply.)

    a. They perform the same function as a backup.

    b. They ensure that the original drive doesn't become corrupt and damage the digital evidence.

    c. They create a copy of the original drive.

    d. They must be run from the command line.

16. The standards for testing forensics tools are based on which criteria?

    a. U.S. Title 18

    b. ISO 5725

    c. ISO 17025

    d. All of the above

17. Which of the following tools can examine files created by WinZip?

    a. FTK

    b. Hex Workshop

    c. Registry Viewer

    d. SMART

18. List four subfunctions of reconstructing drives.

19. When validating the results of a forensics analysis, you should do which of the following?

    a. Calculate the hash value with two different tools.

    b. Use a different tool to compare the results of evidence you find.

    c. Repeat the steps used to obtain the digital evidence, using the same tool, and recalculate the hash value to verify the results.

    d. Do both a and b.

    e. Do both b and c.

    f. Do both a and c.

    g. Do none of the above.

20. NIST testing procedures are valid only for government agencies. True or False?

Hands-On Projects

If necessary, extract all data files in the Chap07\Projects folder on the book's DVD to the *Work*\Chap07\Projects folder on your system. (If necessary, create this folder on your system before starting the projects; it's referred to as "your work folder" in steps.)

Hands-On Project 7-1

In this project, you create and delete files on a USB drive (or small disk partition, if you don't have a USB drive), and then use AccessData FTK to analyze the drive. In Hands-On Project 7-2, you use SecureClean to erase this drive to make sure it contains no data. To download and install SecureClean, follow these steps:

1. Start your Web browser and go to **www.whitecanyon.com/secureclean.php**.

2. Click the **Try Demo** link, scroll down if necessary, and click the **Download Demo** link for SecureClean. Save the **Secureclean.exe** download file in your work folder.

3. Exit your Web browser, closing any download dialog boxes, if necessary.

4. Start Windows Explorer or My Computer, navigate to your work folder, and then double-click **Secureclean.exe**.

5. In the first installation window, click **Next**. Click **Yes** to accept the license agreement, and then click **Next** to accept the default destination folder. Click **Next** to accept the default location for program files, and then click **Next** to accept the default Start menu folder. Finally, click **Finish** to complete the installation.

6. In the "What would you like to try first" dialog box, click **Cancel** to exit SecureClean. Then close any open windows.

Next, you use Microsoft Word and Excel to create and delete files and use FTK to analyze the drive. Follow these steps:

1. Create a **C7Prj01** folder on your USB drive or disk partition.

2. Start a new document in Word and type **This is to test deleting files and then wiping them**. Save the file in the C7Prj01 folder as **Test7-1.doc**. Exit Word.

3. Start a new workbook in Excel. Type a few numbers, and then save the workbook in the C7Prj01 folder on your USB or disk drive as **Test7-2.xls**. Exit Excel.

4. Use Windows Explorer or My Computer to delete both files from the USB or disk drive.

5. Start AccessData FTK, and start a new case. Type your name for the investigator's name, enter **C7Prj01** for the case number and case name, and enter your work folder as the case path. Click **Next** until you reach the Add Evidence dialog box.

6. Click the **Add Evidence** button, click the **Local Drive** option button, and then click **Continue**.

7. In the Select Local Drive dialog box, make sure the USB or disk drive and **Logical Analysis** are selected, and then click **OK**.

8. Read the message in the warning box, and then click **Yes** to continue adding evidence.

9. In the Evidence Information dialog box, click to select your time zone, and then click **OK**. Click **Next**, and then click **Finish**. FTK processes the data on the USB or disk drive.

10. Click the **Deleted Files** button in the Overview tab to display the files deleted from the USB or disk drive (the two test files you created and deleted). The FTK window might also display temporary files that were created.

11. Click any file in the lower pane to view its contents in the upper-right pane.

12. Close all open windows, and exit FTK. If prompted to back up the case, click **No**.

Hands-On Project 7-2

Now you're ready to use SecureClean to remove all traces of data from your USB or disk drive. Follow these steps:

1. Create a **C7Prj02** folder on your USB or disk drive.

2. To start SecureClean, click **Start,** point to **All Programs,** point to **White-Canyon,** point to **SecureClean 4,** and click **Clean My Computer.**

3. If you see the Protected Recycle Bin warning message, click **OK** to continue.

4. In the SecureClean window, click the **Try It Free** button. If you see a notice about checking for online updates, click **No,** and then click **Continue.**

5. In the Drive List section, click to clear the check boxes, if necessary, and then click the check box corresponding to your USB or disk drive. Make sure SecureClean is the only open window, and then click **Deep Clean.**

6. When you see a message about checking the drive for errors, click **OK** to continue.

7. Click the **Start Clean Now** button.

8. In the warning message stating that the data can no longer be recovered, click **OK** to continue. When SecureClean finishes cleaning the drive, click **OK** to exit the program.

9. Start AccessData FTK, and start a new case. Type your name for the investigator's name, enter **C7Prj02** for the case number and case name, and enter your work folder as the case path. Click **Next** until you reach the Add Evidence dialog box.

10. Click the **Add Evidence** button, click the **Local Drive** option button, and then click **Continue.** The Select Local Drive dialog box opens.

11. Make sure the USB or disk drive and **Logical Analysis** are selected, and then click **OK.** If you see a warning message about using live evidence, click **Yes** to continue.

12. In the Evidence Information dialog box, click to select your time zone, and then click **OK** to accept the default settings. Click **Next,** and then click **Finish.**

13. In the Overview tab, click the **Unknown Type** button, click the F~S0001T~P file, and note that it contains no data. The FTK window shows only the root folder, slack/free space, and perhaps an unknown file type. Click the **Unknown Type** button again, if necessary, to see the contents of slack space. If you used SecureClean without deleting any files on the drive, the FTK window shows filenames with hexadecimal values of all 0s. If a SecureClean document appears in the FTK window, the contents are reported as "Nothing to view, document is empty." In the Slack/ Free Space area, the Disk Free, FAT1, and FAT2 columns show 0s, indicating that the drive contains no data.

14. Exit FTK, clicking **No** if prompted to back up the case.

Hands-On Project 7-3

In this project, you create a test drive by planting evidence in the file slack space on a USB drive or small disk partition. Then you use FTK and Hex Workshop (which you downloaded in a previous chapter from *www.hexworkshop.com*) to verify that the drive contains evidence. Follow these steps:

1. First, you format the drive in Windows Explorer. Right-click the drive icon and click **Format,** click to clear the **Quick Format** check box, if necessary, and then click **Start.** If you see a warning message, click **OK** to continue. You can also use SecureClean as described in Hands-On Project 7-2 to wipe the drive. When you're finished, exit Windows Explorer or SecureClean.

2. Create a **C7Prj03** folder on the USB or disk drive. *Warning*: This drive should contain data you no longer need.

3. Start a new document in Word and type **Testing for string Namibia.** Save the file in the C7Prj03 folder as **C7Prj03a.doc.**

4. Close the file, start a new Word document, and type **Testing for string XYZX.** Save the file in the C7Prj03 folder as **C7Prj03b.doc.** Exit Word.

Next, you use Hex Workshop to hide information in file slack space:

1. Start Hex Workshop. On a sheet of paper, create a chart with two columns. Label the columns **Item** and **Sector.**

2. In Hex Workshop, click **Disk, Open Drive** from the menu. Make sure the USB or disk drive is selected, and then click **OK.**

3. Click **File, Open** from the menu. Navigate to and double-click **C7Prj03a.doc.** Scroll down until you see "Testing for string Namibia."

4. Click the tab corresponding to your USB or disk drive, and then click at the beginning of the right column. Click **Edit, Find** from the menu. In the Find dialog box, make sure **Text String** is selected in the Type list box. Type **Namibia** in the Value text box, click the **Either** option button, and then click **OK.** (If Hex Workshop doesn't find "Namibia" the first time, repeat this step.)

5. In the Item column on your chart, write **C7Prj03a.doc.** In the Sector column, write the sector number containing the search text, as shown on the Hex Workshop title bar.

6. Scroll to the bottom of the sector, if necessary. Type **Murder She Wrote** *near* the end of the sector in the right pane, and then click the **Save** toolbar button. (*Note*: If you're asked to enable Insert mode, click **OK,** press **Insert,** click to select the **Disable notification message** check box, and click **OK,** if necessary.)

7. Click the **C7Prj03a.doc** tab. Click **Edit, Find** from the menu, type **Murder** in the Value text box, and then click **OK.** Hex Workshop can't find this text in C7Prj03a.doc. Click **Edit, Find** from the menu, and then click **OK** to verify that Hex Workshop doesn't find "Murder" in the document. Close the file by clicking the lower **Close** button in the upper-right corner.

7

8. Click **File, Open** from the menu. Navigate to and double-click **C7Prj03b.doc**. Scroll down, if needed, until you see the "Testing for string XYZX" text you entered earlier. (*Hint:* You might need to use the Find command more than once to find this text.)

9. Click the tab for your USB or disk drive, if necessary, and then click at the beginning of the right column. Click **Edit, Find** from the menu, type **XYZX** as the value you want to find, and then click **OK**. On your chart, write **C7Prj03b.doc** as the filename in the Item column, and in the Sector column, note the sector number containing the search text, as shown on the Hex Workshop title bar.

10. In the tab for your USB or disk drive, type **I Spy** *near* the end of the sector in the right pane, in the slack space, and then click the **Save** toolbar button.

11. Verify that "I Spy" doesn't appear as part of the file by clicking the **C7Prj03b.doc** tab and searching for this string twice.

12. Close the C7Prj03b.doc file, and exit Hex Workshop.

 In a forensics lab, you would generate the drive's MD5 hash value with a tool such as md5sum, and generate a copy with a tool such as FTK Imager.

Hands-On Project 7-4

Follow these steps to verify your results from Hands-On Project 7-3 with AccessData FTK:

1. Create a **C7Proj04** folder on your USB or disk drive.

2. Start AccessData FTK, and start a new case. Type your name for the investigator's name, enter **C7Prj04** for the case name and case number, and enter your work folder as the case path. Click **Next** until you reach the Add Evidence to Case dialog box.

3. Click the **Add Evidence** button, click the **Local Drive** option button, and then click **Continue**.

4. In the Select Local Drive dialog box, make sure your USB or disk drive and **Logical Analysis** are selected, and then click **OK**. (Click **Yes** in the warning message box, if necessary, to continue working.)

5. In the Evidence Information dialog box, click to select your time zone, and then click **OK**. Click **Next**, and then click **Finish**. FTK processes the files on the drive, and then indicates the evidence items contained on the drive.

6. Click the **Search** tab. Click **Tools, Analysis Tools** from the menu, click to select the **Full Text Indexing** check box, if necessary, and then click **OK**.

7. In the Search Term text box, type **Namibia**, and then click **Add**. Click the **View Cumulative Results** button, and then click **OK** in the Filter Search

Hits dialog box. Repeat this search for the **XYZX**, **Murder**, and **I Spy** keywords. The list under Search Items indicates how many matches (hits) FTK finds on the drive for each keyword. (Note that items in the file slack space aren't listed in the Indexed Search tab.)

8. Click the **Overview** tab, click **Documents**, click **C7Prj03b.doc**, and then scroll the upper-right pane, if necessary, until you can see the "I Spy" text. Make note of the logical sector position displayed at the bottom of the upper-right pane.

9. Click the **Search** tab and then the **Live Search** tab. In the Search Term text box, type **I Spy** and make sure **ASCII** and **Unicode** are selected. Click the **Add** button and then the **Search** button, click to select the **All files** option button if necessary, and then click **OK**. When the search is finished, click **View Results**. A "Search Performed" message and the date are displayed at the upper right.

10. Click the expand (**+**) buttons to find the results of the search, which are displayed as "1 Hit." In the middle pane, scroll until you find "I Spy."

11. Repeat Steps 9 and 10 for "Murder."

12. The bottom pane displays details about the data FTK found on the drive that match your search criteria. Click each occurrence and scroll to the right to see any other information FTK supplies, such as the file's MD5 hash value.

13. Write the filename and sector information for each item found. Note that FTK finds more than one occurrence of each word on the drive. Below your chart, explain why the words appear more than once.

14. Close all open windows, and exit FTK, clicking **No** if prompted to back up the case.

Hands-On Project 7-5

You should test new or updated computer forensics tools to make sure they're performing correctly. When complex software applications are updated, they might create new problems and function failures the vendor wasn't aware of. In this project, you test two competing computer forensics analysis tools to see how they compare in locating and recovering data. To test these tools, you need one or more controlled sample drive images. You should know the contents of these drive images so that you can determine how efficient the tools are at locating data. Developing a good sample test image takes experience in knowing what to look for on a suspect drive.

To prepare for this project, testing FTK against ProDiscover Basic, you need the following:

- ProDiscover Basic installed on your workstation
- FTK installed on your workstation
- The **GCFI-datacarve-NTFS.eve** file you extracted to your work folder

In the following steps, you use ProDiscover to convert the image file to raw (.dd) format and then analyze the two images:

1. Start ProDiscover Basic, click **Tools** from the menu, point to **Image Conversion Tools**, and then click **Convert ProDiscover Image to "DD"**.

2. In the Convert ProDiscover Image to "DD" Image dialog box, click **Browse** next to the Source ProDiscover Image text box. Navigate to your work folder and click **GCFI-datacarve-NTFS.eve**. Click **Open**, and then click **OK**.

3. To start your analysis, click the **New Project** toolbar button. In the New Project dialog box, type **C7Prj05PD** for the project number and project filename, and then click **OK** (*Note*: If you get an error when starting a new project, exit ProDiscover and start it again.)

4. In the tree view, click to expand **Add** and then click **Image File**. In the Open dialog box, navigate to your work folder, click **gcfi-datacarve-ntfs.dd**, and then click **Open**.

5. In the tree view, click to expand **Content View** and then **Images**. Click to expand the. dd image file, and then click **All Files**. If necessary, click **Yes** in the ProDiscover message box that opens.

6. In the work area, right-click any column header, such as Select or File Name, and then click **Field Chooser**. In the right pane of the Field Chooser dialog box, scroll down and click **Modified Date**. Click the **Move Up** button until Modified Date is immediately under File Extension, and then click **OK**.

7. In the work area, click the **Modified Date** column header until the oldest data is displayed at the top of the list.

8. Click the check box next to all deleted files with the date 5/20/2005. For each file, when the Add Comment dialog box opens, type **Deleted date test** for the comment, and then click **OK**.

9. Next, click the **Search** toolbar button. In the Search dialog box, click the **Content Search** tab. In the Search for the pattern(s) text box, type **BM6** (to search for headers for bitmap files). Under Select the Disk(s)/Image(s) you want to search in, click the. dd image file, and then click **OK**.

10. In the Search 1 tab of the search results, click the check box next to deleted files with a **.jpg** extension that have bitmap headers. When the first Add Comment dialog box opens, type **Search results for non-BMP extensions**, click the **Apply to all items** check box, and then click **OK**. Continue selecting the remaining deleted files with .jpg extensions. When you're finished, click **Add to Report**.

11. Click the **Search** toolbar button. In the Search dialog box, click the **Content Search** tab. In the Search for the pattern(s) text box, type **S5000**. Under Select the Disk(s)/Image(s) you want to search in, click the. dd image file, and then click **OK**.

12. In the Search 2 tab of the search results, click the check box next to deleted files with an **.html** extension that contain the search term S5000,

and then click **Add to Report**. Note that the files selected from the first search appear in the second search results, too. Don't clear the check boxes next to these files because they are added to the report for this test.

13. In the tree view, click **Report**, and then click the **Export** toolbar button. In the Export dialog box, click the **RTF Format** option button, click **Browse**, and navigate to and click your work folder. Type **Chap7-5-PD.rtf** in the File Name text box, and then click **Save**. Click **OK** in the Export dialog box, and then click **File, Print Report** from the menu to print your report.

14. When you're finished, click **File, Exit** from the menu. When prompted, click **Yes** to save, and then click **Save**.

Next, you perform the same searches in FTK:

1. Start AccessData FTK, clicking **OK** or **Yes** to any information or warning messages to continue.

2. In the Startup dialog box, click **Start a new case**, and then click **OK**.

3. In the New Case dialog box, enter your name for the investigator, type **C7Prj05FTK** for the case name and number, enter your work folder as the case path, and then click **Next**.

4. In the FTK Report Wizard - Case Information dialog box, fill in your information, and then click **Next**. Continue clicking **Next** until you reach the Add Evidence to Case dialog box.

5. Click the **Add Evidence** button. In the next Add Evidence to Case dialog box, click **Acquired Image of Drive**, and then click **Continue**. In the Open dialog box, navigate to your work folder, click the **gcfi-datacarve-ntfs.dd** image file, and then click **Open**.

6. In the Evidence Information dialog box, click to select your time zone, and then click **OK**. Click **Next**, and then click **Finish** in the Case Summary dialog box.

7. When FTK finishes indexing the image file, click the **Overview** tab, and then click the **Total File Items** button under the File Items column.

8. Click the **File Filter Manager** toolbar button (a purple funnel icon to the left of the Unfiltered menu). In the File Filter Manager dialog box, click the **File Date** check box, and click the **Modified** option button. Click the **between** option button, and type **5/20/2005** in both date range text boxes. Click **Save/Apply**, and in the Save As dialog box, type **Modify Date 5/20/2005** for the filename, and then click **OK**. Click **Close** in the File Filter Manager dialog box.

9. In the File Items column, click **Filtered Out**. Right-click the first file listed in the lower pane and click **Create Bookmark**.

10. In the Create New Bookmark dialog box, type **May 5, 2005 files** in the Bookmark name text box, click the **Include in report** check box, and then click **OK**.

11. Click the **Search** tab and then the **Indexed Search** tab. Type **BM6** in the Search Term text box, click **Add**, click **View Cumulative Results**, and then click **OK** in the Filter Search Hits dialog box.

12. In the Search Hit pane, click to expand the results. Right-click the first file listed in the lower pane and click **Create Bookmark**.

13. In the Create New Bookmark dialog box, type **Index Search BM6** in the Bookmark name text box, click the **Include in report** check box, and then click **OK**.

14. Click the **Live Search** tab. Type **BM6** in the Search Term text box, click **Add** to add this term to the search items, click **Search**, and then click **OK** in the Filter Search Hits dialog box. In the Live Search Progress dialog box, click **View Results**.

15. In the Search Hit pane, click the first search result, click the first file in the lower pane, and then press **Ctrl+A** to highlight all files. Right-click the first file listed in the lower pane and click **Create Bookmark**.

16. In the Create New Bookmark dialog box, type **Live Search BM6** in the Bookmark name text box, click the **Include in report** check box, and then click **OK**.

17. To create a report, click **File, Report Wizard** from the menu, and then click **OK** in the FTK Friendly Reminder message box.

18. In the FTK Report Wizard - Case Information dialog box, enter your name and any additional information, and then click **Next**. In the Bookmarks dialog box, click **Next**.

19. In the Bookmarks - B dialog box, click **Add/Remove File Properties**, and in the Detailed List - Data Items to Include dialog box, click **Unselect All**. Click the **File Name, Full Path, Ext**, and **Mod Date** check boxes, and then click **OK**. In the Bookmarks - B dialog box, click **Next**.

20. Continue clicking **Next** until you reach the FTK Report Wizard - Report Location dialog box, and then click **Finish**.

21. In the Report Wizard dialog box, click **Yes**. Under Selected Bookmarks, click **Index Search BM6, Live Search BM6**, and **May 5, 2005 files**, printing the Web page after you click each item.

22. Exit your Web browser and exit FTK, clicking **No** if prompted to back up the case.

Case Projects

Case Project 7-1

For the arson running case project, the insurance company gives you an image file called Firestarter.dd (extracted to your work folder with the other project files for this chapter). Given the resources you determined you need in Chapter 3, describe the tools you'll use to evaluate and analyze the image.

Case Project 7-2

On the Internet, research two popular GUI tools, Guidance Software EnCase and AccessData FTK, and compare their features to other products, such as ProDiscover (*www.techpathways.com*) and Ontrack EasyRecover Professional (*www.ontrack.com/easyrecoveryprofessional*). Create a chart outlining each tool's current capabilities, and write a one- to two-page report on the features you found most beneficial for your lab.

Case Project 7-3

Research the forensics tools available for Mac OS and Linux. Are tools similar to Hex Workshop available for these OSs? Based on their documentation, how easy would validating these tools be? Select at least two tools, and write a one- to two-page paper describing what you would do to validate them, based on what you have learned in this chapter.

Case Project 7-4

You need to establish a procedure for your corporation on how to verify a new forensics software package. Write two to three pages outlining the procedure you plan to use in your lab.

7

chapter 8

Macintosh and Linux Boot Processes and File Systems

After reading this chapter and completing the exercises, you will be able to:

- Explain Macintosh file structures and the boot process
- Explain UNIX and Linux disk structures and boot processes
- Describe other disk structures

In Chapter 6, you explored Microsoft OSs, including DOS and Windows, and Microsoft file systems. Because computer forensics investigators must understand how most OSs store and manage data, this chapter continues that exploration by examining Linux and Macintosh OSs. Chapters 6 and 8 give you a foundation to build on as you become more knowledgeable about current and legacy OSs and their file systems.

In addition, this chapter discusses media and hardware, such as CDs and DVDs and IDE, SCSI, and SATA drives. You should understand how these devices store data so that you can retrieve evidence as needed. Keep in mind that this chapter is simply an introduction to techniques for examining Linux and Macintosh file systems.

Understanding the Macintosh File Structure and Boot Process

The current Macintosh OS is Mac OS X, version 10.5, known as Leopard. Mac OS X is built on a core called Darwin, which consists of a **Berkeley Software Distribution (BSD) UNIX** application layer built on top of a Mach microkernel. Apple's OSs have been evolving since 1984 with the Apple System 1 and have continued through System 7. In 1997 Apple introduced Mac OS 8 followed by Mac OS 9 before moving on to OS X.

This section focuses primarily on older Mac OS 9 file systems. The next section, "Examining UNIX and Linux Disk Structures and Boot Processes," discusses file systems used by UNIX, Linux, and OS X. The Macintosh is popular with schools and graphics professionals, and Apple's innovations continue to make it popular in the PC market. Because the OS 9 file system was so widely used, mostly in public schools, computer forensics investigators should be familiar with its file and disk structure. In addition, Apple has kept the same GUI, utilities, and application in each major OS release, including OS X. Directory file structures have had only minor changes with each new OS update.

Before OS X, the **Hierarchical File System (HFS)** was used, in which files are stored in directories (folders) that can be nested in other directories. With Mac OS 8.1, Apple introduced **Extended Format File System (HFS+)**, which continues to be an optional format in Mac OS X. The primary difference between HFS and HFS+ is that HFS was limited to 65,536 blocks (512 bytes per block) per volume, and HFS+ raised the number of blocks to more than 4 billion. Consequently, HFS+ supports smaller file sizes on larger volumes, resulting in more efficient disk use. Mac OS X also supports the Unix File System (UFS), which isn't covered in this book. The **File Manager** utility handles reading, writing, and storing data on physical media. It also collects data to maintain the HFS and manipulates files, directories, and other items. The **Finder** is another Macintosh utility that works with the OS to keep track of files and maintain users' desktops.

In older Mac OSs, a file consists of two parts: a **data fork**, where data is stored, and a **resource fork**, where file metadata and application information are stored (see Figure 8-1). Both forks contain the following essential information for each file:

- Resource map
- Resource header information for each file
- Window locations
- Icons

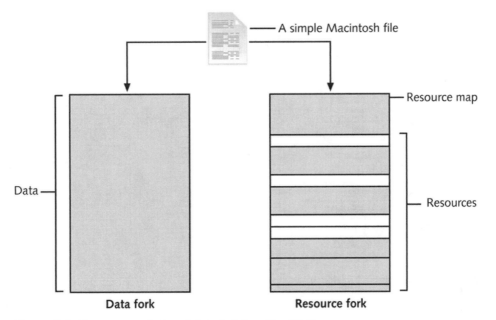

Figure 8-1 The resource fork and data fork in a Mac OS file

The data fork typically contains data the user creates, such as text or spreadsheets. Applications, such as Microsoft Word or Excel, also read and write to the data fork. When you're working with an application file, the resource fork contains additional information, such as menus, dialog boxes, icons, executable code, and controls. In the Mac OS, the resource or data fork can be empty. Because File Manager is in charge of reading and writing information to files, it can access both forks.

Understanding Mac OS 9 Volumes

A volume is any storage medium used to store files. A volume can be all or part of the storage media for hard disks; however, in Mac OS 9 or earlier, a volume on a floppy disk is always the entire floppy. With larger disks, the user or administrator defines a volume.

Volumes have **allocation blocks** and **logical blocks**. A logical block is a collection of data that can't exceed 512 bytes. When you save a file, File Manager assigns the file to an allocation block, which is a group of consecutive logical blocks. On a floppy disk, an allocation block is usually one logical block. As volumes increase in size, one allocation block might be composed of three or more logical blocks. Figure 8-2 shows the relationship between these two types of blocks.

File Manager can access a maximum of 65,535 allocation blocks per volume. If a file contains information, it always occupies one allocation block. For example, if a data fork contains only 11 bytes of data, it occupies one allocation block (512 bytes) on a disk, which leaves more than 500 bytes empty in the data fork.

The Macintosh HFS and HFS+ file systems have two descriptors for the end of file (EOF)—the **logical EOF** and the **physical EOF**. The logical EOF is the actual size of the file, so because file B is 510 bytes, byte 510 is the logical EOF. The physical EOF is the number of allocation blocks for that file, as shown in Figure 8-3, so for file B, it's byte 1023.

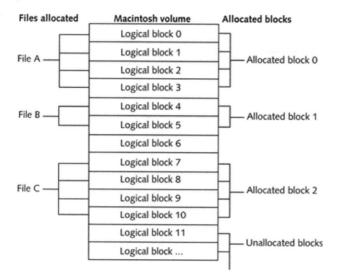

Figure 8-2 Logical and allocation block structures

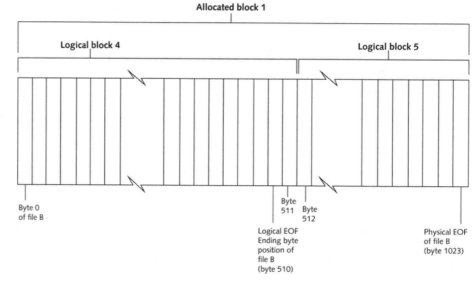

Figure 8-3 Logical EOF and physical EOF

Macintosh reduces file fragmentation by using **clumps**, which are groups of contiguous allocation blocks. As a file increases in size, it occupies more of the clump. Volume fragmentation is kept to a minimum by adding more clumps to larger files.

Exploring Macintosh Boot Tasks

Older Macintosh computers don't use the same type of BIOS firmware commonly found in PCs. Instead, they use **Open Firmware**, a processor- and system-independent boot firmware (part of the boot ROM in most Power PC Macintosh systems). Open Firmware controls the microprocessor after hardware initialization and diagnostics take place before control is passed to the OS. It's responsible for building the device tree, probing for IO devices, and loading the OS kernel from the disk.

Newer Macintosh computers use Intel Core Duo processors with Extensible Firmware Interface (EFI), which replaces BIOS firmware (see *www.intel.com/technology/efi/*).

The boot process for OS 9 is as follows:

1. Power on the computer.
2. Hardware self-test and Open Firmware run.
3. Macintosh OS starts.
4. The startup disk is located.
5. System files are opened.
6. System extensions are loaded.
7. OS 9 Finder starts.

Newer Macintoshes can be booted from a CD, DVD, or FireWire drive. To boot from a CD or DVD, press and hold the C key immediately after powering the system on, and then insert a Macintosh-bootable CD or DVD into the optical drive. To boot from a FireWire drive, connect it to the Macintosh, power it on, and then press and hold the T key. To determine whether an older Macintosh can boot to a FireWire drive, refer to *http://support.apple.com/ kb/HT2699?viewlocale=en_US* for more information.

Tables 8-1 and 8-2 are an overview of how HFS and HFS+ system files handle data.

Table 8-1 HFS system files

HFS block position	HFS structure	Purpose of structure
0 and 1	Boot block	Startup volume containing boot instructions; also stores system files and Finder information.
2	Master Directory Block (MDB)	Contains volume creation date and time and location of other system files, such as Volume Bitmap. A duplicate of this file called the Alternate MDB is located at the second-to-last block on the volume. Its purpose is to provide information to OS disk utilities.
3	Volume Bitmap	Tracks used and unused blocks on the volume.
	Catalog	Lists all files and directories on the volume. It's a B*-tree file that uses the extents overflow file to coordinate all file allocations to the volume.
	Extents overflow file	This B*-tree file lists the extra extents, which are the allocated blocks used to store data files.

Table 8-2 HFS+ system files

HFS+ byte offset (fixed starting position)	HFS+ structure	Purpose of structure
0	Boot blocks	No change from HFS.
1024	Volume Information Block (VIB)	Replaces the MDB used in HFS.
Not fixed	Allocation file	Tracks available free blocks on the volume; replaces the HFS Volume Bitmap.
Not fixed	Extents overflow file	For files with more than eight extents, additional extents are recorded and managed through this B*-tree system file.
Not fixed	Catalog	Similar to an HFS catalog, this improved version allows up to eight extents for each file's forks. It's a B*-tree file.
Not fixed	Attributes file	Stores new file attribute information that isn't available in HFS. The new attributes are inline data attribute records, fork data attribute records, and extension attribute records.
Not fixed	Startup file	New to HFS+, this file can boot non-HFS and non-HFS+ volumes.
Not fixed	Alternate VIB	Same file as the HFS Alternate MDB.
	Reserved (512 bytes)	Last sector of the volume; used by Apple during manufacturing.

For more information on B*-tree and HFS, see *http://tldp.org/HOWTO/Filesystems-HOWTO-7.html*.

For older HFS-formatted drives, the first two logical blocks, 0 and 1, on the volume (or disk) are the boot blocks containing system startup instructions. Optional executable code for system files can also be placed in boot blocks.

Older Macintosh OSs use the **Master Directory Block (MDB)** for HFS, also known as the Volume Information Block (VIB) for HFS+. All information about a volume is stored in the MDB and written to the MDB when the volume is initialized. A copy of the MDB is also written to the next-to-last block on the volume to support disk utility functions. When the OS mounts a volume, some information from the MDB is written to a **Volume Control Block (VCB)**, which is stored in system memory and used by File Manager. When the user no longer needs the volume and unmounts it, the VCB is removed.

The copy of the MDB is updated when the extents overflow file or catalog increases in size. File Manager uses the **extents overflow file** to store any file information not in the MDB or a VCB. The **catalog** is the listing of all files and directories on the volume and is used to maintain relationships between files and directories on a volume.

A system application called **Volume Bitmap** tracks each block on a volume to determine which blocks are in use and which ones are available to receive data. Volume Bitmap has information about the blocks' use but not about their content. Volume Bitmap's size depends on the number of allocated blocks for the volume.

File Manager stores file-mapping information in two locations: the extents overflow file and the file's catalog entry. Mac OS 9 also uses the **B*-tree** file system to organize the directory hierarchy and file block mapping for File Manager. In this file system, files are nodes (records or objects) containing file data. Each node is 512 bytes. The nodes containing actual file data are called **leaf nodes**; they're the bottom level of the B*-tree. The B*-tree also has the following nodes that handle file information:

- The **header node** stores information about the B*-tree file.
- The **index node** stores link information to previous and next nodes.
- The **map node** stores a node descriptor and map record.

TIP

For more information on HFS and HFS+, see *http://developer.apple.com/ technotes/tn/tn1184.html*, *http://developer.apple.com/technotes/tn/tn1150. html*, *http://developer.apple.com/documentation/mac/Files/Files-100. html#HEADING100-0*, and *http://developer.apple.com/referencelibrary/ Carbon/idxFileManagement-date.html*.

8

Using Macintosh Forensics Software

Recently, several computer forensics software vendors have updated or created new tools to investigate Macintosh file systems. This section covers BlackBag Technologies (*www.black bagtech.com/products/overview.htm*). Another product specific to Macintosh forensics is SubRosaSoft MacForensicsLab (*www.macforensicslab.com*). Other vendors, such as Guidance EnCase and X-Ways Forensics, have also added the capability to analyze HFS, HFS+, UFS, and UFS2 file systems. Other forensics software products that can examine UFS and UFS2 are ProDiscover Forensic Edition from Technology Pathways and the freeware tools Sleuth Kit and Autopsy (*www.sleuthkit.org*). Sleuth Kit is discussed in "Examining UNIX and Linux Disk Structures" later in this chapter.

Macintosh Acquisition Methods To examine a Macintosh computer, you need to make an image of the drive, using the same techniques described in Chapter 4. There are some exceptions you should be aware of, however, because of Macintosh design and engineering. For example, a static acquisition of the suspect drive is preferable to a live acquisition. In addition, removing the drive from a Macintosh Mini's CPU case is difficult, and attempting to do so without Apple factory training could damage the computer. You need a Macintosh-compatible forensic boot CD to make an image, which then must be written to an external drive, such as a FireWire or USB drive. Larger Macintoshes are constructed similarly to desktop PCs, making it much easier to remove the hard drive.

NOTE

For Macintosh computers such as the Mac Mini, booting from a forensic boot CD might not be possible because the CD/DVD drive can't be accessed without powering on the computer. For this type of computer, you need a FireWire drive instead of a CD. For additional information on bootable FireWire drives, see *http://support.apple.com/kb/ HT2699?viewlocale=en_US*.

BlackBag Technologies sells acquisition products designed for OS 9 and earlier as well as OS X and offers a forensic boot CD called MacQuisition for making an image of a Macintosh drive (see *www.blackbagtech.com/products/macquisition.htm*). BlackBag Technologies has also written a guide for newer Macintoshes on making an acquisition with a FireWire-connected drive (*www.macforensicslab.com/ProductsAndServices/index.php?main_page=document_general_info&products_id=134*).

After making an acquisition, the next step is examining the image of the file system with a computer forensics tool. The tool you use depends on the image file's format. For example, if you used EnCase, FTK, or X-Ways Forensics to create an Expert Witness (.e01) image, you must use one of these tools to analyze the image because they can read the Expert Witness format and the HFS+ file system. If you made a raw format image, you can use any of the following tools:

- BlackBag Technologies Macintosh Forensic Software (OS X only)
- SubRosaSoft MacForensicsLab (OS X only)
- Guidance Software EnCase (Windows 2000 or later)
- X-Ways Forensics (Windows 2000 or later)

Of these tools, BlackBag Technologies Macintosh Forensic Software and SubRosaSoft MacForensicsLab have a feature for disabling and enabling **Disk Arbitration**. You can configure newer Macintoshes running OS X (10.3 or later) so that they don't automatically mount a drive connected through a FireWire or USB device (see *www.macosxforensics.com/Technologies/DiskArbitration/DiskArbitration.html*). Being able to turn off the mount function in OS X allows you to connect a suspect drive to a Macintosh without a write-blocking device. In the next section, you learn how to use Macintosh forensics tools on an acquired image of an OS 9 drive.

Examining OS 9 Data Structures with BlackBag This section explains how to perform a forensics examination by using BlackBag's tools on an OS 9 image. BlackBag provides demo software to download that's a fully functioning version of its licensed software. For a copy of the demo software, go to *http://blackbagtech.com/store/software/forensic_suite_2.5_-_demo.html*, where you'll find instructions about e-mailing for a username and password to access the download page. You'll have full use of the software until the expiration date listed on this Web page. SubRosaSoft also offers a demo version of MacForensicsLab. If you want to download this demo, contact sales@subrosasoft.com.

 As with any computer forensics software, the more RAM and processor speed your computer has, the more efficiently it can examine a drive. At a minimum, the latest model, Mac Mini, is suitable for running BlackBag.

The activities in this section assume you have a Macintosh running OS X and have installed BlackBag's demo or licensed version on your computer. If you don't have a Macintosh available, read the steps to acquaint yourself with how this application works.

Before starting BlackBag, all data acquisitions (image files) must be configured as **Disk Images** with the correct filename and extensions. Disk Images are copies of entire disks, volumes, or files used by OS X. If you have made a raw image of an OS 9 drive with another tool, such as the dd command-line utility or ProDiscover Basic, you can rename the image file and its segmented files as Disk Image files to make them compatible with OS X. These renamed files are then mounted as virtual drives.

The .dmg extension tells OS X that the file is a Disk Image. If an image file has additional segments, each segment must have a .dmgpart extension. To keep the correct order of each segment, numbers need to be inserted between the filename and the extension, as shown in Table 8-3.

Table 8-3 **Requirements for renaming Disk Image files**

Original filenames for image file and segments	Macintosh Disk Image filenames
GCFI-OS9.001	GCFI-OS9.dmg
GCFI-OS9.002	GCFI-OS9.002.dmgpart
GCFI-OS9.003	GCFI-OS9.003.dmgpart
GCFI-OS9.004	GCFI-OS9.004.dmgpart

After the image and any associated segments have been renamed, they can be loaded as a virtual disk image. Before mounting the image, however, you need to write-protect it to prevent OS X from writing to the virtually mounted drive. When using a Macintosh computer for forensics examinations, images should be placed on a Macintosh drive formatted as Mac OS Extended (with or without the journaling feature) or with a USB-connected NTFS-formatted drive. Do not examine an image from a FAT-formatted drive because the read-only feature can't be used.

To write-protect a Macintosh drive before mounting it, you change permissions for the image and its associated segments by following these steps:

1. In Finder, right-click the image and each segmented associated file and click **Get Info**.
2. In the Info dialog box, click the **Ownership & Permissions** drop-down list, and change all permissions to **Read Only**.
3. In the General section, click the **Locked** check box to complete the write-protection for the image and associated segments.

To mount the .dmg files listed in Table 8-3, in Finder, navigate to the drive and then the directory containing the .dmg files (see Figure 8-4), and double-click the first segmented file, GCFI-OS9.dmg, to load the entire collection of segmented volumes. (Note that OS X Disk Image reads and mounts all associated segments with the .dmgpart extension automatically.)

OS X loads and displays a desktop icon of the virtual mounted disk with the name "untitled." You can rename the icon with the case name, such as GCFI-OS9 DISK, to make it easier to identify. To do this, right-click it and click Get Info. In the Info dialog box, click the Name & Extension drop-down list and type a new name, as shown in Figure 8-5.

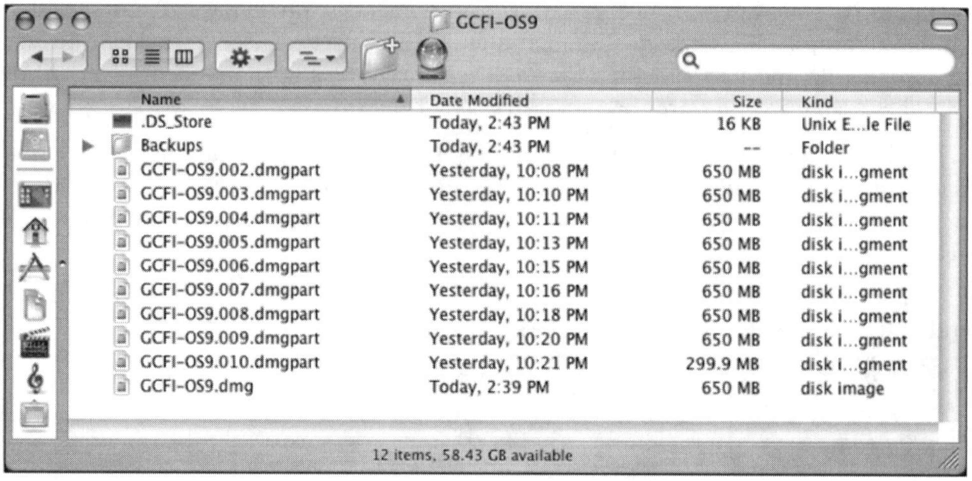

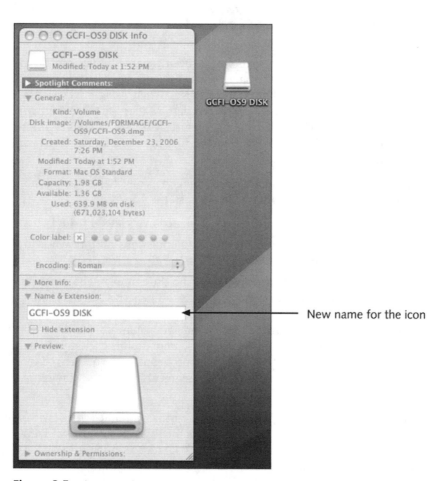

Figure 8-4 OS X Finder showing the renamed raw files as .dmg files

New name for the icon

Figure 8-5 Changing the icon name

Now data is ready for BlackBag to read and examine forensically. To start BlackBag from Finder, navigate to the Applications/BBT Forensic Suite/ directory and double-click the application file BBTFSToolBar_*nnn* (*nnn* is the version number) shown in Figure 8-6.

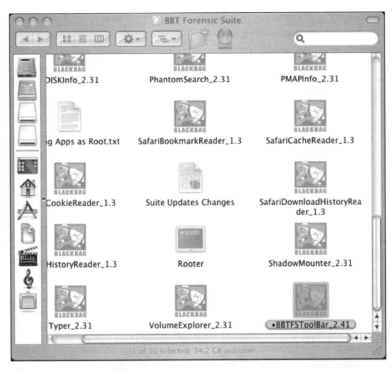

Figure 8-6 Starting BlackBag from Finder

In the BlackBag About dialog box, click OK to display the BlackBag Forensic Suite ToolBar (see Figure 8-7), where you can select a utility to start your analysis.

BlackBag is made up of several utilities for conducting a full analysis of evidence, including PDISKInfo, PMAPInfo, DirectoryScan, FileSearch, MacCarver, and FileSpy. For the latest list of tools that have been integrated into BlackBag and explanations of their uses, see *http://blackbagtech.com/support/documents.html*.

 Before starting the following activity, extract all data files from the Chap08 folder on the book's DVD to the *Work*\Chap08\Chapter folder on your Macintosh system. (You might have to create these folders on your system first.) Then rename the files with .dmg and .dmgpart extensions (as explained in Table 8-3), load the .dmg files on your workstation as a virtual disk, and rename the desktop icon, as described previously.

In this activity, you use the BlackBag DirectoryScan utility, which lists all folders and files, visible and hidden, in the image loaded as a .dmg file:

1. Start BlackBag from Finder, as described previously.

2. In the BlackBag Forensic Suite ToolBar, click **DirectoryScan**. When the Authentication dialog box opens, type the root password for your Macintosh, and then click **OK**.

BLACKBAG
Forensic Suite ToolBar

Minimize
ForensicSettings
DCFLDDAssistant
PDISKInfo
PMAPInfo
IORegInfo
DirectoryScan
FileSearcher
ActiveFileSearcher
GraphView
PhantomSearch
CommentHunter
HeaderBuilder
MacCarver
ImageBuster
VolumeExplorer
FileSpy
SafariCacheReader
SafariCookieReader
SafariBookmarkReader
SafariDownloadHistory...
SafariHistoryReader
LockMaster
Breakup
DeviceChecksum
DMGRename

Figure 8-7 The BlackBag Forensic Suite ToolBar

Many of the utilities in BlackBag require system privileges. These utilities prompt you for the root password the first time you start them.

3. In the DirectoryScan window, click the **Volume** list arrow, and then click to select the .dmg image.

DirectoryScan can scan specific folders as well as an entire volume. To use this option, click the Choose button under Folder.

4. Click the **Select** button to start the directory scanning. When the scanning is done, click **OK** in the Scan Complete! dialog box.

TIP

To locate files of interest, click the appropriate column header to sort in descending or ascending order.

5. Next, survey the listing and click the check boxes next to files of interest to your investigation. If all files and folders are needed for a report, click the small **X** box at the lower left. Figure 8-8 shows the GCFI-OS9 DISK volume selected.

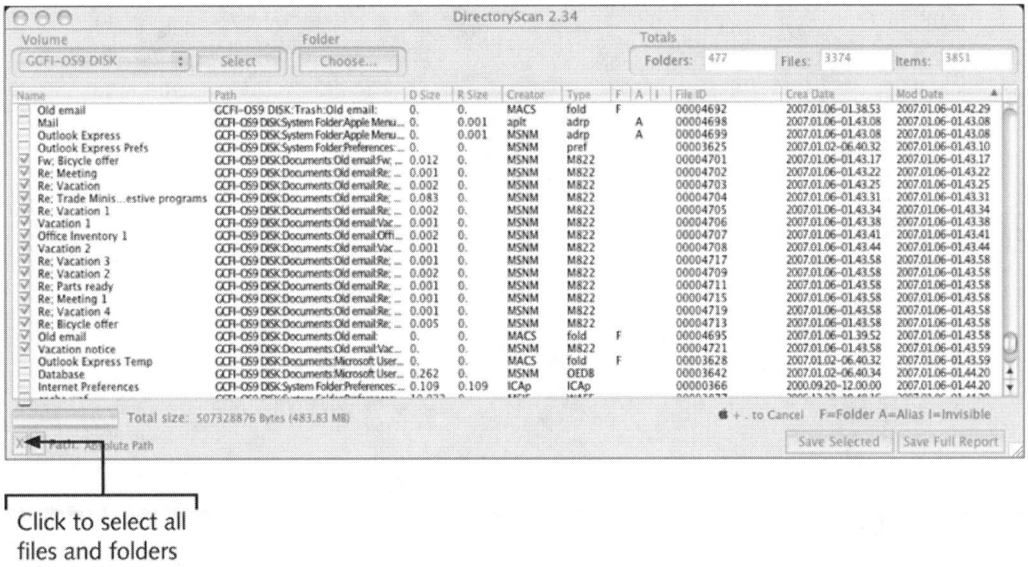

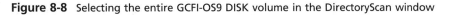

Click to select all
files and folders

Figure 8-8 Selecting the entire GCFI-OS9 DISK volume in the DirectoryScan window

6. Click **Save Selected** or **Save Full Report** to complete this scan.

7. In the Save dialog box, navigate to the folder where you're saving the scan output and click **Save**. In the notification message box, click **OK**.

8. To exit this utility, click the **DirectoryScan** drop-down list and click **Quit Directory Scan** or press **Command+Q**. Leave the BlackBag Forensic Suite ToolBar open for the next activity.

The next activity shows you how to use the FileSearcher utility to locate files by a specific extension:

1. In the BlackBag Forensic Suite ToolBar, click **FileSearcher**. When the Authentication dialog box opens, type the root password for your Macintosh, and then click **OK**.

2. In the FileSearcher dialog box, click the **Select Volume** list arrow, and then click **GCFI-OS9 DISK**.

3. Click the **Name** option button if it's not already selected, click the **right arrow** button to list available extensions, and click **.pdf**. If it's not listed, simply type it in the

Name text box and press **Enter**. When the Search Complete dialog box opens, click **OK**.

4. Next, examine the files listed in the search results output shown in Figure 8-9. Click the check boxes next to the **a9-02.pdf** and **act4.pdf** files.

```
┌──────────────────────────────────────────────────────────────────┐
│ ○ ○ ○                         FileSearcher 2.31                      │
│  ┌─ Search Options ─────────────────────────────────────────────┐  │
│  │ ○ Type: [    ]   Creator: [    ]                              │  │
│  │ ● Name: [.pdf                          ] [.]                  │  │
│  │                                                              │  │
│  │                        [ GCFI-OS9 DISK  ▼]  ( Select Volume ) │  │
│  │                                           ( Choose Folder... ) │  │
│  │  File Name           File Path                               │  │
│  │  ☐ Aladdin_Product_Guide.pdf  GCFI-OS9 DISK:Applications (Mac OS 9):Internet Utilities:Aladdin Folder:Updates & Spe... │
│  │  ☐ a12-02.pdf        GCFI-OS9 DISK:SA:a12-02.pdf            │  │
│  │  ☑ a9-02.pdf         GCFI-OS9 DISK:SA:a9-02.pdf             │  │
│  │  ☑ act4.pdf          GCFI-OS9 DISK:SA:act4.pdf             │  │
│  │  ☐ reg319.pdf        GCFI-OS9 DISK:SA:reg319.pdf           │  │
│  │  ☐ reg543.pdf        GCFI-OS9 DISK:SA:reg543.pdf           │  │
│  │                                                              │  │
│  │  Total size: 12120381 Bytes (11.56 M        Hits: [ 6 ]      │  │
│  │  [                              ]  ☐ Retain Folder Structure │  │
│  │                                    ☐ Path to Comments        │  │
│  │  ● Copy  ○ Move                    ☑ Add Serial Number       │  │
│  │  [X] [ Copy X ][ Copy All ]   ⌘ + . to Cancel  [ Save Report ]│  │
│  └──────────────────────────────────────────────────────────────┘  │
└──────────────────────────────────────────────────────────────────┘
```

Figure 8-9 FileSearcher listing all .pdf documents in the search results

5. Click the **Save Report** button. In the Save dialog box, type the name of the report in the Save As text box. Click the **Where** list arrow, navigate to the **Documents** or **Desktop** folder to save the report, and then click **Save**.

6. Click **Quit FileSearcher** from the FileSearcher menu. To exit BlackBag Forensic Suite ToolBar, click **BBTFSToolBar** and then click **Quit BBTFSToolBar**.

 For more information on performing Macintosh forensics, see *www. macforensicslab.com/ProductsAndServices/index.php?main_page= index&cPath=11*.

Examining UNIX and Linux Disk Structures and Boot Processes

In addition to Windows and Macintosh OSs, contemporary computers and networks use UNIX and Linux. Many flavors of UNIX are available, including System V variants, such as Sun Solaris, IBM AIX, and HP-UX, and BSD variants, such as FreeBSD, OpenBSD, and

NetBSD. Linux is also available in many distributions, such as Red Hat, Fedora, Ubuntu, and Debian. All Linux references in this book are to Fedora because of its popularity and ease of use. Linux is probably the most consistent UNIX-like OS because the Linux kernel is regulated under the **GNU General Public License (GPL)** agreement. The GPL states that anyone is allowed to use, modify, and redistribute software developed under this agreement. It also stipulates that source code for software distributed under the GPL must be publicly available, and any works derived from GPL code must also be licensed under the GPL. BSD variants are released under the BSD license, which is similar to the GPL but makes no requirements for derivative works except that the original copyright remain attached.

GPL and BSD variations are examples of open-source software. Open-source software is popular because it's freely available, can be modified to suit users' needs, and has a reputation for stability and security. This stability and security are possible because anyone can view the source code and make revisions and contributions, so bugs and security vulnerabilities are found and fixed quickly. Open-source software does, however, require a higher level of user skill.

If you're interested in using open-source tools, see *http://sourceforge. net* or *www.gnu.org/software*.

8

Table 8-4 lists several system files in UNIX OSs that you need to examine when dealing with a UNIX or Linux partition. These files can yield information about users and their activities.

Table 8-4 UNIX system files

OS	System files	Purpose
AIX	/etc/exports	Configuration file
	/etc/filesystems	File system table of devices and mount points
	/etc/utmp	Current user's logon information
	/var/adm/wtmp	Logon and logoff history information
	/etc/security/lastlog	User's last logon information
	/var/adm/sulog	Substitute user attempt information
	/etc/group	Group memberships for the local system
	/var/log/syslog	System messages log
	/etc/security/passwd	Master password file for the local system
	/etc/security/failedlogin	Failed logon attempt information
HP-UX	/etc/utmp and /etc/utmpx	Current user's logon information
	/var/adm/wtmp and /var/adm/wtmpx	Logon and logoff history information
	/var/adm/btmp	Failed logon attempt information
	/etc/fstab	File system table of devices and mount points
	/etc/checklist	File system table information (version 9.x)
	/etc/exports	Configuration files

Table 8-4 UNIX system files (*continued*)

OS	System files	Purpose
	/etc/passwd	Master password file for the local system
	/etc/group	Group memberships for the local system
	/var/adm/syslog.log	System messages log
	syslog	System log files
	/var/adm/sulog	Substitute user attempt information
IRIX	/var/adm/syslog	System log files
	/etc/exports	Configuration files
	/etc/fstab	File system table of devices and mount points
	/var/adm/btmp	Failed logon information
	/var/adm/lastlog	User's last logon information
	/var/adm/wtmp and /var/adm/wtmpx	Logon and logoff history information
	/var/adm/sulog	Substitute user attempt information
	/etc/shadow	Master password file for the local system
	/etc/group	Group memberships for the local system
	/var/adm/utmp and /var/adm/utmpx	Current user's logon information
Linux	/etc/exports	Configuration files
	/etc/fstab	File system table of devices and mount points
	/var/log/lastlog	User's last logon
	/var/log/wtmp	Logon and logoff history information
	/var/run/utmp	Current user's logon information
	/var/log/messages	System messages log
	/etc/shadow	Master password file for the local system
	/etc/group	Group memberships for the local system
Solaris	/etc/passwd	Account information for local system
	/etc/group	Group information for local system
	/var/adm/sulog	Switch user log data
	/var/adm/utmp	Logon information
	/var/adm/wtmp, /var/adm/wtmpx, and /var/adm/lastlog	Logon history information
	/var/adm/loginlog	Failed logon information
	/var/adm/messages	System log files
	/etc/vfstab	Static file system information
	/etc/dfs/dfstab and /etc/vfstab	Configuration files

In the following steps, you use standard Linux commands to find information about your Linux system:

1. Start your Linux computer and open a terminal window, if necessary. If your computer starts at a graphical desktop, such as KDE, click the **Fedora** desktop icon, point to **System,** and then click **Terminal.** If you're using GNOME, click the **Applications** drop-down menu, point to **Accessories,** and then click **Terminal.**

2. To find the name of your computer and the Linux kernel revision number, type **uname -a** and press **Enter.** Record the results or capture a screen image.

 To capture a screen image in Linux, use the GIMP graphics program. In Fedora, for example, click the Fedora desktop icon, point to Graphics, and then click The GIMP. From the GIMP menu, click File, Acquire, and then click Screen Shot. In the Screen Shot dialog box, click the Single Window option button, and then minimize the main GIMP window if you want to capture the entire screen. Next, change the setting for Grab After ___ Seconds Delay to 3 seconds, and then click Grab. Now click the window you want to capture. To save the captured image, click File, Save As from the menu in the window containing the captured image. Enter a filename in the Name text box, navigate to and select a location, and then click Save.

3. Type **ls -l** and press **Enter** to list the files in the current directory. Write down the name of one file in the directory.

4. To determine the access time of a file (the last time a command was executed on the file), type **ls -ul** *filename* (substituting the filename you recorded in Step 3 for *filename*) and press **Enter.** Record or capture a screen image of the results.

5. Type **netstat -s** and press **Enter** to see a list of protocols your computer uses to communicate with other systems connected to it.

6. Exit the terminal window.

The standard Linux file system is the **Second Extended File System (Ext2fs),** which can support disks as large as 4 TB and files as large as 2 GB. Ext3fs is a journaling version of Ext2fs that reduces file recovery time after a crash. Of the file structures you have studied so far, Linux is most closely related to Mac OS X because it too uses a BSD file system. The Linux file structure is made up of metadata and data. Metadata includes items such as user ID (UID), group ID (GID), size, and permissions for each file.

Linux is unique in that it uses **inodes,** or information nodes, containing descriptive information about each file or directory. (See "Understanding Inodes" later in this chapter for more in-depth information.) Inodes contain modification, access, and creation (MAC) times, not filenames. To keep track of files and data, Linux assigns an inode number that's linked with the filename in a directory file. (The directory file is where inode information is stored.) The data portion of the Linux file structure contains the file's contents.

In addition to metadata, an inode has a pointer, also referred to as an inode number, to other inodes or blocks where data resides on the disk. Linux can use inodes to store the file in one location and create pointers to it in other locations, such as other directories. For example, suppose you need to access the MyDatabase file when you're working in the Clients, Accounting, and General_Documents directories. Instead of making copies of MyDatabase in each directory, you create the file once in one directory, and then create a symbolic link that points to MyDatabase in the other two directories. To determine an inode's content, you can use the UNIX/Linux ls -l command. To find an inode's pointer number, use the UNIX/Linux ls -i command.

Each inode keeps a symbolic link count. If that number becomes 0, Linux deletes the file. To find deleted files during a forensics investigation, you search for inodes that contain some data and have a link count of 0.

UNIX and Linux Overview

In UNIX and Linux, everything is a file, including disk drives, monitors, any connected tape drives, network interface cards, system memory, directories, and actual files. All UNIX files are defined as objects, which means that a file, like an object in an object-oriented programming language, has properties and methods (actions such as writing, deleting, and reading) that can be performed on it.

UNIX consists of four components that define the file system: boot block, superblock, inode block, and data block. A block is the smallest disk allocation unit in the UNIX file system and can be 512 bytes and up. As explained previously, the boot block contains the bootstrap code—instructions for startup. A UNIX/Linux computer has only one boot block, located on the main hard disk.

The superblock contains vital information about the system and is considered part of the metadata. It indicates the disk geometry, available space, and location of the first inode and keeps track of all inodes. The superblock also manages the UNIX/Linux file system, including configuration information, such as block size for the drive, file system names, blocks reserved for inodes, free inode list, free block starting chain, volume name, and inodes for last update time and backup time. Multiple copies of the superblock are kept in various locations on the disk to prevent losing such important information.

Inode blocks are the first data after the superblock. An inode is assigned to every file allocation unit. As files or directories are created or deleted, inodes are also created or deleted. The link between inodes associated with files and directories controls access to those files or directories.

The data block is where directories and files are stored on a disk drive. This location is linked directly to inodes. As in Microsoft file systems, the Linux file system on a PC has 512-byte sectors. A data block is equivalent to a cluster of disk sectors on a FAT or NTFS volume. Blocks range from 1024 to 4096 bytes each on a Linux volume. Figure 8-10 shows that when you save a file, data blocks are clustered and a unique inode is assigned.

As with other OSs, the size of a data block determines how much disk space is wasted. The larger the data block, the higher the likelihood of fragments. If you create a 512 KB database, 19 data blocks of 8192 bytes are clustered to save the file, and 3648 bytes are left empty but allocated. In addition to keeping track of file size, an inode keeps track of the number of blocks assigned to the file.

All disks have more storage capacity than the manufacturer states. For example, a 20 GB disk might actually have 20.5 GB free space because disks always have bad sectors despite the most careful procedures. DOS and Windows don't keep track of bad sectors, but Linux does in an inode called the **bad block inode**. The root inode is inode 2, and the bad block inode is inode 1. Some forensics tools ignore inode 1 and fail to recover valuable data for

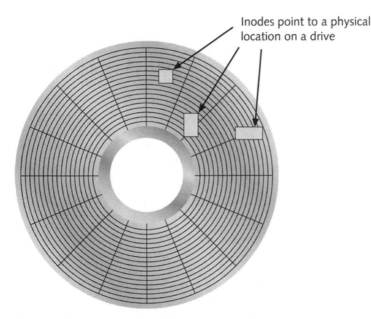

Inodes point to a physical
location on a drive

Figure 8-10 Clustering data blocks to save a file in Linux

8

cases. Someone trying to mislead an investigator can access the bad block inode, list good sectors in it, and then hide information in these supposedly "bad" sectors.

To find bad blocks on your Linux computer, you can use the badblocks command, although you must log on as root to do so. Linux includes two other commands that provide bad block information: mke2fs and e2fsck. The badblocks command can destroy valuable data, but the mke2fs and e2fsck commands include safeguards that prevent them from overwriting important information.

The following activity assumes you have a floppy drive on a Linux computer. If you don't, read the steps to learn how to identify bad blocks on a disk.

In the following steps, you check a floppy disk for bad blocks. These steps assume you're using the KDE GUI available in most Linux distributions. This activity uses the Fedora distribution. You need a blank floppy disk or one containing data you no longer need, and you must log on as root.

1. Boot your Linux computer to a graphical desktop. Insert a floppy disk in the floppy drive, but don't mount it. If your system is set to mount disks automatically, dismount the drive by clicking the **Fedora** desktop icon, pointing to **System,** and clicking **Disk Management.** Make sure the floppy drive is selected, and then click the **Unmount** button. You can also dismount the floppy manually with the umount command.

2. To open a terminal window, click the **Fedora** desktop icon, point to **System,** and click **Terminal.** (If you're using GNOME, click the **Applications** drop-down menu, point to **Accessories,** and then click **Terminal.**)

3. Type **cd /sbin** and press **Enter**, or make sure /sbin is in your .bash_profile path statement. Next, type **mke2fs -c /dev/fd0** and press **Enter**. (If you get a warning message about /dec/fd0 being the entire device, not just a partition, type **y** and press **Enter** to continue.) The /dev/fd0 specifies the location of the first floppy drive on the system. If you're using a different floppy drive, such as fd1, use that location instead. Linux reads and displays disk information, including any bad blocks. After the command prompt appears, record or capture a screen image of the results. (*Note*: Depending on your current location, you might need to type **./mke2fs -c /dev/fd0** and make a similar correction in Step 4.)

4. To compare the results of the mke2fs and e2fsck commands, mount the floppy disk. If necessary, create a mount point in /mnt or /media by typing **mkdir /mnt/floppy** (or **mkdir /media/floppy**) and pressing **Enter**, and then typing **mount /dev/fd0 /mnt/floppy** (or **mount /dev/fd0 /media/floppy**) and pressing **Enter**.

5. (*Note*: Before using the e2fsck command, make sure your floppy drive is dismounted by using the **umount /mnt/floppy** command.) Next, type **e2fsck -c /dev/fd0** and press **Enter**, and then type **y** to start the check. (Replace fd0 with your floppy drive, if necessary.) Linux again reads and displays disk information, including any bad blocks. After the command prompt appears, record or capture a screen image of the results.

6. To find information about the badblocks command, type **man badblocks** and press **Enter**. The first manual page for the badblocks command is displayed. Press **Page Down** to see additional pages. Record or capture a screen image of each page, and then press **q** to exit the man page.

The man command displays pages from the online help manual for information on UNIX and Linux commands and their options.

7. Dismount the floppy disk by typing **umount /dev/fd0** and pressing **Enter**. Leave the terminal window open for the next activity.

You can display information about files and directories by using the Linux ls (list) command along with options for determining the type of information to display. Figure 8-11 shows some of the information you can find with the ls -l command.

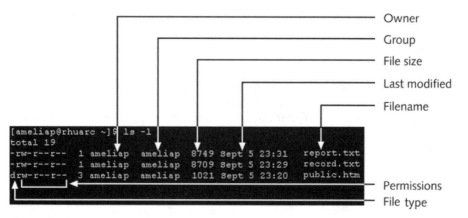

Figure 8-11 Finding information about a file

In the following steps, you use the ls command and some of its options. This activity is performed with Fedora and the KDE GUI. If you're using another Linux distribution, consult its documentation to learn how to start a terminal session.

1. If necessary, start your Linux computer and open a terminal window.

2. Navigate to your home directory, if necessary, by typing **cd /home/*username*** (replacing *username* with the name of your home directory) and pressing **Enter**. Be sure to insert a space after the cd command.

3. At the command prompt, type **ls -A** and press **Enter**. (Be sure to insert a space after the ls command and use an uppercase "A" because Linux commands are case sensitive.) The ls command with the -A option lists all files, including hidden ones, but not the current or parent directories. Write down the files and directories listed, or if too many are listed, scroll to the top of the screen where you entered the ls -A command and note the first filename listed after the command.

4. Next, type **ls -a** and press **Enter**. The ls command with the -a (lowercase "a") option lists all files, including hidden ones and their parent and current directories. Review the results and compare them with the results from Step 3. Note that this option displays "." and ".." immediately after the command.

5. To find the inode number for files in the current directory, type **ls -i** and press **Enter**. What do you notice about the numbering scheme? Record the results. (*Note*: If you're using a fresh install that hasn't been used previously, this step might not produce any results.)

6. To find detailed information about files in the current directory, including size, permission, and modification time, type **ls -l** and press **Enter**. Record the results, and write down the differences and similarities you observed for these commands.

7. You can leave the terminal window open for the next activity, if you like. If not, type **exit** and press **Enter** to close it.

To provide more information about a file or directory, UNIX/Linux file systems have a **continuation inode**, which has more room for detailed information. This information includes the mode and file type, the quantity of links in the file or directory, the file's or directory's access control list (ACL), the least and most significant bytes of the ACL UID and GID, and the file or directory status flag. The status flag is a bit, usually expressed in octal format, containing unique information about how Linux handles permissions for a file or directory. Table 8-5 describes the code values for the status flag bit.

Table 8-5 Code values for an inode

Code values	Description
4000	UID on execution—set
2000	GID on execution—set
1000	Sticky bit—set
0400	Read by owner—allowed
0200	Write by owner—allowed
0100	Execution/search by owner—allowed

Table 8-5 Code values for an inode (*continued*)

Code values	Description
0040	Read by group—allowed
0020	Write by group—allowed
0010	Execution/search by group—allowed
0004	Read by others—allowed
0002	Write by others—allowed
0001	Execution/search by others—allowed

Understanding Inodes

Inodes provide a mechanism for linking data stored in data blocks. Block size depends on how the disk volume was initiated. As mentioned, block sizes can be 512 bytes and up, but many Linux distributions assign 1024 bytes per block.

The Linux Ext2fs and Ext3fs file systems are improvements over the Ext file system in the first Linux release. One major improvement in Ext3fs is that it adds information to each inode that links the other inodes in a chain. Therefore, if one inode becomes corrupt, data can be recovered more easily than in Ext2fs.

When a file or directory is created on a UNIX or Linux file system, an inode is assigned that contains the following information:

- The mode and type of the file or directory
- The number of links to a file or directory
- The UID and GID of the file's or directory's owner
- The number of bytes in the file or directory
- The file's or directory's last access time and last modified time
- The inode's last file status change time
- The block address for the file data
- The indirect, double-indirect, and triple-indirect block addresses for the file data
- Current usage status of the inode
- The number of actual blocks assigned to a file
- File generation number and version number
- The continuation inode's link

This assigned inode has 13 pointers that link to data blocks and other pointers where files are stored. Pointers 1 through 10 link directly to data storage blocks in the disk's data block and contain block addresses indicating where data is stored on the disk. These pointers are direct pointers because each one is associated with one block of data storage.

As a file grows, the OS provides up to three layers of additional inode pointers. In the file's inode, the first 10 pointers are called **indirect pointers**. The pointers in the second layer are called **double-indirect pointers**, and the pointers in the last or third layer are called **triple-indirect pointers**.

To expand storage allocation, the OS initiates the original inode's 11th pointer, which links to 128 pointer inodes. Each pointer links directly to 128 blocks located in the drive's data block. If all 10 pointers in the original inode are consumed with file data, the 11th pointer links to another 128 pointers. The first pointer in this indirect group of inodes points to the 11th block. The last block of these 128 inodes is block 138.

The term "indirect inodes" refers to the 11th pointer in the original inode, which points to another group of inode pointers. In other words, it's linked indirectly to the original inode.

If more storage is needed, the 12th pointer of the original inode is used to link to another 128 inode pointers. From each of these pointers, another 128 pointers are created. This second layer of inode pointers is then linked directly to blocks in the drive's data block. The first block these double-indirect pointers point to is block 139.

If more storage is needed, the 13th pointer links to 128 pointer inodes, each of which points to another 128 pointers, and each pointer in this second layer points to a third layer of 128 pointers. File data is stored in these data blocks, as shown in Figure 8-12.

You work with files and directories at the Linux command line in a shell, which you used in Chapter 4. Table 8-6 lists useful commands for most UNIX and Linux shells, including options that are unique to a UNIX version.

Table 8-6 UNIX and Linux shell commands

Shell command	Associated options	Purpose
cat *file* more *file*		Displays the contents of a file (similar to the MS-DOS Type command)
dd	Refer to man pages for available options	Copies a disk drive by blocks, which is the same as creating an image of a disk drive
df bdf (HP-UX)	-k (Solaris)	Displays partition information for local or NFS mounted partitions
find	Refer to man pages for available options	Locates files matching a specific attribute, such as name, last modification time, or owner
netstat	-a	Identifies other systems connected via the network to a UNIX or Linux system
ps	ax (BSD) -ef (System V)	Displays the status of OS processes
uname	-a	Displays the name of the system

Understanding UNIX and Linux Boot Processes

As a computer forensics investigator, you'll probably need to acquire digital evidence from a UNIX or Linux system that can't be shut down, such as a Web server or file server, so you must understand UNIX/Linux boot processes to identify potential problems. When you power on a UNIX workstation, instruction code stored in firmware on the

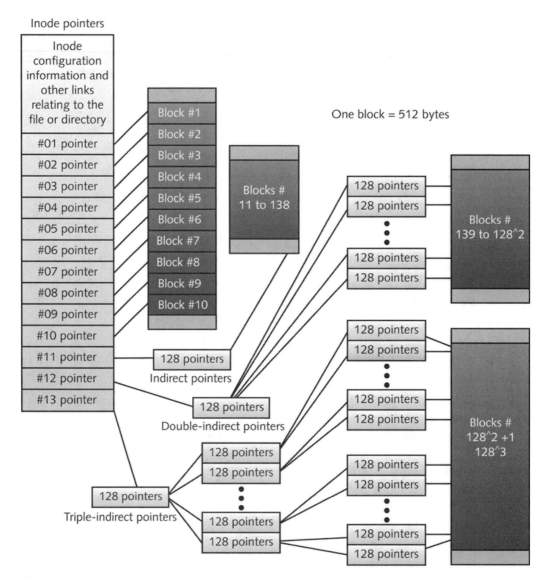

Figure 8-12 Inode pointers in the Linux file system

system's CPU loads into RAM. This firmware is called memory-resident code because it's located in ROM.

As soon as the memory-resident code is loaded into RAM, the instruction code checks the hardware. Typically, the code first tests all components, such as RAM chips, to verify that they're available and capable of running. Then it probes the bus, looking for a device containing the boot program, such as a hard disk, floppy disk, or CD. When it locates the boot device, it starts reading the boot program into memory. The boot program, in turn, reads the kernel into memory. When the kernel is loaded, the boot program transfers control of the boot process to the kernel.

The kernel's first task is to identify all devices. It then configures the identified devices and starts the system and associated processes. After the kernel becomes operational, the system is usually booted to single-user mode, in which only one user can log on. Single-user mode is usually an optional feature that allows users to access other modes, such as maintenance mode. If a user bypasses single-user mode, the kernel runs system startup scripts that are specific to the workstation and then runs in multiuser mode. Users can then log on to the workstation.

As the kernel finishes loading, it identifies the root directory, the system swap file, and dump files. It also sets the hostname and time zone, runs consistency checks on the file system, mounts all partitions, starts network service daemons, sets up the NIC, and establishes user and system accounting and quotas.

Review the documentation for the UNIX system you're examining for more information on the boot process.

Understanding Linux Loader and GRUB

Linux Loader (LILO) is an older Linux utility that initiates the boot process, which usually runs from the disk's MBR. LILO is a boot manager that allows you to start Linux or other OSs, including Windows. If a system has two or more OSs on different disk partitions, LILO can be set up to start any of them. For example, you might have Windows 2000 on one partition and Linux on another. When you turn on the computer, LILO displays a list of available OSs and asks which one you want to load.

LILO uses a configuration file named Lilo.conf in the /etc directory. This file is a script containing the location of the boot device, the kernel image file (such as Vmlinuz), and a delay timer that specifies how much time you have to select the OS you want to use.

Grand Unified Boot Loader (GRUB) is more powerful than LILO. It, too, resides in the MBR and enables you to load a variety of OSs. GRUB can load any kernel to a partition easily. Erich Boleyn created GRUB in 1995 to deal with multiboot processes and a variety of OSs. It works from the command line or can be menu driven. For more details, see *www.gnu. org/software/grub/manual*.

Understanding UNIX and Linux Drives and Partition Schemes

Drives and partitions are viewed in UNIX/Linux much differently than in MS-DOS and Windows. For example, in Windows XP, the primary master disk containing the first boot partition is typically listed as the C drive. In UNIX and Linux, disks and partitions are labeled as paths, with each path starting at the root directory, designated with the / symbol. In IDE drives, the primary master disk is defined as /dev/hda. The first partition on the primary master disk is defined as /dev/hda1; this device is equivalent to drive C in Windows or MS-DOS. If other partitions are located on the primary master disk, their number values are incremented; for example, the second partition on the primary master disk is /dev/hda2. If a disk has a third partition, it's /dev/hda3, and so on.

A drive connected to the primary slave controller is defined as /dev/hdb. If a drive is connected to the secondary master controller, it's listed as /dev/hdc, and the drive connected to the slave controller is /dev/hdd. Any additional controllers and drives are incremented alphabetically. For example, if a drive is mounted to a third additional controller, it's listed as /dev/hde, and so on.

If a SCSI controller is installed on a UNIX or Linux workstation, its designation is similar to that of IDE drives and partitions. The first drive connected to the SCSI controller is defined as /dev/sda and its first partition as /dev/sda1. Any additional partitions are incremented by one; for example, the second partition on a SCSI drive is /dev/sda2.

Linux treats SATA, USB, and FireWire devices the same way as SCSI devices. These plug-and-play devices have the same naming scheme as SCSI drives—/dev/sdb or /dev/sdc—and the partition numbers follow the same sequence as IDE drives.

Examining UNIX and Linux Disk Structures

Several commercial and freeware tools are available for analyzing UNIX and Linux file systems. Most commercial computer forensics tools, such as ASR SMART, X-Ways Forensics, Guidance Software EnCase, AccessData FTK, and ProDiscover Forensic Edition, can analyze UNIX UFS and UFS2 and Linux Ext2, Ext3, ReiserFS, and Reiser4 file systems. (ProDiscover Basic and Windows editions can analyze only FAT and NTFS file systems.)

Freeware tools include Sleuth Kit and its Web browser interface, Autopsy Browser, maintained by Brian Carrier (see *www.sleuthkit.org*). Sleuth Kit, previously called TASK, is partially based on the TCT toolset by Dan Farmer and Wietse Venema and designed as a network analysis tool for investigating attackers.

The U.S. Air Force Office of Special Investigations and the Center for Information Systems Security Studies and Research developed another specialized freeware tool called Foremost (see *http://foremost.sourceforge.net*). Foremost is a carving tool that can read many image file formats, such as raw and Expert Witness. Foremost has a configuration file, foremost.conf, listing the most common file headers, footers, and data structures. If a file format isn't included in the configuration file, it can be added by using a hex editor to determine the new format's header and footer values and a text editor to update foremost.conf. Foremost.conf is typically in the /usr/local/etc directory and contains instructions on updating it. If your installation is different, read the makefile script in the Foremost tarball to see how the current version is installed. A **tarball** is a data file containing one or more files or whole directories and their contents.

Installing Sleuth Kit and Autopsy To begin using Sleuth Kit and Autopsy, you need to install them on a UNIX system, such as Linux, FreeBSD, or Macintosh OS X. Installing Sleuth Kit and Autopsy requires downloading and installing the most recent updates of these tools. You can find current and past versions of Sleuth Kit at *www.sleuthkit.org/sleuthkit/download.php* and Autopsy Browser at *www.sleuthkit.org/autopsy/download.php*.

 Older RPM versions of Sleuth Kit and Autopsy are available at Web sites listed on Sleuth Kit's main page. The **Red Hat Package Manager (RPM)** utility makes installing these tools on Red Hat and Fedora Linux much easier. Several other Linux distributions have tools for installing RPM packages. Check their documentation to see how they handle RPM packages.

For the latest versions of Sleuth Kit and Autopsy Browser, download the most current source code from *www.sleuthkit.org*. The source code for these two tools is packaged into tarballs, which contain installation scripts you run from a terminal window with root privileges. After you have downloaded and extracted the source code and related files, read the README or INSTALL file for instructions explaining how to run the make command to complete the installation. The make command in the latest Sleuth Kit and Autopsy tarballs tests, compiles, and installs each tool.

If your Linux distribution is missing any special libraries used by these tools, the make command displays error messages listing the missing components. Correcting the installation errors can be challenging if you lack skills in UNIX/Linux administration.

Sleuth Kit must be installed before Autopsy Browser, or Autopsy isn't installed correctly.

To run Sleuth Kit and Autopsy Browser, you need to have root privileges. To start Autopsy, follow these steps:

1. If necessary, start your Linux computer and open a terminal window.

2. Change the default location to the Autopsy Browser directory. For example, if you installed Autopsy Browser in /usr/local/autopsy-2.08, type **cd usr/local/autopsy-2.08** and press **Enter**.

3. At the prompt, type **su** and press **Enter**. At the password prompt, enter the root password and press **Enter**.

If you're running Autopsy Browser on a Macintosh or in some Linux distributions, such as Ubuntu, you might not need to switch to superuser. If you don't, make sure you preface all commands with "sudo."

4. To start Autopsy, type **./autopsy** and press **Enter**. Figure 8-13 show the results of this command.

5. Right-click the URL **http://localhost:9999/autopsy**, as indicated in the terminal window, and then click **Copy**.

When copying the Autopsy URL from the terminal window, don't use the Ctrl+C shortcut. This shortcut terminates the privileged URL link needed to run Sleuth Kit from your Web browser.

6. Start your Web browser. Select the current URL in the Address text box, right-click the URL, click **Paste** to insert the Autopsy URL, and then press **Enter**. Figure 8-14 shows the Autopsy main window.

```
[joe@fridaypi ~]$ cd /usr/local/autopsy-2.08
[joe@fridaypi autopsy-2.08]$ su
Password: ******
[joe@fridaypi autopsy-2.08]$ ./autopsy

================================================================

                     Autopsy Forensic Browser
                  http://www.sleuthkit.org/autopsy/
                            ver 2.08

================================================================
Evidence Locker: /home/joe/work
Start Time: Mon Jan 22 07:55:33
Remote Host: localhost
Local Port: 9999

Open an HTML browser on the remote host and paste this URL in it

     http://localhost:9999/autopsy

Keep this process running and use <ctrl-c> to exit
|
```

Figure 8-13 Starting Autopsy from a Linux terminal window

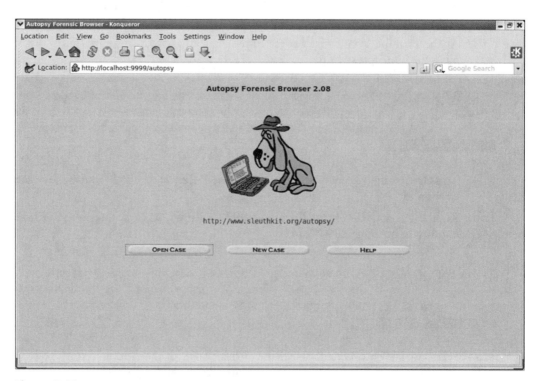

Figure 8-14 The Autopsy main window

If you see a warning message at the top stating that JavaScript is enabled, you have to reconfigure your browser to disable it. After reconfiguring the browser, you might have to exit and restart. If the Autopsy terminal session is still running, simply paste the Autopsy URL into the Address text box again.

7. Leave your Web browser open for the next activity.

Examining a Case with Sleuth Kit and Autopsy In this section, you learn how to use Sleuth Kit and Autopsy Browser to analyze a Linux Ext2 and Ext3 file system. If you closed your Web browser with Autopsy, restart it. Before starting the examination with Sleuth Kit and Autopsy, copy the GCFI-LX.00*n* (with *n* representing a number from 1 to 5) image files from your work folder to the evidence locker, which is the folder designated as the working area for Autopsy when it was installed. Autopsy uses the evidence locker to save results from examinations.

If you don't recall the evidence locker path, navigate to the Autopsy installation folder, open the conf.pl file, and look for the $LOCKDIR parameter to see the current path setting. If you want to change the evidence locker location, update the $LOCKDIR parameter with single quotation marks at the beginning and end of the new path.

The following steps use Sleuth Kit 2.07 and Autopsy Browser 2.08. If you're using different versions, your screens and output might be different from what's shown in this activity.

To start the examination of an acquired image of a Linux disk, follow these steps:

1. In Autopsy's main window, click the **New Case** button. When the Create A New Case dialog box opens, enter the investigation data, using Figure 8-15 as a guide, and then click the **New Case** button to continue.

2. In the Creating Case dialog box, click **Add Host** to continue.

3. In the Add A New Host dialog box, enter your information, using Figure 8-16 as a guide, and then click **Add Host**.

4. In the Adding Host dialog box, click **Add Image** to continue.

5. In the Open Image dialog box, click **Add Image File**.

6. In the Add A New Image dialog box, type the complete path to the evidence locker in the Location text box, click the **Partition** and **Move** option buttons, and then click **Next**. (Remember that UNIX/Linux commands are case sensitive. If you enter a lowercase filename and the filename is uppercase, Autopsy can't find and load the file.)

If you have multiple segment volumes that are sequentially numbered or lettered (the dd command with the split option without the -d switch), use an asterisk as the extension (for example, GCFI-LX.*) so that all segments are read sequentially.

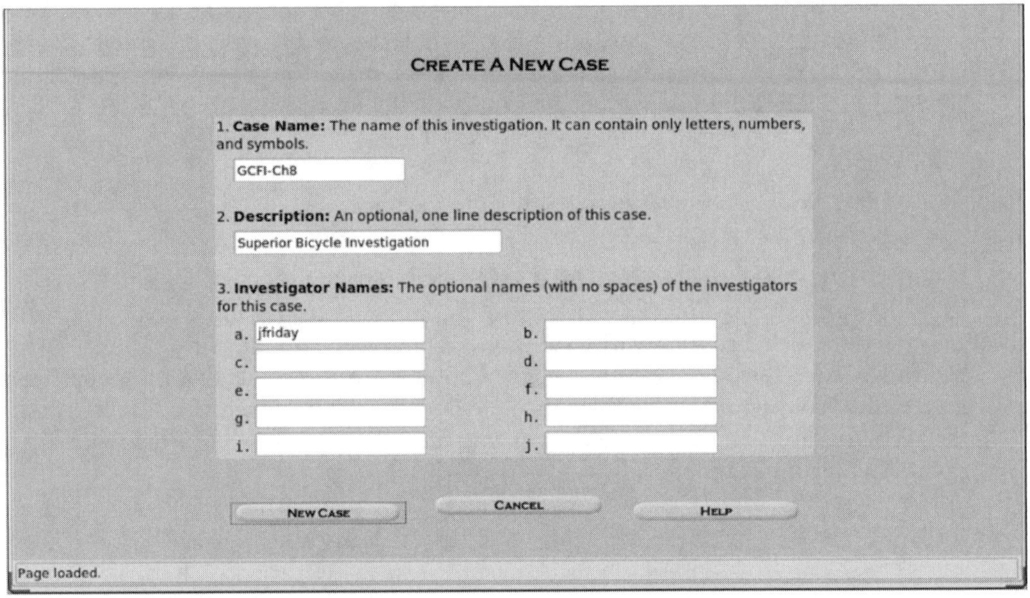

Figure 8-15 The Create A New Case dialog box

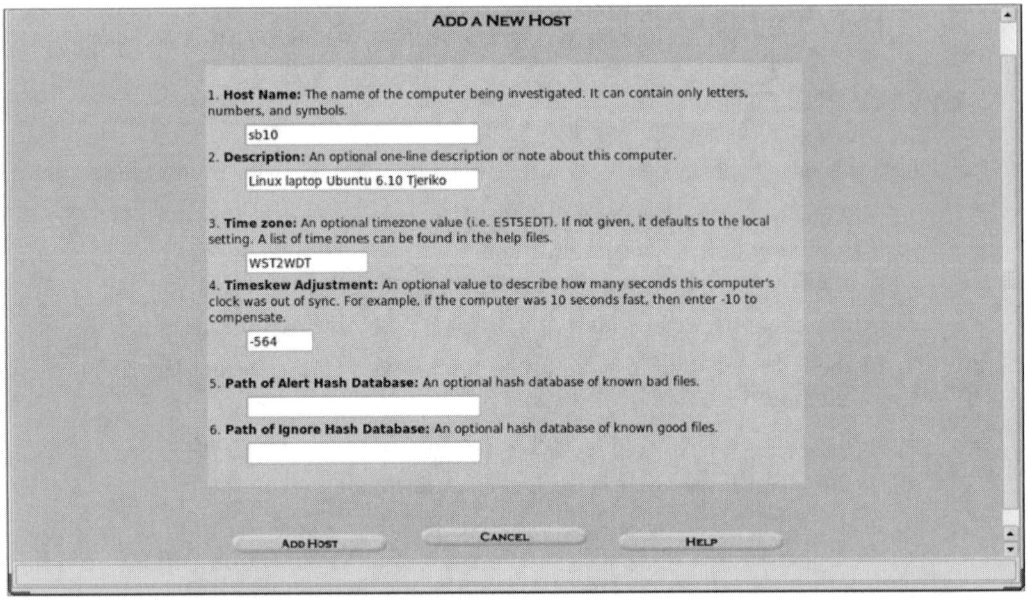

Figure 8-16 The Add A New Host dialog box

7. In the Split Image Confirmation dialog box, verify that all images are correctly loaded; if they are, click **Next**. If not, click **Cancel**. (If this data is incorrect, it's probably caused by an error in the pathname to the evidence locker or image files.)

If you didn't click Partition in Step 6, the image is read as raw data, and file and directory structures aren't visible to Autopsy.

8. In the Image File and File System Detail dialog box, click the **Calculate the hash value for this image** option button, and then click **Add**. In the Calculating MD5 message box, click **OK**.

9. In the Select a volume to analyze or add a new image file dialog box, click **Keyword Search** to initiate a search for keywords of interest to the investigation.

10. In the Keyword Search dialog box, type the name **martha** in the text box, as shown in Figure 8-17, and then click **Search**.

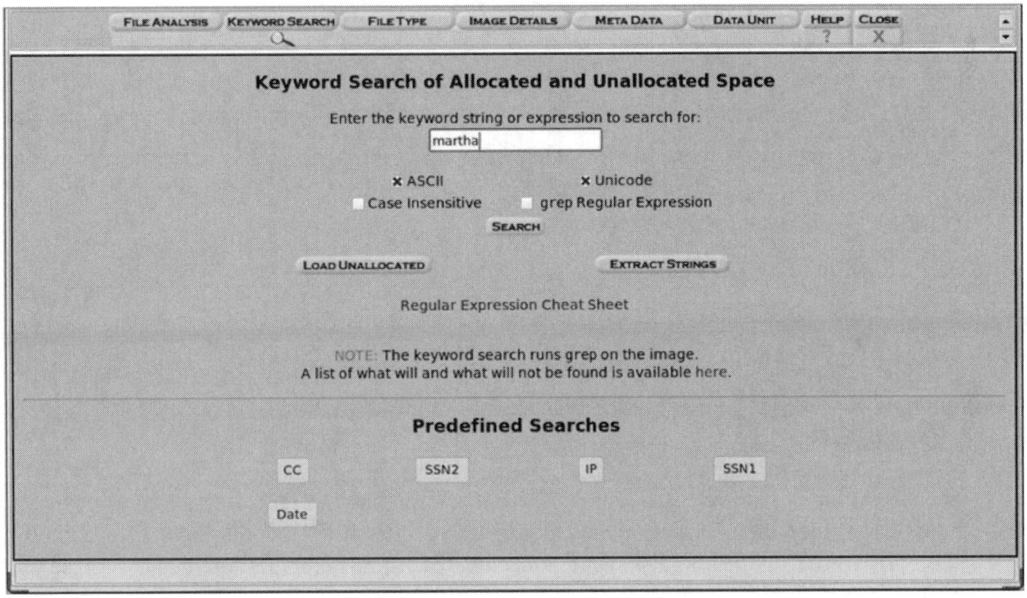

| FILE ANALYSIS | KEYWORD SEARCH | FILE TYPE | IMAGE DETAILS | META DATA | DATA UNIT | HELP | CLOSE |

Keyword Search of Allocated and Unallocated Space

Enter the keyword string or expression to search for:

martha

x ASCII   x Unicode
  Case Insensitive   grep Regular Expression
            SEARCH

LOAD UNALLOCATED   EXTRACT STRINGS

Regular Expression Cheat Sheet

NOTE: The keyword search runs grep on the image.
A list of what will and what will not be found is available here.

Predefined Searches

CC   SSN2   IP   SSN1

Date

Figure 8-17   The Keyword Search dialog box

11. When the search is finished, Autopsy displays a summary of the search results (see Figure 8-18). To see detailed search results, click the **link to results** link at the upper left.

12. Examine the search results by scrolling through the left pane, and then click the **Fragment 236019 "Ascii"** link to view details of the search. Repeat this examination by clicking other ASCII and Hex links for the remaining hits. When you're finished examining the search hits, close the Searching for ASCII and Searching for Unicode dialog box to return to the Select a volume to analyze or add a new image file box. Leave this program open for the next activity.

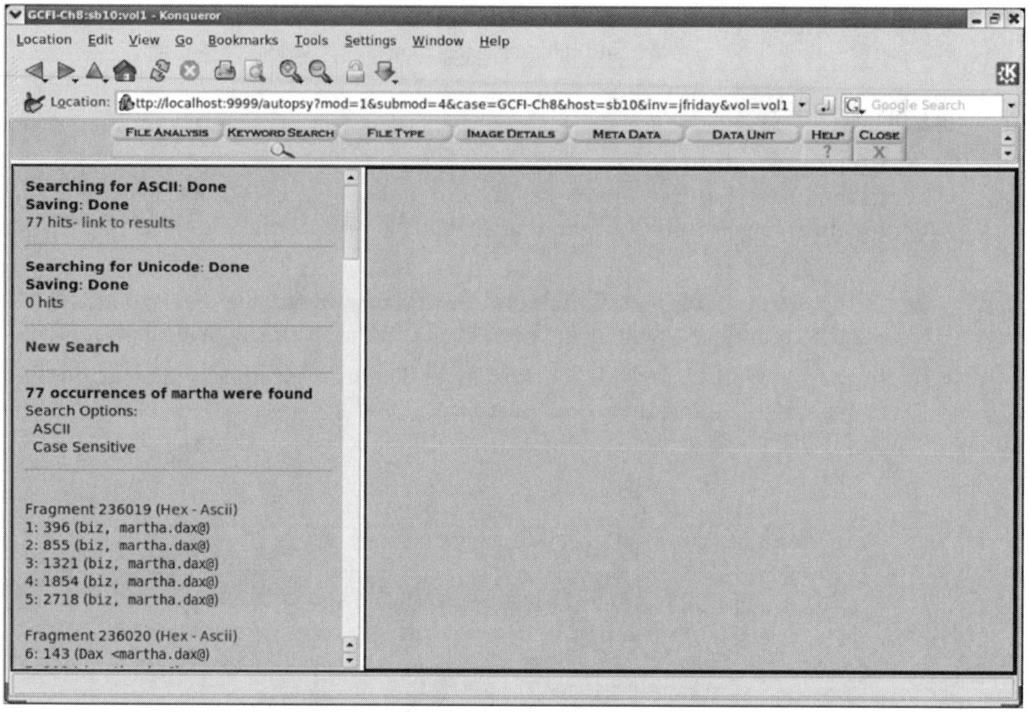

Figure 8-18 Summary of search results

Fragment hits can be exported as a text file for reports by clicking the Export Content button. You can also add notes to each fragment hit by clicking the Add Note button.

Next, you learn how to use the File Activity Time Lines function, which is useful for identifying what files were active at a specific time. This function displays files that might have been corrupted or accessed so that you can examine them further. Follow these steps to see how this function works:

1. To analyze the timelines of the evidence, you need to navigate back to the Select a volume to analyze or add a new image file dialog box, shown in Figure 8-19.

2. Click the **File Activity Time Lines** button.

3. In the File Activity Time Lines dialog box, click **Create Data File**. In the Create Data File dialog box, click the **/1/ gcfi-lx.001-0-0 ext** check box, type **GCFI-LX-body** for the name of the output file, and click **OK**.

4. In the Running fls and Running ils dialog box, click **OK**.

5. In the next dialog box, click the **GCFI-LX-body** option button. Enter the starting date, click the **Specify** option button, and change the date to **Dec 1, 2006**. Then enter the ending date, click the **Specify** option button, and change the date to **Jan 23, 2007** (see Figure 8-20). Then click **OK**.

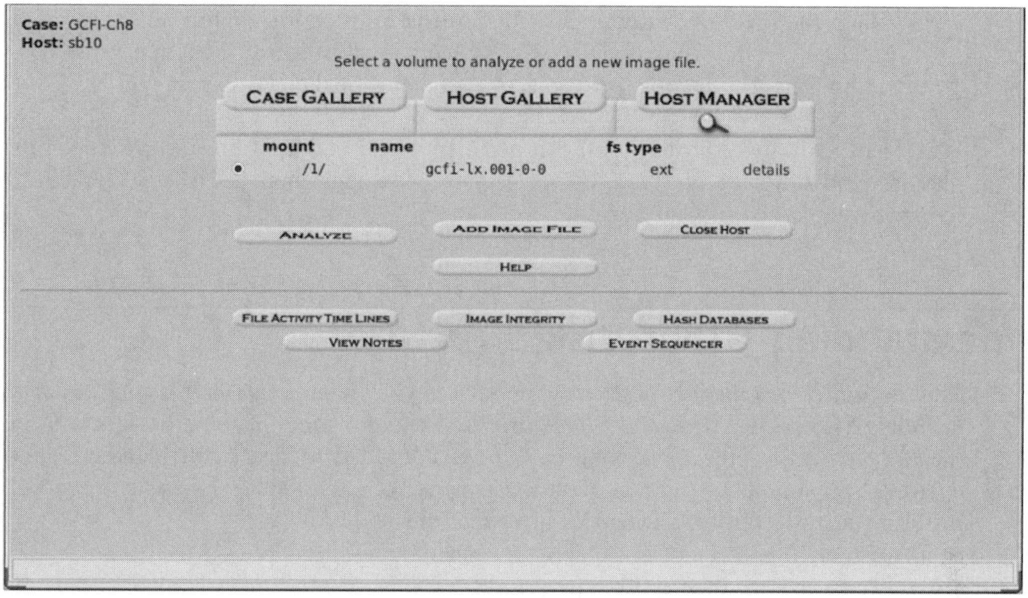

Case: GCFI-Ch8
Host: sb10

Select a volume to analyze or add a new image file.

CASE GALLERY   HOST GALLERY   HOST MANAGER

mount	name	fs type	
• /1/	gcfi-lx.001-0-0	ext	details

ANALYZE   ADD IMAGE FILE   CLOSE HOST

HELP

FILE ACTIVITY TIME LINES   IMAGE INTEGRITY   HASH DATABASES
VIEW NOTES   EVENT SEQUENCER

8

Figure 8-19 The Select a volume to analyze or add a new image file dialog box

For this activity, make sure you use the dates shown in Step 5. If you're analyzing your own Linux disk image instead of using the image file supplied with this book, use a date range that matches the incident you're examining.

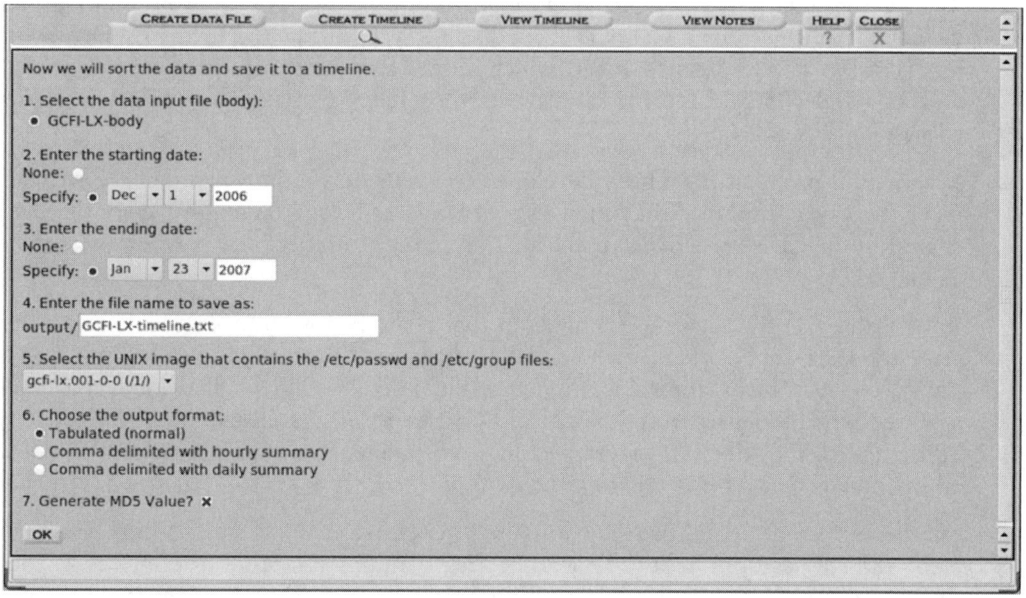

CREATE DATA FILE   CREATE TIMELINE   VIEW TIMELINE   VIEW NOTES   HELP   CLOSE
                                                                                                ?   X

Now we will sort the data and save it to a timeline.

1. Select the data input file (body):
• GCFI-LX-body

2. Enter the starting date:
None: ○
Specify: • Dec ▾ 1 ▾ 2006

3. Enter the ending date:
None: ○
Specify: • Jan ▾ 23 ▾ 2007

4. Enter the file name to save as:
output/ GCFI-LX-timeline.txt

5. Select the UNIX image that contains the /etc/passwd and /etc/group files:
gcfi-lx.001-0-0 (/1/) ▾

6. Choose the output format:
• Tabulated (normal)
○ Comma delimited with hourly summary
○ Comma delimited with daily summary

7. Generate MD5 Value? ✗

OK

Figure 8-20 Entering timeline options

6. When the timeline is done, click **OK** in the notification dialog box to display the timeline results. After reviewing the results, exit Autopsy. You can leave your system running for the Hands-On Projects at the end of the chapter, if you like.

With Sleuth Kit and Autopsy, you can perform additional analysis and produce other output files in subdirectories of the evidence locker. You can then use these files in a narrative report, as explained in Chapter 14.

Understanding Other Disk Structures

This section covers media and hardware devices you might encounter during an investigation, including SCSI, IDE/EIDE, and SATA drives. Although some of these devices were popular in the early days of computing, they have been upgraded to deal with high-end or high-speed devices. You should be familiar with the purpose of each device, its basic operation, and the problems it poses during a forensics investigation.

Examining CD Data Structures

CDs and DVDs are commonly used to store large amounts of data. Many people use CD and DVD burners to transfer digital information from a hard disk to a CD or DVD. As a computer forensics investigator, you might need to retrieve evidence from CDs and DVDs; these optical media store information differently than magnetic media do. To create a CD, a laser burns flat areas (lands) on the top side of the CD (the side without the label). Lower areas not burned by the laser are called pits. The transitions from lands to pits have the binary value of 1, or on. Where there's no transition, the location has a binary value of 0, or off. Figure 8-21 shows the basic structure of a CD.

The **International Organization of Standardization (ISO)** has established standards for CDs, including ISO 9660 for a CD, CD-R, and CD-RW and ISO 13346 for DVDs. ISO 9660 has an extension standard called Joliet, which allows long filenames in Windows 9x, NT, 2000, and XP. Under ISO 13346 for DVDs, the Micro-UDF (M-UDF) function has been added to allow long filenames.

A variety of products have been developed to make CDs more versatile. The writeable CD-R has a dye layer substance that changes when a laser heats it. The heat from the dye causes a change in the CD's reflective capability. This change in reflectivity is what alters the values of 1s and 0s.

Rewriteable CD-RW disks use a medium that changes appearance depending on the temperature the laser applies. This medium, called a **phase change alloy** (also known as a Metal PC layer), changes from amorphic (noncrystalline) to crystalline. The amorphic condition is achieved when the laser heats the Metal PC layer to 600° Celsius. When the laser cools it to 200° Celsius, the Metal PC layer becomes crystalline. Each change reflects or deflects light, which signals that a bit is set to 0 or 1.

On the surface of a CD, data is configured into three regions: the lead-in area, the program area, and the lead-out area. The lead-in area contains the table of contents in the subcode Q-channel. Subcode channels are additional data channels that provide start and end markers for tracks, time codes for each frame, the table of contents in the lead-in area, and graphics

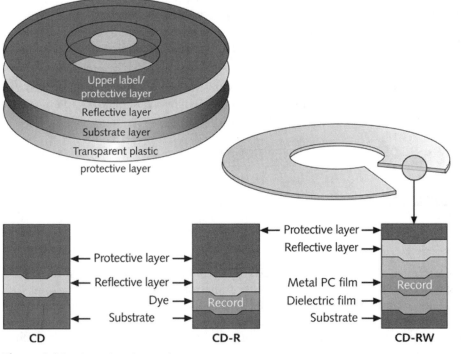

Figure 8-21   Physical makeup of a CD

codes. Up to 99 tracks are available for the table of contents. The lead-in area also synchronizes the CD as it's spinning.

The program area of the CD stores data and, like the lead-in area, has up to 99 tracks available. The lead-out area is the end-of-CD marker for the storage area. Figure 8-22 shows a CD's logical layout.

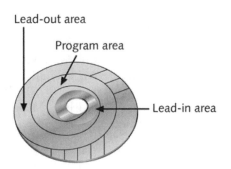

Figure 8-22   Logical layout of a CD

A unit of storage on a CD is called a frame, which includes a synchronized pattern, a control and display symbol, and eight error correction symbols. Each frame contains 24 17-bit symbols, and frames are then combined into blocks that form a sector. A block on a CD is 2352 bytes for music CDs (also called CD-DAs) or 2048 bytes for data CDs. CD players that are 12X or slower use a **constant linear velocity** (**CLV**) method for reading discs, usually music CDs. Newer CD players that are 12X or faster read discs with a **constant angular velocity** (**CAV**) method.

Unlike CDs, DVD disk file structures use a Universal Disk Format (UDF) called Micro-UDF (M-UDF). For backward compatibility, some DVDs have integrated ISO 9660 to allow compatibility with current OSs.

For more information on DVDs, see *http://homepage.mac.com/ wenguangwang/myhome/udf.html*, *www.osta.org/dvdcc/articles.htm*, and *www.osta.org/dvdcc/links.htm*.

Examining SCSI Disks

Small computer system interface (**SCSI**) is an input/output standard protocol device that allows a computer to access devices such as hard drives, tape drives, scanners, CD-ROM drives, and printers. Shugart Systems created SCSI in 1979 to provide a common bus communication device for all computer vendors. As SCSI evolved, it became a standard for PCs, Macintosh, and many UNIX workstations. Older Macintosh systems, such as the Mac SE, shipped with only a SCSI port.

When you examine evidence on a computer system, you need to inventory all connected devices to make sure you collect all possible magnetic media that can help you determine what you need to investigate. During this inventory, you should identify whether the computer uses a SCSI device. If so, determine whether it's an internal SCSI device, such as a hard drive, or an external device, such as a scanner or tape drive. If the computer is using external media devices, such as a tape drive with tapes, or removable disk drives, such as a Jaz drive, examine the content of these devices as part of your investigation. Determine whether you have the right SCSI card, cables, adapters, and terminators to examine a suspect's SCSI drive. You also need the correct software drivers that allow your OS to communicate with a SCSI device.

The **Advanced SCSI Programming Interface** (**ASPI**) provides several software drivers for communication between the OS and SCSI component. Windows versions from 9x and up have integrated ASPI drivers, which make adding a SCSI card to a Windows workstation easy. The Windows 98 Config.sys file, for example, contains ASPI drivers for reading a CD from an emergency boot disk or a Windows 98 startup disk. However, to access a SCSI device from MS-DOS, you must configure MS-DOS to install the correct SCSI driver. Most manuals or textbooks covering A+ certification from CompTIA have information on this procedure.

When connecting a SCSI device to your forensic workstation, you might have to change the port number on the hard disk, for example, to make sure duplicate port numbers aren't assigned to other devices. If you're using a SCSI UltraWide card, such as the Adaptec 29160, port 7 is usually reserved for the SCSI card. Verifying which ports are used for your SCSI device is a good practice to make sure you're prepared to examine SCSI drives.

One characteristic of a SCSI device is proper termination. A SCSI terminator is a resistor that's connected to the end of the SCSI cable or device. Newer SCSI devices typically use an integrated self-terminator. Some newer SCSI cards, such as the Adaptec 29160, self-correct and allow access to a SCSI driver. The device might take several seconds to adjust, however.

One problem with older SCSI drives is identifying which jumper group terminates and assigns a port number. Use Internet search engines to find specification sheets with this information for different types of SCSI drives.

Examining IDE/EIDE and SATA Devices

Most forensic disk examinations involve EIDE and SATA drives. You might, however, encounter older IDE drive versions as well as obsolete versions of MFM and RLL drives. Accessing older drives for the purpose of a forensics acquisition can be a challenge because current technology might not be backward compatible. For these older drives, one of the best resources for information is the Internet. You can often search for a drive's documentation (old and new) by simply using the drive's model number.

All Advanced Technology Attachment (ATA) drives from ATA-33 through ATA-133 IDE and EIDE drives use the standard 40-pin ribbon or shielded cable. ATA-66, ATA-100, and ATA-133 can use the newer 40-pin/80-wire cable, which provides considerably faster data transfer rates.

A pre-ATA-33 IDE drive might not work correctly or be accessible to your workstation, although PCs are usually backward compatible with older IDE drives. When you must access an older IDE drive, you might need to locate an older Pentium I or 486 PC and rely on your technical skills and those of other experts to investigate the disk.

 For more information on ATA drive architecture and future developments, consult the T13 Web site (*www.t13.org*). T13, a committee of the International Committee for Information Technology Standards (*www.incits.org*), is the current authority on ATA standards. For SATA drive architecture and future developments, consult the Serial ATA-International Organization Web site (*www.sata-io.org*). For an overview of most drive standards, see *http://kb.iu.edu/data/adlt.html#current*.

The CMOS on current PCs uses logical block addressing (LBA) and enhanced cylinder, head, and sector (CHS) configurations. When you connect an ATA-33 or newer drive to a PC, the CMOS identifies the disk's correct setting automatically, which is convenient when you're installing hard disks on your workstation. However, this feature can pose problems during an investigation. If you need to make a copy of a pre-ATA-33 256 MB drive, for example, you need its CHS configuration. Suppose you have a spare 4.0 GB drive where you plan to store a copy of the 256 MB drive. When you connect the two drives and power on your workstation, you enter CMOS and manually set it to match the CHS of the 256 MB drive. When you restart your workstation and access CMOS, you find that the CHS setting you changed didn't take effect. To solve this problem, use a disk-imaging tool, such as NTI Safe-Back or Guidance Software EnCase. These tools force the correct CHS configuration onto the target drive so that you can copy evidence data correctly.

Another solution is obtaining a 486 PC. The CMOS and BIOS in the 486 don't adjust the CHS of newer ATA drives automatically but do allow you to set the CHS configuration manually. However, one disadvantage of a 486 PC is that the IDE ATA controller doesn't recognize drives larger than 8.4 GB. If you need to configure the CHS of a drive larger than 8.4 GB manually, you can explore other alternatives. One solution is using an Enhanced Industry Standard Architecture (EISA) card that's engineered to connect to an IEEE 1394 FireWire device. Several vendors make EIDE drive bays that connect to FireWire devices.

Another option with a 486 PC is using an older ISA SCSI card and an A-Card IDE adapter card. A-Card, a Taiwan manufacturer, sells SCSI-to-IDE adapter cards for various SCSI models, including one card designed for UltraWide SCSI that prevents any write accesses to the connected IDE drive. One of many good sources for A-Cards is Microland USA (*www.microlandusa.com*). For the adapter card that prevents data from being written on a disk, locate the model card AEC7720WP that's listed with a write-blocker feature. (When you're searching for these products, enter the product number in a search engine because some might not be listed on the vendor's main site.) With an EISA FireWire card, a FireWire-to-EIDE interface, or a SCSI card with an IDE A-Card adapter, you can change the CHS configuration manually on any EIDE drive from a 486 PC.

Examining the IDE Host Protected Area

In 1998, T13 created a new standard for ATA drives (ATA or ATAPI-5 AT; ATAPI stands for Attachment with Packet Interface-5). This new standard provides a reserved and protected area of an IDE drive that's out of view of the OS. This feature is called Protected Area Run Time Interface Extension Service (PARTIES). Many disk manufacturers also refer to it as host protected area (HPA) in their documentation.

Service technicians use this protected area to store data created by diagnostic and restore programs. Using the HPA eliminates the need for a disaster recovery disk. Accessing the HPA might require a password and always requires special commands that can be run only from the computer's BIOS level. A disk partition utility, such as Fdisk, can't see a disk's HPA because it's accessible only at the BIOS level, not the OS level. As a computer forensics examiner, you should be familiar with the HPA on newer drives because criminals have used it to hide data related to their illegal activities.

One commercial tool for open access to the HPA is X-Ways Replica (see *www.x-ways.net/replica.html*), a DOS utility that fits on a bootable floppy disk or CD. When a suspect computer is booted and Replica is started, it detects whether the HPA is enabled. If it is, Replica notifies you and asks whether you want to turn it off. If you select yes, Replica makes changes to the BIOS to turn HPA off. It then instructs you to reboot to allow access to the HPA. The HPA is also referred to as a BIOS Engineering Extension Record (BEER) data structure.

Exploring Hidden Partitions

Another trick suspects use to conceal evidence is hiding disk partitions. Older tools, such as Norton DiskEdit, can be used to change the disk partition table so that when the drive is viewed from the operating system, as in Windows Explorer, there's no indication that the deactivated partition exists.

Because the hard disk you're investigating might have a hidden partition, use imaging tools that can access unpartitioned areas of a drive. Modern computer forensics tools can identify hidden partitions on most drives. This potential problem is covered in more detail in Chapter 9.

Chapter Summary

- The Macintosh OS uses the Hierarchical File System (HFS), in which files are stored in directories that can be nested in other directories. The File Manager utility handles reading, writing, and storing data to physical media, collects data to maintain the HFS, and is used to manipulate files, directories, and other items. The Finder utility works with the OS to keep track of files and maintain users' desktops.

- In HFS, a file consists of two parts: a data fork and a resource fork. The resource fork contains a resource map and resource header information for each file, window locations, and icons. The data fork contains data the user creates.

- A volume is any storage medium used to store files. Volumes have allocation blocks and logical blocks. A logical block is a collection of data that can't exceed 512 bytes. An allocation block is a group of consecutive logical blocks. When you save a file, File Manager assigns the file to an allocation block.

- HFS files are assigned allocation blocks, which are made of up of one or more logical blocks of 512 bytes each. In allocation blocks, a file has a logical EOF that's the actual end of a file, and the end of allocated blocks is the physical EOF.

- In older Macintosh OSs, the first two logical blocks on each volume (or disk) are the boot blocks, which contain information about system startup. The boot blocks also contain information about system configuration and can store optional executable code for the system file. Typically, system startup instructions are stored in the HFS system file rather than the boot blocks.

- To boot a Macintosh with a Macintosh-bootable CD, press and hold the C key when powering on the computer. To boot to a Macintosh-configured FireWire drive, press and hold the T key when powering on the computer.

- If a write-blocker isn't available, in Mac OS X 10.3 and later, you can disable write capability with Disk Arbitration. This feature prevents a drive from being mounted when it's connected to a computer.

- The Mac OS X Disk Images utility can be used to mount raw image files so that they can be examined with forensics tools. The raw image file must have a .dmg extension, and any additional segments must have a triple-digit sequential number followed by the .dmgpart extension.

- UNIX/Linux file systems have four components: boot block, superblock, inode block, and data block. Block sizes can be 512 bytes and up. Typical block sizes are 1024 to 4096 bytes.

- The Linux Second Extended File System (Ext2fs) uses inodes. Each file's inode contains information about the file, including its location in the volume, which is called the inode number.

- The superblock on a Linux system keeps track of the geometry and available space on a disk, along with the list of inodes.

- Ext3fs is a journaling version of Ext2fs that reduces file recovery time after a crash.

- The Linux file structure is made up of metadata and data. Metadata includes items such as the user ID (UID), group ID (GID), size, and permissions for each file. An inode contains the modification/access/creation (MAC) times, not a filename. An inode is assigned a number that's linked with the filename in the directory file. Pairing the inode number with the filename is how Linux keeps track of files and data. The data portion of the Linux file structure contains the file's contents.

- CDs and DVDs are optical media used to store large amounts of data. They adhere to standards defined by ISO 9660 and ISO 13346, respectively. A unit of storage is called a frame, which contains 24 17-bit symbols.

- SCSI connectors are used for a variety of peripheral devices. They pose unique challenges to a forensics investigation, such as finding the correct device drivers and interfaces.

- IDE/EIDE drives are other physical drives you might run across in investigations. You need to keep older drives in your lab in case you need to restore items from IDE/EIDE drives.

Key Terms

Advanced SCSI Programming Interface (ASPI) A component that provides several software drivers for communication between the OS and SCSI component.

allocation blocks In the Macintosh file system, a group of consecutive logical blocks assembled in a volume when a file is saved.

B*-tree A Macintosh file that organizes the directory hierarchy and file block mapping for File Manager. Files are represented as nodes (objects); leaf nodes contain the actual file data.

bad block inode In the Linux file system, the inode that tracks bad sectors on a drive.

Berkeley Software Distribution (BSD) UNIX A variation of UNIX created at the University of California, Berkeley.

catalog An area of the Macintosh file system used to maintain the relationships between files and directories on a volume.

clumps In the Macintosh file system, groups of contiguous allocation blocks used to keep file fragmentation to a minimum.

constant angular velocity (CAV) The method of reading CDs in CD players that are 12X or faster.

constant linear velocity (CLV) The method of reading CDs in CD players slower than or equal to 12X.

continuation inode An inode containing more detailed information, such as the mode and file type, the quantity of links in the file or directory, the file's or directory's access control list (ACL), the least and most significant bytes of the ACL UID and GID, and the file or directory status flag.

data fork The part of a Macintosh file containing the file's actual data, both user-created data and data written by applications. The data fork also contains the resource map and header information, window locations, and icons, as does the resource fork. *See also* resource fork.

Disk Arbitration The Mac OS X feature for disabling and enabling automatic mounting when a drive is connected via a USB or FireWire device.

Disk Images The format Mac OS X uses for image files (.dmg extension). If the image file has additional segments, these segments must have a .dmgpart extension.

double-indirect pointers The inode pointers in the second layer or group of an OS. *See also* inodes.

Extended Format File System (HFS+) File system used by Mac OS 8.1 and later; the primary difference between HFS and HFS+ is that HFS is limited to 65,536 blocks per volume, and HFS+ raised this number to more than 4 billion. HFS+ supports smaller file sizes on larger volumes, resulting in more efficient disk use.

extents overflow file A file in HFS and HFS+ that's used by the catalog to coordinate all file allocations to the volume. File Manager uses this file when the list of a file's contiguous blocks becomes too long for the catalog. The list's overflow is placed in the extents overflow file. Any file extents not in the MDB or a VCB are also contained in this file. *See also* catalog, Master Directory Block (MDB), *and* Volume Control Block (VCB).

File Manager A Macintosh utility that handles reading, writing, and storing data to physical media. It also collects data to maintain the HFS and is used to manipulate files, folders, and volumes.

Finder A Macintosh utility for keeping track of files and maintaining users' desktops.

GNU General Public License (GPL) An agreement that defines Linux as open-source software, meaning that anyone can use, change, and distribute the software without owing royalties or licensing fees to another party.

header node A node that stores information about the B*-tree file. *See also* B*-tree.

Hierarchical File System (HFS) The system Mac OS uses to store files, consisting of directories and subdirectories that can be nested.

index node A B*-tree node that stores link information to the previous and next nodes. *See also* B*-tree.

indirect pointers The inode pointers in the first layer or group of an OS. *See also* inodes.

inodes A key part of the Linux file system, these information nodes contain descriptive file or directory data, such as UIDs, GIDs, modification times, access times, creation times, and file locations.

International Organization of Standardization (ISO) An organization set up by the United Nations to ensure compatibility in a variety of fields, including engineering, electricity, and computers. The acronym ISO is the Greek word for "equal."

leaf nodes The bottom-level nodes of the B*-tree that contain actual file data in the Macintosh file system. *See also* B*-tree.

logical blocks In the Macintosh file system, a collection of data that can't exceed 512 bytes. Logical blocks are assembled in allocation blocks to store files in a volume.

logical EOF In the Macintosh file system, the number of bytes in a file containing data.

map node A B*-tree node that stores a node descriptor and map record. *See also* B*-tree.

Master Directory Block (MDB) On older Macintosh systems, the location where all volume information is stored. A copy of the MDB is kept in the next-to-last block on the volume. Called the Volume Information Block (VIB) in HFS+.

8

Open Firmware The platform-independent boot firmware Macintosh systems use instead of BIOS firmware to gather information, control boot device selection, and load the OS.

phase change alloy The Metal PC layer of a CD-RW that changes appearance (from noncrystalline to crystalline) depending on the temperature the laser applies. This medium allows writing to the CD several times.

physical EOF In the Macintosh file system, the number of allocation blocks assigned to a file.

Red Hat Package Manager (RPM) A utility that automates installing and uninstalling programs on Red Hat and Fedora Linux distributions.

resource fork The part of a Macintosh file containing file metadata and application information, such as menus, dialog boxes, icons, executable code, and controls. The resource fork also contains the resource map and header information, window locations, and icons, as does the data fork. *See also* data fork.

Second Extended File System (Ext2fs) The standard Linux file system.

small computer system interface (SCSI) An input/output standard protocol device that allows a computer to access devices such as hard drives, tape drives, scanners, CD/DVD-ROM drives, and printers.

tarball A method originally designed to store data on magnetic tapes; the name stands for "*tape ar*chive." This storage method has been used for many years in UNIX computing environments to combine files and directories. In UNIX, BSD, and Linux, tarball files have a .tar extension. The tar command creates an uncompressed continuous file of data. If a tarball file is compressed, another extension is added after .tar, such as .gz or .bz2.

triple-indirect pointers The inode pointers in the third layer or group of an OS. *See also* inodes.

Volume Bitmap A Macintosh application used to track blocks that are in use and blocks that are available.

Volume Control Block (VCB) An area of the Macintosh file system that contains information from the MDB and is used by File Manager. *See also* Master Directory Block (MDB).

Review Questions

1. Explain the differences in resource and data forks in Mac OS 9 and earlier.

2. In Mac OS 9, which of the following is a function of B*-tree nodes? (Choose all that apply.)

   a. The header node stores information about the B*-tree file.

   b. The index node stores link information to the previous and next nodes.

   c. The map node stores a node descriptor and a map record.

   d. The file node stores file metadata.

3. In Mac OS 9 and earlier, storage media are referred to as which of the following?

    a. Segmented blocks

    b. Disks

    c. Inodes

    d. Volumes

4. How does Mac OS 9 reduce disk fragmentation?

    a. Clumps are used to group contiguous allocated blocks.

    b. The MDB is reconfigured by File Manager.

    c. Data is written to the extents overflow file.

    d. Disk Arbitration is used to reorganize data on the volume.

5. What are the boot firmware utilities older Power PC and newer Intel Macintosh computers use? (Choose all that apply.)

    a. Bootstrap code

    b. Open Firmware

    c. Runtime application binaries

    d. Extensible Firmware Interface (EFI)

6. What do you need to do to a raw image file so that Mac OS X sees it and its segments as a virtual disk?

7. How do you mount a .dmg file in Mac OS X?

8. What are the differences in General Public License and BSD agreements for open-source use?

9. What are the differences between the Linux Ext2 and Ext3 file systems?

10. List three pieces of information found in metadata in the Linux file system.

11. How do inodes keep track of a file's name and data?

12. In UNIX OSs, drives, monitors, and NICs are treated as which of the following?

    a. Objects

    b. Tar devices

    c. Files

    d. Mount devices

13. What are the four components of the UNIX file system?

14. Only one copy of the superblock is kept. True or False?

15. What does the superblock in Linux define? (Choose all that apply.)

    a. File system names

    b. Disk geometry

c. Location of the first inode

d. Available space

16. In the UNIX file system, where are directories and files stored?

    a. Superblocks

    b. Data blocks

    c. Inode blocks

    d. Boot blocks

17. The bad block inode can be used to hide data. True or False?

18. The first inode assigned to a file in Linux has 13 pointers that link to which of the following? (Choose all that apply.)

    a. Data blocks

    b. B*-tree nodes

    c. Other pointers where files are stored

    d. Extents overflow file

19. Disk manufacturers use the host protected area for which of the following?

    a. Storing disaster recovery data

    b. Storing BIOS settings

    c. Storing data created by diagnostic and restore programs

    d. Storing OS information

20. What are the ISO standards for CDs, CD-RWs, and DVDs?

Hands-On Projects

If necessary, extract all data files in the Chap08\Projects folder on the book's DVD to the *Work*\Chap08\Projects folder on your system. (You might need to create this folder on your system before starting the projects; it's referred to as "your work folder" in steps.)

Hands-On Project 8-1

In this project, you perform an OS X file system analysis to become familiar with the functions and tools available in BlackBag Technologies Macintosh Forensic Software. You need the following:

- Macintosh G4 or newer running OS X 10.2 or later with 4 GB storage space on the internal drive or an attached work drive to store the analysis output

- BlackBag Technologies demo or licensed version

To prepare for this project, do the following:

1. Make sure the following files have been extracted to your work folder: GCFI-OSX.001 through GCFI-OSX.007.

2. Rename each GCFI-OSX image file in the Macintosh Disk Image format with .dmg and .dmgpart extensions. BlackBag requires the first segment volume to have the segment filename followed by the .dmg extension. All other segmented volumes must have a sequential three-digit extension followed by the .dmgpart extension. In addition, the second segmented file must be .002.dmgpart, not .001.dmgpart. The following chart shows an example of correct renaming:

Uncompressed image files	Macintosh Disk Image name
GCFI-0SX.001	GCFI-0SX.dmg
GCFI-0SX.002	GCFI-0SX.002.dmgpart
GCFI-0SX.003	GCFI-0SX.003.dmgpart
GCFI-0SX.004	GCFI-0SX.004.dmgpart

3. Start Finder, and locate and double-click the first file, **GCFI-OSX.dmg** (previously GCFI-OSX.001), to mount the disk image.

Now follow these steps for the partition mapping data on this OS X drive:

1. Start BlackBag from Macintosh Finder and click **OK** in the Welcome window.

2. To determine what partitions are on this image of an OS X system, click **PDISKInfo** on the BlackBag Forensic Suite ToolBar.

3. In the PDISKInfo window, click the **Suspect Device** list arrow, and then click the .dmg file drive you mounted.

Determining which drive is the .dmg image can be a problem. The Suspect Device list box also displays all connected drives, including the system drive (typically /dev/disk0) and any other drives connected or mounted previously, such as FireWire and USB drives. These additional drives are listed as /dev/disk1, /dev/disk2, and so on. If you have only the main operating drive connected, the .dmg drive is most likely /dev/disk1. If you connected one USB drive before mounting the .dmg drive, the USB drive would be /dev/disk1 and the .dmg drive would be /dev/disk2. Because this tool is read only, you won't harm anything if you access the wrong drive, however.

4. Click the **Partition Map** button to see partition information for the suspect drive. When the Authentication window opens, type the root password for your Macintosh system.

5. Next, save the PDISKInfo output by clicking **Save Report**. In the Save As text box, type **GCFI-OSX-partrpt.txt**, and then click **Save**. In the Where drop-down list box, click the folder where you want to save it. If the Report Saved dialog box opens, click **OK**. When you're finished, exit PDISKInfo.

6. Repeat these steps, clicking the **PMAPInfo** and **IORegInfo** buttons on the BlackBag Forensic Suite ToolBar, and save the report each utility creates. For the IORegInfo utility, click **All Information**.

Continue the analysis of this drive to learn how the DirectoryScan, File-Searcher, and VolumeExplorer utilities work. When you have finished, write a short paper describing the results of each function. You can leave BlackBag running for the next project.

Hands-On Project 8-2

In this project, you test other features of BlackBag and document your findings to learn more about BlackBag's evidence extraction capabilities. You need the following:

- Macintosh G4 or newer running OS X 10.2 or later with a 4 GB storage space on the internal drive or an attached work drive to store the analysis output
- BlackBag Technologies demo or licensed version
- The image files you used in Hands-On Project 8-1

Your report on these functions, which should be three to four pages, should include all items listed on the BlackBag Forensic Suite ToolBar.

Hands-On Project 8-3

On the Internet or in your library, research why Apple decided to change to the BSD UNIX format for its file structure. Write a one- to two-page paper on the reasons for the change and the pros and cons of this decision.

Hands-On Project 8-4

The purpose of this project is to become more familiar with Sleuth Kit and Autopsy. The best way to learn a tool, especially one that isn't well documented, is to explore its functions. You're encouraged to work in teams for this project and share your findings with other students. For this project, you convert the image file GCFI-datacarve-FAT.eve from Chapter 4 to a raw dd image by using ProDiscover Basic, and then analyze it with Sleuth Kit and Autopsy. You need the following:

- A PC running Windows with ProDiscover Basic installed
- A Linux or UNIX system with Sleuth Kit and Autopsy installed
- Disk storage of at least 200 MB to convert the .eve file to a dd file
- Instructions on using the computer forensics tools in this chapter and Chapters 2 and 4

Follow these steps:

1. Start ProDiscover Basic with the **Run as administrator** option. To convert the GCFI-datacarve-FAT.eve file to GCFI-datacarve-FAT.dd on a PC, click **Tools, Image Conversion Tools** from the menu and then click **Convert**

ProDiscover Image to 'DD'. In the Convert ProDiscover Image to 'DD' Image dialog box, click the **Browse** button, navigate to and click the location in your work folder where you saved GCFI-datacarve-FAT.eve, and then click **OK**. Exit ProDiscover Basic.

2. Copy the converted file to a Linux or UNIX system with Sleuth Kit and Autopsy installed. Start Sleuth Kit and Autopsy, as you did earlier in this chapter. In the main window, click **New Case**. In the Create A New Case dialog box, fill in your information (using **GCFI-datacarve-FAT** for the case name), and then click **New Case**.

3. In the Creating Case dialog box, click **Add Host,** and in the Add A New Host dialog box, enter your information, and click **Add Host**.

4. In the Adding Host dialog box, click **Add Image** to continue. In the Open Image dialog box, click **Add Image File**. In the Add A New Image dialog box, type the full pathname and the GCFI-datacarve-FAT.dd image filename in the Location text box, click the **Partition** option button, click the **Copy** option button for the import method, and then click **Next**.

5. In the Image File and File System Detail dialog box, click **Add**, and in the Test Partition dialog box, click **OK**. In the Select a volume to analyze or add a new image file dialog box, click the **Analyze** button.

6. In the Analysis dialog box, click **File Analysis**, and then click **Generate MD5 List of Files**. In the MD5 results window, save the list as **GCFI-datacarve-FAT-MD5.txt** in your work folder, and close the MD5 results window.

7. Next, in the Analysis dialog box, click **File Type**, click **Sort Files by Type,** and then click **OK**. When the analysis is finished, print the Results Summary frame of the Web page.

8. Click **Image Details**, and in the General File System Details dialog box, print the frame containing the results.

9. Write a report describing the information each function asks for and what information it produces so that you can begin building your own user manual for this tool. Leave Sleuth Kit and Autopsy running for the next project.

Hands-On Project 8-5

This project is a continuation of Hands-On Project 8-4, using Sleuth Kit and Autopsy. First, convert the image files C2Prj01.eve and C2Prj04.eve from Chapter 2 to raw dd images in ProDiscover Basic. Second, use Sleuth Kit and Autopsy to perform the same tasks described in Hands-On Project 8-4 for these two image files. When examining these image files, compare the results with your findings in Hands-On Project 8-4, and write a brief report on any similarities or differences to continue adding to your user manual.

Case Projects

Case Project 8-1

You receive a computer system from the officer who tagged and bagged the evidence at a crime scene in a suspect's home. You examine the computer and discover that it uses a SCSI drive on a Windows system. How will you continue the investigation? Write a one-page outline of your options for accessing the SCSI drive and list any additional computer components (including vendors, model numbers, and prices) that might be needed to examine this drive.

Case Project 8-2

You have been asked to review documentation for Sleuth Kit and determine whether the new acquisition format AFF would be practical to use. Your manager instructs you to review the documents at *www.sleuthkit.org/informer/* for any references to AFF, review the Informer documentation, and search the Web to see what information is available on this acquisition format and what computer forensics tools can read it. Your report should be no longer than two pages.

Case Project 8-3

Search the Internet for tools that allow Linux to mount and perform read and write access to an NTFS-formatted drive. The report should list available drivers that can be downloaded and installed with any Linux distribution. The report should be no more than two pages. (*Hint*: See *www.linux-ntfs.org* or *http://sourceforge.net/projects/linux-ntfs/* to start your research.)

chapter 9

Computer Forensics Analysis and Validation

After reading this chapter and completing the exercises, you will be able to:

- Determine what data to analyze in a computer forensics investigation
- Explain tools used to validate data
- Explain common data-hiding techniques
- Describe methods of performing a remote acquisition

This chapter explains how to apply your computer forensics skills and techniques to a computing investigation. One of the most critical functions is validating evidence during the analysis process. In Chapter 4, you learned how data acquisitions are validated for Windows and Linux file systems; in Chapter 5, you were introduced to hashing algorithms; and in Chapter 7, you learned about validating forensics software tools. In this chapter, you learn more about using hashing algorithms in forensics analysis to validate data. You also learn how to refine and modify an investigation plan, use data analysis tools and practices to process digital evidence, determine whether data-hiding techniques have been used, and learn methods for performing a remote acquisition.

Determining What Data to Collect and Analyze

Examining and analyzing digital evidence depend on the nature of the investigation and the amount of data to process. Criminal investigations are limited to finding data defined in the search warrant, and civil investigations are often limited by court orders for discovery. Corporate investigators might be searching for company policy violations that require examining only specific items, such as e-mail. Therefore, investigations often involve locating and recovering a few specific items, which simplifies and speeds processing.

In the corporate environment, however, especially if litigation is involved, the company attorney often directs the investigator to recover as much information as possible. Satisfying this demand becomes a major undertaking with many hours of tedious work. These types of investigations can also result in **scope creep**, in which an investigation expands beyond the original description because of unexpected evidence you find, prompting the attorney to ask you to examine other areas to recover more evidence. Scope creep increases the time and resources needed to extract, analyze, and present evidence. Be sure to document any requests for additional investigation, in case you must explain why the investigation took longer than planned, why the scope widened during the course of the investigation, and so forth.

One reason scope creep has become more common is that criminal investigations increasingly require more detailed examination of evidence just before trial to help prosecutors fend off attacks from defense attorneys. Because defense attorneys typically have the right of full discovery of digital evidence used against their clients, it's possible for new evidence to come to light while complying with the defense request for full discovery. However, this new evidence often isn't revealed to the prosecution; instead, the defense uses it to defend the accused. For this reason, it's become more important for prosecution teams to ensure that they have analyzed the evidence exhaustively before trial. (It should be noted that the defense request for full discovery applies only to criminal cases in the United States; civil cases are handled differently.)

Approaching Computer Forensics Cases

Recall from Chapter 2 that you begin a computer forensics case by creating an investigation plan that defines the investigation's goal and scope, the materials needed, and the tasks to perform. Although there are some basic principles that apply to almost all computer forensics cases, the approach you take depends largely on the specific type of case you're investigating.

For example, gathering evidence for an e-mail harassment case might involve little more than accessing network logs and e-mail server backups to locate specific messages. Your approach, however, depends on whether it's an internal corporate investigation or a civil or criminal investigation carried out by law enforcement. In an internal investigation, evidence collection tends to be fairly easy and straightforward because corporate investigators usually have ready access to the necessary records and files. In contrast, when investigating a criminal cyber-stalking case, you need to contact the ISP and e-mail service. Some companies, such as AOL, have a system set up to handle these situations, but others do not. Many companies don't keep e-mail for longer than 90 days, and some keep it only two weeks.

An employee suspected of industrial espionage can require the most work. You might need to set up a small camera to monitor his or her physical activities in the office. You might also need to plant a software or hardware keylogger (for capturing a suspect's keystrokes remotely), and you need to engage the network administrator's services to monitor Internet and network activities. In this situation, you might want to do a remote acquisition of the employee's drive, and then use another tool to determine what peripheral devices have been accessed.

As a standard practice, you should follow these basic steps for all computer forensics investigations:

For more information on basic processes and recommendations, refer to Chapter 3 for guidelines on setting up a forensic workstation.

9

1. For target drives, use only recently wiped media that have been reformatted and inspected for computer viruses. For example, use ProDiscover Secure Wipe Disk, Digital Intelligence PDWipe, or WhiteCanyon SecureClean to clean all data from the target drive you plan to use.

2. Inventory the hardware on the suspect's computer and note the condition of the computer when seized. Document all physical hardware components as part of your evidence acquisition process.

3. For static acquisitions, remove the original drive from the computer, if practical, and then check the date and time values in the system's CMOS.

4. Record how you acquired data from the suspect drive—note, for example, that you created a bit-stream image and which tool you used. The tool you use should also create an MD5 or SHA-1 or better hash for validating the image.

5. When examining the image of the drive's contents, process the data methodically and logically.

6. List all folders and files on the image or drive. For example, FTK can generate a Microsoft Access database listing all files and folders on a suspect drive. Note where specific evidence is found, and indicate how it's related to the investigation.

7. If possible, examine the contents of all data files in all folders, starting at the root directory of the volume partition. The exception is for civil cases, in which you look for only specific items in the investigation.

8. For all password-protected files that might be related to the investigation, make your best effort to recover file contents. You can use password recovery tools for this purpose, such as AccessData Password Recovery Toolkit (PRTK), NTI Password Recovery, or Passware Kit Enterprise.

9. Identify the function of every executable (binary or .exe) file that doesn't match known hash values. Make note of any system files or folders, such as the System32 folder or its content, that are out of place. If you can't find information on an executable file by using a disk editor, examine the file to see what it does and how it works.

10. Maintain control of all evidence and findings, and document everything as you progress through your examination.

Refining and Modifying the Investigation Plan In civil and criminal cases, the scope is often defined by search warrants or subpoenas, which specify what data you can recover. However, private sector cases, such as employee abuse investigations, might not specify limitations in recovering data. For these cases, it's important to refine the investigation plan as much as possible by trying to determine what the case requires. Generally, you want the investigation to be broad enough to encompass all relevant evidence, yet not so wide-ranging that you waste time and resources analyzing data that's not going to help your case.

Of course, even if your initial plan is sound, at times you'll find that you need to deviate from the plan and follow where the evidence leads you. Even in these cases, having a plan that you deliberately revise along the way is much better than searching for evidence haphazardly.

Suppose, for example, an employee is accused of operating an Internet-based side business using company resources during normal business hours. You use this timeframe to narrow the set of data you're searching, and because you're looking for unauthorized Internet use, you focus the search on temporary Internet files, Internet history, and e-mail communication. Knowing the types of data you're looking for at the outset helps you make the best use of your time and prevents you from casting too wide a net. However, in the course of reviewing e-mails related to the case, you might find references to spreadsheets or Word documents containing financial information related to the side business. In this case, it makes sense to broaden the range of data you're looking for to include these types of files. Again, the key is to start with a plan but remain flexible in the face of new evidence.

Using AccessData Forensic Toolkit to Analyze Data

So far, you have used several different features of FTK; this section goes into more detail on its search and report functions. FTK can perform forensics analysis on the following file systems:

- Microsoft FAT12, FAT16, and FAT32
- Microsoft NTFS (for Windows NT, 2000, XP, and Vista)
- Linux Ext2fs and Ext3fs

FTK can analyze data from several sources, including image files from other vendors. It can also read entire evidence drives or subsets of data, allowing you to consolidate large volumes of data from many sources when conducting a computer forensics analysis. With FTK, you can store everything from image files to recovered server folders on one investigation drive.

FTK also produces a case log file, where you can maintain a detailed record of all activities during your examination, such as keyword searches and data extractions. This log is also handy for reporting errors to AccessData. At times, however, you might not want the log feature turned on. If you're following a hunch, for example, but aren't sure the evidence you recover is applicable to the investigation, you might not want opposing counsel to see a record of this information because he or she could use it to question your methods and perhaps discredit your testimony. (Chapter 15 covers testimony issues in more detail.) Look through the evidence first before enabling the log feature to record searches. This approach isn't meant to conceal evidence; it's a precaution to ensure that your testimony can be used in court.

FTK has two options for searching for keywords. One option is an indexed search, which catalogs all words on the evidence drive so that FTK can find them quickly. This option returns search results quickly, although it does have some shortcomings. For example, you can't search for hexadecimal string values, and depending on how data is stored on the evidence drive, indexing might not catalog every word. If you do use this feature, keep in mind that indexing an image file can take several hours, so it's best to run this process overnight.

The other option is a live search, which can locate items such as text hidden in unallocated space that might not turn up in an indexed search. You can also search for alphanumeric and hexadecimal values on the evidence drive and search for specific items, such as phone numbers, credit card numbers, and Social Security numbers. Figure 9-1 shows the hits found during a live search of an image of a suspected arsonist's laptop. You can right-click a search hit to add it to your bookmarks, which includes the result in your final report.

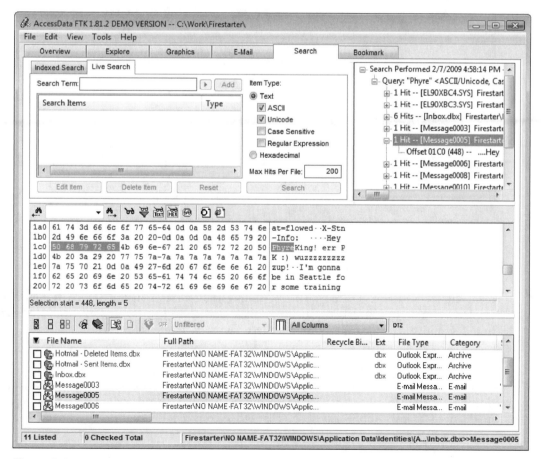

Figure 9-1 Viewing live search results in FTK

In addition to indexed and live searches, FTK has several advanced searching techniques, such as stemming, which enables you to look for words with extensions such as "ing," "ed," and so forth. You can search for similar-sounding words (homonyms, called "Phonics" in FTK), synonyms, and fuzzy representations (words that are close but not exact matches). In an FTK query, a fuzzy search for "raise" would also find "raize," for example.

In the Indexed Search tab, you can also look for files that were accessed or changed during a certain time period. Simply click the Options button to open the Search Options dialog box, and use the settings shown in Figure 9-2. During data processing, FTK also opens compressed files, including Microsoft cabinet (.cab) files, Microsoft personal e-mail folders (.pst or .ost), and .zip files. FTK indexes any compressed files it can open.

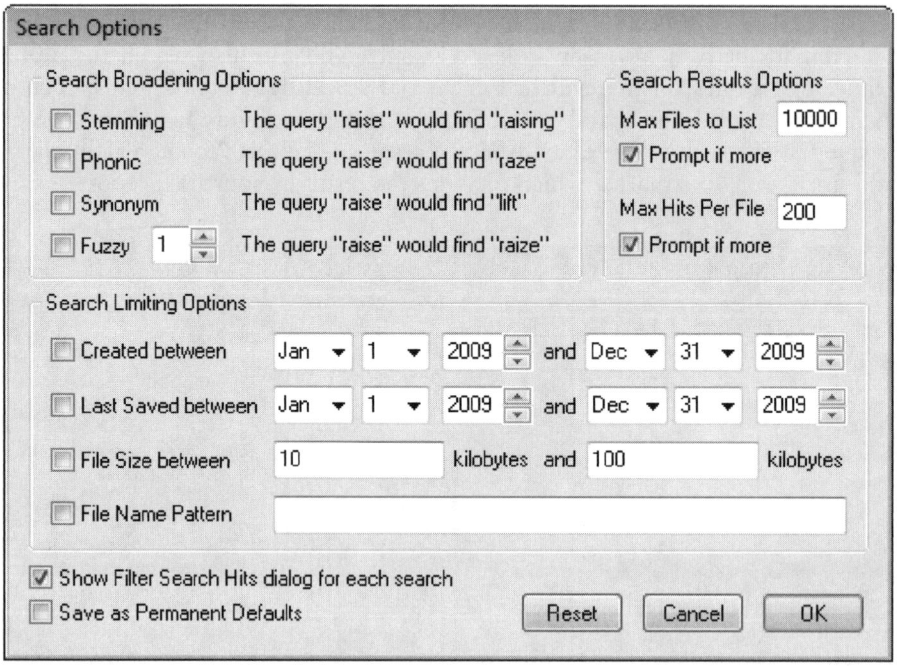

Figure 9-2 Selecting search options in FTK

To generate reports with the FTK Report Wizard, first you need to bookmark files during an examination. FTK and other computer forensics programs use bookmarks to tag and document digital evidence. To tag an item, simply right-click it in the search results and click Bookmark. You can also select an item, click Tools, Add to Bookmark from the menu, fill in a descriptive name for the bookmark (see Figure 9-3), and click OK.

After you have bookmarked data to include in a report, FTK integrates these selected items into an HTML document that you can view in a browser. Each bookmark appears as a hyperlink. You can also use the FTK Report Wizard to insert external files, such as a Word document or an Excel spreadsheet, into the HTML file. Before printing an FTK report, you might need to use Adobe Acrobat or another conversion program to convert the HTML code to a PDF file.

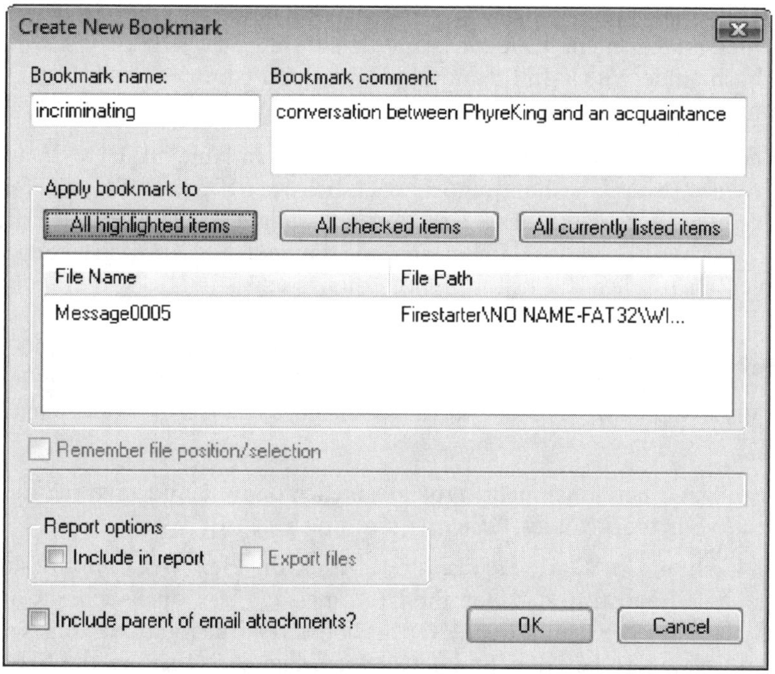

Figure 9-3 Creating a bookmark

Validating Forensic Data

One of the most critical aspects of computer forensics is validating digital evidence because ensuring the integrity of data you collect is essential for presenting evidence in court. Chapter 5 introduced forensic hashing algorithms, and in this section, you learn more about validating an acquired image before you analyze it.

Most computer forensic tools—such as ProDiscover, X-Ways Forensics, FTK, and EnCase—provide automated hashing of image files. For example, when ProDiscover loads an image file, it runs a hash and compares that value to the original hash calculated when the image was first acquired. You might remember seeing this feature when the Auto Image Checksum Verification message box opens after you load an image file in ProDiscover. Computer forensics tools have some limitations in performing hashing, however, so learning how to use advanced hexadecimal editors is necessary to ensure data integrity.

Validating with Hexadecimal Editors

Advanced hexadecimal editors offer many features not available in computer forensics tools, such as hashing specific files or sectors. Learning how to use these tools is important, especially when you need to find a particular file—for example, a known contraband image. With the hash value in hand, you can use a computer forensics tool to search for a suspicious file that might have had its name changed to look like an innocuous file. (Recall that two files with exactly the same content have the same hash value, even if they have different names.) Getting a hash value with a full-featured hexadecimal editor is much faster and easier than with a computer forensics tool.

In previous chapters, you've used the hashing functions available in FTK Imager. Hex Workshop also provides several hashing algorithms, such as MD5 and SHA-1. Sometimes you need the hash value of specific files or sectors to validate whether data or fragments (sectors) match, or you need to verify data during and immediately after an acquisition. To use the hashing functions of Hex Workshop, follow these steps:

Before beginning this activity, extract all data files from the Chap09 folder on the DVD to your *Work*\Chap09\Chapter folder (referred to as "your work folder" in steps). Create this folder on your system first, if necessary.

1. Start Word, and in a new document, type a sentence or two, and save the file as **test_hex.doc** in your work folder. When you're finished, exit Word.

2. Start Hex Workshop. (In Windows Vista, right-click the **Hex Workshop** desktop icon and click **Run as administrator**. When the UAC message box opens, click **Continue**.) Click **File, Open** from the menu. In the Open dialog box, navigate to your work folder, click to select **test_hex.doc**, and click **Open**. Figure 9-4 shows the file open in Hex Workshop.

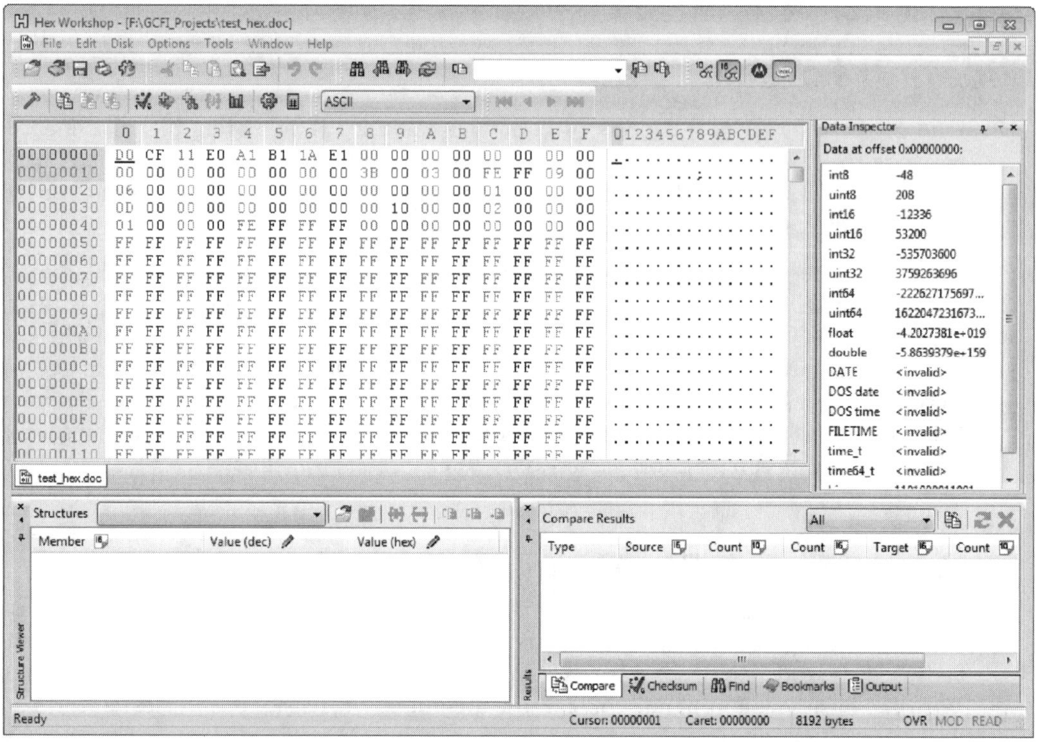

Figure 9-4 Viewing a file opened in Hex Workshop

3. To obtain an MD5 hash of this file, click **Tools, Generate Checksum** from the menu to open the Generate Checksum dialog box (see Figure 9-5).

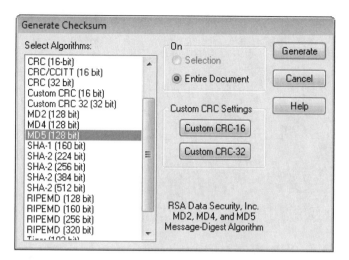

Figure 9-5 The Generate Checksum dialog box

4. In the Select Algorithms list box, scroll down and click **MD5**, and then click the **Generate** button to see the MD5 hash value in the results pane at the lower right (see Figure 9-6).

5. Right-click the hash value and click **Copy**. Start Notepad and paste the hash value into a new text document. Save the file as **test_hex_hashvalue.txt** in your work folder, and exit Notepad. Leave Hex Workshop running for the next activity.

Another feature of Hex Workshop generates the hash value of selected data in a file or sector. To see how this feature works, follow these steps:

1. In Hex Workshop, open the **Jeffersonian quotes.doc** file from your work folder.

2. Place the mouse pointer at the beginning of the byte address **00000000**; the cursor should be positioned on the hexadecimal D0 because you're examining the first sector of the file.

3. Now drag to select a complete sector (512 bytes). To know when you've selected the sector, watch the Offset counter at the lower right in the status bar. It should display "Sel: 00000200" when you've highlighted the entire sector.

As you drag the mouse, note that the Offset counter increments or decrements according to the direction of the mouse's movement across the window. This counter defaults to hexadecimal but can be altered to decimal counting.

4. Click **Tools, Generate Checksum** from the menu.

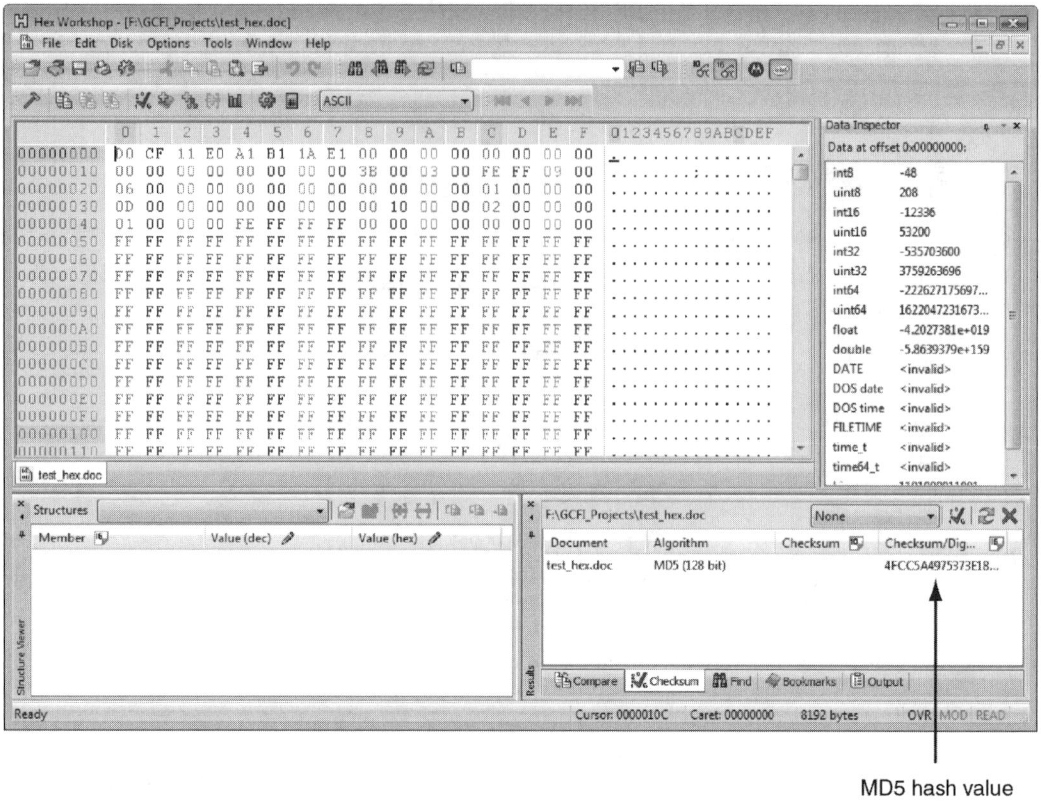

MD5 hash value

Figure 9-6 Hex Workshop displaying the MD5 hash value

5. In the Select Algorithms list box, scroll down and click **MD5**, click to enable the **Selection** option button (if necessary), and then click **Generate**.

6. Right-click the hash value in the results pane and click **Copy**. Start Notepad, and then paste the hash value into a new text document. Save the file as **Quotes_hashvalue.txt** in your work folder, and then exit Notepad and Hex Workshop.

The advantage of recording hash values is that you can determine whether data has changed. As shown in the preceding steps, you can use this method for specific sectors or entire files.

Using Hash Values to Discriminate Data

In Chapter 7, you learned about using the discrimination function to sort known good files from suspicious files. The discrimination function is useful in limiting the amount of data you have to examine, and many current computer forensics tools offer this function.

AccessData has a separate database, **Known File Filter (KFF)**, which is available only with FTK. KFF filters known program files from view, such as MSWord.exe, and identifies known illegal files, such as child pornography. KFF compares known file hash values to files on your evidence drive or image files to see whether they contain suspicious data. Periodically, AccessData updates these known file hash values and posts an updated KFF. As mentioned in Chapter 7, the National Software Reference Library (NSRL; *www.nsrl.nist. gov*) also maintains a national database of updated file hash values for a variety of OSs, applications, and images. Other computer forensics tools, such as X-Ways Forensics, can load the NSRL database and run hash comparisons.

Validating with Computer Forensics Programs

As mentioned, commercial computer forensics programs have built-in validation features. For example, ProDiscover's .eve files contain metadata that includes the hash value. When an image file is loaded in ProDiscover, it's hashed and then compared to the hash value in the stored metadata. If the hashes don't match, ProDiscover notifies you that the acquisition is corrupt and can't be considered reliable evidence. This feature is called Auto Image Checksum Verification.

In ProDiscover and other computer forensics tools, however, raw format image files (.dd extension) don't contain metadata, so you must validate raw format image files manually to ensure the integrity of data. You can also use these hash values to check whether the image file has been corrupted. Sometimes you work on a case for several months, and during that time, files can become corrupted, so you should check for this possibility periodically.

In AccessData FTK Imager, when you select the Expert Witness (.e01) or SMART (.s01) format, additional options for validating the acquisition are available. This validation report also lists MD5 and SHA-1 hash values. The MD5 hash value is added to the proprietary format image file. When this image file is loaded in tools such as FTK, SMART, or X-Ways Forensics, the MD5 hash value is read and compared to the hash value for the original acquisition to verify whether the image file is correct.

Follow these steps to see how ProDiscover's built-in validation feature works:

 In this activity, you use a data file from Chapter 6. Before beginning, move the GCFI-Win98.eve file from your Chapter 6 work folder to this chapter's work folder.

1. Start ProDiscover Basic with the **Run as administrator** option (if you're using Vista), and start a new project. Enter today's date for the project number, **GCFI-Win98** for the project name, and **Denise Robinson, Superior Bicycles - suspected of industrial espionage** for the description, and then click **OK**.

2. In the tree view, click to expand **Add**, and click **Image File**.

3. Navigate to your work folder, click the **GCFI-Win98.eve** file, and click **Open**. (If you're using Windows XP, in the message box about proceeding with the checksum verification, click **Yes**.)

4. After the checksum verification has finished validating the image file, click the **Save Project** button on the toolbar. Save the file as **GCFI-Win98.dft** in your work folder.

5. In the tree view, click to expand **Content View**, if necessary, and then click to expand **Images**.

6. Next, click the **GCFI-Win98** image file, and then click to expand it. You should see the folders on that drive listed.

7. Click to expand the **My Documents** folder and the **New Folder** folder, and then click the first **Temp** folder. Notice that a few files in this folder are graphics files. Click **View, Gallery View** from the menu (see Figure 9-7).

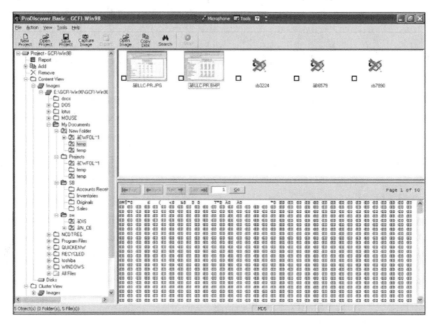

Figure 9-7   ProDiscover's Gallery view

8. In this view, you can right-click any file and export it, view the cluster numbers, compare it to a database containing hashes of known files, mark it as evidence, and so on. When you're finished exploring this view, exit ProDiscover Basic.

Addressing Data-Hiding Techniques

Data hiding involves changing or manipulating a file to conceal information. Data-hiding techniques include hiding entire partitions, changing file extensions, setting file attributes to hidden, bit-shifting, using encryption, and setting up password protection. Some of these techniques are discussed in the following sections.

Hiding Partitions

One way to hide partitions is to create a partition and then use a disk editor, such as Norton DiskEdit, to delete any reference to it manually. To access the deleted partition, users can edit the partition table to re-create the links, and then the hidden partition reappears when the computer is restarted. Another way to hide partitions is with a disk-partitioning utility, such as GDisk, Partition Magic, System Commander, or Linux Grand Unified Bootloader (GRUB), which provides a startup menu where you can select an OS. The system then ignores other bootable partitions.

To circumvent these techniques, be sure to account for all disk space when you're examining an evidence drive. Analyze any disk areas containing space you can't account for so that you can determine whether they contain additional evidence. For example, in the following code, Disk Manager recognizes the extended partition (labeled EXT DOS) as being 5381.1 MB (listed as Mbytes). The LOG DOS labels for partitions E through F indicate that they're logical partitions that make up the extended partition. However, if you add the sizes of drives E and F, the result is only 5271.3 MB, which is your first clue to examine the disk more closely. The remaining 109.8 MB could be a previously deleted partition or a hidden partition. For this example, the following code shows the letter "H" to indicate a hidden partition.

```
Disk    Partitions  Cylinders  Heads   Sectors   Mbytes    Sectors
2            5        11166      16       63      5495.8    11255328
Partition   Status  Type  Volume Label  Mbytes  System   Usage
D:            1                 PRI DOS   109.8   FAT16     2%
              2                 EXT DOS  5381.1             98%
E:            3                 LOG DOS   109.8   FAT16     2%
              4       H         LOG DOS   109.8   FAT16     2%
F:            5                 LOG DOS  5161.5   FAT32     94%
```

Windows creates a partition gap between partitions automatically; however, you might find a gap that's larger than it should be. For example, in Windows 2000/XP, the partition gap is only 63 sectors, so 109.8 MB is too large to be a standard partition gap. In Windows Vista, the gap is approximately 128 sectors.

In Figure 9-8, you can see a hidden partition in Disk Manager, which shows it as an unknown partition. In addition, the drive letters in the visible partitions are nonconsecutive (drive I is skipped), which can be another clue that a hidden partition exists. Most skilled users would make sure this anomaly doesn't occur, however.

Figure 9-8 Viewing a hidden partition in Disk Manager

In ProDiscover, a hidden partition appears as the highest available drive letter set in the BIOS. Figure 9-9 shows four partitions, similar to Figure 9-8, except the hidden partition shows as the drive letter Z. To carve (or salvage) data from the recovered partition gap, you can use other computer forensics tools, such as FTK or WinHex.

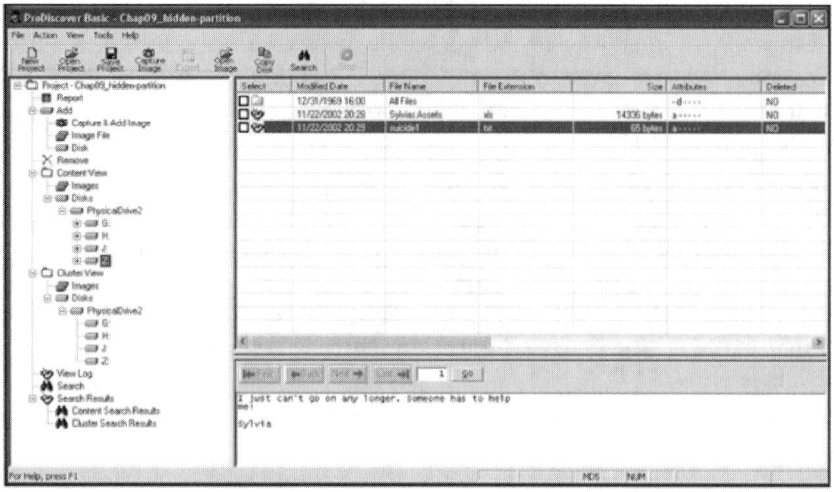

Figure 9-9 Viewing a hidden partition in ProDiscover

Marking Bad Clusters

Another data-hiding technique, more common in FAT file systems, is placing sensitive or incriminating data in free or slack space on disk partition clusters. This technique involves using a disk editor, such as Norton DiskEdit, to mark good clusters as bad clusters. The OS then considers these clusters unusable. The only way they can be accessed from the OS is by changing them to good clusters with a disk editor.

To mark a good cluster as bad in Norton DiskEdit, you type the letter B in the FAT entry corresponding to that cluster. You can then use any DOS disk editor to write and read data to this cluster, which is effectively hidden because it appears as bad to the OS.

> **NOTE** If a FAT partition containing clusters marked as bad is converted to an NTFS partition, the bad clusters remain marked as bad, so the conversion to NTFS doesn't affect the content of these clusters. Most GUI tools skip clusters marked as bad in FAT and NTFS, and these clusters might contain valuable evidence for your investigation.

Bit-Shifting

Some home computer users developed the skill of programming in the computer manufacturer's assembly language and learned how to create a low-level encryption program that changes the order of binary data, making the altered data unreadable when accessed with a text editor or word processor. These programs rearrange bits for each byte in a file. To secure a file containing sensitive or incriminating information, these users run an assembler program (also called a macro) on the file to scramble the bits. To access the file, they run another program that restores the scrambled bits to their original order. Some of these programs are still used today and can make it difficult for investigators to analyze data on a suspect drive. You should start by identifying any files you're not familiar with that might lead to new evidence. Training in assembly language—as well as higher-level programming languages, such as Visual Basic, Visual C++, or Perl—is also helpful.

A related, and well-known, technique for hiding data is shifting bit patterns to alter the byte values of data. **Bit-shifting** changes data from readable code to data that looks like binary executable code. Hex Workshop includes a feature for shifting bits and altering byte patterns of entire files or specified data. To shift bits in a text file, follow these steps:

1. Start Notepad, and in a text document, type **TEST FILE. Test file is to see how shifting bits will alter the data in a file.**

2. Save the file as **Bit_shift.txt** in your work folder, and exit Notepad.

3. Start Hex Workshop. Click **File, Open** from the menu. Navigate to your work folder, and then double-click **Bit_shift.txt**. Figure 9-10 shows the file open in Hex Workshop.

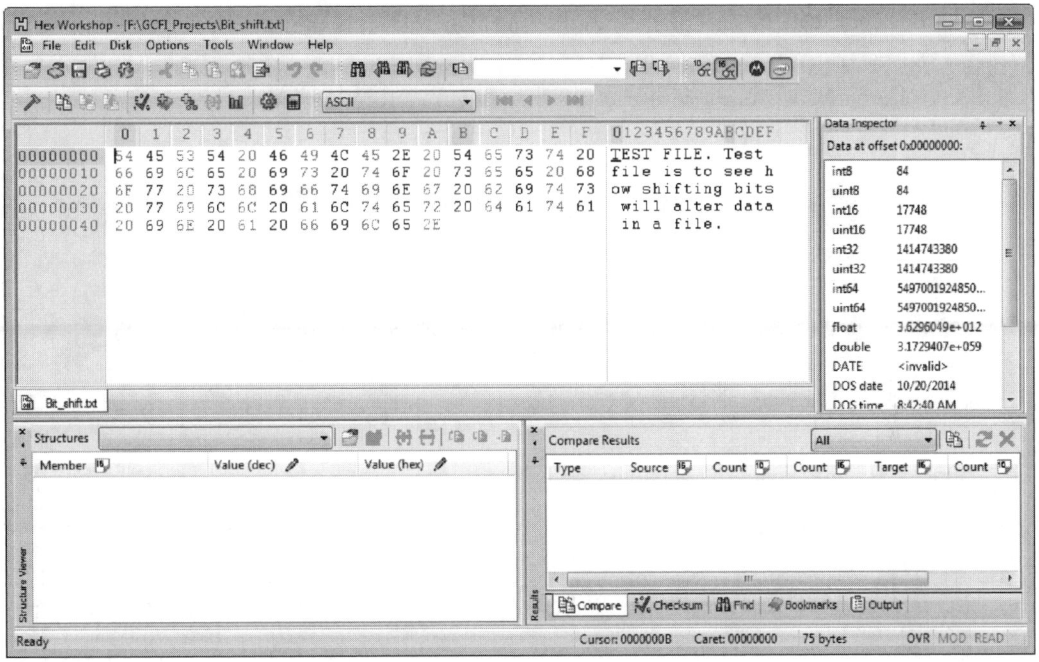

Figure 9-10 Bit_shift.txt open in Hex Workshop

4. To set up Hex Workshop for the bit-shifting exercise, click **Options, Toolbars** from the menu.

5. In the Customize dialog box, click the **Data Operations** check box, and then click **OK**.

6. Click the **Shift Left** button (<< icon) on the Data Operations toolbar. The Shift Left Operation dialog box opens (see Figure 9-11), where you specify how you want to treat the data, the ordering scheme to use for bytes, and whether you shift bits for selected text or the entire file.

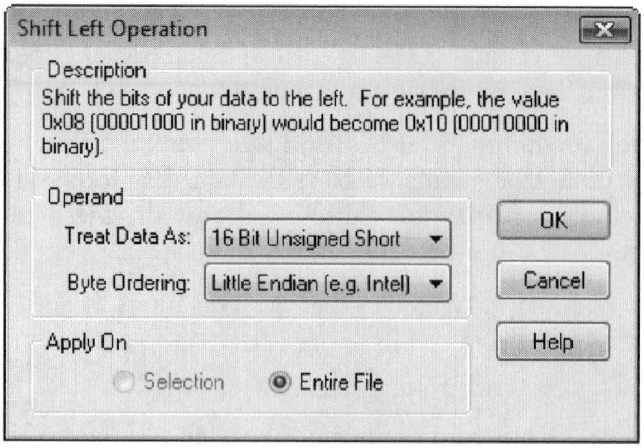

Figure 9-11 The Shift Left Operation dialog box

7. Click **OK** to accept the default settings and shift the bits in Bit_shift.txt to the left.

8. Save the file as **Bit_shift_left.txt** in your work folder. Figure 9-12 shows the file in Hex Workshop, with the @ symbols indicating shifted bits.

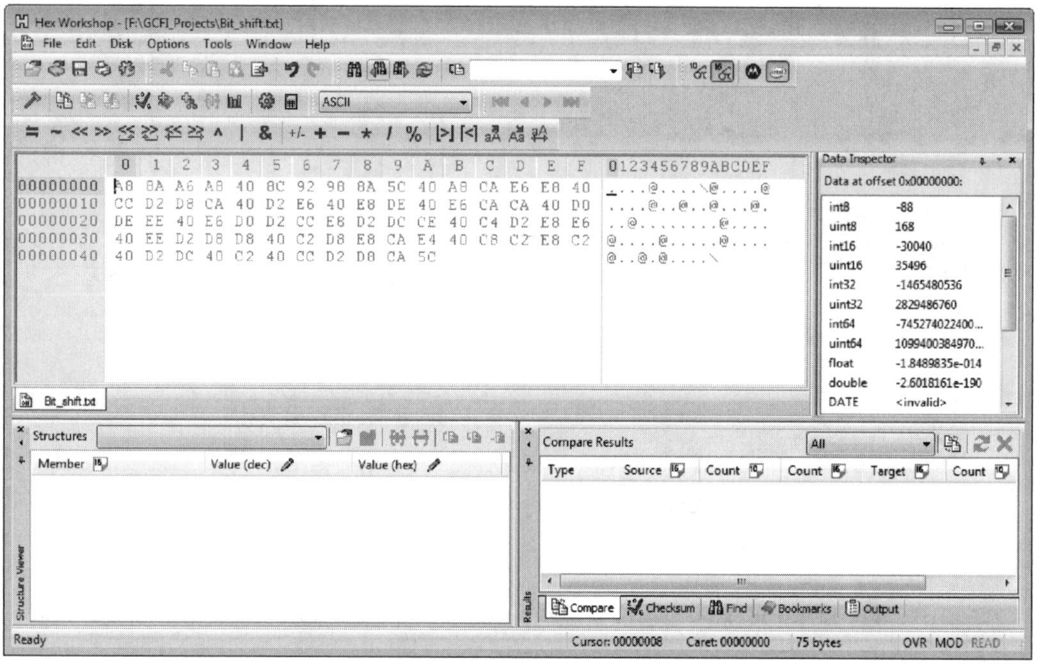

Figure 9-12 Viewing the shifted bits

9. To return the file to its original configuration, shift the bits back to the right by clicking the **Shift Right** button (>> icon) on the Data Operations toolbar. Click **OK**

to accept the default settings in the Shift Right Operation dialog box. The file is displayed in its original format.

10. Save the file as **Bit_shift_right.txt** in your work folder, and leave Hex Workshop open for the next activity.

Now you can use Hex Workshop to find the MD5 hash values for these three files and determine whether Bit_shift.txt is different from Bit_shift_right.txt and Bit_shift_left.txt. (You could also use FTK or ProDiscover to find the MD5 hash values.) To check the MD5 values in Hex Workshop, follow these steps:

1. With Bit_shift_right.txt open in Hex Workshop, click **File, Open** to open **Bit_shift.txt**, and then repeat to open **Bit_shift_left.txt**.

2. Click the **Bit_shift.txt** tab in the upper pane to make it the active file.

3. Click **Tools, Generate Checksum** from the menu to open the Generate Checksum dialog box. In the Select Algorithms list box, click **MD5**, and then click the **Generate** button. Copy the MD5 hash value of Bit_shift.txt, shown in the lower-right pane, and paste it in a new text document in Notepad.

4. Repeat Steps 2 and 3 for Bit_shift_left.txt and Bit_shift_right.txt, pasting their hash values in the same text file in Notepad.

5. Compare the MD5 hash values to determine whether the files are different. When you're finished, exit Notepad and Hex Workshop.

Typically, antivirus tools run hashes on potential malware files, but some advanced malware uses bit-shifting as a way to hide its malicious code from antivirus tools. With the bit-shifting functions in Hex Workshop, however, you can inspect potential malicious code manually. In addition, some malware that attacks Microsoft Office files consists of executable code that's embedded at the end of document files, such as Word documents, and hidden with bit-shifting. When an Office document is opened, the malware reverses the bit-shifting on the executable code and then runs it.

Using Steganography to Hide Data

The term **steganography** comes from the Greek word for "hidden writing." It's defined as hiding messages in such a way that only the intended recipient knows the message is there. Many steganography tools were created to protect copyrighted material by inserting digital watermarks into a file. Some digital watermarks are designed to be visible—for example, to notify users that an image is copyrighted. The digital watermarks used for steganography aren't usually visible, however, when you view the file in its usual application and might even be difficult to find with a disk editor. A nonsteganographic graphics file is the same size as an identical steganographic graphics file, and they look the same when you examine them in a graphics viewing utility, such as IrfanView. However, if you run an MD5 or SHA-1 hash comparison on both files, you'll find that the hash values aren't equal. Chapter 10 discusses a few steganography tools available for lossy graphics files. These tools insert data into the graphics file but often alter the original file in size and clarity.

To hide data, people can use steganography tools, many of which are freeware or shareware, to insert information into a variety of files. If you encrypt a plaintext file with PGP and insert the encrypted text into a steganography file, for example, cracking the encrypted message is extremely difficult. However, most steganography tools can insert only small amounts of data into a file and usually require a password to restrict access to the inserted data.

To detect steganography in evidence, you need information about the case so that you can detect files that might have been used to hide data. During your examination, look for steganography tools on the suspect computer, such as S-Tools, DPEnvelope, jpgx, and tte. If you locate any of these tools, look for files that could be used to hide data—specifically graphics files, but even text documents can be used for steganography. To help identify steganography files, use the following list as a guideline:

1. Locate the last modified date by checking the steganography tool's timestamp.

2. Look for files that appear as both a .bmp and a .jpg file, which might indicate files that started out in one format and then were modified (perhaps by a steganography tool) and saved in another format.

3. Generate a list of all files with a date and time equal to or after the last modified date of the steganography tool, and then examine each file in the generated listing.

If you locate files, especially graphics files, that appear to have been created by a steganography tool, attempt to reverse-engineer the file by re-creating known nonsteganographic images in the steganographic files. This technique is a trial-and-error process and might not be practical unless the investigation is extremely important. Try building a timeline of possible output files that match the last used date of the steganography tools. You can build a timeline with tools such as FTK and Sleuth Kit.

Examining Encrypted Files

People who want to hide data can also use advanced encryption programs, such as PGP or BestCrypt. Encrypted files are encoded to prevent unauthorized access. To decode an encrypted file, users supply a password or passphrase. Without the passphrase, recovering the contents of encrypted files is difficult. Many commercial encryption programs use a technology called **key escrow**, which is designed to recover encrypted data if users forget their passphrases or if the user key is corrupted after a system failure. Forensics examiners can also use key escrow to attempt to recover encrypted data. Although some vendors have developed key recovery tools, the resources needed to crack encryption schemes are usually beyond what's available to small or medium organizations. If you do encounter encrypted data in an investigation, make an effort to persuade the suspect to reveal the encryption passphrase.

Some encryption schemes are so complex that the time to crack them can be measured in days, weeks, years, and even decades. Key sizes of 128 bits to 512 bits make the job of breaking them with a brute-force attack impossible with current technology. The development of quantum computing will probably make today's encryption schemes obsolete. Until then, some will remain unbroken.

Recovering Passwords

Password recovery is a fairly easy task in computer forensics analysis. Several password-cracking tools are available, such as AccessData PRTK, NTI Advanced Password Recovery Software Toolkit, and John the Ripper (*www.openwall.com/john*). These tools use a dictionary or brute-force attack to crack passwords. Brute-force attacks use every possible letter, number, and character found on a keyboard. Eventually, a brute-force attack can crack any password; however, this method can be time and processor intensive. In a dictionary attack, the program uses common words found in the dictionary and tries them as passwords. Most password crackers have dictionaries in a variety of languages, including English, French, Russian, and even Swahili. With some password-cracking tools, you can import additional unique words that are typically extracted from evidence. In FTK, for example, you can export a word list to PRTK.

With other programs, you can build profiles of a suspect to help determine the suspect's password. These programs consider information such as names of relatives or pets, favorite colors, and schools attended. The principle behind these programs is that people have a habit of using things they are comfortable with, especially if it requires memorizing something secret, such as a password.

Using AccessData Tools with Passworded and Encrypted Files AccessData offers a tool called Password Recovery Toolkit (PRTK), which is designed to create possible password lists from many sources so that you can access password-protected files. You can create a password list in many ways, including generating a password list with FTK, as shown in Figure 9-13, or creating a text file of passwords manually, as shown in Figure 9-14.

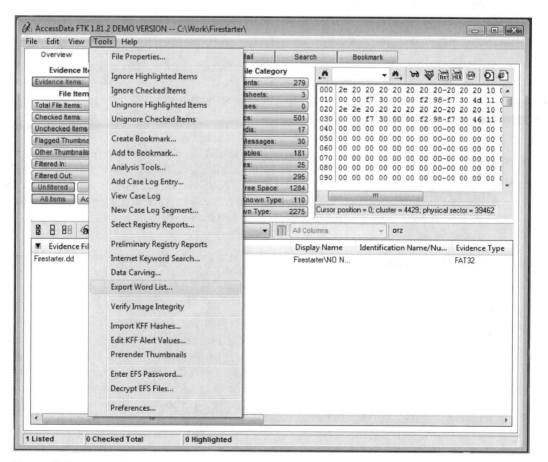

Figure 9-13 Using FTK to generate a password list

```
passwords - Notepad                          [ _ ] [ □ ] [ ✕ ]
File   Edit   Format   View   Help
managerc
managercleschess
managere
managerf
managerg
managerh
manageri
managerk
managerm
managermicrosoft
managerr
managers
managerw
manages
managing
mancanti
manco
mand
mandag
mandated
mandatory
mandatory0
```

Figure 9-14 A partial list of possible passwords

If you haven't installed Password Recovery Toolkit yet, it's available on the book's DVD with the other software. Go ahead and install it now so that you can investigate its features.

To see the variety of dictionaries available in PRTK that you can use for cracking passwords, navigate in Windows Explorer to the main AccessData folder, and open the Dictionaries subfolder (see Figure 9-15). Better yet, you can create your own custom dictionary based on facts in the case. With PRTK, you can also create a profile of a suspect and use that biographical information to generate likely passwords.

Password cracking requires a lot of memory, so the more RAM on your forensic workstation, the better.

FTK can also identify known encrypted files and those that seem to be encrypted. For example, a simple encrypted file is a password-protected WinZip file or PGP file. In the Overview tab of FTK, simply click the Encrypted Files button under the File Status column, and FTK lists all files that appear to be encrypted. For password-protected WinZip or PGP files, select them in the bottom pane. FTK shows you the files contained in the

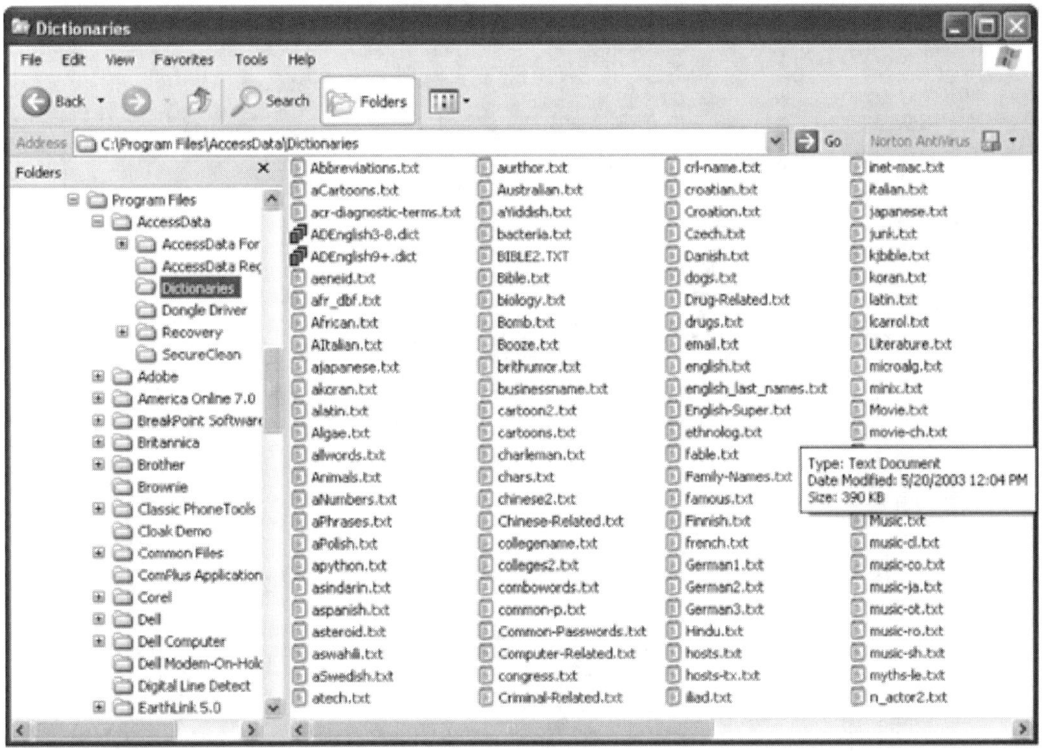

Figure 9-15 is an image of a Windows Explorer window titled "Dictionaries" showing the folder path C:\Program Files\AccessData\Dictionaries with a folder tree on the left and a list of .txt and .dict dictionary files on the right. A tooltip shows "Type: Text Document / Date Modified: 5/20/2003 12:04 PM / Size: 390 KB".

Figure 9-15 Dictionaries available in PRTK

zipped files, and you can them export them for analysis. Figure 9-16 shows a .zip file selected and the file it contains.

As a shortcut, you can export a group of files by selecting them, right-clicking the selection, and clicking Export Files. In the Export Files dialog box, select the All checked files option button (see Figure 9-17). You can then import these files into PRTK and attempt to crack them.

WinZip 9.0 and later password-protected files are almost impossible to crack, so check the suspect's system to determine what version of WinZip was used.

NOTE

Performing Remote Acquisitions

Remote acquisitions are handy when you need to image the drive of a computer far away from your location or when you don't want a suspect to be aware of an ongoing investigation. This method can save time and money, too. Many tools are available for remote acquisitions; in the following sections, you use Runtime Software to learn how remote acquisitions are made.

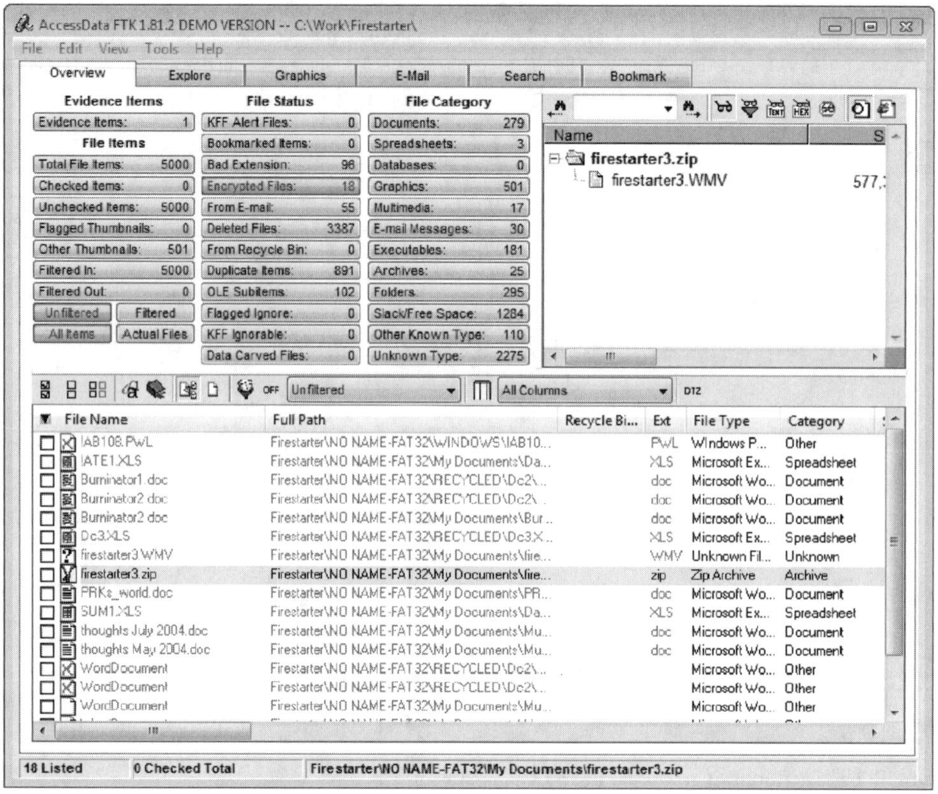

Figure 9-16 FTK displaying encrypted files

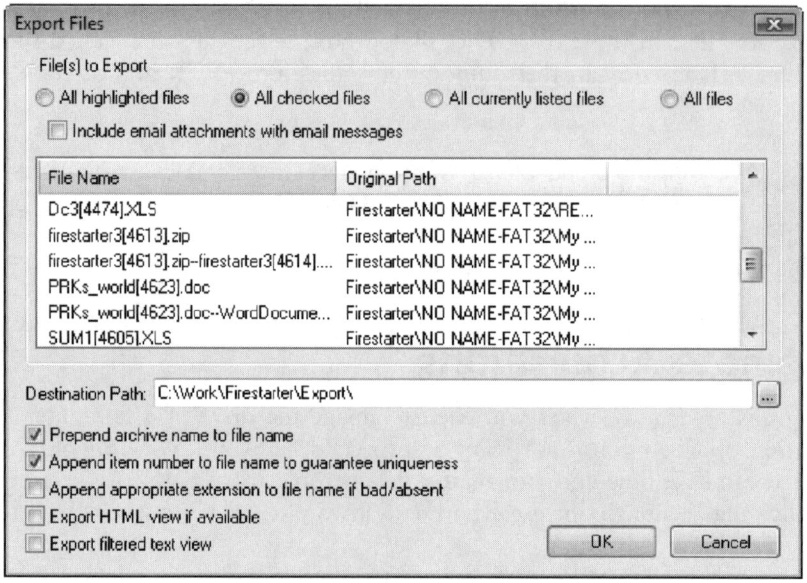

Figure 9-17 Exporting encrypted files

Remote Acquisitions with Runtime Software

Runtime Software (*www.runtime.org*) offers the following shareware programs for remote acquisitions:

- DiskExplorer for FAT
- DiskExplorer for NTFS
- HDHOST

Chapter 4 introduced these tools; remember that they're designed to be file system specific, so there are DiskExplorer versions for both FAT and NTFS that you can use to create raw format image files or segmented image files for archiving purposes.

HDHOST is a remote access program for communication between two computers. The connection is established by using the DiskExplorer program (FAT or NTFS) corresponding to the suspect (remote) computer's file system. The following sections show how to make a live remote acquisition of another computer over a network. To use these tools, it's best to have computers connected on the same local hub or router with minimal network traffic.

When you're using remote access tools, you might have connection difficulties caused by firewall settings on your computer. If so, check firewall settings for the server and client systems.

Preparing DiskExplorer and HDHOST for Remote Acquisitions Preparing for remote access requires the Runtime software, a portable media device (USB drive or floppy disk), and two networked computers. After installing both DiskExplorer programs and HDHOST on your acquisition workstation, copy the installed HDHOST folder to a portable media device, which is used on the suspect's computer. To install the DiskExplorer and HDHOST programs, follow these steps. In this example, a USB drive is used to run HDHOST on the suspect's computer.

1. Copy the Runtime tools from the book's DVD to your workstation, and install DiskExplorer for FAT, DiskExplorer for NTFS, and HDHOST in their default folders.

2. After installing these tools, insert a USB drive. Open Windows Explorer, navigate to the **C:\Program Files\Runtime Software** folder, and copy the **HDHOST** folder to the USB drive.

3. Dismount and remove the USB drive from the workstation.

Your workstation is now ready to connect remotely to a suspect's computer. In the next section, you learn how to set up the host (the suspect's computer).

Making a Remote Connection with DiskExplorer Using HDHOST and DiskExplorer requires running HDHOST on a suspect's computer. To establish a connection with HDHOST, the suspect's computer must be connected to the network, powered on, and logged on to any user account with permission to run uninstalled applications. HDHOST can't be run surreptitiously, as ProDiscover or EnCase Enterprise can. To establish a connection, perform the following steps. This example is for a suspect computer with an NTFS partition.

 Both DiskExplorer programs can acquire entire physical drives; this process isn't file system dependent. To copy specific files remotely, however, you must use the correct DiskExplorer program for the suspect's file system. In addition, you might have to disable any firewalls you have running for these steps to work correctly. Note that some pathnames and filenames in figures might differ from what's on your system.

1. On your acquisition workstation, connect the target drive for receiving the suspect computer's image data (assuming the target drive is a USB or FireWire external hot-swappable drive).

2. After powering on and logging on to the network with the suspect computer, insert the USB drive containing the HDHOST folder.

3. To start HDHOST, open Windows Explorer from the suspect computer. Navigate to the connected USB drive and the HDHOST folder, as shown in Figure 9-18.

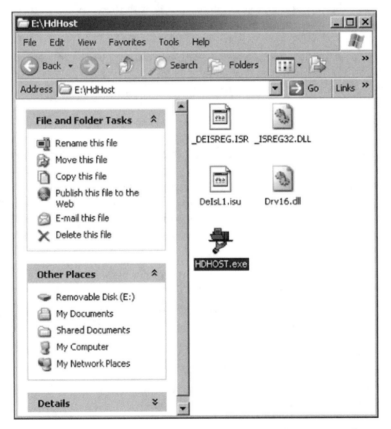

Figure 9-18 Displaying the contents of the HDHOST folder in Windows Explorer

4. Double-click **HDHOST.exe** to start the remote connection. When the HDHOST startup window opens, click the **TCP/IP** option button (see Figure 9-19).

5. On the acquisition workstation, start the correct DiskExplorer program. For example, to start DiskExplorer for NTFS, click **Start**, point to **All Programs**, point to **Runtime Software**, and then click **DiskExplorer for NTFS** to open the window shown in Figure 9-20.

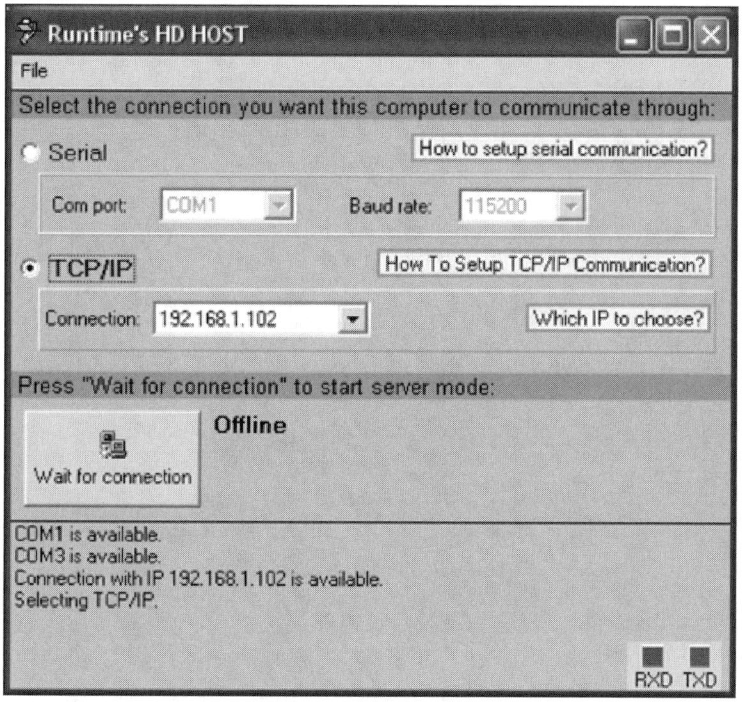

Figure 9-19 Selecting a connection type

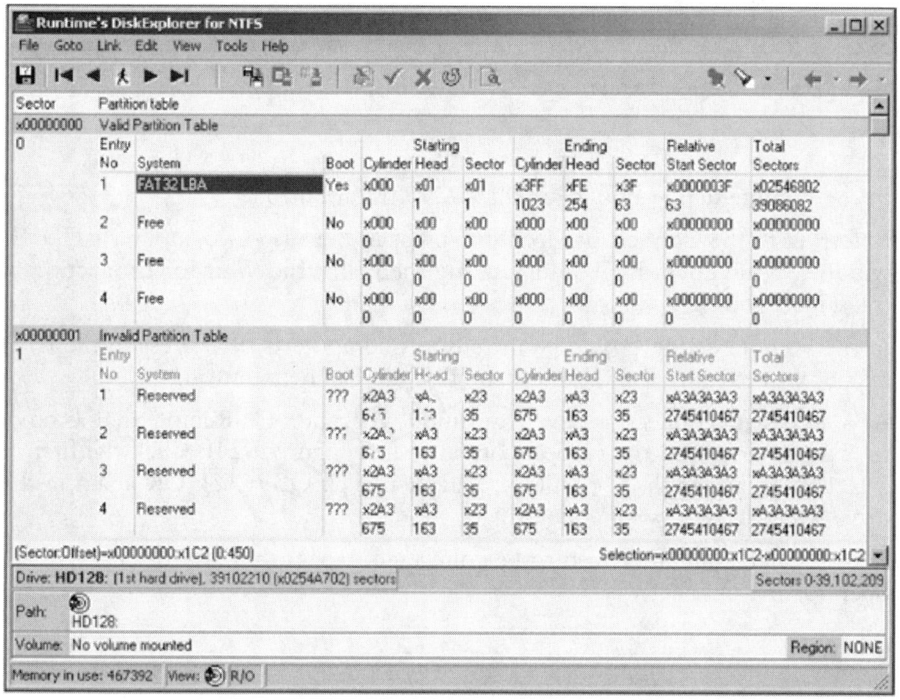

Figure 9-20 The DiskExplorer for NTFS window

6. In the acquisition workstation's DiskExplorer window, click **File, Drive** from the menu.

7. In the Select drive dialog box (see Figure 9-21), click **Remote** at the bottom of the pane listing the drives.

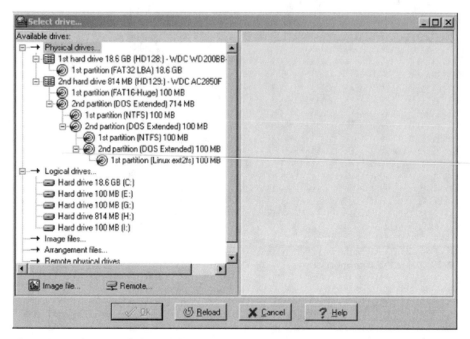

Figure 9-21   The Select drive dialog box

8. In the Remote dialog box, click the **LAN** option button.

9. Referring to the Connection drop-down list in the suspect computer's HDHOST window, write down its IP address, and then click the **Wait for connection** button (see Figure 9-22).

10. In the Remote dialog box, type the suspect computer's IP address in the IP of host text box (see Figure 9-23), and then click the **Connect** button.

11. At a successful connection, the acquisition workstation's Remote dialog box changes to a list of drives on the suspect computer (see Figure 9-24). Click the first drive (HD128) to access the C partition, and then click **OK**. Click **OK** again in the Select drive dialog box.

12. If additional computers need to be connected, repeat these steps. Leave DiskExplorer open for the next activity.

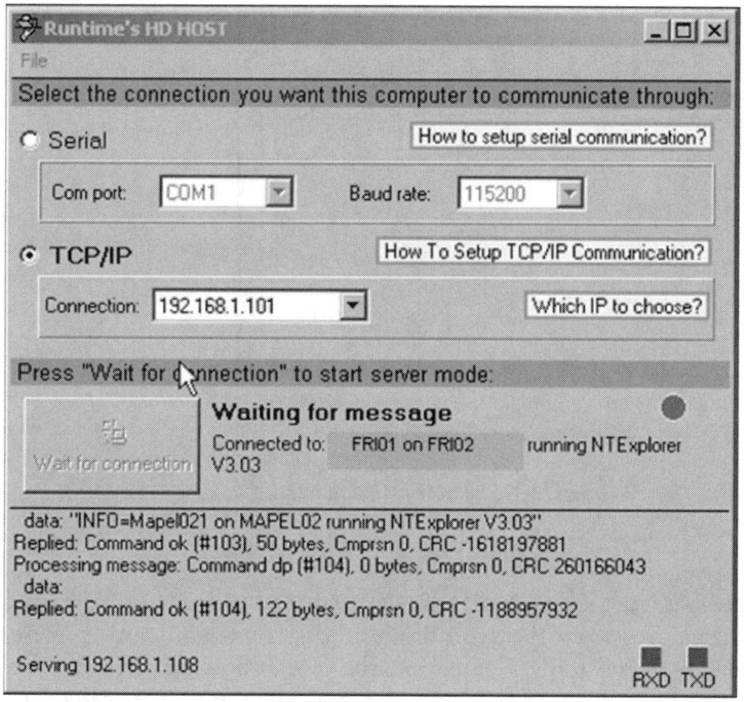

Figure 9-22 The HDHOST remote connection window

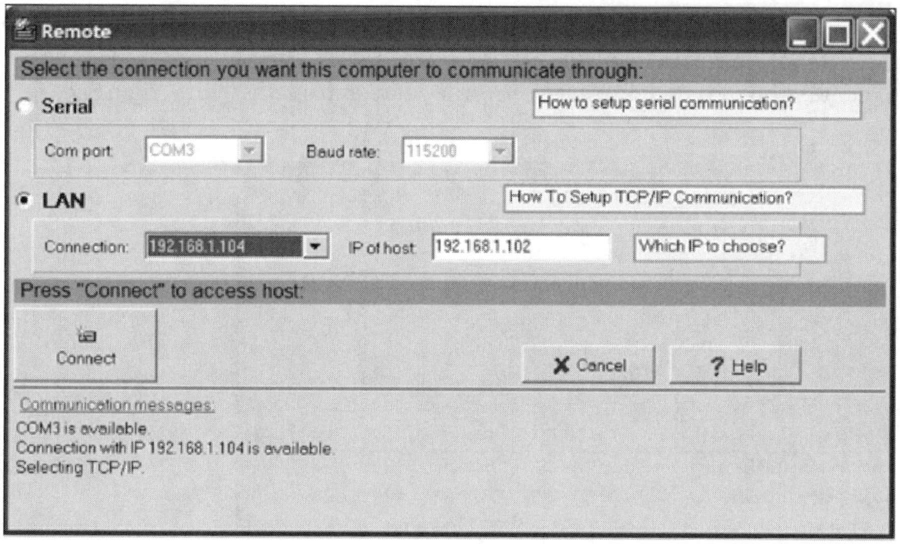

Figure 9-23 Connecting to the remote computer

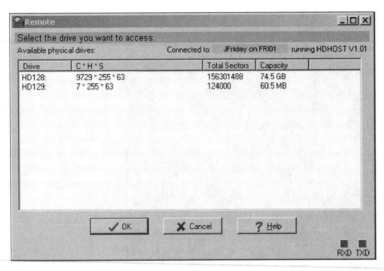

Figure 9-24 Select a drive to access

Making a Remote Acquisition with DiskExplorer After you have established a connection with DiskExplorer from the acquisition workstation, you can navigate through the suspect computer's files and folders or copy data. The following steps explain how to make an acquisition through this remote connection and assume you're using the link you established in the previous steps.

1. To initiate the remote acquisition, in the main window of DiskExplorer, click **Tools**, **Create image file** from the menu.

2. In the Create an Image File dialog box, click the **Lookup** button (the button with three dots). Navigate to the target drive and folder, type **InChp09RT.img** in the File name text box, and click **Save**. Click the **Start** button shown in Figure 9-25.

Figure 9-25 The Create an Image File dialog box

NOTE

Drive acquisition can take a long time, and time management is a critical part of running a forensics lab. For example, acquiring a 2 GB USB drive takes 10 to 20 minutes, depending on your network and processor speed. Plan to be doing other things while the acquisition takes place.

3. Monitor the data copying progress. When the acquisition is finished, click **Cancel** in the Create an Image File dialog box to return to the DiskExplorer main window.

4. Click **File, Exit** from the menu to close the program on the acquisition workstation.

5. On the suspect computer, click **File, Exit** to close HDHOST.

The Runtime tools don't generate a hash for acquisitions; therefore, you need to use another tool, such as Hex Workshop or FTK, to calculate a hash value for the validation. In Chapter 11, you learn more about issues in live acquisitions.

Chapter Summary

- Examining and analyzing digital evidence depend on the nature of the investigation and the amount of data to process. You begin a computer forensics case by creating an investigation plan that defines the investigation's goal and scope, the materials needed, and the tasks to perform. Depending on the evidence you find, you might have to modify your investigation plan at some point.

- For most computer forensics investigations, you follow the same general procedures: Wipe and prepare target drives, document all hardware components on the suspect's computer, check date and time values in the suspect computer's CMOS, acquire data and document your steps, list all folders and files on the suspect system and examine their contents, attempt to open any password-protected files, determine the function of executable files, and document all your steps, making sure to follow evidence preservation procedures.

- One of the most critical aspects of computer forensics is validating digital evidence because ensuring the integrity of data you collect is essential for presenting evidence in court. Computer forensics tools have built-in validation features, but hexadecimal editors offer more advanced features. All data needs to be validated before and during your analysis because digital evidence can be corrupted easily. Use hash values such as MD5 and SHA-1 to verify that data has not changed.

- Data hiding involves changing or manipulating a file to conceal information. Data-hiding techniques include hiding partitions, changing file extensions, setting file attributes to hidden, bit-shifting, using steganography, and using encryption and password protection.

- Remote acquisitions are useful for making an image of a drive when the computer is far away from your location or when you don't want a suspect to be aware of an ongoing investigation.

9

Key Terms

bit-shifting The process of shifting one or more digits in a binary number to the left or right to produce a different value.

key escrow A technology designed to recover encrypted data if users forget their passphrases or if the user key is corrupted after a system failure.

Known File Filter (KFF) A database containing the hash values of known legitimate and suspicious files. It's used to identify files for evidence or eliminate them from the investigation if they are legitimate files.

scope creep The result of an investigation expanding beyond its original description because the discovery of unexpected evidence increases the amount of work required.

steganography A cryptographic technique for embedding information in another file for the purpose of hiding that information from casual observers.

Review Questions

1. Which of the following represents known files you can eliminate from an investigation? (Choose all that apply.)
   a. Any graphics files
   b. Files associated with an application
   c. System files the OS uses
   d. Any files pertaining to the company

2. For which of the following reasons should you wipe a target drive?
   a. To ensure the quality of digital evidence you acquire
   b. To make sure unwanted data isn't retained on the drive
   c. Neither of the above
   d. Both a and b

3. FTK's Known File Filter (KFF) can be used for which of the following purposes? (Choose all that apply.)
   a. Filter known program files from view.
   b. Calculate hash values of image files.
   c. Compare hash values of known files to evidence files.
   d. Filter out evidence that doesn't relate to your investigation.

4. For what legal and illegal purposes can you use steganography?

5. Password recovery is included in all computer forensics tools. True or False?

6. After you shift a file's bits, the hash value remains the same. True or False?

7. Validating an image file once, the first time you open it, is enough. True or False?

8. _____ happens when an investigation goes beyond the bounds of its original description.

9. Suppose you're investigating an e-mail harassment case. Generally, is collecting evidence for this type of case easier for an internal corporate investigation or a criminal investigation?

   a. Criminal investigation because subpoenas can be issued to acquire any needed evidence quickly

   b. Criminal investigation because law enforcement agencies have more resources at their disposal

   c. Internal corporate investigation because corporate investigators typically have ready access to company records

   d. Internal corporate investigation because ISPs almost always turn over e-mail and access logs when requested by a large corporation

10. You're using Disk Manager to view primary and extended partitions on a suspect's drive. The program reports the extended partition's total size as larger than the sum of the sizes of logical partitions in this extended partition. What might you infer from this information?

    a. The disk is corrupted.

    b. There's a hidden partition.

    c. Nothing; this is what you'd expect to see.

    d. The drive is formatted incorrectly.

11. Commercial encryption programs often rely on a technology known as _____ to recover files if a password or passphrase is lost.

12. Steganography is used for which of the following purposes?

    a. Validating data

    b. Hiding data

    c. Accessing remote computers

    d. Creating strong passwords

13. Which FTK search option is more likely to find text hidden in unallocated space: live search or indexed search?

14. Which of the following statements about HDHOST is true? (Choose all that apply.)

    a. It can be used to access a suspect's computer remotely.

    b. It requires installing the DiskExplorer program corresponding to the suspect's file system.

    c. It can run surreptitiously to avoid detection.

    d. It works over both serial and TCP/IP interfaces.

15. Which of the following tools is most helpful in accessing clusters marked as "bad" on a disk?

    a. Norton DiskEdit

    b. FTK

    c. ProDiscover

    d. HDHOST

    e. None of the above

16. The likelihood that a brute-force attack can succeed in cracking a password depends heavily on the password length. True or False?

Hands-On Projects

If necessary, create a C:\Work\Chap09\Projects folder on your system before starting the projects; it's referred to as "your work folder" in steps. Then extract all files from the Chap09\Projects folder on the DVD to your work folder.

Hands-On Project 9-1

In this project, you perform bit-shifting on a file and verify that the file can be restored.

1. Start Notepad and type the following in a new text document: **This document contains very sensitive information. We do not want the competition to be able to read it if they intercept the message.**

2. Save the file as **correspondence.txt** in your work folder, and then exit Notepad.

3. Start Hex Workshop, and open the **correspondence.txt** file.

4. In the chapter, you used the Shift Left and Shift Right buttons on the Data Operations toolbar. Notice as you move your cursor over the toolbar buttons to the right that Rotate Left, Rotate Right, Block Shift Left, and Block Shift Right are also available. Click the **Rotate Right** button. As shown in the Operand section of the Rotate Right Operation dialog box, the data can be treated as an 8-, 16-, 32-, or 64-bit unsigned long. Write down which one it is (assuming little endian is the byte ordering), and then click **OK**.

5. Click the **Rotate Left** button. In the Rotate Left Operation dialog box, make sure the same setting is listed in the Treat Data As text box as for the Rotate Right operation, and then click **OK**. The file should return to its original form. In a rotated shift operation, the bits that "fall off" one end of the number as it's rotated appear on the other end of the number. In this way, no bits are lost, and the process can be reversed to restore the original message.

6. Save the file.

7. Click the **Shift Right** button and click **OK** twice, noting how the data is being treated. Click **OK**.

8. Finally, click the **Block Shift Left** button.

9. Attempt to reverse the procedure by doing the following: Click **Block Shift Right,** click **Shift Left** twice, and click **OK** as needed.

10. Notice that the message is garbled. In a normal (nonrotated) shift operation, the bits that fall off one end of the number when it's rotated are discarded; therefore, the original data is lost or modified. Click **File, Close** from the menu. When prompted to save, click **No.**

11. Open the file again in Hex Workshop, and repeat Steps 7 and 8. Save the file as **correspondence2.txt** in your work folder. If you're prompted to create a backup, click **Yes.**

12. Attempt to undo the procedure by working in reverse, as in Step 9.

13. Write a short paper stating whether you think this method is a reliable one for encrypting. Leave Hex Workshop running for the next project.

Hands-On Project 9-2

In this project, you validate the files used in Hands-On Projects 9-3 and 9-4. Chris Murphy, a Superior Bicycles employee suspected of industrial espionage, had a Windows XP system formatted in NTFS that was seized as part of the investigation. You use the GCFI-NTFS image files for this project, which consist of several .zip files. Extract them to your work folder, if necessary. You need at least 9 GB of storage space for these files.

1. Start Microsoft Word, and open the **GCFI-NTFS hash values.doc** file from your work folder. Print the file so that you can compare it with your results later in this project, and then exit Word.

2. Start Notepad, and open **GCFI-NTFS.pds** (included with the GCFI-NTFS image files). Read this document, which tells ProDiscover how to reassemble the image file from the segments. When you're finished, exit Notepad.

3. In Hex Workshop, open **GCFI-NTFS.eve** from your work folder.

4. Click **Tools, Generate Checksum** from the menu. In the Select Algorithms list box, click **MD5,** and then click the **Generate** button.

5. When the checksum process is finished, check the MD5 hash value in Hex Workshop's lower-right pane, and compare it to the one in the document you printed in Step 1.

6. Repeat Steps 3 through 5 for each remaining GCFI-NTFS file.

7. After you have verified all the files, make a note in your log listing the files you examined and their hash values, and then exit Hex Workshop.

Hands-On Project 9-3

In this project, you search the GCFI-NTFS drive image that belonged to Chris Murphy. You should have completed Hands-On Project 9-2 before beginning this one.

1. Start ProDiscover Basic with the **Run as administrator** option (if you're using Vista), and start a new project. Enter **C9Prj03** for the project number

and **Chris Murphy** for the project filename. In the Description text box, type **suspected of industrial espionage at Superior Bicycles**, and then click **OK**.

2. In the tree view, click to expand **Add,** and then click **Image File**. Navigate to your work folder. Because this image file is segmented, ProDiscover needs the .pds file to reassemble the image. Click **GCFI-NTFS.pds** (in Windows Vista, the .pds extension might not be displayed), and then click **Open**. In the message box prompting you to verify the checksum, click **Yes**. This process takes several minutes.

3. After this process is finished, save the project with its default name in your work folder.

4. In the tree view, click to expand **Project,** if necessary, and then expand **Content View** and **Images**.

5. Click **GCFI-NTFS.eve** and then click to expand it, and then click the **Delorme Docs** folder in the tree view. Browse through this folder in the work area, and mark any files of interest.

6. Chris is known to be a sports fan, and his manager believes the espionage he engaged in was done to support his gambling habit, betting on games' outcomes. Using search terms for the most common U.S. sports—baseball, football, and basketball—ascertain whether any evidence exists to support this claim.

7. Next, examine his Internet history. If necessary, use terms such as "ESPN" during this part of the search.

8. Finally, Chris has been sightseeing in Washington, D.C., so search for terms such as **White House, Lincoln Memorial, George Washington University, Washington Convention Center,** and **National Museum of Women in the Arts**. Exit ProDiscover Basic, saving the project when prompted.

9. Write a short memo to Ileen Johnson, the lead investigator in this case, summarizing your findings and what they indicate.

Hands-On Project 9-4

In this project, you determine what tools Chris used to take pictures of kayak prototypes and smuggle them out of the office. Make sure you have completed Hands-On Project 9-2 before starting this one.

1. Start ProDiscover Basic with the **Run as administrator** option (if you're using Vista), and start a new project. Enter **C9Prj04** for the project number and **Chris Murphy** for the project filename. Enter **suspected of industrial espionage at Superior Bicycles** in the Description text box, and then click **OK**.

2. In the tree view, click to expand **Add,** and then click **Image File**. Navigate to your work folder.

3. Because this image file is segmented, ProDiscover needs the .pds file. If you didn't load this case in Hands-On Project 9-3, perform this step: Click **GCFI-NTFS.pds,** and then click **Open**. In the message box prompting you to verify the checksum, click **Yes**. This process takes several

minutes. After it's finished, save the project with its default name in your work folder.

4. As mentioned, Chris is suspected of taking pictures of the new kayak prototypes, and you need to determine what type of camera he used. If necessary, click to expand **Project** in the tree view.

5. Next, expand **Content View** and then **Images**. Click the **GCFI-NTFS.eve** file, and then expand it.

6. Click the **Special Files** folder, and examine the files in it. You should see some files with the .sxc and .sxw extensions. They were created in Open Office 1.x, but you can open them in Open Office 2.x, too.

7. Using ProDiscover's Search function, search the **GCFI-NTFS.eve** file, using the keyword **kayak**. Right-click any .jpeg files you find and click **View EXIF Data**. (EXIF data is metadata that includes the camera's make and model.) Copy this information to a text file in your work folder.

8. To export any .zip files you find, right-click them and click **Copy File**. In the dialog box that opens, create a folder for this case and save the files there. Then you can expand them with a standard zip utility.

9. When you're finished, exit ProDiscover Basic, and write a one- to two-page report explaining what you found and how this evidence is relevant to the case.

9

Case Projects

Case Project 9-1

Review the facts in the arson running case project (the Firestarter.dd file), and create a list of search terms that apply to the case, such as explosives, bombs, and fires. Run the search in your preferred computer forensics tool, and write a report on any relevant findings.

Case Project 9-2

Several graphics files were transmitted via e-mail from an unknown source to a suspect in an ongoing investigation. The lead investigator gives you these graphics files and tells you that at least four messages should be embedded in them. Use your problem-solving and brainstorming skills to determine a procedure to follow. Write a short report outlining what to do.

Case Project 9-3

A drive you're investigating contains several password-protected files and other files with headers that don't match the extension. Write a report describing the procedures you need to follow to retrieve the evidence. Identify the mismatched file headers to extensions and discuss techniques you can apply to recover passwords from the protected files.

Recovering Graphics Files

After reading this chapter and completing the exercises, you will be able to:

- Describe types of graphics file formats
- Explain types of data compression
- Explain how to locate and recover graphics files
- Describe how to identify unknown file formats
- Explain copyright issues with graphics

Many computer forensics investigations involve graphics, especially those downloaded from the Web and circulated via e-mail. To examine and recover graphics files, you need to understand the basics of computer graphics, including file characteristics, common file formats, and compression methods for reducing file size. This chapter begins with an overview of computer graphics and data compression, and then explains how to locate and recover graphics files based on information stored in file headers. You learn how to identify and reconstruct graphics file fragments, analyze graphics file headers, and repair damaged file headers.

This chapter also explores tools for viewing graphics files you recover and discusses two computer graphics issues: steganography and copyrights. Steganography involves hiding data, including images, in files. Copyrights determine the ownership of media, such as images downloaded from a Web site.

Recognizing a Graphics File

Graphics files contain digital photographs, line art, three-dimensional images, and scanned replicas of printed pictures. You might have used a graphics program, such as Microsoft Paint, Adobe Photoshop, or Gnome GIMP, to create or edit an image. A graphics program creates one of three types of graphics files: bitmap, vector, and metafile. **Bitmap images** are collections of dots, or pixels, in a grid format that form a graphic. **Vector graphics** are based on mathematical instructions that define lines, curves, text, ovals, and other geometric shapes. **Metafile graphics** are combinations of bitmap and vector images.

You can use two types of programs to work with graphics files: graphics editors and image viewers. You use graphics editors to create, modify, and save bitmap, vector, and metafile graphics. You use image viewers to open and view graphics files but not change their contents. When you use a graphics editor or an image viewer, you can open a file in one of many graphics file formats, such as .bmp, .gif, or .eps. Each format has different qualities, including the amount of color and compression it uses. If you open a graphics file in a graphics editor that supports multiple file formats, you can save the file in another file format. However, converting graphics files in this way can change the image quality, as you see in a Hands-On Project at the end of this chapter.

Understanding Bitmap and Raster Images

Bitmap images store graphics information as grids of **pixels**, short for "picture elements." **Raster images** are also collections of pixels, but they store pixels in rows to make images easy to print. In most cases, printing an image converts, or **rasterizes**, it to print pixels line by line instead of processing the complete collection of pixels.

A bitmap's image quality on a monitor is governed by **resolution**, which determines the amount of detail that's displayed. Resolution is related to the density of pixels onscreen and depends on a combination of hardware and software. Monitors can display a range of resolutions; the higher the resolution, the sharper the image. Computers also use a video card containing a certain amount of memory for displaying images. The more advanced the video card's electronics and the more memory it has, the more detailed instructions it can accept, resulting in higher-quality images.

For example, the monitor and video card on your Windows computer might support a 1024 × 768 resolution, which means displaying 1024 pixels horizontally and 768 pixels vertically.

The more pixels displayed, the smaller they must be to fit onscreen and, therefore, the smaller pictures appear onscreen. Because a bitmap image is defined by pixel size, high-resolution images use smaller pixels than low-resolution images do.

Software also contributes to image quality. Software includes drivers, which are coded instructions that set a video card's display parameters, and programs used to create, modify, and view images. With some programs, such as IrfanView (*www.irfanview.com*), you can view many types of images; with other programs, you can view or work with only the graphics files they create. Computer graphics professionals use programs that support high resolutions to have more control over the display of bitmap images. However, bitmaps, especially those with low resolution, usually lose quality when you enlarge them.

Another setting that affects image quality is the number of colors the monitor displays. Graphics files can have different amounts of color per pixel, but each file must support colors with bits of space. The following list shows the number of bits per colored pixel:

- 1 bit = 2 colors
- 4 bits = 16 colors
- 8 bits = 256 colors
- 16 bits = 65,536 colors
- 24 bits = 16,777,216 colors
- 32 bits = 4,294,967,296 colors

Bitmap and raster files use as much of the color palette as possible. However, when you save a bitmap or raster file, the resolution and color might change, depending on the colors in the original file and whether the file format supports these colors.

10

Understanding Vector Graphics

Vector graphics, unlike bitmap and raster images, use lines instead of dots to make up an image. A vector file stores only the calculations for drawing lines and shapes; a graphics program converts these calculations into an image. Because vector files store calculations, not images, they are generally smaller than bitmap files, thereby saving disk space. You can also enlarge a vector graphic without affecting image quality—to make an image twice as large, a vector graphics program, such as CorelDRAW and Adobe Illustrator, computes the image mathematically.

Understanding Metafile Graphics

Metafile graphics combine raster and vector graphics and can have the characteristics of both file types. For example, if you scan a photograph (a bitmap image) and then add text or arrows (vector drawings), you create a metafile graphic.

Although metafile graphics have the features of both bitmap and vector files, they share the limitations of both. For example, if you enlarge a metafile graphic, the area created with a bitmap loses some resolution, but the vector-formatted area remains sharp and clear.

Understanding Graphics File Formats

Graphics files are created and saved in a graphics editor, such as Microsoft Paint, Adobe Freehand MX, Adobe Photoshop, or Gnome GIMP. Some graphics editors, such as Freehand

MX, work only with vector graphics, and some programs, such as Photoshop, work with both.

Most graphics editors enable you to create and save files in one or more of the **standard graphics file formats**. Standard bitmap file formats include Graphics Interchange Format (.gif), Joint Photographic Experts Group (.jpg or .jpeg), Tagged Image File Format (.tif or .tiff), and Windows Bitmap (.bmp). Standard vector file formats include Hewlett Packard Graphics Language (.hpgl) and AutoCad (.dxf).

Nonstandard graphics file formats include less common formats, such as Targa (.tga) and Raster Transfer Language (.rtl); proprietary formats, such as Photoshop (.psd), Illustrator (.ai), and Freehand (.fh10); newer formats, such as Scalable Vector Graphics (.svg); and formats for old or obsolete formats, such as Paintbrush (.pcx). Because you can open standard graphics files in most or all graphics programs, they are easier to work with in a computer forensics investigation. If you encounter files in nonstandard formats, you might need to rely on your investigative skills to identify the file as a graphics file, and then find the right tools for viewing it.

To determine whether a file is a graphics file and to find a program for viewing a nonstandard graphics file, you can search the Web or consult a dictionary Web site. For example, suppose you find a file with a .tga extension during an investigation. None of the programs on your forensic workstation can open the file, and you suspect it could provide crucial evidence. To learn more about this file format, follow these steps:

1. Start your Web browser, and go to **www.webopedia.com**.

2. Type **tga** in the Enter a word for a definition text box, and then press **Enter**. Webopedia lists links to additional Web pages describing the .tga file format.

3. Click the **Webopedia: Data Formats and Their File Extensions** link to open a page with information about different file formats.

4. Scroll down until you find a definition of this format, and write it down. When you're finished, exit your Web browser.

Understanding Digital Camera File Formats

Digital cameras' popularity has had quite an impact on computer forensics because witnesses or suspects can create their own digital photos. As a computer forensics investigator, you might need to examine a digital photo created by a witness to an accident, for example. Crimes such as child pornography might involve hundreds of digital photos of alleged victims, and knowing how to analyze the data structures of graphics files can give you additional evidence for a case. In addition, knowing how digital photos are created and how they store unique information can contribute to your credibility when presenting evidence. Most, if not all, digital cameras produce digital photos in raw or EXIF format, described in the following sections.

Examining the Raw File Format
Referred to as a digital negative, the **raw file format** is typically used on many higher-end digital cameras. The camera performs no enhancement processing—hence the term "raw" for this format. Sensors in the digital camera simply record pixels on the camera's memory card. The advantage of this format is that it maintains the best picture quality.

From a computer forensics perspective, the biggest disadvantage of the raw file format is that it's proprietary, and not all image viewers can display these formats. To view a raw graphics file, you might need to get the viewing and conversion software from the camera manufacturer. Each manufacturer has its own program with an algorithm to convert raw data to other standard formats, such as JPEG or TIF. The process of converting raw picture data to another format is referred to as **demosaicing**.

Adobe (*www.adobe.com/products/photoshop/cameraraw.html*), the maker of Photoshop, is trying to get a standard for the raw format called Digital Negative (DNG).

Examining the Exchangeable Image File Format

Most digital cameras use the Exchangeable Image File (EXIF) format to store digital pictures. The Japanese Electronic Industry Development Association (JEIDA) developed it as a standard for storing metadata in JPEG and TIF files. When a digital picture is taken, information about the camera, such as model, make, and serial number, and settings, such as shutter speed, focal length, resolution, date, and time, are stored in the graphics file. Most digital cameras store graphics files as EXIF JPEG files.

Because the EXIF format collects metadata, investigators can learn more about the type of digital camera and the environment in which pictures were taken. Viewing an EXIF JPEG file's metadata requires special programs, such as Exif Reader (see *www.snapfiles.com/get/exifreader.html*) or ProDiscover, which has a built-in EXIF viewer.

Originally, JPEG and TIF formats were designed to store only digital picture data. EXIF is an enhancement of these formats that modifies the beginning of a JPEG or TIF file so that metadata can be inserted. In the similar pictures in Figure 10-1, the one on the left is an EXIF JPEG file, and the one on the right is a standard JPEG file.

10

Sawtoothmt.jpg   Sawtoothmtn.jpg

Figure 10-1 Similar EXIF and JPEG pictures

Figure 10-2 shows the differences between file headers in EXIF and standard JPEG files. Sawtoothmt.jpg is an EXIF file, and Sawtoothmtn.jpg is a standard JPEG file. The first 160 (hexadecimal 0x9F) bytes are displayed for both files.

All JPEG files, including EXIF, start from offset 0 (the first byte of a file) with hexadecimal FFD8. The current standard header for regular JPEG files is JPEG File Interchange Format

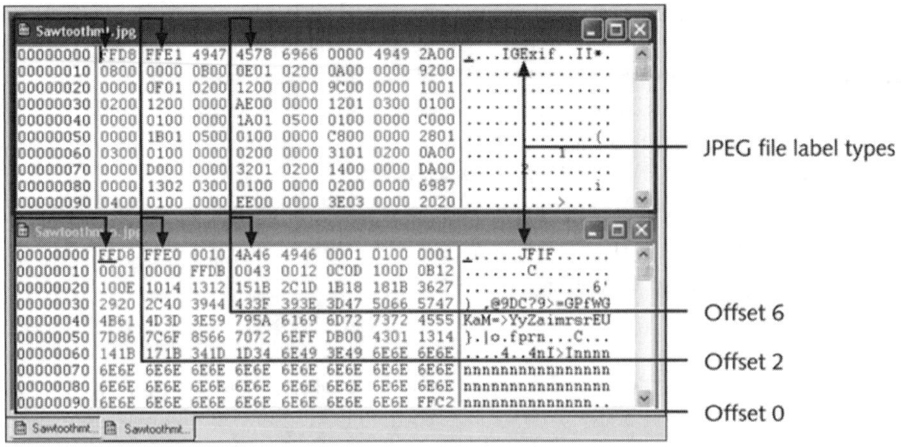

Figure 10-2 Differences in EXIF and JPEG file header information

(JFIF), which has the hexadecimal value FFE0 starting at offset 2. For EXIF JPEG files, the hexadecimal value starting at offset 2 is FFE1. In addition, the hexadecimal values at offset 6 specify the label name (refer to Figure 10-2). For all JPEG files, the ending hexadecimal marker, also known as the end of image (EOI), is FFD9 (see Figure 10-3).

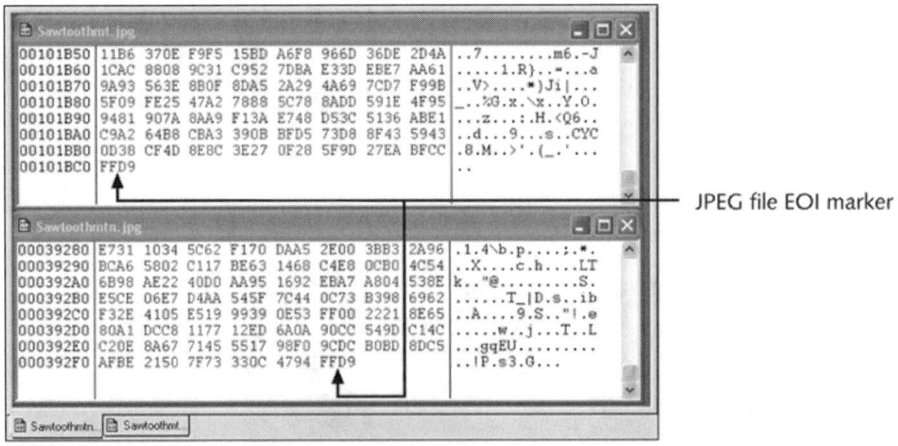

Figure 10-3 EOI marker FFD9 for all JPEG files

With tools such as ProDiscover and Exif Reader, you can extract metadata as evidence for your case. As shown in Figure 10-4, the camera's make and model are Minolta Dimage 2330 Zoom, and the picture was taken on August 12, 2002, at 9:16 p.m.

You might have noticed in Figure 10-1 that there's a lot of sunlight in the photos, but the metadata shows the time of day as after 9:00 p.m. in August. As in any computer forensics investigation, determining date and time for a file is important. Getting this information might not be possible, however, for a variety of reasons, such as suspects losing cameras

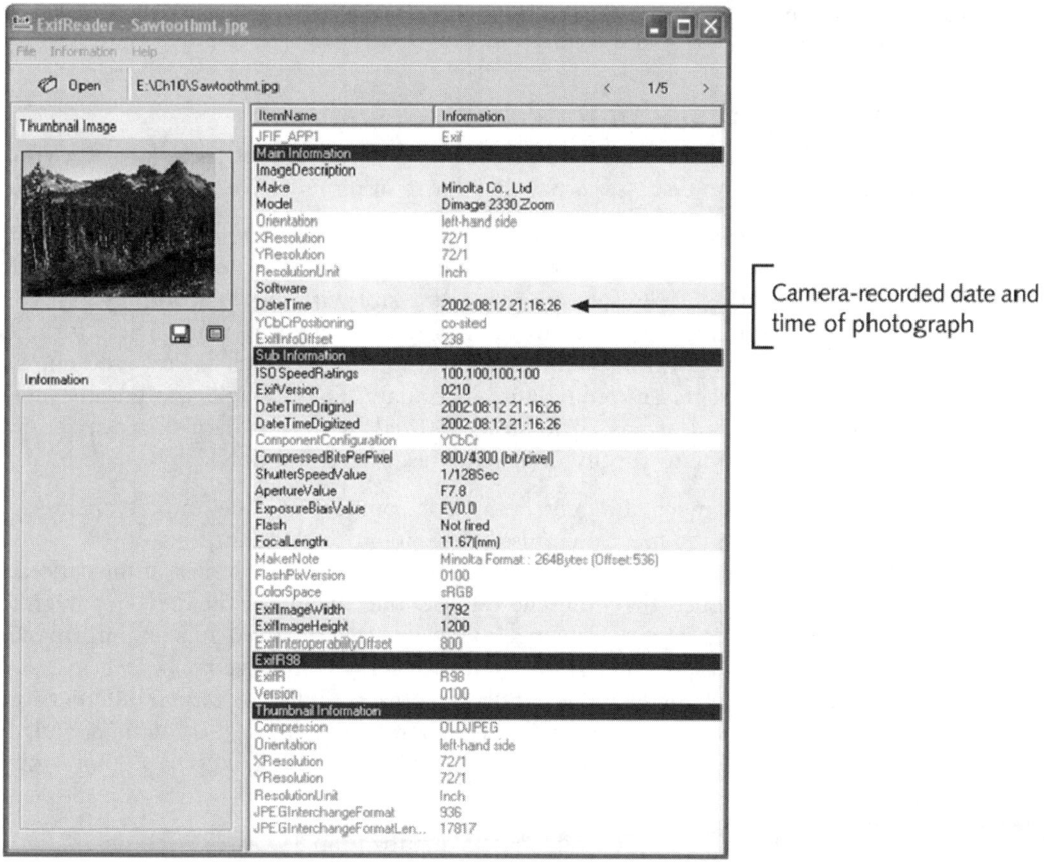

Figure 10-4   Exif Reader displaying metadata from an EXIF JPEG file

after transferring photo files to their computers. You should list this type of evidence as subjective in your report because intentional and unintentional acts make date and time difficult to confirm. For example, suspects could alter a camera's clock intentionally so that an incorrect date and time are recorded when a picture is taken. An unintentional act could be the battery or camera's electronics failing, for example, which causes an incorrect date and time to be recorded. When you're dealing with date and time values in EXIF metadata, always look for corroborating information, such as where the picture was taken, to help support what you find in metadata.

Understanding Data Compression

Most graphics file formats, including GIF and JPEG, compress data to save disk space and reduce the file's transmission time. Other formats, such as BMP, rarely compress data or do so inefficiently. In this case, you can use compression tools to compact data and reduce file size. **Data compression** is the process of coding data from a larger form to a smaller form. Graphics files and most compression tools use one of two data compression schemes: lossless or lossy. You need to understand how compression schemes work to know what happens when an image is altered.

Lossless and Lossy Compression

This section describes how lossless and lossy compression work, explains their advantages and disadvantages, and discusses what they mean in terms of computer forensics.

Lossless compression techniques reduce file size without removing data. When you uncompress a file that uses lossless compression, you restore all its information. GIF and Portable Network Graphics (PNG) file formats reduce file size with lossless compression, which saves file space by using mathematical formulas to represent data in a file. These formulas generally use one of two algorithms: Huffman or Lempel-Ziv-Welch (LZW) coding. Each algorithm uses a code to represent redundant bits of data. For example, if a graphics file contains a large red area, instead of having to store 200 red bytes, the algorithm can set one byte to red and set another byte to specify 200 red bytes. Therefore, only 2 bytes are used.

Lossy compression is much different because it compresses data by permanently discarding bits of information in the file. Some discarded bits are redundant, but others are not. When you uncompress a graphics file that uses lossy compression, you lose information, although most people don't notice the difference unless they print the image on a high-resolution printer or increase the image size. In either case, the removed bits of information reduce image quality. The JPEG format is one that uses lossy compression. If you open a JPEG file in a graphics program, for example, and save it as a JPEG file with a different name, lossy compression is reapplied automatically, which removes more bits of data and, therefore, reduces image quality. If you simply rename a file by using Windows Explorer or the command line, however, the file doesn't lose any more data.

Another form of lossy compression, **vector quantization (VQ)**, uses complex algorithms to determine what data to discard based on vectors in the graphics file. In simple terms, VQ discards bits in much the same way rounding off decimal values discards numbers.

Some popular lossless compression utilities include WinZip, PKZip, StuffIt, and FreeZip. Lzip is a lossy compression utility. You use compression tools to compact folders and files for data storage and transmission. Remember that the difference between lossless and lossy compression is the way data is represented *after* it has been uncompressed. Lossless compression produces an exact replica of the original data after it has been uncompressed, whereas lossy compression typically produces an altered replica of the data.

Locating and Recovering Graphics Files

In a computer forensics investigation involving graphics files, you need to locate and recover all graphics files on the suspect drive and determine which ones are pertinent to your case. Because images aren't always stored in standard graphics file formats, you should examine all files that your computer forensics tools find, even if they aren't identified as graphics files.

Some OSs have built-in tools for recovering graphics files, but they are time consuming, and the results are difficult to verify. Instead, you can use computer forensics tools dedicated to analyzing graphics files. As you work with these tools and built-in OS tools, develop standard procedures for your organization and continue to refine them so that other investigators can benefit from your experience. You should also follow standard procedures for each case to ensure that your analysis is thorough.

As discussed earlier in "Examining the Exchangeable Image File Format," you can use computer forensics tools to analyze images based on information in graphics files. Each graphics file contains a header with instructions for displaying the image; this header information helps you identify the file format. The header is complex and difficult to remember, however; instead of memorizing header information, you can compare a known good file header with that of a suspected file. For example, if you find an image that you suspect is a JPEG file but can't display it with a bitmap graphics program, compare its file header with a known JPEG file header to determine whether the header has been altered. You could then use the information in the known JPEG file header to supply instructions for displaying the image. In other words, you use the known JPEG header information to create a baseline analysis.

Before you can examine a graphics file header, often you need to reconstruct a fragmented graphics file. To do so, you need to identify the data patterns the graphics file uses. If part of the file header has been overwritten with other data, you might also need to repair the damaged header. By rebuilding the file header, you can then perform a forensics analysis on the graphics file. These techniques are described in the following sections.

Identifying Graphics File Fragments

If a graphics file is fragmented across areas on a disk, first you must recover all the fragments to re-create the file. Recovering file fragments is called **carving**, also known as **salvaging** outside North America. To carve a graphics file's data from file slack space and free space, you should be familiar with the data patterns of known graphics file types. Many computer forensics programs, such as ProDiscover or FTK, can recognize these data patterns and carve the graphics files from slack and free space automatically, however. After you recover fragments of a graphics file, you restore them to continue your examination. You use ProDiscover Basic and Hex Workshop later in this chapter to copy known data patterns from files you recover, and then restore this information to view the graphics file.

Repairing Damaged Headers

When you're examining recovered fragments from files in slack or free space, you might find data that appears to be a header for a common graphics file type. If you locate header data that's partially overwritten, you must reconstruct the header to make it readable by comparing the hexadecimal values of known graphics file formats to the pattern of the file header you found.

Each graphics file type has a unique header value. As you become familiar with these header values, you can spot data from partially overwritten headers in file slack or free space. For example, as mentioned earlier, a JPEG file has the hexadecimal header value FFD8, followed by the label JFIF for a standard JPEG or EXIF file at offset 6.

Suppose you're investigating a possible intellectual property theft by a contract employee of Exotic Mountain Tour Service (EMTS). EMTS has just finished an expensive marketing and customer service analysis with Superior Bicycles, LLC. Based on this analysis, EMTS plans to release advertising for its latest tour service with a joint product marketing campaign with Superior Bicycles. Unfortunately, EMTS suspects that a contract travel consultant, Bob

Aspen, might have given sensitive marketing data to another bicycle competitor. EMTS is under a nondisclosure agreement with Superior Bicycles and must protect this advertising campaign material.

An EMTS manager found a USB drive on the desk Bob Aspen was assigned to. Your task is to determine whether the drive contains proprietary EMTS or Superior Bicycles data. The EMTS manager also gives you some interesting information he gathered from the Web server administrator. EMTS filters all Web-based e-mail traffic traveling through its network and detects suspicious attachments. When a Web-based e-mail with attachments is received, the Web filter is triggered. The EMTS manager gives you two screen captures, shown in Figures 10-5 and 10-6, of partial e-mails intercepted by the Web filter that lead him to believe Bob Aspen might have engaged in questionable activities.

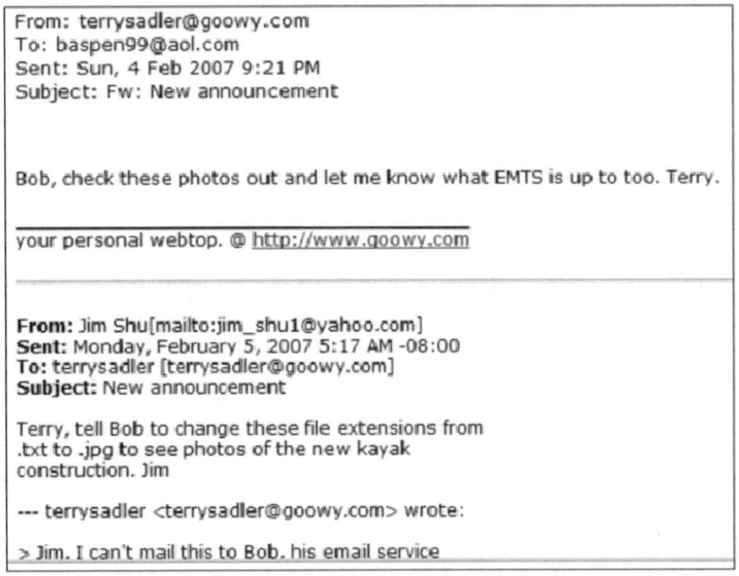

```
From: terrysadler@goowy.com
To: baspen99@aol.com
Sent: Sun, 4 Feb 2007 9:21 PM
Subject: Fw: New announcement


Bob, check these photos out and let me know what EMTS is up to too. Terry.
_____
your personal webtop. @ http://www.goowy.com
_____

From: Jim Shu[mailto:jim_shu1@yahoo.com]
Sent: Monday, February 5, 2007 5:17 AM -08:00
To: terrysadler [terrysadler@goowy.com]
Subject: New announcement

Terry, tell Bob to change these file extensions from
.txt to .jpg to see photos of the new kayak
construction. Jim

--- terrysadler <terrysadler@goowy.com> wrote:

> Jim. I can't mail this to Bob. his email service
```

Figure 10-5 First intercepted capture of an e-mail from Terry Sadler

For this examination, you need to search for all possible places data might be hiding. To do this, in the next section you use ProDiscover's cluster search function with hexadecimal search strings to look for known data.

Searching for and Carving Data from Unallocated Space

At this time, you have little information on what to look for on the USB drive Bob Aspen used. You need to ask some basic questions and make some assumptions based on available information to proceed in your search for information.

In the first message from terrysadler@goowy.com, you see that it's addressed to baspen99@aol.com, which matches the contract employee's name, Bob Aspen. Next, you look at the date and time stamps in this message. The first is 4 Feb 2007 9:21 PM, and the

```
From: denisesuperbic@hotmail.com
To: baspen99@aol.com
Sent: Sun, 4 Feb 2007 9:29 PM
Subject: RE: New announcement

Can you read the attachments yet? Denise

>From: Jim Shu <jim_shu1@yahoo.com>
>To: terrysadler <terrysadler@goowy.com>
>CC: nautieriko@lycos.com
>Subject: New announcement
>Date: Sun, 4 Feb 2007 20:57:37 -0800 (PST)
>
>Terry,
>
>I had a tour of the new kayak factory. I think we can
>run with this to the other party interested in
>competing. I smuggled these files out, they are JPEG
>files I edited with my hex editor so that the email
>monitor won't pick up on them. So to view them you
>have to re-edit each file to the proper JPEG header of
>offset 0x FF D8 FF E0 and offset 6 of 4A. Then you
>have to rename them with a .jpg extention to view
>them.
>
>See attached, Bob Aspen I think is working at EMTS he
```

Figure 10-6   Second intercepted capture of an e-mail from denisesuperbic@hotmail.com

second, farther down, is a header from Jim Shu with a date and time stamp of February 5, 2007, 5:17 AM -08:00.

Therefore, it seems that Jim Shu originally sent the message, which was then forwarded to the terrysadler@goowy.com account. Because the time stamp for Jim Shu is later than the time stamp for terrysadler@goowy.com, Terry Sadler's location might be in a different time zone, somewhere west of Jim Shu, or one of the two e-mail server's time values is off because e-mail servers, not users, provide time stamps. In Chapter 12, you learn more about e-mail header information.

Continuing with the first message, you note that Jim is telling Terry to have Bob alter the file extensions from .txt to .jpg, and the files are about new kayaks. The last line appears to be a previous response from terrysadler@goowy.com commenting that Bob (assuming it's Bob Aspen) can't receive this message.

So far, you have the following facts:

- Jim Shu's e-mail refers to JPEG files.
- Jim Shu's attached JPEG files need to have the extension renamed from .txt to .jpg.
- Jim Shu's attachments might be photographs of new kayaks.
- The e-mail account names in this message are terrysadler@goowy.com, baspen99@aol.com, and jim_shu1@yahoo.com.

Now examine the second e-mail, which contains the following pieces of information:

- Jim Shu had a tour of the new kayak factory.
- Another party might be interested in competing in manufacturing kayaks.
- Jim Shu smuggled out JPEG photos he modified with a hexadecimal editor so that they wouldn't be detected by any Web or e-mail filters.

- Jim Shu provides specific instructions on how to reedit the digital photos and add the .jpeg extension so that they can be viewed.

- Jim Shu thinks Bob Aspen is working at EMTS.

- Jim Shu sent a copy (CC) to nautjeriko@lycos.com.

With these collected facts and your knowledge of JPEG file structures, you can use the steps in the following sections to determine whether these allegations are true.

Planning Your Examination   In the second e-mail from Jim Shu to Terry Sadler, Jim states, "So to view them you have to re-edit each file to the proper JPEG header of offset 0x FF D8 FF E0 and offset 6 of 4A." From this statement, you can assume that any kayak photographs on the USB drive contain unknown characters in the first four bytes and the sixth byte. Because this is all Jim Shu said about the JPEG files, you need to assume that the seventh, eighth, and ninth bytes have the original correct information for the JPEG file.

In "Examining the Exchangeable Image File Format," you learned the difference between a standard JFIF JPEG and an EXIF JPEG file: The JFIF format has 0x FFD8 FFE0 in the first four bytes, and the EXIF format has 0x FFD8 FFE1. In the sixth byte, the JPEG label is listed as JFIF or EXIF. In the second e-mail, Jim Shu mentions 0x FF D8 FF E0, which is a JFIF JPEG format. He also says to change the sixth byte to 0x 4A, which is the uppercase letter "J" in ASCII.

Because the files might have been downloaded to the USB drive, Bob Aspen could have altered or deleted them, so you should be thorough in your examination and analysis. You need to search all sectors of the drive for deleted files, both allocated space (in case Bob didn't modify the files) and unallocated space. In the next section, you use ProDiscover to search for and recover these JPEG files.

Searching for and Recovering Digital Photograph Evidence   In this section, you learn how to use ProDiscover to search for and extract (recover) possible evidence of JPEG files from the USB drive the EMTS manager gave you. The search string to use for this examination is "FIF." Because it's part of the label name of the JFIF JPEG format, you might have several false hits if the USB drive contains several other JPEG files. These false hits, referred to as **false positives**, require examining each search hit to verify whether it's what you are looking for.

It's assumed you have already acquired an image of the USB drive, so the image file is provided on the book's DVD. You should extract all files in the Chap10 folder on the book's DVD to your C:\Work\Chap10\Chapter folder (referred to as "your work folder" in steps). Create this folder on your system first, if necessary.

Remember that the work folder you create most likely has a different name from what's shown in screenshots.

To begin the examination, follow these steps to load the image file:

1. Start ProDiscover Basic (with the **Run as administrator** option if you're using Windows Vista), and click the **New Project** toolbar button. In the New Project dialog box, type **C10InChp** for the project number and filename, and then click **OK**.

2. Click **Action** from the menu, point to **Add**, and click **Image file.**

3. In the Open dialog box, navigate to your work folder, click **C10InChp.eve**, and then click **Open**. If necessary, click **Yes** in the Auto Image Checksum message box.

4. To begin a search, click the **Search** toolbar button or click **Action, Search** from the menu to open the Search dialog box.

5. Click the **Cluster Search** tab, and then click the **Case Sensitive** check box. Under Search for the pattern(s), type **FIF** (see Figure 10-7). Under Select the Disk(s)/Image(s) you want to search in, click the **C10InChp.eve** file, and then click **OK**.

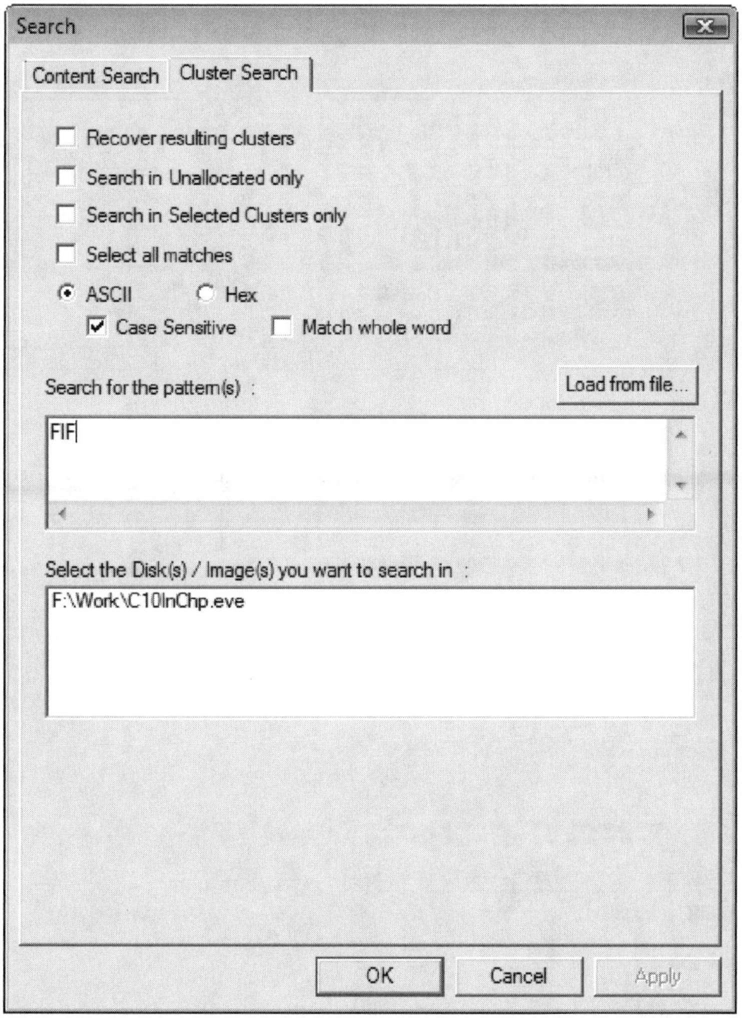

Figure 10-7 Searching clusters in ProDiscover

6. When the search is done, click the first search hit, **4CA(1226)**, to display the cluster's content (see Figure 10-8).

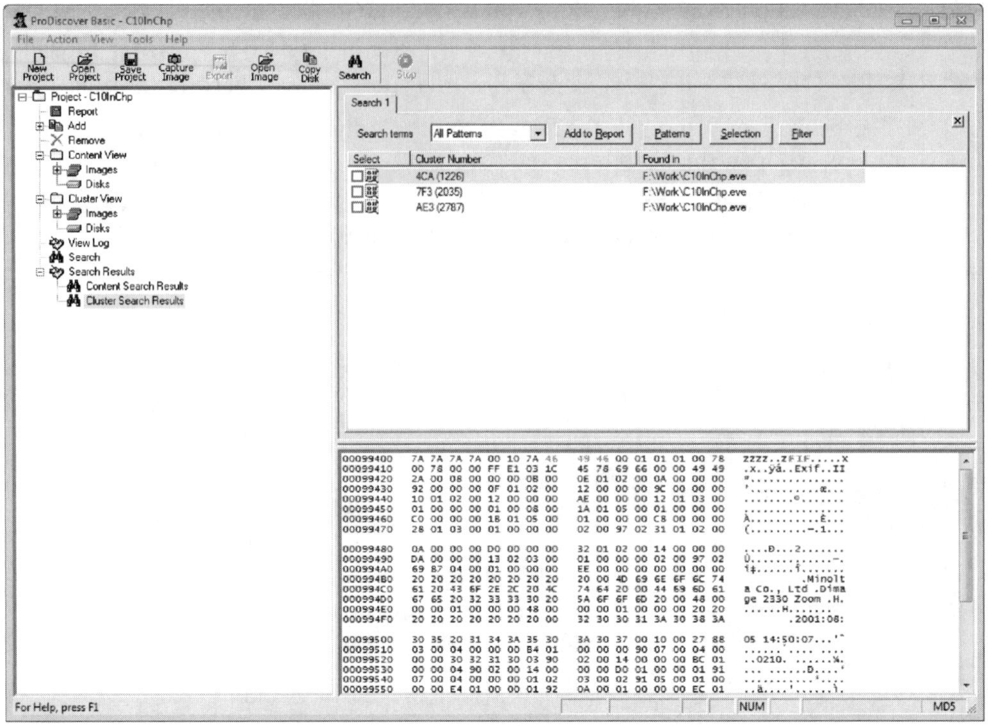

Figure 10-8 Completed cluster search for FIF

7. Double-click the highlighted row **4CA(1226)** to display the cluster view shown in Figure 10-9.

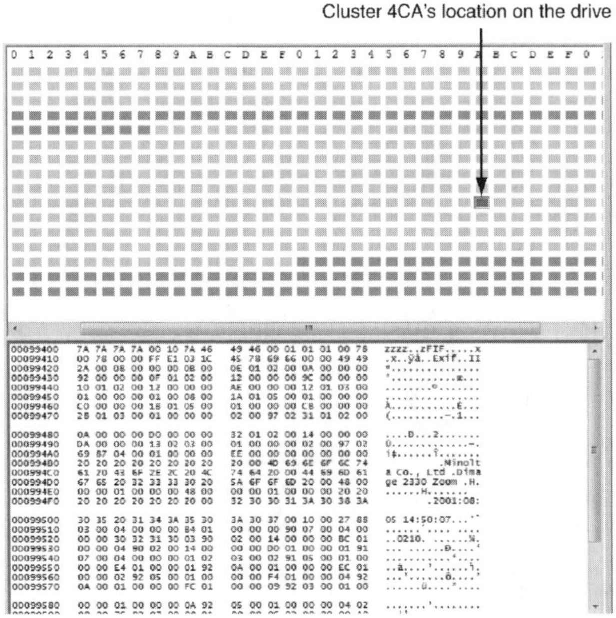

Figure 10-9 Viewing cluster use and location of search hit for 4CA(1226)

In Figure 10-10, the header for this JPEG file has been overwritten with zzzz. This unique header information might give you additional search values that could minimize false-positive hits in subsequent searches.

File header overwritten with zzzz

```
00099400    7A 7A 7A 7A 00 10 7A 46    49 46 00 01 01 01 00 78    zzzz..zFIF.....x
00099410    00 78 00 00 FF E1 03 1C    45 78 69 66 00 00 49 49    .x..ÿá..Exif..II
00099420    2A 00 08 00 00 00 0B 00    0E 01 02 00 0A 00 00 00    *...............
00099430    92 00 00 00 0F 01 02 00    12 00 00 00 9C 00 00 00    '...........Œ...
00099440    10 01 02 00 12 00 00 00    AE 00 00 00 12 01 03 00    ........®.......
00099450    01 00 00 00 01 00 08 00    1A 01 05 00 01 00 00 00    ................
00099460    C0 00 00 00 1B 01 05 00    01 00 00 00 C8 00 00 00    À...........È...
00099470    28 01 03 00 01 00 00 00    02 00 97 02 31 01 02 00    (.........—.1...

00099480    0A 00 00 00 D0 00 00 00    32 01 02 00 14 00 00 00    ....Ð...2.......
00099490    DA 00 00 00 13 02 03 00    01 00 00 00 02 00 97 02    Ú.............—.
000994A0    69 87 04 00 01 00 00 00    EE 00 00 00 00 00 00 00    i‡......î.......
000994B0    20 20 20 20 20 20 20 20    20 00 4D 69 6E 6F 6C 74    .Minolt
000994C0    61 20 43 6F 2E 2C 20 4C    74 64 20 00 44 69 6D 61    a Co., Ltd .Dima
000994D0    67 65 20 32 33 33 30 20    5A 6F 6F 6D 20 00 48 00    ge 2330 Zoom .H.
000994E0    00 00 01 00 00 00 48 00    00 00 01 00 00 00 20 20    ......H.......
000994F0    20 20 20 20 20 20 20 00    32 30 30 31 3A 30 38 3A    .2001:08:

00099500    30 35 20 31 34 3A 35 30    3A 30 37 00 10 00 27 88    05 14:50:07...'ˆ
00099510    03 00 04 00 00 00 B4 01    00 00 00 90 07 00 04 00    ......´.........
00099520    00 00 30 32 31 30 03 90    02 00 14 00 00 00 BC 01    ..0210. .......¼.
00099530    00 00 04 90 02 00 14 00    00 00 D0 01 00 00 01 91    ... .....Ð....'
00099540    07 00 04 00 00 00 01 02    03 00 02 91 05 00 01 00    .........'....
00099550    00 00 E4 01 00 00 01 92    0A 00 01 00 00 00 EC 01    ..ä....'......ì.
00099560    00 00 02 92 05 00 01 00    00 00 F4 01 00 00 04 92    ...'......ô....'
00099570    0A 00 01 00 00 00 FC 01    00 00 09 92 03 00 01 00    ......ü....'....

00099580    00 00 01 00 00 00 0A 92    05 00 01 00 00 00 04 02    .......'.......
```

Figure 10-10   Content of cluster 4CA(1226)

8. Next, you need to locate the file. Right-click cluster block **4CA(1226)** and click **Find File,** and then click **Yes** in the warning message.

9. In the List of Clusters dialog box, click **Show File** (see Figure 10-11), and then click **Close.**

List of Clusters

List of Sectors for the file:

F:\Work\C10InChp.eve\Vacation Pictures\gametour2.exe

```
4ca (1226)
4cb (1227)
4cc (1228)
4cd (1229)
4ce (1230)
4cf (1231)
```

Copy to Clipboard   Show File

Close

Figure 10-11   Viewing all clusters used by the gametour2.exe file

10. In the work area, right-click the **gametour2.exe** file (shown selected in Figure 10-12) and click **Copy File**. In the Save As dialog box, delete the original filename, type **Recover1.jpg**, and then click **Save** to save this file in your work folder.

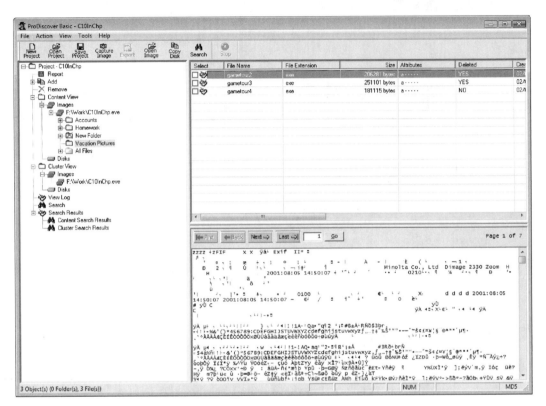

Figure 10-12 Mislabeled file that appears to be altered intentionally

11. Click **File, Exit** from the menu, and then click **Yes** to save this project in your work folder.

The next section shows you how to rebuild header data from this recovered file by using Hex Workshop, although any hexadecimal editor has the capability to examine and repair damaged file headers. From a computer forensics view, this procedure can be considered corrupting the evidence, but knowing how to reconstruct data, as in the preceding example, is part of an investigator's job. When you change data as part of the recovery and analysis process, make sure you document your steps as part of your reporting procedures. Your documentation should be detailed enough that other investigators could repeat the steps, which increases the credibility of your findings. When you're rebuilding a corrupted evidence image file, create a new file and leave the original file in its initial corrupt condition.

Rebuilding File Headers

Before attempting to edit a graphics file you have recovered, try to open it with an image viewer, such as the default Microsoft tool. To test whether you can view the image, double-click the recovered file in its current location in Windows Explorer. If you can open and view the image, you have recovered the graphics file successfully. If the image isn't displayed, you have to inspect and correct the header values manually.

If some of the data you recovered from the graphics file header is corrupt, you might need to recover more pieces of the file before you can view the image, as you'll see in the next section. Because the deleted file you recovered in the previous activity, Recover1.jpg, was altered intentionally, when you attempt to open it, you might see an error message similar to the one in Figure 10-13.

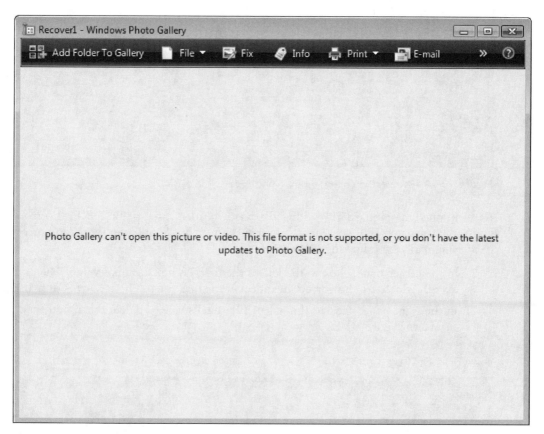

Figure 10-13   Error message indicating a damaged or an altered graphics file

If you can't open a graphics file in an image viewer, the next step is to examine the file's header data to see whether it matches the header in a good JPEG file. If the header doesn't match, you must insert the correct hexadecimal values manually with a hexadecimal editor. To inspect a file with Hex Workshop, follow these steps:

1. Start Hex Workshop. Click **File, Open** from the menu. Navigate to your work folder, and then double-click **Recover1.jpg**. Figure 10-14 shows this file open in Hex Workshop.

2. At the top of the Hex Workshop window, note that the hexadecimal values starting at the first byte position (offset 0) are 7A 7A 7A 7A, and the sixth position (offset 6) is also 7A. Leave Hex Workshop open for the next set of steps.

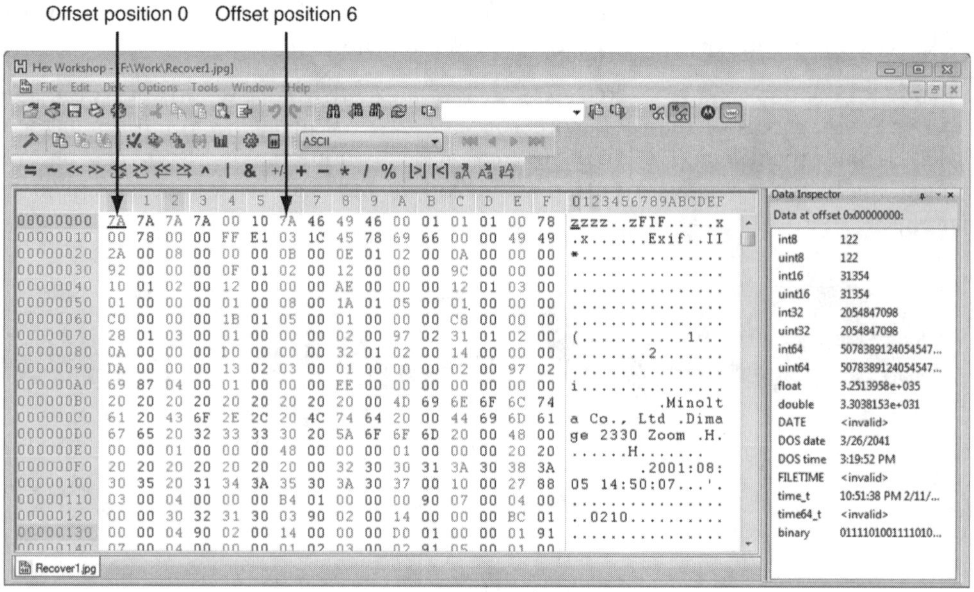

Offset position 0   Offset position 6

Figure 10-14 Recover1.jpg open in Hex Workshop

As mentioned, a standard JFIF JPEG file has a header value of FF D8 FF E0 from offset 0 and the label name JFIF starting at offset 6. Using Hex Workshop, you can correct this file header manually by following these steps:

1. In the center pane, click to the left of the first 7A hexadecimal value. Then type **FF D8 FF E0**, which are the correct hexadecimal values for the first 4 bytes of a JPEG file.

2. In the right pane, click to the left of **FIF**, backspace to delete the **z**, and type **J**, as shown in Figure 10-15.

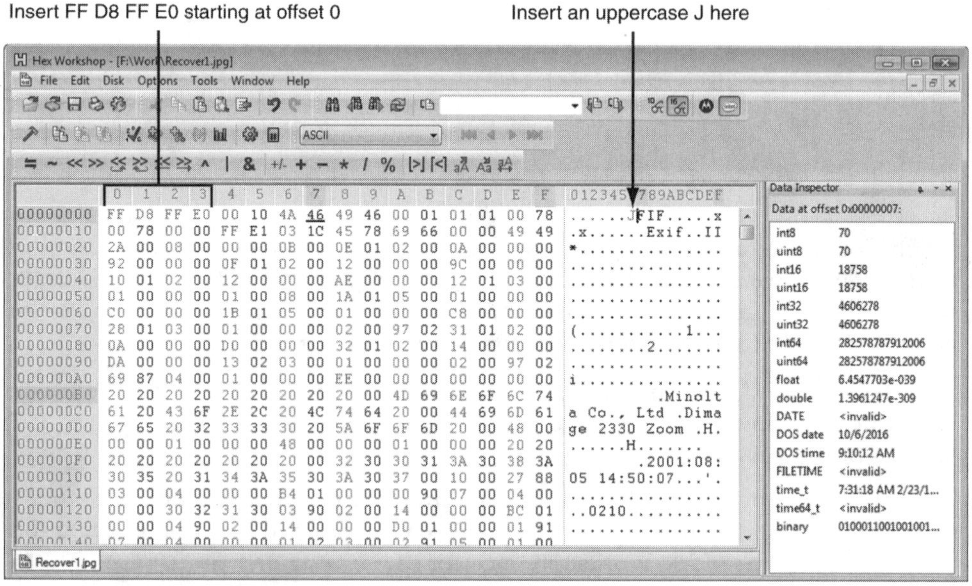

Insert FF D8 FF E0 starting at offset 0   Insert an uppercase J here

Figure 10-15 Inserting correct hexadecimal values for a JPEG file

In Hex Workshop, when you type a keyboard character in the right pane, the corresponding hexadecimal value appears in the center pane. So, for example, when you type J in the right pane, the hexadecimal value 4A appears in the center pane.

3. Click **File, Save As** from the menu. In the Save As dialog box, navigate to your work folder, type **Fixed1.jpg** as the filename, and then click **Save**. Exit Hex Workshop.

Every two hexadecimal values you entered in the previous steps are equivalent to one ASCII character. For example, an uppercase "A" has the hexadecimal value 41, and a lowercase "a" has the hexadecimal value 61. Most disk editors have a reference chart for converting hexadecimal values to ASCII characters, such as Hex Workshop's in Figure 10-16.

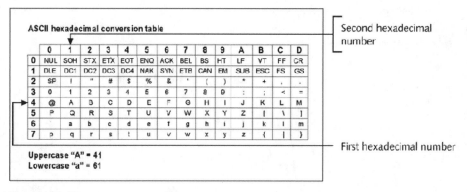

Figure 10-16 ASCII equivalents of hexadecimal values

After you repair a graphics file header, you can test the updated file by opening it in an image viewer, such as Windows Photo Gallery, IrfanView, ThumbsPlus, Quick View, or ACDSee. To test the repaired JPEG file, follow these steps:

1. In Windows Explorer, navigate to your work folder and double-click **Fixed1.jpg**. The file opens in your default image viewer, such as Windows Photo Gallery (see Figure 10-17).

2. Verify that you have recovered the file correctly, and then exit the image viewer.

The process of repairing file headers isn't limited to JPEG files. You can apply the same technique to any file for which you can determine the header value, including Microsoft Word, Excel, and PowerPoint documents and other image formats. You need to know only the correct header format for the type of file you're attempting to repair.

Reconstructing File Fragments

You might occasionally encounter corrupt data that prevents you from recovering data fragments for files. Whether the data corruption is accidental or intentional, you need to know how to examine a suspect drive and extract possible data fragments to reconstruct files for evidentiary purposes. In this section, you learn how to locate noncontiguous clusters from a deleted file. Modern computer forensics tools can typically follow the links between clusters for FAT and NTFS file systems. However, sometimes the pointer information in a FAT or an NTFS MFT file doesn't list this information.

Figure 10-17   Fixed1.jpg open in Windows Photo Gallery

This following activity shows you how to recover a graphics file with a corrupt header that's fragmented on the suspect drive. To perform this data-carving task, you need to locate the starting and ending clusters for each fragmented group of clusters in the corrupted file. Here's an overview of the procedure:

1. Locate and export all clusters of the fragmented file.
2. Determine the starting and ending cluster numbers for each fragmented group of clusters.
3. Copy each fragmented group of clusters in their correct sequence to a recovery file.
4. Rebuild the corrupted file's header to make it readable in a graphics viewer.

Use the project you created previously, C10InChp, to analyze the fragmentation:

1. Start ProDiscover Basic (with the **Run as administrator** option in Windows Vista). Click **File, Open Project** from the menu, navigate to your work folder, click the **C10InChp.dft** file, and then click **Open**.
2. In the tree view, click **Cluster Search Results,** and then in the work area, click **AE3 (2787),** as shown in Figure 10-18.

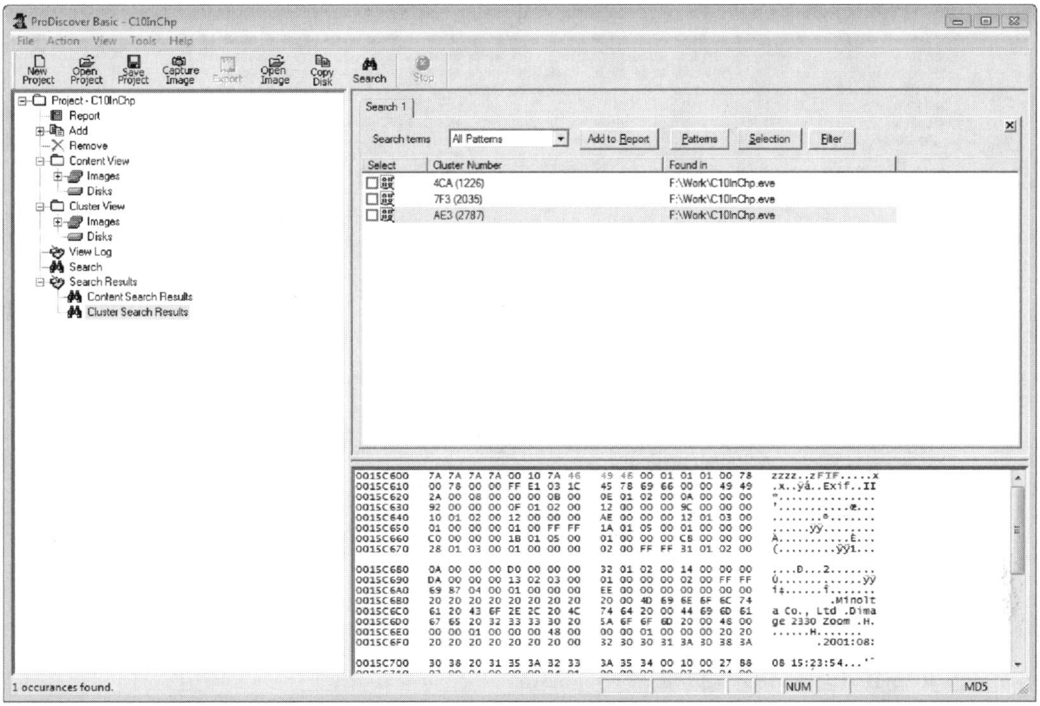

Figure 10-18 Cluster search results for the AE3(2787) cluster

10

3. Right-click the cluster row **AE3(2787)** and click **Find File**.

4. In the List of Clusters dialog box, click **Copy to Clipboard**. Start Notepad, paste the cluster into a new document, and save the file as **AE3-carve.txt** in your work folder. Leave Notepad open for the following steps.

5. In ProDiscover's List of Clusters dialog box, click **Close**.

6. In the tree view, click to expand **Cluster View**, if necessary, click to expand **Images**, and then click the **C10InChp.eve** image file, as shown in Figure 10-19.

7. Examine the AE3-carve.txt file in Notepad to determine the clusters that are grouped together—the range for each cluster group. For example, locate the first cluster number, AE3, and count downward until you locate a cluster number that's not sequential. Make note of the last contiguous cluster number before the change to determine the first cluster group for this fragmented file. Continue through the list of cluster numbers to determine all fragments. The following list shows the cluster groups you should find:

- *Fragment range 1*—AE3 to B3F
- *Fragment range 2*—1F5 to 248
- *Fragment range 3*—3EB to 425
- *Fragment range 4*—16A to 1A1
- *Fragment range 5*—957 to 98C
- *Fragment range 6*—25 to 2C

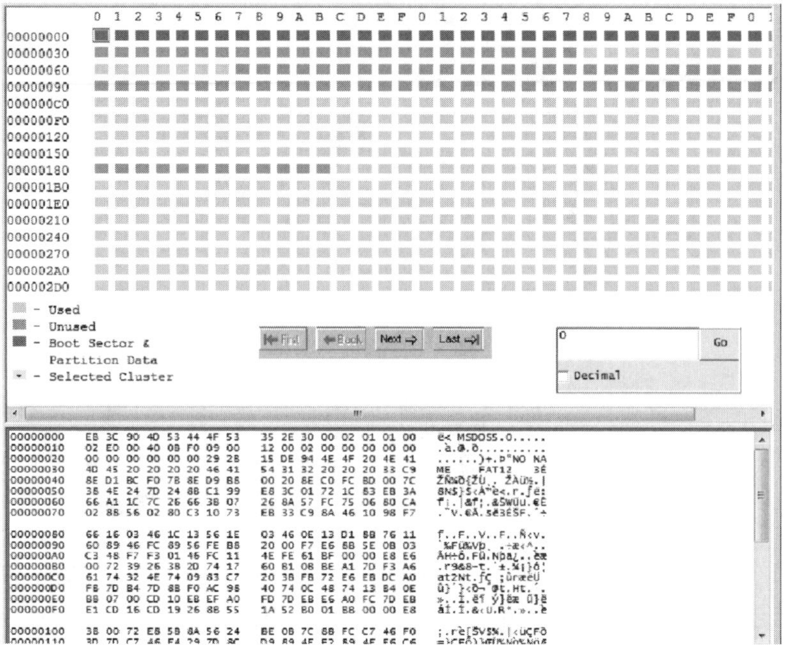

Figure 10-19 Cluster view of C10InChp.eve

The first fragment starts at hexadecimal AE3 (decimal 2787) and continues to hexadecimal B3F. The next fragment starts at 1F5 and continues to 248, and so on until the last segment of fragmented clusters. This file is very fragmented.

8. In ProDiscover's tree view, click **Cluster View, Images,** and the **C10InChp.eve** file, if necessary. In the work area's Sector text box, type **AE3** (see Figure 10-20) and click **Go.**

To view all cluster columns in the work area, as shown in Figures 10-20 and 10-21, you need to maximize ProDiscover Basic's view and increase the work area's size. Drag its left border to the left, into the tree view, until you can see all 30 hexadecimal columns, and then release the mouse button.

9. In the work area, click to select all blocks from **AE3** to **B3F** (see Figure 10-21).

10. Right-click the highlighted blocks (sectors) in the work area and click **Select.** In the Add Comment dialog box, click the **Apply to all items** check box. In the Investigator comments text box, type **Fragment 1 to recover,** and then click **OK.**

11. Repeat Steps 8 through 10 to select the remaining fragmented blocks for these sectors: 1F5 to 248, 3EB to 425, 16A to 1A1, 957 to 98C, and 25 to 2C. In the Add Comment dialog box, increase the comment's fragment number by 1 for each block: Fragment 2 to recover, Fragment 3 to recover, and so on.

12. After all sectors have been selected, click **Tools, Copy Selected Clusters** from the menu.

Row and column position for AE3   Sector text box

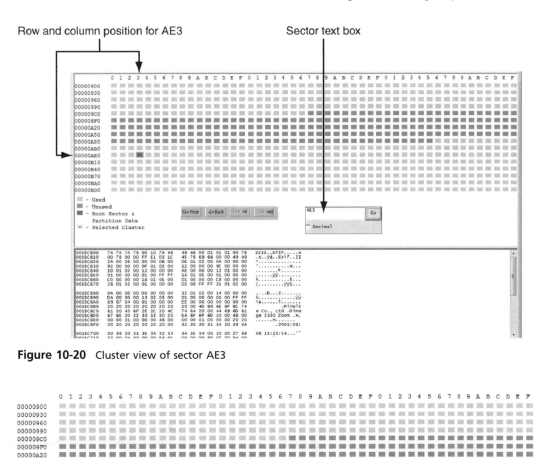

Figure 10-20   Cluster view of sector AE3

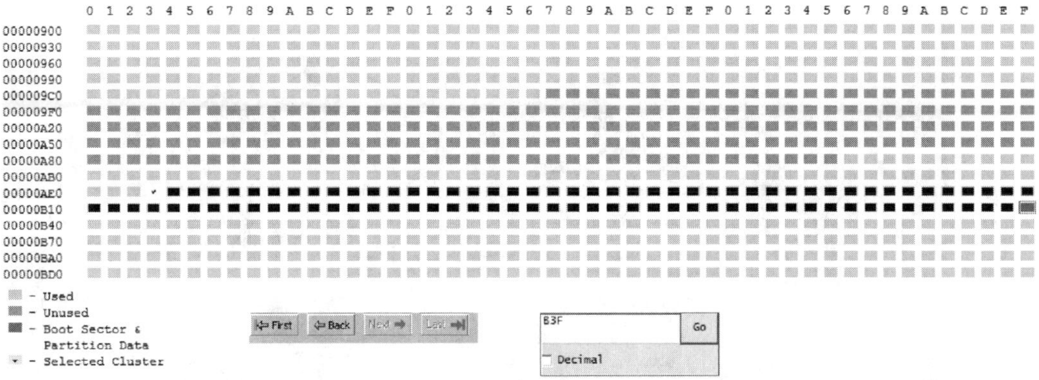

Figure 10-21   Selected blocks from sector AE3 to B3F

13. In the Recover Clusters dialog box, click the **Recover all clusters to a single file** option button and the **Recover Binary** check box (see Figure 10-22). Click **Browse**, navigate to and click your work folder, and then click **OK**.

14. Exit ProDiscover Basic, saving this project in your work folder if prompted. Exit Notepad, saving the file if prompted. The next step would be rebuilding the header of this recovered file, as you did in a previous activity.

When you copy the selected data with ProDiscover's Recover Clusters function, a file named C10InChp-0000-0353.txt is created. ProDiscover adds a .txt extension automatically on all copied sectors or clusters the Recover Clusters function exports.

10

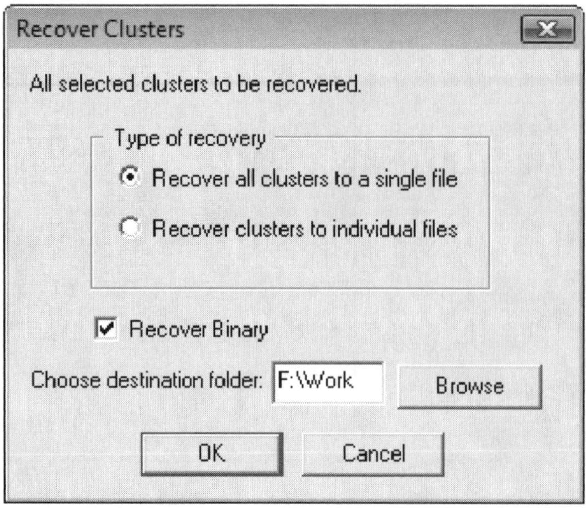

Recover Clusters

All selected clusters to be recovered.

Type of recovery

⦿ Recover all clusters to a single file

◯ Recover clusters to individual files

☑ Recover Binary

Choose destination folder: F:\Work   Browse

OK   Cancel

Figure 10-22 Copying all selected clusters or sectors to a file

In this recovered file, sector AE3 contains "FIF" preceded by the altered header you found at sector 4CA. To view and rebuild C10InChp-0000-0353.txt, you would use the techniques described previously in "Rebuilding File Headers." Remember to save the updated recovered data with a .jpg extension. Figure 10-23 shows the results.

Figure 10-23 Recovered data from starting sector AE3 after Hex Workshop corrects the header

In addition to the natural occurrence of file fragmentation, sometimes suspects intentionally corrupt cluster links in a disk's FAT. Anyone can use a disk-editing tool, such as Norton DiskEdit, to access the FAT and mark specific clusters as bad by typing the letter "B" at the cluster. After you mark a cluster as bad, it's displayed with a 0 value in a disk editor. As Figure 10-24 shows, cluster position 156 has a 0 value, indicating that this cluster doesn't link to any other clusters on the disk. The OS ignores clusters marked in this manner and doesn't use them, which makes it possible to hide data in these clusters.

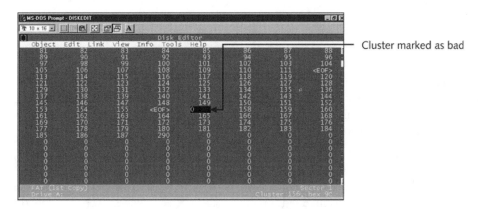

Cluster marked as bad

Figure 10-24   Bad cluster appearing as 0 in Norton DiskEdit

10

Identifying Unknown File Formats

With the continuing changes in technology and computer graphics, eventually you'll encounter graphics file formats you're not familiar with. In addition, suspects might use older computer systems with programs that create files in uncommon or obsolete file formats. Therefore, you must research both old and new file types. Knowing the purpose of each format and how it stores data is part of the investigation process.

The Internet is the best source for learning more about file formats and their extensions. You have already used the Webopedia site to research the TGA file format. You can also use a search engine to search for "file type" or "file format" and find the latest list of Web sites with information on file extensions. If you still can't find a specific file extension, try refining your search by entering the file extension along with the words "file format" in a search engine. One nonstandard graphics file format is XIF. To search for information on this file format, follow these steps:

1. Start your Web browser, and go to **www.google.com**.
2. Type **XIF file format** in the text box and press **Enter**.
3. Click a few links in the search results to learn more about this file format. When you're finished, exit your Web browser.

Nuance PaperPort is a scanning program that produces images in the XIF format, which is derived from the TIF file format. Older versions of PaperPort have a free viewer utility for XIF files; you can also use Windows 2000 Kodak Imaging for Windows. For more information about XIF files, go to *www.scantips.com/pagis1.html*.

The following sites provide information to help you analyze file formats. Keep in mind that information on the Web changes frequently; use a search engine to find graphics file information if you can't access these Web sites:

- *www.digitek-asi.com/file_formats.html*
- *www.wotsit.org*
- *www.martinreddy.net/gfx/*

Analyzing Graphics File Headers

You should analyze graphics file headers when you find new or unique file types that computer forensics tools don't recognize. The simplest way to access a file header is to use a hexadecimal editor, such as Hex Workshop. You can then record the hexadecimal values in the header and use them to define a file type.

For example, suppose you encounter an XIF file, which you learned about in the previous section. Because this format is so old, not much information on it is available. If you need to look for hidden or deleted XIF files, you must build your own header search string. To do this, you need a hexadecimal editor, such as Hex Workshop. To see the differences between XIF and TIF, viewing and comparing header values for these file formats is good practice.

TIF is a well-established file format for transmitting faxes and for use in printed publications. All TIF files start at offset 0 with hexadecimal 49 49 2A. These hexadecimal values translate to the letters "II" in ASCII. Figure 10-25 shows the Sawtooth_050.tif file open in Hex Workshop.

TIF file headers start with hexadecimal 49 49 2A, equivalent to ASCII II

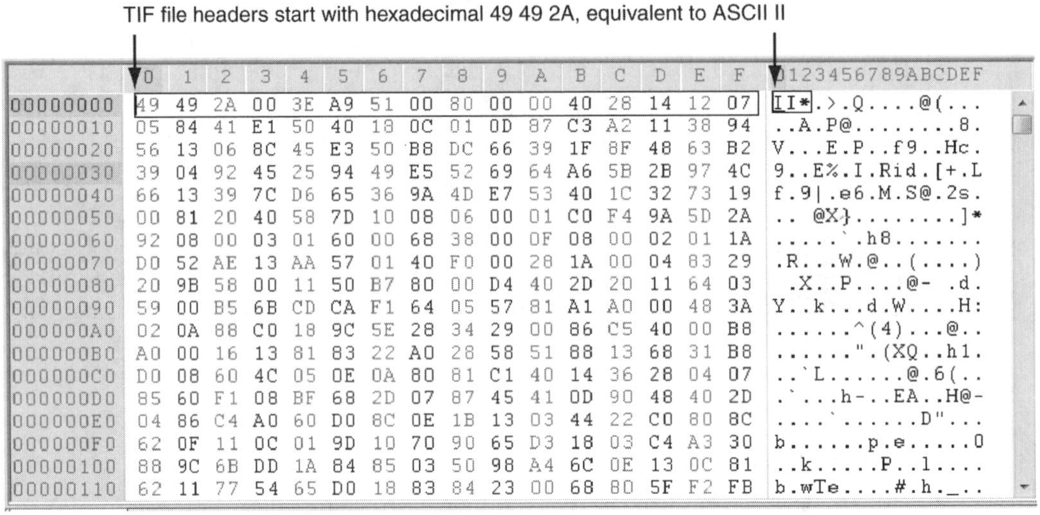

Figure 10-25 A TIF file open in Hex Workshop

The first 3 bytes of an XIF file are the same as a TIF file, followed by other hexadecimal values that distinguish it from a TIF file (see Figure 10-26). As you can see, the XIF header starts with hexadecimal 49 49 2A and has an offset of 4 bytes of 5C 01 00 00 20 65 58 74 65 6E 64 65 64 20 03. (Some values have been cut off in Figure 10-26 to conserve space.) With this information, you can configure your computer forensics tool to detect an XIF file header.

XIF file header   ASCII equivalent shows the same beginning values as a TIF extension

	0	1	2	3	4	5	6	7	8	9	A	B	C	D	E	F	0123456789ABCDEF
00000000	49	49	2A	00	5C	01	00	00	20	65	58	74	65	6E	64	65	II*.\\... eXtende
00000010	64	20	03	00	05	00	01	00	34	00	00	00	02	00	40	00	d ......4.....@.
00000020	00	00	03	00	00	00	00	00	05	00	00	00	00	00	04	00	....
00000030	00	00	00	00	01	00	20	00	01	00	B4	00	00	00	00	00	....
00000040	6F	00	41	75	74	68	6F	72	00	58	65	72	6F	78	20	43	o.Author.Xerox C
00000050	6F	72	70	2E	00	44	61	74	65	00	4A	75	6C	20	32	31	orp..Date.Jul 21
00000060	20	31	39	39	39	00	43	6F	70	79	72	69	67	68	74	00	1999.Copyright.
00000070	43	6F	70	79	72	69	67	68	74	20	28	43	29	20	31	39	Copyright (C) 19
00000080	39	35	2D	31	39	39	36	20	58	65	72	6F	78	20	43	6F	95-1996 Xerox Co
00000090	72	70	6F	72	61	74	69	6F	6E	2C	20	41	6C	6C	20	52	rporation, All R
000000A0	69	67	68	74	73	20	52	65	73	65	72	76	65	64	00	00	ights Reserved..
000000B0	00	00	00	00	01	00	00	5C	01	00	00	00	00	00	00	00	.......\\........
000000C0	00	00	00	00	00	00	00	00	00	00	00	00	00	00	00	00	....
000000D0	00	00	00	00	00	00	00	00	00	00	00	00	00	00	00	00	....
000000E0	00	00	00	00	00	00	00	00	00	00	00	00	00	00	00	00	....
000000F0	00	00	00	00	00	00	00	00	00	00	00	00	00	00	00	00	....
00000100	00	00	00	00	00	00	00	00	00	00	00	00	00	00	00	00	....
00000110	00	00	00	00	00	00	00	00	00	00	00	00	00	00	00	00	....

Figure 10-26 An XIF file open in Hex Workshop

10

Tools for Viewing Images

Throughout this chapter, you have been learning about recognizing file formats, using compression techniques, salvaging header information, recovering graphics files, and saving your modifications. After you recover a graphics file, you can use an image viewer to open and view it. Several hundred image viewers are available that can read many graphics file formats, although no one viewer program can read every file format. Therefore, having many different viewer programs for investigations is best.

Many popular viewer utilities are freeware or shareware programs, such as ThumbsPlus, ACDSee, Quick View, and IrfanView, that can be used to view a wide range of graphics file formats. Most GUI computer forensics tools, such as ProDiscover, EnCase, FTK, X-Ways Forensics, and ILook, include image viewers that display only common image formats, especially GIF and JPEG, which are often found in Internet-related investigations. However, for less common file formats, such as PCX, integrated viewers often simply identify the data as a graphics file or might not recognize the data at all. Being unable to view all formats can prevent you from finding critical evidence for a case. Be sure that you analyze, identify, and inspect every unknown file on a drive.

With many computer forensics tools, you can open files with external viewers.

NOTE

Understanding Steganography in Graphics Files

When you open some graphics files in an image viewer, they might not seem to contain information related to your investigation. However, someone might have hidden information inside the image by using a data-hiding technique called steganography (introduced in Chapter 9), which uses a host file to cover the contents of a secret message.

Steganography has been used since ancient times. Greek rulers used this technique to send covert messages to diplomats and troops via messengers. To protect the message's privacy, rulers shaved their messengers' heads and tattooed messages on their scalps. After their hair grew enough to cover the message, the messengers left for their destinations, where they shaved their heads so that recipients could read the message. This method was a clever way to send and retrieve encrypted information, but it was inefficient because the messengers' hair took a long time to grow back, and only a limited amount of space was available to write messages. However, it enabled the Greeks to send secret messages until their enemies discovered this early form of steganography and began intercepting messengers.

Contemporary steganography is also inefficient because a graphics file can hide only a certain amount of information before its size and structure change. However, it does allow someone to send covert information to a recipient, unless someone else detects the hidden data.

The two major forms of steganography are insertion and substitution. Insertion places data from the secret file into the host file. When you view the host file in its associated program, the inserted data is hidden unless you analyze the data structure carefully. For example, if you create a Web page with HTML, you can display images and text in a Web browser without revealing the HTML code. Figure 10-27 shows a typical Web page as it was

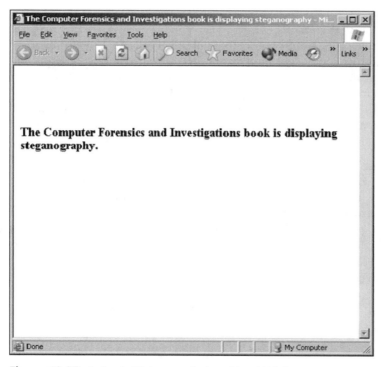

Figure 10-27   A simple Web page displayed in a Web browser

intended to be viewed in a Web browser. This Web page contains hidden text, which is shown in Figure 10-28 along with the source HTML code. To detect hidden inserted text, you need to compare what the file displays and what the file contains. Depending on your skill level, this process can be difficult and time consuming.

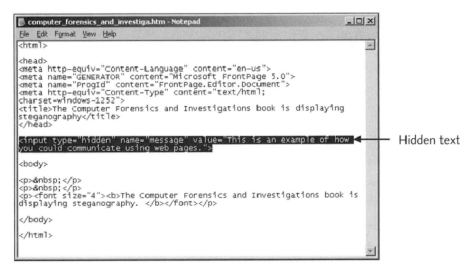

Figure 10-28   The HTML code reveals hidden text

The second type of steganography, substitution, replaces bits of the host file with other bits of data. With a bitmap file, for example, you could replace bits used for pixels and colors with hidden data. To avoid detection, you substitute only those bits that result in the least amount of change.

For example, if you use an 8-bit graphics file, each pixel is represented by 8 bits of data containing information about the color each pixel displays onscreen. The bits are prioritized from left to right, such as 11101100. The first bit on the left is the most significant bit (MSB), and the last bit on the right is the least significant bit (LSB). As the names suggest, changing the MSB affects the pixel display more than changing the LSB does. Furthermore, you can usually change only the last two LSBs in an image without producing a noticeable change in the shade of color the pixel displays. To detect a change to the last two LSBs in a graphics file, you need to use a **steganalysis tool**, which is software designed to identify steganography techniques.

For example, if your secret message is converted to binary form to equal 01101100 and you want to embed this secret message into a picture, you alter the last 2 bits of four pixels. You break the binary form into sections of two, as in 01 10 11 00, and insert the bits into the last 2 bits of each pixel, as shown in Table 10-1.

Table 10-1   Bit breakdown of a secret message

Original pixel	Altered pixel
1010 1010	1010 1001
1001 1101	1001 1110
1111 0000	1111 0011
0011 1111	0011 1100

The sequence of 2 bits is substituted for the last 2 bits of the pixel. This bit substitution can't be detected by the human eye, which can see only about 6 bits of color. Figure 10-29 shows the original picture, a simple line drawing, on the left and the altered image on the right.

Figure 10-29   Original and altered images

The altered image contains the hidden picture shown in Figure 10-30.

Figure 10-30   Hidden picture in the altered image

Whether insertion or substitution is used, graphics files are usually chosen for steganography because they contain enough bits to manipulate for hiding data. Therefore, you should always inspect graphics files for steganography evidence, especially if your suspect is technically savvy.

Steganography can be used with file formats other than graphics files, such as MPEG and AVI files.

Using Steganalysis Tools

You can use several different steganalysis tools (also called "steg tools") to detect, decode, and record hidden data, even in files that have been renamed to protect their contents. If you suspect steganography has been used, search the suspect device for evidence of installed steganalysis tools.

A steganalysis tool can also detect variations of an image. If a graphics file has been renamed, a steganalysis tool can identify the file format from the file header and indicate whether the file contains an image. Although steganalysis tools can help identify hidden data, steganography is generally difficult to detect. In fact, if steganography is done correctly, in most cases you can't detect the hidden data unless you can compare the altered file with the original file. Check to see whether the file size, image quality, or file extensions have changed. If so, you might be dealing with a steganography image. As an example of the complexity of detecting steganography, Niels Provos and Peter Honeyman at the University of Michigan conducted a study of more than two million images used in eBay auctions to see whether hidden data might have been placed in photos (see *www.citi.umich.edu/techreports/reports/citi-tr-01-11.pdf*). They were unable to determine whether any graphics files contained hidden messages.

Steganography and steganalysis tools change as rapidly as some OSs. Current steg tools include Stegowatch, Outguess, StegDetect, and S-Tools. For a list of other steg tools, you can do an Internet search
NOTE on "steganography" or "steganalysis."

10

Steganalysis tools usually compare a suspect file to a known good version or a known bad version of the graphics file. Some recent tools can detect steganography without a known good or bad file, however. Because graphics files are binary, these tools perform complex mathematical calculations to verify a file's authenticity by checking file size and palette color. Other tools compare the hash value of a known good or bad file to the suspect file to determine whether steganography was used.

You can also use steganalysis tools to determine which sectors of a graphics file hide data. Keep in mind that this investigation task can be time consuming. Your first obstacle is obtaining the original graphics file to compare to the suspected steganography file. In some cases, you can find the original file on the suspect's computer or recover it, if it was deleted. If the filename has been changed, you might need to view each graphics file you recover to try to find a match. If you can't find the original file, you can still analyze the suspect file by using a steganalysis tool to detect hidden data. In the Hands-On Projects at the end of this chapter, you analyze a steganography file.

Understanding Copyright Issues with Graphics

Steganography has also been used to protect copyrighted material by inserting digital watermarks into a file. When working with graphics files, computer investigators need to be aware of copyright laws, especially in the corporate environment, where they often work closely with the legal department to guard against copyright violations. Investigators might also need to determine whether a photo is from a known copyrighted source, such as a news photo being posted on a Web page without permission.

The U.S. Copyright Office Web site defines precisely how copyright laws pertain to graphics (see *www.copyright.gov* for information on the 1976 Copyright Act). Copyright laws as they pertain to the Internet, however, aren't as clear. For example, a server in another country might host a Web site, which could mean it's regulated by copyright laws in that country. Because each country has its own copyright laws, enforcement can be difficult. Contrary to what some might believe, there's no international copyright law.

The U.S. Copyright Office identifies what can and can't be covered under copyright law in the United States:

Copyright protects "original works of authorship" that are fixed in a tangible form of expression. The fixation need not be directly perceptible so long as it may be communicated with the aid of a machine or device. Copyrightable works include the following categories:

1. *literary works;*
2. *musical works, including any accompanying words;*
3. *dramatic works, including any accompanying music;*
4. *pantomimes and choreographic works;*
5. *pictorial, graphic, and sculptural works;*
6. *motion pictures and other audiovisual works;*
7. *sound recordings;*
8. *architectural works.*

These categories should be viewed broadly. For example, computer programs and most "compilations" may be registered as "literary works"; maps and architectural plans may be registered as "pictorial, graphic, and sculptural works."

Anything that would ordinarily be copyrighted through noncomputer means and is now being created on digital media is considered to be copyrighted, as long as the process for obtaining a copyright has been followed.

Digital watermarks can be visible or imperceptible in media such as digital photos or audio files. Visible watermarks are usually an image, such as the copyright symbol or a company logo, layered on top of a photo. Imperceptible watermarks don't change the appearance or sound quality of a copyrighted file. Methods used for imperceptible watermarks sometimes involve modifying a file's LSBs into a unique pattern.

Chapter Summary

- A graphics file contains an image, such as a digital photo, line art, a three-dimensional image, or a scanned replica of a printed picture. A graphics program creates and saves one of three types of graphics files: bitmap, vector, and metafile. Bitmap images are collections of dots, or pixels, that form an image. Vector graphics are mathematical instructions that define lines, curves, text, and geometric shapes. Metafile graphics are combinations of bitmap and vector images.

- When you use a graphics editor or an image viewer, you can open a file in one of many graphics file formats. Each format has different qualities, including the amount of color and compression it uses. If you open a graphics file in a program that supports multiple file formats, you can save the file in a different file format. However, converting graphics files this way can change image quality.

- Bitmap images store graphics information as grids of pixels (short for "picture elements"). The quality of a bitmap image displayed onscreen is governed by resolution, which determines the amount of detail displayed. Vector graphics, unlike bitmap and raster files, use lines instead of dots. A vector graphic stores only the calculations for drawing lines and shapes; a graphics program converts these calculations into images. You can enlarge a vector graphic without affecting image quality. Metafile graphics combine bitmap and vector graphics and can have the characteristics of both image types.

- Most graphics editors enable you to create files in one or more of the standard graphics file formats, such as Graphic Interchange Format (.gif), Joint Photographic Experts Group (.jpeg), Windows Bitmap (.bmp), or Encapsulated Postscript (.eps). Nonstandard graphics file formats include less common formats, such as Targa (.tga) and Raster Transfer Language (.rtl); proprietary formats, such as Photoshop (.psd); newer formats, such as Scalable Vector Graphics (.svg); and old or obsolete formats, such as Paintbrush (.pcx).

- Most graphics file formats, including .gif and .jpeg, compress data to save disk space and reduce transmission time. Other formats, such as .bmp, rarely compress data or do so inefficiently. You can use compression tools to compact data and reduce file size. Lossless compression saves file space by using mathematical formulas to represent data in a file. Lossy compression compresses data by permanently discarding bits of information in the file.

- Digital camera photos are typically in raw and EXIF JPEG formats. The raw format is the proprietary format of the camera's manufacturer. The EXIF format is different from the standard JFIF JPEG format because it contains metadata about the camera and picture, such as shutter speed and date and time a picture was taken.

- In a computer forensics investigation involving graphics files, you need to locate and recover all graphics files on a drive and determine which ones are pertinent to your case. Because these files aren't always stored in standard graphics file formats, you should examine all files your computer forensics tools find, even if they aren't identified as graphics files. A graphics file contains a header with instructions for displaying the image. Each type of graphics file has its own header that helps you identify the file format. Because the header is complex and difficult to remember, you can compare a known good file header with that of a suspect file.

- When you're examining recovered data remnants from files in slack or free space, you might find data that appears to be a header for a common graphics file type. If you locate header data that's partially overwritten, you must reconstruct the header to make it readable again by comparing the hexadecimal values of known graphics file formats to the pattern of the file header you found. After you identify fragmented data, you can use a computer forensics tool to recover the fragmented file.

10

- If you can't open a graphics file in an image viewer, the next step is to examine the file header to see whether it matches the header in a known good file. If the header doesn't match, you must insert the correct hexadecimal values manually with a hex editor.

- The Internet is the best source for learning more about file formats and their extensions. You can search for "file type" or "file format" and find a list of Web sites with information on file extensions.

- You should analyze graphics file headers when you find new or unique file types that computer forensics tools don't recognize. The simplest way to do this is with a hex editor. You can record the hexadecimal values in the header for future reference.

- Many popular viewer utilities are freeware or shareware and enable you to view a wide range of graphics file formats. Most GUI forensics tools, such as ProDiscover, EnCase, FTK, X-Ways Forensics, and ILook, include image viewers that display common image formats, especially GIF and JPEG.

- Steganography is a method of hiding data by using a host file to cover the contents of a secret message. The two major techniques are insertion and substitution. Insertion places data from the secret file into the host file. When you view the host file in its associated program, the inserted data is hidden unless you analyze the data structure. Substitution replaces bits of the host file with other bits of data.

- Steganalysis tools can detect hidden data in graphics files, even in files that have been renamed to protect their contents. If the file has been renamed, steganalysis tools can use the file header to identify the file format and indicate whether the file contains an image. Steganalysis tools can also detect variations in a graphics file.

Key Terms

bitmap images Collections of dots, or pixels, in a grid format that form a graphic.

carving The process of recovering file fragments that are scattered across a disk. *See also* salvaging.

data compression The process of coding data from a larger form to a smaller form.

demosaicing The process of converting raw picture data to another format, such as JPEG or TIFF.

Exchangeable Image File (EXIF) A file format the Japanese Electronic Industry Development Association (JEIDA) developed as a standard for storing metadata in JPEG and TIFF files.

false positives The results of keyword searches that contain the correct match but aren't relevant to the investigation.

lossless compression A compression method in which no data is lost. With this type of compression, a large file can be compressed to take up less space and then uncompressed without any loss of information.

lossy compression A compression method that permanently discards bits of information in a file. The removed bits of information reduce image quality.

metafile graphics Graphics files that are combinations of bitmap and vector images.

nonstandard graphics file formats Less common graphics file formats, including proprietary formats, newer formats, formats that most image viewers don't recognize, and old or obsolete formats.

pixels Small dots used to create images; the term comes from "picture element."

raster images Collections of pixels stored in rows rather than a grid, as with bitmap images, to make graphics easier to print; usually created when a vector graphic is converted to a bitmap image.

rasterize The process of converting a bitmap file to a raster file for printing.

raw file format A file format typically found on higher-end digital cameras; the camera performs no enhancement processing—hence the term "raw." This format maintains the best picture quality, but because it's a proprietary format, not all image viewers can display it.

resolution The density of pixels displayed onscreen, which governs image quality.

salvaging Another term for carving, used outside North America. *See* carving.

standard graphics file formats Common graphics file formats that most graphics programs and image viewers can open.

steganalysis tool A program designed to detect and decode steganography techniques.

vector graphics Graphics based on mathematical instructions to form lines, curves, text, and other geometrical shapes.

vector quantization (VQ) A form of compression that uses an algorithm similar to rounding off decimal values to eliminate unnecessary bits of data.

10

Review Questions

1. Graphics files stored on a computer can't be recovered after they are deleted. True or False?

2. When you carve a graphics file, recovering the image depends on which of the following skills?

    a. Recovering the image from a tape backup

    b. Recognizing the pattern of the data content

    c. Recognizing the pattern of the file header content

    d. Recognizing the pattern of a corrupt file

3. Explain how to identify an unknown graphics file format that your computer forensics tool doesn't recognize.

4. What type of compression uses an algorithm that allows viewing the graphics file without losing any portion of the data?

5. When investigating graphics files, you should convert them into one standard format. True or False?

6. Digital pictures use data compression to accomplish which of the following goals? (Choose all that apply.)

    a. Save space on a hard drive.

    b. Provide a crisp and clear image.

    c. Eliminate redundant data.

    d. Produce a file that can be e-mailed or posted on the Internet.

7. Salvaging a file is also known in North America by which of the following terms?

    a. Data recovery

    b. Scavenging

    c. Recycle Bin

    d. Carving

8. In JPEG files, what's the starting offset position for the JFIF label?

    a. Offset 0

    b. Offset 2

    c. Offset 6

    d. Offset 4

9. Each type of graphics file has a unique header containing information that distinguishes it from other types of graphics files. True or False?

10. Copyright laws don't apply to Web sites. True or False?

11. When viewing a file header, you need to include hexadecimal information to view the image. True or False?

12. When recovering a file with ProDiscover, your first objective is to recover cluster values. True or False?

13. Bitmap (.bmp) files use which of the following types of compression?

    a. WinZip

    b. Lossy

    c. Lzip

    d. Lossless

14. A JPEG file uses which type of compression?

    a. WinZip

    b. Lossy

    c. Lzip

    d. Lossless

15. Only one file format can compress graphics files. True or False?

16. A JPEG file is an example of a vector graphic. True or False?

17. JPEG and TIF files:

    a. Have identical values for the first 2 bytes of their file headers

    b. Have different values for the first 2 bytes of their file headers

    c. Differ from other graphics files because their file headers contain more bits

    d. Differ from other graphics files because their file headers contain fewer bits

18. What methods do steganography programs use to hide data in graphics files? (Choose all that apply.)

    a. Insertion

    b. Substitution

    c. Masking

    d. Carving

19. Some clues left on a drive that might indicate steganography include which of the following?

    a. Multiple copies of a graphics file

    b. Graphics files with the same name but different file sizes

    c. S-Tools and Stegowatch in the suspect's All Programs list

    d. All of the above

20. What methods are used for digital watermarking? (Choose all that apply.)

    a. Implanted subroutines that link to a central Web server automatically when the watermarked file is accessed

    b. Invisible modification of the LSBs in the file

    c. Layering visible symbols on top of the image

    d. Using a hex editor to alter the image data

10

Hands-On Projects

If necessary, extract all data files in the Chap10\Projects folder on the book's DVD to the C:\Work\Chap10\Projects folder on your system. (You might need to create this folder on your system before starting the projects; it's referred to as "your work folder" in steps.)

Hands-On Project 10-1

In this project, you use ProDiscover Basic to locate and extract JPEG files with altered extensions. Some of these files are embedded in files with non-JPEG extensions. Find the C10frag.eve file in your work folder, and then follow these steps:

1. Start ProDiscover Basic (with the **Run as administrator** option if you're using Vista) and begin a new project. In the New Project dialog box, type **C10frag** in the Project Number and Project File Name text boxes, and then click **OK**.

2. In the tree view, click to expand **Add**, and then click **Image File**. In the Open dialog box, navigate to your work folder and click **C10frag.eve**. Click **Open**, and then click **Yes**, if necessary, in the Auto Image Checksum message box.

3. Click the **Search** toolbar button. In the Search dialog box, click the **Content Search** tab. Under Search for the pattern(s), type **JFIF**, and under Select the Disk(s)/Image(s) you want to search in, click **C10frag.eve**. Click **OK**.

4. Click each file in the work area's search results that doesn't have a .jpg extension, and in the data area, scroll through each file to find any occurrences of a JFIF label. Click the check box next to each file with a JFIF label. When the Add Comment dialog box opens, type **Recovered hidden .jpg file**, click the **Apply to all items** check box, and then click **OK**.

5. In the tree view, click **Report**, and then click **File, Print Report** from the menu. You can also save your report by clicking the **Export** toolbar button, and in the Export dialog box's File name text box, type **C10Prj01.rtf**, and then click **OK**.

6. Exit ProDiscover Basic, saving your project when prompted.

Hands-On Project 10-2

In this project, you continue the search for files Bob Aspen downloaded. In the in-chapter activity, you recovered three files containing "zzzz" for the first 4 bytes of altered JPEG files. These altered files had different extensions to hide the fact that they're graphics files.

Find the C10carve.eve file in your work folder. This image file is a new acquisition of another USB drive the EMTS manager retrieved. He wants to know whether any similar files on this drive match the files you recovered from the first USB drive. Because you know that the files you recovered earlier have zzzz for the first 4 bytes, you can use it as your search string to see whether similar files exist on this USB drive.

1. Start ProDiscover Basic (with the **Run as administrator** option if you're using Vista) and begin a new project. In the New Project dialog box, type **C10carve** for the project number and project filename, and then click **OK**.

2. In the tree view, click to expand **Add**, and then click **Image File**. In the Open dialog box, navigate to your work folder and click **C10carve.eve**. Click **Open**, and then click **Yes**, if necessary, in the Auto Image Checksum message box.

3. Next, click the **Search** toolbar button. In the Search dialog box, click the **Content Search** tab, and then click the **ASCII** option button and the **Case Sensitive** check box. Under Search for the pattern(s), type **zzzz**, and under Select the Disk(s)/Image(s) you want to search in, click **C10carve.eve**. Click **OK**.

4. Click each file in the work area's search results to display it in the data area. If the file contains zzzz at the beginning of the sector, click the **Select**

check box next to it. In the Add Comment dialog box, type **Sim** **located on first USB drive**, click the **Apply to all items** check bo click **OK.**

5. In the work area, click the **Add to Report** button.

6. Double-click the **gametour5.txt** file. In the work area, click the **File Name** column heading to sort all files in this pane. Scroll through the list of files and click the **Select** check box for the gametour1.txt, gametour2.txt, gametour3.txt, gametour4.txt, and gametour6.txt files. When the Add Comment dialog box opens, type **Additional similar files on USB drive,** and then click **OK.** Repeat this step for each gametour file you find.

7. Right-click the **gametour1.txt** file and click **Copy All Selected Files.** In the Choose Destination dialog box, click **Browse,** navigate to and click your work folder, and then click **OK.**

8. To complete your examination, in the tree view, click **Report,** and then click **File, Print Report** from the menu. You can also save your report by clicking the **Export** toolbar button, and in the Export dialog box's File name text box, type **C10Prj02.rtf.** Then click **OK.**

9. Save the project and exit ProDiscover Basic.

Hands-On Project 10-3

In this project, you use IrfanView to open graphics files and save them in a compressed graphics format different from the original format. You should note any changes in image quality after converting files to a different format. Download IrfanView from *www.irfanview.com* and install it, and then follow these steps:

1. Start IrfanView.

2. Click **File, Open** from the menu. In the Open dialog box, navigate to your work folder, and then double-click **Spider.bmp** to open the file.

3. Click **File, Save as** from the menu. Change the file type to JPG and save the file as **Spider.jpg** in the same location.

4. Save Spider.jpg as **Spider2.bmp** in the same location.

5. Open these three graphics files in new sessions of IrfanView and compare the files. Document any changes you notice.

6. Open **Flower.gif** from your work folder, and save it as **Flower.jpg** in the same location.

If your screen is cluttered with too many open IrfanView windows, close a few that you're no longer working with.

TIP

7. Save Flower.jpg as **Flower2.gif** in the same location.

10

8. Open these three graphics files in new sessions of IrfanView, and document any changes you see when comparing the files.

9. Open **Cartoon.bmp** from your work folder, and save it as **Cartoon.gif** in the same location.

10. Save Cartoon.gif as **Cartoon2.bmp** in the same location.

11. Open these three graphics files in new sessions of IrfanView, and document any changes you see when comparing the files.

12. Exit all instances of IrfanView. Summarize your conclusions in a brief report and submit it to your instructor.

Hands-On Project 10-4

In this project, you use S-Tools4 to create a steganography file for hiding an image. Download S-Tools4 from *www.stegoarchive.com*, install the program, and then follow these steps:

1. In Windows Explorer, navigate to where you installed S-Tools4, and start the program by double-clicking **S-Tools.exe**.

2. Drag **Rushmore.bmp** from your work folder to the S-Tools window.

3. To hide text in the Rushmore.bmp file, drag **findme.txt** from your work folder to the **Rushmore.bmp** image.

4. In the Hiding 99 bytes dialog box, type **FREEDOM** in the Passphrase and Verify passphrase text boxes, and then click **OK**. A hidden data window opens in the S-Tools window.

5. Right-click the hidden data window and click **Save as**. Save the image as **Steg.bmp** in your work folder.

6. Close the Steg.bmp and Rushmore.bmp windows, but leave S-Tools open for the next project.

Hands-On Project 10-5

In this project, you use S-Tools4 to create a secret message in a bitmap file and compare this steganography file to the original file by using the DOS Comp command. You need S-Tools4 and the Mission.bmp and USDECINP.rtf files in your work folder. Follow these steps to create a steganography file:

1. If you have exited S-Tools4, start it by double-clicking **S-Tools.exe** in Windows Explorer.

2. Drag **Mission.bmp** from your work folder to the S-Tools window.

3. Next, drag **USDECINP.rtf** from your work folder to the **Mission.bmp** image.

4. Type **hop10-5** in the Passphrase and Verify passphrase text boxes, and then click **OK**. A hidden data window opens in the S-Tools window.

5. Right-click the hidden data window and click **Save as**. Save the image as **Mission-steg.bmp** in your work folder. Exit S-Tools.

Next, you use the DOS Comp command to compare these two files and redirect the output to a text file for further analysis:

1. Click **Start**, type **cmd** in the Start Search text box, and then press **Enter**. (In Windows XP, click **Start**, **Run**, type **cmd**, and click **OK**.)

2. Change to your work folder by typing **cd \Work\Chap10\Projects** (substituting the path to your work folder) and pressing **Enter**.

3. Type **comp Mission.bmp Mission-steg.bmp > Mission-compare.txt** and press **Enter**, and then at the Compare more files (Y/N) ? prompt, type **n** and press **Enter**.

4. Open the **Mission-compare.txt** file to see what discrepancies were found. When you're finished, close the file, and exit the command prompt window by typing **exit** and pressing **Enter**.

5. To complete this project, write a one-page report on the number of mismatches and the deviation in each mismatch between the two files. In addition, state your observations of the differences in the two files, such as hexadecimal values and their patterns.

Case Projects

CASE PROJECTS

Case Project 10-1

Continue your analysis of the image file for your investigation of the arson running case project. Determine whether any incriminating images are contained in the evidence. Include the location of the file when you document any images you believe to be of evidentiary value.

Case Project 10-2

Do an Internet search to find current steganography tools. Create a spreadsheet listing at least five steganography tools and their features. The spreadsheet should have the following columns: name of tool, vendor (with URL for purchasing or downloading the tool), cost (or note that it's freeware, if applicable), and file formats of data that can be hidden.

Case Project 10-3

You're investigating a case involving an employee who's allegedly sending inappropriate photos via e-mail in attachments that have been compressed with a zip utility. As you examine the employee's hard disk, you find a file named Orkty.zip, which you suspect is a graphics file. When you try to open the file in an image viewer, a message is displayed indicating that the file is corrupt. Write a two- to three-page report explaining how to recover Orkty.zip for further investigation.

Case Project 10-4

You work for a mid-size corporation known for its inventions that does a lot of copyright and patent work. You're investigating an employee suspected of selling and distributing animations created for your corporation. During your investigation of the suspect's drive, you find some files with the unfamiliar extension .cde. The network administrator mentions that other .cde files have been sent through an FTP server to another site. Describe your findings after conducting an Internet search for this file extension.

chapter 11

Virtual Machines, Network Forensics, and Live Acquisitions

After reading this chapter and completing the exercises, you will be able to:

- Describe primary concerns in conducting forensic examinations of virtual machines
- Describe the importance of network forensics
- Explain standard procedures for performing a live acquisition
- Explain standard procedures for network forensics
- Describe the use of network tools

This chapter starts by exploring virtual machines, which are becoming commonplace in business environments. You learn how to detect that a virtual machine has been set up on a host computer and how to acquire an image of a virtual machine. You then move on to an overview of network forensics. Tracing network forensics information can take long, tedious hours of work, but this field overlaps computer forensics in many areas. It's assumed you have had an introductory networking class or Net+ equivalent. The information in this chapter should give you an idea of how computer and network forensics complement each other.

Some of the workload for network administrators involves network forensics. Network forensics differs from network security, in that it deals with tracking down the source and results of an intrusion or attack event, not preventing intrusions or attacks. Recall from Chapter 1 that one part of the investigations triad is network intrusion detection and incident response, which includes determining the intrusion method.

Live acquisitions are becoming more common because they can provide insight on how attackers can access a network, so this chapter explains the process. You also learn about additional tools that both administrators and attackers can use to gain access to network computers. Finally, you learn about the Honeynet Project, a worldwide clearinghouse of information on thwarting network attackers and using honeypots to lure attackers.

Virtual Machines Overview

As mentioned in Chapter 6, virtual machine use is increasing throughout the business world, and virtual machines are even being used to commit crimes. Forensics investigators need to know how to analyze virtual machines and use them to analyze images containing potential malware or unusual software.

As you've learned, virtual machines are handy when you want to run legacy or uncommon OSs and software along with the other software on your computer. For example, you can load a Windows 98 virtual machine on a physical computer (the "host") running Vista. Virtualized networks have become more common, too. Depending on the amount of RAM and hard drive space available, a physical network of 20 computers could have 100 or more virtual machines running.

 Much of the following information on virtual forensics comes from this source: Shavers, B. "Virtual Forensics: A Discussion of Virtual Machines Related to Forensic Analysis." White paper, Seattle, WA, 2008. For more details, download this white paper at *www.forensic focus.com/downloads/virtual-machines-forensics-analysis.pdf*.

An investigation with a virtual machine doesn't differ much from a standard investigation. You begin by acquiring a forensic image of the host computer. Network logs can be helpful in determining what happened on a machine and give clues on what to search for. Even if you know the virtual machine's location on the host, the host might contain shared files that are of interest. Therefore, the best approach is acquiring an image of the host and then exporting associated virtual files.

For forensics investigators, one of the biggest challenges is detecting whether virtual machines are or were loaded on a host computer. On a Windows host, your search for virtual machines should start with the Virtual Machines (My Virtual Machines in Windows XP) folder. Files with a .vmx or .vmc extension (depending on the virtualization software) indicate virtual machines installed on the host.

The next step is to check the Registry for clues that virtual machines have been installed or uninstalled. For example, look in the HKEY_CLASSES_ROOT Registry key and examine the file associations. If a file extension is associated with a virtual device, you know to search for a virtual machine. Another clue is the existence of a VMware network adapter, which means a virtual machine has been installed. To see all network adapters on a system, you can use the Ipconfig (in Windows) or Ifconfig (in Linux) command. Virtual machines can autodetect CDs and DVDs as well as USB devices. As a result, determining what might have been attached to the system is critical. In addition, USB devices are becoming more sophisticated; for example, some even have an OS installed. People with malicious intent could wreak havoc on a system by using a USB OS via a virtual machine.

 Create a *Work*\Chap11\Chapter work folder on your system. The work folder path shown in screenshots might differ slightly from yours.

Before beginning the following activity, download VMware Server from *www.vmware.com/download/server* and install it. You should download version 1.06 or 1.08 because version 2.0 or later might require installing other Windows programs. You also need FTK Imager and AccessData Registry Viewer, which you installed in previous chapters. Then follow these steps to start examining the Registry for clues of virtual machines:

1. Start FTK Imager (with the **Run as administrator** option if you're using Windows Vista).

2. Click **File, Add Evidence Item** from the menu.

3. In the Select Source dialog box, click the **Logical Drive** option button, and then click **Next**.

4. In the Select Drive dialog box, click the **Drive Selection** list arrow, click the drive where you installed VMware Server, and then click **Finish**.

5. In the upper-left pane, navigate to the **Windows** (or **WINNT**)**System32** folder.

6. Right-click the **Config** folder and click **Export Files**.

7. In the Browse For Folder dialog box, navigate to your work folder, and then click **OK**. Exit FTK Imager.

8. Start Registry Viewer. Click the **Open** toolbar button, and navigate to the **Config** subfolder of your work folder. Click the **Software** file, and then click **Open**.

9. In the left pane, expand **VMware, Inc.** and **VMware Server**, and click the **License** folder (see Figure 11-1). The right pane shows detailed license information, including the serial number (deleted in the figure). Exit Registry Viewer.

AccessData Registry Viewer (tm) (Demo Mode) - [SOFTWARE]

File Edit Report View Window Help

Name	Type	Data
StartFields	REG_SZ	Cpt, ProductID, LicenseVersion, LicenseType, Ep...
Cpt	REG_SZ	COPYRIGHT (c) VMware, Inc. 1999-2003
ProductID	REG_SZ	VMware GSX Server for Win32
LicenseVer ..	REG_SZ	3.0
LicenseType	REG_SZ	Site
Epoch	REG_SZ	2003-2-1
Hash	REG_SZ	48f66d56-9aa65173-fa9917c1-74ef1e91-7dff2e11
Serial	REG_SZ	
Name	REG_SZ	Amelia Phillips
CompanyN...	REG_SZ	
LastModified	REG_SZ	2009-03-24 @ 19:53:21 UTC

- Schlumberger
- Secure
- Skype
- Smart-Shopper
- Sun Microsystems
- SupportSoft
- Symantec
- Symantec Technical Support
- SymDebug
- Technology Pathways
- Transparent Language, Inc.
- TrendMicro
- Vantage Software Technologies
- VirtualBookPublications
- VMware, Inc.
  - SID
  - VMnetLib
  - VMware Management Interface
  - VMware Migration Server
  - VMware Player
  - VMware Server
    - Dormant
    - License.vs.1.0-00
    - Private
  - VMware Virtual Machine Importer

Key Properties

Last Written Time	3/24/2009 19:53:21 UTC

```
00 43 00 70 00 74 00 2c 00-20 00 50 00 72 00 6f 00  C·p·t·,· ·P·r·o·
10 64 00 75 00 63 00 74 00-49 00 44 00 2c 00 20 00  d·u·c·t·I·D·,· ·
20 4c 00 69 00 63 00 65 00-6e 00 73 00 65 00 56 00  L·i·c·e·n·s·e·V·
30 65 00 72 00 73 00 69 00-6f 00 6e 00 2c 00 20 00  e·r·s·i·o·n·,· ·
40 4c 00 69 00 63 00 65 00-6e 00 73 00 65 00 54 00  L·i·c·e·n·s·e·T·
50 79 00 70 00 65 00 2c 00-20 00 45 00 70 00 6f 00  y·p·e·,· ·E·p·o·
60 63 00 68 00 00 00 00                             c·h···
```

SOFTWARE\VMware, Inc.\VMware Server\License.vs.1.0-00   Offset: Restore

Figure 11-1 Viewing the VMware license in Registry Viewer

Even if software has been uninstalled, Windows often retains the license information in the Registry. Because of this record in the Registry, when you uninstall a time-limited demo and then attempt to reinstall it, the installation usually fails.

After determining that a virtual machine was or still is installed on the host, the next step is finding it. In VMware, typically you look for files with .vmdk, .vmsd, or .vmx extensions as well as Nvram (virtual RAM) files. In addition, DLL files might be left behind, even after an uninstall. After finding evidence of a virtual machine and its related files, next you need to acquire an image of the virtual machine.

For the next activity, you need a virtual machine you have installed. Follow these steps to acquire an image of a virtual machine:

In these steps, an Ubuntu Linux 8.04 virtual server is used. For this activity, you can download a similar virtual appliance (a virtual machine with an OS already installed) from the Operating Systems category of the VMware Virtual Appliance Marketplace (*http://vmware.com/appliances*).

1. Start FTK Imager (with the **Run as administrator** option, if necessary).

2. Click **File**, **Add Evidence Item** from the menu.

3. In the Select Source dialog box, click the **Image File** option button, and then click **Next**.

4. Click the **Browse** button, navigate to **Documents\Virtual Machines** (in Vista; in XP, the default location is My Documents\My Virtual Machines), and double-click the **.vmdk** file. Click **Finish**.

5. Click to expand the tree at the left. Typically, in an Ubuntu installation, three partitions are listed: partition 1, containing the root partition; partition 5, containing the swap partition; and unallocated space (see Figure 11-2). On Linux systems, the swap partition can be set up to serve as virtual memory.

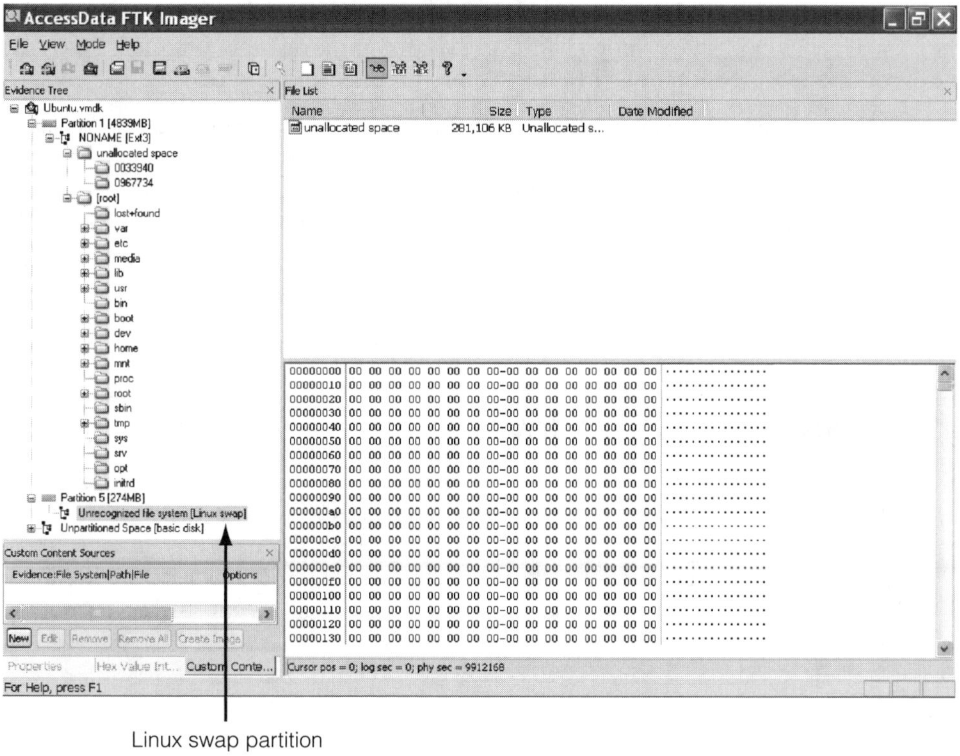

Linux swap partition

Figure 11-2 Examining a virtual machine's swap partition in FTK Imager

6. Next, you acquire an image of this virtual machine. Click **File, Create Disk Image** from the menu.

7. In the Select Source dialog box, click the **Image File** option button, and then click **Next**.

8. In the Select File dialog box, click the **Browse** button, and then navigate to and double-click the **.vmdk** file. Click **Finish**.

9. In the Create Image dialog box, click the **Add** button in the Image Destination section.

10. In the Select Image Type dialog box, verify that **Raw (dd)** is selected for the image format, and then click **Next**.

11. In the Evidence Item Information dialog box, enter today's date for the evidence number, your name, and any other pertinent information, and then click **Next**.

12. In the Select Image Destination dialog box, click the **Browse** button, navigate to and click your work folder, and then click **OK**. In the Image filename (excluding extension) text box, type **C11InChap**. In the Image Fragment Size (MB) text box, type **0** so that FTK Imager doesn't attempt to break the image file into chunks that fit on a CD.

13. Click **Finish**, and then click **Start** to begin the image acquisition. This process might take a few minutes. When it's finished, exit FTK Imager. You can then examine the image with the tool of your choice.

Another option for acquiring an image of a virtual machine is mounting the virtual machine as a physical drive and then acquiring an image of the virtual machine; this method makes the virtual machine behave more like a physical computer. This option is likely to become more common in the future as virtual machines are used more widely.

Virtual machines are also useful when you want to ensure that malware isn't released on your workstation. For example, you can acquire an image of a physical computer, and then load it as a virtual machine. If the image contains malware, you can let it run to see how it behaves without being concerned about its effect on the physical computer or the network it's attached to. As mentioned in Chapter 6, however, some malware can detect that it's running on a virtual machine and won't activate.

Network Forensics Overview

Network forensics is the process of collecting and analyzing raw network data and tracking network traffic systematically to ascertain how an attack was carried out or how an event occurred on a network. Because network attacks are on the rise, there's more focus on this field and an increasing demand for skilled technicians. Labor forecasts predict a shortfall of 50,000 network forensics specialists in law enforcement, legal firms, corporations, and universities.

You might hear the terms cyberforensics or digital forensics; they usually refer to network forensics, not computer forensics.

When intruders break into a network, they leave a trail behind. Being able to spot variations in network traffic can help you track intrusions, so knowing your network's typical traffic patterns is important. For example, the primary ISP in Windhoek, Namibia, has peak hours of use between 6 a.m. and 6 p.m. because most people in that city have Internet access only at work. If a usage spike occurred during the night, the network administrator on duty would recognize it as unusual activity and could take steps to investigate it.

Network forensics can also help you determine whether a network is truly under attack or a user has inadvertently installed an untested patch or custom program, for example. A lot of time and resources can be wasted determining that a bug in a custom program or an untested open-source program caused the "attack."

Network forensics examiners must establish standard procedures for how to acquire data after an attack or intrusion incident. Typically, network administrators want to find compromised machines, get them offline, and restore them as quickly as possible to minimize downtime. However, taking the time to follow standard procedures is essential to ensure that all compromised systems have been found and to ascertain attack methods in an effort to prevent them from happening again. This process is discussed in more detail later in "Developing Standard Procedures for Network Forensics."

Securing a Network

Network forensics is used to determine how a security breach occurred; however, steps must be taken to harden networks before a security breach happens, particularly with recent increases in network attacks, viruses, and other security incidents. Hardening includes a range of tasks, from applying the latest patches to using a **layered network defense strategy**, which sets up layers of protection to hide the most valuable data at the innermost part of the network. It also ensures that the deeper into the network an attacker gets, the more difficult access becomes and the more safeguards are in place. The National Security Agency (NSA) developed a similar approach, called the **defense in depth (DiD)** strategy. DiD has three modes of protection:

- People
- Technology
- Operations

If one mode of protection fails, the others can be used to thwart the attack. Listing people as a mode of protection means organizations must hire well-qualified people and treat them well so that they have no reason to seek revenge. In addition, organizations should make sure employees are trained adequately in security procedures and are familiar with the organization's security policy. Physical and personnel security measures are included in this mode of protection.

The technology mode includes choosing a strong network architecture and using tested tools, such as intrusion detection systems (IDSs) and firewalls. Regular penetration testing coupled with risk assessment can help improve network security, too. Having systems in place that allow quick and thorough analysis when a security breach occurs is also part of the technology mode of protection.

Finally, the operations mode addresses day-to-day operations. Updating security patches, antivirus software, and OSs falls into this category, as does assessment and monitoring procedures and disaster recovery plans.

If you're interested in more information on DiD, visit *www.nsa.gov/ ia/_files/support/defenseindepth.pdf*.

Testing networks is as important as testing servers. You need to be up to date on the latest methods intruders use to infiltrate networks as well as methods internal employees use to sabotage networks. In the early and mid-1990s, approximately 70% of network attacks were caused by internal employees. Since then, this problem has been compounded by contract employees, who often have the same level of network privileges as full-time employees.

In addition, small companies of fewer than 10 employees often don't consider security precautions against internal threats necessary, so they can be more susceptible to problems caused by employees revealing proprietary information to competitors. However, increasing use of the Internet has caused a sharp rise in external threats, so internal and external threats are currently about 50-50.

Performing Live Acquisitions

As you learned in Chapter 4, live acquisitions are especially useful when you're dealing with active network intrusions or attacks or you suspect employees are accessing network areas they shouldn't. Live acquisitions done before taking a system offline are also becoming a necessity because attacks might leave footprints only in running processes or RAM; for example, some malware disappears after a system is restarted. In addition, information in RAM is lost after you turn off a suspect system. However, after you do a live acquisition, information on the system has changed because your actions affect RAM and running processes, which also means the information can't be reproduced. Therefore, live acquisitions don't follow typical forensics procedures.

The problem investigators face is the **order of volatility (OOV)**, meaning how long a piece of information lasts on a system. Data such as RAM and running processes might exist for only milliseconds; other data, such as files stored on the hard drive, might last for years. The following steps show the general procedure for a live acquisition, although investigators differ on exact steps:

1. Create or download a bootable forensic CD, and test it before using it on a suspect drive. If the suspect system is on your network and you can access it remotely, add the appropriate network forensics tools to your workstation. If not, insert the bootable forensics CD in the suspect system.

2. Make sure you keep a log of all your actions; documenting your actions and reasons for these actions is critical.

3. A network drive is ideal as a place to send the information you collect. If you don't have one available, connect a USB thumb drive to the suspect system for collecting data. Be sure to note this step in your log.

4. Next, copy the physical memory (RAM). Microsoft has built-in tools for this task, or you can use available freeware tools, such as memfetch (*www.freshports.org/sysutils/ memfetch*) and BackTrack (discussed in the following section).

5. The next step varies, depending on the incident you're investigating. With an intrusion, for example, you might want to see whether a rootkit is present by using a tool such as RootKit Revealer (*www.microsoft.com/technet/sysinternals/Utilities/ RootkitRevealer.mspx*). You can also access the system's firmware to see whether it has changed, create an image of the drive over the network, or shut the system down and make a static acquisition later.

6. Be sure to get a forensically sound digital hash value of all files you recover during the live acquisition to make sure they aren't altered later.

Performing a Live Acquisition in Windows

Live acquisitions are becoming more necessary, and several tools are available for capturing RAM. Mantech Memory DD (*www.mantech.com/msma/MDD.asp*) can access up to 4 GB RAM in standard dd format. Another freeware tool, Win32dd (*http://win32dd.msuiche.net*), runs from the command line to perform a memory dump in Windows. In addition, commercial tools, such as Guidance Software Winen.exe, can be used.

Another popular tool is BackTrack (*www.remote-exploit.org/backtrack.html*), which combines tools from the White Hat Hackers CD and The Auditor CD (see Figure 11-3). More than 300 tools are available, including password crackers, network sniffers, and freeware forensics tools. BackTrack has become popular with penetration testers and is used at the annual Collegiate Cyber Defense Competitions.

Figure 11-3 Some of the tools available in BackTrack

You can find a review of tools for capturing RAM at SANS Computer Forensics, Investigation, and Response (*http://sansforensics.wordpress. com/2008/12/13/windows-physical-memory-finding-the-right-tool-for-the-job/*).

GUI tools are easy to use, but keep in mind that they require a lot of resources. In addition, some GUI tools might get false readings from Windows OSs. Command-line tools often give you more control. For these reasons, you should become familiar with some command-line network forensics tools (discussed later in this chapter).

Developing Standard Procedures for Network Forensics

Network forensics is a long, tedious process, and unfortunately, the trail can go cold quickly. A standard procedure often used in network forensics is as follows:

1. Always use a standard installation image for systems on a network. This image isn't a bit-stream image but an image containing all the standard applications used. You should also have the MD5 and SHA-1 hash values of all application and OS files.

2. When an intrusion incident happens, make sure the vulnerability has been fixed to prevent other attacks from taking advantage of the opening.

3. Attempt to retrieve all volatile data, such as RAM and running processes, by doing a live acquisition before turning the system off.

4. Acquire the compromised drive and make a forensic image of it.

5. Compare files on the forensic image to the original installation image. Compare hash values of common files, such as Win.exe and standard DLLs, and ascertain whether they have changed.

In computer forensics, you can work from the image to find most of the deleted or hidden files and partitions. Sometimes you restore the image to a physical drive so that you can run programs on the drive. In network forensics, you have to restore the drive to see how malware attackers have installed on the system works. For example, intruders might have transmitted a Trojan program that gives them access to the system and then installed a rootkit, which is a collection of tools that can perform network reconnaissance tasks (using the ls or netstat command to collect information, for instance), keylogging, and other actions.

The problem is that whatever malware the attacker used is now on the system where you restored the drive image. As a responsible investigator, you must make sure you're on an isolated system (not connected to a network) where drives can be wiped to the Department of Defense (DOD) level or destroyed after you've finished your examination. (DOD level requires wiping at least three times.) As mentioned, one solution is restoring the image to a virtual machine, which is isolated from your forensic workstation.

Reviewing Network Logs

Network logs record traffic in and out of a network. Network servers, routers, firewalls, and other devices record the activities and events that move through them. A common way of examining network traffic is running the Tcpdump program (*www.tcpdump.org*), which can produce hundreds or thousands of lines of records. A sample output is shown here:

```
TCP log from 2010-12-16:15:06:33 to 2010-12-16:15:06:34.
Wed Dec 15 15:06:33 2010; TCP; eth0; 1296 bytes; from
    204.146.114.10:1916 to 156.26.62.201:126
Wed Dec 15 15:06:33 2010; TCP; eth0; 625 bytes; from
    192.168.114.30:289 to 188.226.173.122:13
Wed Dec 15 15:06:33 2010; TCP; eth0; 2401 bytes; from
    192.168.5.41:529 to 188.226.173.122:31
Wed Dec 15 15:06:33 2010; TCP; eth0; 1296 bytes; from
    206.199.79.28:1280 to 10.253.170.210:168;first packet
END
```

The first line of the output is simply the header. The rest of the lines follow the format *time; protocol; interface; size; source and destination addresses.* Take another look at the second line from the previous output:

```
Wed Dec 15 15:06:33 2010; TCP; eth0; 1296 bytes; from
   204.146.114.10:1916 to 156.26.62.201:126
```

This line shows that data was transmitted on Wednesday, December 15, 2010 at 15:06:33. It was a TCP packet sent via the Ethernet 0 interface of 1296 bytes. The packet was sent from 204.146.114.10:1916 to 156.26.62.201:126. In these IP addresses, the numbers after the colon represent the port number.

When viewing network logs, port information can give you clues to investigate. For example, you might notice that a particular IP address is coming in frequently on an unusual port. Typically, ports above 1024 should raise a flag. You can check the Internet Assigned Numbers Authority Web site (*www.iana.org/assignments/port-numbers*) for a list of assigned port numbers.

Using a network analysis tool such as Ethereal (which you use later in this chapter), you could generate a list of the top 10 Web sites users in your network are visiting. As shown in the following output, the number of bytes being transferred is listed first, followed by the IP address of the site:

```
Top 10 External Sites Visited:
     4897   188.226.173.122
     2592   156.26.62.201
     4897   110.150.70.190
     4897   132.130.65.172
     4897   192.22.192.204
     4897   83.141.167.38
     1296   167.253.170.210
     1296   183.74.83.174
     625    6.234.186.83
     789    89.40.199.255
```

11

You could also generate a list of the top 10 internal users, as shown:

```
Top 10 Internal Users:
     4897   192.168.5.119
     4897   192.168.5.41
     4897   192.168.5.44
     4897   192.168.5.5
     2401   204.146.114.50
     1296   192.168.5.95
     1296   204.146.114.10
     1296   204.146.114.14
     1296   206.199.79.28
     625    192.168.5.72
```

These network logs can show you patterns, such as an employee transmitting data to or from a particular IP address frequently. Further investigation of the IP address could show that this employee is accessing an online shopping site during company time, for example.

 Automated software packages, such as Tripwire (*www.tripwire.com*), can also tell you when suspicious network activity has occurred. Tripwire is an audit control program that detects anomalies in traffic and sends an alert automatically.

As with all investigations, keep preservation of evidence in mind. Your investigation might turn up other companies that have been compromised. In much the same way you wouldn't turn over proprietary company information to become public record, you shouldn't reveal information discovered about other companies. In these situations, the best course of action is to contact the companies and enlist their aid in tracking down network intruders. Depending on the situation, at some point you might have to report the incident to federal authorities.

Using Network Tools

A variety of tools are available for network administrators to perform remote shutdowns, monitor device use, and more. The tools covered in this chapter are freeware and work in Windows and UNIX. Sysinternals (*www.microsoft.com/technet/sysinternals/*) is a collection of free tools for examining Windows products. They were created by Mark Russinovich and Bryce Cogswell and acquired by Microsoft (see Figure 11-4).

Figure 11-4 Opening page of Sysinternals

As you can see in Figure 11-4, you can choose from file and system, networking, process, and security tools, among others. The following list describes a few examples of the powerful Windows tools available at Sysinternals:

- RegMon shows all Registry data in real time.
- Process Explorer shows what files, Registry keys, and dynamic link libraries (DLLs) are loaded at a specific time.
- Handle shows what files are open and which processes are using these files.
- Filemon shows file system activity.

Far too many tools are available to list here, but you should take some time to explore the site and see what's available. One in particular that's worth investigating is PsTools, a suite created by Sysinternals that includes the following tools:

- *PsExec*—Runs processes remotely
- *PsGetSid*—Displays the security identifier (SID) of a computer or user
- *PsKill*—Kills processes by name or process ID
- *PsList*—Lists detailed information about processes
- *PsLoggedOn*—Displays who's logged on locally
- *PsPasswd*—Allows you to change account passwords
- *PsService*—Enables you to view and control services
- *PsShutdown*—Shuts down and optionally restarts a computer
- *PsSuspend*—Allows you to suspend processes

These tools help you monitor your network efficiently and thoroughly. For example, you can consult records PsTools generates to prove that an employee ran a program without permission. You can also monitor your network and shut down machines or processes that could be harmful.

Although these tools are helpful for network administrators, imagine what would happen if an attacker (or even an internal user) could get administrative rights to the network and start using these tools. For example, in a networking class, students had to install their own servers and then harden their systems. One student was able to use PsShutdown to log on to another student's server and shut it down remotely because that student forgot to create a password for the default user account.

Using UNIX/Linux Tools

Knoppix Security Tools Distribution (STD; *http://s-t-d.org*) is a bootable Linux CD intended for computer and network forensics. To use this tool, you have to adjust the BIOS on the system you're using to make sure it can boot from the CD. Knoppix-STD contains several forensically sound tools put together by Klaus Knopper that are maintained and updated by Knoppix users. (For more detailed information, visit *www.knoppix.net.*) Knoppix offers tools in a variety of categories, including authentication, encryption, forensics, firewalls, IDSs, honeypots, network utilities, password tools, packet sniffers, vulnerability assessment, and wireless tools. A few of the Knoppix-STD tools include the following:

- *dcfldd*—The U.S. DOD computer forensics lab version of the dd command (introduced in Chapter 4)

- *memfetch*—Forces a memory dump
- *photorec*—Retrieves files from a digital camera
- *snort*—A popular IDS that performs packet capture and analysis in real time (*www.snort.org*)
- *oinkmaster*—Helps manage snort rules so that you can specify what items to ignore as regular traffic and what items should raise alarms
- *john*—The latest version of John the Ripper, a password cracker
- *chntpw*—Enables you to reset passwords on a Windows computer, including the administrator password
- *tcpdump* and *ethereal*—Packet sniffers

With the Knoppix-STD tools on a portable CD, you can examine almost any network system. You can also create an image remotely, without the user being aware that you're examining the system's contents.

To see how Knoppix works, go to *http://s-t-d.org* and download the ISO image. (Check with your instructor first.) Following the procedure for copying an ISO image, burn it to a CD and label the CD. Your suspect system can be Windows or Linux and should be on a live network. Then follow these steps:

1. Check the BIOS of your forensic workstation to make sure the first boot device is the CD/DVD-ROM drive, not the hard drive.

2. Because newer machines boot quickly, follow this procedure: Insert the Knoppix-STD CD but leave the CD/DVD-ROM drive door open. Shut down your workstation. Then restart your workstation and close the drive door.

3. The CD should start automatically (or you can press **Enter** at the boot prompt to speed things up). Knoppix usually detects your screen resolution automatically, but you might need to specify it. If you get an error message, try typing **knoppix vga=788** (to select 800 x 600 FrameBuffer mode). If you have any other problems, go to the FAQ section of the Knoppix Web site.

4. When the workstation is fully booted, you see the Knoppix-STD logo in the middle of the screen (see Figure 11-5).

Figure 11-5 The Knoppix-STD logo

5. Right-click anywhere on the screen. When the menu is displayed, point to **XShells**, and then click **Root Aterm**.

6. Type **cd /** to access the root directory. The prompt should change to **root@0[/]#**.

7. To access the hard drive, type **mount -t vfat /dev/hda1 /mnt** and press **Enter**. If you have an NTFS drive, type **mount -t ntfs /dev/hda1 /mnt** and press **Enter**.

8. To begin examining files on the hard drive, type **cd /mnt** and press **Enter**.

9. Type **ls -l** and press **Enter** to get a directory listing.

10. Minimize the Aterm window. Right-click anywhere on the screen, point to **Sniffers**, and click **ethereal**.

 Ethereal is a freeware tool for capturing and analyzing network traffic. It can read Tcpdump, Microsoft Network Analyzer, Cisco Secure IDS iplog, and other files. You download and use a Windows version later in this chapter.

11. When the Ethereal window opens, click **Capture, Start** from the menu. If the Capture Options dialog box opens, click **OK** to accept the defaults. You should see the Ethereal window and the Capture dialog box listing captured frames (see Figure 11-6). If you're not on a live network, ping your neighbor or yourself to generate network traffic, and then try again.

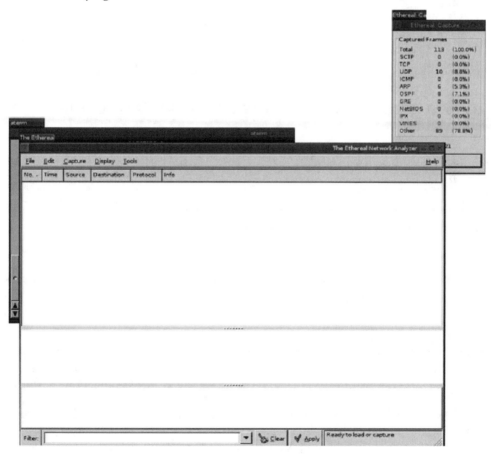

Figure 11-6 Capturing frames in Ethereal

In Ethereal, packets are called frames.

12. After a few minutes, click **Stop**. It takes a few seconds for the network capture to load. When it's finished, you should see a window similar to Figure 11-7. Click a frame in the top pane to view its details in the bottom pane.

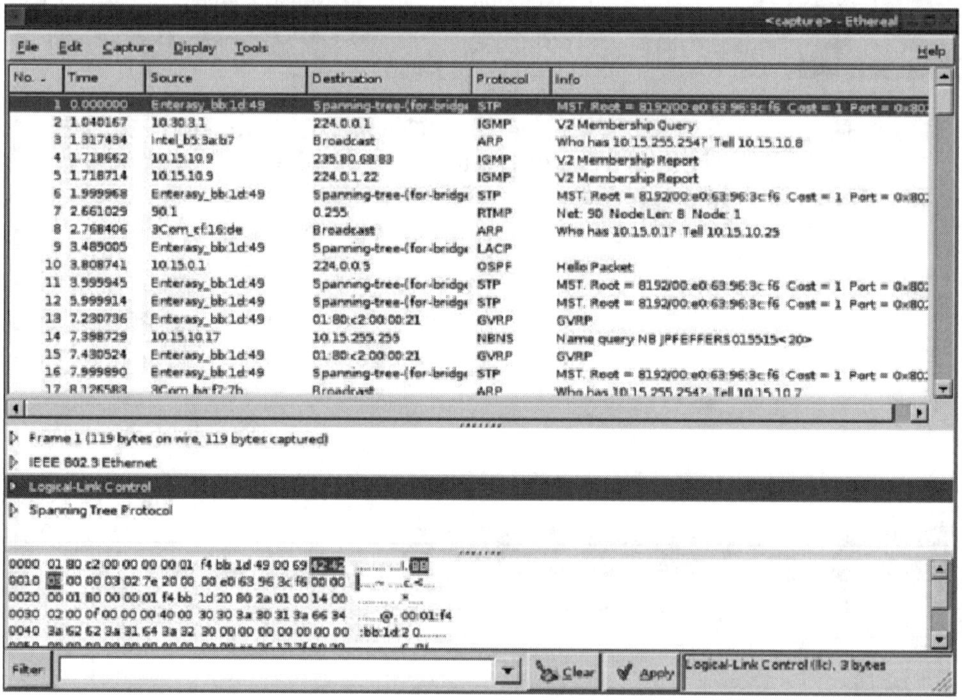

Figure 11-7   Ethereal displaying frame information

13. Click **File, Quit** from the menu. Right-click anywhere on the screen, and click **Reboot**. A message is displayed when Knoppix has been stopped, and the CD/DVD-ROM drive door opens. Remove the CD and close the CD/DVD-ROM drive door. The system then restarts.

Another good Linux tool was The Auditor, a robust security tool that fittingly had a Trojan warrior for its logo. It has been replaced by BackTrack (*http://www.remote-exploit.org/back track_docs.html*), which has tools for network scanning, brute-force attacks, Bluetooth and wireless networks, and more. It also comes with forensics tools, such as Autopsy, Sleuth Kit (which you used in Chapter 8), and ForeMost. BackTrack is designed to be easy to use and is updated frequently. It includes built-in Web browsers, editors, and graphics tools so that you can generate reports. In addition, it contains word lists from many languages (more than 64 million entries) that you can use for password cracking.

Using Packet Sniffers

Packet sniffers are devices and/or software placed on a network to monitor traffic. Most network administrators use sniffers for increasing security and tracking bottlenecks. However, attackers can use them to obtain information illegally. On TCP/IP networks, sniffers examine packets, hence the term "packet sniffers." Most packet sniffers work at Layer 2 or 3 of the OSI model. To understand what's happening on a network, often you have to look at the higher layers by using custom software that comes with switches and routers, however.

Some sniffers perform packet captures, some are used for analysis, and some handle both tasks. Your organization needs to have policies about network sniffing to comply with the new federal laws on digital evidence. Windows has many sniffing tools capable of capturing and analyzing packets, but you can't feed the data they collect directly into other tools. Most tools can read anything captured in Pcap (packet capture) format. (Libpcap is the version for UNIX/Linux, and Winpcap is the version for Windows.) Programs such as Tcpdump, Ethereal, and Snort use the Pcap format, for example.

As a forensics expert, you must choose the tool that best suits your purposes. For example, if your network is being hit with SYN flood attacks, you want to find packets with the SYN flag set. In a SYN flood attack, the attacker keeps asking your server to establish a connection. Although your server can handle thousands of connections, it can handle only a limited number of establishing connections. To find these packets, Tcpdump, Tethereal (the text version of Ethereal), and Snort can be programmed to examine TCP headers to find the SYN flag. Figure 11-8 shows a TCP header; the Flags area contains several flags, including the SYN flag (denoted as S in the figure).

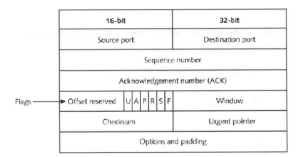

Figure 11-8 A TCP header

Tcpslice (*http://sourceforge.net/projects/tcpslice/*) is a good tool for extracting information from large Libpcap files; you simply specify the time frame you want to examine. It's also capable of combining files. A suite of tools called Tcpreplay (*http://tcpreplay.synfin.net/trac/*) can be used to replay network traffic recorded in Libpcap format; you use this information to test network devices, such as IDSs, switches, and routers. Another tool, Tcpdstat (*www.freebsdsoftware.org/net/tcpdstat.html*), works close to real time to generate Libpcap statistics and break packets down by protocol so that you can get a quick overall view of network traffic, including average and maximum transfer rates.

Ngrep (*http://ngrep.sourceforge.net*) can be used to examine e-mail headers or IRC logs. It collects and hashes data for verification. It's similar to Tcpdump but can be used to identify network communication between worms and viruses. Etherape (*http://etherape.sourceforge. net/*) is a tool for viewing network traffic graphically. Another GUI tool, Netdude (*http://netdude.sourceforge.net/*), was designed as an easy-to-use interface for inspecting and analyzing large Tcpdump files (sometimes several gigabytes). Argus (*www.qosient.com/ argus*) is a session data probe, collector, and analysis tool. This real-time flow monitor can be used for security, accounting, and network management.

Ethereal, which comes with Knoppix-STD, offers a Windows version, shown in Figure 11-9. Ethereal can be used in a real-time environment to open saved trace files from packet captures. An important feature is its capability to rebuild sessions. To use this feature, right-click a frame in the upper pane and click Follow TCP stream. Ethereal then traces the packets associated with an exploit.

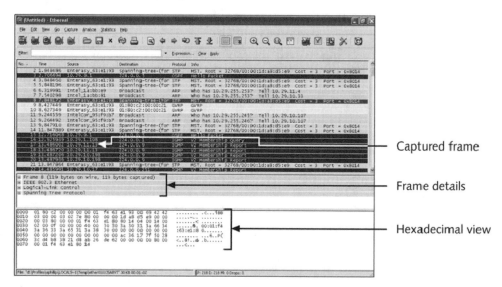

Captured frame

Frame details

Hexadecimal view

Figure 11-9 Ethereal in a Windows environment

To see how this tool works, download Ethereal for Windows (*www.ethereal.com*) and install it on your workstation. Then follow these steps:

Ethereal changed its name to Wireshark recently (*www.wireshark. org*), and several vulnerabilities of Ethereal have been corrected. Although many of the features are the same, steps and screens might differ from what's shown in this chapter if you use the Wireshark version.

1. Start Ethereal, and click **Capture, Interfaces** from the menu to open the Capture Interfaces dialog box (see Figure 11-10).

2. Click the **Capture** button to the right of the network interface that shows traffic. (If you're not on a live network, ping your neighbor or yourself and visit some Web sites to generate traffic. Then start this activity again.)

3. After several frames have been captured, click **Stop**.

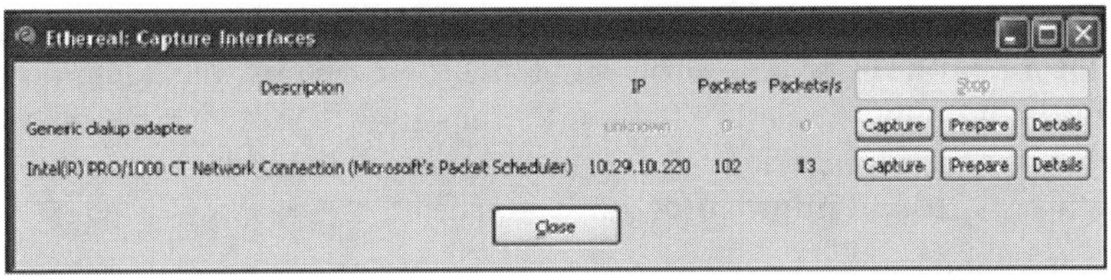

Figure 11-10 The Capture Interfaces dialog box

4. After the trace has been loaded, scroll through the upper pane until you see a TCP frame. Right-click the frame and click **Follow TCP stream**. You should see a window similar to Figure 11-11.

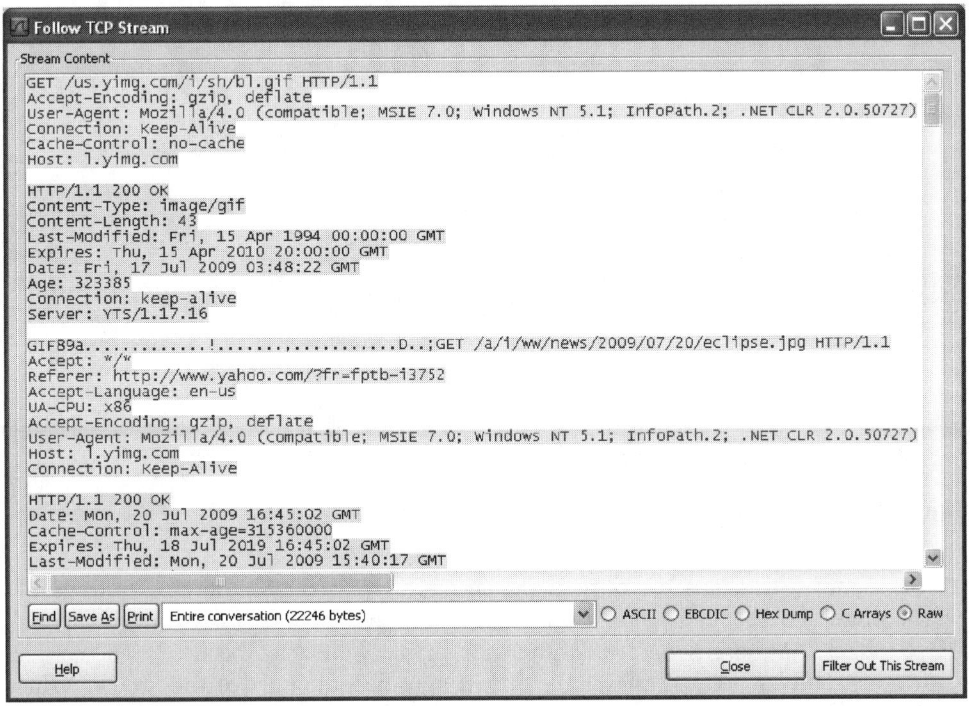

Figure 11-11 Following a TCP stream

5. Note any information displayed in this window, and then exit Ethereal.

You can find additional information on network forensics tools at many of the Web sites mentioned in this chapter. If you're interested in learning even more about network forensics, the next section covers the Honeynet Project.

Examining the Honeynet Project

The Honeynet Project (*www.honeynet.org*) was developed to make information widely available in an attempt to thwart Internet and network attackers. Many people participate in this worldwide project. The objectives are awareness, information, and tools. The first step is to make people and organizations aware that threats exist and they might be targets. The second is to provide information on how to protect against these threats, including how attackers operate, how they communicate, and what tactics they use. Finally, for people who want to do their own research, the Honeynet Project offers tools and methods. Figure 11-12 shows the About page with background information on this project.

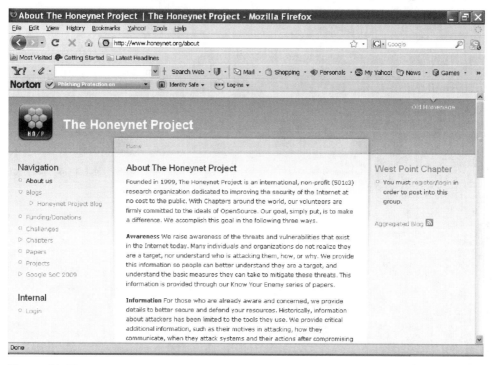

Figure 11-12 The Honeynet Project

A recent major threat is **distributed denial-of-service (DDoS) attacks**. A trace of a DDoS attack might go through other organizations' networks, not just yours or your ISP's. In DDoS attacks, hundreds or even thousands of machines can be used. These machines are known as **zombies** because they have unwittingly become part of the attack. When the first DDoS attacks began, the main concerns were the high monetary impact and the amount of time it took to track down these attacks.

Another major threat is **zero day attacks**. Attackers look for holes in networks and OSs and exploit these weaknesses before patches are available. Vendors usually aren't aware that these vulnerabilities exist, so they haven't developed and released patches for them. Penetration testers attempt to break into networks to find undiscovered vulnerabilities and then predict where the next onslaught of network attacks will come from.

In any corporation, you have to determine the value of the data you're protecting and weigh it against the price of the defense system you plan to install. When an attack strikes, your first response is to stop it and prevent it from going further. Then you need to see what defense procedures worked and what additional procedures might be needed. Training and informing IT staff is critical.

The Honeynet Project was set up as a resource to help network administrators deal with DDoS and other attacks. It involves installing honeypots and honeywalls at various locations in the world. A **honeypot** is a computer set up to look like any other machine on your network; its purpose is to lure attackers to your network, but the computer contains no information of real value. In this way, you can take the honeypot offline and not affect the running of your network. **Honeywalls** are computers set up to monitor what's happening to honeypots on your network and record what attackers are doing (see *www.honeynet.org/ papers/cdrom/*). The legality of honeypots has been questioned, however. Currently, the evidence they produce can't be used in court, but it can certainly be used to determine how culprits are breaking in and create better safeguards for networks.

For organizations that want to put up honeywalls but don't want the financial burden of purchasing extra hardware, the U.K. Honeynet Project has created the **honeystick**. It contains a honeywall and honeypot on a bootable memory stick.

The Manuka Project used the Honeynet Project's principles to create a usable database for students to examine compromised honeypots and determine what happened to them. Some undergraduate and graduate students at Highline Community College, Seattle University, and University of Washington, reporting to Dave Dittrich of the University of Washington, used the Honeynet technique as part of a National Science Foundation (NSF) project.

They went a step further to create a software package that retrieves a compromised drive's image remotely over the network and stores it on the server. They also created software that compares the compromised image with the original drive image. The principle behind honeypots is that they aren't used on the network; they are simply set out to act as bait. The original machine is loaded with the standard software used on that part of the network, a forensic image of it is created, and then the machine is deployed on the network. If the machine is compromised, it's taken offline and another image of it is made. The software then compares the two images to determine what method of attack was used and what files were altered or added. Both images are stored in the database for students at all three schools to use.

For more information on the Manuka Project, see Endicott-Popovsky, B. et al., "The Manuka Project," Information Assurance Workshop, Proceedings from the Fifth Annual IEEE SMC, June 2004, pages 314–320 (ISBN 0-7803-8572-1).

The best part of the Honeynet Project is the Honeynet Challenges (*www.honeynet.org/ challenges*). You can try to ascertain what an attacker did and then post your results online. After a certain amount of time has passed, the solution is posted along with comments from others in the project. It's one of the fastest ways to learn what's happening in the world of network intrusions. If you try any of the challenges, make sure you load them on a nonessential machine because they contain live viruses, worms, and Trojan programs. By attempting to solve the scan of the month, you get a lot of practice in what to look for and how to conduct a network forensics evaluation. Figure 11-13 shows the opening page for the Honeynet Challenges. Many people post solutions for each challenge, and as part of your learning, you could try to re-create their solutions.

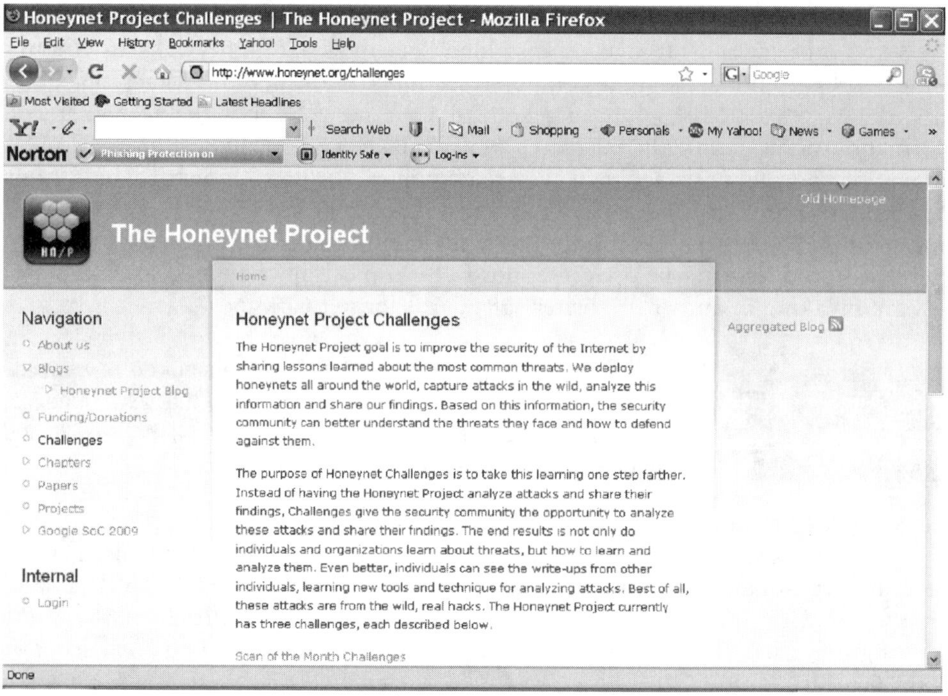

Figure 11-13 The Honeynet Challenges

Chapter Summary

- Virtual machines are important in today's networks, and investigators must know how to detect a virtual machine installed on a host, acquire an image of a virtual machine, and use virtual machines to examine malware.

- Network forensics is the process of collecting and analyzing raw network data and systematically tracking network traffic to ascertain how an attack took place.

- Networks must be hardened by applying layered defense strategies to the network architecture, installing the latest software patches, and making employees aware of security procedures.

- Live acquisitions are necessary to retrieve volatile items, such as RAM and running processes.

- Standard procedures need to be established for how to proceed after a network security event has occurred. As with any digital evidence, live data is fragile and needs to be dealt with accordingly.

- By tracking network logs, you can become familiar with the normal traffic pattern on your network and know when to examine activity that might indicate an attack.

- Network tools can be used to monitor traffic on your network, but they can also be used by intruders who obtain administrative rights to attack your network from the inside.

- Bootable Linux CDs, such as Knoppix-STD, can be used to examine Linux and Windows systems. These CDs provide a wealth of tools for tracking network traffic, cracking passwords, and more.

- The Honeynet Project is designed to help people learn the latest intrusion techniques that attackers are using. The project disseminates information and provides tools for research.

Key Terms

defense in depth (DiD) The NSA's approach to implementing a layered network defense strategy. It focuses on three modes of protection: people, technology, and operations.

distributed denial-of-service (DDoS) attacks A type of DoS attack in which other online machines are used, without the owners' knowledge, to launch an attack.

honeypot A computer or network set up to lure an attacker.

honeystick A honeypot and honeywall combined on a bootable memory stick.

honeywalls Intrusion prevention and monitoring systems that track what attackers do on honeypots.

layered network defense strategy An approach to network hardening that sets up several network layers to place the most valuable data at the innermost part of the network.

network forensics The process of collecting and analyzing raw network data and systematically tracking network traffic to determine how security incidents occur.

order of volatility (OOV) A term that refers to how long an item on a network lasts. RAM and running processes might last only milliseconds; items stored on hard drives can last for years.

packet sniffers Devices and software used to examine network traffic. On TCP/IP networks, they examine packets, hence the name.

zero day attacks Attacks launched before vendors or network administrators have discovered vulnerabilities and patches for them have been released.

zombies Computers used without the owners' knowledge in a DDoS attack.

11

Review Questions

1. What are the potential problems when you discover that another company's machines are being used as part of the same attack your company is dealing with?

2. Why are live acquisitions becoming more common?

3. A layered network defense strategy puts the most valuable data where?

   a. In the DMZ

   b. In the outermost layer

   c. In the innermost layer

   d. None of the above

4. Tcpslice can be used to retrieve specific timeframes of packet captures. True or False?

5. Which of the following tools from Sysinternals monitors Registry data in real time?
   a. PsList
   b. Handle
   c. RegMon
   d. PsUpTime

6. Data gathered from a honeypot is considered evidence that can be used in court. True or False?

7. Name three types of log files you should examine after a network intrusion.

8. List the general procedure for making a live acquisition.

9. Packet sniffers examine what layers of the OSI model?
   a. Layers 2 and 4
   b. Layers 4 through 7
   c. Layers 2 and 3
   d. All layers

10. When do zero day attacks occur? (Choose all that apply.)
    a. On the day the application or OS is released
    b. Before a patch is available
    c. Before the vendor is aware of the vulnerability
    d. On the day a patch is created

11. What are the three modes of protection in the DiD strategy?

12. In what way do live acquisitions violate standard forensics procedures?

13. Having the hash values of standard installation files on a system can help you determine whether an attacker altered the OS. True or False?

14. What are the Pcap versions for UNIX/Linux and Windows?

15. Ethereal can send automated alerts when it encounters anomalies in captured packets. True or False?

16. A honeypot should contain some valuable network data to ensure that it lures attackers successfully. True or False?

Hands-On Projects

The objective of these Hands-On Projects is to give you practice in using freeware tools available for network forensics. Most network forensics tools are created by experienced users, not major vendors that supply extensive documentation. Before beginning, create a *Work*\Chap11\ Projects folder on your system.

Hands-On Project 11-1

If you haven't already done so, download the Knoppix-STD ISO image, burn it to a CD, and then boot your workstation with the CD as described in the chapter. Write a short paper describing how to use five of the available tools and how they would be effective in network forensics. Be prepared to demonstrate them in class. To investigate the available tools, follow these general steps:

1. Right-click the Knoppix desktop, point to **Forensics**, and click **Forensics Shell**.

2. At the prompt, type **ls** and press **Enter**.

3. Select five commands to investigate. First, to see whether Knoppix has a man (manual) page for a command, type **man** *command_name* and press **Enter**. Write down the command's format and a description of what it does.

4. Try to use the tools as explained in the man pages, and note how effective they are.

5. When you're finished, type **exit** and press **Enter** to quit.

6. Right-click the Knoppix desktop, point to **Forensics**, and click **Forensics RTFM** (documentation files).

7. At the prompt, type **ls** and press **Enter**.

8. You should see a list of several README files. To learn more about a command, type **more** *command*.**README** and press **Enter**.

9. Follow the directions to use the command. When you're finished, close the terminal window.

Hands-On Project 11-2

Download the PsTools suite (*www.microsoft.com/technet/sysinternals/Utilities/PsTools.mspx*) and install it on your workstation. Work with another student to test the tools on your lab network. Using the instructions that come with the suite, do the following:

1. Shut down your partner's workstation remotely.

2. Change the password for your partner's account.

3. Retrieve your partner's SID.

Hands-On Project 11-3

BackTrack is intended more as a vulnerability assessment and network penetration-testing suite of tools. In this lab, you examine a vulnerability tool and a penetration-testing tool. Be aware that some of these tools should be used only in an *isolated* lab. Using certain tools on your local ISP, for example, could be considered an attack, and if detected, result in your ISP account being revoked. Before starting this project, download the BackTrack 3 ISO image from *www.remote-exploit.org/backtrack.html* and burn it to a CD.

11

1. BackTrack 3 is a live Linux CD, so you need to do a hard boot with the CD in the drive. It takes a few minutes to load because it's done entirely in RAM. (*Note*: If necessary, type **startx** and press **Enter** at the initial prompt to start BackTrack in graphical mode.)

2. After BackTrack has loaded, click the blue K (referred to as the KDE start button in these steps), point to **Backtrack, Vulnerability Identification,** and **Securityscanner,** and then click **GFI LanGuard 2.0.**

3. Click **File, New scan** from the menu. Click to select the **Scan one computer** option button. In the Hostname/IP address text box, type the IP address of a computer on your network, and then click **Finish.**

4. Click the **Start scanning** button, and after a few minutes, take a screen capture of the resulting scan. Start a report by writing a summary of the results.

5. For the second tool, you use a penetration tester. If you haven't done so, exit LanGuard.

6. Click the KDE start button, point to **Backtrack** and **Penetration,** and then click **FastTrack.** A shell window opens that lists options for this tool.

7. At the prompt, type **./fast-track.py -i** and press Enter to start the program in menu-driven mode.

8. Notice that 10 options are listed. Press the **3** key to select **3 - Internal Hacking,** and then press **Enter.**

9. In the submenu, select **2. Port Scanning** and press **Enter,** and then select **1. Stealth SYN** and press **Enter.**

10. When prompted, type an IP address for a computer on your network, and then press **Enter.**

11. If the program locks up, press **Ctrl+Z.** Otherwise, note the results for your report.

12. Return to the main menu and select three types of scans to perform. Run these three scans, following the prompts, and add the scans' results and a brief description to your report.

13. Close the command window by typing **exit** and pressing **Enter.** Exit BackTrack by clicking the KDE start button, **Logout, Turn Off Computer.**

Hands-On Project 11-4

If you haven't already done so, download Wireshark from *www.wireshark. org*. Start it on a system connected to a live network. Perform a capture for approximately 5 minutes, and then save the trace file in your work folder. If you aren't on a network with traffic, visit several Web sites and ping your classmates to generate traffic. Start FTK Imager and calculate a hash value of the file. Start Wireshark again and examine the trace file. What traffic patterns do you see? Are you on a network using NAT, or are routable IP addresses visible? Do any addresses show up more than others? Is a nonstandard port showing up? Write a short report on your findings and be prepared to present them in class.

Case Projects

Case Project 11-1

You're the owner of a small dental office, with one dentist, five dental hygienists, a nurse, and three office assistants. Your employees must handle confidential patient information, including medical records and financial data, such as credit card numbers. How could you apply DiD principles to your office network?

Case Project 11-2

The Honeynet Project helps monitor network intrusions and attacks worldwide. Go to *www.honeynet.org* and click the Projects link at the left. Select a project that interests you. Write a short paper describing what it does and how it could benefit network security analysts and network administrators.

Case Project 11-3

Go to the Honeynet Project Web site (*www.honeynet.org/challenges*) and locate the page with the most recently solved challenge. Select three solutions that have been submitted. Write a short paper describing these solutions and comparing their findings.

11

chapter 12

E-mail Investigations

After reading this chapter and completing the exercises, you will be able to:

- Explain the role of e-mail in investigations
- Describe client and server roles in e-mail
- Describe tasks in investigating e-mail crimes and violations
- Explain the use of e-mail server logs
- Describe some available e-mail computer forensics tools

This chapter explains how to trace, recover, and analyze e-mail messages by using forensics tools designed for investigating e-mail and general-purpose tools, such as disk editors. Over the past decade, e-mail has become a primary means of communication, and most computer users have e-mail programs to receive, send, and manage e-mail. These programs differ in how and where they store and track e-mail. Some are installed separately from the OS and require their own directories and information files on the local computer. Others take advantage of existing software, such as Web browsers, and install no additional software on the client computer. Throughout this chapter, you see how e-mail programs on the server interact with e-mail programs on the client, and vice versa. You also learn how to recover deleted e-mail from a client computer, regardless of the e-mail program used, and how to trace an e-mail back to the sender.

Exploring the Role of E-mail in Investigations

E-mail evidence has become an important part of many computing investigations, so computer forensics investigators must know how e-mail is processed to collect this essential evidence. In addition, with the increase in e-mail scams and fraud attempts with phishing or spoofing, investigators need to know how to examine and interpret the unique content of e-mail messages.

As a computing investigator, you might be called on to examine a phishing e-mail to see whether it's authentic. Later, in "Tracing an E-mail Message," you learn about resources for looking up e-mail and Web addresses to verify whether they're associated with a spoofed message. Many times, the Internet links in a phishing e-mail appear to be correct, such as the U.S. Internal Revenue Service's Web page, *www.irs.gov*. Typically, **phishing** e-mails are in HTML format, which allows creating links to text on a Web page. By using this technique, a phishing message could redirect the IRS's official Web address to a Web site in a foreign country. To determine whether redirection has been used, you need to view the message's HTML source code and check whether an Internet link is a label with a redirect to a different Web address. For more information on phishing, see *www.wordspy.com/words/phishing.asp*.

One of the most noteworthy e-mail scams was 419, or the Nigerian Scam, which originated as a chain letter from Nigeria, Africa. Fraudsters now need only access to Internet e-mail to solicit victims, thus saving postage costs of international mail. Unlike newer, more sophisticated phishing e-mail frauds, 419 messages have certain characteristic ploys and a typical writing style. For example, the sender asks for access to your bank account so that he can transfer his money to it as a way to prevent corrupt government officials in his homeland from confiscating it. The sender often promises to reward you financially if you make a minor payment or allow access to your bank account. The messages are usually in uppercase letters and use poor grammar. For more information on this scam and other frauds, see *www.snopes.com/crime/fraud/Nigeria.asp*.

One noteworthy example of a lawsuit involving **spoofing** e-mail occurred in February 2001 in the Superior Court of Massachusetts: *Suni Munshani v. Signal Lake Venture Fund II, LP et al.* Suni Munshani claimed he received an e-mail from the CEO of Signal Lake Venture Fund instructing him to purchase options (financial warrants) for a total of $25 million. Signal Lake Venture Fund investigated its e-mail servers and didn't find the e-mail Munshani claimed he received.

In preparation for the trial, Signal Lake Venture Fund conducted a discovery demand for all of Munshani's e-mail. Because of the sensitive information Munshani had on his e-mail server, the court appointed an impartial discovery firm to examine the e-mail. The discovery firm found that Munshani had used a text editor to alter an e-mail the CEO of Signal Lake Venture Fund had sent. The clue to the e-mail being a fake was the **Enhanced Simple Mail Transfer Protocol (ESMTP)** number in the message's header, which is unique to each message an e-mail server transmits. The e-mail Munshani claimed was a legitimate message instructing him to purchase options had the same ESMTP value as the other message the CEO sent. This level of detailed examination revealed that Munshani committed fraud. For more information on this case, see *www.signallake.com/litigation/ma_order_munshani.pdf*.

Exploring the Roles of the Client and Server in E-mail

You can send and receive e-mail in two environments: via the Internet or an intranet (an internal network). In both e-mail environments, messages are distributed from a central server to many connected client computers, a configuration called a **client/server architecture**. The server runs an e-mail server program, such as Microsoft Exchange Server, Novell GroupWise, or UNIX Sendmail, to provide e-mail services. Client computers use e-mail programs (also called e-mail clients), such as Novell Evolution or Microsoft Outlook, to contact the e-mail server and send and retrieve e-mail messages (see Figure 12-1).

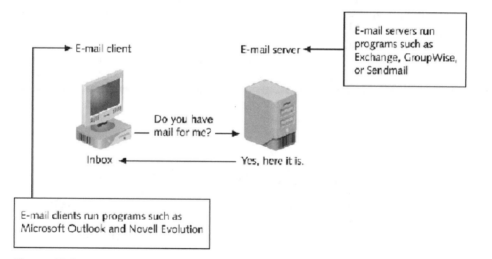

Figure 12-1 E-mail in a client/server architecture

Regardless of the OS or e-mail program, users access their e-mail based on permissions the e-mail server administrator grants. These permissions prevent users from accessing each other's e-mail. To retrieve messages from the e-mail server, users identify themselves to the server, as when logging on to the network. Then e-mails are delivered to their computers.

E-mail services on both the Internet and an intranet use a client/server architecture, but they differ in how client accounts are assigned, used, and managed and in how users access their e-mail. Overall, an intranet e-mail system is for the private use of network users, and Internet e-mail systems are for public use. On an intranet, the e-mail server is generally part of the local network, and an administrator manages the server and its services. In most cases, an intranet e-mail system is specific to a company, used only by its employees, and regulated by its business practices, which usually include strict security and acceptable use policies. For example, network users can't create their own e-mail accounts, and usernames tend to follow a naming convention that the e-mail administrator determines. For example, for John Smith at Some Company, *jsmith* is the username, and it's followed by the company's domain name, *somecompany.com*, to create the e-mail address *jsmith@somecompany.com*.

In an e-mail address, everything after the @ symbol represents the domain name. You need to know the domain information when you investigate e-mail to identify the point of contact at the domain.

In contrast, a company that provides public e-mail services, such as Google, Hotmail, or Yahoo!, owns the e-mail server and accepts everyone who signs up for the service by providing a username and password. E-mail companies also provide their own servers and administrators. After users sign up, they can access their e-mail from any computer connected to the Internet. In most cases, Internet e-mail users aren't required to follow a standardized naming convention for usernames. They can choose their own usernames (but not the domain name), as long as they aren't already in use.

For computer investigators, tracking intranet e-mail is easier because accounts use standard names the administrator establishes. For example, *jane.smith@mycompany.com* is easily recognized as the e-mail address for an employee named Jane Smith. Tracking Internet e-mail users is more difficult because these user accounts don't always use standard naming schemes, and e-mail administrators aren't familiar with all the user accounts on their servers. Identifying the owner of an e-mail account with an address such as *itty_bitty@hotmail.com*, for example, isn't easy.

Investigating E-mail Crimes and Violations

Investigating crimes or policy violations involving e-mail is similar to investigating other types of computer abuse and crimes. Your goal is to find out who's behind the crime or policy violation, collect the evidence, and present your findings to build a case for prosecution or arbitration.

E-mail crimes and violations depend on the city, state, and sometimes country in which the e-mail originated. For example, in Washington State, sending unsolicited e-mail is illegal. However, in other states, it isn't considered a crime. Consult with an attorney for your organization to determine what constitutes an e-mail crime.

Committing crimes with e-mail is becoming commonplace, and more investigators are finding communications that link suspects to a crime or policy violation through e-mail. For example, some people use e-mail when committing crimes such as narcotics trafficking, extortion, sexual harassment, stalking, fraud, child abductions, terrorism, child pornography, and so on. Because e-mail has become a major communication medium, any crime or policy violation can involve e-mail.

Examining E-mail Messages

After you have determined that a crime has been committed involving e-mail, first access the victim's computer to recover the evidence. Using the victim's e-mail client, find and copy any potential evidence. It might be necessary to log on to the e-mail service and access any protected or encrypted files or folders. If you can't actually sit down at the victim's computer, you have to guide the victim on the phone to open and print a copy of an offending message, including the header. The header contains unique identifying numbers, such as the IP address of the server that sent the message. This information helps you trace the e-mail to the suspect.

 Before you work with a victim on the phone, create written procedures for opening and printing an e-mail header and message text with a variety of e-mail programs, according to your state, county, or company's laws or policies. These steps help you give consistent instructions and can be useful when training new investigators.

In some cases, you might have to recover e-mail after a suspect has deleted it and tried to hide it. You see how to recover those messages in "Using AccessData FTK to Recover E-mail" later in this chapter. For now, you continue working with a victim's computer as a cyberdetective.

Copying an E-mail Message Before you start an e-mail investigation, you need to copy and print the e-mail involved in the crime or policy violation. You might also want to forward the message as an attachment to another e-mail address, depending on your organization's guidelines.

The following activity shows you how to use Outlook 2007, included with Microsoft Office, to copy an e-mail message to a USB drive. (*Note*: Depending on the Outlook version you use, the steps might vary slightly.) You use a similar procedure to copy messages in other e-mail programs, such as Outlook Express and Evolution. If Outlook or Outlook Express is installed on your computer, follow these steps:

1. Insert a USB drive into a USB port.

2. Open Windows Explorer or the Computer window, navigate to the USB drive, and leave this window open.

3. Start Outlook by clicking **Start**, pointing to **All Programs**, pointing to **Microsoft Office**, and clicking **Microsoft Office Outlook 2007**.

4. In the Mail Folders pane (see Figure 12-2), click the folder containing the message you want to copy. For example, click the **Inbox** folder. A list of messages in that folder is displayed in the pane in the middle. Click the message you want to copy.

5. Resize the Outlook window so that you can see the message you want to copy and the USB drive icon in Windows Explorer or the Computer window.

6. Drag the message from the Outlook window to the USB drive icon in Windows Explorer or the Computer window.

7. Click **File, Print** from the Outlook menu to open the Print dialog box. After printing the e-mail so that you have a copy to include in your final report, exit Outlook.

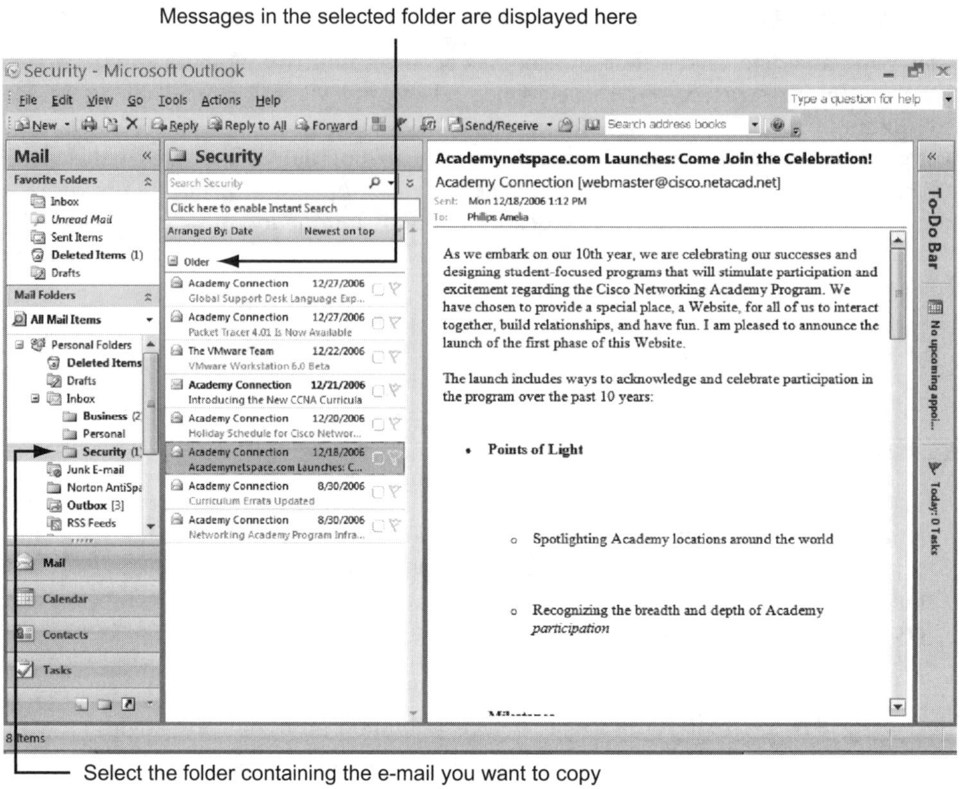

Messages in the selected folder are displayed here

Select the folder containing the e-mail you want to copy

Figure 12-2 Selecting an e-mail to copy

 **TIP** Instead of dragging, you can click a message in the Inbox, and then click File, Save As from the menu. In the Save As dialog box, click the Save in list arrow and navigate to where you want to copy the message, making sure you select the .msg format if you want to make a copy. (For Outlook Express, select the .eml format.) If you select the .txt format, you get only the message contents. Finally, click the Save button.

With many GUI e-mail programs, you can copy an e-mail by dragging it to a storage medium, such as a folder or drive, or by saving it in a different location. For e-mail programs you run from the command line (such as UNIX Pine), however, open the message, and then use the option to copy it, usually located at the bottom of the screen. After you copy an e-mail, work only with the copy, not the original version, to avoid altering the original evidence by mistake.

Viewing E-mail Headers

After you copy and print a message, use the e-mail program that created it to find the e-mail header. This section includes instructions for viewing e-mail headers in a variety of e-mail programs, including Windows GUI clients, a UNIX command-line e-mail program, and some common Web-based e-mail providers. After you open e-mail headers, copy and paste them into a text document so that you can read them with a text editor, such as Windows

Notepad, Linux KEdit or gedit, Pico (used with UNIX), or Apple TextEdit. You examine the headers in the next section.

Whether you're working in a computer lab or elsewhere, installing and becoming familiar with as many e-mail programs as possible is beneficial. Often more than one e-mail program is installed on a computer, and you need to find out which one the suspect is using.

Before beginning the next activity, create a *Work*\Chap12\Chapter work folder on your system. Then extract all files from the Chap12 folder on the book's DVD to your work folder. The work folder path shown in screenshots might differ slightly from yours.

To retrieve an Outlook e-mail header, follow these steps:

1. Start Outlook, and then select the original of the message you copied in the previous section.

2. Right-click the message and click **Message Options** to open the Message Options dialog box. The Internet headers text box at the bottom contains the message header, as shown in Figure 12-3.

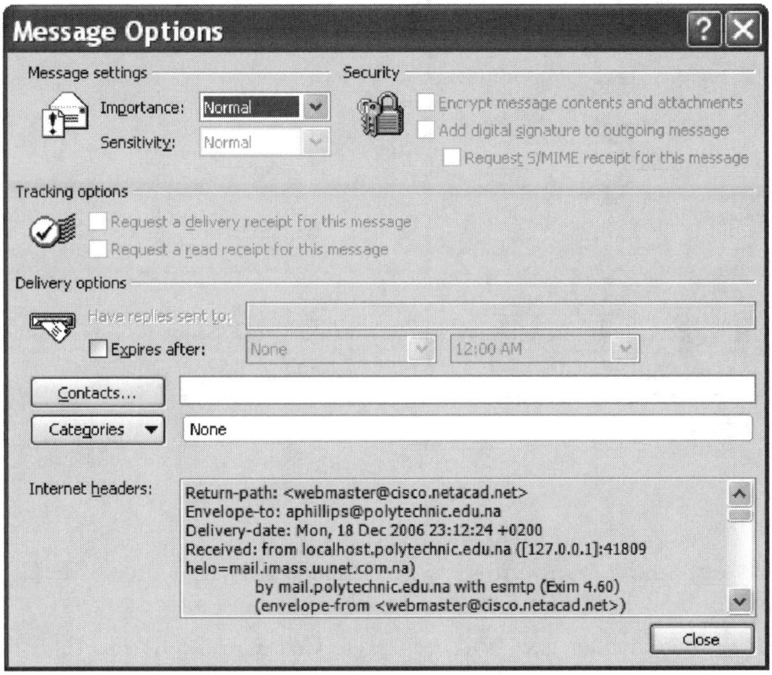

Message Options

Message settings

Importance: Normal

Sensitivity: Normal

Security

☐ Encrypt message contents and attachments

☐ Add digital signature to outgoing message

☐ Request S/MIME receipt for this message

Tracking options

☐ Request a delivery receipt for this message

☐ Request a read receipt for this message

Delivery options

☐ Have replies sent to:

☐ Expires after: None   12:00 AM

Contacts...

Categories ▼   None

Internet headers:

```
Return-path: <webmaster@cisco.netacad.net>
Envelope-to: aphillips@polytechnic.edu.na
Delivery-date: Mon, 18 Dec 2006 23:12:24 +0200
Received: from localhost.polytechnic.edu.na ([127.0.0.1]:41809
helo=mail.imass.uunet.com.na)
        by mail.polytechnic.edu.na with esmtp (Exim 4.60)
        (envelope-from <webmaster@cisco.netacad.net>)
```

Close

Figure 12-3 An Outlook e-mail header

3. Select all the message header text, and then press **Ctrl+C** to copy it to the Clipboard.

4. Start Notepad, and then press **Ctrl+V** in a new document window to paste the message header text.

5. Save the document as **Outlook Header.txt** in your work folder. Then close the document and exit Outlook.

To retrieve an Outlook Express e-mail header, follow these steps:

1. Start Outlook Express, and then display the message you want to examine.
2. Right-click the message and click **Properties** to open a dialog box showing general information about the message.
3. Click the **Details** tab to display the e-mail header (see Figure 12-4).

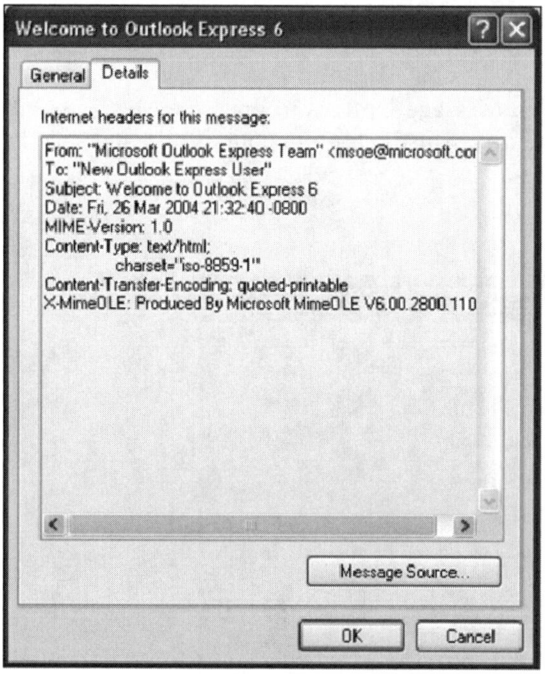

Figure 12-4 An Outlook Express e-mail header

4. Click the **Message Source** button to view the e-mail's HTML source code (see Figure 12-5), which can be helpful in examining possible phishing messages.
5. Select all the message header text, and then press **Ctrl+C** to copy it to the Clipboard.
6. Start Notepad, and then press **Ctrl+V** in a new document window to paste the message header text.
7. Save the document as **Outlook Express Header.txt** in your work folder, and then exit Notepad.
8. Close all open windows and dialog boxes, and then exit Outlook Express.

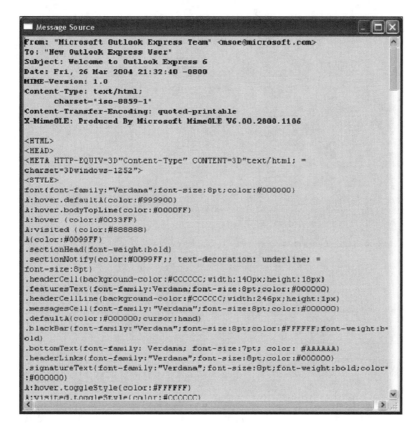

Figure 12-5 Viewing the message's HTML source code

To retrieve an e-mail header in Novell Evolution, follow these steps:

1. Start Evolution, and open the Inbox.

2. Double-click the e-mail message to open it.

3. Click **View, All Message Headers** from the menu to display the e-mail header, shown in Figure 12-6.

4. Select all the message header text, and then press **Ctrl+C** to copy it to the Clipboard. Start a text editor, such as KEdit or gedit, and then press **Ctrl+V** in a new document window to paste the message header text.

5. Save the document as **Evolution Header.txt** in your work folder, close the file, and then exit the text editor and Evolution.

In the previous activities, you used a GUI program to find the header information. Now you see how to find this same information with a command-line e-mail program. If available, follow these steps to retrieve e-mail headers in UNIX Pine:

1. Start Pine by typing **pine** at the command prompt and pressing **Enter**. The Pine e-mail screen appears with available options at the bottom.

2. Type **s** to display setup options.

12

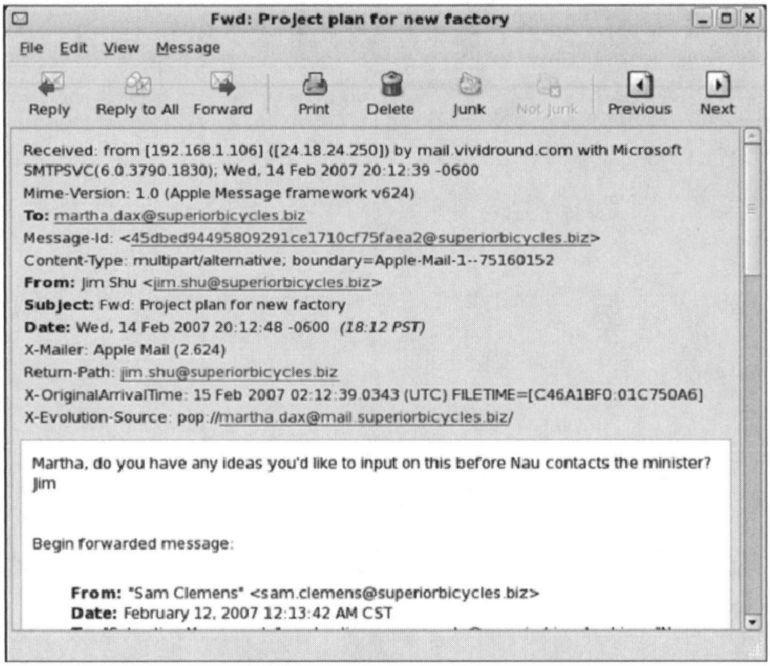

Figure 12-6 An Evolution e-mail header

3. Type **c** to access e-mail configuration options.

4. Scroll the list of options, and use the arrow keys to highlight the [ ] **enable-full-header** option. Then type **x** to select the option.

5. Type **e** to exit configuration mode.

6. When asked whether you want to save or commit the changes, type **y**. You return to the Pine main options.

7. Use the arrow keys to select an e-mail message, and then select **O** in the options at the bottom (see Figure 12-7).

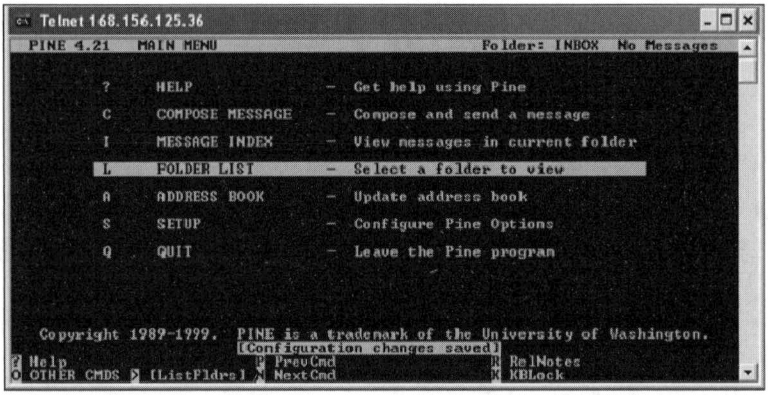

Figure 12-7 E-mail options in Pine

8. Type **h** to open the e-mail header (see Figure 12-8).

9. Type **q** to exit Pine (and **y** to confirm, if necessary).

Figure 12-8 An e-mail header in Pine

These steps also work with elm, another UNIX/Linux command-line e-mail program. For older UNIX applications, such as mail or mailx, you can print e-mail headers by using the print command (an uppercase P). You can also print a saved message with this command:

type *saved e-mail* >> *printer*

Saved e-mail is the message filename and *printer* is the name of the printer. For example, with an e-mail message named Nightmare and a printer called MyPrinter, you use the following command:

type Nightmare >> MyPrinter

Some popular Web-based e-mail service providers are AOL, Hotmail, Gmail, and Yahoo!, and you work with a few in the following activities. You can use any computer connected to the Internet to send and receive e-mail, which makes Web-based e-mail messages more difficult to trace. To view AOL Web e-mail headers, follow these steps:

1. Start your Web browser and log on to AOL.

2. On AOL's main page, click the **Mail** tab, and click **Settings**.

3. Click the **Always show full header** check box, and then click **Save**. Click the **Check Mail** button to return to the mail folders.

4. Select an e-mail, and then click **Action, Print Message** from the menu (see Figure 12-9). Exit AOL.

To view e-mail headers in Apple Mail, follow these steps:

1. Start Mail, and double-click a message to open it.

2. Click **View** from the menu, point to **Message**, and then click **Long Headers**. Figure 12-10 shows the results.

3. Select the message header text, and then click **Edit, Copy** from the menu.

4. Start TextEdit from the Macintosh Applications folder, and click **Edit, Paste** from the menu.

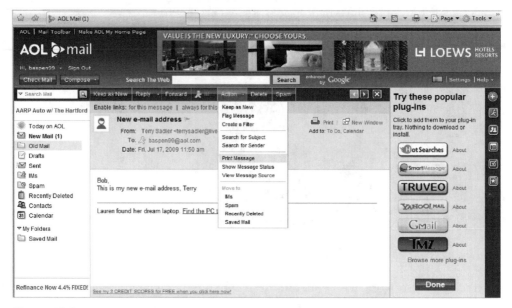

Figure 12-9 Printing an e-mail in AOL

```
O O O                         Fw: Board meeting needs
  ⊘      ⬔      ⬔      ⇥      🖨
Delete  Reply  Reply All  Forward  Print

         From:  Denise Robinson
       Subject:  Fw: Board meeting needs
          Date:  February 14, 2007 8:29:35 PM CST
            To:  Jim Shu
            Cc:  <martha.dax@superiorbicycles.biz>
       Received:  from smtp-sjt-01.vividround.com ([199.249.224.252]) by mail.vividround.com with Microsoft
                  SMTPSVC(6.0.3790.1830); Wed, 14 Feb 2007 20:35:18 -0600
       Received:  from alnrmhc16.comcast.net (alnrmhc16.comcast.net [206.18.177.56]) by smtp-sjt
                  -01.vividround.com (8.12.11/8.12.11) with ESMTP id l1F2UXQU028130 for
                  <jim.shu@superiorbicycles.biz>; Wed, 14 Feb 2007 20:30:33 -0600 (CST)
       Received:  from oemcomputer (c-24-18-24-250.hsd1.mn.comcast.net[24.18.24.250]) by comcast.net
                  (alnrmhc16) with SMTP id <20070215022743b1600ba3e2e>; Thu, 15 Feb 2007 02:28:07 +0000
      Message-Id:  <002c01c750a9$30794ee0$6901a8c0@oemcomputer>
    Mime-Version:  1.0
     Content-Type:  text/plain; charset="iso-8859-1"
Content-Transfer-Encoding:  7bit
       X-Priority:  3
   X-Msmail-Priority:  Normal
        X-Mailer:  Microsoft Outlook Express 5.00.2615.200
       X-Mimeole:  Produced By Microsoft MimeOLE V5.00.2615.200
    X-Eprism-Trap:  Default Trap
    X-Eguard-Score:  () 0.5 BIZ_TLD
    X-Scanned-By:  ePrism email filtering appliance on 199.249.224.252
      Return-Path:  denise.robinson@superiorbicycles.biz
X-Originalarrivaltime:  15 Feb 2007 02:35:18.0203 (UTC) FILETIME=[EE5BB0B0:01C750A9]

Jim,

Tell me what is needed and I'll get started on it.

Denise
```

Figure 12-10 An Apple Mail e-mail header

5. Click **File, Save as** from the menu. Click the **Where** list arrow, and then navigate to and click your work folder.

6. Click **Format, Make Plain Text** from the menu. In the Save As text box, type **Apple Email Header.txt,** and then click **Save.** Exit TextEdit and Apple Mail.

Follow these steps to view e-mail headers in Yahoo!:

1. Log on to your Yahoo! mail account, and click **Inbox** to view a list of messages.

2. Above the message window, click the **Compact Header** down arrow, and click **Full Header** (see Figure 12-11).

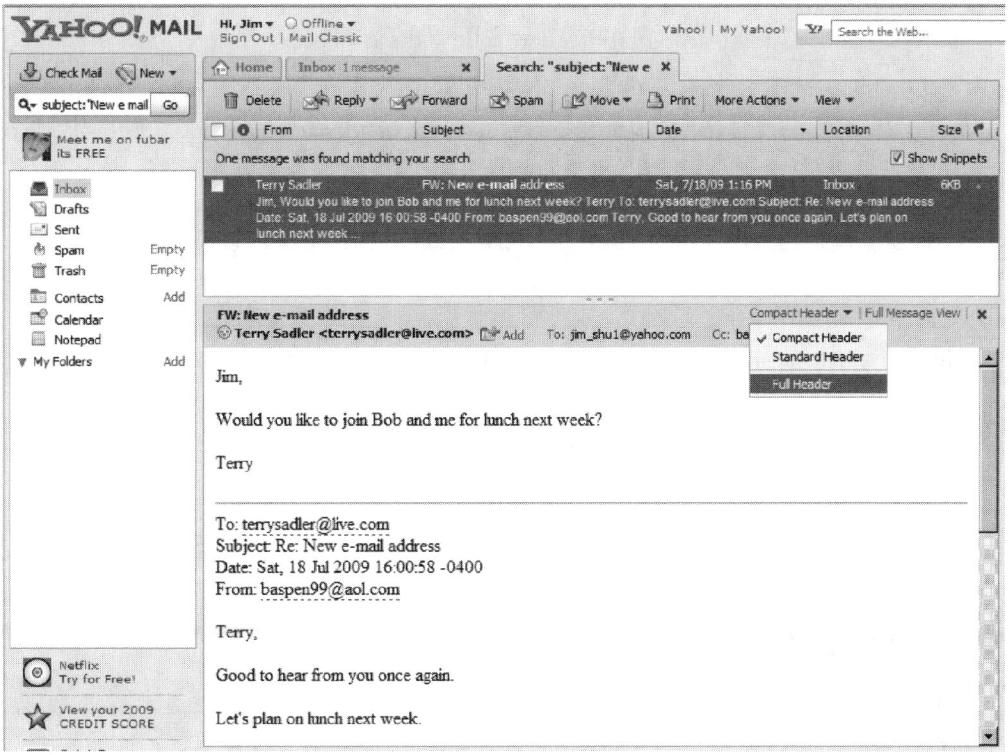

Figure 12-11 Selecting the option to view headers in Yahoo!

3. In the Full Message Headers window, select all the text, press **Ctrl+C** to copy it, and then click **OK**.

4. Start Notepad, and press **Ctrl+V** in a new document window to paste the message header text. Save the document as **Yahoo Header.txt** in your work folder. Log off Yahoo!, and exit your Web browser.

All the e-mail programs reviewed in this section supply the same information in the e-mail header. New e-mail programs might have different options for retrieving e-mail headers. In most cases, however, you can find information about displaying message headers in the program's Help files.

Examining E-mail Headers

The next step is examining the e-mail header you saved to gather information about the e-mail and track the suspect to the e-mail's originating location. The primary piece of information you're looking for is the originating e-mail's domain address or an IP address. Other helpful information includes the date and time the message was sent, filenames of any attachments, and unique message number, if it's supplied.

For more detailed information on e-mail headers, see *www.stopspam. org/index.php?option=com_content&view=article&id=45&Itemid=56.*

To open and examine an e-mail header, follow these steps:

1. Open the Computer window or Windows Explorer and navigate to your work folder.

2. Double-click a .txt file containing message header text, such as **Outlook Header.txt**. The message header opens in Notepad.

Figure 12-12 shows a message header copied from an Outlook e-mail. (The e-mail addresses are not real addresses.) Line numbers have been added for reference.

```
1. Return-Path: <Samspade@myway.com>
2. Delivered To: jim.shu@superiorbicycles.biz
3. Received (qmail 12780 invoked by uid 0); 12 Dec 2010 08:23:37 -
   0000
4. Received from unknown (HELO smtp.superiorbicycles.biz)
   (192.152.64.20) by mail.superiorbicycles.biz with SMTP; 12 Dec
   2010 08:23:37 -0000
5. Received: from Web4009 mail0.myway.com
   (Web4009.mail0.myway.com[192.218.78.27])
        by smtp.superiorbicycles.biz (16.12.6/16.12.6) with SMTP id
        gBC8ILAJ005229
        for <jim.shu@superiorbicycles.biz>; Sun 12 Dec 2010
        00:18:21 -0800
6. Message-ID: <20101212082330.40429.qmail@web4009.mail0.myway.com>
7. Received: from [10.187.241.199] by Web4009.mail0.myway.com via
   HTTP; Sun 12 Dec 2010 00:23:30 PST

   Date: Sun 12 Dec 2010 00:23:30 PST |
   MIME-Version: 1.0
```

Figure 12-12 An e-mail header with line numbers added

The e-mail header in Figure 12-12 provides a lot of information. Lines 1 to 5 show the e-mail servers through which the message traveled. Line 1 shows the return path, which is the address an e-mail program uses for sending a reply, usually indicated as the "Reply to" field in an e-mail. Do *not* rely on the return path to reveal the e-mail's source account, however. Spoofing (faking) an e-mail address in the Return-Path line is easy to do.

Line 2 identifies the recipient's e-mail address. When you're investigating e-mail, you should verify this address by confirming it with the e-mail service provider. Request a bill or log to make sure the account name in Line 2 is the one the victim uses. (Check with your attorney general's office to determine the type of documentation you need.)

Line 3 indicates the type of e-mail service that sent the e-mail, such as qmail (UNIX e-mail), and includes an ID number, such as 12780 in Figure 12-12. With these ID numbers, you can examine logs from the transmitting e-mail server to determine whether the message was actually sent from it. If the transmitting e-mail server doesn't list this unique ID number, there's a good chance the message was spoofed.

Line 4 lists the IP address of the e-mail server that sent the message—192.152.64.20, in this example. It also identifies the name of the server sending the message: in this case, *smtp.superiorbicycles.biz*.

A good indicator of a spoofed e-mail address is the Received from server (in Line 4) and the Return-Path server (in Line 1) being different.

Line 5 contains the name of the e-mail server (or list of e-mail servers) that sent or passed the message to the victim's e-mail server.

Lines 6 and 7 provide information important for e-mail investigators. Line 6 shows a unique ID number that the sending e-mail server assigned to the message. In Figure 12-12, it's 20101212082330.40429. You can use this number to track the message on the originating e-mail server in e-mail logs. Line 7 shows the IP address of the server sending the e-mail and lists the date and time the e-mail was sent. For example, 10.187.241.199 is the IP address of the sending server web4009.mail0.myway.com, and Sun 12 Dec 2010 00:23:30 PST is the date the message was sent. Line 7 might also identify the e-mail as being sent through an HTTP client, as it does in Figure 12-12.

The e-mail header in Figure 12-12 doesn't include a Line 8, which usually identifies attachments. An attachment can be any type of file, from a program to a picture. If a message includes an attachment, investigate it as a supporting piece of evidence. If you're working with the victim, the attachment is usually still attached to the e-mail. If you're investigating a suspect's computer, remember to work with the copied version. On a suspect's computer or forensic image, search for the attached file with a forensics tool, such as FTK, or the OS's Search or Find feature to determine whether the file was saved and still exists on the drive. If you're investigating an e-mail attachment with an unfamiliar file extension, such as .mdf, you can search the Internet to find out what program creates a file of this type.

12

To search for specific files in e-mail headers, use a forensics tool, such as FTK. Forensics tools can also search for unique header information, such as an ID number.

Examining Additional E-mail Files

E-mail programs save messages on the client computer or leave them on the server. How e-mails are stored depends on settings on the client and server. On the client computer, you could save all your e-mail in a separate folder for record-keeping purposes. For example, in Outlook, you can save sent, draft, deleted, and received e-mails in a .pst file, or you can save offline files in an .ost file. With these client files (.pst and .ost), users can access and read their e-mail offline (when their computers aren't connected to the central e-mail server).

Most e-mail programs also include an electronic address book (called Contacts in Outlook), and many offer calendars, tasks list, and memos. A suspect's address book, calendar, task list, and memos can contain valuable information that links e-mail crimes or abuse to other parties and reveal the suspect's physical address and even involvement in other crimes.

In Web-based e-mail, messages are displayed and saved as Web pages in the browser's cache folders. Many Web-based e-mail providers also offer instant messaging (IM) services that can save message contents in proprietary and nonproprietary file formats. These files are usually stored in different folders than Internet data files are. For example, in Windows, you can scan IM files and folders under Documents and Settings*username*\Application Data or under Program Files. IM programs, such as AOL AIM, Windows Messenger, and Yahoo!, usually have their own folder names.

Because some of these programs create proprietary files, you might need special tools to read their contents. For example, Yahoo Message Archive Decoder (*www.ikitek.com*) can open and read files from Yahoo!'s IM program. Some IM programs, such as Windows Messenger, are configured to not save chat content unless users change the default setting, so you might need to search the suspect's Pagefile.sys file to find message fragments. Unlike Yahoo!'s proprietary file format, Windows Messenger stores messages in RTF format that most word processors can read. When you're working on the victim's computer, these files can help you document corroborating evidence for the investigation.

Tracing an E-mail Message

As part of the investigation, you need to determine an e-mail's origin by further examining the header with one of many free Internet tools. Determining message origin is referred to as "tracing." In this section, you learn about some Internet lookup tools that can be used to trace where an e-mail originated.

For example, with the e-mail in Figure 12-12, you can visit *www.superiorbicycles.biz* to find out who administers the domain. If the point of contact isn't listed on the Web site or the domain doesn't have a Web site, you need to use a registry site, such as those in the following list, to determine the point of contact:

- *www.arin.net*—Use the American Registry for Internet Numbers (ARIN) to map an IP address to a domain name and find the domain's point of contact.

- *www.internic.com*—Like *www.arin.net*, you use this site to find a domain's IP address and point of contact.

- *www.freeality.com*—This comprehensive Web site has options for searching for a suspect, including by e-mail addresses, phone numbers, and names.

- *www.google.com*—Use this search engine and others to look for more information and additional postings on discussion boards.

Using one of these Web sites, you can find the suspect's full e-mail address, such as *jim.shu@superiorbicycles.biz*, and contact information. Keep in mind that the suspect might have posted false information, so verify your findings by checking network e-mail logs against e-mail addresses, as described in the next section.

Using Network E-mail Logs

Network administrators maintain logs of the inbound and outbound traffic routers handle. Routers have rules to allow or deny traffic based on source or destination IP address. In most cases, a router is set up to track all traffic flowing through its ports. Using these logs, you can determine the path a transmitted e-mail has taken. The network administrator who manages routers can supply the log files you need. Review the router logs to find the victim's (recipient's) e-mail, and look for the unique ID number, shown in Line 3 in Figure 12-12.

Network administrators also maintain logs for firewalls that filter Internet traffic; these logs can help verify whether an e-mail message passed through the firewall. Firewalls, such as WatchGuard, Cisco Pix, and Check Point, maintain log files that track Internet traffic destined for other networks or the network the firewall is protecting. When the network administrator provides firewall log files, you can open them in a text editor, such as Notepad in Windows or vi in UNIX. Figure 12-13 shows a typical log file for a WatchGuard Firebox II. Although Figure 12-13 shows the log file open in Notepad, some devices use special programs to read log files.

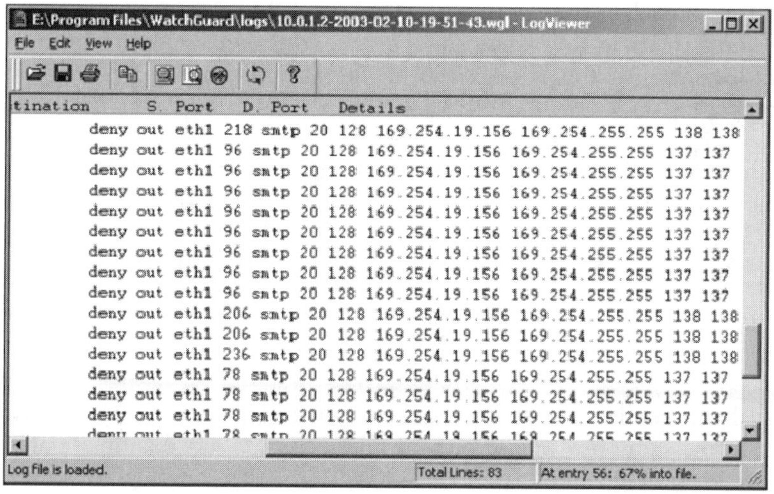

Figure 12-13 A firewall log

Understanding E-mail Servers

An e-mail server is loaded with software that uses e-mail protocols for its services and maintains logs you can examine and use in your investigation. As a computer forensics investigator, you can't know everything about e-mail servers. Your focus is not to learn how a particular e-mail server works but how to retrieve information about e-mails for an investigation. Usually, you must work closely with the network administrator or e-mail administrator, who is often willing to help you find the data or files you need and might even suggest new ways to find this information. If you can't work with an administrator, conduct research on the Internet or use the forensics tools discussed later in this chapter to investigate the e-mail server software and OS.

To investigate e-mail abuse, you should know how an e-mail server records and handles the e-mail it receives. Some e-mail servers use databases that store users' e-mails, and others use a flat file system. All e-mail servers can maintain a log of e-mails that are processed. Some e-mail servers are set up to log e-mail transactions by default; others must be configured to do so. Most e-mail administrators log system operations and message traffic to recover e-mails in case of a disaster, to make sure the firewall and e-mail filters are working correctly, and to enforce company policy.

However, the e-mail administrator can disable logging or use circular logging, which overwrites the log file when it reaches a specified size or at the end of a specified time frame. Circular logging saves valuable server space, but you can't recover a log after it's overwritten. For example, on Monday the e-mail server records traffic in the Mon.log file. For the next six days, the e-mail server uses a log for each day, such as Tues.log, Wed.log, and so forth. On Sunday at midnight, the e-mail server starts recording e-mail traffic in Mon.log, overwriting the information logged the previous Monday. The only way to access the log file information is from a backup file, which many e-mail administrators create before a log file is overwritten.

As shown in Figure 12-14, e-mail logs generally identify the e-mail messages an account received, the IP address from which they were sent, the time and date the e-mail server received them, the time and date the client computer accessed the e-mail, the e-mail contents, system-specific information, and any other information the e-mail administrator wants to track. These e-mail logs are usually formatted in plain text and can be read with a basic text editor, such as Notepad or vi.

```
Administrator@superiorbicycles.biz      -2010-10-16      09:44:22  GMT
10.0.1.205       pegasus.superiorbicycles.biz             PEGASUS   10.0.1.205

Jim.shu@superiorbicycles.biz    1019
5.2.0.9.0.20101016072308.00a543|44@pegasus.superiorbicycles.biz 0         0
407      1      2010-10-16  09:44:22  GMT
```

Figure 12-14 An e-mail server log file

Administrators usually set e-mail servers to continuous logging mode. They can also log all e-mail information in the same file, or use one log file to record, for example, date and time information, the size of the e-mail, and the IP address. These separate log files are extremely useful when you have an e-mail header with a date and time stamp and an IP address, and you want to filter or sort the log files to narrow your search.

After you have identified the source of the e-mail, contact the network or e-mail administrator of the suspect's network as soon as possible. Some e-mail providers, especially Internet e-mail providers, don't keep logs for a long time, and their logs might contain key information for your investigation.

In addition to logging e-mail traffic, e-mail servers maintain copies of clients' e-mail, even if the users have deleted messages from their inboxes. Some e-mail servers don't completely delete messages until the system is backed up. Even if the suspect deletes the e-mail, sometimes the e-mail administrator can recover the e-mail without restoring the entire e-mail system. With other systems, however, the e-mail administrator must recover the entire e-mail server to retrieve one deleted message.

This process is similar to deleting files on a hard drive; the file is marked for deletion, but it's not truly deleted until another piece of data is written in the same place. E-mail servers wait to overwrite disk space until the server has been backed up. If you have a date and time stamp for an e-mail, the e-mail administrator should be able to recover it from backup media if the message is no longer on the e-mail server.

Examining UNIX E-mail Server Logs

This section focuses on the log and configuration files that the Sendmail e-mail server creates by default. Other UNIX e-mail servers produce similar log files in similar locations.

The files that provide helpful information are log files and configuration files. Sendmail creates a number of files on the server to track and maintain the e-mail service. The first one to check is /etc/sendmail.cf, which contains configuration information for Sendmail, so you can determine where log files are stored. Sendmail refers to the sendmail.cf file to find out what to do with an e-mail after it's received. For example, if the server receives an e-mail from an unsolicited site, a line in the sendmail.cf file can tell the Sendmail server to discard it.

Similar to the sendmail.cf file, the syslogd file includes e-mail logging instructions. By viewing this file, you can determine how Sendmail is set up to log e-mail events and which events are logged. The syslogd file's configuration is located in /etc/syslog.conf, which contains three pieces of information that tell you what happened to an e-mail when it was logged: the event, the priority level of concern, and the action taken when it was logged. By default, Sendmail can display an event message, log the event message to a log file, or send an event message to a remote log host. Figure 12-15 shows a typical syslog.conf file. Note that the lines beginning with pound signs (#) are comments describing the commands' purpose.

```
# The following line will send all mail logs to the /var/log/maillog
directory
mail.*                           /var/log/maillog
# Log all emergency messages in the same place
*.emerg                          *
*.emerg                          @superiorbicycles.biz
# This line will put all news and e-mail encoded with uucp with
Critical errors in the #/var/log/spooler
uucp, news.crit
```

Figure 12-15 A typical syslog.conf file

The syslog.conf file simply specifies where to save different types of e-mail log files. The first log file it configures is /var/log/maillog, which usually contains a record of **Simple Mail Transfer Protocol (SMTP)** communication between servers. Figure 12-16 shows a sample of a log monitoring SMTP traffic.

```
May 21 10:10:32 poser sendmail[5365]: NOQUEUE: "wiz" command from
[10.0.1.1] (10.0.1.1)
May 21 10:10:32 poser sendmail[5365]: NOQUEUE: "debug" command from
[10.0.1.1] (10.0.1.1)
```

Figure 12-16 A maillog file with SMTP information

In Figure 12-16, the IP address (10.0.1.1) and the date and time stamp (May 21 10:10:34) in the maillog file are important information in an e-mail investigation. You can compare this information with the header of the e-mail the victim received to confirm the sender. The maillog file also contains information about **Post Office Protocol version 3 (POP3)** events. Figure 12-17 shows the first two lines of a POP3 event. This information includes an IP address and a date and time stamp that you can compare with the e-mail the victim received.

Typically, UNIX systems are set to store log files in the /var/log directory. However, an administrator can change the log location, especially when an e-mail service specifies a differ-

```
May 21 10:12:44 poser ipop3d[5373]: port 110 service init from 10.0.1.1
May 21 10:12:44 poser ipop3d[5373]: Login failure user=rich
host=[10.0.1.1]
```

Figure 12-17 A maillog file with POP3 information

ent location. If you're examining a UNIX computer and don't find the e-mail logs in /var/log, you can use the find or locate command to find them. For example, type "locate .log" at the UNIX command prompt.

The forward slash (/) is used in UNIX/Linux file paths, and the backslash (\) is used in Windows file paths.

If you need more assistance to find where a file is created by default, you can use the UNIX man pages for the e-mail service running on the computer. Be aware that a new directory—/home/*username*/mail—is created on the client computer when a user logs on for the first time and runs Pine or elm. If the server has been configured to deliver e-mail to client machines but not store copies of e-mails on the server, the only copy of the e-mail is on the client computer in the user's mail folder.

If the UNIX e-mail server is set to store all messages on the server, you can access them by requesting that the UNIX administrator create e-mail groups and add you to the same group as the suspect. UNIX e-mail servers don't usually use groups to prevent users from accidentally viewing e-mail that doesn't belong to them. However, e-mail groups can be useful for investigative purposes, as long as you have secured a warrant.

Examining Microsoft E-mail Server Logs

Exchange Server, generally called Exchange, is the Microsoft e-mail server software. Exchange uses a database and is based on the Microsoft Extensible Storage Engine (ESE), which uses several files in different combinations to provide e-mail service. The files most useful to an investigation are .edb and .stm database files, checkpoint files, and temporary files.

In older versions of Exchange, .edb files were the only database files associated with Exchange; newer versions use both the .edb file and the .stm database file. An .edb file is responsible for messages formatted with **Messaging Application Programming Interface (MAPI)**, a Microsoft system that enables different e-mail applications to work together. The .stm database file is responsible for messages that aren't formatted with MAPI properties. These two files constitute the Information Store, a storage area for e-mail messages.

As a database server, Exchange logs information about changes to its data, also called transactions, in a transaction log. To prevent loss of data from the most recent backup, a checkpoint file, or marker, is inserted in the transaction log to mark the last point at which the database was written to disk. With these files, e-mail administrators can recover lost or deleted messages in the event of a disaster, such as a power failure. Exchange also creates .tmp (temporary) files to prevent loss when it's busy converting binary data to readable text.

Like UNIX e-mail servers, Exchange maintains logs to track e-mails. If the Exchange log overflows, data is written to reserve log files, such as res1.log and res2.log. They're used to make sure the database can keep up with the changing environment without losing data. For more information, see *http://technet.microsoft.com/en-us/library/bb331951.aspx*, *http://technet.microsoft.com/en-us/library/bb124452.aspx*, and *http://support.microsoft.com/kb/240145*.

Exchange servers can also maintain a log called Tracking.log that tracks messages. If the Message Tracking feature has been enabled and the e-mail administrator selects verbose (detailed) logging, as shown in Figure 12-18, you can see the date and time stamp, IP address of the sending computer, and the e-mail's contents or body. Except for special forensics tools, the message tracking log in verbose mode provides the most information about messages sent and received in Exchange.

Figure 12-18   A message tracking log in verbose mode

Another log used for troubleshooting and investigating the Exchange environment is the troubleshooting log. You can read this log, also known as a diagnostic log, by using Windows Event Viewer, shown in Figure 12-19, which is available in Administrative Tools. Each event logged has an ID number with a severity level.

To examine the details of an e-mail event, double-click the event to open its Event Properties dialog box (see Figure 12-20). This dialog box provides date and time information, for example, that might be useful if you suspect the e-mail server has been tampered with to alter its contents.

Examining Novell GroupWise E-mail Logs

Novell NetWare's e-mail service, GroupWise, stores user messages in up to 25 proprietary databases. Each database is stored in the Ofuser directory object and referenced by a username followed by a unique identifier and the .db extension, such as JimShu020307.db. In addition, GroupWise uses the Ngwdfr.db database stored in the Ofmsg directory object for delayed or deferred e-mail delivery. This database is similar to how Exchange Server uses .tmp files.

Severity level   Event ID number

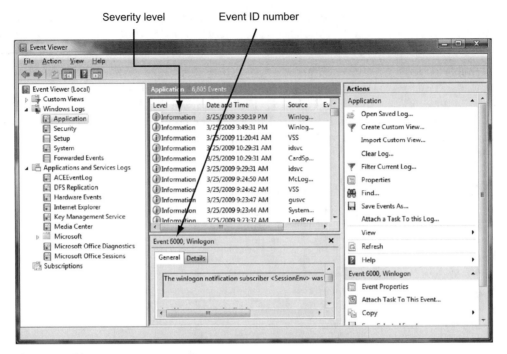

Figure 12-19   Viewing a log in Event Viewer

Figure 12-20   The Event Properties dialog box

 NetWare refers to all entries in its file structure, including directories and users, as "objects."

GroupWise shares resources with the e-mail server databases, as do Microsoft and UNIX e-mail servers. The first folder the GroupWise server shares is PU020101.db. If additional database folders are needed, GroupWise creates and names folders with incremented numbered values, such as PU020102.db for the second folder, PU020103.db for the third folder, and so on. For files that aren't shared by users, GroupWise creates a User.db file in the user's personal account. You can view the user's personal address book by accessing this file.

GroupWise has two ways of organizing mailboxes on the server that make recovering data easy. Permanent index files (.idx extension) that are updated and renamed at the end of every day keep mailboxes in order. Microsoft and UNIX can also sort mailboxes in order, but they don't use an index file to do so. The other method is GroupWise QuickFinder, which uses incremental indexing files to maintain changes to the e-mail server throughout the day, and then writes these changes to the .idx file at a scheduled time.

The GroupWise folder and file structure can be complex because of the Novell directory structure. A number of files are scattered throughout the post office directory, but a specialized database called Guardian, Ngwguard.db, maintains centralized control of the e-mail service and associated files. Guardian is a directory of every database in the GroupWise environment. As its name suggests, Guardian tracks changes in the GroupWise environment and clears any processes before they change a GroupWise database. It also includes other built-in safeguards against data loss. For example, Ngwguard.fbk, Ngwguard.rfl, and Ngwguard.db contain backup copies and log files from the Guardian database, which make it possible to track changes without affecting the server's performance. Although Guardian has these measures to protect e-mail server data, it's still considered a single point of failure. If it's erased or becomes corrupt, you must recover a previous version from a backup and begin your investigation again.

Similar to other e-mail servers, GroupWise generates log files (.log extension) maintained in a standard log format in GroupWise folders. You can use these logs to match an e-mail header with a suspect's IP address.

Using Specialized E-mail Forensics Tools

For many e-mail investigations, you can rely on e-mail message files, e-mail headers, and e-mail server log files. However, if you can't find an e-mail administrator willing to help with the investigation, or you encounter a highly customized e-mail environment, you can use data recovery tools and forensics tools designed to recover e-mail files.

As technology has progressed in e-mail and other services, so have the tools for recovering information lost or deleted from a hard drive. In previous chapters, you have reviewed many tools for data recovery, such as ProDiscover Basic and AccessData FTK. You can also use these tools to investigate and recover e-mail files. Other tools, such as the ones in the following list, are specifically created for e-mail recovery, including recovering deleted attachments from a hard drive:

- DataNumen for Outlook and Outlook Express (*www.datanumen.com/products.htm*)
- FINALeMAIL for Outlook Express and Eudora (*www.finaldata.us/products/products_finalemail.php*)
- Sawmill-GroupWise for log analysis (*www.sawmill.net/formats/groupwise_post_office_agent.html*)
- DBXtract for Outlook Express (*www.oehelp.com/DBXtract/Default.aspx*)

- Fookes Aid4Mail and MailBag Assistant for Outlook, Thunderbird, and Eudora (*www.fookes.com*)

- Paraben E-Mail Examiner, configured to recover several e-mail formats (*www.paraben-forensics.com/catalog/product_info.php?cPath=25&products_id=393*)

- AccessData FTK for Outlook and Outlook Express (*www.accessdata.com*)

- Ontrack Easy Recovery EmailRepair for Outlook and Outlook Express (*www.ontrackdatarecovery.com/email-recovery-software/*)

- R-Tools R-Mail for Outlook and Outlook Express (*www.outlook-mail-recovery.com*)

- OfficeRecovery's MailRecovery for Outlook, Outlook Express, Exchange, Exchange Server, and IBM LotusNotes (*www.officerecovery.com*)

When you use a third-party tool to search for a .db file, for example, you can find where the administrator stores .db files for the e-mail server. To find log files, use .log as the search criteria. You're likely to find at least two logs related to e-mail—one listing logged events for messages and the other listing logged events for accounts accessing e-mail.

FTK, EnCase, and other forensics tools enable you to find e-mail database files, personal e-mail files, offline storage files, and log files. Some tools allow you to view messages and other files with a special viewer; others require using a text editor to compare information, such as the date and time stamp, username, domain, and message contents, to determine whether it matches what was found on the victim's computer.

One advantage of using data recovery tools is that you don't need to know how the e-mail server or e-mail client operates to extract data from these computers. Data recovery tools do the work for you and allow you to view evidence on the computer.

After you compare e-mail logs with the messages, you should verify the e-mail account, message ID, IP address, and date and time stamp to determine whether there's enough evidence for a warrant. If so, you can obtain and serve your warrant for the suspect's computer equipment. Remember to follow the evidence-handling rules and control measures your organization uses, as described in previous chapters.

When requesting a search warrant, consider whether you're looking for evidence of more than one crime. If you intend to investigate different crimes, make sure to include probable cause for each crime so that you need only a single warrant covering all areas of interest. Your investigation might require a second warrant, however. For example, if you're investigating a drive for evidence of harassment and you come across e-mail suggesting that the suspect is also selling controlled substances over the Internet, you need a second warrant to investigate this crime.

After collecting evidence, you begin copying it to another source for the examination while documenting everything you're doing. If you create an image, document the procedure and tool you use. If you're just collecting a specific folder, such as the evolution directory in Novell, document the command you use to copy data. With a tool such as FINALeMAIL, you can scan e-mail database files on a suspect's Windows computer, locate any e-mails the suspect has deleted—these messages don't have data location information—and restore them to their original state. You can also search a computer for other files associated with e-mail, such as databases. Figure 12-21 shows two e-mail databases that FINALeMAIL found—one for Outlook Express and one for Eudora.

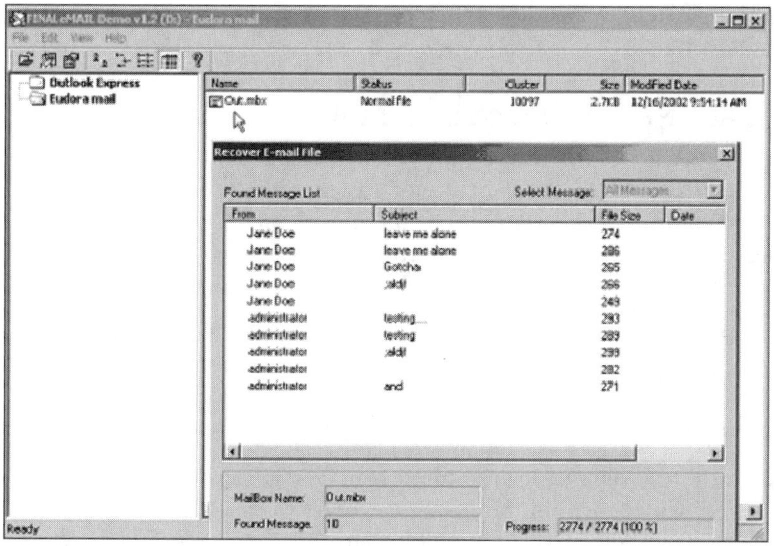

Figure 12-21   E-mail search results in FINALeMAIL

To examine the Eudora database, select it in the left pane, and then double-click Out.mbx in the right pane to open the Recover E-mail File dialog box. As shown in Figure 12-21, there are five Jane Doe messages and five administrator messages. To see the contents, shown in Figure 12-22, double-click the message. In this example, the e-mail's subject line and body

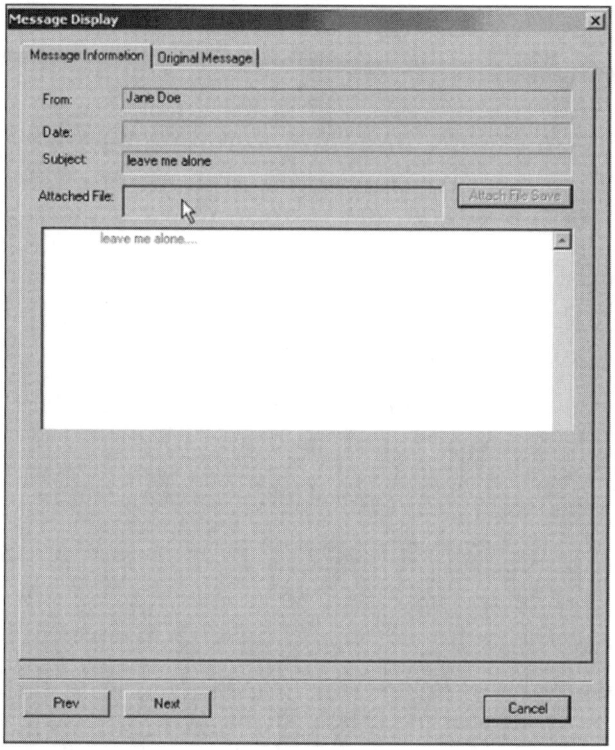

Figure 12-22   Viewing message contents in FINALeMAIL

are the same. FINALeMAIL also enables you to see whether any attachments were sent with the e-mail and view them.

Using AccessData FTK to Recover E-mail

AccessData FTK isn't task or file specific, as are other tools, such as FINALeMAIL. FTK can index data on a disk image or an entire drive for faster data retrieval. Like FINALeMAIL, FTK can filter or find files specific to e-mail clients and servers. You can configure these filters when you enter search parameters. In this section, you learn how to use FTK and a hexadecimal editor to recover e-mails.

To recover e-mail from Outlook and Outlook Express, AccessData integrated dtSearch (*www.dtsearch.com*) into FTK 1.x. dtSearch builds a B*-tree index of all text data in a drive, an image file, or a group of files. One unique feature is its capability to read .pst and .dbx files and index all text information, including attached files.

In this next activity, you're looking for an e-mail from Terry Sadler in the Jim_shu's.pst file. Because of Jim's responses to a poor performance review, the CEO of Superior Bicycles, Martha Dax, suspects he might have obtained sensitive information about the company's business model that he's leaking to a competitor. Martha asked her CIO, Bob Swartz, to have an IT employee copy the Outlook .pst file from Jim Shu's old computer to a USB drive. She gives you a printout of the message from Terry Sadler (see Figure 12-23) along with the USB drive.

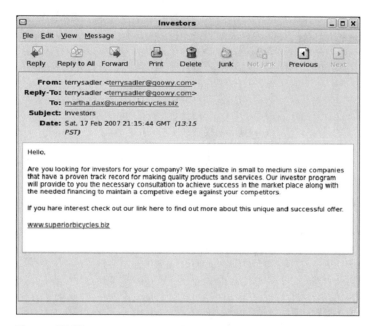

Figure 12-23   Message from Terry Sadler to Martha Dax

To process this investigation, you need to examine the Jim_shu's.pst file, locate the message, and export it for further analysis of its header to see how Jim might have received it. Follow these steps:

If you haven't already installed the demo version of FTK from the book's DVD, do that now. The demo version processes only up to 5000 records or items, including object files, links, duplicate files, or other Windows files. To process more than 5000 records, you need the full licensed version.

1. Start AccessData FTK by right-clicking the **AccessData FTK** desktop icon, clicking **Run as administrator,** and clicking **Continue** in the UAC message box (if you're using Vista). If you're prompted with a warning message and/or notification (see Figure 12-24), click **OK** as needed to continue. If asked whether you want to save the existing default case, click **Yes.**

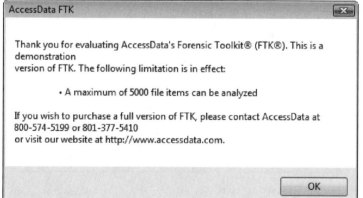

Figure 12-24   KFF warning and AccessData's evaluation notice

The full licensed version of AccessData FTK requires a USB dongle device that uses a special program, CodeMeter.exe. If FTK doesn't detect a licensed dongle, additional messages are displayed. This activity and others in this book work without a licensed dongle, however.

2. When the AccessData FTK Startup dialog box opens, click **Start a new case,** and then click **OK.**

3. In the New Case dialog box, type your name for the investigator name, and type **InChp12-pst** for the case number and case name. Click **Browse**, navigate to and click your work folder, click **OK**, and then click **Next**.

4. In the Case Information dialog box, enter your investigator information, and then click **Next**.

5. Click **Next** until you reach the Refine Case - Default dialog box, shown in Figure 12-25. Click the **Email Emphasis** button, and then click **Next**.

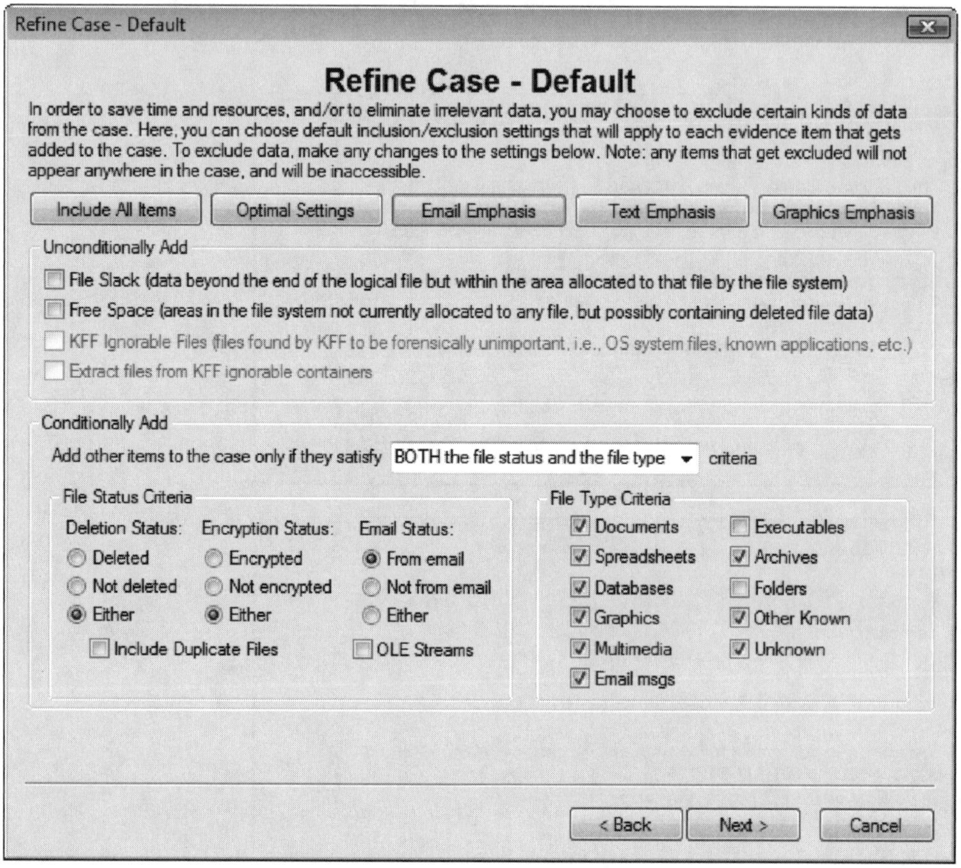

Figure 12-25 The Refine Case - Default dialog box

6. Click **Next** until you reach the Add Evidence to Case dialog box, and then click the **Add Evidence** button.

7. In the Add Evidence to Case dialog box, click the **Individual File** option button (see Figure 12-26), and then click **Continue**.

8. In the Select File dialog box, navigate to your work folder, click the **Jim_shu's.pst** file, and then click **Open**.

9. In the Evidence Information dialog box, click **OK**.

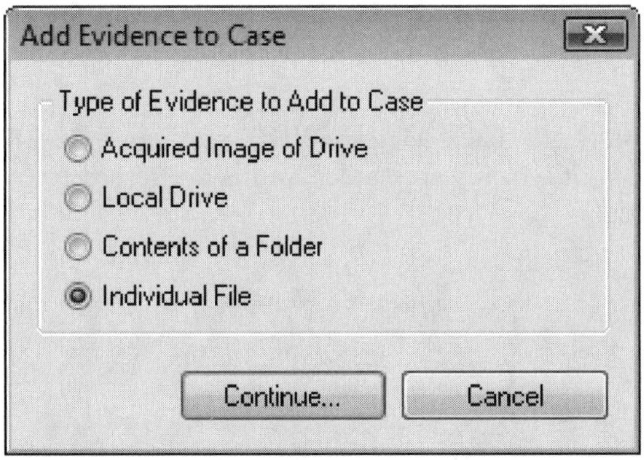

Figure 12-26 Selecting the option for a single file

10. When the Add Evidence to Case dialog box opens, click **Next**. In the Case summary dialog box, click **Finish**.

11. When FTK finishes processing the file, in the main FTK window, click the **E-mail Messages** button, and then click the **Full Path** column header to sort the records (see Figure 12-27).

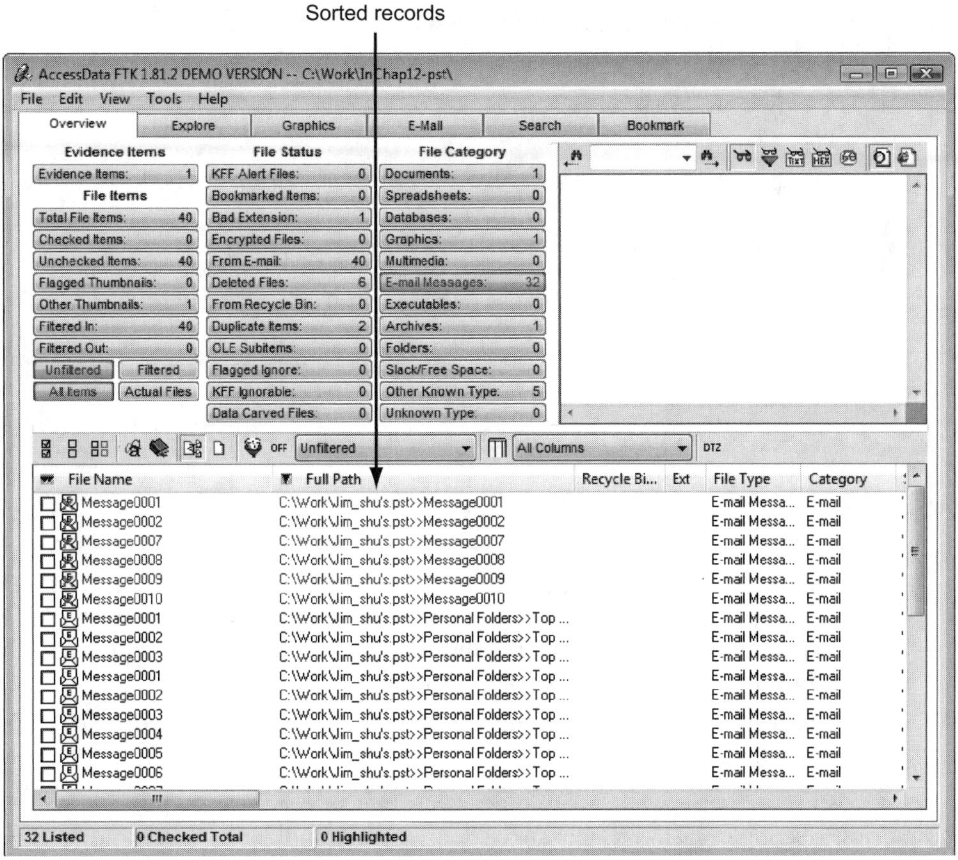

Sorted records

Figure 12-27 Records sorted by full path

12. Click the **E-Mail** tab. In the tree view, click to expand all folders, and then click the **Inbox** folder. If necessary, to view all messages, click the **List all descendants** check box.

13. In the File List pane at the upper right, click **Message0010** (see Figure 12-28); as shown in the pane at the bottom, it's from terrysadler and is addressed to martha.dax@superiorbicycles.biz.

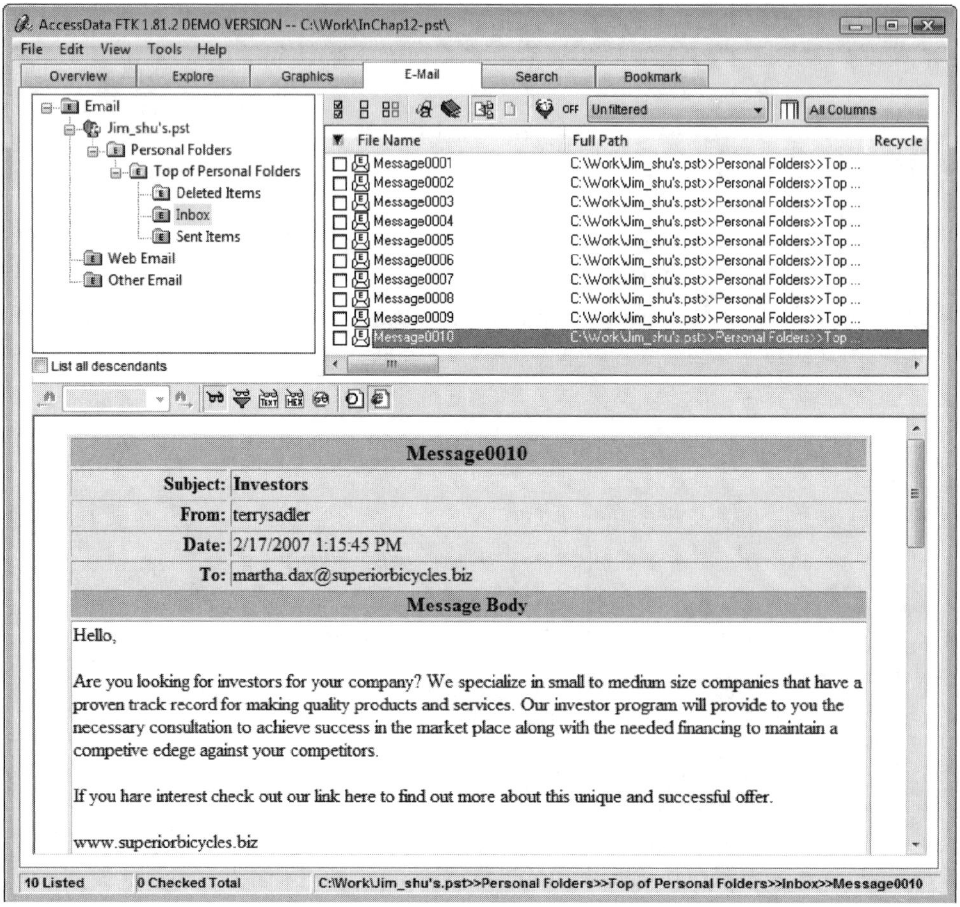

Figure 12-28 The E-Mail tab showing all messages

14. Right-click **Message0010** in the File List pane and click **Export File**. In the Export Files dialog box, click **OK**. If you get a message box about exporting files with a filter applied, click the **Do not remind me anymore** check box, and then click **OK**. Click **OK** again in the Export Files message box.

15. Click **File, Exit** from the menu, and then click **No** in the FTK Exit Backup Confirmation message box.

When you start a case in FTK, a subfolder is created under the case folder to store data. In the previous example, FTK created an InChap12-pst subfolder for this purpose. When you export a file, FTK creates an Export subfolder under this subfolder. So when you exported Message0010, it was saved to InChap12-pst\Export under your work folder. FTK saves exported files in the HTML format with no extension. To view the exported Message0010 file, follow these steps:

1. Open Windows Explorer and navigate to **InChap12-pst\Export** under your work folder.
2. Right-click the **Message0010** file and click **Rename**. Type **Message0010.html** and press **Enter**.
3. Double-click **Message0010.html** to view it in a Web browser.
4. Print this Web page and save it for further analysis. Exit your Web browser and Windows Explorer.

With the information you have found, you can analyze the message header content to see how it compares with other messages. In the next section, you learn how to extract e-mail messages from other types of e-mail clients that FTK can't read.

Using a Hexadecimal Editor to Carve E-mail Messages

Few vendors have products for analyzing e-mail in systems other than Microsoft, such as Apple Mail or Novell Evolution. In this section, you learn about a method for acquiring Evolution e-mail directories and extracting messages with Hex Workshop. These techniques can be used with all e-mail systems that create flat plaintext files, known as an **mbox** format, to store messages. Vendor-unique e-mail file systems, such as Microsoft .pst or .ost, typically use **Multipurpose Internet Mail Extensions (MIME)** formatting, which can be difficult to read with a text or hexadecimal editor.

To carve e-mail messages from Evolution, you need to copy the .evolution directory, its subdirectories, and content to another storage medium that can be transported to your forensic workstation. One way is to export the .evolution directory and subdirectories from an image file to a target directory by using a forensics tool, such as FTK, EnCase, X-Ways Forensics, or Sleuth Kit and Autopsy. These tools export the directory with all subdirectories to the target drive path you designate. For an e-mail recovery that requires extracting only e-mail data from a litigant's computer, the UNIX/Linux tar command is an easy tool to use. You can create a tarball of the entire .evolution directory and uncompress it so that a hexadecimal editor on any OS can read it.

For this case, you're acquiring the .evolution directory from Martha Dax's Linux computer to see whether you can find the same e-mail you found in the Jim_shu's.pst file. Then you compare the message headers of the two e-mails to detect any differences and perhaps discover e-mail addresses other than Terry Sadler's and Martha Dax's. To make a tarball of the .evolution directory, you would follow these steps:

 Because you don't have an .evolution directory on your system, just read through these steps as an example of extracting this file to a USB drive. In the next activity, you use a data file from the book's DVD.

1. Log on to your Linux computer and open a command shell. Type **su** and press **Enter**, and then type the password for root and press **Enter**.

2. Connect a USB drive to your computer and mount it.

3. Navigate to the user's home directory. For this example, you would type **cd /home/martha** and press **Enter**.

4. To determine whether the .evolution directory is in this location, type **ls -a** and press **Enter**. Examine the output. If you don't see an .evolution directory in the home directory, type **ls -aR** to list all subdirectories. When you have located the .evolution directory, use the **cd** command to navigate to the parent directory so that you can copy the .evolution directory and its subdirectories.

5. Type **tar cf martha-evolution.tar .evolution** and press **Enter**.

6. Using File Manager or another GUI directory utility, copy **martha-evolution.tar** to a USB drive, and then unmount and remove it.

7. Type **exit** and press **Enter**, and then log off your Linux computer.

All mbox-formatted messages start with the word "From" followed by a space (the character 0x20). To carve e-mail messages from martha-evolution.tar (which you copied from the DVD to your work folder earlier), follow these steps:

1. Start Hex Workshop. Click **File, Open** from the menu, navigate to your work folder, click **martha-evolution.tar**, and then click **Open**.

2. To locate the e-mail message from Terry Sadler, click **Edit, Find** from the menu. In the Find dialog box, click **Text String** in the Type drop-down list.

3. Type **terrysadler** in the Value text box, make sure the **ASCII String** option button is selected in the Options section, and then click **OK**.

4. Scroll up and place the cursor in front of the letter "F" in the word "From" in the right pane (see Figure 12-29). Notice the offset byte count 000710EF at the bottom.

5. Click at offset **000710EF** in the middle pane and drag down until you reach the end of the message, as shown in Figure 12-30. (Note that your screen might look a little different.)

The ending position of this message is at offset 000720F1. With mbox-formatted files, typically you find the end of the message at the next "From_" occurrence. Because this message is the last in the inbox, it terminates with "0A, 0A, 0A."

6. Right-click the highlighted text and click **Copy**, and then click **File, New** from the menu.

7. In the new Hex Workshop window, click **Edit, Paste** from the menu, and then click **Yes** in the warning message box. Click **File, Save As** from the menu, save the file as **terrysadler-martha-inbox.txt** in your work folder, and exit Hex Workshop.

8. Start Notepad and open the **terrysadler-martha-inbox.txt** file you just saved for reference in the next few paragraphs, and then exit Notepad when you've finished reading this section.

After carving an e-mail message from a tarball .evolution file, you have a plaintext file with no line breaks. The text pasted into Notepad wraps, making it difficult to find reference points (see Figure 12-31).

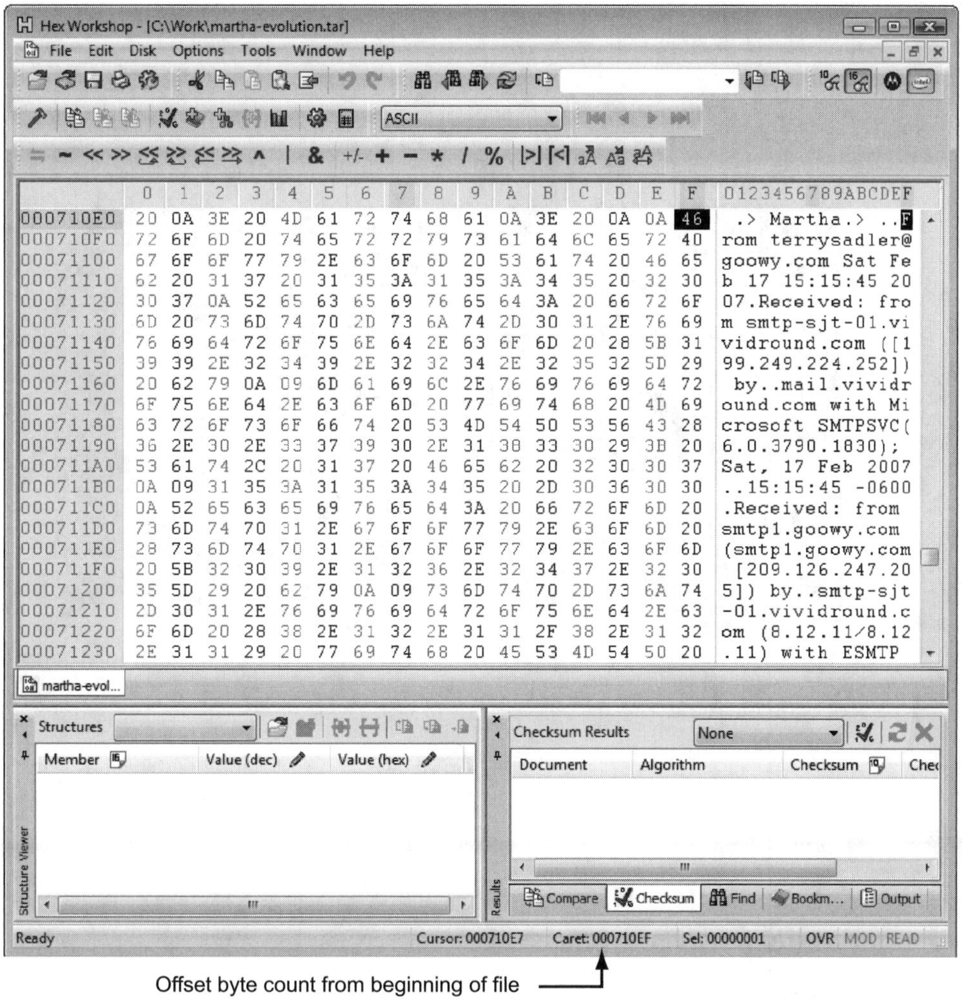

Offset byte count from beginning of file ——→

Figure 12-29 Hex Workshop displaying the beginning of the e-mail from Terry Sadler

To make this file's header and content readable, you need to enter line breaks at logical places, as shown in Figure 12-32, which can be tedious. The effort pays off, however, because you can find information of interest to your investigation more easily.

In Figure 12-32, you can see that the only e-mail addresses visible are *terrysadler@ goowy.com* and *martha.dax@superiorbicycles.biz*. In Figure 12-28, the same message was recovered from the Jim_shu's.pst file with FTK. Note that Jim Shu's e-mail address isn't listed in Figures 12-28, 12-31, or 12-32. By comparing these two messages from the Jim_shu's.pst file and Martha Dax's .evolution inbox, it seems that Terry Sadler had blind copied (Bcc) Jim Shu. This information might be of interest to Martha Dax because it shows that Jim Shu and Terry Sadler have some type of relationship involving a business proposal. By further examining Jim Shu's e-mail and other Superior Bicycles employees' e-mail, you might be able to

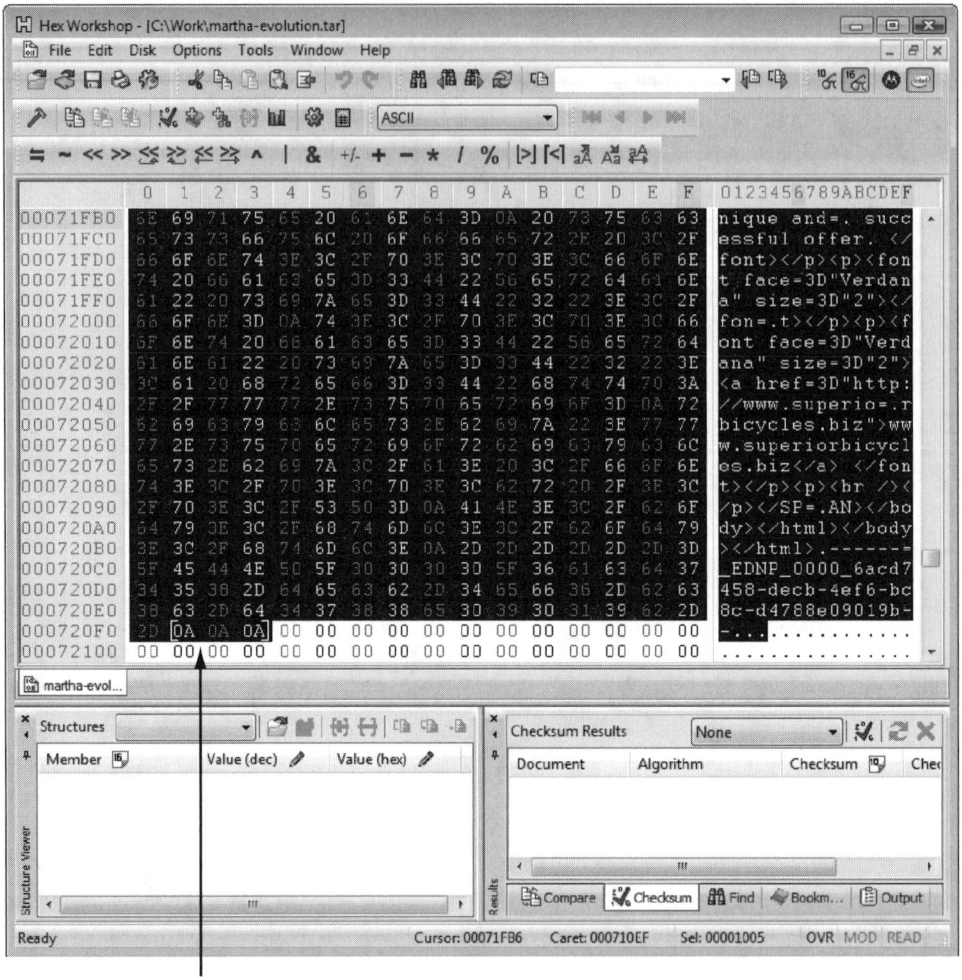

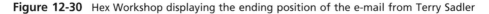

Ending position for this message

Figure 12-30 Hex Workshop displaying the ending position of the e-mail from Terry Sadler

learn what the relationship is and whether it should be of concern to Martha Dax and Superior Bicycles.

Recovering Outlook Files

As a computer forensics examiner recovering e-mail messages from Outlook, you might need to reconstruct .pst files and messages. With many advanced computer forensics tools, such as X-Ways Forensics, AccessData FTK, and Guidance Software EnCase, deleted .pst files can be partially or completely recovered. Typically, additional effort is required to reconstruct these recovered files so that their content can be extracted as part of a data recovery or forensics examination.

The Scanpst.exe recovery tool comes with Microsoft Office and can repair .ost files as well as .pst files. You can run this tool from Windows Explorer or a command prompt and use it

```
terrysadler-martha-inbox - Notepad                    □ ▣ ▨
File  Edit  Format  View  Help
From terrysadler@goowy.com Sat Feb 17 15:15:45 2007Received: from smtp-
sjt-01.vividround.com ([199.249.224.252]) by    mail.vividround.com with
Microsoft SMTPSVC(6.0.3790.1830); Sat, 17 Feb 2007     15:15:45 -0600
Received: from smtp1.goowy.com (smtp1.goowy.com [209.126.247.205]) by
smtp-sjt-01.vividround.com (8.12.11/8.12.11) with ESMTP id l1HLAcgD060105
for <martha.dax@superiorbicycles.biz>; Sat, 17 Feb 2007 15:10:38 -0600
(CST)Received: (qmail 2864 invoked from network); 17 Feb 2007 21:01:53 -
0000Received: by simscan 1.1.0 ppid: 2857, pid: 2859, t: 0.1710s
scanners:       attach: 1.1.0 clamav: 0.88.4/m:38/d:1506 spam: 3.1.2X-
Spam-Checker-Version: SpamAssassin 3.1.2 (2006-05-25) on smtp1.goowy.com
X-Spam-Level: X-Spam-Status: No, score=0.5 required=4.5
tests=ALL_TRUSTED,BIZ_TLD,      HTML_50_60,HTML_MESSAGE
autolearn=disabled version=3.1.2Received: from unknown (HELO
webserver002) ([192.168.25.102])       (envelope-sender
<terrysadler@goowy.com>) by smtp1.goowy.com     (qmail-ldap-1.03) with
SMTP for <martha.dax@superiorbicycles.biz>; 17 Feb    2007 21:01:53 -
0000goowy: id: : 520051From: terrysadler <terrysadler@goowy.com>Reply-To:
terrysadler@goowy.com>To: martha.dax@superiorbicycles.biz
Date: Sat, 17 Feb 2007 21:15:44 GMTMessage-ID:
<2af031584b5c460e95b36ddd6719529f@webserver002>Subject: InvestorsMIME-
Version: 1.0X-Mailer: goowy mail - http://www.goowy.comPriority: NormalX
-Priority: 3Content-Type: multipart/alternative; boundary="----
=_EDNP_0000_6acd7458-decb-4ef6-bc8c-d4788e09019b"X-ePrism-Trap: Default
TrapX-eGuard-Score: () 0.6 BIZ_TLD,HTML_50_60,HTML_MESSAGEX-Scanned-By:
ePrism email filtering appliance on 199.249.224.252Return-Path:
terrysadler@goowy.comX-OriginalArrivalTime: 17 Feb 2007 21:15:45.0640
(UTC)    FILETIME=[C9DBFE80:01C752D8]X-Evolution-Source:
pop://martha.dax@mail.superiorbicycles.biz/X-Evolution: 0000001a-0010This
is a multi-part message in MIME format.------=_EDNP_0000_6acd7458-decb-
4ef6-bc8c-d4788e09019bContent-Type: text/plain; charset="iso-8859-1"
Content-Transfer-Encoding: quoted-printable=0AHello, =0A=0AAre you
looking for investors for your company? We speci=alize in small to medium
size companies that have a proven track record= for making quality
```

Figure 12-31 Carved e-mail message in Notepad

with any data that looks like a .pst or .ost file. Scanpst.exe processes the data and rebuilds it into a .pst file that can be accessed with Outlook or other tools listed in this chapter.

TIP

For more information on Scanpst.exe, see *http://support.microsoft. com/kb/287497*, *www.outlook-tips.net/beginner/scanpst.htm*, *http:// office.microsoft.com/en-us/outlook/HA010563001033.aspx*, and *www. outlook-tips.net/howto/recover_deleted.htm*.

Guidance Software has developed an advanced carving technique used in EnCase to search a drive's (or a drive image's) unallocated space for Outlook data (also known as .pst files). With this technique, EnCase can identify data in unallocated disk space that might be fragments or complete .pst files that have been deleted. You can then extract and reconstruct .pst data in an effort to recover lost e-mail messages. For more information on recovering .pst data with EnCase, see *http://128.175.24.251/forensics/outlookcompencryptionsearch.htm*.

Several other recovery tools are designed to reconstruct e-mail data in Outlook and other e-mail formats. One tool that has been well tested is Advanced Outlook Repair from DataNumen, Inc. (*www.repair-outlook.com*); it's one of the better recovery tools on the market.

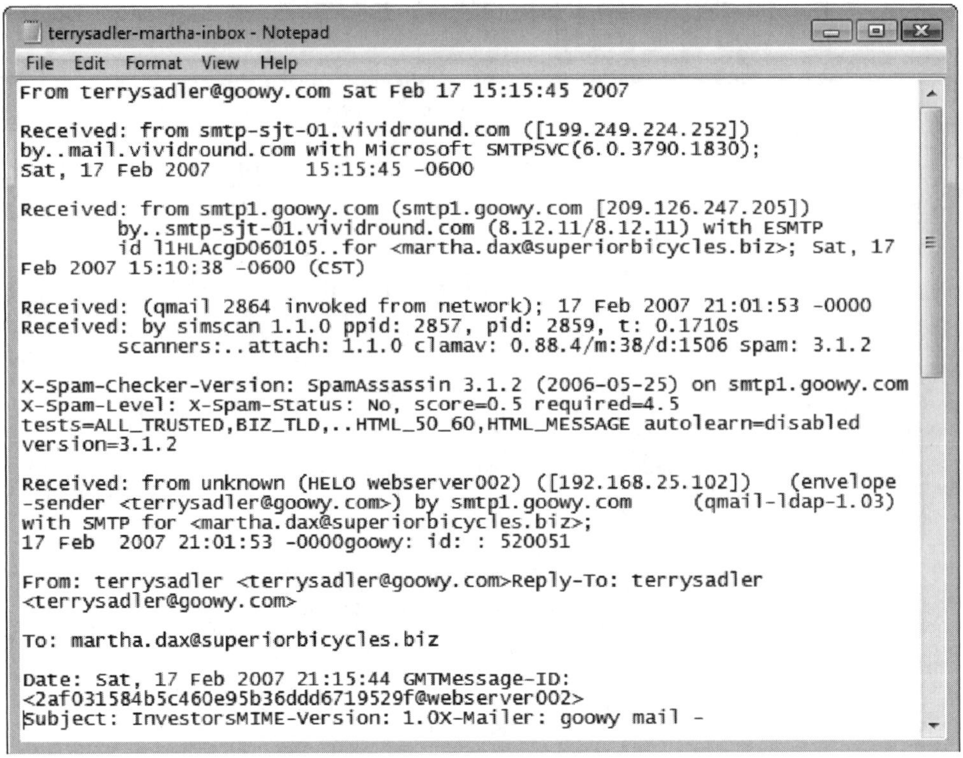

Figure 12-32 After formatting the e-mail message in Notepad

Chapter Summary

- E-mail fraudsters use phishing and spoofing scam techniques. Phishing e-mails typically have links to Web sites that look like legitimate businesses or official government Web sites and solicit personal identity information from victims.

- In both Internet and intranet e-mail environments, e-mail messages are distributed from one central server to connected client computers, a configuration called a client/server architecture. The server uses server e-mail software to provide e-mail services. Client computers use e-mail programs (also called e-mail clients) to contact the e-mail server and send and retrieve e-mails.

- Investigating crimes or policy violations involving e-mail is similar to investigating other types of computer abuse and crimes. Your goal is to find out who's behind the crime, collect the evidence, and build a case.

- After determining that a crime has been committed involving e-mail, access the victim's computer, if possible, and then use the installed e-mail program to find the e-mail the victim received. Next, copy and print the e-mail. You might also want to forward the message to another e-mail address, depending on your organization's guidelines.

- The next step is using the e-mail program that created the message to find the e-mail header, which provides supporting evidence and can help you track the suspect to the e-mail's originating location by finding the domain or IP address. Also helpful are the date and time the message was sent, the filenames of any attachments, and the unique ID number, if it's supplied. When you find the originating e-mail address, you can track the message to a suspect by doing reverse lookups.

- To investigate e-mail abuse, you should know how an e-mail server records and handles e-mail. Some e-mail servers use databases that store users' e-mails; others use a flat file system. E-mail servers also maintain a log (by default or through configuration settings) of all e-mails that are processed.

- For many e-mail investigations, you can rely on e-mail message files, e-mail headers, and e-mail server log files. However, if the e-mail administrator isn't willing to turn over records and files, or you encounter a highly customized e-mail environment, you can use data recovery tools and forensics tools designed to recover e-mail files.

- Currently, only a few forensics tools can recover deleted Outlook and Outlook Express messages. AccessData FTK, for example, uses dtSearch to analyze and create a B*-tree index of data, including e-mails and any attached files.

- For other e-mail applications that use the mbox format, a hexadecimal editor can be used to carve messages manually. This technique requires perseverance because it's tedious and time consuming.

- Advanced tools are available for recovering deleted Outlook files, such as Microsoft Scanpst.exe and Advanced Outlook Recovery from DataNumen.

Key Terms

client/server architecture A network architecture in which each computer or process on the network is a client or server. Clients request services from a server, and a server processes requests from clients.

Enhanced Simple Mail Transfer Protocol (ESMTP) An enhancement of SMTP for sending and receiving e-mail messages. ESMTP generates a unique, nonrepeatable number that's added to a transmitted e-mail. No two messages transmitted from an e-mail server have the same ESMTP value. *See also* Simple Mail Transfer Protocol (SMTP).

mbox A method of storing e-mail messages in a flat plaintext file.

Messaging Application Programming Interface (MAPI) The Microsoft system that enables other e-mail applications to work with each other.

Multipurpose Internet Mail Extensions (MIME) A specification for formatting non-ASCII messages, such as graphics, audio, and video, for transmission over the Internet.

phishing A type of e-mail scam that's typically sent as spam soliciting personal identity information that fraudsters can use for identity theft.

Post Office Protocol version 3 (POP3) A protocol for retrieving e-mail messages from an e-mail server.

Simple Mail Transfer Protocol (SMTP) A protocol for sending e-mail messages between servers.

spoofing Transmitting an e-mail message with its header information altered so that its point of origin appears to be from a different sender. Spoofed e-mails are also referred to as forged e-mail. Spoofing is typically used in phishing and spamming to hide the sender's identity.

Review Questions

1. E-mail headers contain which of the following information? (Choose all that apply.)

   a. The sender and receiver e-mail addresses

   b. An Enhanced Simple Mail Transfer Protocol (ESMTP) or reference number

   c. The e-mail servers the message traveled through to reach its destination

   d. The IP address of the receiving server

   e. All of the above

2. What's the main piece of information you look for in an e-mail message you're investigating?

   a. Sender or receiver's e-mail address

   b. Originating e-mail domain or IP address

   c. Subject line content

   d. Message number

   e. All of the above

3. In Microsoft Outlook, what are the e-mail storage files typically found on a client computer?

   a. .pst and .ost

   b. res1.log and res2.log

   c. PU020102.db

   d. .evolution

4. When searching a victim's computer for a crime committed with a specific e-mail, which of the following provides information for determining the e-mail's originator? (Choose all that apply.)

   a. E-mail header

   b. Username and password

   c. Firewall log

   d. All of the above

5. UNIX, NetWare, and Microsoft e-mail servers create specialized databases for every e-mail user. True or False?

6. Which of the following is a current formatting standard for e-mail?

   a. SMTP

   b. MIME

   c. Outlook

   d. HTML

7. All e-mail headers contain the same types of information. True or False?

8. When you access your e-mail, what type of computer architecture are you using?

    a. Mainframe and minicomputers

    b. Domain

    c. Client/server

    d. None of the above

9. To trace an IP address in an e-mail header, what type of lookup service can you use? (Choose all that apply.)

    a. AT&T AnyWho online directory

    b. Verizon's *superpages.com*

    c. A domain lookup service, such as *www.arin.net, www.internic.com*, or *www.whois.net*

    d. Any Web search engine

10. Router logs can be used to verify what types of e-mail data?

    a. Message content

    b. Content of attached files

    c. Tracking flows through e-mail server ports

    d. Finding blind copies

11. Logging options on many e-mail servers can be:

    a. Disabled by the administrator

    b. Set up in a circular logging configuration

    c. Configured to a specified size before being overwritten

    d. All of the above

12. In UNIX e-mail, the syslog.conf file contains what information?

    a. Logging instructions for the sendmail.cf file

    b. The event, the priority level of concern, and the action taken when an e-mail is logged

    c. SMTP executable code

    d. POP3 executable code

13. What information is *not* in an e-mail header? (Choose all that apply.)

    a. Blind copy (Bcc) addresses

    b. Internet addresses

    c. Domain name

    d. Contents of the message

    e. Type of e-mail server used to send the e-mail

12

14. Which of the following types of files can provide useful information when you're examining an e-mail server?

    a. .dbf files

    b. .emx files

    c. .log files

    d. .slf files

15. Internet e-mail accessed with a Web browser leaves files in temporary folders. True or False?

16. When confronted with an e-mail server that no longer contains a log with the date information you need for your investigation, and the client has deleted the e-mail, what should you do?

    a. Search available log files for any forwarded messages.

    b. Restore the e-mail server from a backup.

    c. Check the current database files for an existing copy of the e-mail.

    d. After it's deleted, the file can no longer be recovered.

17. You can view e-mail headers in all popular e-mail clients. True or False?

18. To analyze e-mail evidence, an investigator must be knowledgeable about an e-mail server's internal operations. True or False?

19. What is the e-mail storage format in Novell Evolution?

    a. MIME

    b. MAPI

    c. Mbox

    d. PDF

20. Sendmail uses which file for instructions on processing an e-mail message?

    a. Sendmail.cf

    b. Syslogd.conf

    c. Mese.ese

    d. Mapi.log

Hands-On Projects

Create a *Work*\Chap12\Projects folder on your system for this chapter's Hands-On Projects. The only data files you need for these projects are from the in-chapter activities.

Hands-On Project 12-1

For this project, start AccessData FTK and open the case file you created earlier in the chapter for the InChp12-pst case. You need to examine the

Jim_shu's.pst file for any messages referring to money. For this project, use FTK's Indexed Search function to look for keywords such as "money," "cash," and so forth.

If you locate messages containing any references to money, export each one into an HTML file in AccessData's Export subfolder, as described in the chapter. Then open each message in a Web browser and examine its header information to determine its actual source and sender.

When you have finished this examination, write a one-page report of your findings. Keep this session of FTK open for the next project.

Hands-On Project 12-2

This project is a continuation of Hands-On Project 12-1. You need to locate any messages with file attachments. Follow these steps:

1. If FTK isn't running, start it and open the case file from the InChp12-pst case.
2. If the Overview window isn't displayed, click the **Overview** tab.
3. Click the **From E-mail** button under the File Status column.
4. In the File List pane, click the **Full Path** column to sort all records by pathname.
5. Next, scroll through the File List pane and look at each message. When you have located messages with identical ID numbers, export each one to the AccessData Export subfolder.

> FTK displays attached messages with the same complete path and filename as the message it's attached to. It's also followed by >> and the attachment's filename.

6. Open Windows Explorer to examine the files (messages and attachments) you have exported. Write a one-page memo stating the contents of each message and the nature of each attachment. Print all attachments and include them with the memo, and then close Windows Explorer. Leave FTK running for the next project.

Hands-On Project 12-3

In this project, a continuation of the previous two projects, you locate and export all deleted messages that FTK locates in the Jim_shu's.pst file. Follow these steps:

1. If FTK isn't running, start it and open the case file from the InChp12-pst case.
2. If the Overview window isn't displayed, click the **Overview** tab.
3. Click the **Deleted Files** button under the File Status column.

4. In the File List pane, hold down **Ctrl** as you click each message to select them as a group. Then right-click the group of files, and export them to your work folder.

5. Open Windows Explorer to examine the files you have exported, and write a one-page memo describing what they contain. Close Windows Explorer, and leave FTK running for the next project.

Hands-On Project 12-4

The attorney assigned to this investigation has asked you to list all Internet addresses and e-mail addresses in the Jim_shu's.pst file. Follow these steps:

1. If FTK isn't running, start it and open the case file from the InChp12-pst case.

2. If the Overview window isn't displayed, click the **Overview** tab.

3. Click **Tools, Internet Keyword Search** from the menu. In the Internet Keyword Search Options dialog box, click **OK** to start the search.

4. In the search results, click the **Add List to Evidence** button.

5. Record the filename and path of the Web Scan *yyyymmdd-hhmmss*.htm file created from this search, and then click **OK** in the Evidence Added Successfully dialog box. Click **Close** in the Internet Address Search Results dialog box.

6. Exit FTK and open Windows Explorer. Navigate to the path where the Web Scan *yyyymmdd-hhmmss*.htm file was saved, such as C:*Work*\Chap12\Projects\InChap12-pst\Attach.

7. Double-click the **Web Scan *yyyymmdd-hhmmss*.htm** file to open it in your Web browser.

8. Print the Web Scan *yyyymmdd-hhmmss*.htm file, exit your browser and Windows Explorer, and submit the printout to your instructor.

Hands-On Project 12-5

The attorney for Superior Bicycles, Ileen Johnson, has asked you to examine Martha Dax's Evolution e-mail data for any messages referring to the words "special projects." To perform this task, you need Hex Workshop and the martha-evolution.tar file you used earlier in the chapter. Follow these steps:

If you didn't download and install Hex Workshop (*www.hexworkshop. com*) earlier in the book, do so before beginning this project.

1. Start Hex Workshop. Click **File, Open** from the menu, navigate to your work folder, and double-click **martha-evolution.tar**.

2. Click the **Find** toolbar button. In the Find dialog box, click the **Type** list arrow, and then click **Text String**. In the Value text box, type **special projects**, and then click **OK**.

3. In the main Hex Workshop window, scroll up until you find the first occurrence of **From:**. Click the letter **F**, and then drag down in the right pane, highlighting all text until you reach the next From: statement.

4. Right-click the text highlighted in the right pane and click **Copy**.

5. Start Notepad. Click **Edit, Paste** to copy the selected text into a new text document. Click **File, Save As** from the menu, save it as **Special-projects1.txt** in your work folder, and then click **Save**. Click **File, Print** from the menu to print this document. Close the file, and leave Notepad open.

6. Continue the search by clicking the **Find Again** toolbar button in Hex Workshop and repeat Steps 2 through 5 (without restarting Notepad).

7. Exit Hex Workshop and Notepad when you have finished your searches. Submit the recovered e-mail messages you printed to your instructor.

Case Projects

CASE PROJECTS

Case Project 12-1

You get a call from a high school student named Marco who claims he has just received an e-mail from another student threatening to commit suicide. Marco isn't sure where the student sent the e-mail from. Write a brief report on how you should proceed, including what you should do first in this situation.

Case Project 12-2

A mother calls you to report that her 15-year-old daughter has run away from home. She has access to her daughter's e-mail account and says her daughter has a number of e-mails in her inbox suggesting she has run away to be with a 35-year-old woman. Write a brief report on how you should proceed.

Case Project 12-3

The Research and Development Department of a large manufacturing firm contacts you to conduct an e-mail investigation, claiming that an employee is violating International Traffic in Arms Regulations (ITAR) by sending missile-guidance specifics to a party outside the continental United States. Write a brief report on how you should proceed.

Case Project 12-4

Billy Williams at the local city hall contacts your supervisor, Mike Mackenzie, with a complaint of sexual harassment that involves the city's e-mail system. You're assigned to find the suspect and build a case to terminate the city employee. When interviewing Billy, you discover he was involved with the sus-

12

pect, Mary Jane, but ended the relationship against Mary Jane's wishes. Both he and Mary Jane still work for the city. Billy has kept several e-mails from Mary Jane and offers them for your review. When you interview Mary Jane, she denies any wrongdoing and claims she is being set up. After your investigation, you confirm that the e-mails Billy submitted were falsified and Mary Jane was set up. Write a brief report on how your investigation would prove Mary Jane's innocence.

Cell Phone and Mobile Device Forensics

After reading this chapter and completing the exercises, you will be able to:

- Explain the basic concepts of mobile device forensics
- Describe procedures for acquiring data from cell phones and mobile devices

This chapter explains how to retrieve information from a cell phone or mobile device. Although some freeware is used in projects, much of the software discussed in this chapter is expensive and not provided on the book's DVD. Check with your instructor to see whether any is available at your facility.

Cell phone and mobile device forensics is a rapidly changing field that poses challenges in trying to retrieve information. Unlike what you might see in television shows, you don't just start scrolling through contact lists or most recent calls. As with all digital investigations, you need to follow forensics procedures, as described in this chapter.

Understanding Mobile Device Forensics

People store a wealth of information on cell phones, and the thought of losing your cell phone and, therefore, the information stored on it can be a frightening prospect. Despite this concern, not many people think about securing their cell phones, although they routinely lock and secure laptops or desktops. Depending on your phone's model, the following items might be stored on it:

- Incoming, outgoing, and missed calls
- Text and Short Message Service (SMS) messages
- E-mail
- Instant messaging (IM) logs
- Web pages
- Pictures
- Personal calendars
- Address books
- Music files
- Voice recordings

Many people store more information on their cell phones than they do on their computers, and with this variety of information, piecing together the facts of a case is possible. Recent cases, such as the rape allegations at Duke University and the Scott Peterson murder trial, show that cell phone data is used increasingly in court as evidence. (For more information, see *www.time.com/time/health/article/0,8599,1653267,00.html.*) In some countries, cell phones are even used to log in to bank accounts and transfer funds from one cell phone to another, which provides even more potential evidence. This handheld device is one of the most versatile pieces of equipment invented yet.

Despite the usefulness of these devices in providing clues for investigations, investigating cell phones and mobile devices is one of the most challenging tasks in digital forensics. No single standard exists for how and where cell phones store messages, although many phones use similar storage schemes. In addition, new phones come out about every six months, and they're rarely compatible with previous models. Therefore, the cables and accessories you have might become obsolete in a short time. Also, cell phones are often combined with PDAs, which can make forensics investigations more complex.

Mobile Phone Basics

Since the 1970s, when Motorola introduced cell phones, mobile phone technology has advanced rapidly. Gone are the days of two-pound cell phones that only the wealthy could afford. In the past 40 years, mobile phone technology has developed far beyond what the inventors could have imagined.

Up to the end of 2008, there have been three generations of mobile phones: analog, digital personal communications service (PCS), and **third-generation** (3G). 3G offers increased bandwidth, compared with the other technologies:

- 384 Kbps for pedestrian use
- 128 Kbps in a moving vehicle
- 2 Mbps in fixed locations, such as office buildings

 The use of 3G phones for illicit activities—such as identity theft, child pornography, and bank fraud—is expected to rise quickly, given 3G's rapid adoption around the world. For example, according to market research firm In-Stat, 92% of the phones sold in Japan in 2006 were 3G phones (*www.instat.com/press.asp?Sku=IN0703679AW&ID=2040*). In addition, Deutsche Bank Research predicts that 3G will have more than 60% market penetration in Western Europe by 2010 (*www.dbresearch.com*).

Sprint Nextel introduced the **fourth-generation** (4G) network in 2009, and other major carriers, such as AT&T, are expected to follow suit between now and 2012. Several technologies can be used for 4G networks and are discussed later in this section.

Many digital networks are used in the mobile phone industry, and Table 13-1 lists the main ones. Much of this table is taken from the National Institute of Standards and Technology (NIST) document "Guidelines on Cell Phone Forensics" (Special Publication [SP] 800-101, May 2007; *http://csrc.nist.gov/publications/nistpubs/800-101/SP800-101.pdf*). You can download this document to learn more.

13

Table 13-1 Digital networks

Digital network	Description
Code Division Multiple Access (CDMA)	Developed during WWII, this technology was patented by Qualcomm after the war. One of the most common digital networks, it uses the full radio frequency spectrum to define channels. Sprint and Verizon, for example, use CDMA networks.
Global System for Mobile Communications (GSM)	Another common digital network, it's used by AT&T and T-Mobile and is the standard in Europe and Asia.
Time Division Multiple Access (TDMA)	This digital network uses the technique of dividing a radio frequency into time slots; GSM networks use this technique. It also refers to a specific cellular network standard covered by Interim Standard (IS) 136.
Integrated Digital Enhanced Network (iDEN)	This Motorola protocol combines several services, including data transmission, into one network.

Table 13-1 Digital networks (*continued*)

Digital network	Description
Digital Advanced Mobile Phone Service (D-AMPS)	This network is a digital version of the original analog standard for cell phones.
Enhanced Data GSM Environment (EDGE)	This digital network, a faster version of GSM, is designed to deliver data.
Orthogonal Frequency Division Multiplexing (OFDM)	This technology for 4G networks uses energy more efficiently than 3G networks and is more immune to interference.

Most **Code Division Multiple Access (CDMA)** networks conform to IS-95, created by the **Telecommunications Industry Association (TIA)**. These systems are referred to as cdmaOne, and as they go to 3G services, they will become cdma2000.

Global System for Mobile Communications (GSM) uses the **Time Division Multiple Access (TDMA)** technique, so multiple phones take turns sharing a channel, much like token ring networks. As noted in Table 13-1, TDMA also refers to the IS-136 standard, which introduced sleep mode to enhance battery life. TDMA can operate in the cell phone (800 to 1000 MHz) or PCS (1900 MHz) frequency, so it's compatible with several cell phone networks.

The 3G standard was developed by the **International Telecommunication Union (ITU)** under the United Nations. It's compatible with CDMA, GSM, and TDMA. The **Enhanced Data GSM Environment (EDGE)** standard was developed specifically for 3G.

 Typically, phones developed for use on a GSM network aren't compatible with phones designed for a CDMA network. Until recently, users who traveled frequently between the United States and Europe needed separate phones for each place. Even today, many carriers charge a roaming fee for using your phone outside its primary country.

4G networks can use the following technologies:

- *Orthogonal Frequency Division Multiplexing (OFDM)*—The **Orthogonal Frequency Division Multiplexing (OFDM)** technology uses radio waves broadcast over different frequencies, uses power more efficiently, and is more immune to interference ("What You Need to Know About 4G," *www.networkworld.com/news/2007/052107-special-focus-4g.html*).

- *Mobile WiMAX*—This technology uses the IEEE 802.16e standard and Orthogonal Frequency Division Multiple Access (OFDMA) and is expected to support transmission speeds of 12Mbps. Sprint has chosen this technology for its 4G network, although some argue it's not true 4G.

- *Ultra Mobile Broadband (UTMS)*—Also known as CDMA2000 EV-DO, this technology is expected to be used by CDMA network providers to switch to 4G and support transmission speeds of 100 Mbps.

- *Multiple Input Multiple Output (MIMO)*—This technology, developed by Airgo and acquired by Qualcomm, is expected to support transmission speeds of 312 Mbps.

- *Long Term Evolution (LTE)*—This technology, designed for GSM and UMTS technology, is expected to support 45 Mbps to 144 Mbps transmission speeds.

Many of these technologies are still in testing phases but with further development should enhance existing 3G networks. As an investigator, you should research them to make sure you stay up to date. So far, the only standard for 4G is IEEE 802.16e for Mobile WiMAX. An actual 4G standard isn't expected for several years.

Although digital networks use different technologies, they operate on the same basic principles. Basically, geographical areas are divided into cells resembling honeycombs. As described in NIST SP 800-101 (mentioned earlier in this section), three main components are used for communication with these cells:

- *Base transceiver station (BTS)*—This component is made up of radio transceiver equipment that defines cells and communicates with mobile phones; it's sometimes referred to as a cell phone tower, although the tower is only one part of the BTS equipment.

- *Base station controller (BSC)*—This combination of hardware and software manages BTSs and assigns channels by connecting to the mobile switching center.

- *Mobile switching center (MSC)*—This component connects calls by routing digital packets for the network and relies on a database to support subscribers. This central database contains account data, location data, and other key information needed during an investigation. If you have to retrieve information from a carrier's central database, you usually need a warrant or subpoena.

Inside Mobile Devices

Mobile devices can range from simple phones to small computers, also called **smart phones**. The hardware consists of a microprocessor, ROM, RAM, a digital signal processor, a radio module, a microphone and speaker, hardware interfaces (such as keypads, cameras, and GPS devices), and an LCD display. Many have removable memory cards, and Bluetooth and Wi-Fi are now included in some mobile devices, too.

Most basic phones have a proprietary OS, although smart phones use the same OSs as PCs (or stripped-down versions of them). These OSs include Linux, Windows Mobile, RIM OS, Palm OS, Symbian OS, and, with the introduction of the Apple iPhone, a version of Mac OS X. Typically, phones store system data in **electronically erasable programmable read-only memory (EEPROM)**, which enables service providers to reprogram phones without having to access memory chips physically. Many users take advantage of this capability by reprogramming their phones to add features or switch to different service providers. Although this reprogramming isn't supported officially by service providers, instructions on how to do so are readily available on the Internet.

The OS is stored in ROM, which is nonvolatile memory, so along with other items, it's available even if the phone loses power. Acquiring data from ROM is covered in more detail later in "Understanding Acquisition Procedures for Cell Phones and Mobile Devices."

SIM Cards Subscriber identity module (SIM) cards are found most commonly in GSM devices and consist of a microprocessor and 16 KB to 4 MB EEPROM. There are also high-capacity, high-density, super, and mega SIM cards that boast as high as 1 GB EEPROM. SIM cards are similar to standard memory cards, except the connectors are aligned differently. To find the SIM card, pop open the panel covering the battery. You usually need to take the battery out to get to the SIM card underneath it.

13

GSM refers to mobile phones as "mobile stations" and divides a station into two parts: the SIM card and the mobile equipment (ME), which is the remainder of the phone. The SIM card is necessary for the ME to work and serves these additional purposes:

- Identifies the subscriber to the network
- Stores personal information
- Stores address books and messages
- Stores service-related information

SIM cards come in two sizes, but the most common is the size of a standard U.S. postage stamp and about 0.75 mm thick. Portability of information is what makes SIM cards so versatile. By switching a SIM card between compatible phones, users can move their information to another phone automatically without having to notify the service provider. For example, if you travel between neighboring countries often, you could have a GSM phone and two SIM cards. When you travel to another country, you simply switch to the other SIM card. Another common practice is switching to another SIM card when you have used most of your monthly minutes on your main SIM card.

Older CDMA phones don't use SIM cards; they incorporate the card's functions into the phone. Newer TDMA phones in North America do use SIM cards, however, and they are sealed so that users must contact the service provider when changing phones or providers.

Inside PDAs

Personal digital assistants (PDAs) can still be found as separate devices from mobile phones. Most users carry them instead of a laptop to keep track of appointments, deadlines, address books, and so forth. Palm Pilot and Microsoft Pocket PC were popular models when PDAs came on the market in the 1990s, and standalone PDAs are still made by companies such as Palm, Sharp, and HP. However, because cellular connectivity is becoming so widespread and is often an expected feature in recent PDAs, the number of PDAs that don't have integrated phones is likely to decrease steadily. Similar to smart phones, PDAs house a microprocessor, flash ROM, RAM, and various hardware components. As with smart phones, the amount of information on a PDA varies depending on the model. Usually, you can retrieve a user's calendar, address book, Web access, and other items.

A number of peripheral memory cards are used with PDAs:

- *Compact Flash (CF)*—CF cards are used for extra storage and work much the same way as PCMCIA cards.
- *MultiMedia Card (MMC)*—MMC cards are designed for mobile phones, but they can be used with PDAs to provide another storage area.
- *Secure Digital (SD)*—SD cards are similar to MMCs but have added security features to protect data.

Most PDAs are designed to synchronize with a computer, so they have built-in slots for that purpose (whether hard-wired or wireless synchronization). The importance of this feature is discussed in the following section.

Understanding Acquisition Procedures for Cell Phones and Mobile Devices

Proper search and seizure procedures for cell phones and mobile devices are as important as procedures for computers. The main concerns with mobile devices are loss of power and synchronization with PCs.

All mobile devices have volatile memory, so making sure they don't lose power before you can retrieve RAM data is critical. At the investigation scene, determine whether the device is on or off. If it's off, leave it off, but find the recharger and attach it as soon as possible. Note this step in your log if you can't determine whether the device was charged at the time of seizure. If the device is on, check the LCD display for the battery's current charge level.

Because mobile devices are often designed to synchronize with applications on a user's PC, any mobile device attached to a PC via a cable or cradle/docking station should be disconnected from the PC immediately. This precaution helps prevent synchronization that might occur automatically on a preset schedule and overwrite data on the device. In addition, collect the PC and any peripheral devices to determine whether the hard drive contains any information that's not on the mobile device.

Depending on the warrant or subpoena, the time of seizure might be relevant. In addition, messages might be received on the mobile device after seizure that may or may not be admissible in court. If you determine that the device should be turned off to preserve battery power or a possible attack, note the time and date at which you take this step. The alternative is to isolate the device from incoming signals with one of the following options:

- Place the device in a paint can, preferably one that previously contained radio wave–blocking paint.
- Use the Paraben Wireless StrongHold Bag (*www.paraben-forensics.com/catalog*), which conforms to Faraday wire cage standards.
- Use eight layers of antistatic bags (for example, the bags that new hard drives are wrapped in) to block the signal.

The drawback of using these isolating options is that the mobile device is put into roaming mode, which accelerates battery drainage. NIST suggests supplying a portable means of power, such as a battery-powered charger, to prevent this problem. Newer mobile devices shut themselves off or enter a "sleep state" after reaching a certain low battery level.

 Make sure you handle all components with care and protect them from environmental factors and sources of electromagnetic interference (EMI).

When you're back in the forensics lab, you need to assess what can be retrieved. Knowing where information is stored is critical. You should check these four areas:

- The internal memory
- The SIM card
- Any removable or external memory cards
- The system server

13

Because of wiretap laws, checking system servers requires a search warrant or subpoena, so you need one if you want to check voicemail, for example. (Note that some newer phones and phone plans store voicemail on the phone.) You might also need information from the service provider to ascertain where the suspect or victim was at the time of a call, to access backups of address books, and more.

Memory storage on a mobile device is usually implemented as a combination of volatile and nonvolatile memory. Volatile memory requires power to maintain its contents, but nonvolatile memory does not. Although the specific locations of data vary from one phone model to the next, volatile memory usually contains data that changes frequently, such as missed calls, text messages, and sometimes even user files. Nonvolatile memory, on the other hand, contains OS files and stored user data, such as a personal information manager (PIM) and backed-up files.

As mentioned, memory resides in the phone itself and in the SIM card, if the device is equipped with one. The file system for a SIM card is a hierarchical structure (see Figure 13-1). This file structure begins with the root of the system (MF). The next level consists of directory files (DF), and under them are files containing elementary data (EF). In Figure 13-1, the EFs under the GSM and DCS1800 DFs contain network data on different frequency bands of operation. The EFs under the Telecom DF contain service-related data.

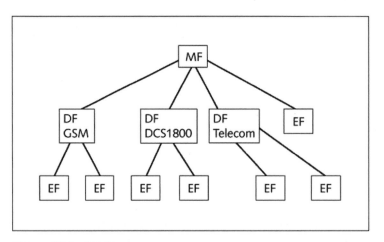

Figure 13-1 SIM file structure

You can retrieve quite a bit of data from a SIM card. The information that can be retrieved falls into four categories:

- Service-related data, such as identifiers for the SIM card and subscriber
- Call data, such as numbers dialed
- Message information
- Location information

If power has been lost, you might need PINs or other access codes to view files. Typically, users keep the original PIN assigned to the SIM card, so when you're collecting evidence at the scene, look for users' manuals and other documentation that can help you access the SIM card. With most SIM cards, you have three attempts at entering an access code before the device is locked, which then requires calling the service provider or waiting a certain amount of time before trying again. Common codes to try are 1-1-1-1 or 1-2-3-4.

Mobile Forensics Equipment

Mobile forensics is such a new science that many of the items you're accustomed to retrieving from computers, such as deleted files, aren't available on mobile devices. The biggest challenge is dealing with constantly changing models of cell phones. What works today might not work on a model that comes out tomorrow. This section gives you an overview of procedures for working with mobile forensics software, and specific tools are discussed in the following sections. Remember that when you're acquiring evidence, generally you're performing two tasks: acting as though you're a PC synchronizing with the device (to download data) and reading the SIM card.

The first step is identifying the mobile device. Most users don't alter their devices, but some file off serial numbers, change the display to show misleading data, and so on. When attempting to identify a phone, you can make use of several online sources, such as *www.cellphoneshop.com*, *www.phonescoop.com*, and *www.mobileforensicscentral.com*.

Make sure you have installed the mobile device software on your forensic workstation. As mentioned, not all facilities are equipped with the necessary software because many tools are cost prohibitive. Some vendors offer tools that simply take pictures of screens as you scroll through them. Forensically, this approach isn't the best, but you can use it if no other alternatives are available.

The next step is to attach the phone to its power supply and connect the correct cables. Often you have to rig cables to connect to devices because cables for the model you're investigating are not available. U.S. companies usually don't supply cables for phones not commonly used in the United States, but the reverse is true for companies based in Europe. Some vendors have toolkits with an array of cables you can use (discussed later in "Mobile Forensics Tools").

After you've connected the device, start the forensics program and begin downloading the available information. If your forensics software doesn't support the model you're investigating, you might need to look into acquiring other tools. Your main concern should be that the software is forensically sound.

13

SIM Card Readers With GSM phones and many newer models of mobile devices, the next step is accessing the SIM card, which you can do by using a combination hardware/software device called a SIM card reader. To use this device, you should be in a forensics lab equipped with antistatic devices. In addition, biological agents, such as fingerprints, might be present on the inside of the case, so you should consult the lead investigator when you're ready to proceed to this step. The general procedure is as follows:

1. Remove the back panel of the device.
2. Remove the battery.
3. Under the battery, remove the SIM card from its holder.
4. Insert the SIM card into the card reader, which you insert into your forensic workstation's USB port.

A variety of SIM card readers are on the market. Some are forensically sound and some are not; make sure you note this feature of the device in your investigation log. Another problem with SIM card readers is dealing with text and SMS messages that haven't been read yet. After you view a message, the device shows the message as opened or read. For this reason, documenting messages that haven't been read is critical. Using a tool that takes pictures of each screen can be valuable in this situation. These screen captures can provide additional documentation.

 Keep in mind that many SIM card readers for cell phones can't read BlackBerries. You need to determine whether your lab or company investigates BlackBerries often enough to justify purchasing special software for this purpose.

iPhone Forensics Because the iPhone is so popular, its features are copied in many other mobile devices. The wealth of information that can be stored on this device makes iPhone forensics particularly challenging. At first, many researchers and hackers tried to find a way to "crack" the iPhone but were unsuccessful because the device is practically impenetrable. A more fruitful approach was hacking backup files. However, this method does have limitations: You can access *only* files included in a standard backup, so deleted files, for example, can't be accessed.

The best method, of course, is acquiring a forensic image, which enables you to recover deleted text messages and similar data. iPhone acquisition procedures are, in general, similar to procedures for other mobile devices. You should acquire data directly from the iPhone instead of the host device it's synced with; however, you should also acquire a forensic image of the device's data. A recent white paper on iPhone forensics goes into more detail on examination and acquisition procedures ("iPhone Forensics—Annual Report on iPhone Forensic Industry," March 2, 2009, Andrew Hoog; download available by registering at *http://chicago-ediscovery.com*). To acquire a forensic image, this report recommends the following tools geared to iPhones or the Mac OS:

- MacLockPick II (*www.macforensicslab.com/ProductsAndServices/index.php?main_page=product_info&cPath=12&products_id=2*)—This tool uses backup files, such as MDBackup, stored by iPhones. So although it can recover quite a bit of data, it can't recover deleted files, for example.
- MDBackUp Extract (*www.blackbagtech.com*)—This tool, developed by Black Bag Technologies, a leader in Macintosh forensic tools, analyzes the iTunes mobile sync backup directory. As of this writing, it's in beta form.

Mobile Forensics Tools Paraben Software (*www.paraben.com*), a leader in mobile forensics software, offers several tools, including Device Seizure, used to acquire data from a variety of phone models. Paraben also has the Device Seizure Toolbox containing assorted cables, a SIM card reader, and other equipment for mobile device investigations. DataPilot (*www.datapilot.com*) has a similar collection of cables that can interface with Nokia, Motorola, Ericsson, Samsung, Audiovox, Sanyo, and others.

Another popular tool is BitPim (*www.bitpim.org*), used to view data on many CDMA phones, including LG, Samsung, Sanyo, and others. It offers versions for Windows, Linux, and Mac OS X. It's not a forensics tool, however, so you should note this fact in your investigation log. BitPim stores files in My Documents\BitPim by default, so when you start a new case, make sure you move these files to another location first so that they're not overwritten. A new tool, BitPim Cleaner by Mobile Forensics, Inc. (MFI, *http://mobileforensicsinc. com/store_files/Products.htm*), moves these files for you. MFI is a new vendor of mobile forensics software and offers several affordable products as well as training. Another new vendor, Susteen Inc. (*www.mobileforensics.com/Products/Secure-View-for-Forensics.php*) claims to be FBI approved.

Keep in mind that you should validate any new tool and verify its claims with rigorous testing.

Cellebrite UFED Forensic System (*www.cellebrite.com/UFED-Standard-Kit.html*) works with cell phones and PDAs. This kit comes with several cables, includes handset support for phones from outside the United States, and handles multiple languages.

MOBILedit! (*www.mobiledit.com*) is a forensics software tool containing a built-in write-blocker. It can connect to phones directly via Bluetooth, irDA, or a cable and can read SIM cards by using a SIM reader. It's also notable for being very user friendly.

Another tool is SIMCon (*www.simcon.no*), used to image files on a GSM/3G SIM or USIM card, including stored numbers and text messages. SIMCon's features include the following:

- Reads files on SIM cards
- Analyzes file content, including text messages and stored numbers
- Recovers deleted text messages
- Manages PIN codes
- Generates reports that can be used as evidence
- Archives files with MD5 and SHA-1 hash values
- Exports data to files that can be used in spreadsheet programs
- Supports international character sets

In the Superior Bicycles case used throughout this book, Sebastian Mwangonde and Nau Tjeriko are known as close friends. Nau is a nurse who provides ergonomic specifications to Superior Bicycles, and Sebastian is an employee of the company; both are suspected of drug dealing. In addition to all the computer evidence collected so far, their cell phones have been seized during the investigation. You can use SIMCon to see the file structure of Sebastian's SIM card (see Figure 13-2). Figure 13-3 shows the actual SMS messages Nau sent to Sebastian. In Hands-On Project 13-1, you use SIMCon to examine files on Sebastian's SIM card.

13

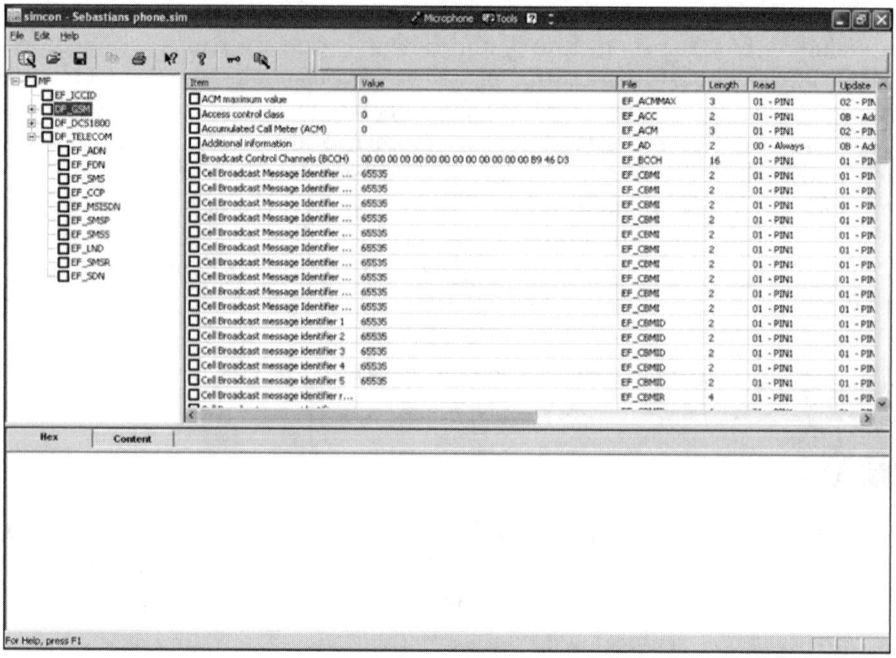

Figure 13-2 File structure of a SIM card viewed in SIMCon

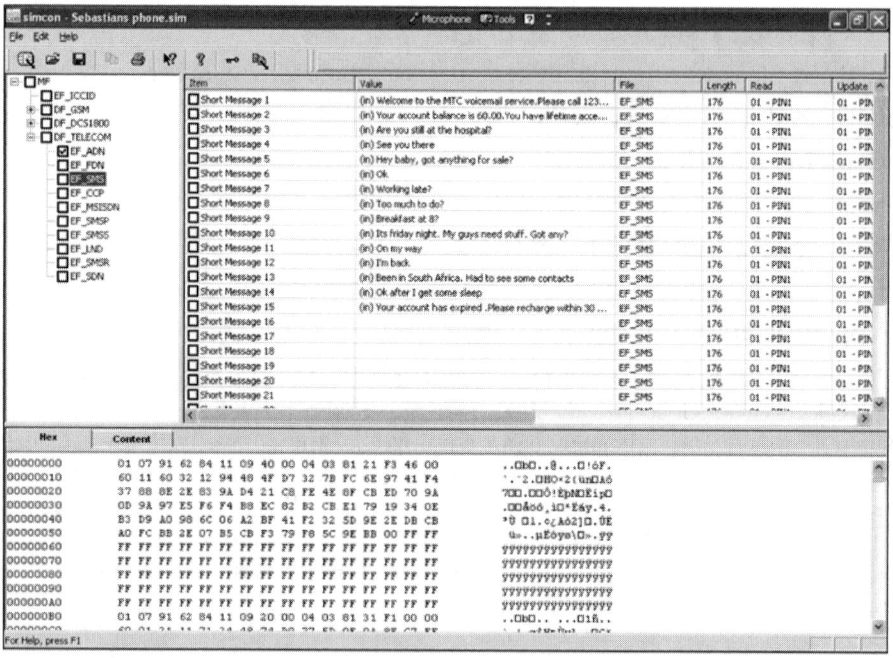

Figure 13-3 SMS messages viewed in SIMCon

Software tools differ in the items they display and the level of detail. For example, Figure 13-4 shows information from the same phone used in Figure 13-3 but viewed in a different software tool, Sim Card Reader. As you might guess from this figure, which displays less information than SIMCon does, this program is more useful as a tool for updating files than as a tool for data retrieval. In general, tools designed to edit information, although they are user friendly, usually aren't forensically sound. You might be able to view some data with one of these tools that you can't view with a forensics tool, but note this step in your log and state that the tool isn't typically used for forensics purposes.

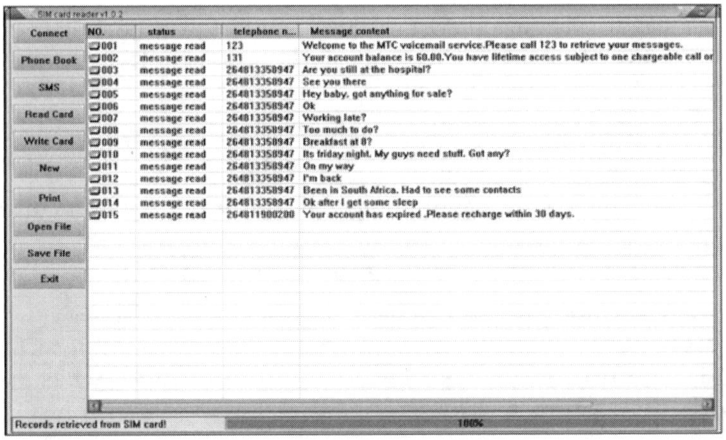

Figure 13-4 Information available in Sim Card Reader

Every program has its idiosyncrasies, so be aware of the shortcomings of the tools you use, and document every step you take during an investigation.

Chapter Summary

- People store a wealth of information on cell phones, including calls, text messages, picture and music files, address books, and more. These files can give you a lot of information when investigating cases.

- Mobile phones have gone through three generations: analog, digital personal communications service (PCS), and third-generation (3G). Two major digital networks currently used in the United States are Code Division Multiple Access (CDMA) and Global System for Mobile Communications (GSM).

- 4G technology is the next generation of mobile phones. Orthogonal Frequency Division Multiplexing (OFDM) is expected to yield faster and higher quality mobile communication.

- Mobile devices range from basic, inexpensive phones used primarily for phone calls to smart phones that integrate a phone, PDA, camera, music player, and more into one device.

- Data can be retrieved from several different places in phones, including volatile memory, nonvolatile memory, SIM cards, and Secure Digital, MultiMedia Card, and Compact Flash cards.

- Personal digital assistants (PDAs) are still in widespread use and often contain a lot of personal information, such as appointments, calendars, contact information, notes, and more. However, their use is likely to decline in coming years, as smart phones have added all these features and more.

- As with computers, proper search and seizure procedures must be followed for mobile devices. In particular, investigators must take care to ensure that mobile devices remain connected to a power source so that they don't lose data in volatile memory. Also, suspect devices should be disconnected from PCs as soon as possible to prevent any synchronization that might overwrite data on the device.

- To isolate a mobile device from incoming messages, you can place it in a specially treated paint can, a wave-blocking wireless evidence bag, or eight layers of antistatic bags.

- SIM cards store data in a hierarchical file structure, containing a system root, which holds directory files, which in turn hold elementary data.

- iPhone forensics is becoming more important as these devices grow in popularity. Accessing backup files is the easiest way to retrieve information from these devices, but acquiring an image is more accurate and produces more detailed data.

- Many software tools are available for reading data stored in mobile devices. Typically, these devices connect to the phone wirelessly (through Bluetooth or irDA) or with a cable. Some also read SIM cards by using a SIM card reader, which is a combination hardware/software device.

Key Terms

Code Division Multiple Access (CDMA) A widely used digital cell phone technology that makes use of spread-spectrum modulation to spread the signal across a wide range of frequencies.

electronically erasable programmable read-only memory (EEPROM) A type of nonvolatile memory that can be reprogrammed electrically, without having to physically access or remove the chip.

Enhanced Data GSM Environment (EDGE) An improvement to GSM technology that enables it to deliver higher data rates. *See also* Global System for Mobile Communications (GSM).

fourth-generation (4G) The next generation of mobile phone standards and technologies promises higher speeds and improved accuracy. Sprint Nextel introduced 4G in 2009, and other major carriers intend to follow suit between now and 2012.

Global System for Mobile Communications (GSM) A second-generation cellular network standard; currently the most popular cellular network type in the world.

International Telecommunication Union (ITU) An international organization dedicated to creating telecommunications standards.

Orthogonal Frequency Division Multiplexing (OFDM) A 4G technology that uses radio waves broadcast over different frequencies; it's considered to use power more efficiently and be more immune to interference.

personal digital assistants (PDAs) Handheld electronic devices that typically contain personal productivity applications used for calendaring, contact management, and note taking. Unlike smart phones, PDAs don't have telephony capabilities.

smart phones Mobile telephones with more features than in a traditional phone, including a camera, an e-mail client, a Web browser, a calendar, contact management software, an instant-messaging program, and more.

subscriber identity module (SIM) cards Removable cards in GSM phones that contain information for identifying subscribers. They can also store other information, such as messages and call history.

Telecommunications Industry Association (TIA) A U.S. trade association representing hundreds of telecommunications companies that works to establish and maintain telecommunications standards.

third-generation (3G) The most recent generation of mobile phone standards and technology; provides for more advanced features and higher data rates than the older analog and personal communications service (PCS) technologies.

Time Division Multiple Access (TDMA) The technique of dividing a radio frequency into time slots, used by GSM networks; also refers to a specific cellular network standard covered by Interim Standard (IS) 136. *See also* Global System for Mobile Communications (GSM).

Review Questions

1. List four places where mobile device information might be stored.

2. Typically, you need a search warrant to retrieve information from a system server. True or False?

3. The term TDMA refers to which of the following? (Choose all that apply.)

   a. A technique of dividing a radio frequency so that multiple users share the same channel

   b. A proprietary protocol developed by Motorola

   c. A specific cellular network standard

   d. A technique of spreading the signal across many channels

4. What is the most popular cellular network worldwide?

5. Which of the following relies on a central database that tracks account data, location data, and subscriber information?

   a. BTS

   b. MSC

   c. BSC

   d. None of the above

13

6. GSM divides a mobile station into _____ and _____.

7. SIM cards have a capacity up to which of the following?
   a. 100 MB
   b. 4 MB
   c. 1 GB
   d. 500 MB

8. List two ways you can isolate a mobile device from incoming signals.

9. Which of the following categories of information is stored on a SIM card? (Choose all that apply.)
   a. Volatile memory
   b. Call data
   c. Service-related data
   d. None of the above

10. Most SIM cards allow _____ access attempts before locking you out.

11. SIM card readers can usually read both cell phone and BlackBerry SIM cards. True or False?

12. List two peripheral memory cards used with PDAs.

13. When acquiring a mobile device at an investigation scene, you should leave it connected to a PC so that you can observe synchronization as it takes place. True or False?

Hands-On Projects

If necessary, extract all data files in the Chap13\Projects folder on the book's DVD to the C:\Work\Chap13\Projects folder on your system. (You might need to create this folder on your system before starting the projects; it's referred to as "your work folder" in steps.)

Hands-On Project 13-1

In this project, you use SIMCon (*www.simcon.no*) to investigate Sebastian's SIM card. This program isn't free, so check with your instructor before downloading it. If you don't have access to this software, skip to the next project.

1. Start your Web browser, if necessary, and go to **www.simcon.no**. Download and install the program.

2. Start SIMCon by clicking **Start**, pointing to **All Programs**, pointing to **simcon**, and then clicking **simcon**.

3. Click **OK** in the About SIMCon dialog box.

4. To open the file containing Sebastian's messages, click **File, Open** from the menu, navigate to your work folder, click the **Sebastians_phone.sim** file, and then click the **Open** button.

5. Examine the file structure of the SIM card, and note whether it seems consistent with the file structure shown in the chapter.

6. Locate the area listing SMS messages. Click several messages in the list in the upper-right pane, and note that when you click a message, details about it are displayed in the lower pane.

7. Continue to examine messages, including information such as delivery and receipt times, and write a short report stating what you found and how it might be useful to the investigation. Submit this report to your instructor.

8. When you're finished, click **File**, **Exit** from the menu to exit SIMCon.

Hands-On Project 13-2

Recall that Sebastian's and Nau's cell phones were seized with the other digital evidence. One of your colleagues has a licensed version of SIMCon. You were able to go to her forensics lab and examine the SIM cards of both phones. In this project, you examine the exported Excel files.

1. Start Excel, and open the **Messages_Sebastian's_phone.xls** and **Messages_Nau's_phone.xls** files.

2. These two employees are suspected of drug dealing. If the messages aren't currently in chronological order, change the display to sort them in this order.

3. Establish the timeline for what transpired between the two. Note items such as when they respond to each other's messages, dates and times, and what numbers they call.

4. Write a short report summarizing the data you examined and stating any conclusions you can draw from the SMS messages.

Hands-On Project 13-3

SIMCon is a forensics software tool that generates a lot of information for cell phone investigations. In Hands-On Project 13-2, you examined SMS messages on two phones. In this project, you view the report with additional details that was generated. Be prepared to do research for this assignment.

1. Start Notepad, and open **Report_Nau's_phone.txt**. Start a second instance of Notepad, and open **Report_Sebastian's_phone.txt**.

2. As you examine the reports, determine definitions for the following items: International Mobile Subscriber Identity (IMSI), PLMN selector, HPLMN search period, and Cell Broadcast Message Identifier (CBMI). Note any other items of interest.

3. Determine what "SIM Phase: phase 2 - profile download required" means.

4. You notice "Originating Address (TP-OA): 264813358948" in the report for Nau's phone. The number breaks down into 264-81-3358948. Determine what the first two numbers—264 and 81—designate.

5. What do the following originating addresses mean?
   - Originating Address (TP-OA): 123
   - Originating Address (TP-OA): 131

6. Next, compare the two files. If you didn't complete Hands-On Project 13-2, create a timeline of the SMS messages.

7. Write a report with answers to the preceding questions, and include any conclusions you drew about the messages' contents.

Hands-On Project 13-4

As mentioned in the chapter, many SIM card reader tools aren't forensically sound. In this project, you use one of these tools to examine SIM cards.

1. Start your Web browser, go to **www.dekart.com/products/card_management/ sim_manager**, and download SIMManager.exe. Note that it has a 30-day free trial.

2. Install SIMManager and start the program. If you get a message stating that this copy of the program isn't registered, click **OK**.

3. Click the **Open** toolbar icon, navigate to your work folder, click the **Phonebook_Sebastian's.phn** file, and click **OK**.

4. Click to select **Phonebook_Sebastian's** on the left; his name and the cell phone number are then displayed on the right.

5. Click the **SMS Messages** icon on the left. Examine the messages displayed on the right.

6. Click the **Print** toolbar icon to print the messages. Accept the default selections, and then click **Print**.

7. Examine the menu items, and notice that this tool is used for altering or updating a SIM card, not for investigative purposes. Click **File**, **Close** from the menu.

8. Click the **Open** toolbar icon, navigate to your work folder, click the **Phonebook_Nau's.phn** file, and then click **OK**.

9. Determine Nau's full first name. Next, click the **SMS Messages** icon on the left.

10. Notice that two different SMS Centers are listed on the left. Draw a conclusion as to what the difference might be.

11. Print the messages, following the procedure in Step 6.

12. Compare the two sets of messages, and correlate the timestamps. Create a timeline based on this information.

13. Write a short report on your findings and any relevant conclusions.

Hands-On Project 13-5

Acquire 10 to 12 antistatic bags. Wrap a cell phone (yours or another student's) in eight layers of bags, and then attempt to call the phone. If the phone rings, add another layer. When it no longer responds, make a note of how many layers were needed. You can also experiment to see whether fewer layers or the phone model makes a difference. Next, try the same experiment with a BlackBerry device. Write a short summary of your findings.

Case Projects

Case Project 13-1

You have been called in on a case involving a particular cell phone, but you don't have the equipment to conduct a forensics analysis of it. Do online research to find possible resources, and write a one- to two-page paper explaining what tools you could use to analyze the cell phone.

Case Project 13-2

For this project, you need access to a mobile forensics toolkit. Select a cell phone model for which you have no cable. After doing Internet research for possible options, write a plan for approaching the problem. Remember that you don't want to destroy data, so make sure you include a step to test the equipment before using it.

13

Report Writing for High-Tech Investigations

After reading this chapter and completing the exercises, you will be able to:

- Explain the importance of reports
- Describe guidelines for writing reports
- Explain how to use forensics tools to generate reports

This chapter gives you guidelines on writing reports of your findings in computer forensics investigations. You learn about different types of reports and what to include in a typical report. You also examine how to generate report findings with forensics software tools.

Understanding the Importance of Reports

You write a report to communicate the results of your forensic examination of a computer or network system. A forensics report presents evidence in court, at an administrative hearing, or as an affidavit used to support issuing an arrest or a search warrant. A report can also provide justification for collecting more evidence and be used at a probable cause hearing, as evidence in a grand jury hearing, or at a civil motion hearing. Besides presenting facts, reports can communicate expert opinion. You should look at your report as your first testimony in a case. You must expect to be examined and cross-examined about it. Opposing counsel will look for an opportunity to attack the facts you present, whether you determined them yourself or extracted them from other reports or the expected testimony of other witnesses. You need to know what facts affect your opinion and what facts do not.

For civil cases, including those involving computer forensics investigations, U.S. district courts require that expert witnesses submit written reports; state courts are also starting to require reports from expert witnesses, although the details of these requirements vary. Therefore, if you're a computer forensics examiner involved in a civil case, you must write a report explaining your investigation and findings. Specifically, Rule 26, Federal Rules of Civil Procedure (FRCP; see *www.law.cornell.edu/rules/frcp/Rule26.htm*), requires that parties who anticipate calling an expert witness to testify must provide a copy of the expert's written report that includes all opinions, the basis for the opinions, and the information considered in coming to those opinions. The report must also include related exhibits, such as photographs or diagrams, and the witness's curriculum vitae listing all publications the witness contributed to during the preceding 10 years. (These publications don't have to be relevant to the case.)

In addition, federal courts, as a matter of rule, require all technical, scientific, or expert witnesses to provide a report before trial in civil cases. See FRCP 26 (a) (2); Federal Rules of Evidence (FRE) 702, 703, and 705; and the rule stated in *Daubert v. Merrell Dow Pharmaceuticals, Inc.*, 509 U.S. 579, which is that testimony is based on sufficient facts or data, testimony is the product of reliable principles and methods, and the witness has applied the principles and methods reliably to the facts of the case. This rule is followed in more than half the states. The remaining states generally follow the rule established in *Frye v. United States*, 293 F. 1013 (D.C. Cir. 1923), which states that testimony is inadmissible unless it is "testimony deduced from a well-recognized scientific principle or discovery; the thing from which the deduction is made must be sufficiently established to have gained general acceptance in the particular field in which it belongs."

In addition to opinions and exhibits, the written report must specify fees paid for the expert's services and list all other civil or criminal cases in which the expert has testified (in trials and depositions) for the preceding 4 years. This list doesn't need to include cases in which the expert acted as a consulting expert and didn't provide expert testimony or cases in which the expert testified as a **lay witness** (a witness testifying to personally observed facts).

Although the requirements for information in reports aren't specific, you should keep a copy of any deposition notice or subpoena so that you can include the following information:

- Jurisdiction (for example, United States District Court for Eastern District of Washington)
- Style of the case (the format used for official court documents—for example, using a header such as *John Smith, Plaintiff v. Paul Jones, Defendant*)
- Cause number (case file number)
- Date and location of the deposition
- Name of the deponent (the person testifying at deposition)

There are no requirements to include details of testimony in a report, although you should summarize key points of your testimony for future reference and keep transcripts of your previous testimony, if available.

As an expert witness, you should be aware that lawyers use services called **deposition banks** (libraries), which store examples of expert witnesses' previous testimony. Some of these services have hundreds of thousands of depositions on file and might have several depositions for expert witnesses who testify regularly. After a case is resolved, a lawyer sends copies of the opposing expert witnesses' depositions to the bank to be stored. In preparation for a trial, when the opposing party has identified an expert witness, the attorney might request copies of this witness's previous testimony. Lawyers might also request transcripts of previous testimony by their own potential experts to ensure that the experts haven't previously testified to a contrary position. Lawyers who are members of associations also use electronic mailing lists to ask other members for copies of previous depositions by a specific expert witness.

Attorneys can now submit documents electronically in many courts; the standard format in federal courts is Portable Document Format (PDF).

14

Limiting a Report to Specifics

The client (who might be an attorney, a detective, or an investigator) should define the investigation's goal or mission. All reports to the client should start by stating this mission or goal, which is usually to find information on a specific subject, recover certain important documents, or recover certain types of files or files with specific dates and times. Clearly defining the goals reduces the time and cost of the examination and is especially important with the increasing size of hard drives and networks.

Before you begin writing, identify your audience and the purpose of the report to help you focus on specifics. Remember that if the audience has little technical knowledge, you might have to dedicate part of the report to educating readers on technical issues. You can do this with a set of several stock paragraphs that you keep on hand, although you should update these stock definitions periodically.

Types of Reports

Computer forensics examiners are required to create different types of reports, such as a formal report consisting of facts from your findings, a preliminary written or verbal report to your attorney, and an examination plan for the attorney who has retained you.

An **examination plan** is a document that serves as a guideline for knowing what questions to expect when you're testifying (see Figure 14-1). Your attorney uses the examination plan to guide you in your testimony. You can propose changes to clarify or define information or to include substantive information the attorney might have omitted. You can also use the examination plan to help your attorney learn the terms and functions used in computer forensics.

WITNESS EXAMINATION PLAN

WITNESS:_Karen Stolz_____/Factors:____Expert and Treating for P.

Direct Examination - Expected Testimony   Objection/Rule/

Testimony on CV

Identity and Address Iowa Bureau of Criminal Investigation

Position (Current) Computer Forensic Examiner

Undergraduate   Iowa State University summa cum laude 1990 BS Computer Engineering

Summer Internship 1989 Des Moines Police Department

Neurology residency, University of Massachusetts MC 86-89

Chief resident in neurology, UM MC 88-89____explain neurology

Fellowship in Electroencephalography and Clinical Neurophysiology, UWMC-Seattle 89-90

Fellowship in Sleep Disorders Medicine, Univ. Michigan MC, 90-91

Academic Appointments

Lecturer, Dept of Computer Science, University of Iowa 1998-Current

Instructor, Iowa Police Academy, 1999-Current

Professional Society Certifications

P.E.   1999

CISSP 2001

Membership

American Society for Industrial Security

Publications

      Journal of the Iowa State Bar Association, May 1999, "Computer Forensics on Raid Servers-Testifying to a Reasonable Certainty"

How many systems have you conducted forensic examination on?

What is your relationship to the Plaintiff? Retained by his attorney to examine the hard drive of his computer for all financial records. I have never actually met or talked with Mr. Smith.

How long did it take you conduct this examination?

What types of files were you looking for?   Why those file types?   Where did you find those file types?

What condition were the files in?

What is your opinion as to the cause of that condition?

Can you say for a reasonable certainty that the financial data files were deleted intentionally? Yes.

Are you able to state to a reasonable certainty who deleted the financial data files? Yes.

What is your fee for examining the hard drive, preparing a report and testifying?

Cross Examination - Expected Testimony

How many times have you worked for Mr. Sawyer as an expert witness? I've had 16 contracts as consulting expert or expert witness.

Have you ever previously testified that overwrite utilities are not 100% reliable? Yes, but that was in 1994 and utilities are so far as I can tell 100% reliable today.

Figure 14-1 A sample examination plan

A verbal report is less structured than a written report. Typically, it takes place in an attorney's office, where the attorney requests your consultant's report. As an expert hired as a trial consultant, you'll use verbal reports often. Keep in mind that others can't force your attorney to repeat what you've told him or her in a verbal report. A verbal report is usually a preliminary report and addresses areas of investigation yet to be completed, such as the following:

- Tests that haven't been concluded

- Interrogatories that the lawyer might want to address to opposing parties

- Document production, either requests for production (to parties) or subpoenas (to non-parties, people who have information but aren't a named party in the case)

- Determining who should be deposed and the plan for deposing them

With preliminary reports, mention to your client that your factual statement and opinion are still tentative and subject to change as more information comes in.

A written report is frequently an affidavit or a declaration. Because this type of report is sworn to under oath (and penalty of perjury or comparable false swearing statute), it demands attention to detail, carefully limiting what you write, and thorough documentation and support of what you write. See the following section for more guidelines on written reports.

To minimize the chance of being deposed, avoid producing a written report for as long as you can. If you must produce an informal or preliminary report in written form, understand that statements you don't make are as important as ones you do include.

Guidelines for Writing Reports

In the past, the method for expressing an opinion was to have an attorney frame a hypothetical question based on available factual evidence. The law required that an expert who doesn't have personal knowledge about the system or occurrence must state opinions by response to hypothetical questions, which ask the expert witness to express an opinion based on hypothetical facts without referring specifically to a particular system or situation. In this regard, you as a forensics investigator (an expert witness) differ from an ordinary witness. You didn't see or hear the incident in dispute; you're giving evidence as an opinion based on professional knowledge and experience, even if you might never have seen the system, data, or scene.

Although the rules of evidence have relaxed requirements on the way an expert renders an opinion, structuring hypothetical questions for your own use helps ensure that you're basing your opinion on facts expected to be supported by evidence. State the facts needed to answer the question, and don't include any unnecessary facts. You might want to address alternative facts, however, if they allow your opinion to remain the same. The expression "alternative facts" might seem contradictory, but it simply means competing facts. If there weren't alternative possible facts, the case would not be at trial; it would have been decided at summary judgment.

An expert's opinion is governed by FRE, Rule 705, and the corresponding rule in many states. For more information on Rule 705, visit *www.law.cornell.edu/rules/fre/rules.htm#Rule705*.

14

The following text from a court transcript illustrates an exchange using a hypothetical question between an attorney and a computer forensics expert. Note that the word "presented" is used in this transcript; it means that the attorney handed the expert something while asking a question.

Mr. Stiubhard: Mr. Noriki, presented with a hard drive of 40 GB, an attached Maxtor manufacturer's data sheet that indicated it was manufactured in May 2002, previous testimony by a detective that the notebook computer in which this drive was found was manufactured by Dell Computer Corporation in June 2002 and purchased by the owner in June 2002. Based on those facts testified to, do you have an opinion whether this is original equipment on this system?

Mr. Noriki: Yes.

Mr. Stiubhard: Mr. Noriki, what is your opinion on whether this hypothetical hard drive would be the original equipment with the system?

Mr. Noriki: Based on facts you have provided, it is my professional opinion that the hard drive would....

Hypothetical questions can be abused and made so complex that the finder of fact (the expert) might not be able to remember enough of the question to evaluate the answer. Another abuse of the hypothetical question is that it effectively allows attorneys to recite their favored facts to the jury repeatedly and in the order and with the emphasis they want to use.

As an expert witness, you can testify to an opinion or conclusion, if these basic conditions are met:

- The opinion, inferences, or conclusions depend on special knowledge, skill, or training not within the ordinary experience of lay witnesses or jurors.

- The witness must be shown to be qualified as a true expert in the field (which is why a curriculum vitae is important).

- The witness must testify to a reasonable degree of certainty (probability) regarding his or her opinion, inference, or conclusion.

- Generally, expert witnesses must first describe the data (facts) on which their opinion, inference, or conclusion is based, or they must testify in response to a hypothetical question that sets forth the underlying evidence.

What to Include in Written Preliminary Reports

Remember that anything you write down as part of your examination for a report is subject to **discovery** from the opposing attorney. Therefore, a written preliminary report is considered a **high-risk document** because opposing counsel can demand discovery on it. If the written preliminary report states a contrary or more equivocal position than you take in your final report or testimony, you should expect opposing counsel to try to discredit your testimony by using the written report. It's simply better if there's no written report to provide. If you must write a preliminary report, don't use words such as "preliminary copy," "draft copy," or "working draft." These words give opposing counsel an opening for discrediting you and make it seem as though the attorney who retained you contributed to what should be your independent professional judgment. In addition, if you do write a preliminary report, don't destroy it before a final resolution of the case or any discovery issue related to the report. Destroying the report could be considered destroying or concealing evidence; among lawyers, this action is called **spoliation**, and it could subject your client to monetary or evidentiary sanctions.

For written preliminary reports, therefore, include the same information you would supply in an informal verbal report. First, restate the assignment to confirm with your client that the work you have done is focused correctly. Next, summarize what has been accomplished. Identify the systems you have examined, what tools you have used, and what you have seen. State evidence preservation or protection processes you have used. (See Chapters 5 and 9 for more information on these processes.) The following list shows additional items to include in your report:

- Summarize your billing to date and estimate costs to complete the effort.
- Identify the tentative conclusion (rather than the preliminary conclusion).
- Identify areas for further investigation and obtain confirmation from the attorney on the scope of your examination.

Report Structure

A report usually includes the sections shown in the following list, although the order varies depending on organizational guidelines or case requirements:

- Abstract
- Table of contents
- Body of report
- Conclusion
- References
- Glossary
- Acknowledgments
- Appendixes

Each section should have a title indicating what you're discussing, so make sure it conveys the essential point of the section. For example, the body of your report might be titled "Investigation Findings for ABC Bicycle, Inc.: Intellectual Property Theft."

If the report is long and complex, you should provide an abstract. More people read the abstract than the entire report, so writing one for your report is important. The abstract and table of contents give readers an overview of the report and its points so that they can decide what they need to review. An abstract simply condenses the report to concentrate on the essential information. It should be one or two paragraphs totaling about 150 to 200 words. Remember that the abstract should describe the examination or investigation and present the report's main ideas in a summarized form. Informative abstracts don't duplicate references or tables of results. As with any research paper, write the abstract last.

The body consists of the introduction and discussion sections. The introduction should state the report's purpose and show that you're aware of its terms of reference. You should also state any methods used and any limitations and indicate how the report is structured. It's important to justify why you are writing the report, so make sure you answer the question "What is the problem?" You should also give readers a map of what you're delivering. Introduce the problem, moving from broader issues to the specific problem, finishing the introduction with the precise aims of the report (key questions). Craft this introduction carefully, setting up the processes you used to develop the information in logical order. Refer to

14

relevant facts, ideas, and theories as well as related research by other authors. Organize discussion sections logically under headings to reflect how you classify information and to ensure that your information remains relevant to the investigation.

Two other main sections are the conclusion and supporting materials (references and appendixes). The conclusion starts by referring to the report's purpose, states the main points, draws conclusions, and possibly renders an opinion. References and appendixes list the supporting material to which your work refers. Follow a style manual's guidelines on format for presenting references, such as *Gregg Reference Manual: A Manual of Style, Grammar, Usage, and Formatting*; *The Chicago Manual of Style: The Essential Guide for Writers, Editors, and Publishers*; or the *MLA Style Manual and Guide to Scholarly Publishing* from the Modern Language Association. Appendixes provide additional resource material not included in the body of the report.

Writing Reports Clearly

To produce clear, concise reports, you should assess the quality of your writing, using the following criteria:

- *Communicative quality*—Is it easy to read? Think of your readers and how to make the report appealing to them.
- *Ideas and organization*—Is the information relevant and clearly organized?
- *Grammar and vocabulary*—Is the language simple and direct so that the meaning is clear and the text isn't repetitive? However, technical terms should be used consistently; you shouldn't try to use variety for these terms. Using different words for the same thing might raise questions.
- *Punctuation and spelling*—Are they accurate and consistent?

Good expert reports share many of the qualities of other kinds of writing. To write is to think, so a report should lay out ideas in a logical order that facilitates logical thinking. Make each sentence follow from the previous one, building an argument piece by piece. Group related ideas and sentences into paragraphs, and group paragraphs into sections. Create a flow from the beginning of the report to the end.

The report should be grammatically sound, use correct spelling, and be free of writing errors. Avoid jargon, slang, or colloquial terms. Most lawyers, judges, and jurors aren't technically trained, so if technical terms must be used, define them in ordinary language (or refer readers to your glossary). Defining acronyms and any abbreviations not used as standard measurement units is particularly important. If there's any possibility of misinterpreting an abbreviation, define it or use the full expression. For example, "m" is used routinely in scientific/technical writing as an abbreviation for "meter," but nontechnical readers (especially in the United States) might assume it's an abbreviation for "mile."

Considering Writing Style
Style means the tone of language you use to address the reader. When writing a report, use a natural language style. For instance, talk about yourself in the first person, not the third person; for example, don't call yourself "Your Affiant" when "I" is appropriate and clearly more natural. (However, keep in mind that too many sentences containing "I" can become repetitive.) A natural language style helps keep readers interested in what you have to say. However, you should also follow formal writing guidelines, so pay attention to word usage, grammar, and spelling.

Be sure to avoid vague language and generalizations, as in "There was a problem." Instead, state the problem specifically and describe what you or others did to solve it. Be careful about repetition, too; repeat only what's necessary, such as key words or technical terms.

Most of the report describes what you did, so it should be in past tense, but use present or future tense as appropriate. Use active rather than passive voice to avoid boring writing and contorted phrases. For example, "the software recovered the following data" is more direct and, therefore, more interesting to read than "the following data was recovered by the software."

Avoid presenting too many details and personal observations. Your only agenda should be finding the truth, so don't think in terms of catching somebody or proving something. It's not your job to win the case. Don't become an advocate for anything other than the truth and your honest objective opinion.

A final caution in writing style: Project objectivity. You must communicate calm, detached observations in your report, so don't become emotionally involved in the investigation. Always try to identify the flaws in your thinking or examination; it's better to identify flaws than allow opposing counsel to do it for you at an embarrassing moment.

Including Signposts Another aspect of writing clearly is choosing language that gives your readers signposts to what you're trying to communicate, draws their attention to a point, and shows them the sequence of a process. Signposts assist readers in scanning the text quickly by highlighting the main points and logical development of information.

For example, the first substantive section of your report could start with "This is the report of findings from the forensic examination of computer SN 123456." The discussion of your examination procedures could be introduced with "The first step in this examination was," "The second step in this examination was," and so on. "First" and "second" are signposts that show the sequence of information or tasks. When you want to evaluate something, you might include a signpost such as "The problem with this is …" To show that you're drawing a conclusion, introduce the point with "This means that …" or "The result shows that …"

Designing the Layout and Presentation of Reports

Layout and presentation involve many factors, including using clear titles and section headings. A numbering system is also part of the layout. Typically, report writers use one of two numbering systems: decimal numbering or legal-sequential numbering. After you choose a system, be sure to follow it consistently throughout the report.

A report using the decimal numbering system divides material into sections and restarts numbering with each main section, as shown in the following example. With this system, readers can scan the headings and understand how one part of the report relates to the other.

I. Abstract

1.1. This report includes a review of data found on hard drives on Computer A and Computer B. Both systems were Dell desktop computers. Computer A had no image files other than those that would have been found in routine office applications. Computer B had more than 60 GB of image data (approximately 120,000 JPG files with dates from January 30, 2008, to March 15, 2009).

14

II. Detailed Analysis

Computer A

2.1. The hard drives of Computer A are designated drive C and drive D.

2.2. Both hard drives are 100 GB Maxtor drives.

2.3. Both hard drives are less than 20% full.

Computer B

2.4 The hard drives of Computer B are designated drive C and drive D.

2.5. Both hard drives are 80 GB Seagate drives.

2.6. Both drives are more than 90% full.

The legal-sequential numbering system is often used in legal pleadings. Each Roman numeral represents a major aspect of the report, and each Arabic numeral is an important piece of supporting information, as shown in the following example. This system is meaningful to lawyers but might not be as effective with nonlawyers because the sequential numbering doesn't indicate a hierarchy that shows the relative importance of information in the report.

I. Abstract

1. This report includes a review of data found on hard drives on Computer A and Computer B. Both systems were Dell desktop computers. Computer A had no image files other than those that would have been found in routine office applications. Computer B had more than 60 GB of image data (approximately 120,000 JPG files with dates from January 30, 2008, to March 15, 2009).

II. Detailed Analysis

Computer A

2. The hard drives of Computer A are designated drive C and drive D.

3. Both hard drives are 100 GB Maxtor drives.

4. Both hard drives are less than 20% full.

Computer B

5. The hard drives of Computer B are designated drive C and drive D.

6. Both hard drives are 80 GB Seagate drives.

7. Both drives are more than 90% full.

Providing Supporting Material Use material such as figures, tables, data, and equations to help tell the story as it unfolds. Refer to this material in the text and integrate the points they make into your writing. Number figures and tables sequentially as they're introduced (for example, Figure 1, Figure 2, and so forth with another sequence for Table 1, Table 2, and so on).

Figure captions should supply descriptive information. In charts, label all axes and include units of measure. Insert a figure or table after the paragraph in which it's first mentioned, or gather all supporting material in one place after the references section (before any appendixes).

Formatting Consistently How you format text is less important than being consistent in applying formatting. For example, if you indent paragraphs, be sure to indent them all. Use fonts consistently, and use a consistent style of headings throughout (for example, major headings in bold with initial capitals, minor headings in italics, and so forth). Follow the same guideline throughout for units of measure; for example, use "%" or "percent," but don't use both. In other words, establish a template and stick to it.

Explaining Examination and Data Collection Methods Explain how you studied the problem, which should follow logically from the report's purpose. Depending on the kind of data, this section might contain subsections on examination procedures, materials or equipment, data collection and sources, and analytical or statistical techniques. Supply enough detail for readers to understand what you did.

Data collection is a critical portion of the report. Without good data recording in a lab notebook or record, completing a report beyond this point is futile. If your data collection process becomes the subject of discovery or examination, presenting data in a well-organized manner is important. Use tables in your report to illustrate how data was handled and examined. As mentioned, tables should be labeled clearly as to their content and numbered for easy referral.

Including Calculations In most cases, hashing algorithms are calculated in computer forensics investigations. If you use any hashing algorithms, be sure to give the common name, such as "Message Digest 5 (MD5) hash." Generally, you don't need to give examples of each type of hash if you're using standard tools; you explain generally what they do and cite the authority or policy you rely on for using the tool. For example, to explain why you're using the MD5 hash, you might cite the National Software Reference Library (NSRL; *www.nsrl.nist.gov*) as an authority. You could also cite a court case in which a tool's validity had been accepted previously.

Providing for Uncertainty and Error Analysis In computer forensics, many results can be absolutely true if stated conservatively but might be a guess if you overreach. Therefore, a statement of limitations of knowledge and uncertainty is necessary to protect your credibility. For example, if you're using the timestamp for a file in a Windows OS to indicate that the file was created at a certain time, you need to acknowledge that a PC clock could be reset easily. In addition, you should state that there's no absolute assurance that a file's timestamp is a reflection of its creation time, but there might be other reliable indicators, such as timestamps of other files, creation timestamps for directories, creation order of certain files, and information in automatic backups.

14

Explaining Results and Conclusions Explain your findings, using subheadings to divide the discussion into logical parts. Make comments on results as they're presented, discussing the importance of what you found in light of the overall report objectives. Take a step back from the details and synthesize what has (and has not) been learned about the problem and what the information means. Describe what you actually found, not what you hoped to find. Including this discussion as you present results can often improve clarity and readers' understanding.

Link your discussion to figures and tables as you present results, and describe and interpret what these supporting materials show. If you have many similar figures, select representative examples for the main report and put the rest in an appendix.

Save broader generalizations and summaries for the report's conclusion. The conclusion should restate the objectives, aims, and key questions and summarize your findings with clear, concise statements. Keep the conclusion brief and to the point.

Providing References When you write a report, you must cite references to all material you have used as sources for the content of your work. These citations are made wherever you quote, paraphrase, or summarize someone else's opinions, theories, or data. References can include books, periodicals, newspapers, Web sites, conference proceedings, personal communications, and interviews.

In the main section of your report, you typically cite references with the author's last name and year of publication enclosed in parentheses. (Sometimes page numbers are required, too; check the style manual you're following for specific guidance.) In the references section, you list sources alphabetically by author and provide publication information. Give enough detail so that someone else could track down the information. Follow a standard format, such as the one shown in the following examples, for use of italics, capitalization, volume and page numbers, publisher address, and other style concerns. Many good style manuals are available, and having one handy is worthwhile.

The following examples show how different sources are presented in the references section; keep in mind that formatting might differ slightly depending on the style manual you follow:

Personal (unpublished) communications:

> Cited in the text only, as in "x is recoverable by using tool A (Koenick, F., pers. comm.)."

Lecture notes:

> Stiubhard, C. K. "The Curriculum Vitae." Lecture for CIS 411/511, CTIN and City University, Seattle, WA, May 1, 2009.

Web site:

> Law Office of Christopher K. Stiubhard. *www.stiubhardlaw.com*, 2009.

Single-author journal article:

> O'Herlighy, T. A. "Development of Relationships on the Internet." *Journal of the Advocate* 7, 2004, pp. 130–142.

Multiple-author journal article:

> Noriki, H. W., C. K. Stiubhard, and M. D. Clay. "Investigation of Counterfeiting of Spare Parts—A Statistical Analysis." *The Frontline Journal of Aviation* 8, 2007, pp. 150–152.

Book:

> Clark, Franklin and Ken Diliberto. *Investigating Computer Crime*. CRC Press, New York, 1996.

Government/technical report:

> U.S. Department of Justice. "The Examination of Computers." Report XYZ-001, Washington, DC, 2005.

Chapter in an edited volume:

> Pellegrino, A. "Investigation of the Automated Backup Copies of Microsoft Application Files." In Noriki, H. W. et al, *Computer Forensics*. Learning Technology, Springfield, MA, 2006.

Including Appendixes If necessary, you can include appendixes containing material such as raw data, figures not used in the body of the report, and anticipated exhibits. Arrange them in the order referred to in the report. They are considered additional material and might not be examined by readers. Some portions of appendixes might be considered optional, but others are required. For example, exhibits are required under FRCP, Rule 26, as is your curriculum vitae (unless bona fides are integrated into the report).

Whether you're working for a law firm, computer forensics firm, research laboratory, or law enforcement agency, these organizations have established formats for reports. Be sure to get samples from them before beginning your report.

Generating Report Findings with Forensics Software Tools

With many computer forensics software tools, such as ProDiscover, X-Ways Forensics, FTK, ILook, and EnCase, log files and reports are generated when you perform an analysis. Although forensics software reports what was found and where, remember that it's your responsibility to explain the significance of the evidence you recover and, if necessary, define any limitations or uncertainty that applies to your findings. These reports and logs are typically in text, word processing, or HTML format. In this section, you learn how to integrate a software-generated report into the official investigation report that you present to your attorney or client.

As an example of a report from a computing investigation, you re-examine a case from Chapter 6. Before starting the activity, create a *Work*\Chap14\Chapter folder on your system (referred to as "your work folder" in steps). Your folder name will likely differ from what's shown in screenshots.

For this activity, the general counsel for Superior Bicycles, Ileen Johnson, has asked you to look for correspondence to Superior Bicycles employee Denise Robinson. Specifically, Ileen wants to know what messages Denise has received from Terry Sadler and whether she has any accounting data, such as spreadsheets, on her computer. Ileen informs you that she doesn't know Mr. Sadler's full e-mail address, only that it starts with "terrysadler." Because Denise is in a different city, Ileen had an outside computer forensics consultant capture data from Denise's computer. She gives you a CD containing an image file, GCFI-Win98.eve, from Denise's computer and tells you that she believes Denise uses OpenOffice as her office application.

14

Using ProDiscover Basic to Generate Reports

You need to look for spreadsheet accounting information that might have been created with OpenOffice Calc and e-mail correspondence created in Outlook Express. For OpenOffice Calc, search for files with .ods and .sxc extensions. For Outlook Express, look for files with a .dbx extension. When you have located files matching these extensions, bookmark them and generate a report in ProDiscover. Then you export the files for further examination in FTK Demo. To begin this activity, follow these steps:

1. Copy **GCFI-Win98.eve** from where you moved it in Chapter 9 to this chapter's work folder.

2. Start ProDiscover Basic with the **Run as administrator** option (if you're using Vista). If the Launch Dialog dialog box opens, click **Cancel**.

3. Click **File, New Project** from the menu. In the New Project dialog box, type **InChap14** for the project number and filename, and then click **OK**. Save the project in your work folder.

4. In the tree view, click to expand **Add** and then click **Image File**.

5. In the Open dialog box, navigate to your work folder, click the **GCFI-Win98.eve** file, and click **Open**. If the Auto Image Checksum message box opens, click **Yes**.

6. Click to expand **Images** under Content View, and then expand the **GCFI-Win98.eve** file path so that you can see the folders and files in the work area.

7. Click the **Search** toolbar button. In the Search dialog box, click the **Search for files named** option button, and in the text box underneath, type the following extensions (see Figure 14-2), pressing **Enter** after each one: **.ods, .sxc,** and **.dbx.**

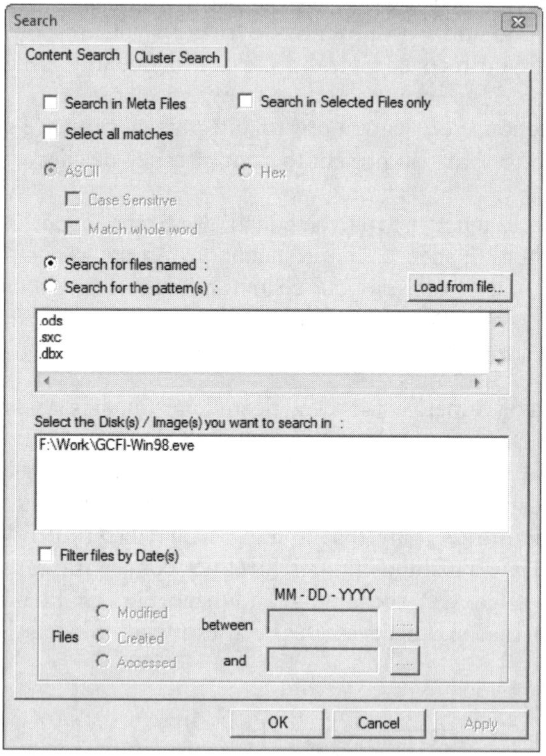

Figure 14-2 Searching for file extensions

8. Under Select the Disk(s)/Image(s) you want to search in, click the **GCFI-Win98.eve** image file, and then click **OK**.

9. In the search results, click the check box next to the **Inbox.dbx** file. In the Add Comment dialog box, type **Files for case report InChap14** in the Investigator comments text box, click the **Apply to all items** check box, and then click **OK**.

10. In the search results, click the check boxes next to **Sent Items.dbx, Speedy Financials2.sxc, Speedy Financials 1.sxc, Speedy Financials.sxc,** and **Speedy Financials3.sxc**, as shown in Figure 14-3.

Select	File Name	Found in
☐🐝	soffice.sxc	F:\Work\GCFI-Win98.eve\..\WINDOWS\Shell...
☐🐝	Folders.dbx	F:\Work\GCFI-Win98.eve\..\WINDOWS\Applic...
☑🐝	Inbox.dbx	F:\Work\GCFI-Win98.eve\..\WINDOWS\Applic...
☐🐝	Offline.dbx	F:\Work\GCFI-Win98.eve\..\WINDOWS\Applic...
☐🐝	Outbox.dbx	F:\Work\GCFI-Win98.eve\..\WINDOWS\Applic...
☐🐝	Pop3uidl.dbx	F:\Work\GCFI-Win98.eve\..\WINDOWS\Applic...
☐🐝	Deleted Items.dbx	F:\Work\GCFI-Win98.eve\..\WINDOWS\Applic...
☑🐝	Sent Items.dbx	F:\Work\GCFI-Win98.eve\..\WINDOWS\Applic...
☐🐝	Speedy Financials3.sxc.lnk	F:\Work\GCFI-Win98.eve\..\WINDOWS\Recent
☐🐝	Speedy Financials 1.sxc.lnk	F:\Work\GCFI-Win98.eve\..\WINDOWS\Recent
☐🐝	Speedy Financials2.sxc.lnk	F:\Work\GCFI-Win98.eve\..\WINDOWS\Recent
☐🐝	Speedy Financials.sxc.lnk	F:\Work\GCFI-Win98.eve\..\WINDOWS\Recent
☑🐝	Speedy Financials2.sxc	F:\Work\GCFI-Win98.eve\..\My Documents\SB...
☑🐝	Speedy Financials 1.sxc	F:\Work\GCFI-Win98.eve\..\My Documents\SB...
☑🐝	Speedy Financials.sxc	F:\Work\GCFI-Win98.eve\..\My Documents\SB...
☑🐝	Speedy Financials3.sxc	F:\Work\GCFI-Win98.eve\..\My Documents\SB...

Figure 14-3 Selecting files in the search results

11. Click the **Add to Report** button, and then double-click **Inbox.dbx** to return to the work area.

12. In the work area, right-click **Inbox.dbx** and click **Copy All Selected Files**.

13. In the Choose Destination dialog box, click the **Browse** button, browse to your work folder, click **OK**, and then click **OK** again.

14. In the tree view, click **Report**, and then click **Action**, **Export** from the menu to open the Export dialog box.

15. In the File Name text box, type **InChp14-prodiscover**. Click **Browse**, navigate to and double-click your work folder, click **Save**, and then click **OK** to save the report.

16. Exit ProDiscover. If you're prompted to save the project, click **Yes**.

In the following section, you see how to integrate the ProDiscover report into an FTK report that can be used as part of an investigation's findings.

Using AccessData FTK to Generate Reports

AccessData FTK has some unique features that aren't available in ProDiscover Basic. The following steps show you how to further analyze the Outlook Express .dbx files you exported with ProDiscover. First, load the case data for processing by performing these steps:

1. Start FTK with the **Run as administrator** option (if you're using Vista). If you're prompted with a warning dialog box and/or notification message, click **OK** to continue, and click **OK**, if necessary, in the message box thanking you for evaluating the program.

2. In the AccessData FTK Startup dialog box, click the **Start a new case** option button, and then click **OK**.

3. In the New Case dialog box, enter your name in the Investigator's name text box and **InChp14** in the Case Number and Case Name text boxes. Next to the Case Path text box, click **Browse**, navigate to your work folder where you exported the data files, click **OK**, and then click **Next**.

4. In the Case Information dialog box, enter your school or group name in the Agency/Company text box and your name in the Examiner's Name text box, and then click **Next**.

14

5. Click **Next** until you reach the Refine Case - Default dialog box. Click the **Email Emphasis** button, and then click **Next**. In the Refine Index Default dialog box, click **Next** again.

6. In the Add Evidence dialog box, click **Add Evidence**, and in the Add Evidence to Case dialog box, click the **Contents of a Folder** option button, and then click **Continue**. In the Browse for Folder dialog box, navigate to the folder where you exported the .dbx files, such as *Work*\Chap14\Chapter\GCFI-Win98.eve\Windows (see Figure 14-4), and then click **OK**.

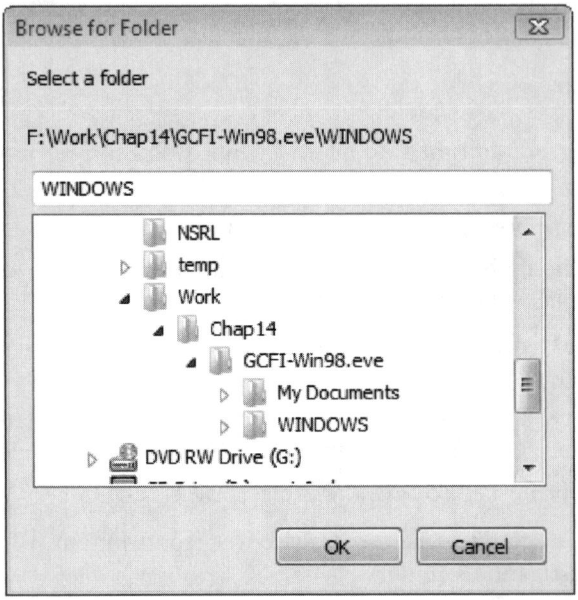

Figure 14-4 Selecting the folder for extracted e-mail files

7. In the Evidence Information dialog box, click **OK**, and in the Add Evidence dialog box, click **Next**.

8. To start the processing, click **Finish** in the Case Summary dialog box. Leave FTK running for the next set of steps.

Next, you look at e-mail messages for information about Terry Sadler. Follow these steps to search for references to "terrysadler" and bookmark them for your report:

1. In the main FTK window, click the **Search** tab, and then click the **Indexed Search** tab. In the Search Term text box, type **terrysadler**. Click **Add**, and then click the **View Cumulative Results** button.

2. In the Filter Search Hits dialog box, click **OK**. In the upper-right pane of the main FTK window, expand the list of hits, as shown in Figure 14-5.

3. Next, you need to select all messages with the name terrysadler. In the File List pane at the bottom, click the check box next to each message (see Figure 14-6).

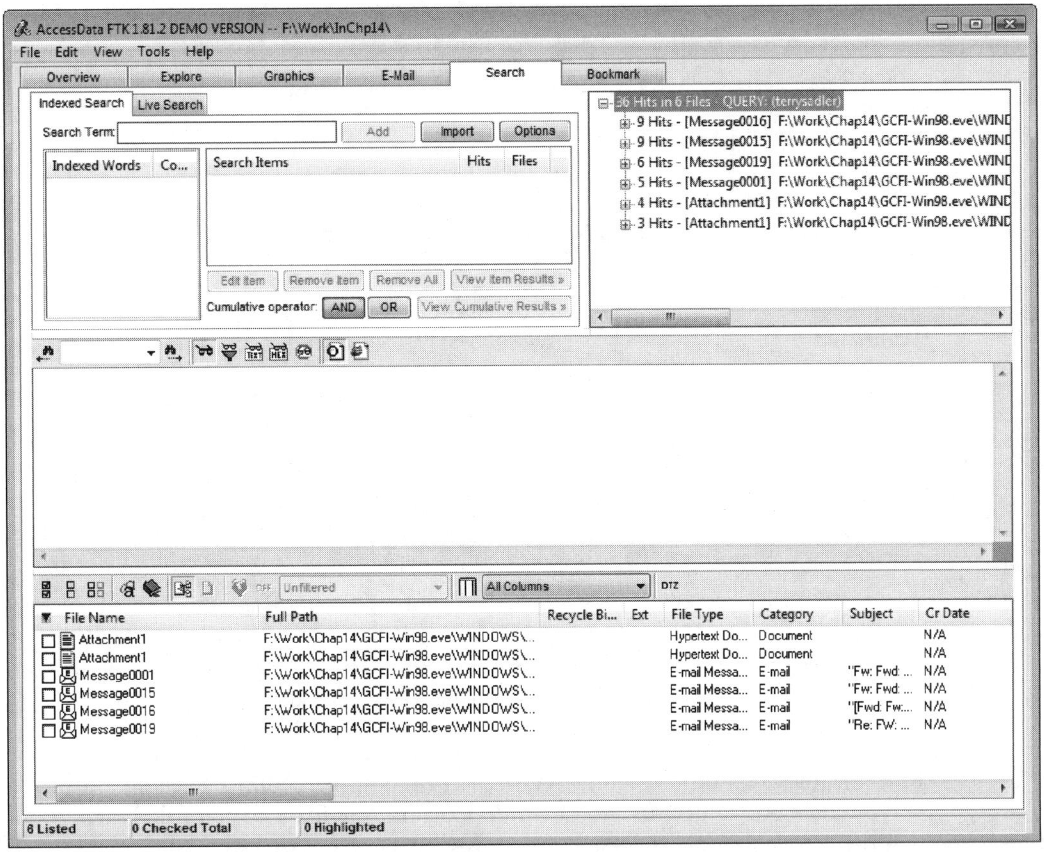

Figure 14-5 Indexed search results for the name terrysadler

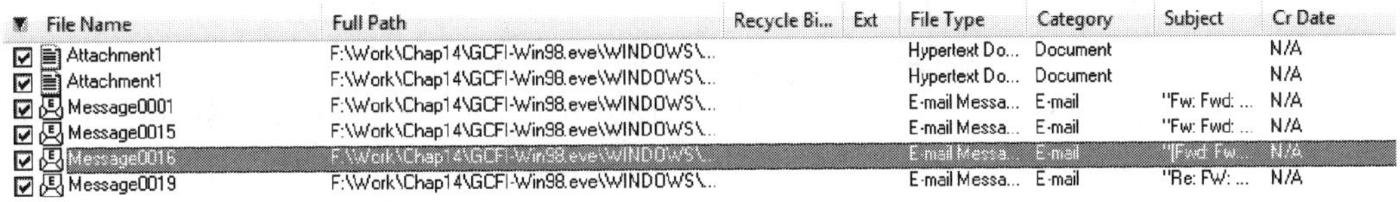

Figure 14-6 Files selected to be bookmarked

14

4. Click **Tools**, **Create Bookmark** from the menu. In the Create New Bookmark dialog box, type **Terry Sadler E-mail** in the Bookmark name text box, and click the **All checked items** button. Click the **Include in report** and **Export files** check boxes (see Figure 14-7), and then click **OK**.

5. To create a report, click **File**, **Report Wizard** from the menu. If the FTK Friendly Reminder message about filtered data opens, click **OK**.

6. In the Case Information dialog box, update or add information if necessary, and then click **Next**.

7. In the Bookmarks dialog box, click **Yes, include all bookmarks** and **Yes, export all bookmarked files**, and then click **Next**.

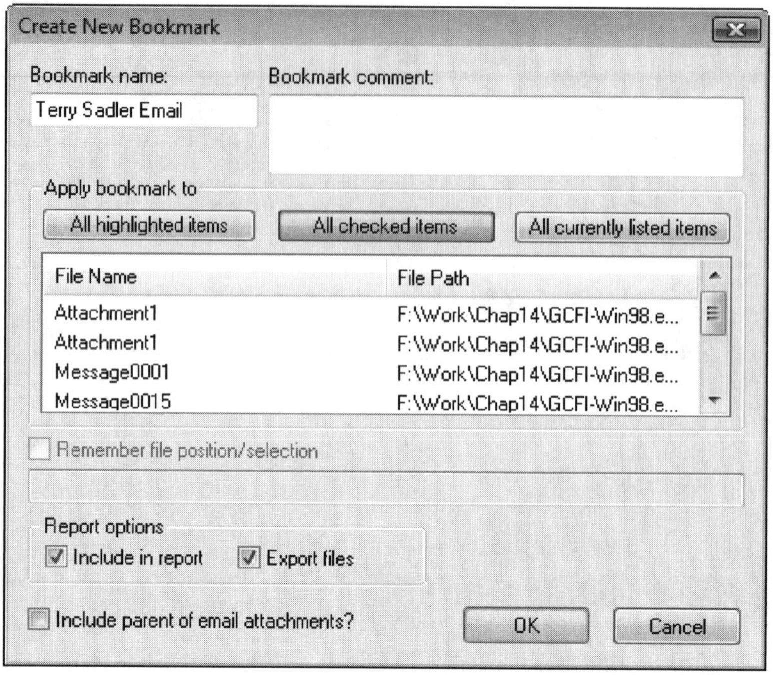

Create New Bookmark

Bookmark name: Bookmark comment:

Terry Sadler Email

Apply bookmark to

[All highlighted items] [All checked items] [All currently listed items]

File Name	File Path
Attachment1	F:\Work\Chap14\GCFI-Win98.e...
Attachment1	F:\Work\Chap14\GCFI-Win98.e...
Message0001	F:\Work\Chap14\GCFI-Win98.e...
Message0015	F:\Work\Chap14\GCFI-Win98.e...

☐ Remember file position/selection

Report options
☑ Include in report   ☑ Export files

☐ Include parent of email attachments?   [OK]   [Cancel]

Figure 14-7   Selecting settings in the Create New Bookmark dialog box

8. Continue clicking **Next** until you reach the Supplementary Files dialog box, where you click **Add Files**. In the Open dialog box, navigate to the folder where the ProDiscover report is located, click **InChp14-prodiscover.rtf**, click **Open**, and then click **Next**.

9. In the Report Location dialog box, click **Finish**. When you see the Report Wizard message box, click **Yes**. FTK opens the report in your Web browser (see Figure 14-8).

10. Exit FTK by clicking **File, Exit** from the menu. In the FTK Backup Confirmation dialog box, click **No**. Leave your Web browser open for the projects at the end of this chapter.

If you need to close your Web browser, you can open the report later by navigating to the C:\Work\Chap14\Chapter\InChp14\report folder in Windows Explorer and double-clicking the Index.htm file.

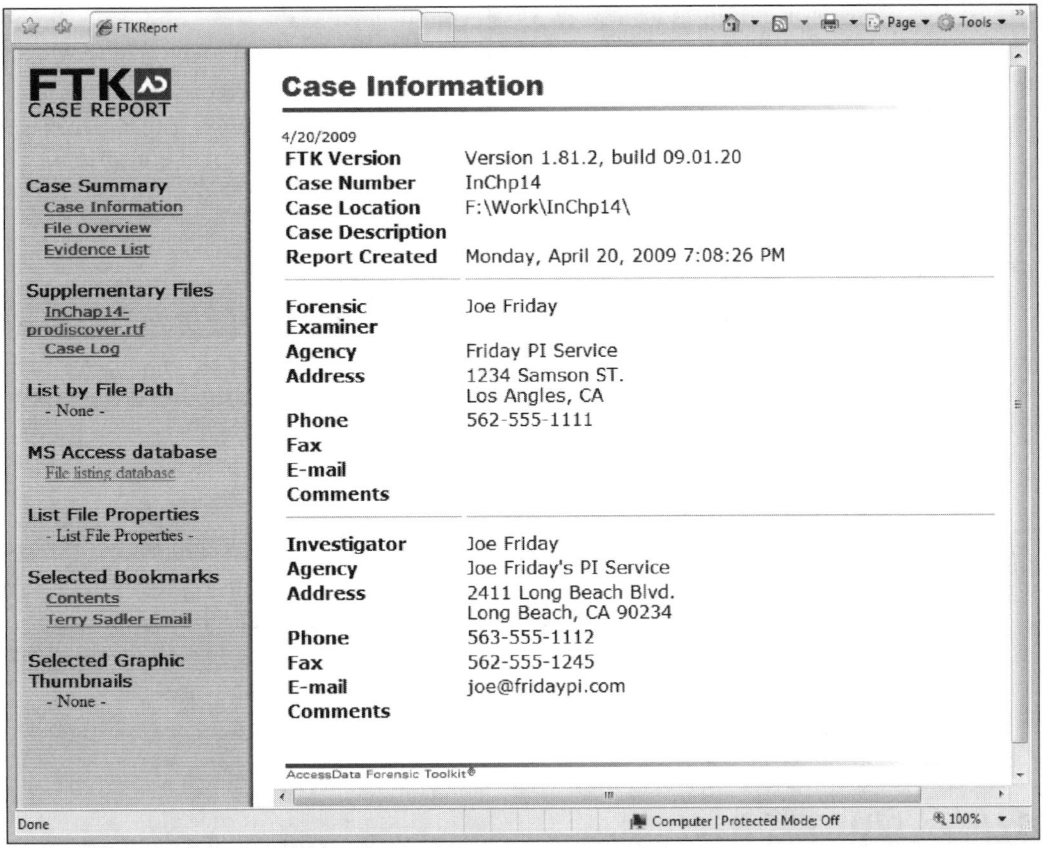

Figure 14-8 The completed case report

Chapter Summary

■ All U.S. district courts and many state courts require expert witnesses to submit written reports.

■ Rule 26, FRCP in the United States requires expert witnesses who anticipate that they will have to testify to submit written reports. The report must include the expert's opinion along with the basis for the opinion.

■ Attorneys use deposition banks to research expert witnesses' previous testimony and to learn more about expert witnesses hired by opposing counsel.

■ Reports should answer the questions you were retained to answer and keep information that doesn't support specific questions to a minimum.

■ A well-defined report structure contributes to readers' ability to understand the information you're communicating. Make sure your report includes clearly labeled sections and follows a numbering scheme consistently. Ensure that supporting materials, such as figures and tables, are numbered and labeled clearly.

14

- Clarity of writing is critical to a report's success. Make sure to include signposts to give readers clues about the sequence of information, and avoid vague wording, jargon, and slang.

- Convey a tone of objectivity, and be detached in your observations. Synthesize what has (and has not) been learned about the problem and what the information means.

Key Terms

deposition banks Libraries of previously given testimony that law firms can access.

discovery Efforts to obtain information before a trial by demanding documents, depositions, interrogatories (written questions answered in writing under oath), and written requests for admissions of fact.

examination plan A document that lets you know what questions to expect when you are testifying.

high-risk document A written report containing sensitive information that could create an opening for the opposing attorney to discredit you.

lay witness A person whose testimony is based on personal observation; not considered to be an expert in a particular field.

spoliation Destroying or concealing evidence; this action is subject to sanctions.

Review Questions

1. Which of the following rules or laws requires an expert to prepare and submit a report?
   a. FRCP 26
   b. FRE 801
   c. Neither
   d. Both

2. For what purpose have hypothetical questions traditionally been used in litigation?
   a. To frame the factual context of rendering an expert witness's opinion
   b. To define the case issues for the finder of fact to determine
   c. To stimulate discussion between the consulting expert and the expert witness
   d. To deter the witness from expanding the scope of his or her investigation beyond the case requirements
   e. All of the above

3. If you were a lay witness at a previous trial, you shouldn't list that case in your written report. True or False?

4. Which of the following is an example of a written report?

   a. A search warrant

   b. An affidavit

   c. Voir dire

   d. Any of the above

5. What is destroying a report before the final resolution of a case called?

6. An expert witness can give an opinion in which of the following situations?

   a. The opinion, inferences, or conclusions depend on special knowledge, skills, or training not within the ordinary experience of laypeople.

   b. The witness is shown to be qualified as a true expert in the field.

   c. The witness testifies to a reasonable degree of certainty (probability) about his or her opinion, inference, or conclusion.

   d. All of the above

7. Which of the following is the standard format for reports filed electronically in federal courts?

   a. Word

   b. Excel

   c. PDF

   d. HTML

   e. Any of the above

8. When writing a report, what's the most important aspect of formatting?

   a. A neat appearance

   b. Size of the font

   c. Clear use of symbols and abbreviations

   d. Consistency

9. Automated tools help you collect and report evidence, but you're responsible for doing which of the following?

   a. Explaining your formatting choices

   b. Explaining the significance of the evidence

   c. Explaining in detail how the software works

   d. All of the above

10. What can be included in report appendixes?

14

11. Which of the following statements about the legal-sequential numbering system in report writing is true?

    a. It's favored because it's easy to organize and understand.

    b. It's most effective for shorter reports.

    c. It doesn't indicate the relative importance of information.

    d. It's required for reports submitted in federal court.

12. What is a major advantage of automated forensics tools in report writing?

Hands-On Projects

In this chapter's projects, several of the data files have been used in previous chapters. Because some of these extracted files are very large and might take up too much room on your computer's drive, move them from these previous folders to this chapter's *Work*\Chap14\Projects folder. If necessary, create this folder on your system before beginning the projects.

Hands-On Project 14-1

This project is a continuation of the in-chapter activities. The general counsel for Superior Bicycles, Ileen Johnson, has asked you to list extracted e-mail metadata from the FTK report. Open the HTML report you generated from this in-chapter activity. If you have closed the file, you can open it from Windows Explorer by navigating to the C:*Work*\Chap14\Chapter\InChp14\report path and double-clicking Index.htm.

Your report should be created on a spreadsheet. You use this spreadsheet in subsequent projects so that you can analyze two or more sources of e-mail correspondence. Your report should have the following information:

- Project number
- FTK message number
- Message origin, such as Return (Re:), Forward (Fw:), or other
- Subject
- From (e-mail address of sender)
- Date
- Time
- Time zone
- To E-mail #1, #2, and so on
- Cc E-mail #1, #2, and so on
- Attachments, if applicable
- Message ID number
- A brief summary of each e-mail's content

Save the report as Chap14hop1.xls (if you're using Excel) or Chap14hop1.ods (if you're using OpenOffice Calc) in your work folder. After completing this spreadsheet, review the contents of each message and write a brief summary memo (listing at least sender, receiver, subject, and date) to Ileen Johnson. Turn the spreadsheet and memo in to your instructor.

Hands-On Project 14-2

Ileen Johnson has sent you another image file collected from employee Chris Murphy's computer, which uses a different file system from Denise Robinson's computer. (For this project, you use the GCFI-NTFS image files, and you might have to move them from a previous chapter's work folder to this chapter's work folder.) In processing these files, you need to look for spreadsheet accounting information created with OpenOffice Calc (files with .ods and .sxc extensions) and e-mail correspondence created with Outlook Express (.dbx and .pst extensions). When you have located any files with these extensions, bookmark them and generate a report with ProDiscover, and then export the files for further examination in FTK. Follow these steps:

1. Start ProDiscover Basic with the **Run as administrator** option (if you're using Vista). If the Launch Dialog dialog box opens, click **Cancel**.

2. Click **File, New Project** from the menu. In the New Project dialog box, type **C14Prj02** for the project number and project filename, and then click **OK**. Save the project in your work folder.

3. In the tree view, click to expand **Add** and then click **Image File**.

4. In the Open dialog box, navigate to your work folder, click the **GCFI-NTFS.pds** (or **GCFI-NTFS.eve**) file, and click **Open**. If the Auto Image Checksum message box opens, click **Yes**.

5. Click to expand **Images** under Content View, if necessary, and then expand the **GCFI-NTFS.eve** file path so that you can see the folders and files in the work area.

6. Click the **Search** toolbar button. In the Search dialog box, click the **Search for files named** option button. In the text box under it, type the following file extensions, pressing **Enter** after each one: **.ods, .sxc, .dbx,** and **.pst**.

7. Under Select the Disk(s)/Image(s) you want to search in, click the **GCFI-NTFS.eve** image file, and then click **OK**.

8. In the search results, click the check box next to the **Inbox.dbx** file. In the Add Comment dialog box, type **Files for case report C14Prj02** in the Investigator comments text box, click the **Apply to all items** check box, and then click **OK**.

9. In the search results, click the check boxes next to **Sent Items.dbx, Superior Financials2.sxc, Superior Financials 1.sxc, Superior Financials.sxc,** and **Superior Financials3.sxc**.

10. Click the **Add to Report** button, and then double-click **Inbox.dbx** to return to the work area.

14

11. In the work area, right-click **Inbox.dbx** and click **Copy All Selected Files**.

12. In the Choose Destination dialog box, click the **Browse** button, browse to your work folder, click **OK**, and then click **OK** again.

13. In the tree view, click **Report**, and then click **Action**, **Export** from the menu to open the Export dialog box.

14. Type **C14Prj02-prodiscover** in the File Name text box. Click **Browse**, navigate to and click your work folder, click **Save**, and then click **OK** to save the report. Exit ProDiscover Basic. If you're prompted to save the project, click **Yes**.

Next, you integrate this ProDiscover report into an FTK report, analyze the files you extracted, and bookmark these files for your report:

1. Start FTK with the **Run as administrator** option (if you're using Vista), and click **OK** or **Yes** in any warning or message boxes. In the AccessData FTK Startup dialog box, click the **Start a new case** option button, and then click **OK**.

2. In the New Case dialog box, type your name in the Investigator Name text box and **C14Prj02** in the Case Number and Case Name text boxes. Click **Browse**, navigate to and click your work folder, click **OK**, and then click **Next**.

3. In the Case Information dialog box, type your school or group name in the Agency/Company text box and your name in the Examiner's Name text box, and then click **Next**.

4. Click **Next** until you reach the Refine Case - Default dialog box. Click the **Email Emphasis** button, and then click **Next**. In the Refine Index Default dialog box, click **Next** again.

5. In the Add Evidence dialog box, click **Add Evidence**. In the Add Evidence to Case dialog box, click the **Contents of a Folder** option button, and then click **Continue**. In the Browse for Folder dialog box, navigate to and click the folder where you exported the files, and then click **OK**.

6. In the Evidence Information dialog box, click **OK**, and then in the Add Evidence dialog box, click **Next**.

7. To start the processing, click **Finish** in the Case Summary dialog box.

8. In the main FTK window, click the **Search** tab, and then click the **Indexed Search** tab. Type **terrysadler** in the Search Term text box, click **Add**, and then click the **View Cumulative Results** button.

9. In the Filter Search Hits dialog box, click **OK**. In the upper-right pane, expand the list of hits. In the File List pane, click the check box next to each message containing Terry Sadler's e-mail address.

10. Click **Tools**, **Create Bookmark** from the menu. In the Create New Bookmark dialog box, type **Terry Sadler E-mail** in the Bookmark name text box, click the **All checked items** button, click to select the **Include in report** and **Export files** check boxes, and then click **OK**.

11. To create a report, click **File**, **Report Wizard** from the menu. If you see the FTK Friendly Reminder message about filtered data, click **OK**.

12. In the Case Information dialog box, update or add information if necessary, and then click **Next**.

13. In the Bookmarks dialog box, click **Yes, include all bookmarks** and **Yes, export all bookmarked files**, and then click **Next**.

14. In the Open dialog box, navigate to the folder where you saved the Pro-Discover report, click **C14Prj02-prodiscover.rtf**, click **Open**, and then click **Next**.

15. In the Report Location dialog box, click **Finish**, and in the Report Wizard message box, click **Yes** to view the report in your Web browser. Print the report and submit it to your instructor, and leave the report open for the next project.

Hands-On Project 14-3

In this project, you examine the e-mail contents from the files you extracted in Hands-On Project 14-2 and add information to the spreadsheet you created in Hands-On Project 14-1 (Chap14hop1.xls or Chap14hop1.ods). Use the HTML report you generated to list extracted e-mail messages in your spreadsheet. After completing this spreadsheet, review the contents of each message and write a brief summary (listing at least sender, receiver, subject, and date) in a memo to Ileen Johnson. Submit the spreadsheet and memo to your instructor.

Hands-On Project 14-4

For this project, print all e-mail messages and spreadsheets from the two cases you processed in the previous Hands-On Projects. Then write a one- to two-page report addressed to Ileen Johnson that explains the steps you have taken and the evidence you found in your examination. In the conclusion, state your opinion about the nature of the correspondence, based on the e-mails you collected and compared for these cases. Include any supporting materials as appendixes, and be sure to follow the writing guidelines described in this chapter for your report.

14

Case Projects

CASE PROJECTS

Case Project 14-1

The county prosecutor has hired you to investigate a case in which the county treasurer has been accused of embezzlement. What additional resources, such as other experts, might you need to collect data for this investigation? Write a one-page paper outlining what resources you should consider to help you with the evidence collection process.

Case Project 14-2

Your computer investigation firm has been hired to verify the local police department's findings on a current case. Tension over the case is running high in the city. What do you need to ask the police investigator for, and what procedures should you follow? Consider what test you might use to validate the police department's findings. Write a one- to two-page report outlining what you need to do.

Case Project 14-3

Your manager has asked you to research and recommend a writing guide that examiners in your computer forensics organization will use for all official written reports. Conduct research on the Internet to find information about style manuals and technical and legal writing guides. You should also research writing guides from professional associations, such as the IEEE and the American Psychological Association. Write a two- to three-page report recommending a style manual and/or technical/legal writing guide for your organization to use and explain the reasons for your recommendations. Note that you might want to combine guidelines from different sources in coming up with recommendations for computer forensics reports.

chapter 15

Expert Testimony in High-Tech Investigations

After reading this chapter and completing the exercises, you will be able to:

- Explain guidelines for giving testimony as a technical/scientific or expert witness

- Describe guidelines for testifying in court

- Explain guidelines for testifying in depositions and hearings

- Describe procedures for preparing forensics evidence for testimony

This chapter explains the rules of evidence and procedure as they apply to testimony. You learn about the types of testimony—for trials, depositions, and hearings—and the difference between a technical/scientific witness and an expert witness. In addition, you learn how to avoid some common problems of testimony and learn some techniques you can use to increase the value of your testimony. This chapter also offers an example of how to prepare forensics evidence for testimony.

Preparing for Testimony

When cases go to trial, you as a forensics examiner can play one of two roles: You are called as a **technical/scientific witness** or as an **expert witness**. As a technical/scientific witness, you provide only the facts you have found in your investigation—any evidence that meets the relevance standard and is more probative than prejudicial. When you give technical/scientific testimony, you present this evidence and explain what it is and how it was obtained. You don't offer conclusions, only the facts. However, as an expert witness, you have opinions about what you have found or observed. You form these opinions from experience and deductive reasoning based on facts found during an investigation. In fact, it's your opinion that makes you an expert witness.

For either type of testimony in a computer forensics case, you need to prepare thoroughly. Establish communication early with your attorney. Before you start processing evidence, learn about the victim, the complainant, opposing experts or technical/scientific witnesses, and the opposing attorney as soon as possible. Learn the basic points of the dispute. As you learn about the case, take notes, but keep them in rough draft form and record only the facts, keeping your opinions to a minimum. (As explained in Chapter 14, any written material is subject to discovery, so use caution in what you put in written form.)

Your attorney can give you specific guidelines in preparing for the case. Remember that as an expert witness, you work for the attorney, not the client (plaintiff or defendant), so if you discover negative findings, communicate them as soon as possible to your attorney.

As part of your preparation, confirm your findings with your own documentation and by corroborating with other computer forensics professionals. Return to the notes you took during your investigation. If you're working with electronic notes, use care in storing them. In your analysis and reporting, develop and maintain a standard method of processing to minimize confusion and help you prepare for testimony later. Computer forensics is only now developing a peer review process. To get peer review, often you have to search outside your region. Learn to take advantage of your professional network and request peer reviews to help support your findings.

You might also want to use the Internet to learn about opposing experts and try to find their strengths and weaknesses in previous testimony. Review their curriculum vitae, if possible, and see how they present themselves. Your attorney might be able to get copies of depositions they have given in other cases, usually from the deposition banks mentioned in Chapter 14. Some organizations of forensics investigators also maintain electronic mailing lists that you can use to query members about other expert witnesses.

Review the following questions when preparing your testimony:

- What is my story of the case (the central facts relevant to my testimony)?
- What can I say with confidence?
- What is the client's overall theory of the case?
- How does my opinion support the case?
- What is the scope of the case? Have I gone too far?
- Have I identified the client's needs for how my testimony fits into the overall theory of the case?

Documenting and Preparing Evidence

As emphasized in previous chapters, document your steps in gathering and preserving evidence to make sure they are repeatable, in case you're challenged. If your findings can't be repeated, they lose credibility as evidence. In addition, validate your tools and verify your evidence with hashing algorithms to ensure its integrity. (Refer to Chapter 5 for guidelines on using hashing algorithms.) The following guidelines are also useful in ensuring the integrity of your evidence:

- If you need a checklist to analyze evidence, create it only for a specific case. Don't create a formal checklist of your procedures that's applied to all your cases or include such a checklist in your report. If opposing counsel obtains this checklist through discovery, you might be challenged during cross-examination about inconsistencies in your performance, if you deviated from the checklist.

- As a standard practice, collect evidence and record the tools you used in designated file folders or evidence containers. This method helps organize your evidence and tools. Follow a system to record where items are kept for each case and how documentation is stored.

- Remember that the chain of custody of evidence supports the integrity of your evidence; do whatever you can to prevent contamination of the evidence. You should also document any lapse or gap in evidence preservation or custody. Lapses and gaps don't necessarily result in evidence being inadmissible, but they might affect the weight given to the evidence.

- When collecting evidence, be careful not to get too little or too much information. For litigation, you're responsible for collecting only what's asked for, no more. In some circumstances, collecting and identifying evidence on facts unrelated to the case could cause problems for your attorney.

- Make sure you note the date and time of your forensic workstation when starting your analysis. If precise time is an issue, consider using an Internet clock, such as the one at *www.time.gov*, or an atomic clock to verify the accuracy of your workstation's clock. Many retailers, such as Wal-Mart and Radio Shack, now sell atomic clocks.

- Keep only successful output when running analysis tools; don't keep previous runs, such as those missing necessary switch or output settings. Note that you used the tool, but it didn't generate results because of these missing settings.

- When searching for keyword results, rerun searches with well-defined keywords and search parameters. You might even want to state how they relate to the case, such as

15

being business or personal names. Narrow the search to reduce false hits, and eliminate search results containing false-positive hits.

- When taking notes of your findings, keep them simple and specific to the investigation. You should avoid any personal comments so that you don't have to explain them to opposing counsel.

- When writing your report, list only the evidence that's relevant to the case; do not include unrelated findings.

- Define any procedures you use to conduct your analysis as scientific and conforming to your profession's standards. Listing textbooks, technical books, articles by recognized experts, and procedures from authoritative organizations that you relied on or referenced during your examination is a common way to prove your conformity with scientific and professional standards.

Reviewing Your Role as a Consulting Expert or an Expert Witness

Depending on your attorney's needs, you might provide only your opinion and technical expertise to him or her instead of testifying in court; this role is called a consulting expert. If your role changes from consulting expert to expert witness later, however, your previous work as a consulting expert is subject to discovery by opposing counsel. For this reason, don't record conversations or telephone calls.

When presenting yourself to a federal court as an expert witness, Federal Rules of Civil Procedure (FRCP) 26 (2) (B) requires that you provide the following information:

- Other cases in which you have testified as an expert at trial or deposition in the preceding four years

- Ten years of any published writings

- Previous compensation you have received when giving testimony

In addition, the court can appoint its own expert witnesses. Court-appointed expert witnesses must be neutral in their opinions, and they must be knowledgeable in their field. As an expert hired by the defense or plaintiff, you need to evaluate the court's expert. Make sure you brief your attorney on your findings and opinion of the court's expert to help your attorney deal with any testimony the court-appointed expert provides.

When approached to give expert testimony, find out whether you are the first one asked. If you aren't, find out why other experts might have been contacted but not retained.

Creating and Maintaining Your CV

Your **curriculum vitae** (CV) lists your professional experience and is used to qualify your testimony. For forensics specialists, keeping this document updated and complete is crucial to supporting your role as an expert and showing that you're constantly enhancing your skills through training, teaching, and experience.

Your CV should describe tasks you've performed that define specific accomplishments and your basic and advanced skills. You should also list your general and professional education and professional training. If the list of training is extremely lengthy, use a heading such as "Selected Training Attended." Be sure to include coursework sponsored by government agencies or organizations that train government agency personnel and courses sponsored or approved by professional associations, such as bar associations. Also, note any professional training you provided or contributed to. You must also include a testimony log that reflects every testimony you have given as an expert.

Make sure your CV reflects your professional background. Unlike a job resume, it should not be geared toward a specific trial. Most important, keep your CV current and date it for version control. If your CV is more than three months old, you probably need to update it to reflect new cases and additional training.

Keep a separate list of books you've read on your area of expertise, but don't include this list in your CV because it might suggest that you approve of everything written in these books.

Preparing Technical Definitions

Before you testify in court, prepare definitions of technical concepts that you can use when questioned by your attorney and the opposing attorney. Make sure you use your own words, and remember that you're explaining these concepts for a nontechnical audience. You don't need to make the jury subject matter experts; you're simply explaining the general meaning of these terms. The following are examples of definitions to prepare ahead of time for your testimony:

- Computer forensics
- CRC-32, MD5, and SHA-1 hashing algorithms
- Image and bit-stream backups
- File slack and unallocated (free) space
- File timestamps
- Computer log files
- Folder or directory
- Hardware
- Software
- Operating system

Preparing to Deal with the News Media

Some legal actions generate interest from the news media, but you should avoid contact with news media, especially during a case, for the following reasons:

- Your comments could harm the case and create a record that can be used against you.
- You have no control over the context of the information a journalist publishes.
- You can't rely on a journalist's promises of confidentiality. Journalists have been known to be aggressive in getting information, and their interests do not coincide with

15

yours or your client's. Be on guard at all times because your comments could be interpreted in a manner that taints your impartiality in this case and future cases. Even after the case is resolved, avoid discussing details with the press.

If you're solicited for information or opinions by journalists (or anyone else), refrain from saying anything, and refer them to your client (the attorney who retained you). If you can't avoid a journalist, consult with your attorney and determine how to handle the situation. Plan to record any attempted interviews so that you have your own record of what occurred. (Note, however, that state laws on consent for recording vary.) This recording can be important if you're misquoted or quoted out of context. Reporters often look for a sensational sound bite or controversial quote.

Testifying in Court

Before you're called to testify in court, you should become familiar with the usual procedures followed during a trial. First, your attorney examines you about your qualifications to demonstrate to the court that you're competent as an expert or technical witness. The opposing counsel might then cross-examine you on your qualifications (perhaps in an attempt to discredit you). Next, your attorney leads you through the evidence, and then opposing counsel cross-examines you. After your testimony, you might be called back to update your testimony, or you might be called as a rebuttal witness.

Understanding the Trial Process

The typical order of trial proceedings, whether civil or criminal, is as follows:

- *Motion in limine*—A pretrial motion to exclude certain evidence because it would prejudice the jury. Effectively, a **motion in limine** is a written list of objections to certain testimony or exhibits. It allows the judge to decide whether certain evidence should be admitted when the jury isn't present. Some evidence is so prejudicial that the jury simply knowing it exists is enough to damage the case. In this situation, getting a ruling on the evidence before trial is crucial.

- *Empaneling the jury*—This process includes voir dire of venireman (questioning potential jurors to see whether they're qualified), strikes (rejecting potential jurors), and seating of jurors.

- *Opening statements*—Both attorneys provide an overview of the case.

- *Plaintiff*—Plaintiff presents the case.

- *Defendant*—Defendant presents the case.

- *Rebuttal*—Rebuttal from both plaintiff and defense is an optional phase of the trial. Generally, it's allowed to cover an issue raised during cross-examination.

- *Closing arguments*—Statements that organize the evidence and state the applicable law.

- *Jury instructions*—The attorneys propose instructions to the jury on how to consider the evidence, and then the judge approves or disapproves; if the instructions are approved, the judge reads them to the jury.

Providing Qualifications for Your Testimony

During the qualification phase of your testimony, your attorney asks questions to elicit the qualifications that make you an expert witness. This qualification phase is called **voir dire** (from the French, literally "to see, to say"). Typically, your attorney guides you through your CV. The amount of detail in this examination depends on several factors, but they all relate to how much advantage the attorney sees in your qualifications. After your attorney has completed this examination, he or she asks the court to accept you as an expert on computer forensics. However, opposing counsel might object and is allowed to examine you, too; usually, cross-examination happens only if the opposing attorney thinks there's something to gain from it.

If you know that the opposing expert witness taught or took a course that used a publication you wrote or co-authored, tell your attorney about it. He could emphasize that you're the author and examine the opposing witness on this fact.

The following example is a short direct-examination voir dire:

Q: Please state your name and spell your last name for the record.
A: William Nokiki, N-O-K-I-K-I.
Q: What is your profession?
A: I am a computer forensics examiner.
Q: How long have you been a computer forensics examiner?
A: Twelve years.
Q: Where are you currently employed?
A: I am currently employed by IT Forensics, Incorporated, of Seattle, Washington.
Q: How long have you been with IT Forensics?
A: Eight years.
Q: What is your title with IT Forensics?
A: I am a senior case manager.
Q: What training have you received in computer forensics?
A: I have been trained at the Federal Law Enforcement Training Center in 2000, I trained with NTI in 1996, and I have received training from the International Association of Computer Investigative Specialists since 1999, most recently training on large disk acquisition and network monitoring. I have taken dozens of short courses with many different investigative training organizations over the past fifteen years.
Q: Where have you been an instructor?
A: I have taught classes on computer forensics at City College, Highline Community College, Bellevue Community College, and Lake Washington Technical College. I taught the computer forensics instructors for the state of Washington in 2002. I have made many shorter presentations, including continuing legal education programs approved by the Washington State Bar Association.
Q: Have you been published?
A: Yes, I am co-author of the college textbook Computer Investigations and Forensics.
Q: Have you testified previously?
A: Yes, I have most recently in United States v. Smith. A detailed list of occasions in which I have testified is in my CV.

15

Plaintiff's Attorney:	Your witness.
Defense Attorney:	No questions for the witness.
Plaintiff's Attorney:	Your honor, Plaintiff would move that Mr. Nokiki be accepted as an expert witness on computer forensics.
Judge:	Any objection, Mr. Defense Attorney?
Defense Attorney:	No objection, Your Honor.
Judge:	Mr. Nokiki is accepted as an expert witness on computer forensics. You may proceed, Mr. Plaintiff's Attorney.

If you have especially strong qualifications and have been qualified as an expert on several occasions, opposing counsel might offer to accept you as an expert without your qualifications being stated formally. Generally, your attorney bypasses that offer in favor of impressing the jury with your qualifications.

General Guidelines on Testifying

Whether you're serving as an expert or a scientific/technical witness, be professional and polite when presenting yourself to any attorney or the court. Before the trial, try to learn the jury, judge, and attorneys' level of knowledge on and attitudes toward computers and technology. Talk to local attorneys to learn more about the type of people typically serving on local juries. With this knowledge, you can gauge your presentation to your audience's educational level, and incorporate appropriate analogies into your explanations. Remember that the judge is well educated but not necessarily in the field of digital evidence. Jurors typically average around 12 years of education and an eighth-grade reading level. The attorneys might have a thorough background in the field, but you're the expert with experience. You could also be dealing with an arbiter or mediator who may or may not have a background in computer forensics.

There are two responses you use often as a witness. First, if asked a question you can't answer, respond by saying, "That is beyond the scope of my expertise" or "I was not requested to investigate that." These statements make it clear that you understand your limitations. You won't seem less of an expert for knowing and expressing your limitations. If anything, acknowledging your limitations enhances your standing with a jury. Second, if you don't understand a question or find it confusing, simply say, "Can you please rephrase the question?" Typically, this response gets the attorney to reorganize the question and is one method you can use to control the pace and direction of the examination. If the question is stated awkwardly or you aren't sure of the intent, ask the attorney for clarification.

Another aspect of acknowledging your limitations is making sure you avoid overstating opinions. Part of what you have to deliver to the jury is a person they can trust to help them figure out something that's beyond their expertise. Overstating an opinion creates the potential for the jury to mistrust or doubt you; like a teacher, you should admit your limitations and the limitations of your results.

Your delivery is an important part of how you answer questions and affects the impact you have on the jury. The following list offers some general guidelines on delivery and presentation:

- Always acknowledge the jury and direct your testimony to them, using an enthusiastic, sincere tone to keep the jury interested in what you have to say. When an attorney or the judge asks you a question, turn toward the questioner, and then turn back to the jury to give the answer.

- If a microphone is present, place it 6 to 8 inches from you, and remember to speak loudly and clearly so that the jury can hear and understand you.

- Use simple, direct language to help the jury understand you. For example, use "test" instead of "analyze," as in "I ran a test on the files I found." Also, make sure you use specific, articulate speech when speaking; for clarity, avoid contractions and slang, unless you're quoting a fact related to the case.

- Avoid humor. What one person thinks is funny, another won't. In addition, limit your responses to what you perceive as attempts at humor from anybody else.

- Build repetition into your explanations and descriptions for the jury.

- Use chronological order to describe events when testifying, and use hand gestures to help the audience understand what you're emphasizing. For example, point to graphics while talking. (Graphics are discussed more later in "Using Graphics During Testimony.")

- If you're using technical terms, identify and define these terms for the jury, using analogies and graphics as appropriate. List any important technical elements, showing how you verified and validated each element.

- When giving an opinion, cite the source of the evidence the opinion is based on. Then express your opinion and explain your methodology—how you arrived at your opinion.

- If the witness chair is adjustable, make sure the height is comfortable, and turn the chair so that it faces the jury.

- To enhance your image with the jury, dress in a manner conforming to the community's dress code. In a small town, dress like the attorneys in the case. If your testimony is being videotaped, avoid fine stripes in suits or ties because they can generate a strobing effect in video recordings under artificial light. Men should wear conservative ties with a base color of red; women should wear suits in conservative colors or a dress that allows freedom of movement. A somewhat dated opinion for expert witnesses recommends dressing in the same fashion as the local bank manager so that the jury associates you with a respected figure in the community. A similarly dated opinion proposes that black, dark green, or yellow clothing isn't appropriate.

- Don't memorize your testimony; you should strive for a natural, extemporaneous tone. Also, make sure you have alternative ways to describe or explain key facts.

- For direct examinations, state your opinion, identify evidence to support your opinion, explain the method you used to arrive at your opinion from your analysis, and then restate your opinion.

As mentioned previously, have definitions and explanations aimed at a nontechnical audience ready for technical terms you must use in your testimony. Learn how to describe the tools you use as a standardized process for your work. Make sure you're knowledgeable about the fallibility of computer forensics so that you can resist counterattacks from opposing counsel. Lengthy explanations might be good for some jury cases but not for others, so seek your attorney's opinion.

Prepare your testimony with the attorney who hired you. The following are specific questions you should prepare for:

- How is data (or evidence) stored on a hard drive?

- What is an image or a bit-stream copy of a drive?

- How is deleted data recovered from a drive?
- What are Windows temporary files and how do they relate to data or evidence?
- What are system or network log files?

Using Graphics During Testimony Graphical exhibits, such as charts and tables, illustrate and clarify your findings. As a general rule, memory retention is much weaker for audio material and slightly stronger for visual material. Therefore, oral testimony supported by graphical presentations is an effective way to impart information and help your listeners retain it. Your exhibits must be clear and easy to understand. Graphics should be big, bold, and simple so that the jury can see them easily, and consider factors such as glare and adequate contrast to ensure easy visibility. If necessary, make smaller copies of graphics for jurors so that they can see details better.

The goal of using graphics is to provide information the jury needs to know, such as how hardware and software work, an explanation of your findings, and the role the evidence plays in the case. Make sure each graphic conveys only one concept or point; don't try to include too much information in a single graphic. If you're using graphics to explain a complex technical concept or procedure, use two or more graphics, with the first graphic providing an overview.

Don't include vendor logos on your charts, and don't use charts created by someone else, unless you commissioned someone to create them, to avoid possible copyright issues. Another advantage of creating your own charts is to make sure you're comfortable with what's in them and can explain the material in them.

Review all graphics with your attorney before trial, and make sure you've practiced using your graphics so that you appear comfortable and confident. In most courts, you need at least three additional copies of your graphics: one for your attorney, one for the opposing attorney, and one for the judge. However, it's the attorney's responsibility to have graphical exhibits admitted into evidence.

Courtrooms are becoming more audiovisual capable, and you might be able to use a projector system. If one is available, discuss using it with your attorney. You might also talk about the possibility of giving jurors copies of your presentation on CD or DVD.

Make sure the jury can see your graphics, and face the jury during your presentation. If your graphics haven't been placed near the jury box, ask the judge if you can move them so that the jury can see them better. When you're talking about specific areas of an illustration, use a pointer to direct jurors' attention to details. You can also use your hands to help emphasize certain information or direct attention to specific points. Make sure any gestures are above the waist so that the jury can see them. If an attorney asks you questions as you explain the graphics, face the jury and answer the questions in full sentences.

When you're standing in front of the jury, leave your jacket unbuttoned and keep your elbows bent to show that you're comfortable, confident, and at ease.

Avoiding Testimony Problems Although you should recognize when conflict-of-interest issues apply to your case and discuss any concerns with the attorney who hires you, be aware of a practice called **conflicting out**. It's an attempt by opposing attorneys to prevent you from serving on an important case and is most common in the private sector when you work as an independent consultant. Opposing attorneys might call to discuss the case with you and then claim you can't testify because of a conflict of interest caused by you discussing the case with another attorney besides the one who hired you. As a result, you might be excluded from working for an attorney needing your services. (The issue of conflict is raised by motion after witness lists are exchanged.)

In addition, avoid agreeing to review a case unless you're under contract with that person. Also, avoid conversations with opposing attorneys—there's no such thing as an "off the record" conversation with opposing attorneys after you have been retained; refer them to the attorney who retained you. Have a fee agreement ready to e-mail or fax to opposing attorneys to protect yourself from this practice; this agreement documents that they didn't want to retain you. If you aren't retained, you're in a better position to collect a fee for the service you did provide, and it deters them from attempting to manufacture a conflict issue.

Early in direct examination, your attorney should ask whether you were hired to perform an analysis and testify. He or she might ask how much you charged for your services and whether you have already been paid; you should receive payment before testifying. If you haven't been paid, it might seem that you have a contingent interest in the litigation—that your payment depends on the resolution of the case. Fees and payment schedules are an appropriate subject for examination, although the judge might limit these questions. If your attorney doesn't ask you questions about payment, the opposing counsel could examine you on it in an effort to discredit you or lessen your credibility as a witness. However, opposing counsel knows that this tactic might be used on his expert witnesses, too, so he might touch on the subject but not dwell on it, unless you say you haven't been paid completely.

When you're testifying, don't talk to anyone during court recess. If the opposing attorney sees you having a conversation with anyone, including the attorney who retained you, the opposing attorney could cross-examine you again and demand that you explain and repeat your conversation. However, be aware that your attorney might want to notify you of updates during breaks, so make sure you conduct any conferences in a private setting. If a juror approaches and says anything to you, decline to talk with him or her and promptly report the contact to the attorney who retained you. This event must be reported to the court.

Understanding Prosecutorial Misconduct If you're working for a prosecutor in a criminal case and believe you have found exculpatory evidence (evidence that exonerates or diminishes the defendant's liability), you have an obligation to ensure that the evidence isn't concealed. Initially, you should report the evidence (emphasizing its exculpatory nature) to the prosecutor handling the case. Be sure you document the communication of your concern to the prosecutor. If this information isn't disclosed to the defense attorney in a reasonable time, you can report it to the prosecutor's supervisor. Be sure to document this communication, too. Documentation of each attempt to induce disclosure and your reasoning is important to protect your reputation.

If these efforts still don't result in disclosure, you can report the lack of disclosure to the judge. Be sure you have documented your attempts to bring the matter to the prosecutor's attention before bringing it to the judge. Don't communicate directly with the defense attorney; reporting evidence to the judge fulfills your obligation.

15

Testifying During Direct Examination

You provide direct testimony when you answer questions from the attorney who hired you. This direct examination is the most important part of testimony at a trial. Cross-examination is not as important, even if the opposing attorney is attempting to discredit you.

When preparing your testimony for direct examination, keep some guidelines and techniques in mind. You should work with your attorney to get the right language that communicates your message to the jury effectively. Also, your attorney might advise you to be wary of your inclination to be helpful. This trait is natural, but it can hurt your testimony. You shouldn't volunteer any information or be overly friendly (or hostile) to the opposing attorney.

Review the examination plan your attorney has prepared to see whether you can make any suggestions for improvement; this plan is structured to ensure that questions elicit relevant evidence during direct examination. Make sure you've prepared a clear overview of your findings and have a systematic and easy-to-follow plan for describing your evidence-collection methods. Practice testifying with your graphics so that you're comfortable using them.

Your attorney might also help you develop a theme to follow when presenting your testimony, but make sure you use your own words when answering questions. Generally, the best approach your attorney can take in direct examination is to ask you open-ended questions and let you give your testimony.

In addition, make sure you know the following terms before giving testimony because your attorney will likely use them during the direct examination:

- *Independent recollection*—Information you know about this case and others without being prompted
- *Customary practice*—Procedures that are traditionally followed in similar cases
- *Documentation of the case*—The written records you have maintained

When your attorney questions you about your background and qualifications, your answers should show why you are an expert able to give testimony. Give answers that emphasize your factual findings and opinions. Remember to tailor your language to the jury's educational level, and try to strike a balance between technical language and layperson language when describing complex matters.

Avoid vagueness in your wording choices, too. For example, don't use expressions such as "very large" or "a long time." The meaning of these expressions varies, depending on what they're compared to, and that comparison might be different for every juror. Use precise numbers and units of measurement, and if relevant, cite numbers' statistical position, relationship to the mean, or an expected value or range.

When you're using graphics in a presentation, keep in mind that you're instructing the jury in what you did to collect evidence, so follow some of the same guidelines teachers would use in a classroom to make sure the jury understands your explanations.

Testifying During Cross-Examination

When answering questions from the opposing attorney, use your own words. Keep in mind that certain words have additional meanings that an opposing attorney can exploit. For example, the word "suspicious" is more value laden than the more neutral "concerned."

During cross-examination, opposing attorneys sometimes use the trick of interrupting you as you're answering a question. In a trial, a judge usually doesn't allow this trick, but in a deposition, there's no independent arbiter of procedure. Be aware of leading questions from the opposing attorney, too. An ambiguous question, such as "Isn't it true that forensics experts always destroy their handwritten notes?" is an attempt to lead you to say something that could be construed as wrong. (The answer to that question should be "I don't know.") Leading questions call for yes or no answers and are sometimes referred to as "setup questions"—setting you up for a response that could be damaging to your client's case. They are often phrased in a complex structure, designed to limit your freedom in answering. Getting to the real question opposing counsel is asking might take many questions.

If opposing attorneys ask you a question such as "Did you use more than one tool to verify the evidence?" they are checking to make sure you validated the findings from one tool by using another tool. Opposing attorneys often ask the following questions, too:

- What are the tools you used and what are their known problems or weaknesses?
- Are the tools you used reliable? Are they consistent, and do they produce the same results?
- Have other professionals called on you as a consultant on how to use tools?
- Do you keep up with the latest technologies applied to computer forensics, such as by reading journal articles?

During examinations, lawyers aren't supposed to ask another question until you have finished answering the current question. However, opposing counsel sometimes uses rapid-fire questions meant to throw you off. Taking a moment to turn toward the jury before you answer gives you time to maintain control over the speed of the opposing attorney's examination. Even though your attorney should object by saying, "Counsel has not allowed the witness to answer the question," don't be afraid to regroup and restate your answers if you get confused during your testimony. Jurors will sympathize because often they are confused by the opposing attorney's questions, too.

If the opposing attorney declares that you aren't answering the questions, he could be making an attempt to get you to change your testimony. You aren't giving the answer he wants, or he's attempting to get you to say something that contradicts part of your previous testimony. Don't take this attempt personally, but think carefully about what the opposing attorney is trying to do.

During a jury trial, keep eye contact with the jury. You might find yourself competing with the opposing attorney, but do your best to keep the jury's attention on you during your testimony. As the opposing attorney asks you questions, avoid strict yes or no answers, if possible; add facts to clarify your answer, when appropriate, before opposing counsel can hit you with a "killer question." This type of question, contrived based on a change in a basic underlying fact, is one that you seemingly can't answer or deny. It can derail your testimony and your client's case; however, the judge will usually support you in stating conditions or limits.

Sometimes opposing attorneys ask several questions inside one question; this practice is called a compound question, and your attorney should object to it. If your attorney doesn't, you can respond by saying "Could you please break your last question into separate questions?" Another tactic opposing attorneys use in cross-examinations is to make a speech and phrase it as a question. You have no obligation to respond to statements by opposing counsel. The judge usually catches this error, and your attorney should also object. Other methods

15

opposing attorneys use to challenge your credibility are putting words in your mouth and summarizing your testimony to fit their needs, creating assumptions or speculation, and controlling the pace of your testimony. Other tactics are stating minor inconsistencies that cause you to make conflicting statements and encouraging you to volunteer information.

Your response to questioning tactics should challenge the opposing attorney to be more sensible, a response that often plays well with juries. Take your time answering questions. Be thoughtful, professional, and courteous in your responses. The more patient you are during the cross-examination, the better you'll weather any possible attacks. If the opposing attorney becomes assertive or upset with your testimony, be as professional and courteous as possible. If he continues to lose control, staying calm and professional strengthens your image by comparison. Responding to a question with a sentence that communicates limitations or qualifications might be important, if a simple yes or no doesn't answer the question completely and accurately. If you feel the need to have your attorney expand a line of questions on redirect, have an agreed-on expression you can use to signal him, such as "This question requires a more complex answer, but the short answer is yes (or no)."

In addition to direct examination and cross-examination, most jurisdictions now allow the judge and jurors to ask questions. These questions are subject to the rules of evidence just as any other question is. Attorneys can object to these questions but generally won't unless they are an especially serious breach of the rules, such as a question that was specifically excluded in a motion in limine. Answering a question from the judge or a juror should be viewed as an opportunity. As a witness, you usually have to guess at what's important to the judge and jury, but a question from them is one you don't have to guess about.

Many factors contribute to your stress on the stand, including the judge, the attorneys, the jury, and the feeling of losing control. Don't think you're responsible for the outcome. If you make a mistake, correct it, and get back on track with your testimony. You want to avoid showing that you have lost control, such as by the following behaviors:

- Being argumentative when being badgered by the opposing attorney or feeling nervous about testifying
- Having poor listening skills or using defensive body language, such as crossing your arms
- Being too talkative or talking too fast when answering questions
- Being too technical for the jury to understand your testimony
- Acting surprised and unprepared to respond when presented with unknown or new information

Never have unrealistically high self-expectations when testifying; everyone makes mistakes. Who controls the testimony is the most important part for the attorney, in both direct examination and cross-examination. The key to successful cross-examination is to continue selling yourself to the jury, no matter how much the opposing attorney tries to discredit you or your testimony.

Preparing for a Deposition or Hearing

A **deposition** differs from trial testimony because there's no jury or judge. Both attorneys are present and ask you questions. The purpose of the deposition is for the opposing attorney to preview your testimony before trial. The attorney who requests a deposition usually establishes its location, which might be in his or her office or your forensics laboratory.

There are two types of depositions: discovery and testimony preservation. A **discovery deposition** is part of the discovery process for trial. The opposing attorney who requested the deposition frequently conducts the equivalent of a direct examination and a cross-examination. Your attorney usually asks only questions needed to clarify a point that could be subject to misinterpretation in your direct testimony. Although a discovery deposition can be videotaped, a written transcript is more common. If the deposition *is* videotaped, rules require a longer notice period to schedule it than a stenographically recorded one.

A **testimony preservation deposition** is usually requested by your client to preserve your testimony in case of schedule conflicts or health problems. These depositions are often videotaped in addition to the written transcript, and your testimony is entered by playing the videotape for the jury. In some cases, you can set the deposition at your laboratory or have lab facilities available, which can make it easier to conduct demonstrations and produce better testimony. This deposition follows the pattern of trial testimony, with your attorney calling you as a witness and conducting a direct examination, opposing counsel conducting cross-examination, and redirect and recross examination if necessary. The judge rules on objections and, based on objections that are sustained, decides which portions of the testimony are omitted from the copy presented to the jury.

Guidelines for Testifying at Depositions

Often attorneys are more combative during discovery depositions than they are during trial (or videotaped depositions). For this reason, a deposition can be more stressful than trial testimony. Therefore, strive to stay calm and convey a relaxed, confident appearance during a deposition. For example, try to keep your hands on top of the table, and make sure your chair is at the right height to avoid sitting below the opposing attorney's eye level. Maintain a professional demeanor and try not to be influenced by the opposing attorney's tone, expression, or tactics. Learn the opposing attorney's name before the deposition and include it in your responses to project a sense of equality in position between you and opposing counsel. Look the opposing attorney directly in the eyes, even if he attempts to avoid eye contact.

Remember that during a deposition, opposing attorneys use all the techniques available to them at trial, so keep the guidelines for testimony in mind when answering questions, and be assertive in your responses. If you're particularly concerned about the deposition, ask your attorney to videotape a practice session, and then evaluate your performance. Here are some general rules to follow during depositions:

- Be professional and polite.
- Use facts when describing your opinion.
- Understand that being deposed in a discovery deposition is an unnatural process; it's intended to get you to make mistakes.

15

If you prepared a written report, the opposing attorney might attempt to use it against you by leading you to testify contrary to what you had previously written. If the attorney is concealing the report or any other document from your view, ask to see the document. When the opposing attorney asks you about something specific in your written report, ask what page number he's referring to. If you don't have the report in your hands, you can ask to review it.

If your attorney objects to a question from the opposing attorney, pause and think of what direction your attorney might want you to go in your answer. Keep your answers short and simple. Strive for a relaxed, friendly demeanor, especially if you're being videotaped. To gain time and control, ask the opposing attorney questions to clarify what he's asking for, such as asking him to repeat the question.

Be prepared at the end of a deposition to spell any specialized or technical words you used. To aid court reporters, provide them with a list of technical or scientific words you use often, including definitions and correct spellings.

Recognizing Deposition Problems Discuss any potential problems with your attorney before the deposition. Identify anything that might affect your client negatively and could be used by opposing counsel. If you don't disclose this information, the opposing attorney might use it against you in court. Be prepared to defend yourself if there are problems. The following guidelines can also help you avoid problems during depositions:

- Avoid omitting information in your testimony; omissions can cause major problems. Although you don't have to volunteer more information than an attorney asks for, make sure you're telling the truth at all times.

- To respond to difficult questions that could jeopardize your client's case, pause before answering, allowing your attorney to object before you answer.

- To avoid having the opposing attorney box you into a corner or lead you to contradict previous statements, answer only the questions you're asked, using short answers that are narrow in scope when possible.

- Recognize that excessively detailed questions from opposing counsel are an attempt to get you to contradict yourself. Avoid trying to educate the opposing attorney, especially if the questions seem to be beyond the scope of your expertise or the questions you were retained to answer. Feel free to give answers such as "I don't know" or "I don't understand."

- When asked whether you know about an opposing expert witness, your response should be as professional as possible. A good standard answer is "I have heard Mr. Smith is a competent examiner, but I have not reviewed his work." If you have specific and verifiable information that's damaging to the opposing expert's reputation, you can note it, but do it in an understated manner. This technique emphasizes your professional demeanor, especially if you have negative information about the opposing expert's skills or competency.

- Keep in mind that you can correct any minor errors you make during your examination by referring back to the error and correcting it. You also have an opportunity after the deposition, but you have to ask for it. You'll be asked at the end of the deposition if you waive signature; if you want to review the deposition, you shouldn't waive signature because you then get a chance to review, make corrections on the corrections page, and sign the deposition.

- Also, discovery deposition testimony often doesn't make it to the jury; however, it might be presented to the jury, usually as part of an attempt to discredit the witness. This process is called "publishing the deposition."

Guidelines for Testifying at Hearings

Testifying at a hearing is generally comparable to testifying at a trial, so follow the same general guidelines you would for courtroom testimony. A hearing can be before an administrative agency or a legislative body or in a court (when it typically addresses specific issues). An administrative hearing generally addresses the agency's subject matter and seeks evidence in your testimony on a subject for which it's contemplating making a rule. A presiding officer is present, and the format of questioning depends on the agency's rules and the purpose of the hearing. Often administrative or legislative hearings are related to events that resulted in litigation. Testifying at administrative hearings isn't as common as testifying in depositions or trials.

The federal government has thousands of administrative agencies, and states often have hundreds of administrative agencies.

A judicial hearing is held in court to determine the admissibility of certain evidence before trial. No jury is present, but evidentiary suppression hearings are usually held early in the case to determine whether a criminal case moves forward or is dismissed. Generally, they focus more on your procedure in obtaining and preserving evidence than on the substance of the evidence or your opinion. They can also include the basis or authority (warrant or probable cause) for you conducting the examination. In most criminal cases, the defense attorney seeks to suppress any evidence for which there's an arguable basis for rejection.

Preparing Forensics Evidence for Testimony

In this section, you learn the steps for extracting information to be presented to a court. You also learn how to prepare to testify on digital evidence you have collected. You should be ready to answer specific questions from your attorney as well as opposing counsel.

In the following example, the general counsel for Superior Bicycles, Ileen Johnson, has asked you to collect all known e-mail addresses from employee Chris Murphy's computer. Ms. Johnson also needs the message contents of e-mail for her paralegal staff to review and all e-mail from Mr. Murphy's computer image with addresses that aren't from Superior Bicycles. Ms. Johnson advises you that you need to testify on data you extracted to show the chain of custody for your findings.

Before beginning the following activity, create a folder called *Work\Chap15\Chapter* for your work folder, and move all GCFI-NTFS image file segments, including the GCFI-NTFS.pds file, you used in previous chapters to this folder.

To perform this task, you use ProDiscover Basic to extract e-mail folders and FTK Demo to extract and analyze e-mail metadata and messages. Follow these steps:

1. Start ProDiscover Basic with the **Run as administrator** option (if you're using Vista), and click the **New Project** toolbar button. Type **C15InChp** for the project number and filename, and then click **OK**.

2. Click **Action** from the menu, point to **Add**, and click **Image File**.

3. In the Open dialog box, navigate to your work folder, click **GCFI-NTFS.pds**, and then click **Open**. If necessary, click **Yes** in the Auto Image Checksum message box.

4. To begin a search for Outlook and Outlook Express folders, click the **Search** toolbar button or click **Action, Search** from the menu to open the Search dialog box.

5. Click the **Content Search** tab, and then click the **Search for files named** option button. Under Search for the pattern(s), type **.dbx** and **.pst**, pressing **Enter** after each entry. Under Select the Disk(s)/Image(s) you want to search in, click the **GCFI-NTFS.eve** file, and then click **OK**.

6. At the top of the search results, click the **Selection** button, and then click **Select All**. When the Add Comment dialog box opens, click the **Apply to all items** check box, type **Extracted Outlook folders** in the Investigator comments text box, and then click **OK**.

7. At the top of the search results, click the **Add to Report** button, and then double-click **Inbox.dbx** (twice, if necessary) to return to the work area.

8. Right-click **Inbox.dbx** and click **Copy All Selected Files**.

9. In the Choose Destination dialog box, click the **Browse** button, browse to your work folder, click **OK**, and then click **OK** again.

10. Click **File, Save Project** from the menu. In the Save As dialog box, navigate to and click your work folder, and then click **Save**. Exit ProDiscover Basic.

For the next part of the testimony preparation, you use FTK Demo. Follow these steps to locate e-mail addresses and metadata that can be copied into a spreadsheet:

1. Start FTK with the **Run as administrator** option (if you're using Vista). If you're prompted with warning dialog boxes and/or notification messages, click **OK** to continue.

2. Click **Start a new case**, and then click **OK**. In the New Case dialog box, enter your name in the Investigator's name text box and **InChp15** in the Case Number and Case Name text boxes. Next to the Case Path text box, click **Browse**, navigate to and click your work folder, click **OK**, and then click **Next**.

3. In the Case Information dialog box, enter your school or group name in the Agency/ Company text box, enter your name in the Examiner's Name text box, and then click **Next**.

4. Click **Next** until you reach the Refine Case - Default dialog box. Click the **Email Emphasis** button, and then click **Next**.

5. Click **Next** until you reach the main Add Evidence to Case dialog box, and then click the **Add Evidence** button. In the Add Evidence to Case dialog box, click the **Contents of a Folder** option button, and then click **Continue**.

6. In the Browse for Folder dialog box, navigate to and click your work folder, and then click **OK**. In the Evidence Information dialog box, click **OK**, and in the main Add Evidence to Case dialog box, click **Next**.

7. To start the processing, click **Finish** in the Case summary dialog box.

Next, you locate all non-Superior Bicycles e-mail messages and extract them into HTML files. Superior Bicycles e-mail addresses have a .biz extension, so you shouldn't search for this extension. Instead, search for the standard e-mail address extensions of .com, .net, and .org.

1. Click **Tools, Internet Keyword Search** from the FTK menu. In the Internet Keyword Search Options dialog box, click to clear all **URL Searches** check boxes, leave the default **E-mail Address Searches** check boxes selected, and then click **OK**.

2. In the Internet Address Search Results dialog box shown in Figure 15-1, click the **Internet Address** column heading to sort all addresses by message.

Internet Address Search Results

```
SMTPSVC(6.0.3790.1830);
  Thu, 11 Jan 2007 13:13:12 -0600
Received: from myway.com (nn4.excitenetwork.com [207.159.120.58])
  by smtp-sjt-01.vividround.com (8.12.11/8.12.11) with ESMTP id I0BJCti7057068
  for <chris.murphy@superiorbicycles.biz>; Thu, 11 Jan 2007 13:12:55 -0600 (CST)
Received: by mprdmxin.myway.com (Postfix, from userid 110)
  id EC834676A4; Thu, 11 Jan 2007 13:52:49 -0500 (EST)
To: chris.murphy@superiorbicycles.biz
Subject: Plans
Received: from [24.18.24.250] by mprdmailfe10.nwk.myway.com via HTTP; Thu, 11 Jan 2007 13:52:49 EST
X-AntiAbuse: This header was added to track abuse, please include it with any abuse report
X-AntiAbuse: ID = f869dfbea97fe07b9eab2f865d19b540
Reply-to: 5amspade@myway.com
From: "Sam"<5amspade@myway.com>
```

Internet Address	File Name	Full Path	File Type
5amspade@myway.c...	Message0020	F:\Work\InChp15\G...	E-mail Message
"Sam"<5amspade...	Message0020	F:\Work\InChp15\G...	E-mail Message
5amspade@myway.c...	Message0020	F:\Work\InChp15\G...	E-mail Message
<20070111185249.E...	Message0020	F:\Work\InChp15\G...	E-mail Message
5amspade@myway.c...	Message0020	F:\Work\InChp15\G...	E-mail Message
<terrysadler@goo...	Message0020	F:\Work\InChp15\G...	E-mail Message
5amspade@mprdmai...	Message0020	F:\Work\InChp15\G...	E-mail Message
<terrysadler@goo...	Message0020	F:\Work\InChp15\G...	E-mail Message
<5amspade@mprd...	Message0020	F:\Work\InChp15\G...	E-mail Message
<terrysadler@goo...	Message0020	F:\Work\InChp15\G...	E-mail Message
<5amspade@myw...	Message0020	F:\Work\InChp15\G...	E-mail Message

[Create bookmark...] [Add List to Evidence]   [Close]

Figure 15-1 The Internet Address Search Results dialog box

---

3. To create a listing of all addresses, click the **Add List to Evidence** button at the bottom. When the Evidence Added Successfully message box opens, click **OK**.

4. Click the first e-mail address—**"Sam"<5amspade@myway.com>**—in the Internet Address column that's associated with Message0020 in the File Name column, and then click the **Create bookmark** button at the bottom. If you don't see "Sam"<5amspade@myway.com> at the top, scroll down the list to find it.

5. In the Create New Bookmark dialog box, type **spade0020** in the Bookmark name text box, click the **Include in report** and **Export files** check boxes, and then click **OK**.

15

The bookmark name includes the message number to make it easier to locate and identify later.

TIP

6. Repeat Steps 4 and 5 for **5amspade@myway.com** associated with Message0042, and use **spade0042** for the bookmark name.

FTK displays all search results for e-mail address in all messages. Typi-cally, the same e-mail address appears several times in a message, as Figure 15-1 showed. When bookmarking multiple search results, you NOTE need to select one message instead of each e-mail address search hit.

7. Find the next occurrence of **<5amspade@myway.com>** associated with Message0008, and repeat Steps 4 and 5, using the bookmark name **spade0008**.

8. Continue scrolling and bookmarking these messages and e-mail accounts: **<baspen99@aol.com>**, **<jim_shu1@yahoo.com>**, **<Jim_shu@comcast.net>**, **<terrysadler@goowy.com>**, and **murphy10@hotmail.com**. Select e-mail addresses associated with messages, and ignore filenames listed as attachments.

9. When you're done bookmarking messages and e-mail accounts, click **Close** in the Internet Address Search Results dialog box.

10. In the main FTK window, click the **Overview** tab, if necessary. Click the **Uncheck all files in the current list** button on the File List toolbar, and then click **Yes** in the FTK confirmation message box.

11. Under the File Status heading, click the **Bookmarked Items** button. On the File List toolbar, click the **Check all files in the current list** button (see Figure 15-2), and then click **Yes** in the FTK confirmation message box.

Figure 15-2 The FTK File List toolbar

12. In the File List pane, right-click the first file, **Message0001**, and click **Export File**. In the Export Files dialog box, click **All checked files**, make sure the **Include email attachments with email messages** and **Append appropriate extension to file name if bad/absent** check boxes are selected, and then click **OK**. Click **OK** again in the Export Files dialog box.

13. Next, click **File, Report Wizard** from the FTK menu. In the Case Information dialog box, type your school's name in the Agency/Company text box and your name in the Investigator's Name text box, and then click **Next**.

14. In the Bookmarks - A dialog box, click **Yes, include all bookmarks,** and then click **Next**.

15. In the Bookmarks - B dialog box, click **Add/Remove File Properties**. In the Detailed List - Data Items to Include dialog box, click **Unselect all**. Then click the **Subject, Email Date, From, To, CC,** and **Attachment** check boxes, and then click **OK**.

16. Click **Next** until you reach the Report Location dialog box, and then click **Finish**.

17. In the Report Wizard dialog box, click **Yes** to view the HTML report.

18. Inspect the report, and then exit your Web browser.

19. Print the FTK report and all HTML files created with the Internet Address Search Results function. Note that the HTML files are in the InChp15\Attach subfolder of your work folder. The e-mail message saved as an HTML file is stored in the InChp15\Export subfolder of your work folder. When you're finished, exit FTK, saving your project if prompted.

Preparing Explanations of Your Evidence-Collection Methods

To prepare for court testimony, you should prepare answers for questions on what steps you took to extract e-mail metadata and messages from the image of Chris Murphy's computer. You might also be asked to explain specific features of the computer, OS, and applications (such as Outlook) and explain how these applications and computer forensics tools work.

Ms. Johnson plans to ask you the following questions when you're called to testify. Prepare your answers, referring to these examples as guidelines, so that you can answer the questions with confidence and professionalism.

Question 1: How did you locate e-mail messages from the image of Mr. Murphy's computer?

Answer 1: I used Technology Pathways ProDiscover Basic to access and search the GCFI-NTFS image of Mr. Murphy's computer.

Question 2: What e-mail files did you search for on Mr. Murphy's computer?

Answer 2: I searched for all files with Microsoft Outlook and Outlook Express extensions of .pst and .dbx.

Question 3: Can you please explain what .pst and .dbx files are?

Answer 3: Microsoft e-mail programs maintain personal e-mail storage files with a file extension of .pst for Outlook and .dbx for Outlook Express. These files are specially formatted to store e-mail messages and attachments.

Question 4: Did you use ProDiscover Basic to examine the e-mail messages?

Answer 4: No, I used another tool called AccessData FTK.

Question 5: What is FTK?

Answer 5: FTK is Forensics Toolkit.

Question 6: What does FTK do differently from ProDiscover?

Answer 6: FTK can read and recover e-mail messages and attachments from Microsoft Outlook and Outlook Express. It can also recover deleted messages from .pst and .dbx files that usually can't be recovered from Outlook or Outlook Express.

Question 7: After you extracted the e-mail files from Mr. Murphy's computer, how did you locate the non-Superior Bicycles e-mail addresses?

Answer 7: FTK has a built-in function that can search for Internet URLs and e-mail addresses. Using this function, I was able to separate the messages to locate all non-Superior Bicycles e-mail addresses.

Question 8: What is a URL?

Answer 8: A URL is a Uniform Resource Locator; it's an Internet address, such as www.whitehouse.gov or www.fbi.gov.

Question 9: How many e-mail addresses did you find in Mr. Murphy's computer?

Answer 9: FTK reported finding 73 e-mail messages.

Question 10: How many of these messages were non-Superior Bicycles e-mail addresses?

Answer 10: I located a total of 16 non-Superior Bicycles e-mail addresses from this forensics examination.

15

Chapter Summary

- When cases go to trial, you as the forensics expert play one of two roles: a technical/scientific witness or an expert witness. As a technical/scientific witness, you're providing only the facts you have discovered in your investigation. However, as an expert witness, you have opinions about what you have observed. In fact, it's your opinion that makes you an expert witness.

- If you're called as a technical or expert witness in a computer forensics case, you need to prepare for your testimony thoroughly. Establish communication early with your attorney. Substantiate your findings with your own documentation and by collaborating with other computer forensics professionals.

- When you're called to testify in court, your attorney examines you on your qualifications to establish your competency as an expert or a technical witness. Opposing counsel might attempt to discredit you based on your past record. Your attorney then leads you through the evidence, followed by the opposing counsel cross-examining you. Redirect examinations and recross examinations of limited scope might follow.

- Make sure you're prepared for questions opposing counsel might use to discredit you, confuse you, or throw you off the track. Stay calm and project professionalism in your behavior and appearance.

- A deposition differs from a trial because there's no jury or judge. Both attorneys and a court reporter are present, and the attorney asks you questions. There are two types of depositions: discovery and testimony preservation.

- Know whether you're being called as a scientific/technical witness or expert witness (or both) and whether you're being retained as a consulting expert or expert witness. Also, be familiar with the contents of your curriculum vitae.

- Depositions usually fall into two categories: discovery depositions and testimony preservation depositions. Testimony preservation depositions are often videotaped. Hearings are typically administrative hearings or judicial hearings.

- Guidelines for testifying at depositions and hearings are much the same as guidelines for courtroom testimony. Keep in mind that attorneys at discovery depositions might be more combative, so striving to maintain a calm, professional appearance can be critical.

- Make sure you prepare answers for questions on what steps you took to collect and analyze evidence and questions on what tools you used and how they work.

Key Terms

conflicting out The practice of opposing attorneys trying to prevent you from testifying by claiming you have discussed the case with them and, therefore, have a conflict of interest.

curriculum vitae (CV) An extensive outline of your professional history that includes your education, training, work, and what cases you have worked on as well as training you have conducted, publications you have contributed to, and professional associations and awards.

deposition A formal examination in which you're questioned under oath with only the opposing parties, your attorney, and a court reporter present. There's no judge or jury. The purpose of a deposition is to give opposing counsel a chance to preview your testimony before trial.

discovery deposition The opposing attorney sets the deposition and frequently conducts the equivalent of both direct and cross-examination. A discovery deposition is considered part of the discovery process. *See also* deposition.

expert witness This type of testimony reports opinions based on experience and facts gathered during an investigation.

motion in limine A pretrial motion made to exclude mentioning certain evidence because it would prejudice the jury.

technical/scientific witness This type of testimony reports only the facts (findings of an investigation); no opinion is given in court.

testimony preservation deposition A deposition held to preserve your testimony in case of schedule conflicts or health problems; it's usually videotaped as well as recorded by a stenographer. *See also* deposition.

voir dire In this qualification phase of testimony, your attorney asks you questions to establish your credentials as an expert witness. The process of qualifying jurors is also called voir dire.

Review Questions

1. Which of the following describes scientific/technical testimony?

    a. Factual testimony describing information recovered during an examination

    b. Testimony by law enforcement officers

    c. Testimony based on observations by lay witnesses

    d. None of the above

2. Which of the following describes expert witness testimony? (Choose all that apply.)

    a. Testimony designed to assist the jury in determining matters beyond the ordinary person's scope of knowledge

    b. Testimony that defines issues of the case for determination by the jury

    c. Testimony resulting in the expression of an opinion by a witness with scientific, technical, or other professional knowledge or experience

    d. Testimony designed to raise doubt about facts or witnesses' credibility

3. When using graphics while testifying, which of the following guidelines applies? (Choose all that apply.)

    a. Make sure the jury can see your graphics.

    b. Practice using charts for courtroom testimony.

    c. Your exhibits must be clear and easy to understand.

    d. Make sure you have plenty of extra graphics, in case you have to explain more complex or supporting issues.

15

4. What kind of information do scientific/technical witnesses provide during testimony? (Choose all that apply.)

   a. Their professional opinion on the significance of evidence

   b. Definitions of issues to be determined by the finder of fact

   c. Facts only

   d. Observations of the results of tests they performed

5. What expressions are acceptable to use in testimony to respond to a question for which you have no answer? (Choose all that apply.)

   a. No comment.

   b. That's beyond the scope of my expertise.

   c. I don't want to answer that question.

   d. I was not requested to investigate that.

   e. That is beyond the scope of my investigation.

6. What should you do if you realize you have made a mistake or misstatement during a deposition? (Choose all that apply.)

   a. If the deposition is still in session, refer back to the error and correct it.

   b. Decide whether the error is minor, and if so, ignore it.

   c. If the deposition is over, make the correction on the corrections page of the copy provided for your signature.

   d. Call the opposing attorney and inform him of your mistake or misstatement.

   e. Request an opportunity to make the correction at trial.

7. List two types of depositions.

8. At trial as a technical, scientific, or expert witness, what must you always remember about your testimony?

   a. You're responsible for the outcome of the case.

   b. Your duty is to report your technical or scientific findings or render an honest opinion.

   c. Avoid mentioning how much you were paid for your services.

   d. All of the above

9. Before testifying, you should do which of the following? (Choose all that apply.)

   a. Create an examination plan with your attorney.

   b. Make sure you've been paid for your services and the estimated fee for the deposition or trial.

   c. Get a haircut.

   d. Type all the draft notes you took during your investigation.

10. Voir dire is the process of qualifying a witness as an expert. True or False?

11. What is a motion in limine?

    a. A motion to dismiss the case

    b. The movement of molecules in a random fashion

    c. A pretrial motion for the purpose of excluding certain evidence

    d. A pretrial motion to revise the case schedule

12. During your cross-examination, you should do which of the following? (Choose all that apply.)

    a. Maintain eye contact with the jury.

    b. Pay close attention to what your attorney is objecting to.

    c. Help the attorneys, judge, and jury in understanding the case, even if you have to go a bit beyond the scope of your expertise.

    d. Pay close attention to opposing counsel's questions.

    e. Answer opposing counsel's questions as briefly as is practical.

13. Your curriculum vitae is which of the following? (Choose all that apply.)

    a. A necessary tool to be an expert witness

    b. A generally required document to be made available before your testimony

    c. A detailed record of your experience, education, and training

    d. Focused on your skills as they apply to the current case

14. The most reliable way to ensure that jurors recall testimony is to do which of the following?

    a. Present evidence using oral testimony supported by hand gestures and facial expressions.

    b. Present evidence combining oral testimony and graphics that support the testimony.

    c. Wear bright clothing to attract jurors' attention.

    d. Emphasize your points with humorous anecdotes.

    e. Memorize your testimony carefully.

15. If you're giving an answer that you think your attorney should follow up on, what should you do?

    a. Change the tone of your voice.

    b. Argue with the attorney who asked the question.

    c. Use an agreed-on expression to alert the attorney to follow up on the question.

    d. Try to include as much information in your answer as you can.

15

16. In answering a question about the size of a hard drive, which of the following responses is appropriate? (Choose all that apply.)

    a. It's a very large hard drive.

    b. The technical data sheet indicates it's a 250 gigabyte hard drive.

    c. It's a 250 gigabyte hard drive configured with 235 gigabytes of accessible storage.

    d. I was unable to determine the drive size because it was so badly damaged.

17. List three items you should include in your CV.

18. While working for a prosecutor, what should you do if the evidence you found appears to be exculpatory and isn't being released to the defense?

    a. Keep the information on file for later review.

    b. Bring the information to the attention of the prosecutor, then his or her supervisor, and finally to the judge (the court).

    c. Destroy the evidence.

    d. Give the evidence to the defense attorney.

Hands-On Projects

The Hands-On Projects in this chapter have you acting as an expert witness and rendering an opinion on a case. It's assumed that you know how to retrieve data from an image file and document your evidence. Current certification exams also take this approach.

For these projects, you need GCFI-Win98.eve from Chapter 14 and the GCFI-NTFS image and project files used earlier in this chapter. Before beginning, create a *Work*\Chap15\Projects folder, and move all image files and ProDiscover project files to this subfolder, if necessary.

HANDS-ON PROJECTS

Hands-On Project 15-1

After reviewing the e-mail messages and metadata produced from the in-chapter activity, Ileen Johnson has determined that Chris Murphy appears to have a Hotmail e-mail address of murphy10@hotmail.com, and he's receiving and sending messages from this account to other non-Superior Bicycles e-mail addresses. Ms. Johnson has asked you to examine the GCFI-NTFS image file and search for any additional e-mail correspondence from any Web e-mail account.

For this project, you search the GCFI-NTFS image file for messages in allocated and unallocated space containing the keywords "yahoo.com" and "hotmail.com":

1. Start ProDiscover Basic with the **Run as administrator** option (if you're using Vista), and click the **Open Project** toolbar button (or the **Open Project** tab, if the Launch Dialog dialog box opens). In the Open dialog box, navigate to your work folder, click **C15InChp.dft**, and then click **Open**. (Remember that you moved your in-chapter project files to the work folder path *Work*\Chap15\Projects before starting these projects.) Click **Yes** in the Auto Image Checksum message box, if necessary.

2. To prepare a report so that the information is easier to read when you present it to the requesting attorney, you need to delete data that might have already been written to ProDiscover's report. To clear this previously collected information, click **Action** from the menu, point to **Clear Report,** and click **Clear All.**

3. Click the **Search** toolbar button or click **Action, Search** from the menu to open the Search dialog box.

4. Click the **Content Search** tab, and then click the **Search for the pattern(s)** option button. In the Search for the pattern(s) text box, type **yahoo.com** and **hotmail.com** (to search for Web e-mail accounts), pressing **Enter** after each one. Under Select the Disk(s)/Image(s) you want to search in, click the **GCFI-NTFS.eve** file, and then click **OK.**

5. Click the **wbk19.tmp** file in the Documents and Settings\Chris\Local Settings\Temporary Internet Files\Content.IE5 path in the search results to view its contents in the data area.

6. Examine the contents of wbk19.tmp, and note that it appears to be the narrative of a message. Then examine the contents of **wbk1B.tmp** and **wbk1F.tmp.** They also appear to be e-mail messages that have been stored in temporary files with a "wbk" prefix. Double-click the **wbk19.tmp** file to return to the main window.

7. In the tree view, note that you're in Documents and Settings\Chris\Local Settings\Temporary Internet Files\Content.IE5\G3KJKH63. Scroll up in the work area, and click **wbk11.tmp** to display its content in the data area.

8. Select the file's contents by clicking in the data area and pressing **Ctrl+A** or dragging across the text with your mouse. Then right-click the selected text, point to **Add to Subsets,** and click **Add Raw.** In the Add Comment dialog box, type **Web e-mail recovered** in the Investigator comments text box, and then click **OK.**

9. Inspect other temporary wbk files and repeat Step 8 when you find what seem to be e-mail messages. *Hint*: Of special interest are messages from Terry Sadler in the wbk48.tmp file.

10. When you've finished examining the temporary files, click **Report** in the tree view. Right-click in the report window and click **Select All.** Right-click the selected text and click **Copy.** Open a new document in your word processing program, and paste this text in it.

11. Move to the end of the document and enter your name below "This Report was created by ProDiscover." Save the report as **C15Prj01,** and submit an electronic copy to your instructor. Exit the word processing program and ProDiscover Basic. Click **No** if asked to save the project.

Hands-On Project 15-2

Ileen Johnson needs additional information from Chris Murphy's image file in preparation for pretrial planning. She's asked you to search for any occurrences of the keywords "carbon fiber" and "titanium mesh" and needs your findings included in another report.

1. Start ProDiscover Basic with the **Run as administrator** option (if you're using Vista), and click the **Open Project** toolbar button (or the **Open Project** tab, if the Launch Dialog dialog box opens). In the Open dialog box, navigate to your work folder, click **C15InChp.dft**, and then click **Open**.

2. Click **Action** from the menu, point to **Clear Report**, and click **Clear All**. Click the **Search** toolbar button or click **Action, Search** from the menu to open the Search dialog box.

3. Click the **Content Search** tab, and then click the **Search for the pattern(s)** option button. In the Search for the pattern(s) text box, type **carbon fiber** and **titanium mesh**, pressing **Enter** after each one. Under Select the Disk(s)/Image(s) you want to search in, click the **GCFI-NTFS.eve** file, and then click **OK**.

4. In the search results, click the **wbk48.tmp** file. In the data area, scroll down to find the keywords contained in this file. In the search results, click the **Select** check box next to this file. In the Add Comment dialog box, type **Keyword hits for carbon fiber and titanium** in the Investigator comments text box, click the **Apply to all items** check box, and then click **OK**.

5. Repeat Step 4 for the **wbk4A.tmp, wbk4C.tmp, wbk4E.tmp, A0000334.dll,** and **A0000340.dll** files.

6. When you're finished, double-click the **wbk48.tmp** file to return to the main window. In the data area, select the file's contents. Right-click the selected text, point to **Add to Subsets**, and click **Add Raw**.

7. In the tree view, click **Report**. Right-click in the report window and click **Select All**. Copy this text to a new document in your word processing program.

8. Move to the end of the document and enter your name below "This Report was created by ProDiscover." Save the report as **C15Prj02**, and submit an electronic copy to your instructor.

9. Exit the word processing program and ProDiscover Basic. Click **No** if asked to save the project.

Hands-On Project 15-3

Ileen Johnson needs all e-mail on Denise Robinson's computer image that has a non-Superior Bicycles address listed in a spreadsheet. She plans to submit this spreadsheet and e-mail HTML files to the court as additional evidence. In this project, you extract Outlook Express e-mail folders in ProDiscover Basic and use FTK to examine the e-mail content.

1. Start ProDiscover Basic with the **Run as administrator** option (if you're using Vista), and click the **New Project** toolbar button. In the New Project dialog box, type **C15Prj03** for the project number and filename, and then click **OK**. (If the Launch Dialog dialog box opens, enter this information in the New Project tab, and then click **Open**.)

2. Click **Action** from the menu, point to **Add**, and click **Image File**.

3. In the Open dialog box, navigate to your work folder, click **GCFI-Win98.eve,** and then click **Open.** If necessary, click **Yes** in the Auto Image Checksum message box.

4. To begin a search for Outlook Express folders, click the **Search** toolbar button or click **Action, Search** from the menu.

5. In the Search dialog box, click the **Content Search** tab, and then click the **Search for files named** option button. In the Search for the pattern(s) text box, type **.dbx** and press **Enter.** Under Select the Disk(s)/Image(s) you want to search in, click the **GCFI-Win98.eve** file, and then click **OK.**

6. In the search results, click the **Selection** button, and then click **Select All.** When the Add Comment dialog box opens, click the **Apply to all items** check box, type **Extracted Outlook Express folders** in the Investigator comments text box, and then click **OK.**

7. In the search results, click the **Add to Report** button, and then double-click **Inbox.dbx** (twice, if necessary) to return to the work area.

8. Right-click **Inbox.dbx** and click **Copy All Selected Files.**

9. In the Choose Destination dialog box, click the **Browse** button, browse to and click your work folder, click **OK,** and then click **OK** again.

10. Click **File, Save Project** from the menu, and save this project in your work folder. Exit ProDiscover Basic.

For the next part of the testimony preparation, you use FTK. Follow these steps to locate e-mail addresses that can be copied into a spreadsheet:

1. Start FTK with the **Run as administrator** option (if you're using Vista). If you see any warning or evaluation messages, click **OK** to continue.

2. When the AccessData FTK Startup dialog box opens, click **Start a new case,** and then click **OK.**

3. In the New Case dialog box, enter your name in the Investigator's name text box and, **C15Prj03** in the Case Number and Case Name text boxes. Next to the Case Path text box, click **Browse** and navigate to your work folder. Click **OK,** and then click **Next.**

4. In the Case Information dialog box, enter your school or group name in the Agency/Company text box and your name in the Examiner's Name text box, and then click **Next.**

5. Click **Next** until you reach the Refine Case - Default dialog box. Click the **Email Emphasis** button, and then click **Next.** In the Refine Index Default dialog box, click **Next** again.

6. In the main Add Evidence to Case dialog box, click **Add Evidence.** In the Add Evidence to Case dialog box, click the **Contents of a Folder** option button, and then click **Continue.** In the Browse for Folder dialog box, navigate to and click your work folder, and then click **OK.**

7. In the Evidence Information dialog box, click **OK,** and in the main Add Evidence to Case dialog box, click **Next.**

8. To start the processing, click **Finish** in the Case summary dialog box.

15

In the next portion of this examination, you copy e-mail addresses to an HTML file that can be copied into a spreadsheet later if needed:

1. Click **Tools, Internet Keyword Search** from the menu. In the Internet Keyword Search Options dialog box, click to clear all **URL Searches** check boxes. Click to select the last **E-mail Address Searches** check box, type **biz** in the text box next to it (see Figure 15-3), and then click **OK**.

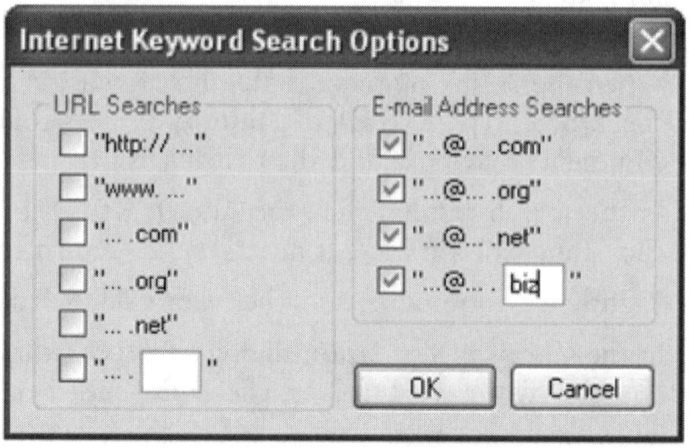

Figure 15-3   Adding an e-mail extension to the search

2. When the Internet Address Search Results dialog box opens, click **Add List to Evidence**, click **OK** in the message box, and then click **Close**.

3. In the main window, click the **Overview** tab, if necessary. Under the File Category heading, click the **E-mail Messages** button.

4. On the File List toolbar, click the **Check all files in the current list** button, and then click **Yes** in the FTK confirmation message box.

5. Click **Edit, Copy Special** from the menu. In the Copy Special dialog box, click the **All Checked Items** option button, click the **Unselect all** button, and then click the **Subject** check box. Scroll down to the bottom of the list box, and click the **Email Date, From, To, CC,** and **Attachment** check boxes (see Figure 15-4), and then click the **Copy** button.

6. Start your spreadsheet program, and in a new spreadsheet file, click **Edit, Paste Special** from the menu. In the Paste Special dialog box, click **HTML** (in Excel), and then click **OK**.

7. Save the spreadsheet as **C15-3CopySpecial-results.xls** in your work folder. Exit the spreadsheet program, but leave FTK running for the next set of steps.

Next, you locate all non-Superior Bicycles e-mail messages and extract them to HTML files. Superior Bicycles e-mail addresses have a .biz extension, so you shouldn't search on this extension. Instead, search for the standard e-mail address extensions of .com, .net, and .org.

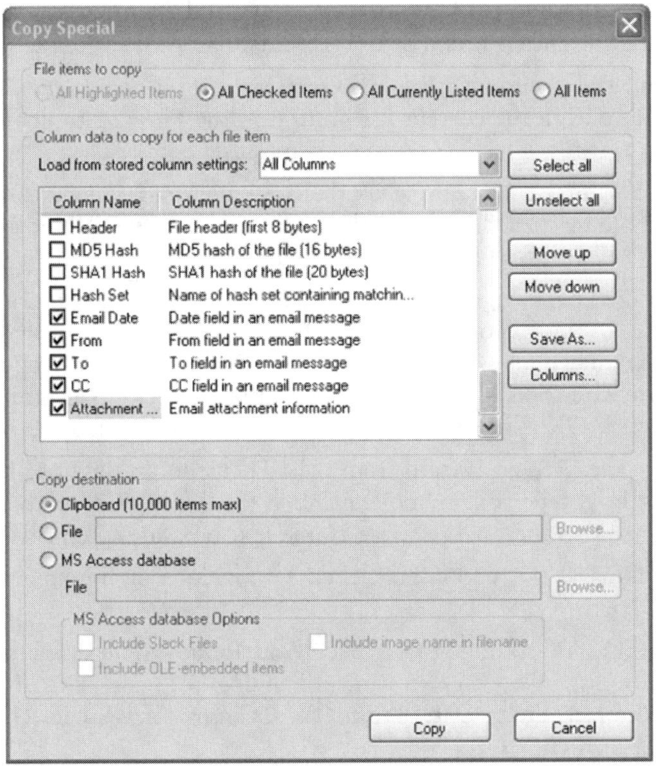

Figure 15-4 The Copy Special dialog box

1. Click **Tools, Internet Keyword Search** from the FTK menu. In the Internet Keyword Search Options dialog box, click to clear all **URL Searches** check boxes, leave the default **E-mail Address Searches** check boxes selected, and then click **OK**.

2. In the Internet Address Search Results dialog box, click the **Internet Address** column heading to sort all addresses by message.

3. To create a listing of all addresses, click the **Add List to Evidence** button at the bottom. When the Evidence Added Successfully message box opens, click **OK**.

4. Click the first e-mail address—**"Sam"<5amspade@myway.com>**—in the Internet Address column that's associated with Message0019 in the File Name column, and then click the **Create bookmark** button at the bottom. If "Sam"<5amspade@myway.com> isn't at the top, scroll down the list to find it.

5. In the Create New Bookmark dialog box, type **spade0019** in the Bookmark name text box, click the **Include in report** and **Export files** check boxes, and then click **OK**.

6. Scroll down the list to Message0016 with an address of terrysadler@goowy.com, click to select this message, and click the **Create bookmark** button. Repeat Step 5, using **sadler0016** for the bookmark name.

7. Repeat Step 6 for other messages from terrysadler@goowy.com. *Hint*: Seven messages should be bookmarked.

15

8. When you're finished bookmarking messages and e-mail accounts, click **Close** in the Internet Address Search Results dialog box.

9. In the main FTK window, click the **Overview** tab, if necessary. Click the **Uncheck all files in the current list** button on the File List toolbar, and then click **Yes** in the FTK confirmation message box.

10. Under the File Status heading, click the **Bookmarked Items** button. On the File List toolbar, click the **Check all files in the current list** button, and then click **Yes** in the FTK confirmation message box.

11. In the File List pane, right-click the first file, **Message0001**, and click **Export File**. In the Export Files dialog box, click **All checked files**, verify that the **Include email attachments with email messages** and **Append appropriate extension to file name if bad/absent** check boxes are selected, and then click **OK**. Click **OK** again in the Export Files dialog box.

12. Next, click **File**, **Report Wizard** from the FTK menu. In the Case Information dialog box, type your school's name in the Agency/Company text box and your name in the Investigator's Name text box, and then click **Next**.

13. In the Bookmarks - A dialog box, click **Yes, include all bookmarks**, and then click **Next**.

14. In the Bookmarks - B dialog box, click **Add/Remove File Properties**. In the Detailed List - Data Items to Include dialog box, click **Unselect all**. Click the **Subject, Email Date, From, To, CC,** and **Attachment** check boxes, and then click **OK**.

15. Click **Next** until you reach the Report Location dialog box, and then click **Finish**.

16. In the Report Wizard dialog box, click **Yes** to view the HTML report. Inspect the report, and then exit your Web browser and FTK.

17. Submit electronic copies of the FTK report, all HTML files created with the Internet Address Search Results function, and spreadsheets containing the e-mail metadata Ms. Johnson requested. Note that the HTML files are in the C15Prj03\Attach subfolder of your work folder. The e-mail message saved as an HTML file is stored in the C15Prj03\Export subfolder of your work folder.

Hands-On Project 15-4

Ileen Johnson needs you to collect information from the GCFI-Win98.eve image file of Denise Robinson's computer. She informs you that she received word from another source that Denise Robinson transmitted faxed spreadsheets and other files from her computer. These spreadsheets are for a new startup competitor named Speedy Bicycle. The source also mentioned that some of these spreadsheet files have a prefix of "sb" in their names. Search for all spreadsheet and graphics files that might have been sent to a fax machine. You need to search for OpenOffice version 1.0 spreadsheet files (.sxc extension), any zip files containing archives of files of interest, and possibly any renamed files. To locate this data, perform the following steps.

1. Start ProDiscover Basic with the **Run as administrator** option (if you're using Vista), and click the **Open Project** toolbar button (or the **Open Project** tab, if the Launch Dialog dialog box opens). In the Open dialog box, navigate to your work folder, click **C15Prj03.dft**, and then click **Open**. If necessary, click **Yes** in the Auto image Checksum message box.

2. Click **Action** from the menu, point to **Clear Report**, and click **Clear All**.

3. Click the **Search** toolbar button or click **Action, Search** from the menu to open the Search dialog box.

4. Click the **Content Search** tab, and then click the **Search for files named** option button. In the Search for the pattern(s) text box, type **.sxc**. Under Select the Disk(s)/Image(s) you want to search in, click the **GCFI-Win98.eve** file, and then click **OK**.

5. In the search results, click the **Select** check box next to Speedy Financials2.sxc. In the Add Comment dialog box opens, type **Speedy OpenOffice spreadsheet files**, click the **Apply to all items** check box, and then click **OK**.

6. Repeat Step 5 for **Speedy Financials 1.sxc, Speedy Financials.sxc**, and **Speedy Financials3.sxc**.

7. Open the Search dialog box. Click the **Content Search** tab, and then click the **Search for files named** option button. In the Search for the pattern(s) text box, type **.zip**. Under Select the Disk(s)/Image(s) you want to search in, click the **GCFI-Win98.eve** file, and then click **OK**.

8. In the search results, scroll down and locate SBLLC.ZIP and five Recycle Bin files: DC4.ZIP, DC5.ZIP, DC6.ZIP, DC7.ZIP, and DC8.ZIP. Click the **Select** check box next to each file.

9. Open the Search dialog box. Click the **Content Search** tab, and then click the **Search for files named** option button. In the Search for the pattern(s) text box, type **sb**. Under Select the Disk(s)/Image(s) you want to search in, click the **GCFI-Win98.eve file**, and then click **OK**.

10. In the search results, scroll down and click the **Select** check box next to SBLLC-PR.BMP, SBLLC-PR.JPG, and SBLLC-PR.TIF. If the Add Comment dialog box opens, type **Keyword hits for files with sb prefix** in the Investigator comments text box, click the **Apply to all items** check box, and then click **OK**.

11. Double-click the **SBLLC-PR.TIF** file to switch to the main window. In the work area, right-click **SBLLC-PR.BMP** and click **Copy All Selected Files**.

12. In the Choose Destination dialog box, click **Browse** and navigate to your work folder. In the Browse for Folder dialog box, click **Make New Folder**, type **C15-4ExportData**, and then click **OK** twice.

13. Exit ProDiscover Basic, saving the project when prompted. Open Windows Explorer and navigate to **Chap15\Projects\C15-4ExportData\ GCFI-Win98.eve** (substituting your work folder name, if necessary). Locate and examine all files exported from these steps, and then send electronic copies to your instructor.

15

Case Projects

Case Project 15-1

For this project, you create a brief outline of the steps you used for the in-chapter activity and Hands-On Projects. This project helps you review your work so that you can testify competently on your findings and the procedures you used. The outline doesn't need detailed steps; it serves as a way to trigger your memory about what you did.

Case Project 15-2

You have been approached by an attorney who needs you as a technical and possibly an expert witness in a criminal case. The attorney has requested your curriculum vitae so that she can review it and prepare questions for you to answer during the pretrial qualifications. Prepare a draft of your CV and turn it in to your instructor for review. Your CV will be an ongoing project in your career.

Case Project 15-3

The attorney from Case Project 15-2 has given you a list of computer forensics terms and asked you to write definitions for these terms. These definitions will be given to the jury to help them better understand the case's subject matter. Conduct Internet research to define the following terms, making sure you target your definitions to nontechnical readers:

- Hashes for Cyclic Redundancy Check, Message Digest, and Secure Hash Algorithm
- An image of a drive
- Static versus live data acquisition of drives
- Data carving
- Computer forensics tool validation

When you're finished, submit the definitions to your instructor.

Case Project 15-4

Ileen Johnson has asked you to create a Microsoft PowerPoint, OpenOffice Impress, or Web HTML presentation on the work you did for the in-chapter activity and Hands-On Projects. She plans to have you make this presentation to the jury during the trial. Integrate portions of your ProDiscover and FTK reports and findings from e-mail or spreadsheet data that might be of use for testimony. When you're finished, submit the PowerPoint, Impress, or HTML files to your instructor.

16

Ethics for the Expert Witness

After reading this chapter and completing the exercises, you will be able to:

- Explain how ethics and codes apply to expert witnesses
- Explain how other organizations' codes of ethics apply to expert testimony
- Describe ethical difficulties in expert testimony
- Explain the process of carving data manually

For computer forensics examiners, maintaining the highest level of ethical behavior in their work is essential. In this chapter, you learn how computer forensics experts and other professionals apply ethics and codes of conduct to their work and to giving expert testimony. Computer forensics examiners are responsible for meeting the highest standards when conducting examinations, preparing reports, and giving testimony to ensure that evidence is accurate, reliable, and impartial. In addition, you must know when to disqualify yourself from an investigation. Knowing what to look for when taking a new case helps you avoid potential ethical problems.

Applying Ethics and Codes to Expert Witnesses

Ethics are the rules you internalize and use to measure your performance. The standards that others apply to you or that you're compelled to adhere to by external forces, such as licensing bodies, can be called ethics, but they are more accurately described as laws. Many professions now call these laws **codes of professional conduct or responsibility**. Both concepts of ethics are addressed in this chapter.

People need ethics to help maintain their balance, especially in difficult and contentious situations, and for guidance on their values. Ethics also help you maintain self-respect and the respect of your profession. Because computer forensics examiners don't have the same formal, detailed codes of conduct that professions such as medicine and the law have, relying on an internal code of ethics might be more critical. In addition, your internal standards, related to a philosophical, religious, or moral position, can be higher than standards established by codes of professional conduct. Laws governing codes of professional conduct or responsibility define the lowest level of action or performance required to avoid liability. Even with these low standards, there are still violations.

One of the most effective mechanisms for protecting yourself at a personal level and a legal level is to have nothing to hide. This ethical position allows people to be self-critical and critical of others. People who fear having their improper acts revealed feel as though they must protest the improper acts of others being revealed. Being able to engage in criticism of yourself or others, however, makes it possible to refine and strengthen personal codes of ethics or codes of professional responsibility.

Expert witnesses are expected to present unbiased, specialized, and technical evidence to a jury. However, experts, like the attorneys who hire them, bring their biases and other ethical failings to court. As a professional, you must control your biases, not allow them to control you. Ethics are a tool you can use to identify and control your biases or prejudices.

Currently, expert witnesses testify in more than 80% of trials, and in many trials, multiple expert witnesses testify. The courts are clearly aware of the importance of expert witnesses to the legal system and are concerned about expert witnesses' ethics and the challenges experts face in reconciling their ethical standards and court practice. Awareness of this challenge is evident in the following statement from *Kenneth C. v. Delonda R.* (814 N.Y.S.2d 562, 2006):

> ... the topic of expert witness ethics and professionalism is largely undeveloped and there are few definitive statements about what exactly the expert witness's ethical obligations are and how they are to handle the subtle as well as the more

blatant attempts to influence them. While some expert witnesses belong to professions that have an established code …, many experts come from professions that are not self-governing with a uniform code of ethics…. Even where professional associations have established ethical guidelines for conducting investigations, forming opinions … very few explain how the ethical boundaries imposed on judges and lawyers may bear on the performance of their role in the legal system….

Included in most professions' codes of professional conduct is an admonition to adhere to or comply with the law. The most important laws applying to attorneys and witnesses are the rules of evidence. As mentioned in Chapter 15, the Federal Rules of Evidence (FRE) prescribe the methods by which experts appear at trial. Codes of professional conduct or responsibility affect attorneys who hire experts, but experts are bound by their personal ethics and the ethics of their professional organizations. Professional organizations' guidelines are often vague and broad and might do little to enforce experts' ethical conduct, however. Finding examples of experts' ethically questionable behavior in court isn't difficult. For example, in an investigation of the West Virginia State Police Crime Lab (438 S.E.2d 501, W. Va. 1993), a former officer in the Serology Division was found to have falsified evidence in criminal prosecutions. In addition, the article "Geoffrey Campbell, Erdmann Faces New Legal Woes: Pathologist Indicted for Perjury in Texas Murder Trial" (*American Bar Association Journal*, November 1995) describes how a former Texas pathologist faked autopsies to aid in criminal trials.

In the United States, there's no state or national licensing body for computer forensics examiners. Some states have licensing requirements for private investigators and classify computer forensics examiners with private investigators, but the work private investigators usually do bears little resemblance to the work of computer forensics examiners. Therefore, your sources for ethical standards are your internal values (ethics) and codes of professional associations you belong to and certifying bodies that have granted you a certification as well as your employer's rules of professional conduct. Most examiners rely on a combination of these standards to construct their professional ethical codes.

Computer Forensics Examiners' Roles in Testifying

As you learned in Chapter 15, in testifying, computer forensics examiners have two roles: testifying to the facts found during evidence recovery (scientific/technical witness) and rendering an opinion based on education, training, and experience (expert witness).

As an expert witness, you can testify even if you weren't present when the event occurred or didn't handle the data storage device personally. Because of an expert's important role in litigation, attorneys often shop for experts who can support their cases, and experts' fees might be only a secondary consideration. Criticism of expert witnesses is widespread in the legal community because it's possible to find and hire an expert to testify to almost any opinion on any topic. As a result, the impartiality of expert testimony and the potential for misconduct have become concerns.

16

If you're going to have a long and productive career as an expert witness, beware of attorneys' opinion shopping. An attorney might be willing to risk your career to improve the prospect of success in a case—and can always find another expert for the next case. The most effective way to prevent opinion shopping is to require that the attorney retaining your services send you enough material on the case for you to make an evaluation. Distinguishing opinion shopping from the process of attempting to disqualify experts by creating conflicts can be difficult, however.

Conversely, attorneys should be cautious of expert witnesses who will tailor an opinion. If witnesses will tailor opinions for you, they might have tailored opinions for somebody else. When an expert witness is discredited, it can affect the attorney's credibility, too.

Considerations in Disqualification

One of the effects of violating court rules or laws is **disqualification**. This outcome isn't usually punitive, but it can be embarrassing for you as a professional and potentially for the attorney who retained you.

Opposing counsel might attempt to disqualify you based on any deviations from opinions you've given in previous cases. Any testimony you give at trials or depositions is on record and available to attorneys. (As mentioned in Chapter 14, attorneys search deposition banks for information on expert witnesses.) If there's a change in your position on a point, be sure to explain why you have changed it, such as recent developments in technology, new tools with new capabilities, or the facts of the current case differing from a previous case. An apparent change of position could be a subject for cross-examination, and you must be able to explain what appears to be contradictory opinions, or you'll be seen as tailoring testimony to your client's needs.

Some attorneys contact many experts as a ploy to disqualify them or prevent opposing counsel from hiring them; as explained in Chapter 15, this practice is called "conflicting out." Although attorneys might merely be scouting the field for information, you should always note calls from attorneys and the nature of the communication. Have a standard response, such as "Before we go beyond the general nature of the case and my expertise, you need to complete a client questionnaire and send me an investigation retainer." The retainer can be small, perhaps 2 to 8 hours of your usual billable rate for a simple case; the purpose of requesting the retainer is to deter attorneys from communicating with you solely for the purpose of discrediting or disqualifying you. No explicit rule in the code of professional conduct prohibits attorneys from engaging in this process, but there are general prohibitions on engaging in actions designed to delay or be obstructive without legitimate purpose. These types of actions are unlikely to result in a bar association taking disciplinary action against attorneys, however.

Before allowing an attorney to describe any case details, determine who the parties are to reduce the possibility of a conflict. Although you aren't bound by the rigid rules on conflict of interest that bind attorneys, you might be working for an attorney on a case opposing the attorney who called you, and that conflict could reflect on the attorney.

Whenever you're aware of a possible disqualification issue, bring it to the attention of the attorney who has retained you. The attorney then can get an early determination on the disqualification issue. There are rules to determine whether you can be disqualified from working on a case merely because you discussed general aspects of it. The rules for disqualification are derived from court decisions. Factors courts have used in determining whether to disqualify an expert include the following:

- Whether the attorney informed the expert that their discussions were confidential
- Whether the expert reviewed materials marked as confidential or attorney work product

- Whether the expert was asked to sign a confidentiality agreement
- Number of discussions held over a period of time
- The type of documents that were reviewed (publicly filed or confidential)
- The type of information conveyed to the expert—whether it included general or specific data or included confidential information, trial strategies, plans for method of proof, and so forth
- The amount of time involved in discussions or meetings between the expert and attorney
- Whether the expert provided the attorney with confidential information
- Whether the attorney formally retained the expert
- Whether the expert voiced concerns about being retained
- Whether the expert was requested to perform services for the attorney
- Whether the attorney compensated the expert

Numerous cases describe disqualification under the communication standards. For example, in *Wang Laboratories, Inc. v. Toshiba Corp.* (762 F. Supp. 1246 [E.D. Va. 1991]), the court summarized the process of determining whether an expert should be disqualified because of previous contact with an opposing party. The test is in two parts. First, was it objectively reasonable for the first party who claims to have previously retained the consultant to conclude that a confidential relationship existed? Second, was any confidential or privileged information disclosed by the first party to the consultant?

Similarly, there's extensive case law in which experts were not disqualified and allowed to testify over the objection of opposing counsel. For example, in *Hewlett-Packard Co. v. EMC Corp.* (330 F. Supp. 2d 1087 [N.D. Cal. 2004]) and *Tidemann v. Nadler Golf Car Sales, Inc.* (224 F.3d 719 [7th Cir. 2000]), the other side's lawyer merely served a subpoena on the expert to get factual testimony. If you don't know which standards for disqualification are being applied or how they are being applied in your jurisdiction, you should research the applicable state's court rulings on these issues. States often refer to already established rulings in other states or federal courts, and you can use an online search to find cases in the applicable jurisdiction. You might also want to have a standing relationship with an attorney who can advise you on these issues.

Traps for Unwary Experts

Expert witnesses should be cautious about the following potential traps, even though some aren't laid deliberately:

- What are some differences between the attorney's motives and the investigator's duty that may affect how the investigator acts, or is expected to act, as an expert witness?
- Is the function of the expert witness in conflict with the investigator's code of professional responsibility?
- Attorneys look at witnesses' codes of professional responsibility based on organizations that they are members of. As an expert witness, you should anticipate that the opposing counsel will look at your organization memberships and those organizations' codes of professional responsibility.

16

Contingency fees aren't allowed except in certain limited circumstances; for example, consultants who don't testify can earn a contingency fee for locating testifying experts or investigative leads. However, an expert's activities leading to testimony can't be compensated on a contingent basis. Even the appearance of testimony on a contingent basis is dangerous. Therefore, experts should be paid in full for all previous work and for the anticipated time required for testimony.

It's unlikely you will encounter these situations, but if you do, it's wise to ask the hiring attorney to file a motion with the court requesting a ruling on disqualification. This process protects you from future liability or ethical complaints. If the attorney doesn't want to follow this procedure, consider withdrawing from the employment.

In addition, avoid obvious ethical errors, such as the following:

- Don't present false data or alter data.
- Don't report work that was not done.
- Don't ignore available contradictory data.
- Don't do work beyond your expertise or competence.
- Don't allow the attorney who retained you to influence your opinion in an unauthorized way. (Keep in mind that there are authorized points of influence, such as the attorney framing a hypothetical question for you or asking you to answer specific questions.)
- Don't accept an assignment if it can't be done reasonably in the allowed time.
- Don't reach a conclusion before doing complete research.
- Don't fail to report possible conflicts of interest.

Determining Admissibility of Evidence

Although stating hypothetical questions during examination is no longer required in court, these questions can give you the factual structure to support and defend your opinion. You owe your client a full understanding of the facts relevant to your opinion, and you can ask him or her to establish that there's evidence supporting the facts on which your opinion is based.

Although expert opinions can be presented without stating the underlying factual basis, the testimony isn't admissible if the facts on which the opinion is based are inadequate or there's insufficient evidence to allow stating a legitimate opinion. FRE 702 (whether the expert is qualified and whether the expert opinion can be helpful) and FRE 703 (whether basis for the testimony is adequate) are considered in determining admissibility. If a question on admissibility arises under FRE 702 or 703, the court might require underlying facts or data to determine whether or to what extent the expert should be permitted to testify. Obviously, opposing counsel has an opportunity to explore and challenge the underlying facts and data on cross-examination. However, experts who provide explanations for how they reached their conclusions are far more persuasive to a judge or jury.

Organizations with Codes of Ethics

No single source offers a definitive code of ethics for expert witnesses, so you must draw on standards from other organizations to form your own ethical standards. This section discusses the impact that other organizations' ethical guidelines can have on expert testimony. Many professional organizations have rules to guide their members in areas such as interaction with patients/clients, objectivity, role in society, fees, solicitation, independence, and contractual relationships. The more restrictive and specific the ethical rules are, the more impact they have in curbing unethical expert testimony.

International Society of Forensic Computer Examiners

The International Society of Forensic Computer Examiners (ISFCE) Code of Ethics and Professional Responsibility provides guidelines for its members on how they are expected to perform their duties as computer forensics examiners. These guidelines include specific instructions on how members must maintain their professional standing and define what members must do and not do when performing their duties as computer forensics examiners. For example, the ISFCE code of ethics includes guidelines such as the following:

- Maintain the utmost objectivity in all forensic examinations and present findings accurately.
- Conduct examinations based on established, validated principles.
- Testify truthfully in all matters before any board, court, or proceeding.
- Avoid any action that would appear to be a conflict of interest.
- Never misrepresent training, credentials, or association membership.
- Never reveal any confidential matters or knowledge learned in an examination without an order from a court of competent jurisdiction or the client's express permission.

In addition, members are expected to maintain their integrity by reporting other members who violate the code of conduct to the ISFCE.

NOTE
The ISFCE also offers a Certified Computer Examiner (CCE) certification and includes ethical standards for examiners holding this certification. For more information on the ISFCE Code of Ethics and Professional Responsibility, see *www.isfce.com/ethics2.htm*.

International High Technology Crime Investigation Association

In its bylaws, the International High Technology Crime Investigation Association (HTCIA) provides a detailed Code of Ethics of Professional Standards Conduct for its members. HTCIA core values include the following requirements related to testifying:

- The HTCIA values the Truth uncovered within digital information and the effective techniques used to uncover that Truth, so that no one is wrongfully convicted.
- The HTCIA values the Integrity of its members and the evidence they expose through common investigative and computer forensic best practices, including specialized techniques used to gather digital evidence.

16

NOTE
For more information on the HTCIA code of ethics, see *www.htcia. org/bylaws.shtml*.

International Association of Computer Investigative Specialists

The International Association of Computer Investigative Specialists (IACIS) provides a well-defined, simple guide for expected behavior of computer forensics examiners. These standards follow the principles defined by other professional organizations for investigations and testimony. The standards for IACIS members that apply to testifying include the following:

- Maintain the highest level of objectivity in all forensic examinations and accurately present the facts involved.

- Examine and analyze evidence in a case thoroughly.

- Conduct examinations based on established, validated principles.

- Render opinions having a basis that is demonstratively reasonable.

- Not withhold any findings, whether inculpatory or exculpatory, that would cause the facts of a case to be misrepresented or distorted.

For more information on the IACIS code of ethics, see *www.iacis.com/new_membership/code_of_ethics*.

American Bar Association

As a computer forensics examiner, you will be dealing with attorneys, so you should be aware of the basic rules of professional conduct they must follow. The American Bar Association (ABA) is not a licensing body, but the ABA's Model Code of Professional Responsibility (Model Code) and its successor, the Model Rules of Professional Conduct (Model Rules), are the basis of state licensing bodies' codes. In the United States, attorneys are licensed by states.

These codes are quite extensive, so only a few relevant sections are given here. To read the codes in their entirety, go to *www.abanet.org/cpr/mrpc/mcpr.pdf* for the Model Code and *www.abanet.org/cpr/mrpc/mrpc_toc.html* for the Model Rules.

Both the Model Rules and the Model Code contain provisions limiting the fees experts can receive for their services. Model Rule 3.4(b) states that unlike other witnesses who can be reimbursed only for their expenses, an expert is permitted to receive a fee for preparation and for testimony in court. However, paying expert witnesses contingency fees for their services is considered improper. The Model Code also prevents payment to experts on a contingency basis, although it does permit reasonable fees for their professional services. Model Code EC 7-28 reiterates the ban on contingency fees and adds that "[W]itnesses should always testify truthfully and should be free from any financial inducements that might tempt them to do otherwise." These legal guidelines apply a restraint on possibly unethical expert witness behavior, with the burden on the attorney hiring the expert; the attorney is subject to these ethical guidelines, not the expert.

The ABA has stated that, unlike attorneys, expert witnesses do not owe a duty of loyalty to their clients. Experts must remain independent from their clients and not become a client advocate. In essence, experts must analyze, explain, and offer accurate opinions of the relevant issue before the court, not strive to advocate and persuade the judge and jury toward a certain point of view.

Model Rule 3.4 also prevents attorneys from falsifying evidence or assisting a witness in false testimony. This rule could affect expert testimony in two ways. First, attorneys must not permit expert witnesses to testify in an area that's not scientifically valid. Second, attorneys must not coax opinions from experts that are beyond the realm of their specialized knowledge. Coaxing would result in unreliable testimony because the expert would be testifying in an area in which he or she has no expertise.

American Medical Association

The first known expert witness was a civil engineer testifying in a port silting case in 1782, but medical professionals are the experts who testify most often. Almost every case involving an injury requires a report or testimony from the treating physician and the opposing independent medical examiner. Therefore, the medical profession has developed detailed rules on how to be a witness. Although the Hippocratic Oath is the foundation of medical ethics, the American Medical Association (AMA) has supplemented it with the Principles of Medical Ethics (*www.ama-assn.org/ama/pub/physician-resources/medical-ethics/code-medical-ethics/ principles-medical-ethics.shtml*). The AMA's policy on expert witness testimony sets out five recommendations:

- The physician is a professional with special training and experience and has an ethical obligation to assist the administration of justice.

- The physician may not become a partisan during the legal proceeding.

- The medical witness should testify truthfully and be adequately prepared.

- The physician must make the attorney calling him or her aware of favorable and unfavorable information uncovered in the physician's assessment.

- The physician may not accept a contingency fee.

To see the AMA's complete policy on expert witness testimony, go to *www.ama-assn.org/apps/pf_new/pf_online* and search on "testimony."

Several other provisions address the ethical constraints of testifying physicians. First, the AMA's Council on Ethical and Judicial Affairs has issued an opinion to clarify the relationship of law and ethics. The opinion states that although ethical and legal principles are intertwined, ethical obligations exceed legal duties. Further, the Council has issued an opinion stating that contingency fees are not acceptable and condemning any type of fee that doesn't relate to the value of the medical service.

In addition, Principles I and II of the Principles of Medical Ethics require that physicians provide competent medical service, deal honestly in their profession, and seek to expose other physicians who are engaged in fraud or are lacking in character. To meet the reliability and validity standard at trial, a testifying medical expert must be competent and deal honestly in his or her profession. Principle III states that a physician must "respect the law"; a physician who respects the law testifies truthfully as to his or her specialized knowledge. Principle V requires physicians to maintain and advance their scientific knowledge and to make relevant information available to society, so physicians must remain current with scientific knowledge and publish in peer-reviewed publications.

16

The AMA also sets goals in dealing with its members. In 1998, the AMA proposed additional guidelines for expert witness testimony. Among these guidelines was a provision encouraging the AMA to work with local licensing boards to devise disciplinary measures for physicians who give fraudulent testimony. Other provisions suggested continuing to educate physicians testifying as expert witnesses about their ethical responsibilities and encouraged the formation of state expert witness programs to address the difficulties in monitoring expert testimony. However, in practice, the responsibility usually falls on physicians to regulate themselves and their ethical behavior.

American Psychological Association

For psychologists, the most broadly accepted set of guidelines governing their conduct as experts is the American Psychological Association's (APA's) Ethical Principles of Psychologists and Code of Conduct (commonly referred to as the Ethics Code). These guidelines offer the most comprehensive regulations of any professional organization and devote an entire section to forensics activities. The Ethics Code (*www.apa.org/ethics/code2002.html*) consists of standards that are enforceable rules for the conduct of psychologists and applies only to psychologists' activities that are part of their scientific and professional functions or activities that are psychological in nature.

Several standards in the APA's Ethics Code apply to psychologists' expert testimony and are supported by the court's decision in *Daubert v. Merrill Dow*. The Ethics Code requires a basis for scientific and professional judgments. When psychologists are testifying in a legal proceeding, they must rely on scientifically and professionally derived knowledge when making scientific or professional judgments (expert opinion). When selecting assessment techniques or instruments, psychologists must consider the questions they are addressing and previous research on applying these techniques or instruments correctly. Psychologists are also instructed to strive to prevent the misuse or abuse of assessment techniques and instruments.

The Ethics Code also cautions psychologists about the limitations of assessment tools. Psychologists must be familiar with their reliability, validity, and proper application and recognize the limitations on the certainty of diagnoses, judgments, and predictions they make with these tools. Recognizing these limitations is particularly crucial to expert witness testimony. Therefore, psychologists must reveal any reservations they have about the accuracy or limitations of tests they used. In addition, they're prohibited from using obsolete tests or outdated results as a basis for their assessments and opinions. This prohibition helps protect the validity and reliability of their test results and expert testimony.

Other Ethics Code standards are related to expert testimony, too. Psychologists must provide services and conduct research only within the confines of their competence and ability. In addition, when psychologists want to participate in a new practice area or technique, they must first qualify themselves with appropriate study, research, or consultation. From a legal perspective, this standard protects opposing parties from experts who might be tempted to testify in an area in which they have little expertise. Also, psychologists are cautioned to avoid false or deceptive statements in all aspects of their testimony, whether it's related to their expertise, experience, or results.

Section 7.0 of the Ethics Code, governing forensics activities, states several important rules for psychological experts to follow. Standard 7.01 states that psychologists who perform assessments and provide expert testimony must comply with all provisions of the Ethics Code, be truthful and candid in their testimony and reports, and base their work on their specialized knowledge and competence. All assessments, reports, and recommendations must be based on information and techniques (personal interviews are especially favored) that generate enough evidence to substantiate their findings. The Ethics Code also states that psychologists can provide written or oral testimony on a person's psychological characteristics only after conducting an examination that's thorough enough to support their conclusions. If they can't examine a person after making a reasonable effort to do so, they're required to clarify the impact this lack of an examination has on the validity and reliability of their expert testimony and state the resulting limits on the nature and extent of their conclusions and recommendations.

Ethical Difficulties in Expert Testimony

Despite the professional guidelines described in the previous section, problems still exist with expert witness testimony. There are inherent conflicts between the goals of attorneys and the goals of scientists or technicians (experts). Attorneys work in an adversarial system and look to sway the judge or jury with the most articulate, understandable expert, who is generally the most persuasive expert rather than the best scientist. In contrast, science requires experts to focus on the evidence without the influence of others' objectives.

As a result, *Daubert* and the APA's forensics guidelines can challenge experts to choose between complete impartiality and responsible advocacy. On one hand, an expert may appear in the role of impartial educator, whose purpose is to help the judge or jury understand a fact or an issue. According to *Daubert*, to provide reliable and valid testimony, the expert has the "ethical responsibility to present a complete and unbiased picture of the … research relevant to the case at hand." With an adversarial system, pressures from hiring attorneys, and a tendency to identify with the side for whom you're working, educating impartially is difficult. Therefore, experts should accept the position they have been placed in and act as responsible advocates. Ethical problems surface when experts decide to advocate for one side, as they must consider the line between using research to argue one side of an issue fairly and distorting and misrepresenting available research. *Daubert* cautions that if an expert falsifies, distorts, or misrepresents the facts while advocating his or her position, opinion testimony will not be deemed reliable or valid.

Enforcing any professional organization's ethical guidelines is difficult. The principles can be enforced only against members of the organization, and if the expert chooses to withdraw from the organization, there's no effective mechanism to enforce the guidelines. For computer forensics examiners testifying as experts, this means an organization has limited influence over examiners as witnesses in the form of peer pressure and reputation among peers. In addition, without a specific organization to oversee and comment on current expert testimony standards or transgressions, it's difficult to identify and investigate violations or to apprise an organization's members of acceptable methodologies and standards.

As a result, even the most specific guidelines, such as Section 7.0 of the APA Ethics Code, are as challenging to enforce as the broader restrictions the AMA has established. All guidelines rely primarily on internalization of the codes and witnesses' analysis of when and how they will participate in a case. The available guidelines also fail to ensure superior quality expert testimony because along with applicable laws, they set only a minimum level of acceptable performance or competence as the standard.

16

Ethical Responsibilities Owed to You

The attorney who has retained you, opposing counsel, and the court also owe you ethical responsibilities as an expert witness. Your attorney owes you a fair statement of the case or situation, adequate time to review evidence and prepare your report, and a reasonable opportunity to examine data, conduct testing, and investigate the matter before rendering an opinion. If the attorney wants you to render an opinion quickly and without adequate opportunity to review, be cautious. He might be trying to get you to commit based on inadequate information, or he's trying to rush you because he hasn't kept track of critical dates and is under pressure to meet a deadline. The attorney might also hold you under subpoena for an excessive amount of time waiting to testify. This might reflect difficulties in anticipating the amount of time required for other witnesses' testimony; however, you should be paid for the waiting time per the fee agreement. Making any portion of your fee dependent on a favorable report is inappropriate and should be a breach of the fee agreement. You are owed fair compensation for your time and work under the terms of the fee agreement.

Most attorneys, including opposing counsel, are competent, courteous professionals, but if they aren't, you can expect abuses that might include inquiry into your personal finances; unless this inquiry is about the terms of compensation for the current case, it's inappropriate. In addition, some opposing counsel attempt to make discovery depositions physically uncomfortable, such as using an excessively warm or cool room, having you face into the sun, or refusing to take comfort breaks. You don't need to endure the situation in silence, but you should be practical. Note the conditions to the attorney who set the deposition and ask him or her to correct the situation. If the situation is not corrected, you should note these conditions into the record, and continue noting them as long as the conditions persist.

After you have noted the problem into the record, you can refuse to continue with the deposition; however, these situations are rare and even more rare in court. Generally, you should consult with an attorney before taking that last step. If you think the behavior was serious enough that you can justify refusing to continue, you should also consider reporting the attorney to the state bar association. Other tactics include the attorney who set the deposition neglecting to have payment ready for you; you can refuse to attend the deposition if payment isn't tendered. An opposing attorney might also ask repetitive questions; the attorney who retained you should object to these techniques. For a testimony preservation deposition, however, you can expect that the attorney calling for your testimony will try to make you as comfortable as possible because he or she wants your best performance.

As a measure of protection, you might want to have your personal attorney attend the deposition; this attorney can't object to questions but is available to advise the attorney who retained you or to advise you during breaks. A less costly alternative is arranging to have your attorney available by phone during the deposition. In this case, you could bring your own recorder to the deposition and play back portions to your attorney, unless there's an order to the contrary. In most jurisdictions, attendees are allowed to record depositions, so unless somebody objects, record your testimony. A recording is also useful when you review your deposition testimony before signing the transcript.

Standard and Personally Created Forensics Tools

The tools you use to recover, control, and track evidence are subject to review by opposing parties. If the court deems them unreliable, the evidence you recovered with those tools might not be admitted or be admitted with a limiting instruction. If you use standard tools—commonly used tools or commercially available tools—you simplify the process of validating them.

Personally created tools, if they're designed to serve a specific purpose and have been adequately tested to validate their accuracy for that purpose, might have advantages that you can demonstrate to a judge, who ultimately determines whether evidence is admissible. For example, a tool you've created could be more compact or run more efficiently than other comparable tools. You're still required to validate these tools, however, and might have to share their source code for analysis. Remember that "borrowing" code from other products or incorporating other tools into your own without acknowledgment or paying royalties could be a violation of copyright and is considered theft. In addition, it can result in a major embarrassment for you, could have serious criminal and civil liability implications, and could adversely affect the attorney who retained you.

An Ethics Exercise

For this final chapter, you're given a forensics image that Ileen Johnson acquired from an anonymous source. It was sent with no return address and a typed note stating that Superior Bicycles would be interested in correspondence and spreadsheet files with the filenames JimShu and Baidar that the image might contain. Your task is to analyze all possible data values in this image and report your findings to Ileen Johnson, General Counsel for Superior Bicycles.

Before beginning these activities, refer to the information in the "Examining NTFS Disks" section of Chapter 6 that describes FILE0 records in the MFT file. Then extract compressed files from the Chap16 folder on the book's DVD to your *Work*\Chap16\Chapter folder. If necessary, create the folder first. The work folder pathname you see in screenshots might differ.

The tools on this book's DVD have limitations in searching for Unicode data strings. The following information guides you on how to search for Unicode text with the hex search function in ProDiscover Basic. To build search strings for this purpose, you must also use a hexadecimal editor, such as WinHex or Hex Workshop, to convert text characters to their hexadecimal values.

Determining Hexadecimal Values for Text Strings

16

A computer forensics examiner's technical capability requires the ability to work around problems and challenges when dealing with digital evidence. ProDiscover Basic is an introductory tool with limitations that the licensed versions of ProDiscover Windows, Forensics, Investigator, and Incident Response don't have. Specifically, you can't search for Unicode text data in ProDiscover Basic. As a workaround, however, you can search for the hexadecimal equivalents of string text values. When converting plain text to hexadecimal, remember to place null (00) values between each character's hexadecimal values because Unicode values stored on NTFS drives are 16 bits each. The first 8 bits are equivalent to ASCII; the remaining 8 bits are used by other languages.

To begin examining the anonymous disk image, you start by determining the hexadecimal values for the text strings "JimShu" and "Baidar." Follow these steps to convert the text values into hexadecimal values:

> For this activity, search for only the first six hexadecimal values to locate the data of interest for this analysis.

1. Start WinHex Demo. Click **File, New** from the menu, type **200** in the Desired file size text box, and then click **OK**.

2. Move the cursor to the input area on the right, and type **J i m S h u** and **B a i d a r** on separate lines, as shown in Figure 16-1. Make sure you insert a null (0x00) space between each character.

Unicode text has a null (0x00) value between each character

Figure 16-1 Determining hexadecimal values

3. Write down these two hexadecimal values: **4A 00 69 00 6D 00 53 00 68 00 75 00** for JimShu and **42 00 61 00 69 00 64 00 61 00 72 00** for Baidar.

4. Save this file as **InChp16-unicode.txt** in your work folder, and exit WinHex.

Searching for Unicode Data in ProDiscover Basic

With the collected information from the previous steps, now it's time to examine the anonymous user's disk image:

1. Start ProDiscover Basic (with the **Run as administrator** option if you're using Vista), and start a new project, using **C16InChp01** for the project number and filename.

2. Click **Action** from the menu, point to **Add**, and click **Image File**.

3. In the Open dialog box, navigate to and click the image file **C16InChp.dd**, and then click **Open**.

4. Click **Action, Search** from the menu. In the Search dialog box, click the **Content Search** tab, and then click the **Hex** option button. Click the **Search for the pattern(s)** option button, if necessary, and in the Search text box, type the hexadecimal value for Baidar that you wrote down in the preceding activity. Under Select the Disk(s)/Image(s) you want to search in, click the image file, and then click **OK**.

5. In the search results, click **pagefile.sys**, the first file listed, and examine its contents (shown in Figure 16-2) for string data matching the search criteria.

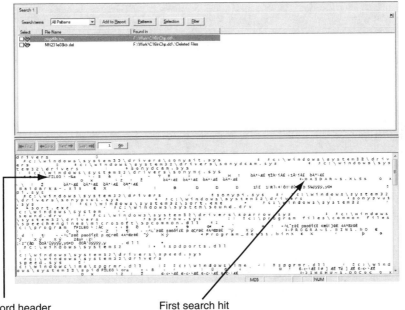

MFT record header   First search hit

Figure 16-2 Viewing search results

The lower pane of the search results contains MFT records with a FILE0 header that appear to be associated with files starting with "Baidar" and "JimShu." This finding could mean that an MFT file occupied this space where Pagefile.sys is located now. How this might occur varies; the cause might be a reformatted disk or a new OS installation. Reformatting or reinstalling an OS doesn't completely overwrite previous data on a disk, thus revealing residual data, such as MFT records and their associated files.

6. Next, double-click **pagefile.sys** to view the file in the main ProDiscover window. Right-click the **pagefile.sys** file and click **Copy File** to copy it to your work folder.

7. Exit ProDiscover Basic, saving when prompted.

Interpreting Attribute 0x80 Data Runs

The next task is a detailed examination of Pagefile.sys in WinHex Demo. You learn how to interpret data runs from the MFT file's fragments found in the Pagefile.sys file.

16

Navigating Through an MFT Record   For this task, you need WinHex Demo and a
spreadsheet program, such as Microsoft Excel or OpenOffice Calc. To examine the
Pagefile.sys file with WinHex Demo, follow these steps:

1. Start WinHex Demo. Click **File, Open** from the menu, navigate to and click
   Pagefile.sys, and then click **Open**.

2. Click **Search, Find Text** from the menu. In the Find Text dialog box, type **BAIDAR**
   in the text box at the top. Click the **Match case** check box, click **Unicode** in the list
   box underneath (see Figure 16-3), and then click **OK**.

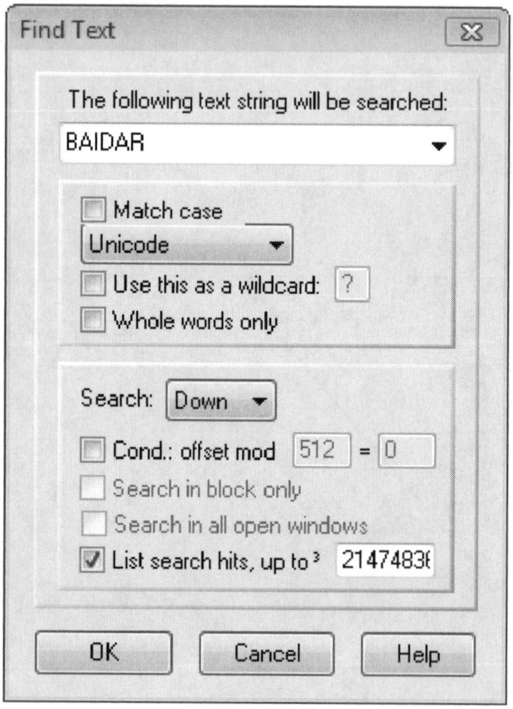

Figure 16-3   The Find Text dialog box

3. In the main window, the cursor is placed in the right pane at the start of the first
   occurrence of the Unicode string BAIDAR. From this position, scroll upward until
   you see FILE0.

4. To position the cursor at the start of the next attribute, place the cursor in the middle
   pane where FILE0 starts, and drag down 0x38 hexadecimal bytes (see Figure 16-4),
   using the offset counter in the lower-right corner as a guide.

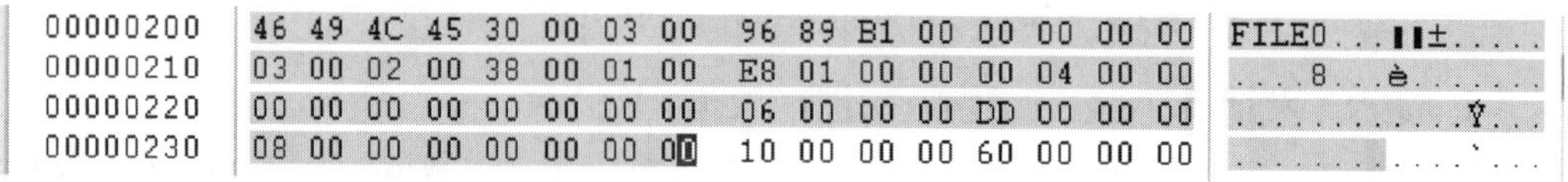

```
00000200   46 49 4C 45 30 00 03 00   96 89 B1 00 00 00 00 00   FILE0...▌▌±.....
00000210   03 00 02 00 38 00 01 00   E8 01 00 00 00 04 00 00   ....8...è...
00000220   00 00 00 00 00 00 00 00   06 00 00 00 DD 00 00 00   ............Ÿ...
00000230   08 00 00 00 00 00 00 00   10 00 00 00 60 00 00 00
```

Figure 16-4   MFT record header

All numeric values in these steps are hexadecimal. If the offset counter is in decimal mode, click the row of numbers to the right of the hexadecimal section once. Each time you click here, WinHex toggles between decimal and hexadecimal modes.

5. Place the cursor at the beginning of attribute 0x10, and drag down 0x60 hexadecimal byte until you reach the next attribute, 0x30 (see Figure 16-5).

```
00000230   08 00 00 00 00 00 00 00   10 00 00 00 60 00 00 00   ............`...
00000240   00 00 00 00 00 00 00 00   48 00 00 00 18 00 00 00   ........H.......
00000250   00 F2 C4 B3 03 C6 C9 01   B6 CE C0 13 ED C5 C9 01   .òÄ³.ÆÉ.¶ÎÀ.íÅÉ.
00000260   10 31 C3 13 ED C5 C9 01   00 F2 C4 B3 03 C6 C9 01   .1Ã.íÅÉ..òÄ³.ÆÉ.
00000270   20 00 00 00 00 00 00 00   00 00 00 00 00 00 00 00    ...............
00000280   00 00 00 00 09 01 00 00   00 00 00 00 00 00 00 00   ................
00000290   00 00 00 00 00 00 00 00   30 00 00 00 78 00 00 00   ........0...x...
```

Figure 16-5 Viewing attribute 0×10

6. The next two sections of the file are the short and long filename attribute 0x30. Figure 16-6 shows the short filename attribute. Both have lengths of 0x78 hexadecimal bytes. Repeat the previous step until you reach attribute 0x80.

```
00000290   00 00 00 00 00 00 00 00   30 00 00 00 78 00 00 00   ........0...x...
000002A0   00 00 00 00 00 00 03 00   5A 00 00 00 18 00 01 00   ........Z.......
000002B0   8E 00 00 00 00 00 01 00   00 F2 C4 B3 03 C6 C9 01   Ž........òÄ³.ÆÉ.
000002C0   00 F2 C4 B3 03 C6 C9 01   00 F2 C4 B3 03 C6 C9 01   .òÄ³.ÆÉ..òÄ³.ÆÉ.
000002D0   00 F2 C4 B3 03 C6 C9 01   00 00 00 00 00 00 00 00   .òÄ³.ÆÉ.........
000002E0   00 00 00 00 00 00 00 00   20 00 00 00 00 00 00 00   ...............
000002F0   0C 02 42 00 41 00 49 00   44 00 41 00 52 00 7E 00   ..B.A.I.D.A.R.~.
00000300   31 00 2E 00 58 00 4C 00   53 00 73 00 00 00 00 00   1...X.L.S.s.....
```

Figure 16-6 Attribute 0×30: short filename

7. From the starting position of attribute 0x80, count 0x40 hexadecimal bytes to the beginning of the first data run, as shown in Figure 16-7. Leave WinHex Demo open for the next activity.

```
00000380   6C 00 73 00 00 00 00 00   80 00 00 00 58 00 00 00   l.s.....l...X...
00000390   01 00 00 00 00 00 05 00   00 00 00 00 00 00 00 00   ................
000003A0   21 00 00 00 00 00 00 00   40 00 00 00 00 00 00 00   !.......@.......
000003B0   00 44 00 00 00 00 00 00   00 44 00 00 00 00 00 00   .D.......D......
000003C0   00 44 00 00 00 00 00 00   31 14 CB 01 01 31 04 52   .D......1.Ë..1.R
000003D0   6C 02 11 04 F4 21 04 D8   FB 21 02 2E FE 00 35 89   l...ô!.Øû!..þ.5‰
000003E0   FF FF FF FF 82 79 47 11   00 00 00 00 00 00 00 00   ÿÿÿÿ‚yG.........
```

Figure 16-7 Attribute 0×80, the beginning of the first data run

Now that you have located the data run's starting position, the next task is to calculate the starting and ending cluster positions of each data run fragment. (For more detailed information on calculating data runs, refer back to Figures 6-20, 6-21, and 6-22.)

Configuring the Data Interpreter Window in WinHex Typically, when WinHex starts, the Data Interpreter window opens, where you can convert data formats into easy-to-read values, such as converting hexadecimal values into decimal values. For the following activities, you need to know how to configure the Data Interpreter window to perform data run calculations. Follow these steps:

1. Start WinHex Demo, if necessary. If the Data Interpreter window doesn't open, click **View** from the menu, point to **Show**, and click the check box next to **Data Interpreter**.

2. Click **Options, Data Interpreter** from the menu to open the Data Interpreter Options dialog box. Click the **8 bit, signed**, **16 bit, signed**, and **24 bit, signed** check boxes, click the **Win32 FILETIME (64 bit)** check box on the right (clearing any other check boxes that are selected), as shown in Figure 16-8, and then click **OK**. Leave WinHex Demo open for the next activity.

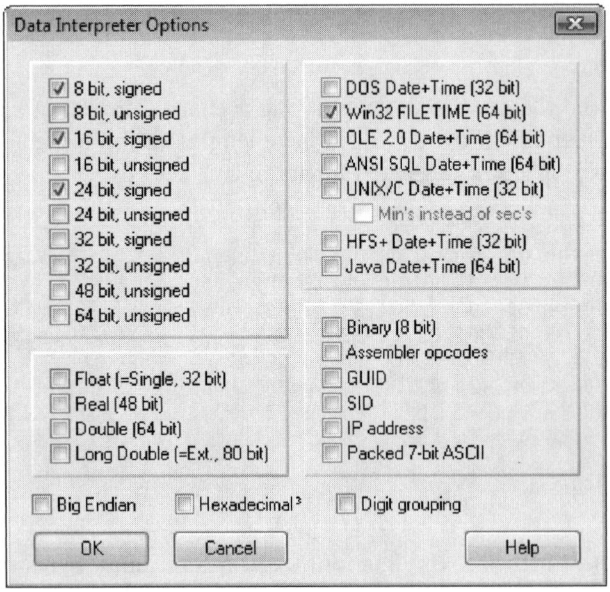

Figure 16-8 The Data Interpreter Options dialog box

Calculating Data Runs Next, you determine the starting and ending cluster numbers for the MFT record's data run. The length of this MFT record is less than 512 bytes (0x200 hexadecimal), so the data runs don't have an update sequence array value, as described in Chapter 6. To calculate the data runs for this example, follow these steps:

1. To determine the number of clusters for the first data run, place the cursor on the data run position immediately to the right of the first data run position 31, as shown in Figure 16-9. Because it's only 1 byte long, the 0x14 converts to 20 in decimal (as shown in the Data Interpreter window), which indicates 20 clusters in the first data run.

2. To determine the starting logical cluster number (LCN) position for this data run, place the cursor to the left of the "C" in the string **CB 01 01**. Note that this address

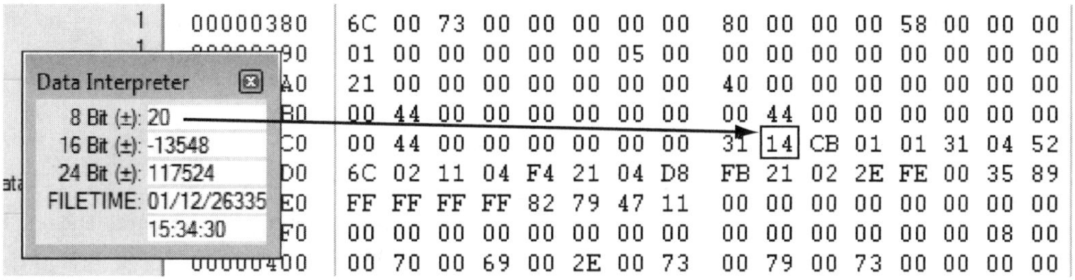

```
   1 | 00000380  6C 00 73 00 00 00 00 00   80 00 00 00 58 00 00 00
   1 | 00000390  01 00 00 00 00 00 05 00   00 00 00 00 00 00 00 00
┌─────────────────────────┐A0  21 00 00 00 00 00 00 00   40 00 00 00 00 00 00 00
│ Data Interpreter    ☒  │B0  00 44 00 00 00 00 00 00   00 44 00 00 00 00 00 00
│   8 Bit (±): 20 ────────│    00 44 00 00 00 00 00 00   31 [14] CB 01 01 31 04 52
│  16 Bit (±): -13548   C0│D0  6C 02 11 04 F4 21 04 D8   FB 21 02 2E FE 00 35 89
│  24 Bit (±): 117524   D0│E0  FF FF FF FF 82 79 47 11   00 00 00 00 00 00 00 00
│  FILETIME: 01/12/26335 E0│F0  00 00 00 00 00 00 00 00   00 00 00 00 00 00 08 00
│          15:34:30     F0│00  00 70 00 69 00 2E 00 73   00 79 00 73 00 00 00 00
└─────────────────────────┘
```

Figure 16-9 Number of clusters in the first data run

location is 3 bytes, or 24 bits, as shown in Figure 16-10. Therefore, the starting LCN position for the first data run is 65995, as shown in the Data Interpreter window.

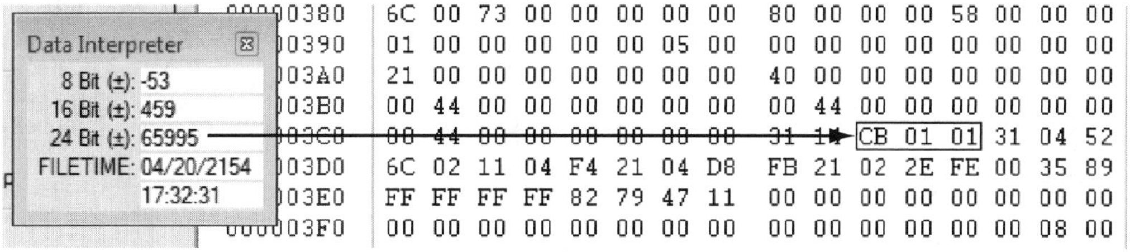

```
              00000380  6C 00 73 00 00 00 00 00   80 00 00 00 58 00 00 00
┌───────────────────────┐0390  01 00 00 00 00 00 05 00   00 00 00 00 00 00 00 00
│ Data Interpreter   ☒ │03A0  21 00 00 00 00 00 00 00   40 00 00 00 00 00 00 00
│   8 Bit (±): -53      │03B0  00 44 00 00 00 00 00 00   00 44 00 00 00 00 00 00
│  16 Bit (±): 459      │03C0  00 44 00 00 00 00 00 00   31 14 CB 01 01 31 04 52
│  24 Bit (±): 65995 ───│03D0  6C 02 11 04 F4 21 04 D8   FB 21 02 2E FE 00 35 89
│  FILETIME: 04/20/2154 │03E0  FF FF FF FF 82 79 47 11   00 00 00 00 00 00 00 00
│          17:32:31     │03F0  00 00 00 00 00 00 00 00   00 00 00 00 00 00 08 00
└───────────────────────┘
```

Figure 16-10 Starting LCN position for the first data run

3. Next, move the cursor to the next data run's cluster count position; it has a hexadecimal value of 0x04 that converts to decimal 4. The next 3 bytes (24 bits) display the virtual cluster number (VCN) 52 6C 02, which converts to 158802 in decimal.

4. Repeat Steps 1 to 3 to find the remaining clusters per fragment and the VCN values, as shown in Figure 16-11. (Refer to Chapter 6 for information on how NTFS manages MFT records.)

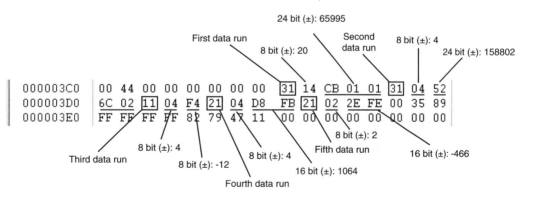

Figure 16-11 Data runs for the Baidarka-.xls file

5. To simplify the calculations, enter the LCN and VCN values in a spreadsheet, as shown in Figure 16-12. When you're finished, exit WinHex Demo.

Enter VCNs here

Enter LCNs here

Calculated VCN per
fragment for
column B

Assigned number of
clusters per fragment
for column D

	A	B	C	D	E
1	Filename: Baidarka-.xls		Tradesecret folder		
2	Fragment	VCN	Starting Cluster	Clusters per fragment	Ending Cluster
3	1	LCN starting no.	65995	20	66014
4	2	158802	224797	4	224800
5	3	-12	224785	4	224788
6	4	-1064	223721	4	223724
7	5	-466	223255	2	223256

Formulas for column C

= C3 starting LCN
= C3+B4 for cell C4
= C4+B5 for cell C5
= C5+B6 for cell C6
= C6+B7 for cell C7

Formulas for column E

= (C3+D3)-1 for cell E3
= (C4+D4)-1 for cell E4
= (C5+D5)-1 for cell E5
= (C6+D6)-1 for cell E6
= (C7+D7)-1 for cell E7

Figure 16-12 Converted data run values in a spreadsheet

Carving Data Run Clusters Manually

Now that you have calculated the starting and ending cluster positions for the Baidarka-.xls file, it's time to recover the fragments in ProDiscover Basic. To begin data carving, follow these steps:

1. Start ProDiscover Basic, and click the **Open Project** toolbar icon. In the Open dialog box, navigate to and click the **C16Inchp01.dft** project, and then click **Open**.

2. In the tree view, click to expand **Cluster View, Images,** and then click **C16InChp.dd.**

3. In the spreadsheet you created in the previous activity, locate the starting cluster position (65995) in cell C3, and then locate the clusters per fragment (20) in cell D3.

4. In ProDiscover's work area, click the **Decimal** check box under the Cluster text box, type the decimal value **65995** in the text box, and then click **Go**.

5. Click cluster position 65995, hold the **Shift** key down, and press the **down arrow** key once to highlight additional clusters. Then press the **left arrow** key until the value **66014** is shown in the Cluster text box (see Figure 16-13).

When extracting fragments, it's important to recover only the clusters from the starting and ending cluster positions. Adding extra clusters produces a corrupted file that the intended application, such as Microsoft Word or Excel, can't read.

6. In the work area, right-click the highlighted cluster blocks and click **Recover**.

7. In the Recover Clusters dialog box, click the **Recover all clusters to a single file** option button, if necessary, and then click the **Recover Binary** check box (see Figure 16-14). Click **Browse**, navigate to and click your work folder, and then click **OK** twice. Leave ProDiscover Basic open.

Starting fragment 65995

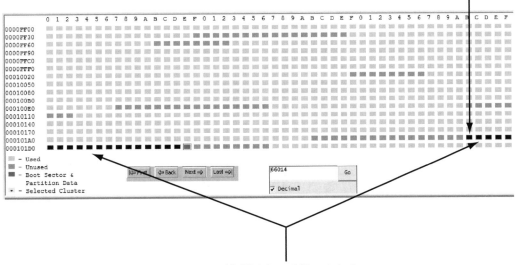
Highlighting additional clusters

Figure 16-13 Highlighted cluster for the first fragment

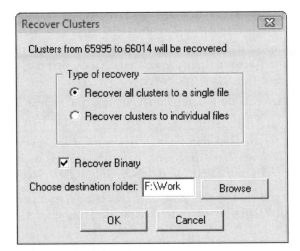

Figure 16-14 The Recover Clusters dialog box

Return to the spreadsheet and locate the starting cluster for the second, third, fourth, and fifth data run fragments. Follow these steps for each remaining data run fragment:

1. Enter the starting cluster position in the Cluster text box, and click **Go**.

2. Click this starting cluster position, hold the **Shift** key down, and press the **right arrow** key until you reach the ending cluster position for the data run (see Figure 16-15).

16

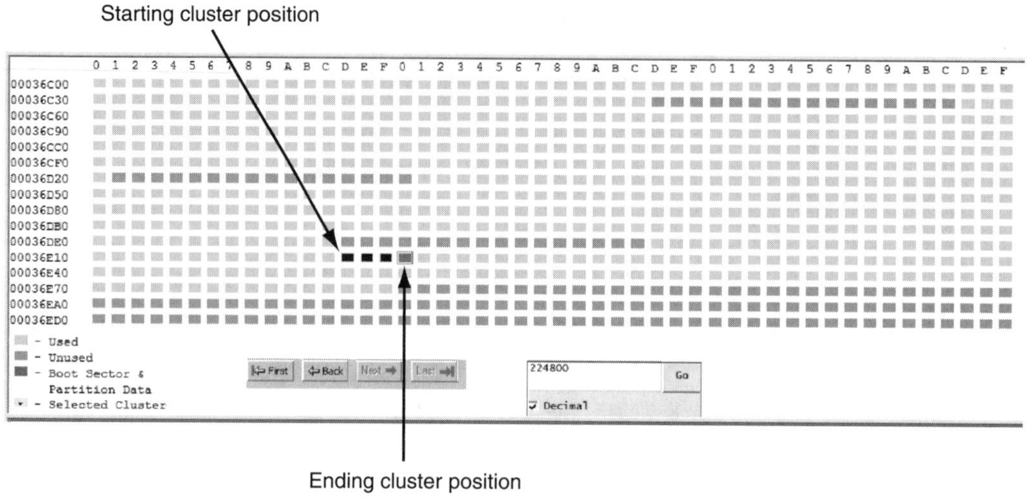

Starting cluster position

Ending cluster position

Figure 16-15 Highlighting clusters for the data run fragment

TIP

If you're using Windows Vista, when you hold down the Shift key and press an arrow key, additional cluster blocks might be highlighted. If this occurs, release the Shift key and press the arrow key to return to the starting cluster position. Then try highlighting the correct clusters again.

3. In the work area, right-click the highlighted cluster blocks and click **Recover**.

4. In the Recover Clusters dialog box, click the **Recover all clusters to a single file** option button, if necessary, and click the **Recover Binary** check box. Click **Browse**, navigate to and click your work folder, and then click **OK** twice.

5. Refer to your spreadsheet for the remaining data run fragments, and repeat Steps 1 through 4 to recover them.

When you have finished carving the fragmented data runs, the next step is appending the fragments into one file. To combine all fragments, they must be in the correct order. If you switch the order of any fragment, the recovered file is unreadable. Follow these steps:

1. In Windows Vista, click **Start**, type **cmd** in the Start Search text box, and press **Enter**. (In Windows XP, click **Start**, **All Programs**, point to **Accessories**, and click **Command Prompt**.)

2. In the DOS command prompt window, change to your work folder with the **cd** command. For example, type **cd \work** and press **Enter**. To make sure you're in the correct folder, type **dir C16InChp-*** and press **Enter** to see a listing of the fragments you recovered.

3. Use the following commands to append the fragments into one file. Make sure you type each command in the correct fragment order listed in the spreadsheet you created, and press **Enter** after each command:

```
type C16InChp-65995-66014.txt > Baidarka-.xls
type C16InChp-224797-224800.txt >> Baidarka-.xls
```

```
type C16InChp-224785-224788.txt >> Baidarka-.xls
type C16InChp-223721-223724.txt >> Baidarka-.xls
type C16InChp-223255-223256.txt >> Baidarka-.xls
```

4. Exit the DOS command prompt window, and test your work by opening the Baidarka-.xls file from Windows Explorer. If it fails to open in your spreadsheet program, review your steps to make sure you collected the correct clusters and have appended them in the correct order.

You've completed the data-carving procedure in ProDiscover Basic and WinHex. In the Hands-On Projects, you carve additional files and see whether there are any ethics concerns.

Chapter Summary

- Ethics can be defined as rules you internalize and use to measure your performance (internal standards) or standards that you're compelled to adhere to by external forces, such as licensing bodies (codes of professional conduct or responsibility). Laws governing codes of professional conduct or responsibility typically define the lowest level of action or performance required to avoid liability.

- There's no U.S. licensing body for computer forensics examiners. Therefore, sources for ethical standards are your own internal values (ethics), codes of professional associations you belong to and certifying bodies that have granted you a certification, and your employer's rules of professional conduct. Most examiners rely on a combination of these standards to construct their professional ethical codes.

- Be aware of attempts to disqualify you as an expert. Opposing counsel might attempt to disqualify you based on any deviations from opinions you've given in previous cases, so be prepared to explain the reason for any changes in your position. Some attorneys might contact you solely for the purpose of discrediting or disqualifying you ("conflicting out"). Always note calls from attorneys and the nature of the communication, and require that the attorney complete a client questionnaire and send you an investigation retainer.

- Courts use many factors in determining whether to disqualify an expert, such as whether an expert was formally retained and compensated, whether an expert was informed that discussions were confidential, and so on.

- Be aware of obvious ethical errors, such as ignoring contradictory data, performing work beyond your expertise or competence, allowing the attorney who hired you to influence your opinion improperly, and reaching a conclusion before completing your research.

- No single source offers a definitive code of ethics for expert witnesses, so you must draw on standards from other organizations to form your own ethical standards. Many professional organizations, such as the ABA and AMA, have rules to guide their members in areas such as interaction with patients/clients, objectivity, role in society, fees, solicitation, independence, and contractual relationships.

- The inherent conflict between the needs of the justice system and your obligations for professional conduct can create ethical difficulties. With an adversarial legal system, pressures from hiring attorneys, and a tendency to identify with the side for whom you're

16

working, maintaining impartiality can be difficult. Computer forensics examiners should consider their personal values, review the codes of conduct that apply to other professions, and develop a personal code of conduct that will protect them from ethical errors.

- The attorney who has retained you, opposing counsel, and the court owe you ethical responsibilities as an expert witness. For example, your attorney owes you a fair statement of the case or situation, adequate time to review evidence and prepare your report, and a reasonable opportunity to examine data, conduct testing, and investigate the matter before rendering an opinion.

- The tools you use to recover, control, and track evidence are subject to review by opposing parties. If the court deems them unreliable, the evidence you recovered with those tools might not be admitted or be admitted with a limiting instruction. If you create tools for your own use, you must still validate them and submit them for review.

- After carving data artifacts, analyzing as much of the information as possible is critical. This information includes the create, modified, last access, and record timestamps in a recovered MFT record in addition to any recovered data runs. Collecting as many facts as possible provides more complete findings for your final report.

Key Terms

codes of professional conduct or responsibility External rules that often have the effect of law in limiting professionals' actions; breach of these rules can result in discipline, including suspension or loss of a license to practice and civil and criminal liability.

contingency fees Payments that depend on the content of the expert's testimony or the outcome of the case.

disqualification The process by which an expert witness is excluded from testifying.

ethics Rules that you internalize and use to measure your performance; sometimes refers to external rules (codes of professional conduct or responsibility).

Review Questions

1. Describe two types of ethical standards.

2. Ethical obligations are duties that you owe only to others. True or False?

3. List three sound reasons for offering a different opinion from one you testified to in a previous case.

4. List three or more factors courts have used in determining whether to disqualify an expert.

5. All expert witnesses must be members of associations that license them. True or False?

6. Contingency fees can be used to compensate an expert under which circumstances?

    a. When the expert is too expensive to compensate at the hourly rate

    b. When the expert is willing to accept a contingency fee arrangement

    c. When the expert is acting only as a consultant, not a witness

    d. All of the above

7. List three organizations that have a code of ethics or conduct.

8. In the United States, no state or national licensing body specifically licenses computer forensics examiners. True or False?

9. When you begin a conversation with an attorney about a specific case, what should you do? (Choose all that apply.)

    a. Ask to meet with the attorney.

    b. Answer his or her questions in as much detail as possible.

    c. Ask who the parties in the case are.

    d. Refuse to discuss details until a retainer agreement is returned.

10. What purpose does making your own recording during a deposition serve?

    a. It shows the court reporter that you don't trust him or her.

    b. It assists you with reviewing the transcript of the deposition.

    c. It allows you to review your testimony with your attorney during breaks.

    d. It prevents opposing counsel from intimidating you.

11. Externally enforced ethical rules, with sanctions that can restrict a professional's practice, are more accurately described as which of the following?

    a. Laws

    b. Objectives

    c. A higher calling

    d. All of the above

12. Describe an unethical technique opposing counsel might use to make a deposition difficult for you.

13. What are some risks of using tools you have created yourself?

    a. The tool might not perform reliably.

    b. The judge might be suspicious of the validity of results from the tool.

    c. You might have to share the tool's source code with opposing counsel for review.

    d. The tool doesn't generate reports in a standard format.

14. List four steps you should take, in the correct order, to handle a deposition in which physical circumstances are uncomfortable.

15. List three obvious ethical errors.

16

16. Codes of professional conduct or responsibility set the highest standards for professionals' expected performance. True or False?

Hands-On Projects

The following projects produce correspondence that might contain attorney-client privileged information. Your task is to locate and recover the data and report to Ileen Johnson on your findings. Before beginning these projects, create a C:*Work*\Chap16\Projects folder on your system and move the file used with in-chapter activities to this folder.

HANDS-ON PROJECTS

Hands-On Project 16-1

For this project, you calculate data runs for the following files from an anonymous user's disk image. All the MFT records for the files of interest are in the Pagefile.sys file recovered during the in-chapter activity. The files of interest are as follows:

- JimShuMemo.doc (two or more versions of this file might exist)
- Kayak4.jpg
- Baidarka.xls

Using WinHex Demo, locate the MFT records and determine the data runs for each record, as described in the in-chapter activity. Create a spreadsheet listing the starting and ending cluster positions for each file, and turn it in to your instructor for review.

Hands-On Project 16-2

After you have calculated data runs for all known recoverable files in the previous project, you need to carve out the data runs and rebuild each file in ProDiscover Basic, as you did in the in-chapter activity. When you're finished, submit the rebuilt files to your instructor for review.

Hands-On Project 16-3

After reviewing the files you recovered, Ileen Johnson needs to know the create dates for each file. Using the information in Chapter 6 (refer to Figure 6-13), locate the create date value for all files, including the file recovered from the in-chapter activity. For this task, use WinHex's Data Interpreter window. After determining this information, write a short report listing each file's create date, and turn it in to your instructor.

When using the Data Interpreter for data and time values, place the cursor at the beginning of the date field. For example, if the date and time string is 62 16 9B 68 0A 7C C9 01, place the cursor on the 62 value.

TIP

Hands-On Project 16-4

Based on the information you have extracted so far, Ileen Johnson wants to know whether there are any additional files of interest, such as PDF documents. Using ProDiscover Basic, reopen the in-chapter case file C16InChp01.dft. Using the Content Search tab, enter *.pdf as the search criteria, as shown in Figure 16-16. When you have located all PDF files, copy them and hand them in to your instructor.

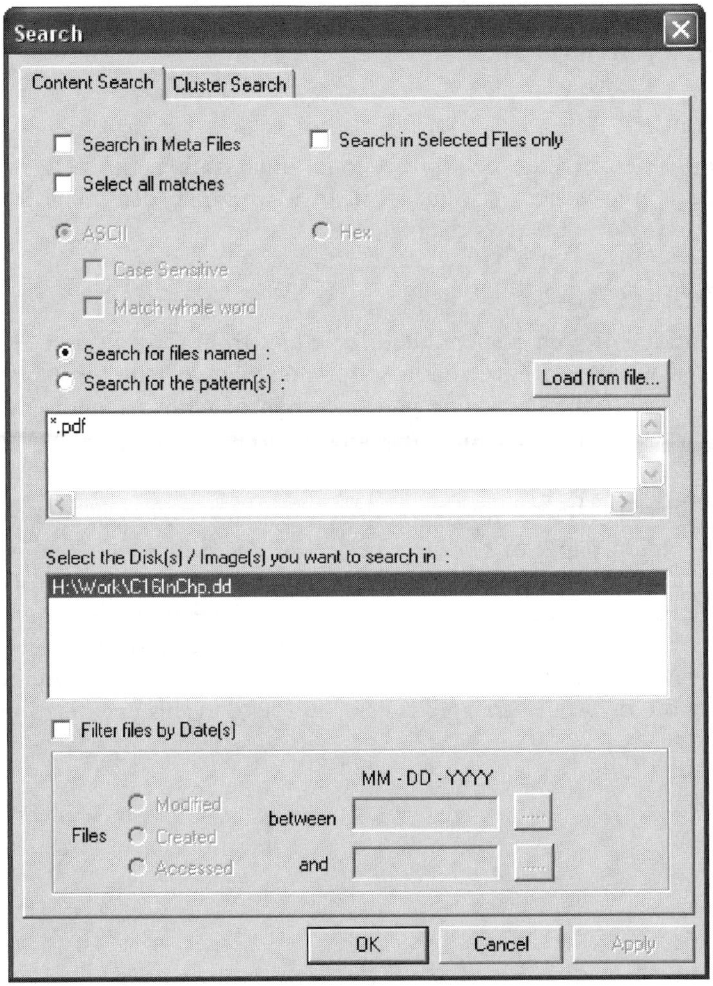

16

Figure 16-16 Searching for PDF files in ProDiscover

Case Projects

CASE PROJECTS

Case Project 16-1

Write a code of ethics for an organization you belong to or a school you attend, and explain the purpose of the code. Your code of ethics should have at least three items of expected ethical behavior.

Case Project 16-2

Write a one- to two-page paper on the basic tenets of your personal ethical code and the sources your code is based on. It should be based on your personal experiences with ethical conflicts and how your understanding of ethics has played a part in your life.

Case Project 16-3

Examine a code of ethics for a professional organization, business, or government agency, and write a critique of it. In your paper, determine the entity's priorities and whose interests the code serves.

Case Project 16-4

Write a critique of your personal code of ethics from Case Project 16-2. How can you tell when you have followed (or not followed) the precepts of your personal code of ethics? Include your experiences with personal ethical conflicts and whether you were able to resolve them.

Case Project 16-5

Write an opinion paper of two or more pages describing your findings in the in-chapter activities and Hands-On Projects. Review the contents of the files you extracted, and make your own conclusion on what Jim Shu might be up to, based on this collected data. You should also take into consideration date and time values as part of your opinion on the files' validity. In addition, give an opinion on any legal correspondence you found in this examination.

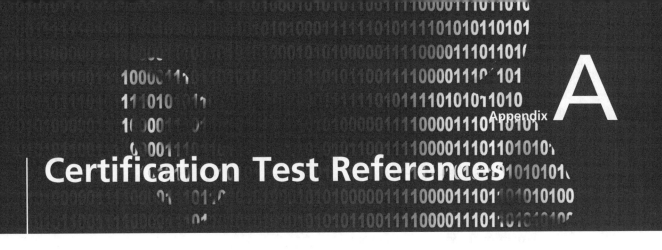

Appendix A

Certification Test References

This appendix gives you an overview of National Institute of Standards and Technology (NIST) testing processes for certification of computer forensics tools and computer forensics training programs offering certificates.

NIST Computer Forensics Tool Testing

NIST provides several resources on computer forensics tool testing. Check these resources regularly for the latest updates and test results. The following links on the NIST Web site are of specific interest to computer forensics examiners:

- The Computer Forensics Tool Testing (CFTT) Project (*www.cftt.nist.gov*)
- The National Software Reference Library (NSRL) Project (*www.nsrl.nist.gov/index. html*)

The CFTT Project was developed to give the legal community, law enforcement, and forensics tool vendors a program to validate the reliability of these tools. As part of the validation, this project is intended to help vendors improve their products to ensure that their results stand up in court.

The NSRL is a repository of known software and files from computer vendors. OS and application files are identified by their unique hash values, usually MD5 and SHA-1 hashes. Computer forensics examiners can filter out known files by their hash values, which reduces the number of files they need to inspect for possible digital evidence. The NSRL also contains hash values for known bad files, typically computer viruses and contraband material.

Types of Computer Forensics Certifications

Several organizations, both public and private, have developed certification programs for computer forensics examiners. Some organizations specialize in certain areas, and others take a general overview approach, but all provide a baseline for what examiners are supposed to be proficient in when conducting computer investigations. These organizations typically have fees for membership and certification exams.

Some of these organizations have come and gone for a variety of reasons. If you decide to obtain a certification, examine the sponsoring organization's history and management and check the board of directors or advisers' credentials. With this information, you can determine an organization's orientation. For example, if an organization's members are well known for disk and media forensics, you know the certification is oriented toward standalone computing exams. If an organization's members are well known for network and intrusion forensics, you know the certification focuses on network firewalls and other related network intrusion topics. In addition, the older the organization is, the better the chances are that it will be around for future support.

Computer forensics certification organizations can be divided into three categories:

- Professional certifying organizations
- Application vendor certifying companies
- Computer forensics public and private training groups

The following sections describe some well-known certifying organizations, but many other organizations provide certification. When selecting a certification program, research it thoroughly to make sure it fits your needs. All these programs require a sizable investment of your time and money.

Professional Certifying Organizations

These organizations are typically nonprofit or not-for-profit groups that have specific missions to provide guidelines and training for computer forensics.

IACIS Certification   The International Association of Computer Investigative Specialists (IACIS) is a nonprofit organization formed to promote professional standards and certify computer forensics examiners. Through IACIS, you can become a Certified Forensic Computer Examiner (CFCE). To qualify to take the CFCE exam, you must be an active law enforcement officer or other person qualified to be an IACIS member. For more information on qualification requirements, visit *www.iacis.com*.

IACIS offers an extensive testing program to verify competence in performing a computing investigation. The examination process is not a training program; it's strictly a testing program. Applicants are screened before acceptance into the certification program, and IACIS is the sole decision maker for all applicants. IACIS offers two ways to obtain CFCE certification. The first is to attend an annual training conference that allows you to complete the certification. The second is to apply for the examination through an external certificate program that requires completion within 13 months. Applying for the certification requires completing an application form and paying the associated fee. For the latest information on fees, go to *www.iacis.com/certification*. If you're rejected for any reason, your fee is returned. If you're accepted into the program, a monitor (an IACIS CFCE member) directs you through the testing.

ISFCE Certification   Similar to IACIS, the International Society of Forensic Computer Examiners (ISFCE) provides guidelines for training for its Certified Computer Examiner (CCE) certification. You can find current information on ISFCE at *www.isfce.com* and more information on the CCE certification at *www.certified-computer-examiner.com*. Presently, several universities and colleges sponsor credited and noncredited computer forensics classes for this certification. In addition, many commercial computer forensics training companies offer CCE training.

GIAC Certification The SysAdmin, Audit, Network, Security (SANS) Institute offers extensive training in all aspects of computing security, including forensics. The SANS certification program is called Global Information Assurance Certification (GIAC; *www.giac.org/overview*) and has several training tracks. One track, Global Certified Forensic Analyst (GCFA), provides unique training in network intrusion response forensics for computer media. Tools used for GCFA training are open source and require extensive knowledge of UNIX and Linux. For more information on this program, visit *www.giac.org/certifications/security/gcfa.php*.

Application Vendor Certifying Companies

Several computer forensics application vendors have developed their own certification programs. These programs follow standard guidelines for practices used in all computer forensics investigations and examinations. In addition, these vendor-specific exams certify that people achieving these certifications are competent in using their forensics tools. Two well-established vendor certification programs are Guidance Software EnCase Certified Engineer (EnCE) and AccessData Certified Examiner (ACE).

EnCE Certification For acceptance into the EnCE certification program, you must meet one of several prerequisite options defined at *www.guidancesoftware.com/computer-forensics-training-ence-certification.htm*. Testing for this certification is divided into two phases. The first phase requires passing a test successfully (80% or higher score) at a Thomson Prometric testing facility. The second phase is a practical test of computer evidence and requires an 85% or better score to pass.

ACE Certification For acceptance into the ACE certification program, you must meet one of several prerequisite options defined at *www.accessdata.com/acePreparation.html*. This program also has two phases with similar scoring requirements. The first phase is administered through Thomson Prometric. For more information on Thomson Prometric testing methods and facility locations, see *www.prometric.com/default.htm*.

Computer Forensics Public and Private Training Groups

Several small businesses, universities, and colleges have developed program certificates for successful completion of their coursework; these organizations can be divided into academic institutions and private training companies. The programs range from one day to several months of classroom work. Most academic institutions offer college credit for their courses, and private training companies typically offer continuing education credits. For more information on these programs, refer to the Web sites listed in the following sections. To locate other programs, do an Internet search on "computer forensics certificates."

Academic Institutions Here are some of the leading schools offering computer forensics certificates:

- British Columbia Institute of Technology, *www.bcit.ca/study/programs/525gascert*
- Caldwell College, *www.caldwell.edu/academics/Business/cert_computer_forensics.aspx*
- California State at Fullerton, *www.csufextension.org/Classes/certificate/CertDetail. aspx?GN=3298&GV=2*
- Canberra Institute of Technology, *www.cit.act.edu.au/future/courses/computer_ forensics_advanced_diploma/*

- Champlain College, *http://digitalforensics.champlain.edu/*
- College of San Mateo, *www.smccd.net/csmcis/cert_of_comp_in_cis.php*
- George Washington University, *http://nearyou.gwu.edu/htc/index1.html*
- Kent State University, *www.kent.edu/regional/Programs/descriptions/ computerforensics.cfm*
- Oregon State University, *www.bus.oregonstate.edu/services/nti.htm*
- Spokane Falls Community College, *www.spokanefalls.edu/TechProf/InfoSys/ CertForensics.aspx*
- University of Alabama at Birmingham, *http://main.uab.edu/show.asp?durki=69261*
- University of Central Florida, *www.cs.ucf.edu/csdept/info/gccf/*
- University of Melbourne, *www.mccp.unimelb.edu.au/courses/award-courses/graduate-certificate/digital-forensics*
- University of Rhode Island, *http://forensics.cs.uri.edu/*
- University of Washington, *www.extension.washington.edu/ext/certificates/cpf/cpf_gen.asp*
- West Virginia University, *www.lcsee.cemr.wvu.edu/forensics/*
- Wilber Wright College, *http://wright.ccc.edu/Programs/csfi.asp*

Private Training Companies The following list shows a few of the top private training companies offering computer forensics certificates:

- Gatlin Education Services, *www.gatlineducation.com/forensic_computer_training_ overview.html*
- Key Computing Services, *www.cftco.com/staff.htm*
- NTI, *www.forensics-intl.com/osu3day.html*
- NWC3C, *www.nw3c.org/ocr/courses_desc.cfm*
- Stroz Friedberg, LLC, *www.strozllc.com/trainingcenter/xprGeneralContent1. aspx?xpST=TrainingCenter*
- Technological Crime Learning Institute, *www.cpc.gc.ca/courses-cours/descript/ cmpfor-infjud-eng.html*

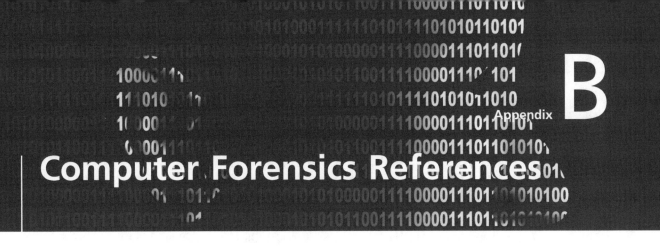

Computer Forensics References

This book is only the beginning of computer forensics and investigations. To master all levels of computer forensics, you should familiarize yourself with the works of many other authors who have made significant contributions to this profession. This appendix lists several computer forensics books, operating system books, and legal references that can expand your skills and understanding of conducting computing investigations. In addition, you'll find helpful Web links, e-mail lists, and professional journals.

Computer Forensics Reference Books

In recent years, several books specifically on computer forensics have been published. The following sections list a variety of books that can expand your technical skills and understanding of computing investigations.

Brown, Christopher L.T. *Computer Evidence: Collection & Preservation*. Course Technology, 2006 (ISBN 1584504056).

Bunting, Steve and William Wei. *EnCase Computer Forensics: The Official EnCE: EnCase Certifed Examiner Study Guide*. Sybex, 2006 (ISBN 0782144357).

Caloyhannides, Michael A. *Computer Forensics and Privacy*. Artrech House Publishers, 2001 (ISBN 1580532837).

Carrier, Brian. *File System Forensic Analysis*. Addison-Wesley Professional, 2005 (ISBN 0321268172).

Carvey, Harlan. *Windows Forensic Analysis DVD Toolkit*, 2nd ed. Syngress, 2009 (ISBN 1597494224).

Casey, Eoghan, ed. *Digital Evidence and Computer Crime*. Academic Press, 2003 (ISBN 0121631044).

Casey, Eoghan, ed. *Handbook of Computer Crime Investigation, Forensic Tools and Technology*. Academic Press, 2002 (ISBN 0121631036).

Clark, Franklin and Ken Diliberto. *Investigating Computer Crime*. CRC Press, 1996 (ISBN 0849381584).

Fowler, Kevvie. *SQL Server Forensic Analysis*. Addison-Wesley Professional, 2008 (ISBN 0321544366).

Icove, David, Karl Seger, and William VonStorch. *Computer Crime, A Crimefighter's Handbook*. O'Reilly & Associates, Inc., 1995 (ISBN 1565920864).

Jones, Keith J., Richard Bejtlich, and Curtis W. Rose. *Real Digital Forensics: Computer Security and Incident Response*. Addison-Wesley Professional, 2005 (ISBN 0321240693).

Kruse II, Warren G. and Jay G. Heiser. *Computer Forensics: Incident Response Essentials*. Pearson Education, 2001 (ISBN 0201707195).

Kubansiak, Ryan R., Sean Morrissey, and Jesse Varsalone (tech. ed.). *Mac OS X, iPod, and iPhone Forensic Analysis DVD Toolkit*. Syngress, 2008 (ISBN 1597492973).

Malin, Cameron H., James M. Aquilina, and Eoghan Casey. *Malware Forensics: Investigating and Analyzing Malicious Code*. Syngress, 2008 (ISBN 159749268X).

Mel, H.X. and Doris Baker. *Cryptography Decrypted*. Addison-Wesley, 2001 (ISBN 0201616475).

Pogue, Chris, Cory Altheide, and Todd Haverkos. *UNIX and Linux Forensic Analysis DVD Toolkit*. Syngress, 2008 (ISBN 1597492698).

Prosise, Chris, Kevin Mandia, and Matt Pepe. *Incident Response: Computer Forensics*. McGraw-Hill, 2003 (ISBN 007222696X).

Rosenblatt, Kenneth S. *High-Technology Crime*. KSK Publications, 1995 (ISBN 0964817101).

Sammes, A.J. and Brian Jenkinson. *Forensic Computing*, 2nd ed. Springer, 2007 (ISBN 1846283973).

Stephenson, Peter. *Investigating Computer-Related Crime*. CRC Press, 2000 (ISBN 0849322189).

MS-DOS Reference Books

The following books are good references on how to use MS-DOS and how to create your own DOS batch files. Some of these books might be out of print. If you can't find them at a local bookstore, try searching for them on eBay or at *www.half.com.*

Cooper, Jim. *Special Edition Using MS-DOS 6.22, 3rd Edition*. Que, 2002 (ISBN 078972573).

Gookin, Dan. *DOS for Dummies, 3rd Edition*. Wiley Publishing, Inc., 1999 (ISBN 0764503618).

Menefee, Craig and Nick Anis. *Harnessing DOS 6.0, Batch File and Command Macro Power*. Bantam Computer Books, 1993 (ISBN 0553351885).

Windows Reference Books

The better you understand the many versions of Windows operating systems, the better you understand what data you're looking for and recovering. The following standard Microsoft Windows books are useful for computer forensics examiners:

Bott, Ed, Carl Siechert, and Craig Stinson. *Microsoft Windows XP Inside Out, Second Edition*. Microsoft Press, 2004 (ISBN 073562044X).

Honeycutt, Jerry. *Microsoft Windows Registry Guide, Second Edition*. Microsoft Press, 2005 (ISBN 0735622183).

Osborne, Sandra. *Windows NT Registry: A Settings Reference.* Sams Publishing, 1998 (ISBN 1562059416).

Tulloch, Mitch, et al. *Windows Vista Resource Kit.* Microsoft Press, 2007 (ISBN 0735622833).

Linux Reference Books

Linux is becoming more popular with end users and computing forensics examiners. The more you know and understand about Linux, the easier it is to use. Linux as an operating system provides more dynamic control of processes, which is beneficial to computing forensics examiners.

Rankin, Kyle. *Knoppix Hacks: 100 Industrial-Strength Tips and Tools.* O'Reilly Media, Inc., 2004 (ISBN 0596007876).

Siever, Ellen, et al. *Linux in a Nutshell: A Desktop Quick Reference.* O'Reilly Media, Inc., 2005 (ISBN 0596009305).

Sobell, Mark G. *A Practical Guide to Linux Commands, Editors, and Shell Programming.* Prentice Hall PTR, 2005 (ISBN 0131478230).

Tyler, Chris. *Fedora Linux: A Complete Guide to Red Hat's Community Distribution.* O'Reilly Media, Inc., 2006 (ISBN 0596526822).

Legal Reference Books

The following books are guides on expert testimony:

Babitsky, Steven and James J. Mangraviti, Jr. *How to Become a Dangerous Expert Witness: Advanced Techniques and Strategies.* SEAK, Inc., 2005 (ISBN 1892904276).

Babitsky, Steven, James J. Mangraviti, Jr., and Christopher J. Todd. *The Comprehensive Forensic Services Manual: The Essential Resources for All Experts.* SEAK, Inc., 2000 (ISBN 1892904071).

Babitsky, Steven, James J. Mangraviti, Jr., and Christopher J. Todd. *The Comprehensive Forensic Services Manual: The Essential Resources for All Experts.* SEAK, Inc., 2002 Supplement (ISBN 18929040225).

Smith, Fred Chris and Rebecca Gurley Bace. *A Guide to Forensic Testimony: The Art and Practice of Presenting Testimony as an Expert Technical Witness.* Addison-Wesley Professional, 2002 (ISBN 0201752794).

For additional information on legal subjects, visit *http://west.thomson.com/westlaw/*.

Web Links

Association of Certified Fraud Examiners, *www.acfe.com*

CERIAS, *www.cerias.purdue.edu/site/research/forensics/*

CERT, *www.cert.org*

Champlain College, Computer & Digital Forensics, *http://digitalforensics.champlain.edu*

Computer Crime Research Center, *www.crime-research.org*

Computer Forensic Analysis, *www.porcupine.org/forensics/*

Computer Forensics, Cybercrime and Steganography Resources, *www.forensics.nl*

Computer Technology Investigators Network, *www.ctin.org*

Digital Forensic Investigator, *www.dfinews.com*

Digital Forensic Research Workshop, *www.dfrws.org*

FBI Laboratory, *www.fbi.gov/hq/lab/org/cart.htm*

FBI's Forensic Science Communications, *www.fbi.gov/hq/lab/fsc/current/index.htm*

Forensic Focus, *www.forensicfocus.com*

High Tech Crime Consortium, *www.hightechcrimecops.org*

IFIP, *www.cis.utulsa.edu/ifip119*

International High Technology Crime Investigation Association, *www.htcia.org*

Journal of Digital Forensics, Security and Law, *www.jdfsl.org*

NTI, *www.forensics-intl.com*

Open Source Digital Forensics, *www.opensourceforensics.org*

Penguin Sleuth, *http://penguinsleuth.org*

SANS, *www.sans.org*

Sleuth Kit, *www.sleuthkit.org*

Source Forge, Digital Forensics Tool Testing Images, *http://dftt.sourceforge.net*

US-CERT, *www.us-cert.gov*

E-mail Lists
Computer Forensics World, *www.computerforensicsworld.com/index.php*

Mobile Phone Forensics, *www.mobilephoneforensics.com*

X-Ways Support Forum, *www.x-ways.net/cgi-bin/discus/discus.cgi*

Yahoo! Groups
Computer Forensics Tool Testing (CFTT), *http://tech.groups.yahoo.com/group/cftt/*

Forensic Focus, *http://tech.groups.yahoo.com/group/ForensicFocus/*

Linux Forensics, *http://tech.groups.yahoo.com/group/linux_forensics/*

Macintosh OS Forensics, *http://tech.groups.yahoo.com/group/macos_forensics/*

Phone Forensics, *http://tech.groups.yahoo.com/group/phoneforensics/*

Windows Forensics, *http://tech.groups.yahoo.com/group/windowsforensics/*

Professional Journals

Information Forensics and Security, University of Illinois-Urbana, 2265 Beckman Institute, MC 251, 405 N. Mathews Avenue, Urbana, IL 61801.

International Journal of Digital Evidence, IJDE Editor, Utica College, 1600 Burrstone Road, Utica, NY 13502.

International Journal of Digital Forensics and Incident Response, 6277 Sea Harbor Drive, Orlando, FL 32887-4800.

Journal of Digital Forensic Practice, Taylor & Francis, Inc., 325 Chestnut Street, Suite 800, Philadelphia, PA 19106.

The Journal of Digital Forensics, Security and Law, JDFSL Editor, Association of Digital Forensics, Security and Law, Longwood University, 201 High Street, Farmville, VA 23909.

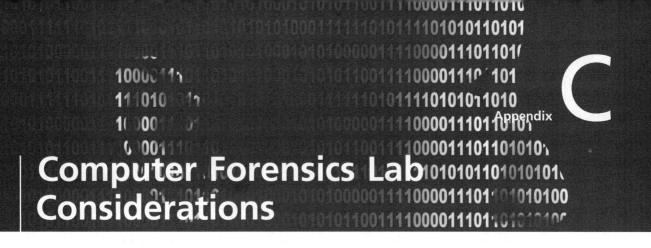

Computer Forensics Lab Considerations

In Chapter 3, you learned what's needed for a computer forensics lab. This appendix addresses some additional considerations for planning and operating of a lab.

International Lab Certification

In addition to the American Society of Crime Laboratory Directors (ASCLD; *www.ascld. org*), the International Organization of Standards (ISO) has requirements for standard processes that transcend national boundaries. An organization can become ISO certified when it has integrated processes to ensure that established requirements in products and services are met consistently. Of special interest to computer forensics examiners are the following ISO standards that can be applied to lab operation:

- ISO 9000: Quality management system in production environments
- ISO 9001: Quality management
- ISO 9069: Software quality model
- ISO 9241: Ergonomic requirements for office work with visual display
- ISO 17025: General requirements for competence of test and calibration laboratories
- ISO 27001: Information technology–Security techniques–Information security management systems

For more information on ISO standards, visit *www.iso.org*, *www. ansi.org/standards_activities/iso_programs/overview.aspx?menuid=3*, and *www.fasor.com/iso25*.

Considering Office Ergonomics

Because computer investigations often require hours of processing drives for evidence, your workspace should be as comfortable as possible to prevent repetitive-motion injuries and other computer work–related injuries. Ergonomics is the study of designing equipment to meet the human need for comfort and allow improved productivity and involves psychology, anatomy, and physiology. Understanding psychology helps designers create equipment that people can easily understand how to use. Ergonomic design also considers anatomy to make sure the equipment correctly fits the person using it. Physiology helps determine how much effort or energy the person using the equipment must expend.

To ensure an ergonomic workspace, review the following questions when arranging your workspace and selecting lab furniture:

- *Desk or workstation table*—Is the desk placed at the correct height for you? Do you need a chair that's lower or higher than normal to make the desktop easy to reach and comfortable to use? Are your wrists straight when sitting? Is this position comfortable? Are the heels of your hands in a comfortable position? Do they exert too much pressure on the desktop? Do you need a keyboard or mouse pad?

- *Chair*—Can your chair's height be adjusted? Is the back of the chair too long or too short? Is the seat portion too long or too short for your thighs? Are the seat and back padded enough to be comfortable? Can you sit up straight when viewing the computer monitor? Are your elbows in a comfortable position while working? How do your shoulders and back feel while sitting and working at the workstation? Is your head facing the computer's monitor, or do you have to turn your head because you can't position the chair in front of the monitor?

- *Workbench*—Is the workbench for your lab facility at the correct height when you're standing in front of it? Can you reach the back of the bench easily without having to stand on a stool?

Besides furniture, consider the ergonomics of your keyboard and mouse. These two items probably contribute to more repetitive-motion injuries than any other devices because they were designed for moderate but not extensive use. Using the keyboard for several hours at a time can be painful and cause physical problems. Make sure your wrists are straight when you're working with a keyboard or mouse, even if these items are ergonomically designed.

If you work with computers for hours in one position, you'll injure yourself. No matter how well the furniture, keyboard, or mouse is designed, always take breaks to stretch and rest your body.

Considering Environmental Conditions

Your lab's ventilation and temperature also contribute to your comfort and productivity. Although a typical desktop computer uses standard household electricity, computers get warm as they run. Unless you invest in a liquid-cooled computer case for your forensic workstation, a standard desktop computer generates heat. The more workstations you're running, the hotter your lab, so the room needs adequate air conditioning and ventilation. Consult with your building's facility coordinator to determine whether the room can be upgraded to handle your current and expected computing needs.

Use the following checklist of heating, ventilation, and air-conditioning (HVAC) system questions when planning your computer forensics laboratory:

- How large is the room, and how much air moves through it per minute?
- Can the room handle the increased heat that workstations generate?

- How many workstations will be placed in this room? What's the maximum number of workstations the room can handle?

- Can the room handle the heat output from a small RAID server?

Lighting

Lighting is often an overlooked environmental issue in computer forensics labs. Most offices have too many lights at the wrong illumination, which can cause headaches and eyestrain. Several vendors offer natural or full-spectrum lighting, which is less fatiguing than standard incandescent or fluorescent lights, although it doesn't have any health benefits.

In 1986, the Food and Drug Administration (FDA) issued a Health Fraud Notice about "false and misleading" claims and "gross deceptions" by light bulb and lamp manufacturers on the benefits of full-spectrum lighting (*FDA Enforcement Report: Health Fraud Notice,* 1986, WL 59812).

If the lighting in your lab is a problem, consult with facility management and find out what products can best meet your needs. For additional information on dealing with eyestrain, see *www.apple.com/about/ergonomics/vision.html.*

Considering Structural Design Factors

The physical construction of your computer forensics lab is another factor to consider. Your lab should be a safe, secure, lockable room. Processing a drive or creating an image can take anywhere from a few hours to several days or weeks. When you must leave evidence unattended overnight, you need a secure location—a room that no unauthorized people can access without your control.

The National Industrial Security Program Operating Manual (NISPOM), Chapter 5, Section 8, page 1, "Construction Requirements," gives an overview of how to build a secure lab. See *http://nsi.org/Library/Govt/Nispom.html* for details.

To ensure physical security, examine the facility's hardware, walls, ceiling, floors, and windows. Make sure only heavy-duty building material has been used in the construction. All hardware, such as door hinges on the outside of the lab, should be peened, pinned, brazed, or spot-welded to prevent removal.

Walls can be constructed of plaster, gypsum wallboard, metal panels, hardboard, wood, plywood, glass, wire mesh, expanded metal, or other materials offering resistance to and evidence of unauthorized entry. If you use insert panels, you need to install material that can reveal evidence of an attempt to gain entry.

Ceilings, like walls, can be constructed of plaster, gypsum wallboard, acoustic ceiling panels, hardboard, wood, plywood, ceiling tile, or other material that offers some sort of resistance and makes detection possible if access is attempted. False or drop ceilings in which the walls don't extend to the true ceiling because of hanging ceiling tile must be reinforced with wire mesh or 18-gauge expanded metal that extends from the top of the false wall to the true ceiling. This material must overlap adjoining walls and should provide resistance so that attempted access can be detected.

If you have raised floors, which are common in data centers, look for large openings in the perimeter walls. If you find any, use the same types of material described for ceilings to make sure the floor provides resistance and shows evidence of someone attempting to access the lab.

Avoid windows on the lab exterior. If you're assigned a room with exterior windows, install additional material, such as wire mesh, on the inside to improve security. If your lab must be placed on an exterior wall, request an upper floor, not a ground floor. Also, make sure computer monitors face away from windows to prevent unauthorized people from being able to see what you're working on.

Doors can be wood (solid core) or metal and shouldn't have windows. If the door does have a window, it should have wire mesh in the glass for resistance so that attempted entries can be detected. The door's locking device should have a heavy-duty, built-in combination device or a high-quality key-locking doorknob. If you're using a key-locking doorknob, only authorized personnel should have a copy of the key.

Depending on your lab's location, you might need to install intrusion detection systems and fire alarms. Consult and contract with a bonded alarm company.

Determining Electrical Needs

You need enough electrical power to run workstations and other equipment; 15- and 20-amp service is preferred for electrical outlets. In addition, you should have enough electrical outlets spaced throughout the lab for easy access, eliminating the need for extension cords or electrical plug strips, which are potential fire hazards.

If you have adequate electrical power for your operation, power fluctuations aren't usually a problem unless you're in an area with poor electrical service. Most computers are fairly tolerant of power fluctuations, although they do cause electrical wear and tear on computer components. However, all electrical devices eventually fail, usually because of accumulated electrical voltage spikes. If your lab equipment exhibits unexplained failures, consult with your facilities manager to check for problems in electrical power.

In addition, uninterruptible power supply (UPS) units must be connected to all forensic workstations to reduce electrical problems. If a power failure occurs, a UPS unit enables you to continue working until you can shut down your computer safely. Most UPS units also block or filter electrical fluctuations, which helps minimize computer component problems that might corrupt and destroy evidence stored on sensitive magnetic media.

Planning for Communications

When you're planning voice and data communications, note that each examiner needs a telephone. Unless you're working in a TEMPEST environment, which has special voice and data access requirements, you can install a multiline Integrated Services Digital Network (ISDN) phone system in the lab. ISDN is the easiest way for lab personnel to handle incoming calls.

You also need dial-up or broadband Internet access. Computer forensics software vendors often provide updates and patches on their Web sites, and you need to be able to download them. You also need Internet access to conduct research on evidence you find and to consult with other forensics professionals. However, don't keep your workstation connected to the Internet while conducting your analysis unless it's absolutely required. Internet connections can compromise your system's security, even with a firewall installed.

Setting up a local area network (LAN) for workstations in a lab enables you to transfer data to other examiners easily and makes operations run more smoothly. For example, you can share a RAID file server and printers on a LAN. This setup is especially useful when you have specialty printers connected to a print server. Using a central RAID server also saves time when you're copying large files, such as image files.

If your organization is part of a wide area network (WAN), consider having a separate computer used only to connect to the WAN to protect the security of your forensic workstations. By keeping your forensic workstations physically separate from the WAN, you eliminate any intentional or unintentional access to your evidence or work product. For example, although workstations on a WAN can receive notices to upgrade software, doing so while your forensic workstation is connected to the WAN can corrupt evidence. Isolating systems prevents this corruption.

Installing Fire-Suppression Systems

Any electrical device can cause a fire, although it's not common with computers. However, an electrical short in a computer might destroy a cable. If the power on a low-voltage cable is high enough, it could ignite other combustible items nearby. Computers can also cause fires if a hard disk's servo-voice coil actuators freeze because of damage to the drive. When this happens, the head assembly can't move. The disk's circuit card then applies more electrical power to actuators to try to move the head assembly, which passes too much power through the disk. Disk components can handle only so much power before they fail and overload the cables connecting the drive to the computer. When too much power is applied to these low-voltage cables, especially ribbon cables, sparks can fly, causing a fire.

Most offices are equipped with fire sprinkler systems and dry chemical fire extinguishers (B rated). For most forensics lab operations, these fire-suppression systems work well, and no additional protection is required. However, if your lab facility has raised floors, you might need to install a dry chemical fire-suppression system. If you have any concerns, contact your facility coordinator or the local fire marshal. For additional information on best practices for fire extinguishers, see *www.fire-extinguisher101.com/fireprotectionproduct.html*. For information on computer room fire-suppression systems, see *www.fssa.net*.

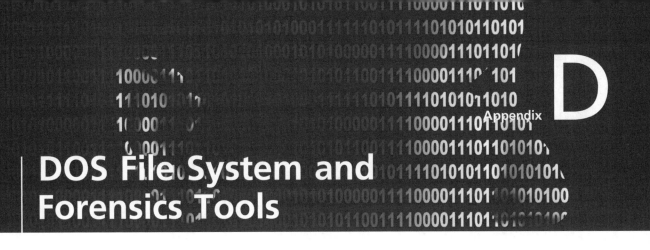

DOS File System and Forensics Tools

Many computer forensics tools have migrated to a Windows GUI environment. Before Windows NT, however, computer forensics examinations were conducted with tools that worked in MS-DOS. Mastering these tools can give you a unique understanding of how newer, more advanced tools work. In addition, some DOS tools, such as DriveSpy, enable you to perform tasks that you can't perform as easily with recent GUI tools. Learning about these tools is also important because you'll likely run across legacy systems in investigations. This appendix is an overview of the FAT file system used in DOS and some commercial MS-DOS data acquisition and analysis tools designed for FAT.

Overview of FAT Directory Structures

When Microsoft created the MS-DOS operating system, data was stored on floppy disks. Floppy disks have a limited maximum size, so the addressable storage space is small compared to modern hard disks. All floppy disks for Microsoft OSs use the FAT12 file system. (FAT file systems are explained in more detail in Chapter 6.) Because of the limited disk and memory space on older computers, Microsoft engineered FAT12 so that directory names could be only one to eight characters. Filenames could be up to eight characters, and file extensions could be zero to three characters. This naming scheme is often called the "8.3 naming convention." The characters in file extensions identify the file type, such as .doc for a Word document or .xls for an Excel spreadsheet.

When larger drives were developed, Microsoft reengineered FAT and created FAT16, which allows up to 2 GB of addressable storage space for drive partitions. With further advances in disk technologies, Microsoft created FAT32, which can access up to 2 terabytes (TB) or more of storage space. In MS-DOS 6.22, the same directory and filename conventions from FAT12 were carried over to FAT16. In Windows 95 and later, FAT32 maintains the eight-character maximum for filenames and three-character limit for file extensions.

When larger filenames than FAT12 and FAT16 allowed were needed, Microsoft developed Virtual FAT (VFAT). VFAT provides two filenames for every file: a long filename in what looks like Unicode format, displayed in a hexadecimal editor with null (00) values between each character, and a short filename that uses eight-character filenames and three-character extensions. The purpose of having both filenames is backward compatibility with older Microsoft OSs and file systems. For example, Figure D-1 shows four files, one with a long filename (Market_Plan-31.txt) and three with short filenames. When you view Market_Plan-31.txt in MS-DOS with the Dir command, you see its name converted to the short filename: Market~1.txt (see Figure D-2).

Figure D-1 Viewing filenaming in Windows Explorer

```
A:\WORK>DIR

 Volume in drive A is APP_B
 Volume Serial Number is 1C36-19E4

 Directory of A:\WORK

.              <DIR>         01-12-2005     06:39p
..             <DIR>         01-12-2005     06:39p
PICS           <DIR>         01-12-2005     06:39p
MARKET~1  TXT      167,123  09-12-2004     06:50p
MP-32     TXT       78,985  09-12-2004     06:50p
MT-1      TXT       28,533  09-12-2004     06:51p
MT-2      TXT       23,802  09-12-2004     06:52p
        7 file(s)          298,443 bytes
                         1,157,005 bytes free



A:\WORK>|
```

Figure D-2 Viewing filenaming in MS-DOS with the Dir command

You can view and examine directory contents with many different tools, but only DriveSpy, a command-line utility, is designed to run in DOS. Using DriveSpy to examine a directory structure requires locating the directory's cluster position first. Continuing with the previous example, you locate the cluster number for the Work directory with the Dir command (see Figure D-3).

Cluster number for the
Work directory's location

```
DAP1:\>DIR /S

The following output could be lengthy...
(Displaying files in a recursive directory listing)
Would you like to disable PAGE mode until this command completes[Y/N]? Y


Directory of: \

                     Create         Modify (DOS)  Last       Start
Name        Attrib   Date    Time   Date    Time  Access     Cluster        Size
----------- ------  --------------- ------------- --------   ---------  ----------
WORK        -d----  -------- -----  01-12-05 18:39 09-12-05        2              0

Directory of: \WORK

                     Create         Modify (DOS)  Last       Start
Name        Attrib   Date    Time   Date    Time  Access     Cluster        Size
----------- ------  --------------- ------------- --------   ---------  ----------
.           -d----  -------- -----  01-12-05 18:39 --------        2              0
..          -d----  -------- -----  01-12-05 18:39 --------        0              0
PICS        -d----  -------- -----  01-12-05 18:39 09-12-05        3              0
MT-1   TXT  a-----  -------- -----  09-12-04 18:51 --------     2451          29544
MARKET~1 TXT a-----  -------- -----  09-12-04 18:50 --------     1965         167123
(Market_Plan-31.TXT)
```

Figure D-3 Finding the Work directory's cluster number

Next, to display information listed in the directory, use the Cluster command. Note that the cluster number for the Work directory is 2 in Figure D-3. To view this cluster's content, type Cluster 2 and press Enter (see Figure D-4).

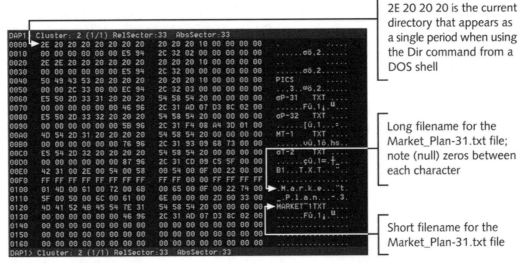

2E 20 20 20 is the current directory that appears as a single period when using the Dir command from a DOS shell
Long filename for the Market_Plan-31.txt file; note (null) zeros between each character
Short filename for the Market_Plan-31.txt file
DAP1> Cluster: 2 (1/1) RelSector:33 AbsSector:33

Figure D-4 Viewing the directory cluster content

NOTE

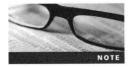

For more information on using these commands, refer to "Quick References for DriveSpy" later in this appendix.

Another useful tool that can run in Windows is the shareware Directory Snoop from Briggs Softworks (*www.briggsoft.com*). Directory Snoop is a convenient GUI tool for inspecting and recovering deleted data from disks. Figure D-5 shows an example of using Directory Snoop for FAT partitions.

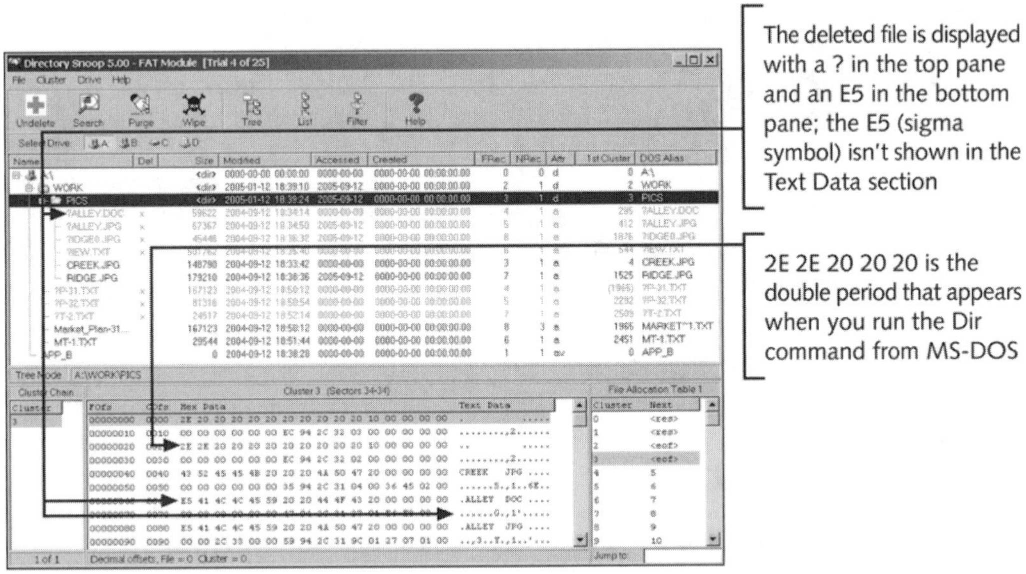

The deleted file is displayed with a ? in the top pane and an E5 in the bottom pane; the E5 (sigma symbol) isn't shown in the Text Data section
2E 2E 20 20 20 is the double period that appears when you run the Dir command from MS-DOS
Directory Snoop 5.00 - FAT Module [Trial 4 of 25]

Figure D-5 Using Directory Snoop

Note that no long filenames are listed in the bottom pane, which indicates that MS-DOS 6.22 or earlier was used to format the floppy disk and write data to it.

FAT directories contain specific information about the files stored in them. All FAT directories start with a hexadecimal 2E followed by several hexadecimal 20 values. A hexadecimal 2E converts to the ASCII value for a period, and a hexadecimal 20 represents a space. The following information is listed for all files in a directory:

- Long filename for Windows 95 or later FAT disks
- Short filename (8.3 naming convention)
- Attributes assigned to the file
- Case and creation time in milliseconds
- Creation time of the file
- Creation date of the file
- Last access date of the file
- Starting cluster high-word for FAT32 file systems
- Modified timestamp
- Modified date stamp
- Starting cluster of the file (assigned by FAT when all links to the file are listed)
- File size

When a file is deleted in a FAT directory, a hexadecimal E5 is inserted as the filename's first character (see callout in Figure D-5). If the file is renamed, an entry with the new filename is created, and the old filename is marked as deleted with the E5 value, just as though the file had been deleted. These entries aren't usually deleted from the directory. Figure D-6 shows a renamed file in a directory on a FAT12 drive.

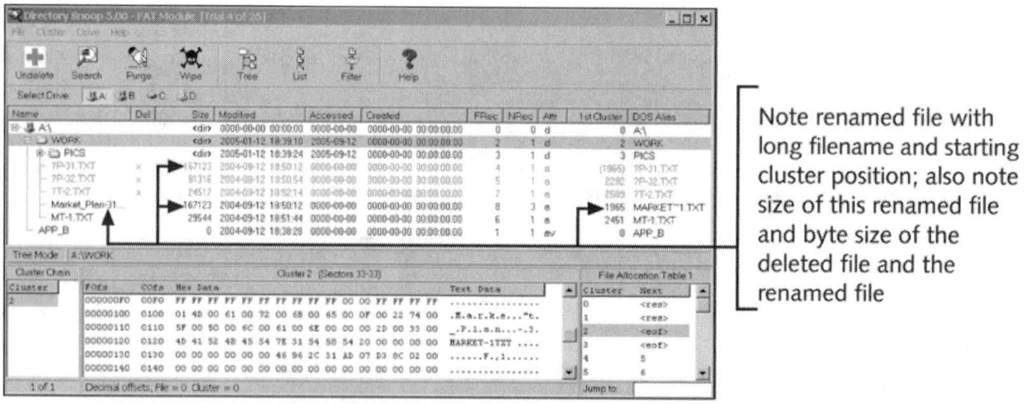

Note renamed file with long filename and starting cluster position; also note size of this renamed file and byte size of the deleted file and the renamed file

Figure D-6 Using Directory Snoop with a FAT12 drive

You can also reverse-engineer the starting cluster position and file size. These values are listed in hexadecimal format in the directory. To convert hexadecimal values to decimal, use the Windows scientific calculator:

1. In Windows, click **Start**, point to **All Programs**, point to **Accessories**, and click **Calculator**.

2. Click **View, Scientific** from the Calculator menu.

3. In the Scientific Calculator window, click the **Hex** option button.

4. Using the keyboard or number buttons in this window, enter the hexadecimal value you want to convert, and then click the **Dec** option button.

As shown in Figure D-7, the last four hexadecimal numbers are the byte size for the Market~1.txt file. When converting these numbers from hex to decimal, you read them from right to left: 00 02 8C D3, in this example. What's displayed with the Dir command or in Windows Explorer might be slightly smaller than what's converted. Figure D-7 also shows Market~1.txt's starting cluster number in hex. To convert these numbers to decimal, you enter them from right to left, too: 07 AD.

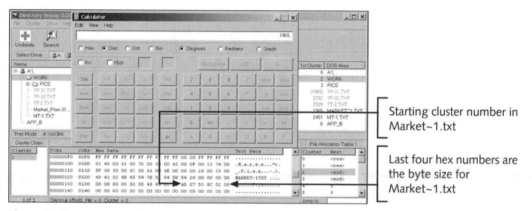

Starting cluster number in Market~1.txt

Last four hex numbers are the byte size for Market~1.txt

Figure D-7 Converting from hexadecimal to decimal

Note the decimal value 1965 that's been entered in the scientific calculator in Figure D-7. In FAT directory entries, the file's starting cluster position is at offset 1A hexadecimal or 26 decimal from the first position where the filename is displayed. Remember, the first position where the filename appears has the starting value of 0. The file's byte size is located starting at offset 1C hexadecimal or 28 decimal. These values are read from right to left.

In computer forensics investigations, often you need to determine the size of a file that has been deleted and overwritten by a newer file. This information can give you clues about copies of the deleted file on other disks.

Sample DOS Scripts

When you're performing repetitive tasks in DOS, building scripts (called "batch programs") to automate these tasks is helpful and can help you avoid data entry mistakes. This section covers two useful batch program examples with the Goto, For...In...Do, and Choice commands.

Goto is a simple branching command that instructs the batch program to jump to a defined location specified by a unique name preceded with a colon, as in this example:

```
:go_loop
echo sample goto loop
goto go_loop
```

A loop structure repeats commands until a specified condition is met. The preceding Go_Loop command runs indefinitely because it doesn't specify a condition that stops the loop. To specify a condition, you can use the If command to test three possible conditions: Errorlevel, the value of two strings to see whether they are equal, and whether a file exists.

The If Errorlevel command has five numeric error codes. The following commands return the error codes explained in Table D-1: Backup, Diskcomp, Diskcopy, Format, Graftable, Keyb, Replace, Restore, and Xcopy.

Table D-1 Error codes

Code	Result
0	Indicates a successful operation
1	Error of a read or write operation
2	The user initiated Ctrl+C (a common method to interrupt a command)
3	Fatal termination of read or write
4	Error during initialization

The following code is an example of how to use Errorlevel in a batch file with Xcopy, used to copy files and any subfolders to a specified location:

```
xcopy c:\temp a:\
iferrorlevel 1 goto go_error
Other code skipped when the above error is encountered.
:go_error
echo Command failed! Check for floppy in drive A
```

The following code uses Errorlevel with the Exist command. You use this command in the format If Exist *Filename* to verify whether *Filename* exists. If it does, the next command or function on the same line is performed. If *Filename* doesn't exist, the command on the same line is skipped, and the command on the next line is performed.

```
cd \mydocu~1
if exist text.doc goto go_del
Other code skipped when the above error is encountered.
:go_del
del text.doc
```

In MS-DOS, you can also compare strings. The following example shows how to use the If command to compare two values and then branch to another command:

```
rem test_if.bat
if "%1"=="" goto err_msg
if %1==copyfile goto go_copy
if %1==bye goto end
:err_msg
echo You need to enter something!
echo Run this batch file again!
goto :end
:go_copy
copy c:\temp\text.doc a:
:end
exit
```

To run this batch file, be sure to enter a matching parameter, as in the following code:

```
test_if copyfile
```

or

```
test_if bye
```

This example shows that if the user enters no parameters, which MS-DOS interprets as a null value, DOS tells the user to run the file again with the correct input. It stops running the file with the Exit command and returns to the MS-DOS prompt.

MS-DOS parameters are case-sensitive. If you use all uppercase characters in a batch file, for example, you must type uppercase letters when you enter the parameters.

The For...In...Do command is used to define a group of variables and process those variables to perform a task. A parameter can also be passed to refine the batch file. A double percent sign with a single letter (%%A) defines a variable in MS-DOS batch files, as in the following example:

```
rem cpfloppy.bat
for %%a in (A: a: B: b:) do if "%%A"=="%1" goto cp_file
echo You forgot to specify which floppy drive to use.
echo Remember the floppy drive is either A: or B:
goto end
:cp_file
echo You have selected the %1 drive.
copy c:\temp\text.doc a:
:end
```

With the For command, a batch file repeats a command or function until the correct value is entered. In the preceding example, the For %%A command branches to the Do If statement if the user types the correct floppy drive letter. The allowed values for this example are a, A, b, and B. Use the Choice command if you want to build a batch file to accept input after the file has started running. This command limits you to the options you've listed in the batch file and doesn't pass a parameter. This command also uses the Errorlevel command, although not like the other previously listed DOS commands. In the steps that follow, you create a batch file that uses these options to format a floppy disk. The Choice command can branch to up to 255 different labels defined in its key switch value. This is the syntax of the Choice command:

```
choice /C:key /N /S /T:choice,seconds prompt
```

Table D-2 defines each switch and option for the Choice command.

Table D-2 Switches and options for the Choice command

Switch or option	Function
/C:key	Defines the keys, or labels, displayed at the Choice prompt
/N	Suppresses key list and question mark, which are normally displayed by the DOS prompt
/S	Makes the input at the Choice prompt case sensitive
/T:choice, seconds	Provides a delay in seconds for any previously defined /C:key value
prompt	Defines choices for the user

The Errorlevel command has five basic responses from 0 to 4, as shown previously in Table D-1. Used with the Choice command, Errorlevel responds with exit codes, defined in Table D-3, to allow you to branch to a specific label.

Table D-3 Errorlevel codes for the Choice command

Code	Results
0	Terminated by user pressing Ctrl+C or Ctrl+Break
1	First key parameter is selected with the /C:key switch
2	Second key parameter is selected with the /C:key switch
3–254	nth key parameter is selected with the /C:key switch
255	Error parameter is selected with the /C:key switch

The Choice command is an external MS-DOS command. Windows 9x stores the command in the Windows\Command folder; MS-DOS 6.22 stores it in the DOS directory. To build a batch file on a floppy disk, you must copy the Choice command to the disk along with the batch file. To use the Choice command in a batch file, follow these steps:

Before beginning this activity, create a work folder for this appendix, such as *Work*\AppD.

1. On a Windows 98 computer, start Notepad, and in a new text document, type the following code:

```
@echo off
cls
echo.
echo *** Floppy Disk Format Batch Job ***
echo.
echo Choose the drive containing the disk you want to format.
echo.
echo Floppy disk drives available:
echo.
echo "A:"
echo "B:"
echo.
echo Select drive and type of format:
echo.
echo Option        Drive & Format
echo ------        ----------------
echo    A          A:  Quick Format
echo    B          A:  Unconditional Format
echo    C          A:  Quick Format with System Files
echo    D          B:  Quick Format
echo    E          B:  Unconditional Format
echo    F          B:  Quick Format with System Files
choice /c:ABCDEF "Choose drive and format option"
if errorlevel  255    goto Error
if errorlevel  6      goto F_for
if errorlevel  5      goto E_for
if errorlevel  4      goto D_for
if errorlevel  3      goto C_for
if errorlevel  2      goto B_for
if errorlevel  1      goto A_for

:Error
echo.
echo Run this batch file again,
echo but next time,
echo make a different selection.
echo.
goto end

:F_for
echo.
echo "B: Quick format with system files."
format b: /q /s
echo.
goto end

:E_for
rem "B: Unconditional format."
format b: /u
goto end
```

```
:D_for
echo "B: Quick format."
format b: /q
goto end

:C_for
echo "A: Quick format with system files."
format a: /q
goto end

:B_for
echo "A: Unconditional format."
format a: /u
goto end

:A_for
echo "A: Quick format."
pdblock 0
:end
```

2. Save the file as **MyChoice.bat** in your work folder, and exit Notepad.

3. Open a command prompt window. Using the **cd** command, navigate to your work folder.

4. Type **MyChoice.bat** and press **Enter**.

The batch file displays commands on the screen that you can use to format the disk in the A or B drive in a variety of formats—quick, unconditional, or quick with system files.

5. In drive A or B, insert a floppy disk containing files you no longer need. Then type **c** or **f**, depending on the floppy drive you're using. Your choice is confirmed, and the floppy disk is formatted.

6. When the formatting is finished, close the command prompt window.

For more information on batch programming, see the "MS-DOS Reference Books" section in Appendix B.

Setting Up Your Workstation for Computer Forensics

Before using DOS forensics tools, you need to configure a workstation to boot to MS-DOS. This section explains how to set up a workstation so that a Windows 98 OS can boot to DOS.

It's assumed you have a full-featured DOS forensics tool from Digital Intelligence DriveSpy and Image (see *www.digitalintelligence.com*). If not, read along to see how to configure a DOS forensic workstation.

The C drive (root directory) in Windows 98 contains a system file named Msdos.sys. Its properties are usually set to Hidden and Read-only so that it can't be changed inadvertently. You can add two commands to this file so that it displays the Windows Startup menu, also called the Startup Boot menu. To add commands to the Msdos.sys file, follow these steps:

1. Start Windows 98, if necessary. Click **Start, Run,** type **msconfig** in the Open text box, and then click **OK** to open the System Configuration Utility dialog box (see Figure D-8).

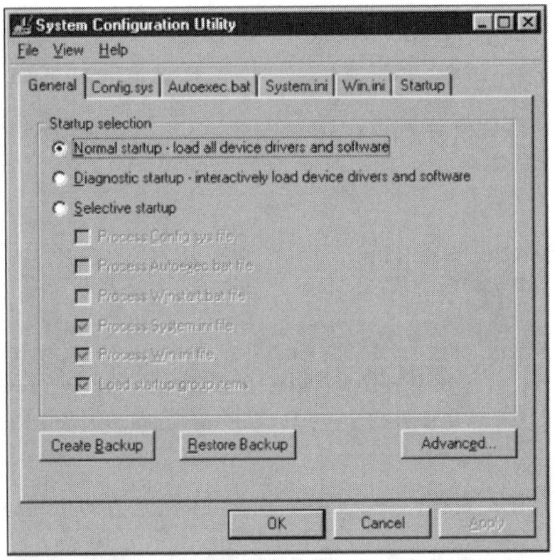

Figure D-8 The System Configuration Utility dialog box

2. In the General tab, you select startup settings. Configuring the Startup menu is an advanced setting, so click the **Advanced** button to open the Advanced Troubleshooting Settings dialog box (see Figure D-9).

3. Click the **Enable Startup Menu** check box so that Windows displays the Startup menu when you start the computer.

4. Click **OK** twice to close the Advanced Troubleshooting Settings dialog box and System Configuration Utility dialog box. Windows modifies the Msdos.sys file by turning on the Boot Menu switch.

5. If you're prompted to restart so that changes can take effect, click **Yes.** Because the Startup menu has been enabled, verify that **1. Normal** is selected for the boot option, and press **Enter.**

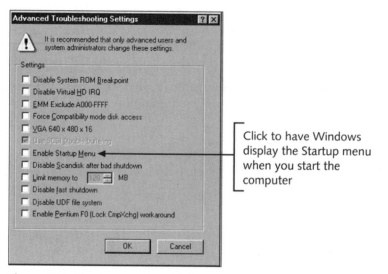

Click to have Windows display the Startup menu when you start the computer

Figure D-9 The Advanced Troubleshooting Settings dialog box

Now you can open the Msdos.sys file, examine its settings, and add a command to the file to extend how long the Startup menu is displayed before it closes and Windows starts as usual. Before you can modify the Msdos.sys file, you must change its Read-only and Hidden properties. Follow these steps:

1. If necessary, change the Windows view setting to show hidden files. To do this, open My Computer, and then click **View, Folder Options** from the menu. In the Folder Options dialog box, click the **View** tab. Under the Hidden files folder, click the **Show all files** option button, and then click **OK**.

2. In the My Computer window, navigate to the root drive on your hard disk, which is usually C. (If the drive where Windows is installed has a different drive letter, use it instead of C.) Right-click **Msdos.sys** and click **Properties** to open the Msdos.sys Properties dialog box.

3. In the Attributes section, click to clear the **Read-only** and **Hidden** check boxes, and then click **OK**.

4. Start Notepad, and then click **File, Open** from the menu. In the Open dialog box, navigate to the root drive, click **All Files** (*.*), if necessary, in the Files of type list box, and then double-click **Msdos.sys**. The Msdos.sys file opens in Notepad.

The BootMenu command is set to 1, which means it's enabled. A setting of 0 means it's disabled. (You might need to scroll to see the BootMenu command in this window.) If the Msdos.sys file contains a BootMenuDelay command, it's set to 5 seconds by default.

5. If the Msdos.sys file doesn't include a BootMenuDelay line, press **Enter** at the end of the file to add a new line, and then type **BootMenuDelay=59**, as shown in Figure D-10. If the file does have a BootMenuDelay line, extend the amount of time the Startup

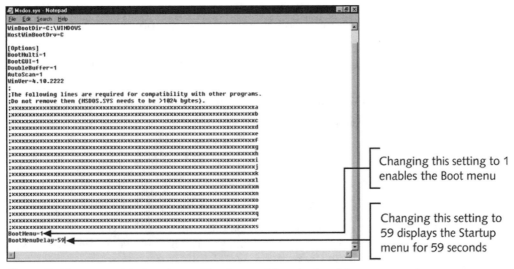

Figure D-10   The modified Msdos.sys file after enabling the BootMenu command

menu is displayed by changing the setting to 59, which is the maximum setting for displaying the Startup menu.

6. Click **File**, **Save** from the menu, and then exit Notepad.

7. Next, you need to restart your computer with the Normal boot option. If you're working in a computer lab, check with your instructor or technical support person to make sure you have permission to restart your computer. Click **Start**, **Shut Down**, **Restart**, **OK**.

8. Install your DOS forensics tool, such as DriveSpy and Image, on your computer.

Creating Forensic Boot Media

Your goal in a computer forensics examination is to not alter the original data, so you should never examine the original evidence drive, if possible. In this section, you make a boot floppy disk to serve as your forensic boot media. Whenever a computer starts, it accesses files on the hard drive, even if the computer boots from a floppy disk containing system files. When the boot process accesses files on the hard drive, it changes their date stamps and timestamps, which can jeopardize an investigation, especially if you're trying to determine when the computer was last used. Booting the computer without a specially configured floppy disk destroys information important to an investigation. Windows 9x can also alter other files, especially if DriveSpace is used on a FAT16 drive. The boot floppy disk you create is configured so that the boot process doesn't alter any files on the hard drive when the computer starts, thus preserving the suspect's drive. Having access to a software or hardware write-blocker for the suspect's drive is always a good precaution.

Assembling Tools for a Forensic Boot Floppy Disk

The steps in this section describe how to make a boot floppy disk. Many CD/DVD burner programs can create a bootable CD/DVD. These burner programs typically require a bootable floppy disk that's read by the burner program copied to the CD/DVD. If your CD/DVD burner program requires a bootable floppy, use this procedure. To make a boot floppy disk for forensics acquisitions, you need the following items:

- A disk editor, such as WinHex (the demo version doesn't work for this procedure) or Hex Workshop
- A floppy disk containing files you no longer need
- MS-DOS operating system, such as MS-DOS 6.22, Windows 95B (OSR2), or Windows 98 (not Windows XP, 2000, Me, or NT)
- A computer that can boot to a true MS-DOS level (one of the OSs listed previously)
- A DOS forensics acquisition tool, such as Replica, DriveSpy, EnCase, or SafeBack
- A write-blocking hardware device to protect the evidence drive (recommended)

The first task is to make the floppy disk bootable from the MS-DOS prompt, meaning it contains the system files needed to start the computer. The following steps use a Windows 98 computer. The process is similar in Windows 95.

1. Boot into DOS mode. Insert the floppy disk into the floppy drive, which is usually drive A.
2. At the C:\> prompt, format the floppy disk by typing **format a: /u /s**, pressing **Enter**, and then pressing **Enter** again when ready. When the system has finished formatting, it prompts you for a volume name. Type **Bootdisk** and press **Enter**. When prompted to format another disk, type **n** (for no) and press **Enter**.
3. At the DOS prompt, type **attrib -r -h -s a:*.*** and press **Enter** to remove the Read-only and Hidden attributes for all files on the floppy disk.
4. Delete the Drvspace.bin file on the A drive by typing **del a:\drvspace.bin** and pressing **Enter**.

To make the floppy disk bootable from Windows Explorer, follow these steps:

1. Boot into Windows 98. (*Note*: If your workstation's BIOS is set to boot from the A drive first, remember to remove the bootable floppy disk from the drive before you start Windows.) Insert the floppy disk into your computer's floppy drive.
2. Open Windows Explorer. Right-click the 3½" **Floppy (A:)** icon and click **Format**.
3. Click **Full** in the upper pane, and then click to select the **Copy system files** check box in the lower pane. Click **Start**. When you're done, change the file attributes by right-clicking the files and clicking **Properties**. Click to clear the **Hidden** and **Read-only** check boxes, and then click **OK**. Click **Close** in the Format Results dialog box and the Format dialog box.
4. Right-click the **Drvspace.bin** file, click **Delete**, and then click **Yes** in the Confirm File Delete message box.

After you create a bootable floppy disk, update the OS files to remove any reference to the hard drive, which is usually the C drive. This step ensures that when you're acquiring a FAT16 or FAT32 evidence disk, your boot floppy disk doesn't contaminate it. You need to modify the Command.com and Io.sys files to make a forensic boot disk. The following steps show you how to use Hex Workshop for this task. Hex Workshop should already be installed on your computer before you perform these steps.

 If you have updated Command.com and Io.sys correctly, there's no need for a hardware write-blocking device.

1. If necessary, boot into Windows. Insert the boot floppy disk you created in the previous set of steps into the floppy drive.

2. The changes from this point can be done in Windows 98 or in Windows 2000. (Screenshots in these steps were taken in Windows 2000.) In Windows 2000, open Windows Explorer, and click **Tools, Folder Options** from the menu. Click the **View** tab, if necessary, and in the Advanced settings section, click **Show Hidden files and folders,** and then click **OK.** In Windows 98, click **View, Folder Options** from the Windows Explorer menu. Click the **View** tab. Under Hidden files, click the **Show all files** option button (if necessary), and then click **OK.**

3. Start Hex Workshop. The opening window shown in Figure D-11 might differ slightly from yours, depending on the version.

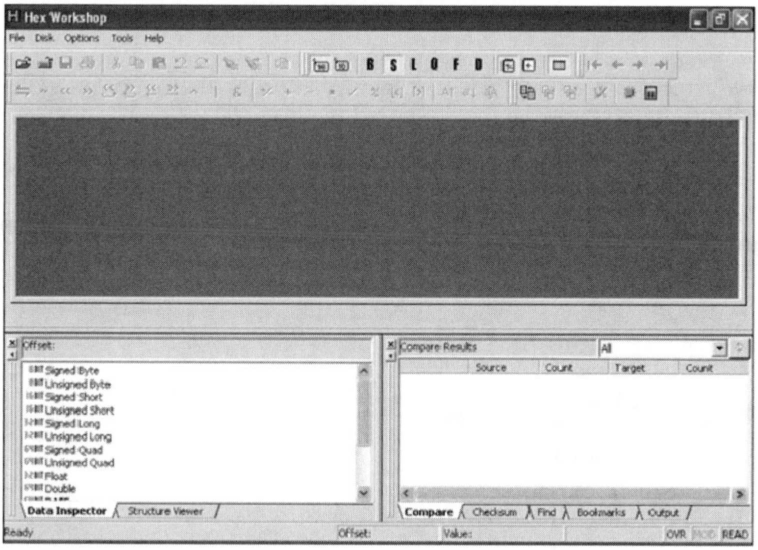

Figure D-11 The opening window in Hex Workshop

4. Click **File, Open** from the menu. In the Open dialog box, navigate to the A drive. Click **Command.com,** and then click **Open.**

5. To replace references to the hard drive (drive C) in Command.com, start by clicking **Edit, Replace** from the menu. In the Replace dialog box, click the **Type** list arrow in the Replace section. A list of data you can replace is displayed. Click **Text String.**

6. In the Find text box, type **c:** or the letter of your primary hard drive. In the Replace text box, type **a:** (see Figure D-12).

7. Click **OK.** The Replace dialog box opens, which you use to search for and replace the specified text. Click the **Replace All** button, and then click **OK.**

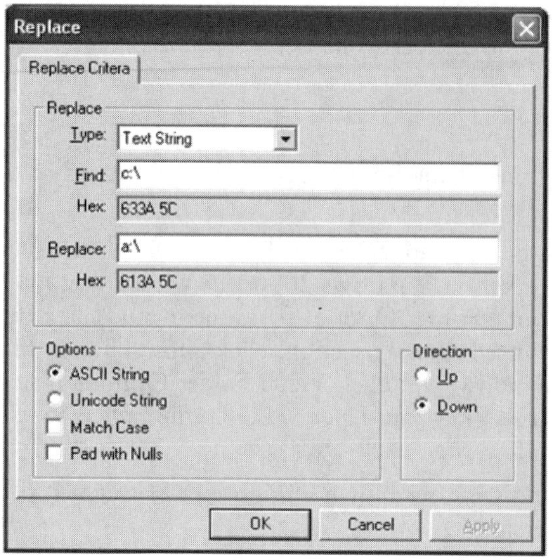

Figure D-12 Specifying what text to replace in the Command.com file

8. Click **File, Save** from the menu to save the changes you made to Command.com on the floppy disk. If you're prompted to make a backup of Command.com, click **No**.

In the following steps, you modify the Io.sys file to change all references to the C drive and the DriveSpace utility. You don't want to activate DriveSpace because it can corrupt data.

1. Click **File, Open** from the Hex Workshop menu. In the Open dialog box, navigate to the A drive, and then click **Io.sys**. Click the **Open** button to open the file in Hex Workshop (see Figure D-13).

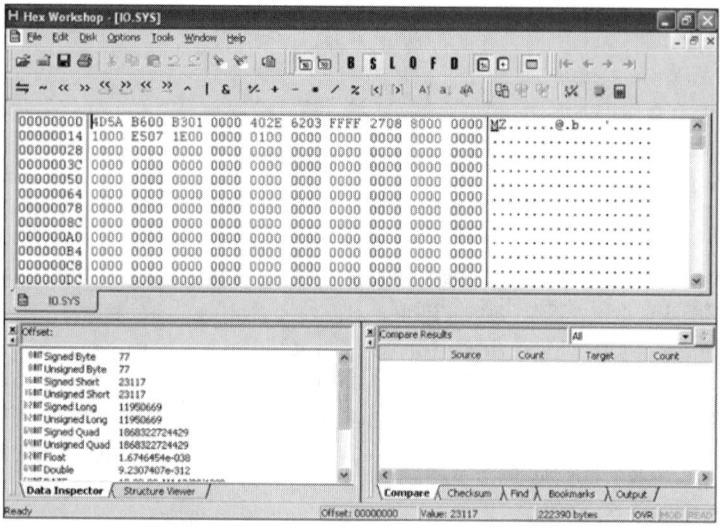

Figure D-13 Io.sys open in Hex Workshop

2. Click **Edit, Replace** from the menu. In the Replace dialog box, click the **Type** list arrow, and then click **Text String**, if necessary. In the Find text box, type **c:**. In the Replace text box, type **a:**, and then click **OK**.

3. In the Replace dialog box, click the **Replace All** button, and then click **OK**.

4. Click **Edit, Replace** from the menu. In the Find text box, delete the current text, and then type **.bin**. In the Replace text box, type **.zzz** (see Figure D-14). Replacing .bin with .zzz prevents Io.sys from referencing DriveSpace. Note that the .zzz extension isn't associated with any program; it's used here simply to change .bin to something else.

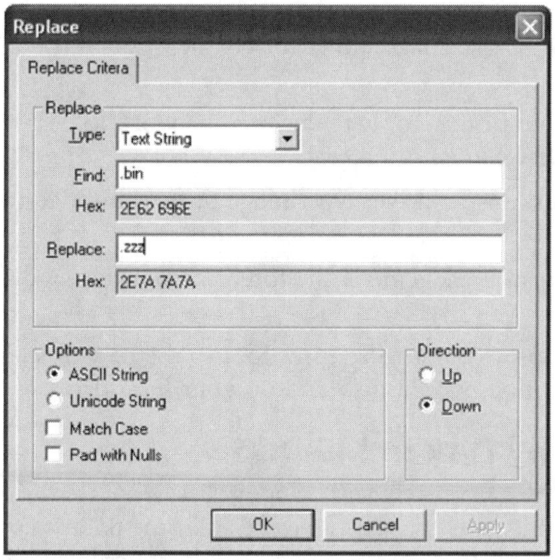

Figure D-14 Replacing the file extension

5. Click **OK**. In the Replace dialog box, click the **Replace All** button, and then click **OK**.

6. Click **File, Save** from the menu to save your changes to Io.sys on the floppy disk. If you're prompted to make a backup of Io.sys, click **No**.

7. Click **File, Exit** from the menu to close Hex Workshop. Restart your computer with the forensic boot floppy disk to test it. Make sure your forensic boot floppy disk is stored in a safe place.

You can use the floppy disk to boot a suspect's computer without contaminating evidence on the hard drive. Next, you add forensics software to the floppy disk so that you can use it to acquire an evidence drive. The forensics software you add depends on the tools you have available. In the following steps, you copy Digital Intelligence tools to the boot floppy disk:

1. Open a command prompt window, and navigate to the **Tools** folder in your work folder.

2. Place your forensic boot floppy disk in the floppy drive. You need both DriveSpy and Image on the boot disk.

3. At the command prompt, type **copy *.* a:** and press **Enter**.

4. Verify that the files have been copied to the floppy disk by typing **dir a:** and pressing **Enter**. Exit the command prompt window.

You should make a backup copy of this floppy disk. You can use the MS-DOS Diskcopy command, or you can make an image with the Digital Intelligence Image utility. You need your original forensic boot floppy disk and an extra blank floppy disk. To make a duplicate disk with Diskcopy, follow these steps:

1. Insert the original forensic boot floppy disk in the floppy drive (for example, drive A).

2. Open a command prompt window. Type **diskcopy a: a: /v** and press **Enter**.

3. Follow the prompts to make the duplicate copy, inserting the blank formatted floppy disk when requested.

4. To make an image of the disk with the Image utility, insert the original forensic boot floppy disk in the floppy drive.

5. At the command prompt, navigate to the **Tools** folder in your work folder, which is where you originally installed DriveSpy and Image.

6. With the forensic boot floppy disk in the drive, type **image a: for_boot.dat** and press **Enter**.

7. When the command prompt is displayed, remove the forensic boot floppy disk and place the blank disk in the drive.

8. Type **image for_boot.dat a:** and press **Enter** to transfer files to the new disk. You now have a copy of the forensic boot floppy on a disk and on your hard drive.

Making an Image of a Floppy Disk in MS-DOS

One method of making a duplicate copy of your evidence floppy disk is to use the MS-DOS command Diskcopy with the verification switch /v, which verifies that the data is copied correctly. This command copies one floppy disk to another floppy disk. Its only disadvantages are that it doesn't create a separate image file of the original floppy disk and doesn't generate a hash value. Use the Diskcopy command only if you have no other tools to preserve the original data. The Digital Intelligence Image tool gives you a reliable backup of your floppy disk evidence. It generates a verifiable hash value but doesn't generate a hash value that's admissible in court as proof of nontampering.

To make an image of a floppy disk, retrieve the floppy disk from your secure evidence container, and write the necessary information on your evidence custody form. Then perform the following steps at the DOS prompt on your forensic workstation to make an image of a floppy disk in MS-DOS:

1. Because the evidence floppy disk is the original storage medium, you must write-protect it. Move the write-protect tab on the floppy disk to the open position. (When working with multiple disks, be sure to specify, in your working notes, on which disks you moved the write-protect tab. Some judges have required investigators to return the evidence to the owner in exactly the same condition in which it was seized, which includes correct repositioning of the write-protect tabs.)

2. If necessary, boot your computer to the MS-DOS prompt.

3. Insert the evidence floppy disk into the floppy drive. The original disk is your source disk.

4. At the MS-DOS prompt, type **diskcopy a: a: /v** and press **Enter**. If you're prompted to insert the source disk, do so and press **Enter**.

5. After the disk is copied, you're prompted to place a target disk in the floppy drive. This is where you want to store a copy of the evidence disk. Remove the evidence disk and insert a blank unformatted or formatted disk into the floppy drive. The software overwrites everything automatically. Follow the onscreen instructions and proceed with the data copy.

6. As data is copied to the target floppy disk, place the original floppy disk in your secure evidence container. When prompted to create another duplicate of the disk, type **n** for no. When prompted to copy another disk, type **n** for no.

7. Place a label on the working copy of the floppy disk, if necessary, and then write **Working copy #1** on the label.

Remember to maintain the chain of custody for evidence.

In a live investigation, you should place the original floppy disk in your secure evidence container as the data is being copied to the target disk.

Using MS-DOS Acquisition Tools

In the past, tools for computing investigations were created for MS-DOS. Many of these tools are still commercially available and are easy to use. Because they fit on a forensic boot floppy disk, they require fewer resources to make an image of evidence data. Computer forensics examiners should know how to use DOS tools, such as DriveSpy or Replica. This section focuses on DriveSpy, and Replica is discussed later in this appendix.

DriveSpy has two types of commands for saving digital evidence from a source disk and writing to a target disk: data-preservation commands and data-manipulation commands. Each type has special applications for acquiring and re-creating digital evidence. Before you learn more about DriveSpy data-acquisition commands, you should understand how DriveSpy refers to and accesses sector ranges.

Understanding How DriveSpy Accesses Sector Ranges

DriveSpy has two methods of accessing disk sectors. The first method defines the absolute starting sector followed by a comma and the total number of sectors to read on a drive. For example, if the starting sector is 1000 on the primary master drive (drive 0), and you want to copy the next 100 sectors, DriveSpy uses the following format:

```
0:1000,100
```

With this command, DriveSpy copies from absolute sector 1000 to absolute sector 1099 because sector 1000 is the first sector, and sector 1099 is 100 sectors after that. DriveSpy uses this format for designating disk sectors with the CopySect, WriteSect, SaveSect, and Wipe commands, which you explore later in this chapter. CopySect, WriteSect, and SaveSect work similarly to the UNIX/Linux dd command.

The second way of specifying sectors is to list the absolute starting and ending sectors. An absolute sector starts at the beginning of a disk; a relative sector starts at the beginning of the current partition. The concept is similar to absolute and relative cell referencing in a spreadsheet. To designate a start and end sector value, you include a hyphen between the sector values. For example, if the starting sector is 1000 on the primary master drive (drive 0), and you need to copy through absolute sector 1100 (the next 101 sectors), this is the format:

```
0:1000-1100
```

With some DriveSpy commands, you can direct data from a specified sector range to another sector, which can be on the same disk or a different disk. For example, if you're recovering data from a damaged part of a disk, you can transfer the data to a good part of the disk. To designate the target location, list the drive number followed by a colon and the starting absolute sector number. For example, to copy data from absolute sectors 1000 to 1099 on the primary master drive to absolute sectors 2000 to 2099 on a secondary drive, use this CopySect command:

```
CopySect 0:1000,100 1:2000,100
```

If you're working in DriveSpy Partition mode, the DriveSpy screen shows a logical sector number and an absolute sector number. Be sure to use the absolute sector number. In the following steps, you use DriveSpy to examine absolute and logical sectors. Use a Windows 98 computer, boot into DOS, and then follow these steps:

1. From the DOS command prompt, navigate to the **Tools** folder in your work folder.

2. At the command prompt, type **drivespy** and press **Enter** to start DriveSpy.

3. At the SYS prompt, type **d0** and press **Enter** to access your hard disk. Note the numbers for the start and end sectors of the disk and select a number between them, such as 2344.

4. At the D0 prompt, type **sector 2344** and press **Enter**. A sector map is displayed (see Figure D-15).

```
D0> AbsSector: 2344
0000   00 00 00 00 00 00 00 00    00 00 00 00 00 00 00 00    ................
0010   00 00 00 00 00 00 00 00    00 00 00 00 00 00 00 00    ................
0020   00 00 00 00 00 00 00 00    00 00 00 00 00 00 00 00    ................
0030   00 00 00 00 00 00 00 00    00 00 00 00 00 00 00 00    ................
0040   00 00 00 00 00 00 00 00    00 00 00 00 00 00 00 00    ................
0050   00 00 00 00 00 00 00 00    00 00 00 00 00 00 00 00    ................
0060   00 00 00 00 00 00 00 00    00 00 00 00 00 00 00 00    ................
0070   00 00 00 00 00 00 00 00    00 00 00 00 00 00 00 00    ................
0080   00 00 00 00 00 00 00 00    00 00 00 00 00 00 00 00    ................
0090   00 00 00 00 00 00 00 00    00 00 00 00 00 00 00 00    ................
00A0   00 00 00 00 00 00 00 00    00 00 00 00 00 00 00 00    ................
00B0   00 00 00 00 00 00 00 00    00 00 00 00 00 00 00 00    ................
00C0   00 00 00 00 00 00 00 00    00 00 00 00 00 00 00 00    ................
00D0   00 00 00 00 00 00 00 00    00 00 00 00 00 00 00 00    ................
00E0   00 00 00 00 00 00 00 00    00 00 00 00 00 00 00 00    ................
00F0   00 00 00 00 00 00 00 00    00 00 00 00 00 00 00 00    ................
0100   00 00 00 00 00 00 00 00    00 00 00 00 00 00 00 00    ................
0110   00 00 00 00 00 00 00 00    00 00 00 00 00 00 00 00    ................
0120   00 00 00 00 00 00 00 00    00 00 00 00 00 00 00 00    ................
0130   00 00 00 00 00 00 00 00    00 00 00 00 00 00 00 00    ................
0140   00 00 00 00 00 00 00 00    00 00 00 00 00 00 00 00    ................
0150   00 00 00 00 00 00 00 00    00 00 00 00 00 00 00 00    ................
0160   00 00 00 00 00 00 00 00    00 00 00 00 00 00 00 00    ................
D0> AbsSector: 2344
```

Figure D-15 A sector map in Drive mode

5. Press **Esc** to return to the D0 prompt. Type **p1** and press **Enter** to use Partition mode.

6. At the D0P1 prompt, type **sector 2344** and press **Enter**. (Replace 2344 with the sector number you used in Step 5, if necessary.) A map of sector 2344 in Partition 1 appears, as shown in Figure D-16.

```
DOP1>RelSector: 2344   AbsSector: 2407
0000   00 00 00 00 00 00 00 00   00 00 00 00 00 00 00 00   ................
0010   00 00 00 00 00 00 00 00   00 00 00 00 00 00 00 00   ................
0020   00 00 00 00 00 00 00 00   00 00 00 00 00 00 00 00   ................
0030   00 00 00 00 00 00 00 00   00 00 00 00 00 00 00 00   ................
0040   00 00 00 00 00 00 00 00   00 00 00 00 00 00 00 00   ................
0050   00 00 00 00 00 00 00 00   00 00 00 00 00 00 00 00   ................
0060   00 00 00 00 00 00 00 00   00 00 00 00 00 00 00 00   ................
0070   00 00 00 00 00 00 00 00   00 00 00 00 00 00 00 00   ................
0080   00 00 00 00 00 00 00 00   00 00 00 00 00 00 00 00   ................
0090   00 00 00 00 00 00 00 00   00 00 00 00 00 00 00 00   ................
00A0   00 00 00 00 00 00 00 00   00 00 00 00 00 00 00 00   ................
00B0   00 00 00 00 00 00 00 00   00 00 00 00 00 00 00 00   ................
00C0   00 00 00 00 00 00 00 00   00 00 00 00 00 00 00 00   ................
00D0   00 00 00 00 00 00 00 00   00 00 00 00 00 00 00 00   ................
00E0   00 00 00 00 00 00 00 00   00 00 00 00 00 00 00 00   ................
00F0   00 00 00 00 00 00 00 00   00 00 00 00 00 00 00 00   ................
0100   00 00 00 00 00 00 00 00   00 00 00 00 00 00 00 00   ................
0110   00 00 00 00 00 00 00 00   00 00 00 00 00 00 00 00   ................
0120   00 00 00 00 00 00 00 00   00 00 00 00 00 00 00 00   ................
0130   00 00 00 00 00 00 00 00   00 00 00 00 00 00 00 00   ................
0140   00 00 00 00 00 00 00 00   00 00 00 00 00 00 00 00   ................
0150   00 00 00 00 00 00 00 00   00 00 00 00 00 00 00 00   ................
0160   00 00 00 00 00 00 00 00   00 00 00 00 00 00 00 00   ................
DOP1>RelSector: 2344   AbsSector: 2407
```

Figure D-16 A sector map in Partition mode

DriveSpy displays a relative sector (RelSector) and an absolute sector (AbsSector).

7. Press **Esc** to return to the D0P1 prompt, and then type **exit** and press **Enter** to exit DriveSpy.

Compare the sector numbers in the two figures. In Figure D-15, the absolute sector is 2344, and in Figure D-16, the relative sector is 2344. Note that the absolute sector in Figure D-16 is not the same as in Figure D-15.

Using DriveSpy Data Preservation Commands

You can preserve and re-create digital evidence with the DriveSpy SavePart and WritePart commands. These two commands restore only FAT16 or FAT32 disk partitions. When restoring a FAT16 saved partition, use a partition utility, such as Fdisk, to partition the target drive as FAT16. For a FAT32 saved partition, use a partition utility to partition the target drive as FAT32.

The SavePart command acquires an entire partition allocated on a disk, regardless of the file system. In other words, it acquires an image of a non-DOS partition, such as an NTFS or a

Linux partition. The WritePart command re-creates the saved partition in its original form. Restoring a non-DOS partition to a DOS partition re-creates the data, although the partition's format isn't exactly the same as the original non-DOS partition. The partition contains the data but appears to be a DOS FAT partition with unreadable file and directory structures.

 The CopySect command, used to copy an absolute sector range from one disk to another, is limited when trying to match source and target disks. To make an exact copy of a suspect's drive, you need a drive of the same make, model, and size. CopySect doesn't adjust the target drive's geometry to match the source drive. Instead, use the SavePart and WritePart commands to duplicate partitions for FAT16 and FAT32 disks. For all other file systems, see "Using the SaveSect Command" and "Using the WriteSect Command" later in this chapter.

Using the SavePart Command Use the SavePart command in DriveSpy Partition mode to create an image of a specified disk partition of a suspect's drive. This command uses lossless data compression to reduce the size of the image file. It then saves every sector of the disk partition in the image file you specify. You can redirect the image file's output to another disk to preserve the image file. If the target disk for the image file is too small for the entire image, DriveSpy requests another disk automatically. For example, if you have a 40 GB suspect drive and two 20 GB target drives connected to your forensic workstation, you can use the SavePart command to write data to the first 20 GB drive. When space runs out on the first drive, DriveSpy asks for another. You can then specify the path to redirect the image file output to the second 20 GB drive.

You can also use the SavePart command to save image data to removable media, such as a Jaz disk or USB drive. SavePart requests additional drives as necessary. After saving a partition, DriveSpy generates an MD5 hash and stores it in the image file. When the image is restored, the MD5 hash is verified.

In the following steps, you use DriveSpy to save a partition. Normally, you use the SavePart command on a hard drive with multiple partitions. However, because using SavePart on a large partition can take several hours, you examine your hard drive and save a partition from a floppy disk. You need a floppy disk containing a few files to complete these steps. The following steps must be performed in Windows 98 DOS:

1. If you have a licensed copy of DriveSpy and Image, copy these two tools and their associated .ini files to your work folder.

2. Change to your work folder, and at the command prompt, type **drivespy** and press **Enter**.

3. At the SYS prompt, type **output App_Drp1.txt** and press **Enter** to create an output file for recording your actions and results.

4. At the SYS prompt, type **drives** and press **Enter** to list all drives connected to your workstation. Figure D-17 shows a system with one hard drive. The drives and partitions on your system might be different.

```
SYS> DRIVES
Physical Drives on this System:

Drive | Mode | Cylinders      Heads      Sectors |   Length  Size (Mb)
----- | ---- | ----------    ----------  ---------- | ---------- ----------
    0 | LBA  |     -              -            - |  23579136     11513
      | CHS  |    1023           255           63 |  16494495      8024

Note: CHS values are not displayed for LBA drives which do not provide
      the associated information via Interrupt 13 Extensions.  This will
      in no way adversely effeCt the performance or accuracy of DRIVESPY.

SYS>_
```

Figure D-17 Listing drives on your system

NOTE The computer in Figure D-17 has an older 11 GB drive that doesn't show logical block addressing (LBA). Newer disks show LBA along with CHS values. Your forensics tool can interpret these older drives in the same way it interprets newer drives.

5. At the SYS prompt, type **d0** and press **Enter** to select the drive containing the partition you want to copy, such as drive 0. The partitions on drive 0 are displayed (see Figure D-18).

```
Drive 1 Partition Summary:

      PRI   Part   Part                 Boot          Start        End
Num   EXT   Code   Type        HID      Code   ACT    Sector       Sector    Size (Mb)
---   ---   ----   --------    ---      ----   ---    ----------   --------- ----------
  1   PRI   0x0c   FAT32                0x80    *         63        29567954     11507

D1>_
```

Figure D-18 Listing partitions on a drive

6. At the D0 prompt, type **part 1** and press **Enter** to select the partition you want to save, such as partition 1. The contents of this partition, including sectors, are displayed (see Figure D-19).

7. Although you normally use the SavePart command at this point to save the contents of the current partition, here you switch to a floppy disk and acquire its partition to save time. Insert a floppy disk containing a few files into the floppy disk drive. At the D0P1 prompt, type **drive a** and press **Enter** to access the floppy disk.

8. At the DA prompt, type **part 1** and press **Enter** to access the partition level.

9. At the DAP1 prompt, type **savepart C:*Work*\\App_D.ima** and press **Enter** to copy the partition on the floppy disk to an image file named App_D.ima on your hard drive. (Replace *Work* with the work folder you're using.)

10. DriveSpy creates the image file, listing details about the partition and displaying a progress indicator. Depending on the disk size, creating the image file might take a few minutes or several hours. When finished, DriveSpy generates an MD5 hash value (see Figure D-20). At the DAP1 prompt, type **exit** and press **Enter**.

```
PARTITION Mode Selected.

Partition 1: Primary, FAT32 (0x0C)
Defined in Partition Table at Absolute Sector: 0 (Entry Number 1)

Sectors/Cluster:       16
Total Sectors:         23567292
Total Clusters:        1741516
Raw Capacity           11507 Mb
Formatted Capacity:    11507 Mb

                   |  Start      End   |
                   |  Sector    Sector |
----------------   | -------- -------- |
Partition          |        0 23567291 |
Boot Sector        |        0       31 |
FAT1               |       32    11528 |
FAT2               |    11529    23021 |
Data Area          |    23026 23567281 |
Partition Slack    |23567282 23567291 |

* Root Directory at Cluster: 2

DOP1:\>_
```

Figure D-19   Listing the contents of a partition

```
DAP1:\>SavePart C:\WORK\APP_D\APP_D.IMA

Drive:                  A
Partition:              1
OS Type                 0x01 (FAT12)
Absolute Start Sector:  0
Absolute End Sector:    2879
Total Sectors:          2880
Time Stamp:             Mon Jul 01 08:32:54 2007

Processing Relative Sector:        2879

MD5 Hash:    a4f43ee25b3503728eb6df9797f994d5

Done!

DAP1:\>_
```

Figure D-20   Using SavePart to create an image file

Drives with multiple partitions have a partition gap, which is the space between the end of one partition and the start of another. (In the early days of computer crime, criminals attempting to hide data used these partition gaps to store incriminating evidence.) For example, suppose one disk has three partitions. The first partition, partition 1, ends on absolute sector 8610839, as shown in Figure D-21. Partition 2 starts on absolute sector 8610903 and ends on absolute sector 17221679. Partition 3 starts on absolute sector 17221743 and ends on absolute sector 39070079. Each partition ends on one sector, and the next partition starts 64 sectors later. On this system, 64 sectors between each partition aren't used by the file system.

```
DO>PARTS

Drive 0 Partition Summary:

      PRI  Part  Part              Boot        Start      End
Num   EXT  Code  Type        HID   Code  ACT   Sector     Sector    Size (Mb)
---   ---  ----  --------    ---   ----  ---   --------   --------   --------
  1   PRI  0x0B  FAT32             0x80   *         63     8610839       4204
  2   EXT  0x0B  FAT32             0x80          8610903  17221679       4204
  3   EXT  0x0B  FAT32             0x80         17221743  39070079      10668

DO>_
```

Figure D-21   A partition table

You can't use the SavePart command to inspect or extract data from partition gaps, although you can use other DriveSpy commands to do so. You learn how to use these other DriveSpy commands later in this appendix.

Using the WritePart Command   The counterpart to the SavePart command is WritePart, which you use in DriveSpy Partition mode to re-create the saved partition image file created with the SavePart command. For example, the following command restores the App_D.ima image file to the AppD folder on the D drive:

```
WritePart D:\AppD\App_D.ima
```

The WritePart command uncompresses the SavePart image file and writes it to a specified drive. WritePart checks the target drive and writes to that drive only if it's equal to or larger than the original drive. When WritePart creates the partition on the target drive, it changes the partition number to match the source drive. If the image file spans more than one volume (disk), DriveSpy prompts you in the same manner as the SavePart command for the location of the next image volume.

In the following activity, you restore the App_D.ima file you created with the SavePart command. If you were doing this activity on an actual hard drive with multiple partitions, you would have to be extremely careful that you're working on the correct drive and partition. Note that you can't use the WritePart command in Windows, so reboot to an MS-DOS prompt, if necessary. These steps show how to use the WritePart command with a floppy disk, but typically, you use WritePart for a hard disk partition.

You can use a blank floppy disk in the following steps. However, because WritePart was developed for use on a hard drive, your system might lock if you use a floppy disk. If this happens, create a small hard drive partition that's larger than the floppy disk, and then restore the image to that partition. Use a partition tool such as Fdisk, Partition Magic, or Norton Gdisk to create a 1.5 MB partition, for example. Then substitute all references to drive A (or DA) in the following steps with the newly created drive and partition, such as D1P1.

1. At the MS-DOS prompt, navigate to your work folder. Type **drivespy** and press **Enter**.

2. At the SYS prompt, type **output App_Drp2.txt** and press **Enter** to create an output file.

3. At the SYS prompt, type **drive a** and press **Enter** to access the floppy drive. (If you're using a hard drive partition, use the partition number, such as **drive 1**.) At the DA prompt, type **part 1** and press **Enter** to access the partition level of the floppy disk.

4. At the DAP1 prompt, type **writepart App_D.ima** and press **Enter** to restore the image file you created in your work folder to a floppy disk. When a warning is displayed, type **y** to continue. DriveSpy takes a few minutes to restore the image file. Together, Figures D-22 and D-23 show the output of the WritePart command.

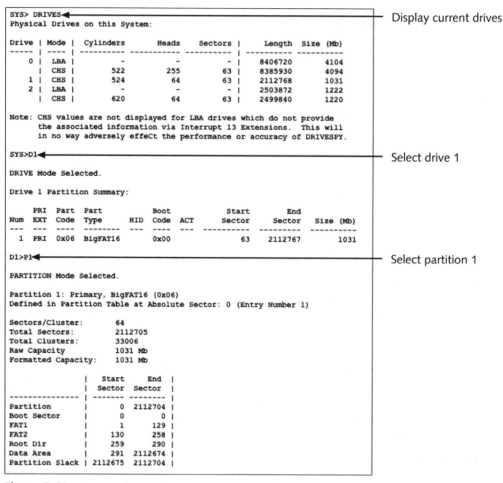

Figure D-22   Output of using the WritePart command

5. At the DAP1 prompt, type **exit** and press **Enter**.

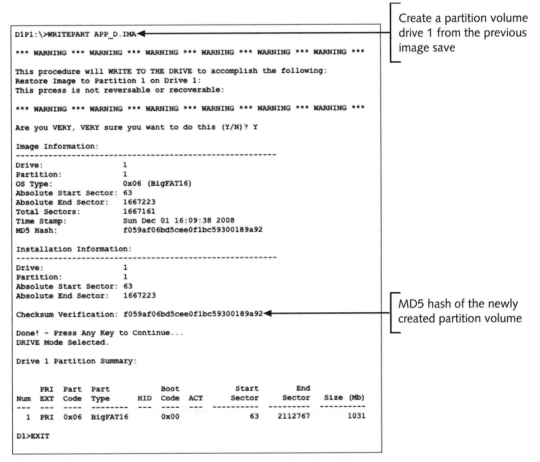

Figure D-23 ⟶ Create a partition volume drive 1 from the previous image save

⟶ MD5 hash of the newly created partition volume

Figure D-23 Output of using the WritePart command (continued)

Using DriveSpy Data Manipulation Commands

DriveSpy has two additional sector-copying commands that help you collect and preserve data: SaveSect and WriteSect. With these two commands, you can isolate specific areas of a disk and preserve them for later examination. The activities in the following sections assume you have three additional drives, each one larger than 230 MB, connected to your workstation. However, the steps can be performed with one additional drive connected to your workstation; in that case, change drive 3 (d3) to drive 1 (d1) in the steps.

Using the SaveSect Command The SaveSect command copies specific sectors on a disk to a file. It copies the sectors as an image so that the file is an exact duplicate of the original sectors. Because the created file isn't compressed, it's called a "flat" file. You can also use SaveSect to collect any sector data located in partition gaps. If a partition is hidden or deleted, use this command to copy the entire hidden section or deleted partition to a flat file.

You can use the SaveSect command in DriveSpy Drive and Partition modes; you list only the source sector values and specify a file as the target. For example, the following command saves sectors 40000 to 49999 to a file named Part_gap.dat:

```
SaveSect 1:40000-49999 C:\Work\AppD\Part_gap.dat
```

To save a sector in DriveSpy, follow these steps in Windows 98 DOS:

1. At the DOS command prompt, type **drivespy** and press **Enter**.

2. At the SYS prompt, type **output C:*Work*\App_Drp3.txt** and press **Enter** to create an output file for recording your actions and results. (Replace *Work* with your work folder name.)

3. At the SYS prompt, type **drives** and press **Enter** to determine which drive to copy.

4. At the SYS prompt, type **d3** (or **d1** if you're using only one extra drive) and press **Enter** to access the drive you want to copy. Substitute the number for your drive, if necessary.

5. At the D3 prompt, type **p1** and press **Enter** to select the partition containing the sectors you want to copy. (Note that typing "p1" is the same as typing "part 1.")

6. At the D3P1 prompt, type **savesect 3:0-415232 C:*Work*\App_Ds.dat** and press **Enter** to copy sectors 0 to 415232 to the App_Ds.dat file. See an example in Figure D-24, although the filename differs. (*Note*: If you're using only one extra drive, use this command for drive 1: **savesect 1:0-415232 C:*Work*\App_Ds.dat**.)

7. At the D3P1 prompt, type **exit** and press **Enter**.

Using the WriteSect Command   With the WriteSect command, you can re-create the data acquired with SaveSect. You use this command in DriveSpy Drive or Partition mode to re-create an absolute sector range from a SaveSect file to a target drive. For example, the following command writes a flat file named Part_gap.dat starting at absolute sector 10000 on drive 2:

```
WriteSect C:\Work\AppD\Part_gap.dat 2:10000
```

The disadvantage of using the WriteSect command is that if you aren't careful, you can overwrite data on a target drive. Always review commands to verify where you're sending data. If you're using only one extra drive, change d3 to d1, as described previously. To write a sector data file in DriveSpy, follow these steps:

1. At the DOS command prompt, navigate to the **Tools** folder in your work folder. At the command prompt, type **drivespy** and press **Enter**.

2. At the SYS prompt, type **output C:*Work*\App_Drp4.txt** and press **Enter** to create an output file. (Replace *Work* with your work folder.)

3. At the SYS prompt, type **drives** and press **Enter** to list the drives the system recognizes. Select the drive to which you want to copy data, and make sure it doesn't contain any important data.

4. At the SYS prompt, type **d3** and press **Enter** to access the drive you want. Substitute the number for your drive, if necessary.

5. At the D3 prompt, type **writesect C:*Work*\App_D.dat 3:0** and press **Enter** to start transferring data to absolute sector 0 on drive 3. See Figure D-25 for an example,

```
SYS> DRIVES ◄────────────────────────────────────────────── Display current drives
Physical Drives on this System:

Drive | Mode |  Cylinders       Heads       Sectors |   Length    Size (Mb)
----- | ---- | ----------- ----------- ----------- | ----------- -----------
    0 | LBA  |       -            -            -    |   8406720      4104
      | CHS  |      522          255           63   |   8385930      4094
    1 | CHS  |      524           64           63   |   2112768      1031
    2 | LBA  |       -            -            -    |   2503872      1222
      | CHS  |      620           64           63   |   2499840      1220
    3 | LBA  |       -            -            -    |   1667232       814
      | CHS  |      826           32           63   |   1665216       813


Note: CHS values are not displayed for LBA drives which do not provide
      the associated information via Interrupt 13 Extensions.  This will
      in no way adversely effeCt the performance or accuracy of DRIVESPY.

SYS>D3 ◄──────────────────────────────────────────────────── Select drive 3

DRIVE Mode Selected.

Drive 3 Partition Summary:

     PRI  Part  Part                Boot             Start        End
Num  EXT  Code  Type        HID     Code  ACT       Sector      Sector     Size (Mb)
---  ---  ----  ---------   ---     ----  ---      ----------  ----------  ----------
  1  PRI  0x06  BigFAT16            0x80   *            63       415295         202

D3>P1 ◄──────────────────────────────────────────────────── Select partition 1

PARTITION Mode Selected.

Partition 1: Primary, BigFAT16 (0x06)
Defined in Partition Table at Absolute Sector: 0 (Entry Number 1)

Sectors/Cluster:      8
Total Sectors:      414925
Total Clusters:      51810
Raw Capacity:       202 Mb
Formatted Capacity: 202 Mb

                  |  Start     End   |
                  | Sector   Sector  |
----------------- | -------  -------- |
Partition         |     0     415232  |
Boot Sector       |     0         0   |
FAT1              |     1       203   |
FAT2              |   204       406   |
Root Dir          |   407       438   |
Data Area         |   439     414918  |
Partition Slack   | 414919    415232  |

D3P1:\>SAVESECT 3:0-415232 C:\WORK\APP_D\APP_D.IMA ◄──────── Save sectors to file

Done:

D3P1:\>EXIT
```

Figure D-24 Using the SaveSect command

although the filename differs. (*Note*: If you're using only one extra drive, use this command for drive 1: **writesect C:*Work*\\App_Ds.dat 1:0.**)

6. Type **y** when a warning is displayed. At the D3 prompt, type **exit** and press **Enter**.

Like the SavePart command, SaveSect can save an entire drive to a data file. The SaveSect and WriteSect commands are useful if you need to acquire an image from a non-Microsoft FAT file system. For example, you can use SavePart and WritePart on a Linux Ext2fs disk. Make sure the target drive where you plan to save the SavePart output file is larger than the source drive.

```
SYS> DRIVES ◄─────────────────────────────────────────────────────────  Display current drives

Physical Drives on this System:

Drive | Mode | Cylinders       Heads       Sectors |      Length   Size (Mb)
----- | ---- | ----------  ------------  ----------- | ---------- ----------
    0 | LBA  |          -            -            - |    8406720       4104
      | CHS  |        522          255           63 |    8385930       4094
    1 | CHS  |        524           64           63 |    2112768       1031
    2 | LBA  |          -            -            - |    2503872       1222
      | CHS  |        620           64           63 |    2499840       1220
    3 | LBA  |          -            -            - |    1667232        814
      | CHS  |        826           32           63 |    1665216        813


Note: CHS values are not displayed for LBA drives which do not provide
      the associated information via Interrupt 13 Extensions.  This will
      in no way adversely effeCt the performance or accuracy of DRIVESPY.

SYS>D3 ◄──────────────────────────────────────────────────────────────  Select drive 3

DRIVE Mode Selected.

Drive 3 Partition Summary:

      PRI  Part  Part          Boot            Start       End
Num   EXT  Code  Type     HID  Code  ACT      Sector     Sector      Size (Mb)
---   ---  ----  -------- ---  ----  ---   ----------- ----------   ----------

D3>WRITESECT C:\WORK\APP_D\APP_D.IMA 3:0 ◄─────────────────────────────  Write the sector data file
                                                                        to the disk
*** WARNING *** WARNING *** WARNING *** WARNING *** WARNING *** WARNING ***

This procedure will WRITE TO THE DRIVE to accomplish the following:
Write to physical sectors on drive 3:
This prcess is not reversable or recoverable:

*** WARNING *** WARNING *** WARNING *** WARNING *** WARNING *** WARNING ***

Are you VERY, VERY sure you want to do this (Y/N)? Y

Done:

D3P1:\>EXIT
```

Figure D-25   Using the WriteSect command

Quick References for DriveSpy

This section contains references to the commands used with the software tools described in this book. Table D-4 lists switches and attributes for DriveSpy commands, and Table D-5 lists switches for the Wipe command.

Table D-4   DriveSpy command switches and attributes

Category and switch	Attribute	Description	Example
Wildcards	Asterisk (*)	Represents one or more characters	To copy all .txt files to the AppD folder on Drive D, use Copy *.txt D:\AppD\
	Question mark (?)	Represents a single character	To copy all files named Mydoc with an extension beginning with "do," such as .doc and .dot, use Dir Mydoc.do?

Table D-4   DriveSpy command switches and attributes (*continued*)

	Attribute	Description	Example
File attributes (/A)	A D E V S H R	Archived files Directories Erased files Disk volumes or partitions System files Hidden files Read-only files	To list all the attributes of archived files, use Dir *.* /AA To list only directories on a disk partition, use Dir /AD To copy hidden files, use Copy *.* /AH D:\AppD\
Sorting (/O)	N E G S D A X -	Sort by name Sort by extension Sort by directory Sort by file size Sort by modification date and time Sort by last access date Sort deleted files when using Dir Before an attribute, reverses the sort order	To get a directory listing sorted by date, use Dir *.gif /OD To display files by date and time in descending order, use Dir *.* /O-A
Recursion (/S)		Access subdirectory data when using other DriveSpy commands	To list files in the current directory and all subdirectories, use Dir /S To copy specific files from current directories and all subdirectories, use Copy *.txt \D:\AppD\ /S
File types (/T)		Select file types defined in DriveSpy.ini	To use the Unerase command to recover Excel files: Unerase *.* /T:xls D:\AppD\
File groups (/G)		Access or recover defined groups	To copy files defined in the Intel_Prop group: Copy *.* /G:Intel_Prop D:\AppD\

To negate the output of any attribute, add a hyphen in front of it. For example, Dir /-AD displays files but not directories.

Table D-5 Wipe command switches

Switch	Description
Sector range, such as Wipe 0-1000	List specific sectors to overwrite
/L	Overwrite only a logical partition
/FREE	Overwrite only unallocated disk space
/SLACK	Overwrite only file slack space
/UNUSED	Overwrite unallocated and file slack space
/C:[*value*]	Overwrite a specified character value, which can be hexadecimal or decimal, as in /C:0xF6 or /C:246
/RAND	Random characters generated for the overwrite
/MBR	Overwrite the Master Boot Record
/SA	Display sector addresses while overwriting the disk

A Sample Script for DriveSpy

With the DriveSpy SaveSect and WriteSect commands, you can create multiple volume segments of drives and then re-create the saved volumes on a new target drive. Because SaveSect and WriteSect work in Drive mode, they can copy and write data from non-FAT drives. For example, the sample script in this section is for a Macintosh running OS 8.2 on an 8 GB SCSI drive. Figure D-26 shows the output of using SaveSect to create multiple volume segments of a drive.

```
OUTPUT MAC_SAV.LOG
PAGE OFF
DRIVE 1
SAVESECT 00000000-00999999 MAC_SAV.000
SAVESECT 01000000-01999999 MAC_SAV.001
SAVESECT 02000000-02999999 MAC_SAV.002
SAVESECT 03000000-03999999 MAC_SAV.003
SAVESECT 04000000-04999999 MAC_SAV.004
SAVESECT 05000000-05999999 MAC_SAV.005
SAVESECT 06000000-06999999 MAC_SAV.006
SAVESECT 07000000-07999999 MAC_SAV.007
SAVESECT 08000000-08999999 MAC_SAV.008
SAVESECT 09000000-09999999 MAC_SAV.009
SAVESECT 10000000-10999999 MAC_SAV.010
SAVESECT 11000000-11999999 MAC_SAV.011
SAVESECT 12000000-12999999 MAC_SAV.012
SAVESECT 13000000-13999999 MAC_SAV.013
SAVESECT 14000000-14999999 MAC_SAV.014
SAVESECT 15000000-15999999 MAC_SAV.015
SAVESECT 16000000-16957030 MAC_SAV.016
```

Figure D-26 Output of the SaveSect command

This script creates volume segments of 512,000,000 bytes each, except the last volume segment, which is only 489,999,872 bytes because the end of the drive is at block position 16957030. (Remember that each block is 512 bytes.) Figure D-27 shows using WriteSect to restore multiple volumes from a SaveSect script.

```
OUTPUT MAC_WRT.LOG
PAGE OFF
DRIVE 1
WRITESECT MAC_SAV.000 00000000-00999999
WRITESECT MAC_SAV.001 01000000-01999999
WRITESECT MAC_SAV.002 02000000-02999999
WRITESECT MAC_SAV.003 03000000-03999999
WRITESECT MAC_SAV.004 04000000-04999999
WRITESECT MAC_SAV.005 05000000-05999999
WRITESECT MAC_SAV.006 06000000-06999999
WRITESECT MAC_SAV.007 07000000-07999999
WRITESECT MAC_SAV.008 08000000-08999999
WRITESECT MAC_SAV.009 09000000-09999999
WRITESECT MAC_SAV.010 10000000-10999999
WRITESECT MAC_SAV.011 11000000-11999999
WRITESECT MAC_SAV.012 12000000-12999999
WRITESECT MAC_SAV.013 13000000-13999999
WRITESECT MAC_SAV.014 14000000-14999999
WRITESECT MAC_SAV.015 15000000-15999999
WRITESECT MAC_SAV.016 16000000-16957030
```

Figure D-27 Output of the WriteSect command

Using X-Ways Replica

X-Ways Software Technology AG, the creator of WinHex, offers an MS-DOS program called Replica, a compact imaging program that's small enough to load on a forensic boot floppy. Replica produces a dd-like or Expert Witness image of a drive. Similar to the UNIX/Linux dd command, Replica has options for acquiring an entire drive or specific sectors. Replica copies data from one drive to image segment files or from one disk to another disk.

 An important feature of Replica is its capability to identify and access a drive's host protected area. Replica is included with the purchase of X-Ways Forensics or X-Ways Evidor. For more information on X-Ways products, see *www.x-ways.net*.

To use Replica, create a forensic boot floppy disk as described previously or load it on your forensic workstation. To run Replica, you must use an MS-DOS shell, not Windows DOS, because it needs to access the computer's BIOS. When Replica starts, it checks the computer's BIOS to see whether the host protected area (HPA) is enabled. If HPA is on, Replica asks whether you want to turn it off. If you answer yes, it disables HPA and then instructs you to restart the computer. When the computer restarts in MS-DOS, HPA is opened, which allows copying all sectors of the drive. Follow these steps to disable HPA and then acquire an image of a drive:

1. At the DOS prompt, type **replica** and press **Enter**.
2. If you're prompted to disable HPA, type y for yes, and then restart the computer and restart Replica.
3. In the Select the source screen, enter the number of the drive to copy (for example, 2).
4. In the Select the partition screen, enter the number of the partition or enter 0 to copy an entire drive.

5. Next, in the Select the Destination screen, enter the number corresponding to the type of acquisition; for example, enter 0 to create an image file.

6. In the next screen, type the name of the image file, including the full path, and press **Enter**.

 With Replica image filenaming conventions, you can leave the extension blank or add a number or letter value. Replica increments the extension automatically for each new volume segment.

7. At the segment split prompt, type the size for each volume segment (such as 650).

8. In the Ready to clone screen, type **y** to create a Replica log file that records errors and other information for the acquisition.

9. At the hash prompt, type **m** (for MD5) and press **Enter** to record the MD5 value of the suspect's drive (see Figure D-28).

```
X-Ways Replica 2.0    (c)2002-2004 X-Ways Software Technology AG

Ready to clone ...

Source     : Hard disk 2 (2.9 GB)
Destination : C:\Work\App_D\Apreplic.00 (image file, segment size 681,674,400 bytes)
6,185,088 sectors will be copied

Log errors silently in file "replica.log"?
[Y/N]  Y

Would you like the source data to be hashed?

[M]D5, [C]RC32, [N]o M
```

Figure D-28 Selecting the type of hashing

10. In the Proceed screen, type **y** for yes and press **Enter** to start the acquisition.

You see the screen shown in Figure D-29 when Replica finishes copying all sectors to the image file.

```
X-Ways Replica 2.0    (c)2002-2004 X-Ways Software Technology AG

If the image base file or any subsequent segment exists already, it will be LOST. PROCEED?
[Y/N] Y
Copying sectors No. 6,185,088 ...        100%
Total bad sectors so far: none
Total destigation image file segments so far: 5

6,185,088 sectors were copied

C:\_
```

Figure D-29 Completed cloning of the drive

4-mm DAT Magnetic tapes that store about 4 GB of data, but like CD-Rs, are slow to read and write data.

acquisition The process of creating a duplicate image of data; one of the five required functions of computer forensics tools.

Advanced Forensic Format (AFF) A new data acquisition format developed by Simson L. Garfinkel and Basis Technology. This open and extensible format stores image data and metadata. File extensions include .afd for segmented image files and .afm for AFF metadata.

Advanced SCSI Programming Interface (ASPI) A component that provides several software drivers for communication between the OS and SCSI component.

affidavit The document, given under penalty of perjury, that investigators create to detail their findings. This document is often used to justify issuing a warrant or to deal with abuse in a corporation.

allegation A charge made against someone or something before proof has been found.

allocation blocks In the Macintosh file system, a group of consecutive logical blocks assembled in a volume when a file is saved.

American Society of Crime Laboratory Directors (ASCLD) A national society that sets the standards, management, and audit procedures for labs used in crime analysis, including computer forensics labs used by the police, FBI, and similar organizations.

American Standard Code for Information Interchange (ASCII) An 8-bit coding scheme that assigns numeric values to up to 256 characters, including letters, numerals, punctuation marks, control characters, and other symbols.

approved secure container A fireproof container locked by a key or combination.

areal density The number of bits per square inch of a disk platter.

attorney-client privilege (ACP) Communication between an attorney and client about legal matters is protected as confidential communications. The purpose of having confidential communications is to promote honest and open dialogue between an attorney and client. This confidential information must not be shared with unauthorized people.

attribute ID In NTFS, an MFT record field containing metadata about the file or folder and the file's data or links to the file's data.

authorized requester In a corporate environment, the person who has the right to request an investigation, such as the chief security officer or chief intelligence officer.

Autoexec.bat A batch file containing customized settings for MS-DOS that runs automatically. It includes the default path and environmental variables, such as temporary directories.

Automated Fingerprint Identification Systems (AFIS) A computerized system for identifying fingerprints that's connected to a central database; used to identify criminal suspects and review thousands of fingerprint samples at high speed.

B*-tree A Macintosh file that organizes the directory hierarchy and file block mapping for File Manager. Files are represented as nodes (objects); leaf nodes contain the actual file data. **bad block inode** In the Linux file system, the inode that tracks bad sectors on a drive.

Berkeley Software Distribution (BSD) UNIX A variation of UNIX created at the University of California, Berkeley.

bitmap images Collections of dots, or pixels, in a grid format that form a graphic.

bit-shifting The process of shifting one or more digits in a binary number to the left or right to produce a different value.

bit-stream copy A bit-by-bit duplicate of data on the original storage medium. This process is usually called "acquiring an image" or "making an image."

bit-stream image The file where the bit-stream copy is stored; usually referred to as an "image," "image save," or "image file."

Boot.ini A file that specifies the Windows path installation and a variety of other startup options.

BootSect.dos If a machine has multiple booting OSs, NTLDR reads BootSect.dos, which is a hidden file, to determine the address (boot sector location) of each OS. *See also* NT Loader (Ntldr).

bootstrap process Information contained in ROM that a computer accesses during startup; this information tells the computer how to access the OS and hard drive.

brute-force attack The process of trying every combination of characters—letters, numbers, and special characters typically found on a keyboard—to find a matching password or passphrase value for an encrypted file.

business case A document that provides justification to upper management or a lender for purchasing new equipment, software, or other tools when upgrading your facility. In many instances, a business case shows how upgrades will benefit the company.

carving The process of recovering file fragments that are scattered across a disk. *See also* salvaging.

catalog An area of the Macintosh file system used to maintain the relationships between files and directories on a volume.

Certified Electronic Evidence Collection Specialist (CEECS) A certificate awarded by IACIS at completion of the written exam.

Certified Forensic Computer Examiner (CFCE) A certificate awarded by IACIS at completion of all portions of the exam.

chain of custody The route evidence takes from the time the investigator obtains it until the case is closed or goes to court.

client/server architecture A network architecture in which each computer or process on the network is a client or server. Clients request services from a server, and a server processes requests from clients.

clumps In the Macintosh file system, groups of contiguous allocation blocks used to keep file fragmentation to a minimum.

clusters Storage allocation units composed of groups of sectors. Clusters are 512, 1024, 2048, or 4096 bytes each.

Code Division Multiple Access (CDMA) A widely used digital cell phone technology that makes use of spread-spectrum modulation to spread the signal across a wide range of frequencies.

codes of professional conduct or responsibility External rules that often have the effect of law in limiting professionals' actions; breach of these rules can result in discipline, including suspension or loss of a license to practice and civil and criminal liability.

Command.com This system file provides a command prompt when booting to MS-DOS mode.

computer forensics The process of applying scientific methods to collect and analyze data and information that can be used as evidence.

computer forensics lab A computer lab dedicated to computing investigations; typically, it has a variety of computers, OSs, and forensics software.

Computer Forensics Tool Testing (CFTT) A project sponsored by the National Institute of Standards and Technology to manage research on computer forensics tools.

computer-generated records Data generated by a computer, such as system log files or proxy server logs.

computer investigations Conducting forensic analysis of systems suspected of containing evidence related to an incident or a crime.

computer-stored records Digital files generated by a person, such as electronic spreadsheets.

Computer Technology Investigators Network (CTIN) A nonprofit group based in Seattle–Tacoma, WA, composed of law enforcement members, private corporation security professionals, and other security professionals whose aim is to improve the quality of high-technology investigations in the Pacific Northwest.

Config.sys A text file containing commands that typically run only at system startup to enhance the computer's DOS configuration.

configuration management The process of keeping track of all upgrades and patches you apply to your computer's OS and applications.

conflicting out The practice of opposing attorneys trying to prevent you from testifying by claiming you have discussed the case with them and, therefore, have a conflict of interest.

constant angular velocity (CAV) The method of reading CDs in CD players that are 12X or faster.

constant linear velocity (CLV) The method of reading CDs in CD players slower than or equal to 12X.

contingency fees Payments that depend on the content of the expert's testimony or the outcome of the case.

continuation inode An inode containing more detailed information, such as the mode and file type, the quantity of links in the file or directory, the file's or directory's access control list (ACL), the least and most significant bytes of the ACL UID and GID, and the file or directory status flag.

covert surveillance Observing people or places without being detected, often using electronic equipment, such as video cameras or key stroke/screen capture programs.

criminal case A case in which criminal law must be applied.

criminal law Statutes applicable to a jurisdiction that state offenses against the peace and dignity of the jurisdiction and the elements that define these offenses.

curriculum vitae (CV) An extensive outline of your professional history that includes your education, training, work, and what cases you have worked on as well as training you have conducted, publications you have contributed to, and professional associations and awards.

Cyclic Redundancy Check (CRC) A mathematical algorithm that translates a file into a unique hexadecimal value.

cylinder A column of tracks on two or more disk platters.

data compression The process of coding data from a larger form to a smaller form.

data fork The part of a Macintosh file containing the file's actual data, both user-created data and data written by applications. The data fork also contains the resource map and header information, window locations, and icons, as does the resource fork. *See also* resource fork.

data recovery A specialty field in which companies retrieve files that were deleted accidentally or purposefully.

data runs Cluster addresses where files are stored on a drive's partition outside the MFT record. Data runs are used for nonresident MFT file records. A data run record field consists of three components; the first component defines the size in bytes needed to store the second and third components' content.

data streams Ways in which data can be appended to a file (intentionally or not). In NTFS, data streams become an additional file attribute.

defense in depth (DiD) The NSA's approach to implementing a layered network defense strategy. It focuses on three modes of protection: people, technology, and operations.

demosaicing The process of converting raw picture data to another format, such as JPEG or TIFF.

deposition A formal examination in which you're questioned under oath with only the opposing parties, your attorney, and a court reporter present. There's no judge or jury. The purpose of a deposition is to give opposing counsel a chance to preview your testimony before trial.

deposition banks Libraries of previously given testimony that law firms can access.

device drivers Files containing instructions for the OS for hardware devices, such as the keyboard, mouse, and video card.

digital evidence Evidence consisting of information stored or transmitted in electronic form.

disaster recovery A specialty field in which companies perform real-time backups, monitoring, data recovery, and hot site operations.

discovery Efforts to obtain information before a trial by demanding documents, depositions, interrogatories (written questions answered in writing under oath), and written requests for admissions of fact.

discovery deposition The opposing attorney sets the deposition and frequently conducts the equivalent of both direct and cross-examination. A discovery deposition is considered part of the discovery process. *See also* deposition.

discrimination The process of sorting and searching through investigation data to separate known good data from suspicious data; along with validation, one of the five required functions of computer forensics tools.

Disk Arbitration The Mac OS X feature for disabling and enabling automatic mounting when a drive is connected via a USB or FireWire device.

Disk Images The format Mac OS X uses for image files (.dmg extension). If the image file has additional segments, these segments must have a .dmgpart extension.

disqualification The process by which an expert witness is excluded from testifying.

distributed denial-of-service (DDoS) attacks A type of DoS attack in which other online machines are used, without the owners' knowledge, to launch an attack.

DOS protected-mode interface (DPMI) Used by many computer forensics tools that don't operate in the Windows environment. It allows DOS programs to access extended memory while protecting the system.

double-indirect pointers The inode pointers in the second layer or group of an OS. *See also* inodes.

drive slack Unused space in a cluster between the end of an active file and the end of the cluster. It can contain deleted files, deleted e-mail, or file fragments. Drive slack is made up of both file slack and RAM slack. *See also* file slack and RAM slack.

electronically erasable programmable read-only memory (EEPROM) A type of nonvolatile memory that can be reprogrammed electrically, without having to physically access or remove the chip.

Encrypting File System (EFS) A public/private key encryption first used in Windows 2000 on NTFS-formatted disks. The file is encrypted with a symmetric key, and then a public/private key is used to encrypt the symmetric key.

Enhanced Data GSM Environment (EDGE) An improvement to GSM technology that enables it to deliver higher data rates. *See also* Global System for Mobile Communications (GSM).

Enhanced Simple Mail Transfer Protocol (ESMTP) An enhancement of SMTP for sending and receiving e-mail messages. ESMTP generates a unique, nonrepeatable number that's added to a transmitted e-mail. No two messages transmitted from an e-mail server have the same ESMTP value. *See also* Simple Mail Transfer Protocol (SMTP).

enterprise network environment A large corporate computing system that can include formerly independent systems.

ethics Rules that you internalize and use to measure your performance; sometimes refers to external rules (codes of professional conduct or responsibility).

evidence bags Nonstatic bags used to transport removable media, hard drives, and other computer components.

evidence custody form A printed form indicating who has signed out and been in physical possession of evidence.

examination plan A document that lets you know what questions to expect when you are testifying.

Exchangeable Image File (EXIF) A file format the Japanese Electronic Industry Development Association (JEIDA) developed as a standard for storing metadata in JPEG and TIFF files.

exculpatory Evidence that indicates the suspect is innocent of the crime.

exhibits Evidence used in court to prove a case.

expert witness This type of testimony reports opinions based on experience and facts gathered during an investigation.

Extended Format File System (HFS+) File system used by Mac OS 8.1 and later; the primary difference between HFS and HFS+ is that HFS is limited to 65,536 blocks per volume, and HFS+ raised this number to more than 4 billion. HFS+ supports smaller file sizes on larger volumes, resulting in more efficient disk use.

extensive-response field kit A portable kit designed to process several computers and a variety of operating systems at a crime or incident scene involving computers. This kit should contain two or more types of software or hardware computer forensics tools, such as extra storage drives.

extents overflow file A file in HFS and HFS+ that's used by the catalog to coordinate all file allocations to the volume. File Manager uses this file when the list of a file's contiguous blocks becomes too long for the catalog. The list's overflow is placed in the extents overflow file. Any file extents not in the MDB or a VCB are also contained in this file. *See also* catalog, Master Directory Block (MDB), and Volume Control Block (VCB).

extraction The process of pulling relevant data from an image and recovering or reconstructing data fragments; one of the five required functions of computer forensics tools.

false positives The results of keyword searches that contain the correct match but aren't relevant to the investigation.

File Allocation Table (FAT) The original Microsoft file structure database. It's written to the outermost track of a disk and contains information about each file stored on the drive. PCs use the FAT to organize files on a disk so that the OS can find the files it needs. The variations are FAT12, FAT16, FAT32, and FATX.

File Manager A Macintosh utility that handles reading, writing, and storing data to physical media. It also collects data to maintain the HFS and is used to manipulate files, folders, and volumes.

file slack The unused space created when a file is saved. If the allocated space is larger than the file, the remaining space is slack space and can contain passwords, logon IDs, file fragments, and deleted e-mails.

file system The way files are stored on a disk; gives an OS a road map to data on a disk.

Finder A Macintosh utility for keeping track of files and maintaining users' desktops.

forensic copy Another name for a bit-stream image.

forensic workstation A workstation set up to allow copying forensic evidence, whether on a hard drive, USB drive, CD, or Zip disk. It usually has software preloaded and ready to use.

Fourth Amendment The Fourth Amendment to the U.S. Constitution in the Bill of Rights dictates that the government and its agents must have probable cause for search and seizure.

fourth-generation (4G) The next generation of mobile phone standards and technologies promises higher speeds and improved accuracy. Sprint Nextel introduced 4G in 2009, and other major carriers intend to follow suit between now and 2012.

geometry A disk drive's internal organization of platters, tracks, and sectors.

Global System for Mobile Communications (GSM) A second-generation cellular network standard; currently the most popular cellular network type in the world.

GNU General Public License (GPL) An agreement that defines Linux as open-source software, meaning that anyone can use, change, and distribute the software without owing royalties or licensing fees to another party.

Hal.dll The Hardware Abstraction Layer dynamic link library allows the OS kernel to communicate with hardware.

hash value A unique hexadecimal value that identifies a file or drive.

hazardous materials (HAZMAT) Chemical, biological, or radiological substances that can cause harm to people.

head The device that reads and writes data to a disk drive.

head and cylinder skew A method manufacturers use to minimize lag time. The starting sectors of tracks are slightly offset from each other to move the read-write head.

header node A node that stores information about the B*-tree file. *See also* B*-tree.

Hierarchical File System (HFS) The system Mac OS uses to store files, consisting of directories and subdirectories that can be nested.

High Performance File System (HPFS) The file system IBM uses for its OS/2 operating system.

high-risk document A written report containing sensitive information that could create an opening for the opposing attorney to discredit you.

High Tech Crime Network (HTCN) A national organization that provides certification for computer crime investigators and computer forensics technicians.

High Technology Crime Investigation Association (HTCIA) A nonprofit association for solving international computer crimes.

honeypot A computer or network set up to lure an attacker.

honeystick A honeypot and honeywall combined on a bootable memory stick.

honeywalls Intrusion prevention and monitoring systems that track what attackers do on honeypots.

hostile work environment An environment in which employees cannot perform their assigned duties because of the actions of others. In the workplace, these actions include sending threatening or demeaning e-mail or a co-worker viewing pornographic or hate sites.

inculpatory Evidence that indicates a suspect is guilty of the crime with which he or she is charged.

index node A B*-tree node that stores link information to the previous and next nodes. *See also* B*-tree.

indirect pointers The inode pointers in the first layer or group of an OS. *See also* inodes.

industrial espionage Selling sensitive or proprietary company information to a competitor.

Info2 file In Windows NT through Vista, the control file for the Recycle Bin. It contains ASCII data, Unicode data, and date and time of deletion.

initial-response field kit A portable kit containing only the minimum tools needed to perform disk acquisitions and preliminary forensics analysis in the field.

innocent information Data that doesn't contribute to evidence of a crime or violation.

inodes A key part of the Linux file system, these information nodes contain descriptive file or directory data, such as UIDs, GIDs, modification times, access times, creation times, and file locations.

International Association of Computer Investigative Specialists (IACIS) An organization created to provide training and software for law enforcement in the computer forensics field.

International Organization of Standardization (ISO) An organization set up by the United Nations to ensure compatibility in a variety of fields, including engineering, electricity, and computers. The acronym ISO is the Greek word for "equal."

International Organization on Computer Evidence (IOCE) A group that sets standards for recovering, preserving, and examining digital evidence.

International Telecommunication Union (ITU) An international organization dedicated to creating telecommunications standards.

interrogation The process of trying to get a suspect to confess to a specific incident or crime.

interview A conversation conducted to collect information from a witness or suspect about specific facts related to an investigation.

Io.sys This MS-DOS file communicates between a computer's BIOS, the hardware, and the OS kernel.

key escrow A technology designed to recover encrypted data if users forget their passphrases or if the user key is corrupted after a system failure.

keyed hash set A value created by an encryption utility's secret key.

keyword search A method of finding files or other information by entering relevant characters, words, or phrases in a search tool.

Known File Filter (KFF) A database containing the hash values of known legitimate and suspicious files. It's used to identify files for evidence or eliminate them from the investigation if they are legitimate files.

lay witness A person whose testimony is based on personal observation; not considered to be an expert in a particular field.

layered network defense strategy An approach to network hardening that sets up several network layers to place the most valuable data at the innermost part of the network.

leaf nodes The bottom-level nodes of the B*-tree that contain actual file data in the Macintosh file system. *See also* B*-tree.

limiting phrase Wording in a search warrant that limits the scope of a search for evidence.

line of authority The order in which people or positions are notified of a problem; these people or positions have the legal right to initiate an investigation, take possession of evidence, and have access to evidence.

litigation The legal process leading to a trial with the purpose of proving criminal or civil liability.

live acquisitions A data acquisition method used when a suspect computer can't be shut down to perform a static acquisition. Data is collected from the local computer or over a remote network connection. The captured data might be altered during the acquisition because it's not write-protected. Live acquisitions aren't repeatable because data is continually being altered by the suspect computer's OS.

logical acquisition This data acquisition method captures only specific files of interest to the case or specific types of files, such as Outlook PST files. *See also* sparse acquisition.

logical addresses When files are saved, they are assigned to clusters, which the OS numbers sequentially starting at 2. Logical addresses point to relative cluster positions, using these assigned cluster numbers.

logical blocks In the Macintosh file system, a collection of data that can't exceed 512 bytes. Logical blocks are assembled in allocation blocks to store files in a volume.

logical cluster numbers (LCNs) The numbers sequentially assigned to each cluster when an NTFS disk partition is created and formatted. The first cluster on an NTFS partition starts at count 0. LCNs become the addresses that allow the MFT to read and write data to the disk's nonresident attribute area. *See also* virtual cluster number (VCN) and data runs.

logical EOF In the Macintosh file system, the number of bytes in a file containing data.

lossless compression A compression method in which no data is lost. With this type of compression, a large file can be compressed to take up less space and then uncompressed without any loss of information.

lossy compression A compression method that permanently discards bits of information in a file. The removed bits of information reduce image quality.

low-level investigations Corporate cases that require less effort than a major criminal case.

map node A B*-tree node that stores a node descriptor and map record. *See also* B*-tree.

Master Boot Record (MBR) On Windows and DOS computers, this boot disk file contains information about partitions on a disk and their locations, size, and other important items.

Master Directory Block (MDB) On older Macintosh systems, the location where all volume information is stored. A copy of the MDB is kept in the next-to-last block on the volume. Called the Volume Information Block (VIB) in HFS+.

Master File Table (MFT) NTFS uses this database to store and link to files. It contains information about access rights, date and time stamps, system attributes, and other information about files.

mbox A method of storing e-mail messages in a flat plaintext file.

Message Digest 5 (MD5) An algorithm that produces a hexadecimal value of a file or storage media. Used to determine whether data has been changed.

Messaging Application Programming Interface (MAPI) The Microsoft system that enables other e-mail applications to work with each other.

metadata In NTFS, this term refers to information stored in the MFT. *See also* Master File Table (MFT).

metafile graphics Graphics files that are combinations of bitmap and vector images.

motion in limine A pretrial motion made to exclude mentioning certain evidence because it would prejudice the jury.

Msdos.sys A hidden text file containing startup options for Windows 9x. In MS-DOS 6.22 and earlier, it was an actual OS executable.

multi-evidence form An evidence custody form used to list all items associated with a case. *See also* evidence custody form.

Multipurpose Internet Mail Extensions (MIME) A specification for formatting non-ASCII messages, such as graphics, audio, and video, for transmission over the Internet.

National Institute of Standards and Technology (NIST) One of the governing bodies responsible for setting standards for various U.S. industries.

National Software Reference Library (NSRL) A NIST project with the goal of collecting all known hash values for commercial software and OS files.

network forensics The process of collecting and analyzing raw network data and systematically tracking network traffic to determine how security incidents occur.

network intrusion detection and incident response Detecting attacks from intruders by using automated tools; also includes the manual process of monitoring network firewall logs.

New Technology File System (NTFS) The file system Microsoft created to replace FAT. NTFS uses security features, allows smaller cluster sizes, and uses Unicode, which makes it a more versatile system. NTFS is used mainly on newer OSs, starting with Windows NT.

nonkeyed hash set A unique hash numbered generated by a software tool and used to identify files.

nonstandard graphics file formats Less common graphics file formats, including proprietary formats, newer formats, formats that most image viewers don't recognize, and old or obsolete formats.

notarized Having a document witnessed and a person clearly identified as the signer by a notary public.

NT Loader (Ntldr) A program located in the root folder of the system partition that loads the OS. *See also* Bootsect.dos.

NTBootdd.sys A device driver that allows the OS to communicate with SCSI or ATA drives that aren't related to the BIOS.

NTDetect.com A 16-bit program that identifies hardware components during startup and sends the information to Ntldr.

Ntoskrnl.exe The kernel for the Windows XP OS.

one-time passphrase A password used to access special accounts or programs requiring a high level of security, such as a decryption utility for an encrypted drive. This passphrase can be used only once, and then it expires.

Open Firmware The platform-independent boot firmware Macintosh systems use instead of BIOS firmware to gather information, control boot device selection, and load the OS.

order of volatility (OOV) A term that refers to how long an item on a network lasts. RAM and running processes might last only milliseconds; items stored on hard drives can last for years.

Orthogonal Frequency Division Multiplexing (OFDM) A 4G technology that uses radio waves broadcast over different frequencies; it's considered to use power more efficiently and be more immune to interference.

packet sniffers Devices and software used to examine network traffic. On TCP/IP networks, they examine packets, hence the name.

Pagefile.sys At startup, data and instruction code are moved in and out of this file to optimize the amount of physical RAM available during startup.

partition A logical drive on a disk. It can be the entire disk or part of the disk.

Partition Boot Sector The first data set of an NTFS disk. It starts at sector [0] of the disk drive and can expand up to 16 sectors.

partition gap Unused space or void between the primary partition and the first logical partition.

password-cracking software Software used to match the hash patterns of passwords or to simply guess passwords by using common combinations or standard algorithms.

password dictionary attack An attack that uses a collection of words or phrases that might be passwords for an encrypted file. Password recovery programs can use a password dictionary to compare potential passwords to an encrypted file's password or passphrase hash values.

password protected The method of requiring a password to limit access to certain files and areas of storage media; this method prevents unintentional or unauthorized use.

person of interest Someone who might be a suspect or someone with additional knowledge that can provide enough evidence of probable cause for a search warrant or arrest.

personal digital assistants (PDAs) Handheld electronic devices that typically contain personal productivity applications used for calendaring, contact management, and note taking. Unlike smart phones, PDAs don't have telephony capabilities.

personal identity information (PII) Any information that can be used to create bank or credit card accounts, such as name, home address, Social Security number, and driver's license number.

phase change alloy The Metal PC layer of a CD-RW that changes appearance (from noncrystalline to crystalline) depending on the temperature the laser applies. This medium allows writing to the CD several times.

phishing A type of e-mail scam that's typically sent as spam soliciting personal identity information that fraudsters can use for identity theft.

physical addresses The actual sectors in which files are located. Sectors reside at the hardware and firmware level.

physical EOF In the Macintosh file system, the number of allocation blocks assigned to a file.

pixels Small dots used to create images; the term comes from "picture element."

plain view doctrine When conducting a search and seizure, objects in plain view of a law enforcement officer, who has the right to be in position to have that view, are subject to seizure without a warrant and can be introduced as evidence. As applied to executing searches of computers, the plain view doctrine's limitations are less clear.

police blotter A log of criminal activity that law enforcement personnel can use to review the types of crimes currently being committed.

Post Office Protocol version 3 (POP3) A protocol for retrieving e-mail messages from an e-mail server.

private key In encryption, the key used to decrypt the file. The file owner keeps the private key.

probable cause The standard specifying whether a police officer has the right to make an arrest, conduct a personal or property search, or obtain a warrant for arrest.

professional conduct Behavior expected of an employee in the workplace or other professional setting.

professional curiosity The motivation for law enforcement and other professional personnel to examine an incident or crime scene to see what happened.

protected-mode GUI Provides the same functional startup process for Windows that Config.sys provided for DOS. It loads all the device drivers.

public key In encryption, the key used to encrypt a file; it's held by a certificate authority, such as a global registry, network server, or company such as VeriSign.

RAM slack The unused space between the end of the file (EOF) and the end of the last sector used by the active file in the cluster. Any data residing in RAM at the time the file is saved, such as logon IDs and passwords, can appear in this area, whether the information was saved or not. RAM slack is found primarily in older Microsoft OSs.

raster images Collections of pixels stored in rows rather than a grid, as with bitmap images, to make graphics easier to print; usually created when a vector graphic is converted to a bitmap image.

rasterize The process of converting a bitmap file to a raster file for printing.

raw file format A file format typically found on higher-end digital cameras; the camera performs no enhancement processing—hence the term "raw." This format maintains the best picture quality, but because it's a proprietary format, not all image viewers can display it.

raw format A data acquisition format that creates simple sequential flat files of a suspect drive or data set.

reconstruction The process of rebuilding data files; one of the five required functions of computer forensics tools.

recovery certificate A method NTFS uses so that a network administrator can recover encrypted files if the file's user/creator loses the private key encryption code.

Red Hat Package Manager (RPM) A utility that automates installing and uninstalling programs on Red Hat and Fedora Linux distributions.

redundant array of independent disks (RAID) Two or more disks combined into one large drive in several configurations for special needs. Some RAID systems are designed for redundancy to ensure continuous operations if one disk fails. Another configuration spreads data across several disks to improve access speeds for reads and writes.

Registry A Windows database containing information about hardware and software configurations, network connections, user preferences, setup information, and other critical information.

repeatable findings Being able to obtain the same results every time from a computer forensics examination.

resolution The density of pixels displayed onscreen, which governs image quality.

resource fork The part of a Macintosh file containing file metadata and application information, such as menus, dialog boxes, icons, executable code, and controls. The resource fork also contains the resource map and header information, window locations, and icons, as does the data fork. *See also* data fork.

right of privacy The belief employees have that their transmissions at work are protected.

risk management The process of determining how much risk is acceptable for any process or operation, such as replacing equipment.

salvaging Another term for carving, used outside North America. *See* carving.

Scientific Working Group on Digital Evidence (SWGDE) A group that sets standards for recovering, preserving, and examining digital evidence.

scope creep The result of an investigation expanding beyond its original description because the discovery of unexpected evidence increases the amount of work required.

search and seizure The legal act of acquiring evidence for an investigation. *See also* Fourth Amendment.

search warrants Legal documents that allow law enforcement to search an office, a place of business, or other locale for evidence related to an alleged crime.

Second Extended File System (Ext2fs) The standard Linux file system.

sector A section on a track, typically made up of 512 bytes.

secure facility A facility that can be locked and allows limited access to the room's contents.

Secure Hash Algorithm version 1 (SHA-1) A forensic hashing algorithm created by NIST to determine whether data in a file or on storage media has been altered.

silver-platter doctrine A policy no longer in effect that allowed a state law enforcement officer to pass illegally obtained evidence to the federal government and allowed federal prosecution to use that evidence.

Simple Mail Transfer Protocol (SMTP) A protocol for sending e-mail messages between servers.

single-evidence form A form that dedicates a page for each item retrieved for a case. It allows investigators to add more detail about exactly what was done to the evidence each time it was taken from the storage locker. *See also* evidence custody form.

small computer system interface (SCSI) An input/output standard protocol device that allows a computer to access devices such as hard drives, tape drives, scanners, CD/DVD-ROM drives, and printers.

smart phones Mobile telephones with more features than in a traditional phone, including a camera, an e-mail client, a Web browser, a calendar, contact management software, an instant-messaging program, and more.

sniffing Detecting data transmissions to and from a suspect's computer and a network server to determine the type of data being transmitted over a network.

sparse acquisition Like logical acquisitions, this data acquisition method captures only specific files of interest to the case, but it also collects fragments of unallocated (deleted) data. *See also* logical acquisition.

special-interest groups (SIGs) Associated with various operating systems, these groups maintain electronic mailing lists and might hold meetings to exchange information about current and legacy operating systems.

spoliation Destroying or concealing evidence; this action is subject to sanctions.

spoofing Transmitting an e-mail message with its header information altered so that its point of origin appears to be from a different sender. Spoofed e-mails are also referred to as forged e-mail. Spoofing is typically used in phishing and spamming to hide the sender's identity.

standard graphics file formats Common graphics file formats that most graphics programs and image viewers can open.

static acquisitions A data acquisition method used when a suspect drive is write-protected and can't be altered. If disk evidence is preserved correctly, static acquisitions are repeatable.

steganalysis tool A program designed to detect and decode steganography techniques.

steganography A cryptographic technique for embedding information in another file for the purpose of hiding that information from casual observers.

subscriber identity module (SIM) cards Removable cards in GSM phones that contain information for identifying subscribers. They can also store other information, such as messages and call history.

tarball A method originally designed to store data on magnetic tapes; the name stands for "tape archive." This storage method has been used for many years in UNIX computing environments to combine files and directories. In UNIX, BSD, and Linux, tarball files have a .tar extension. The tar command creates an uncompressed continuous file of data. If a tarball file is compressed, another extension is added after .tar, such as .gz or .bz2.

technical/scientific witness This type of testimony reports only the facts (findings of an investigation); no opinion is given in court.

Telecommunications Industry Association (TIA) A U.S. trade association representing hundreds of telecommunications companies that works to establish and maintain telecommunications standards.

TEMPEST A term referring to facilities that have been hardened so that electrical signals from computers, the computer network, and telephone systems can't be monitored or accessed easily by someone outside the facility.

testimony preservation deposition A deposition held to preserve your testimony in case of schedule conflicts or health problems; it's usually videotaped as well as recorded by a stenographer. *See also* deposition.

third-generation (3G) The most recent generation of mobile phone standards and technology; provides for more advanced features and higher data rates than the older analog and personal communications service (PCS) technologies.

Time Division Multiple Access (TDMA) The technique of dividing a radio frequency into time slots, used by GSM networks; also refers to a specific cellular network standard covered by Interim Standard (IS) 136. *See also* Global System for Mobile Communications (GSM).

track density The space between tracks on a disk. The smaller the space between tracks, the more tracks on a disk. Older drives with wider track densities allowed the heads to wander.

tracks Concentric circles on a disk platter where data is stored.

triple-indirect pointers The inode pointers in the third layer or group of an OS. *See also* inodes.

Trusted Computing Group (TCG) A nonprofit organization that develops support standards for trusted computer access across multiple platforms.

Trusted Platform Module (TPM) A microchip that stores encryption key data used to encrypt and decrypt drive data.

unallocated disk space Partition disk space that isn't allocated to a file. This space might contain data from files that have been deleted previously.

Unicode A character code representation that's replacing ASCII. It's capable of representing more than 64,000 characters and non-European-based languages.

Uniform Crime Report Information collected at the federal, state, and local levels to determine the types and frequencies of crimes committed.

UTF-8 (Unicode Transformation Format) One of three formats Unicode uses to translate languages for digital representation.

validation The process of checking the accuracy of results; along with discrimination, one of the five required functions of computer forensics tools.

vector graphics Graphics based on mathematical instructions to form lines, curves, text, and other geometrical shapes.

vector quantization (VQ) A form of compression that uses an algorithm similar to rounding off decimal values to eliminate unnecessary bits of data.

verdict The decision returned by a jury.

virtual cluster number (VCN) When a large file is saved in NTFS, it's assigned a logical cluster number specifying a location on the partition. Large files are referred to as nonresident files. If the disk is highly fragmented, VCNs are assigned and list the additional space needed to store the file. The LCN is a physical location on the NTFS partition; VCNs are the offset from the previous LCN data run. *See also* logical cluster numbers (LCNs) and data runs.

virtual machines Emulated computer environments that simulate hardware and can be used for running OSs separate from the physical (host) computer. For example, a computer running Windows Vista could have a virtualWindows 98 OS, allowing the user to switch between OSs.

voir dire In this qualification phase of testimony, your attorney asks you questions to establish your credentials as an expert witness. The process of qualifying jurors is also called voir dire.

volume Any storage media, such as a floppy disk, a partition on a hard drive, the entire drive, or several drives. On Intel systems, a volume is any partitioned disk.

Volume Bitmap A Macintosh application used to track blocks that are in use and blocks that are available.

Volume Control Block (VCB) An area of the Macintosh file system that contains information from the MDB and is used by File Manager. *See also* Master Directory Block (MDB).

vulnerability assessment and risk management The group that determines the weakest points in a system. It covers physical security and the security of OSs and applications.

warning banner Text displayed on computer screens when people log on to a company computer; this text states ownership of the computer and specifies appropriate use of the machine or Internet access.

whole disk encryption An encryption technique that performs a sector-by-sector encryption of an entire drive. Each sector is encrypted in its entirety, making it unreadable when copied with a static acquisition method.

write-blocker A hardware device or software program that prevents a computer from writing data to an evidence drive. Software write-blockers typically alter interrupt 13 write functions to a drive in a PC's BIOS. Hardware write-blockers are usually bridging devices between a drive and the forensic workstation.

zero day attacks Attacks launched before vendors or network administrators have discovered vulnerabilities and patches for them have been released.

zombies Computers used without the owners' knowledge in a DDoS attack.

zoned bit recording (ZBR) The method most manufacturers use to deal with a platter's inner tracks being shorter than the outer tracks. Grouping tracks by zones ensures that all tracks hold the same amount of data.

Numerics

3DES (Triple Data Encryption Standard) encryption, 136–137

3G (third-generation), 497–499, 509

4G (fourth-generation), 497–499, 508

4-mm DAT magnetic tapes, 175, 190

419 messages (Nigerian Scam), 452

486 PCs, 334

A

ABA (American Bar Association), 582

abstracts, report, 521

access to crime scene, 168

AccessData Certified Examiner (ACE), 78

AccessData Distributed Network Attack (DNA), 269

AccessData FTK Demo, 154–156

AccessData FTK (Forensic Toolkit)

　acquiring evidence with, 183–188

　analyzing data with, 348–351

　e-mail forensics, 476–481, 490–492

　overview, 154–155

　pretrial preparation, 558–561, 569–572

　report generation, 529–533, 538–539

　testing, 291–294

　verification of evidence on USB drives, 290–291

AccessData FTK Imager

　capturing images with, 123–126

　hash values, 178–179, 193–194

　validation, 129, 355

　virtual machines, 425–428

AccessData FTK Report Wizard, 350

AccessData Password Recovery Toolkit (PRTK) dictionary, 268–269, 363–365

AccessData Registry Viewer, 233–234, 236–237, 425–426

AccessData Ultimate Toolkit, 271–272

ACE (AccessData Certified Examiner), 78

ACP (attorney-client privilege), 39–40, 60

acquisition

　defined, 261–263, 284

　overview, 28–29

adapter cards, SCSI-to-IDE, 334

Add A New Host dialog box, Autopsy, 325–326

Add A New Image dialog box, Autopsy, 325

Add Comment dialog box, ProDiscover Basic, 234–235, 402, 418–419, 528, 537, 558

Add Evidence dialog box, AccessData FTK, 530

Add Evidence to Case dialog box, AccessData FTK, 183, 185, 478–479, 530, 538, 558

Advanced Forensic Format (AFF), 100–102, 140

Advanced Outlook Repair, 485

Advanced SCSI Programming Interface (ASPI), 332, 336

AFF (Advanced Forensic Format), 100–102, 140

affidavits, 13, 21

AFIS (Automated Fingerprint Identification Systems), 169, 190

alarms, forensics lab, 83

allegations, 12, 21

allocation blocks, 299–300, 336

American Bar Association (ABA), 582

American Medical Association (AMA), 583–585

American Psychological Association (APA), 584–585

American Society of Crime Laboratory Directors (ASCLD), 72, 94

American Standard Code for Information Interchange (ASCII), 249

antistatic bags, 501, 508, 512

antistatic pads, 82

AOL, 461–462

APA (American Psychological Association), 584–585

appedixes, including in reports, 526–527

Apple Mail, 461–462

approved secure containers, 33, 36–37, 60, 80–82

areal density, 200–201, 249

Argus, 440

Arizona v. Hicks, 162–163

ASCII (American Standard Code for Information Interchange), 249

ASCLD (American Society of Crime Laboratory Directors), 72, 94

ASPI (Advanced SCSI Programming Interface), 332, 336

ASRData SMART, 139, 274–275

attachments, e-mail, 390, 465, 491

attorney-client privilege (ACP), 39–40, 60

attribute 0x10, 216–217

attribute 0x30, 217–218

attribute 0x40, 217–219

attribute 0x80, 218–220, 589–593

attribute ID, 211, 249

auditing forensics labs, 83

Australian Department of Defence PyFlag, 139

authorized requesters, 17, 21

authorship of digital evidence, 153–154

MFT file, 211–224

overview, 208–210

Recovery Key Agent, 227

system files, 210–211

file types, identification of, 204–205

File_Name attribute 0x30, 217–218

FileSearcher utility, 309–310

Filter Search Hits dialog box, AccessData FTK, 530

FINALeMAIL tool, 473–476

Find dialog box, AccessData Registry Viewer, 236

Find Text dialog box, WinHex, 590

Finder utility, 298, 337

firewall log files, 467

FireWire drives, 301, 303

floor plans, forensics lab, 83–85

floppy disks, 315–316

FOIA (Freedom of Information Act) laws, 157

Foremost tool, 322

forensic copies, 47, 60

Forensic Examiner Information dialog box, AccessData FTK, 183

Forensic Suite ToolBar, 307–308

Forensic Toolkit. *See* AccessData FTK

forensics laboratories

business case for developing

acceptance testing, 93

acquisition, 92

approval, 92

budget development, 90

correction for acceptance, 93

cost, 90–91

hardware requirements, 91

implementation, 92–93

justification, 90

overview, 88–90

preparing, 90

production, 93

software requirements, 91–92

certification requirements

AccessData Certified Examiner, 78

acquiring certification and training, 76

budget planning, 73–76

duties of manager and staff, 72–73

EnCase Certified Examiner certification, 78

High-Tech Crime Network, 77–78

International Association of Computer Investigative Specialists, 76–77

defined, 94

physical requirements for

auditing, 83

conducting high-risk investigations, 80

evidence containers, 80–82

floor plans, 83–85

maintenance, overseeing, 82

physical security needs, 82–83

security needs, identifying, 79–80

workstations

building, 278–279

for corporate labs, 86

defined, 60

disaster recovery plan, 87–88

equipment upgrades, planning for, 88

hardware peripherals, 86–87

laptop, 88

operating systems, 87

overview, 44–45

for police labs, 85–86

for private labs, 86

recommendations for, 280

setting up, 45–46

software inventories, 87

forensics workstations. *See* workstations, forensic

formatting, report, 525

Fourth Amendment, 2–3, 10, 22, 161

fourth-generation (4G), 497–499, 508

fragmentation, file, 399–405

frames, CD, 331–332

FRCP (Federal Rules of Civil Procedure), 516, 544

FRE (Federal Rules of Evidence), 151–157, 577

Freedom of Information Act (FOIA) laws, 157

FreeOTFE, 230

freeware tools, 322

F-Response, 137

Frye v. United States, 516

FTK. *See* AccessData FTK

G

"General Test Methodology for Computer Forensic Tools" article, 281

Generate Checksum dialog box, Hex Workshop, 353–354, 361

geometry, 199, 250

GIMP graphics program, 313

Global System for Mobile Communications (GSM), 497–500, 508

GNU General Public License (GPL), 311, 337

Grand Unified Boot Loader (GRUB), 321

graphics, using in testimony, 550

graphics editors, 382–384

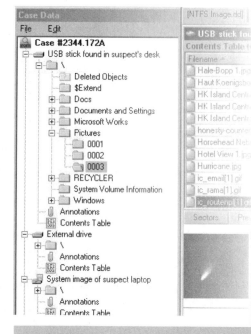